Politics

ANDREW HEYWOOD

MACMILLAN

First published 1997 by
MACMILLAN PRESS LTD
Houndmills, Basingstoke, Hampshire RG21 6XS
and London
Companies and representatives
throughout the world

ISBN 0–333–71250–1 hardcover
ISBN 0–333–64510–3 paperback

A catalogue record for this book is available
from the British Library.

This book is printed on paper suitable for recycling and
made from fully managed and sustained forest sources.

10   9   8   7   6   5   4   3   2   1
06   05   04   03   02   01   00   99   98   97

Typeset by Footnote Graphics, Warminster, Wilts
Printed in Great Britain by
The Bath Press, Bath

For Mark and Robin

Contents

PART 2

Nations and Globalisation

PART 3

Political Interaction

PART 5

Policy and Performance

Preface

THIS book provides a comprehensive and up-to-date introduction to the study of politics. It is designed to be of use to students taking courses in any field of the discipline, as well as general readers with an interest in the subject.

Politics stubbornly (and splendidly) refuses to stand still. The idea that history is 'speeding up' is not just a symptom of *fin de siècle* anxiety; in a sense, history *is* speeding up. For instance, the final decades of the twentieth century have seen the collapse of communism, the end of the Cold War, the emergence of a global economy, a technological revolution in production and communications and the rise of political Islam. Indeed, we appear to be living in a kind of 'post-world'; ideas such as postmodernism, postmaterialism, post-Fordism, post-socialism and postindustrialism vie with one another to demonstrate how much and which bits of the familiar world have now disappeared. And yet not all is flux and confusion. The pace of change may have increased, but certain aspects of social existence and important features of the political landscape have proved to be remarkably resilient to change. Therefore, while this book gives full weight to modern developments such as globalisation, the growth of feminism and Green politics, the upsurge of ethnic nationalism and the emergence of new social movements, conventional approaches to the discipline are not neglected, and the contribution of classical thinkers such as Plato, Aristotle, Marx and Mill is not ignored.

The task of providing a comprehensive guide to political analysis is made more difficult by the disparate nature of the discipline itself. All too frequently, politics resembles a collection of disciplines (political theory, comparative government, international relations, policy analysis and so on) rather than a single, coherent field of study. Undoubtedly, justice must be done to the various branches of the discipline, each of which has developed its own conceptual tools and, to some extent, its own methodology. Nevertheless, whenever possible, a holistic approach is adopted that tries to bring out what is distinctive about political analysis as a whole, and also highlights concerns that are shared by all who are interested in the subject. In an attempt to bridge the political philosophy–political science divide, links are thus drawn between normative and empirical theory, and a genuinely international perspective is adopted in preference to a country-by-country or system-by-system one.

The book is organised around five central themes. Part 1 on the theories of politics examines the conceptual and methodological issues that underpin the study of politics, and thus serves as an introduction to theories and ideas that are addressed throughout the book. Part 2 on nations and globalisation discusses the role and significance of the nation-state, particularly in the light of internationalisation and the emergence of global politics. Part 3 on political interaction looks at links between the political and nonpolitical worlds and at channels of communication between government and the governed. Part 4 on the machinery of government considers the institutional and political processes that affect both the nature of government and its style of operation. Part 5 on policy and performance analyses how policy is made and how the performance of political systems can be judged, thus linking back to the theoretical and ideological issues examined in Part 1.

Each chapter starts with an outline of its major themes and a series of questions that indicate the central topics that are addressed in the chapter. At the end of each chapter, there is a summary, a list of questions for discussion, and suggestions for further reading. Additional material is provided throughout the text in the form of glossary panels and boxed information. Brief biographies are provided of key political thinkers and significant political figures, together with a discussion of their theoretical role or importance. Concept boxes offer a fuller discussion of important political terms and concepts, particularly those with meanings that are complex or contested. Focus boxes give either further insight into particular theories or approaches, or an overview of relevant debates and arguments. These boxes are comprehensively cross-referenced, emphasising the interlocking character of the discipline. A glossary containing definitions of all the significant terms and concepts in the text is included at the end of the book. The bibliographical details of the references in the text (except for works only referred to in the boxes) are given in the bibliography at the end of the book, in addition to details of other relevant works.

I would like to express my sincere gratitude to the academic reviewers who commented on earlier drafts of this work, namely John Greenaway, Wyn Grant, Chris Brown and Gerry Stoker. Their advice and criticism was both constructive and insightful, and undoubtedly improved the book at a number of points. Discussions with colleagues and friends, particularly Karon and Doug Woodward, also helped to sharpen the ideas and arguments developed here. My publishers Frances Arnold and Steven Kennedy have been a constant source of support and encouragement, leavened, I am glad to say, by patience when necessary. My most heart-felt thanks, however, go, as ever, to my wife Jean. Not only did she take sole responsibility for the preparation of the typescript of this book, but she also offered advice on both style and content, which was especially useful when I was in danger of lapsing into incoherence. This book is dedicated to my sons, Mark and Robin.

Andrew Heywood, 1997

Acknowledgements

The author and publishers wish to thank the following for permission to use copyright material:

Associated Press p. 322; Jerry Bauer p. 29; Columbia University Press p. 56; Communist Party Library pp. 55, 177, 191; Duckworth p. 192; Harvard University pp. 56, 94; Hulton–Getty Picture Collection pp. 200, 208; Macmillan Archive p. 172; Mansell Collection pp. 6, 7, 13, 43, 45, 72, 73, 105, 110, 124, 168, 247, 285, 294, 302, 331; Merseyside County Galleries p. 59; MIT/Donna Coveney p. 150; H. Roger-Viollet pp. 155, 201; John Topham Picture Collection pp. 126, 173, 181, 267; Ullstein Bilderdienst pp. 9, 48, 54, 84, 194, 197; Yale University Office of Public Affairs p. 256.

Every effort has been made to trace all the copyright holders, but if any have been inadvertently overlooked the publishers will be pleased to make the necessary arrangement at the first opportunity.

PART

I

Theories of Politics

CHAPTER 1

What is Politics?

'Man is by nature a political animal.'

ARISTOTLE *Politics*, 1

Politics is exciting because people disagree. They disagree about how they should live. Who should get what? How should power and other resources be distributed? Should society be based on cooperation or conflict? And so on. They also disagree about how such matters should be resolved. How should collective decisions be made? Who should have a say? How much influence should each person have? And so forth. For Aristotle, this made politics the 'master science', that is, nothing less than the activity through which human beings attempt to improve their lives and create the Good Society. Politics is, above all, a social activity. It is always a dialogue, and never a monologue. Solitary individuals such as Robinson Crusoe may be able to develop a simple economy, produce art, and so on, but they cannot engage in politics. Politics only emerges with the arrival of a Man (or Woman) Friday. Nevertheless, the disagreement that lies at the heart of politics also extends to the nature of the subject and how it should be studied. People disagree about both what it is that makes social interaction 'political', and how political activity can best be analysed and explained.

The central issues explored in this chapter are as follows:

Contents

Key issues

▶ What are the defining features of politics as an activity?

▶ How has 'politics' been understood by various thinkers and traditions?

▶ Does politics take place within all social institutions, or only in some?

▶ What approaches to the study of politics as an academic discipline have been adopted?

▶ Can the study of politics be scientific?

▶ What roles do concepts, models and theories play in political analysis?

■ Defining politics

Politics, in its broadest sense, is the activity through which people make, preserve and amend the general rules under which they live. Although politics is also an academic subject (sometimes indicated by the use of 'Politics' with a capital P), it is then clearly the study of this activity. Politics is thus inextricably linked to the phenomena of **conflict** and **cooperation**. On the one hand, the existence of rival opinions, different wants, competing needs and opposing interests guarantees disagreement about the rules under which people live. On the other hand, people recognise that, in order to influence these rules or ensure that they are upheld, they must work with others, hence Hannah Arendt's (see p. 9) definition of political power as 'acting in concert'. This is why the heart of politics is often portrayed as a process of conflict resolution, in which rival views or competing interests are reconciled with one another. However, politics in this broad sense is better thought of as a search for conflict resolution than as its achievement, as not all conflicts are, or can be, resolved. Nevertheless, the inescapable presence of diversity (we are not all alike) and scarcity (there is never enough to go around) ensure that politics is an inevitable feature of the human condition.

Any attempt to clarify the meaning of 'politics' must nevertheless address two major problems. The first is the mass of associations that the word has when used in everyday language; in other words, politics is a 'loaded' term. Whereas most people think of, say, economics, geography, history and biology simply as academic subjects, few people come to politics without preconceptions. Many, for instance, automatically assume that students and teachers of politics must in some way be biased, finding it difficult to believe that the subject can be approached in an impartial and dispassionate manner. To make matters worse, politics is usually thought of as a 'dirty' word: it conjures up images of trouble, disruption and even violence on the one hand, and deceit, manipulation and lies on the other. There is nothing new about such associations. As long ago as 1775, Samuel Johnson dismissed politics as 'nothing more than a means of rising in the world', while in the nineteenth century the US historian Henry Adams summed up politics as 'the systematic organisation of hatreds'. Any attempt to define politics therefore entails trying to disentangle the term from such associations. Not uncommonly, this has meant attempting to rescue the term from its unsavoury reputation by establishing that politics is a valuable, even laudable, activity.

The second and more intractable difficulty is that even respected authorities cannot agree what the subject is about. Politics is defined in such different ways: as the exercise of power, the exercise of authority, the making of collective decisions, the allocation of scarce resources, the practice of deception and manipulation, and so on. The virtue of the definition advanced in this text, 'the making, preserving and amending of general social rules', is that it is sufficiently broad to encompass most, if not all, of the competing definitions. However, problems arise when the definition is unpacked, or when the meaning is refined. For instance, does 'politics' refer to a particular way in which rules are made, preserved or amended (that is, peacefully, by debate), or to all such processes? Similarly, is politics practised in all social contexts and institutions, or only in certain ones (that is, government and public life)?

From this perspective, politics may be treated as an 'essentially contested' concept (see p. 18), in the sense that the term has a number of acceptable or legitimate mean-

Conflict: Competition between opposing forces, reflecting a diversity of opinions, preferences, needs or interests.

Cooperation: Working together; achieving goals through collective action.

ings. On the other hand, these different views may simply consist of contrasting conceptions of the same, if necessarily vague, concept. Whether we are dealing with rival concepts or alternative conceptions, the debate about 'what is politics?' is worth pursuing because it exposes some of the deepest intellectual and ideological disagreements in the academic study of the subject. The different views of politics examined here are as follows:

- politics as the art of government
- politics as public affairs
- politics as compromise and consensus
- politics as power and the distribution of resources.

Politics as the art of government

'Politics is not a science ... but an art', Chancellor Bismarck is reputed to have told the German Reichstag. The art Bismarck had in mind was the art of government, the exercise of control within society through the making and enforcement of collective decisions. This is perhaps the classical definition of politics, developed from the original meaning of the term in Ancient Greece.

The word 'politics' is derived from *polis*, literally meaning city-state. Ancient Greek society was divided into a collection of independent city-states, each of which possessed its own system of government. The largest and most influential of these city-states was Athens, often portrayed as the cradle of democratic government. In this light, politics can be understood to refer to the affairs of the *polis*, in effect, 'what concerns the *polis*'. The modern form of this definition is therefore 'what concerns the state'. This view of politics is clearly evident in the everyday use of the term: people are said to be 'in politics' when they hold public office, or to be 'entering politics' when they seek to do so. It is also a definition which academic political science has helped to perpetuate.

In many ways, the notion that politics amounts to 'what concerns the state' is the traditional view of the discipline, reflected in the tendency for academic study to focus upon the personnel and machinery of government. To study politics is in essence to study government, or, more broadly, to study the exercise of authority. This view is advanced in the writings of the influential US political scientist David Easton (1979, 1981), who defined politics as the 'authoritative allocation of values'. By this he meant that politics encompasses the various processes through which government responds to pressures from the larger society, in particular by allocating benefits, rewards or penalties. 'Authoritative values' are therefore ones that are widely accepted in society, and considered binding by the mass of citizens. In this view, politics is associated with 'policy' (see p. 382), that is, with formal or authoritative decisions that establish a plan of action for the community.

However, what is striking about this definition is that it offers a highly restricted view of politics. Politics is what takes place within a **polity**, a system of social organisation centred upon the machinery of government. Politics is therefore practised in cabinet rooms, legislative chambers, government departments and the like, and it is engaged in by a limited and specific group of people, notably politicians, civil servants and lobbyists. This means that most people, most institutions and most social activities can be regarded as being 'outside' politics. Businesses, schools and other educational institutions, community groups, families and so on are in this sense 'nonpolitical',

Concept

The state

The state is a political association that establishes sovereign (see p. 143) jurisdiction within defined territorial borders and exercises authority through a set of permanent institutions. These institutions are those that are recognisably 'public' in that they are responsible for the collective organisation of communal life and are funded at the public's expense. The state thus embraces the various institutions of government, but it also extends to the courts, nationalised industries, social-security system, and so forth; it can be identified with the entire 'body politic'. For the German sociologist Max Weber (see p. 194), the state was defined by its monopoly of the means of 'legitimate violence' (see Chapter 5).

Polis: (*Greek*) City-state; classically understood to imply the highest or most desirable form of social organisation.

Polity: A society organised through the exercise of political authority; for Aristotle, rule by the many in the interests of all.

Niccolo Machiavelli (1469–1527)

Italian politician and author. The son of a civil lawyer, Machiavelli's knowledge of public life was gained from a sometimes precarious existence in politically unstable Florence. He served as Second Chancellor (1498–1512), and was despatched on missions to France, Germany and throughout Italy. After a brief period of imprisonment and the restoration of Medici rule, Machiavelli embarked on a literary career. His major work, *The Prince*, published in 1531, drew heavily upon his first-hand observations of the statecraft of Cesare Borgia and the power politics that dominated his period. It was written as a guide for the future prince of a united Italy. The adjective 'Machiavellian' subsequently came to mean 'cunning and duplicitous'.

Concept

Authority

Authority can most simply be defined as 'legitimate power'. Whereas power is the *ability* to influence the behaviour of others, authority is the *right* to do so. Authority is therefore based on an acknowledged duty to obey rather than on any form of coercion or manipulation. In this sense, authority is power cloaked in legitimacy or rightfulness. Weber (see p. 194) distinguished between three kinds of authority, based on the different grounds upon which obedience can be established: *traditional* authority is rooted in history, *charismatic* authority stems from personality, and *legal–rational* authority is grounded in a set of impersonal rules (see the section on legitimising power, p. 193–6).

Anti-politics: Disillusionment with formal and established political processes, reflected in nonparticipation, support for antisystem parties, or the use of direct action.

---

because they are not engaged in 'running the country'. By the same token, to portray politics as an essentially state-bound activity is to ignore the increasingly important international or global influences upon modern life, such as the impact of transnational technology and multinational corporations. In this sense, this definition of politics is a hangover from the days when the nation-state (see p. 117) could still be regarded as an independent actor in world affairs.

This definition can, however, be narrowed still further. This is evident in the tendency to treat politics as the equivalent of party politics. In other words, the realm of 'the political' is restricted to those state actors who are consciously motivated by ideological beliefs, and who seek to advance them through membership of a formal organisation such as a political party. This is the sense in which politicians are described as 'political', whereas civil servants are seen as 'nonpolitical', as long as, of course, they act in a neutral and professional fashion. Similarly, judges are taken to be 'nonpolitical' figures while they interpret the law impartially and in accordance with the available evidence, but they may be accused of being 'political' if their judgement is influenced by personal preferences or some other form of bias.

The link between politics and the affairs of the state also helps to explain why negative or pejorative images have so often been attached to politics. This is because, in the popular mind, politics is closely associated with the activities of politicians. Put brutally, politicians are often seen as power-seeking hypocrites who conceal personal ambition behind the rhetoric of public service and ideological conviction. Indeed, this perception has become more common in the modern period as intensified media exposure has more effectively brought to light examples of corruption and dishonesty, giving rise to the phenomenon of **anti-politics**. This rejection of the personnel and machinery of conventional political life is rooted in a view of politics as a self-serving, two-faced and unprincipled activity, clearly evident in the use of derogatory phrases such as 'office politics' and 'politicking'. Such an image of politics is sometimes traced back to the writings of Niccolo Machiavelli, who, in *The Prince* ([1531] 1961), developed a strictly realistic account of politics which drew attention to the use by political leaders of cunning, cruelty and manipulation.

Such a negative view of politics reflects the essentially liberal perception that, as individuals are self-interested, political power is corrupting, because it encourages those 'in power' to exploit their position for personal advantage and at the expense of others. This is famously expressed in Lord Acton's (1834–1902) aphorism: 'power tends to corrupt, and absolute power corrupts absolutely'. Nevertheless, few who

Aristotle (384–22 BCE)

Greek philosopher. Aristotle was a student of Plato and tutor of the young Alexander the Great. He established his own school of philosophy in Athens in 335 BCE; this was called the 'peripatetic school' after his tendency to walk up and down as he talked. His 22 surviving treatises, compiled as lecture notes, range over logic, physics, metaphysics, astronomy, meteorology, biology, ethics and politics. In the Middle Ages, Aristotle's work became the foundation of Islamic philosophy, and it was later incorporated into Christian theology. His best known political work is *Politics*, a study of the ideal constitution.

Concept

Power

Power, in its broadest sense, is the ability to achieve a desired outcome, and it is sometimes referred to in terms of the 'power *to*' do something. This includes everything from the ability to keep oneself alive to the ability of government to promote economic growth. In politics, however, power is usually thought of as a relationship, that is, as the ability to influence the behaviour of others in a manner not of their choosing. It is referred to in terms of having 'power *over*' people. More narrowly, power may be associated with the ability to punish or reward, bringing it close to force or manipulation, in contrast to 'influence', which also encompasses rational persuasion (see the faces of power focus box, p. 11).

view politics in this way doubt that political activity is an inevitable and permanent feature of social existence. However venal politicians may be, there is a general, if grudging, acceptance that they are always with us. Without some kind of mechanism for allocating authoritative values, society would simply disintegrate into a civil war of each against all, as the early social-contract theorists argued (see p. 87). The task is therefore not to abolish politicians and bring politics to an end, but rather to ensure that politics is conducted within a framework of checks and constraints that ensure that governmental power is not abused.

Politics as public affairs

A second and broader conception of politics moves it beyond the narrow realm of government to what is thought of as 'public life' or 'public affairs'. In other words, the distinction between 'the political' and 'the nonpolitical' coincides with the division between an essentially *public* sphere of life and what can be thought of as a *private* sphere. Such a view of politics is often traced back to the work of the famous Greek philosopher Aristotle. In *Politics*, Aristotle declared that 'man is by nature a political animal', by which he meant that it is only within a political community that human beings can live 'the good life'. From this viewpoint, then, politics is an ethical activity concerned with creating a 'just society'; it is what Aristotle called the 'master science'.

However, where should the line between 'public' life and 'private' life be drawn? The traditional distinction between the public realm and the private realm conforms to the division between the state and civil society. The institutions of the state (the apparatus of government, the courts, the police, the army, the society-security system and so forth) can be regarded as 'public' in the sense that they are responsible for the collective organisation of community life. Moreover, they are funded at the public's expense, out of taxation. In contrast, civil society consists of what Edmund Burke (see p. 45) called the 'little platoons', institutions such as the family and kinship groups, private businesses, trade unions, clubs, community groups and so on that are 'private' in the sense that they are set up and funded by individual citizens to satisfy their own interests, rather than those of the larger society. On the basis of this 'public/private' division, politics is restricted to the activities of the state itself and the responsibilities which are properly exercised by public bodies. Those areas of life that individuals can and do manage for themselves (the economic, social, domestic, personal, cultural and artistic spheres, and so on) are therefore clearly 'nonpolitical'.

Civil society

The term civil society has been defined in a variety of ways. Originally, it meant a 'political community', a society governed by law, under the authority of a state. More commonly, it is distinguished from the state, and the term is used to describe institutions that are 'private' in that they are independent from government and organised by individuals in pursuit of their own ends. 'Civil society' therefore refers to a realm of autonomous groups and associations: businesses, interest groups, clubs, families and so on. Hegel (see p. 84), however, distinguished between the family and civil society, viewing the latter as a sphere of egoism and selfishness.

An alternative 'public/private' divide is sometimes defined in terms of a further and more subtle distinction, namely that between 'the political' and 'the personal' (see Figure 1.1). Although civil society can be distinguished from the state, it nevertheless contains a range of institutions that are thought of as 'public' in the wider sense that they are open institutions, operating in public, to which the public has access. One of the crucial implications of this is that it broadens our notion of the political, transferring the economy in particular from the private to the public realm. A form of politics can thus be found in the workplace. Nevertheless, although this view regards institutions such as businesses, community groups, clubs and trade unions as 'public', it remains a restricted view of politics. According to this perspective, politics does not, and should not, infringe upon 'personal' affairs and institutions. Feminist thinkers in particular have pointed out that this implies that politics effectively stops at the front door; it does not take place in the family, in domestic life, or in personal relationships. This view is illustrated, for example, by the tendency of politicians to draw a clear distinction between their professional conduct and their personal or domestic behaviour. By classifying, say, cheating on their partners or treating their children badly as 'personal' matters, they are able to deny the political significance of such behaviour on the grounds that it does not touch on their conduct of public affairs.

The view of politics as an essentially 'public' activity has generated both positive and negative images. In a tradition dating back to Aristotle, politics has been seen as a noble and enlightened activity precisely because of its 'public' character. This position was firmly endorsed by Hannah Arendt, who argued in *The Human Condition* (1958) that politics is the most important form of human activity because it involves interaction amongst free and equal citizens. It thus gives meaning to life and affirms the uniqueness of each individual. Theorists such as Jean-Jacques Rousseau (see p. 73) and John Stuart Mill (see p. 44) who portrayed political participation as a good in itself have drawn similar conclusions. Rousseau argued that only through the direct and continuous participation of all citizens in political life can the state be bound to the common good, or what he called the 'general will' (see p. 72). In Mill's view, involvement in 'public' affairs is educational in that it promotes the personal, moral and intellectual development of the individual.

In sharp contrast, however, politics as public activity has also been portrayed as a form of unwanted interference. Liberal theorists in particular have exhibited a preference for civil society over the state, on the grounds that 'private' life is a realm of choice, personal freedom and individual responsibility. This is most clearly demonstrated by attempts to narrow the realm of 'the political', commonly expressed as the

Public	Private
The state: apparatus of government	Civil society: autonomous bodies: businesses, trade unions, clubs, families, and so on

Public	Private
Public realm: politics, commerce, work, art, culture, and so on	Personal realm: family and domestic life

Fig. 1.1 Two views of the public/private divide

Hannah Arendt (1906–75)

German political theorist and philosopher. Hannah Arendt was brought up in a middle-class Jewish family. She fled Germany in 1933 to escape from Nazism, and finally settled in the USA, where her major work was produced. Her wide-ranging, even idiosyncratic, writing was influenced by the existentialism of Heidegger (1889–1976) and Jaspers (1883–1969); she described it as 'thinking without barriers'. Her major works include *The Origins of Totalitarianism* (1951), *The Human Condition* (1958), *On Revolution* (1963) and *Eichmann in Jerusalem* (1963), which she described as a study of the 'banality of evil'.

wish to 'keep politics out of' private activities such as business, sport and family life. From this point of view, politics is unwholesome quite simply because it prevents people acting as they choose. For example, it may interfere with how firms conduct their business, or with how and with whom we play sports, or with how we bring up our children.

Politics as compromise and consensus

The third conception of politics relates not so much to the arena within which politics is conducted as to the way in which decisions are made. Specifically, politics is seen as a particular means of resolving conflict, that is, by compromise, conciliation and negotiation, rather than through force and naked power. This is what is implied when politics is portrayed as 'the art of the possible'. Such a definition is inherent in the everyday use of the term. For instance, the description of a solution to a problem as a 'political' solution implies peaceful debate and arbitration, as opposed to what is often called a 'military' solution. Once again, this view of politics has been traced back to the writings of Aristotle and, in particular, to his belief that what he called 'polity' is the ideal system of government, as it is 'mixed' in the sense that it combines both aristocratic and democratic features (see p. 25–6). One of the leading modern exponents of this view is Bernard Crick. In his classic study *In Defence of Politics*, Crick offered the following definition:

Politics [is] the activity by which differing interests within a given unit of rule are conciliated by giving them a share in power in proportion to their importance to the welfare and the survival of the whole community. (Crick, 1993:21)

In this view, the key to politics is therefore a wide dispersal of power. Accepting that conflict is inevitable, Crick argued that when social groups and interests possess power they must be conciliated; they cannot merely be crushed. This is why he portrayed politics as 'that solution to the problem of order which chooses conciliation rather than violence and coercion' (p. 30). Such a view of politics reflects a deep commitment to liberal–rationalist principles. It is based on resolute faith in the efficacy of debate and discussion, as well as on the belief that society is characterised by consensus rather than by irreconcilable conflict. In other words, the disagreements that exist *can* be resolved without resort to intimidation and violence. Critics, how-

◆   Concept

Consensus

The term consensus means
agreement, but it usually
refers to an agreement of a
particular kind. It implies,
first, a broad agreement,
the terms of which are
accepted by a wide range of
individuals or groups.
Secondly, it implies an
agreement about
fundamental or underlying
principles, as opposed to a
precise or exact agreement.
In other words, a
consensus permits
disagreement on matters of
emphasis or detail. The
term 'consensus politics' is
used in two senses. A
procedural consensus is a
willingness to make
decisions through
consultation and
bargaining, either between
political parties or between
government and major
interests. A *substantive*
consensus is an overlap of
the ideological positions of
two or more political
parties, reflected in
agreement about
fundamental policy goals.
Examples are the UK's
postwar social-democratic
consensus, and Germany's
social-market consensus.)

ever, point out that Crick's conception of politics is heavily biased towards the form
of politics that takes place in western pluralist democracies; in effect, he equated
politics with electoral choice and party competition. As a result, his model has little
to tell us about, say, one-party states or military regimes.

This view of politics has an unmistakeably positive character. Politics is certainly
no utopian solution (compromise means that concessions are made by all sides,
leaving no one perfectly satisfied), but it is undoubtedly preferable to the alternatives: bloodshed and brutality. In this sense, politics can be seen as a civilised and
civilising force. People should be encouraged to respect politics as an activity, and
should be prepared to engage in the political life of their own community. Nevertheless, Crick saw politics as an embattled and often neglected activity. He saw its principal enemy as 'the desire for certainty at any cost', and he warned that this is
demonstrated in many forms, including the seductive influence of political ideologies, blind faith in democracy, the impact of rabid nationalism and the promise of
science to disclose objective truth.

Politics as power

The fourth definition of politics is both the broadest and the most radical. Rather
than confining politics to a particular sphere (the government, the state or the 'public' realm) this view sees politics at work in all social activities and in every corner of
human existence. As Adrian Leftwich proclaimed in *What is Politics? The Activity
and Its Study* (1984:64), 'politics is at the heart of *all* collective social activity, formal
and informal, public and private, in *all* human groups, institutions and societies'. In
this sense, politics takes place at every level of social interaction; it can be found
within families and amongst small groups of friends just as much as amongst nations
and on the global stage. However, what is it that is distinctive about political activity?
What marks off politics from any other form of social behaviour?

At its broadest, politics concerns the production, distribution and use of
resources in the course of social existence. Politics is, in essence, power: the ability to
achieve a desired outcome, through whatever means. This notion was neatly
summed up in the title of Harold Lasswell's book *Politics: Who Gets What, When,
How?* (1936). From this perspective, politics is about diversity and conflict, but the
essential ingredient is the existence of scarcity: the simple fact that, while human
needs and desires are infinite, the resources available to satisfy them are always limited. Politics can therefore be seen as a struggle over scarce resources, and power can
be seen as the means through which this struggle is conducted.

Advocates of this view of power include feminists and Marxists. Modern
feminists have shown particular interest in the idea of 'the political'. This arises from
the fact that conventional definitions of politics effectively exclude women from
political life. Women have traditionally been confined to a 'private' sphere of
existence, centred on the family and domestic responsibilities. In contrast, men have
always dominated conventional politics and other areas of 'public' life. Radical
feminists have therefore attacked the 'public/private' divide, proclaiming instead
that 'the personal is the political'. This slogan neatly encapsulates the radical-
feminist belief that what goes on in domestic, family and personal life is intensely
political, and indeed that it is the basis of all other political struggles. Clearly, a more
radical notion of politics underlies this position. This view was summed up by Kate
Millett in *Sexual Politics* (1969:23), in which she defined politics as 'power-

Focus on . . .

'Faces' of power

Power can be said to be exercised whenever A gets B to do something which B would not otherwise have done. However, A can influence B in various ways. This allows us to distinguish between different dimensions or 'faces' of power:

▶ **Power as decision-making:** This face of power consists of conscious actions that in some way influence the content of decisions. The classic account of this form of power is found in Robert Dahl's *Who Governs? Democracy and Power in an American City* (1961), which made judgements about who had power by analysing decisions in the light of the known preferences of the actors involved. Such decisions can nevertheless be influenced in a variety of ways. In *Three Faces of Power* (1989), Keith Boulding distinguished between the use of force or intimidation (the stick), productive exchanges involving mutual gain (the deal), and the creation of obligations, loyalty and commitment (the kiss).

▶ **Power as agenda setting:** The second face of power, as suggested by Bachrach and Baratz (1962), is the ability to prevent decisions being made, that is, in effect, 'non-decision-making'. This involves the ability to set or control the political agenda, thereby preventing issues or proposals from being aired in the first place. For instance, private businesses may exert power both by campaigning to defeat proposed consumer-protection legislation (first face), and by lobbying parties and politicians to prevent the question of consumer rights being publicly discussed (second face).

▶ **Power as thought control:** The third face of power is the ability to influence another by shaping what he or she thinks, wants, or needs (Lukes, 1974). This is power expressed as ideological indoctrination or psychological control. An example of this would be the ability of the advertising industry to remove pressure for stiffer consumer-protection laws by persuading consumers that their interests had already been looked after by business (in the form of, for example, 'planet-friendly' products). In political life, the exercise of this form of power is seen in the use of propaganda and, more generally, in the impact of ideology (see p. 41).

structured relationships, arrangements whereby one group of persons is controlled by another'. Feminists can therefore be said to be concerned with 'the politics of everyday life'. In their view, relationships within the family, between husbands and wives, and between parents and children, are every bit as political as relationships between employers and workers, or between governments and citizens.

Marxists have used the term 'politics' in two senses. On one level, Marx (see p. 51) used 'politics' in a conventional sense to refer to the apparatus of the state. In the *Communist Manifesto* ([1848] 1967), he thus referred to political power as 'merely the organised power of one class for oppressing another' (p. 105). For Marx, politics, together with law and culture, are part of a 'superstructure' that is distinct from the economic 'base' which is the real foundation of social life. However, he did not see the economic 'base' and the legal and political 'superstructure' as entirely separate. He believed that the 'superstructure' arose out of, and reflected, the economic 'base'.

At a deeper level, political power, in this view, is therefore rooted in the class system; as Lenin (see p. 75) put it, 'politics is the most concentrated form of economics'. As opposed to believing that politics can be confined to the state and a narrow public sphere, Marxists can be said to believe that 'the economic is political'. From this perspective, civil society, characterised as Marxists believe it to be by class struggle, is the very heart of politics.

Views such as these portray politics in largely negative terms. Politics is, quite simply, about oppression and subjugation. Radical feminists hold that society is patriarchal, in that women are systematically subordinated and subjected to male power. Marxists traditionally argued that politics in a capitalist society is characterised by the exploitation of the proletariat by the bourgeoisie. On the other hand, these negative implications are balanced against the fact that politics is also seen as the means through which injustice and domination can be challenged. Marx, for instance, predicted that class exploitation would be overthrown by a proletarian revolution, and radical feminists proclaim the need for gender relations to be reordered through a sexual revolution. However, it is also clear that when politics is portrayed as power and domination it need not be seen as an inevitable feature of social existence. Feminists look to an end of 'sexual politics' achieved through the construction of a nonsexist society, in which people will be valued according to personal worth rather than on the basis of gender. Marxists believe that 'class politics' will end with the establishment of a classless communist society. This, in turn, will eventually lead to the 'withering away' of the state, bringing politics in the conventional sense also to an end.

■ Studying politics

Approaches to the study of politics

Disagreement about the nature of political activity is matched by controversy about the nature of politics as an academic discipline. One of the most ancient spheres of intellectual enquiry, politics was originally seen as an arm of philosophy, history or law. Its central purpose was to uncover the principles upon which human society should be based. From the late nineteenth century onwards, however, this philosophical emphasis was gradually displaced by an attempt to turn politics into a scientific discipline. The high point of this development was reached in the 1950s and 1960s with an open rejection of the earlier tradition as meaningless metaphysics. Since then, however, enthusiasm for a strict science of politics has waned, and there has been a renewed recognition of the enduring importance of political values and normative theories. If the 'traditional' search for universal values acceptable to everyone has largely been abandoned, so has been the insistence that science (see p. 16) alone provides a means of disclosing truth. The resulting discipline is today more fertile and more exciting, precisely because it embraces a range of theoretical approaches and a variety of schools of analysis.

The philosophical tradition

The origins of political analysis date back to Ancient Greece and a tradition usually referred to as 'political philosophy'. This involved a preoccupation with essentially ethical, prescriptive or *normative* questions, reflecting a concern with what 'should',

Plato (427–347 BCE)

Greek philosopher. Plato was born of an aristocratic family. He became a follower of Socrates, who is the principal figure in his ethical and philosophical dialogues. After Socrates' death in 399 BCE, Plato founded his own academy in order to train the new Athenian ruling class. Plato taught that the material world consists of imperfect copies of abstract and eternal 'ideas'. His political philosophy, expounded in *The Republic* and *The Laws*, is an attempt to describe the ideal state in terms of a theory of justice. Plato's work has exerted wide influence on Christianity and on European culture in general.

'ought' or 'must' be brought about, rather than what 'is'. Plato and Aristotle are usually identified as the founding fathers of this tradition. Their ideas resurfaced in the writings of medieval theorists such as Augustine (354–430) and Aquinas (1225–74). The central theme of Plato's work, for instance, was an attempt to describe the nature of the ideal society, which in his view took the form of a benign dictatorship dominated by a class of philosopher kings.

Such writings have formed the basis of what is called the 'traditional' approach to politics. This involves the analytical study of ideas and doctrines that have been central to political thought. Most commonly, it has taken the form of a history of political thought that focuses on a collection of 'major' thinkers (that spans, for instance, Plato to Marx) and a canon of 'classic' texts. This approach has the character of literary analysis: it is primarily interested in examining what major thinkers said, how they developed or justified their views, and the intellectual context within which they worked. Although such analysis may be carried out critically and scrupulously, it cannot be **objective** in any scientific sense, as it deals with **normative** questions such as 'why should I obey the state?', 'how should rewards be distributed?' and 'what should the limits of individual freedom be?'.

The empirical tradition

Although it was less prominent than normative theorising, a descriptive or empirical tradition can be traced back to the earliest days of political thought. It can be seen in Aristotle's attempt to classify constitutions (see p. 25–6), in Machiavelli's realistic account of statecraft, and in Montesquieu's (see p. 294) sociological theory of government and law. In many ways, such writings constitute the basis of what is now called comparative government, and they gave rise to an essentially institutional approach to the discipline. In the USA and the UK in particular, this developed into the dominant tradition of analysis. The empirical approach to political analysis is characterised by the attempt to offer a dispassionate and impartial account of political reality. The approach is 'descriptive' in that it seeks to analyse and explain, whereas the normative approach is 'prescriptive' in the sense that it makes judgements and offers recommendations.

Descriptive political analysis acquired its philosophical underpinning from the doctrine of empiricism, which spread from the seventeenth century onwards through the work of theorists such as John Locke (see p. 43) and David Hume (1711–76). The doctrine of empiricism advanced the belief that experience is the

Objective: External to the observer, demonstrable; untainted by feelings, values or bias.

Normative: The prescription of values and standards of conduct; what 'should be' rather than what 'is'.

only basis of knowledge, and that therefore all hypotheses and theories should be tested by a process of observation. By the nineteenth century, such ideas had developed into what became known as positivism, an intellectual movement particularly associated with the writings of Auguste Comte (1798–1857). This doctrine proclaimed that the social sciences, and, for that matter, all forms of philosophical enquiry, should strictly adhere to the methods of the natural sciences. Once science was perceived to be the only reliable means of disclosing truth, the pressure to develop a science of politics became irresistible.

The scientific tradition

The first theorist to attempt to describe politics in scientific terms was Karl Marx. Using his so-called materialist conception of history (see p. 51), Marx strove to uncover the driving force of historical development. This enabled him to make predictions about the future based upon 'laws' that had the same status in terms of proof as laws in the natural sciences. The vogue for scientific analysis was also taken up in the nineteenth century by mainstream analysis. In the 1870s, 'political science' courses were introduced in the universities of Oxford, Paris and Columbia, and by 1906 the *American Political Science Review* was being published. However, enthusiasm for a science of politics peaked in the 1950s and 1960s with the emergence, most strongly in the USA, of a form of political analysis that drew heavily upon **behaviouralism**. For the first time, this gave politics reliably scientific credentials, because it provided what had previously been lacking: objective and quantifiable data against which hypotheses could be tested. Political analysts such as David Easton proclaimed that politics could adopt the methodology of the natural sciences, and this gave rise to a proliferation of studies in areas best suited to the use of quantitative research methods, such as voting behaviour, the behaviour of legislators, and the behaviour of municipal politicians and lobbyists.

Behaviouralism, however, came under growing pressure from the 1960s onwards. In the first place, it was claimed that behaviouralism had significantly constrained the scope of political analysis, preventing it from going beyond what was directly observable. Although behavioural analysis undoubtedly produced, and continues to produce, invaluable insights in fields such as voting studies, a narrow obsession with quantifiable data threatens to reduce the discipline of politics to little else. More worryingly, it inclined a generation of political scientists to turn their backs upon the entire tradition of normative political thought. Concepts such as 'liberty', 'equality', 'justice' and 'rights' were sometimes discarded as being meaningless because they were not **empirically** verifiable entities. Dissatisfaction with behaviouralism grew as interest in normative questions revived in the 1970s, as reflected in the writings of theorists such as John Rawls (see p. 56) and Robert Nozick (see p. 94).

Moreover, the scientific credentials of behaviouralism started to be called into question. The basis of the assertion that behaviouralism is objective and reliable is the claim that it is 'value-free', that is, that it is not contaminated by ethical or normative beliefs. However, if the focus of analysis is observable behaviour, it is difficult to do much more than describe the existing political arrangements, which implicitly means that the *status quo* is legitimised. This conservative value bias was demonstrated by the fact that 'democracy' was, in effect, redefined in terms of observable behaviour. Thus, instead of meaning 'popular self government' (literally, government *by* the people), democracy came to stand for a struggle between competing elites to win power through the mechanism of popular election. In other

Behaviouralism: The belief that social theories should be constructed only on the basis of observable behaviour, providing quantifiable data for research.

Empirical: Based on observation and experiment; empirical knowledge is derived from sense data and experience.

words, democracy came to mean what goes on in the so-called democratic political systems of the developed West.

Recent developments

Amongst recent theoretical approaches to politics is what is called formal political theory, variously known as 'political economy', 'public-choice theory' (see p. 258) and 'rational-choice theory'. This approach to analysis draws heavily upon the example of economic theory in building up models based upon procedural rules, usually about the rationally self-interested behaviour of the individuals involved. Most firmly established in the USA, and associated in particular with the so-called Virginia School, formal political theory provides at least a useful analytical device which may provide insights into the actions of voters, lobbyists, bureaucrats and politicians, as well as into the behaviour of states within the international system. This approach has had its broadest impact on political analysis in the form of what is called institutional public-choice theory. The use of such techniques by writers such as Anthony Downs, Mancur Olson and William Niskanen, in fields such as party competition, interest-group behaviour and the policy influence of bureaucrats, is discussed in later chapters. The approach has also been applied in the form of game theory, which has been developed more from the field of mathematics than from economics. It entails the use of first principles to analyse puzzles about individual behaviour. The best known example in game theory is the 'prisoners' dilemma' (see Figure 1.2).

By no means, however, has the rational-choice approach to political analysis been universally accepted. While its supporters claim that it introduces greater rigour into the discussion of political phenomena, critics have questioned its basic assumptions. It may, for instance, overestimate human rationality in that it ignores the fact that people seldom possess a clear set of preferred goals and rarely make decisions in the light of full and accurate knowledge. Furthermore, in proceeding from an abstract model of the individual, rational-choice theory pays insufficient attention to social and historical factors, failing to recognise, amongst other things, that human self-interestedness may be socially conditioned, and not merely innate. As a result, a variety of approaches have come to be adopted for the study of politics as an academic discipline. This has made modern political analysis both richer and more diverse. To established normative, institutional and behavioural approaches have been added not only rational-choice theory, but also, more recently, feminism and **discourse** theory. In particular, political philosophy and political science are now less likely to be seen as distinct modes of enquiry, and still less as rivals. Instead, they have come to be accepted simply as contrasting ways of disclosing political knowledge.

Can the study of politics be scientific?

Although it is widely accepted that the study of politics should be scientific in the broad sense of being rigorous and critical, some have argued, as has been pointed out, that it can be scientific in a stricter sense, that is, that it can use the methodology of the natural sciences. This claim has been advanced by Marxists and by positivist social scientists, and it was central to the 'behavioural revolution' of the 1950s. The attraction of a science of politics is clear. It promises an impartial and reliable means of distinguishing 'truth' from 'falsehood', thereby giving us access to objective knowledge about the political world. The key to achieving this is to distinguish between

Discourse: Human interaction, especially communication; discourse may disclose or illustrate power relationships.

Concept

Science, scientism

Science (from the Latin *scientia*, meaning 'knowledge') is a field of study that aims to develop reliable explanations of phenomena through repeatable experiments, observation and deduction. The 'scientific method', by which hypotheses are verified (proved true) by testing them against the available evidence, is therefore seen as a means of disclosing value-free and objective truth. Karl Popper (1902–94), however, suggested that science can only falsify hypotheses, since 'facts' may always be disproved by later experiments. Scientism is the belief that the scientific method is the only source of reliable knowledge, and so should be applied to fields such as philosophy, history and politics, as well as the natural sciences. Doctrines such as Marxism, utilitarianism (see p. 383) and racialism (see p. 114) are scientist in this sense.

Focus on . . .

The prisoners' dilemma

Two criminals, held in separate cells, are faced with the choice of 'squealing' or 'not squealing' on one another. If only one of them confesses, but he provides evidence to convict the other, he will be released without charge, while his partner will take the whole blame and be jailed for ten years. If both criminals confess, they will each be jailed for six years. If both refuse to confess, they will only be convicted of a minor crime, and they will each receive a one-year sentence. The options are shown in Figure 1.2.

In view of the dilemma confronting them it is likely that both criminals will confess, fearing that if they do not the other will 'squeal' and they will receive the maximum sentence. Ironically, the game shows that rational behaviour can result in the least favourable outcome (in which the prisoners jointly serve a total of 12 years in jail). In effect, they are punished for their failure to cooperate or trust one another. However, if the game is repeated several times, it is possible that the criminals will learn that self-interest is advanced by cooperation, which will encourage both to refuse to confess.

Fig. 1.2 Options in prisoners' dilemma

	Prisoner B	
	Confesses	Does not confess
Confesses	A: B: 6, 6	A: B: 6, 10
Does not confess	A: B: 10, 0	A: B: 1, 1

(Prisoner A on the left axis; Prisoner B across the top)

'facts' (empirical evidence) and 'values' (normative or ethical beliefs). Facts are objective in the sense that they can be demonstrated reliably and consistently; they can be proved. Values, by contrast, are inherently subjective, a matter of opinion.

However, any attempt to construct a science of politics must confront three difficulties. The first of these is the problem of data. For better or worse, human beings are not tadpoles that can be taken into a laboratory or cells that can be observed under a microscope. We cannot get 'inside' a human being, or carry out repeatable experiments on human behaviour. What we can learn about individual behaviour is therefore limited and superficial. In the absence of exact data, we have no reliable means of testing our hypotheses. The only way round the problem is to ignore the thinking subject altogether by subscribing to the doctrine of **determinism**. One example would be behaviourism (as opposed to behaviouralism), the school of psychology associated with John B. Watson (1878–1958) and B. F. Skinner

Determinism: The belief that human actions and choices are entirely conditioned by external factors; determinism implies that free will is a myth.

(1904–90). This holds that human behaviour can ultimately be explained in terms of conditioned reactions or reflexes. Another example is 'dialectical materialism', the crude form of Marxism that dominated intellectual enquiry in the USSR.

Secondly, there are difficulties that stem from the existence of hidden values. The idea that models and theories of politics are entirely value-free is difficult to sustain when examined closely. Facts and values are so closely intertwined that it is often impossible to prise them apart. This is because theories are invariably constructed on the basis of assumptions about human nature, human society, the role of the state and so on that have hidden political and ideological implications. A conservative value **bias**, for example, can be identified in behaviouralism, rational-choice theories and systems theory (see p. 19). Similarly, feminist political theories are rooted in assumptions about the nature and significance of gender divisions.

Thirdly, there is the myth of neutrality in the social sciences. Whereas natural scientists may be able to approach their studies in an objective and impartial manner, holding no presuppositions about what they are going to discover, this is difficult and perhaps impossible to achieve in politics. However politics is defined, it addresses questions relating to the structure and functioning of the society in which we live and have grown up. Family background, social experience, economic position, personal sympathies and so on thus build into each and every one of us a set of preconceptions about politics and the world around us. This means that scientific objectivity, in the sense of absolute impartiality or neutrality (see p. 287), must always remain an unachievable goal in political analysis, however rigorous our research methods may be. Perhaps the greatest threat to the accumulation of reliable knowledge thus comes not from bias as such, but from the failure to acknowledge bias, reflected in bogus claims to political neutrality.

Concepts, models and theories

Concepts, models and theories are the tools of political analysis. However, as with most things in politics, the analytical tools must be used with care. First, let us consider concepts. A concept is a general idea about something, usually expressed in a single word or a short phrase. A concept is more than a proper noun or the name of a thing. There is, for example, a difference between talking about a cat (a particular and unique cat) and having a concept of a 'cat' (the idea of a cat). The concept of a cat is not a 'thing' but an 'idea', an idea composed of the various attributes that give a cat its distinctive character: 'a furry mammal', 'small', 'domesticated', 'catches rats and mice', and so on. The concept of 'equality' is thus a principle or ideal. This is different from using the term to say that a runner has 'equalled' a world record, or that an inheritance is to be shared 'equally' between two brothers. In the same way, the concept of 'presidency' refers not to any specific president, but rather to a set of ideas about the organisation of executive power.

What, then, is the value of concepts? Concepts are the tools with which we think, criticise, argue, explain and analyse. Merely perceiving the external world does not in itself give us knowledge about it. In order to make sense of the world we must, in a sense, impose meaning upon it, and this we do through the construction of concepts. Quite simply, to treat a cat as a cat, we must first have a concept of what it is. Concepts also help us to classify objects by recognising that they have similar forms or similar properties. A cat, for instance, is a member of the class of 'cats'. Concepts are therefore 'general'; they can relate to a number of objects, indeed to any object

Bias: Sympathies or prejudices that (often unconsciously) affect human judgement; bias implies distortion.

◆▮▮▮▮▮▮▮▮ **Concept** ▮▮▮

Ideal type

An ideal type (sometimes 'pure type') is a mental construct in which an attempt is made to draw out meaning from an otherwise almost infinitely complex reality through the presentation of a logical extreme. Ideal types were first used in economics, for instance, in the notion of perfect competition. Championed in the social sciences by Max Weber, ideal types are explanatory tools, not approximations of reality; they neither 'exhaust reality' nor offer an ethical ideal. Weberian examples include types of authority (see p. 6) and bureaucracy (see p. 341).

that complies with the characteristics of the general idea itself. It is no exaggeration to say that our knowledge of the political world is built up through developing and refining concepts which help us make sense of that world. Concepts, in that sense, are the building blocks of human knowledge.

Nevertheless, concepts can also be slippery customers. In the first place, the political reality we seek to understand is constantly shifting and is highly complex. There is always the danger that concepts such as 'democracy', 'human rights' and 'capitalism' will be more rounded and coherent than the unshapely realities they seek to describe. Max Weber tried to overcome this problem by recognising particular concepts as 'ideal types'. This view implies that the concepts we use are constructed by singling out certain basic or central features of the phenomenon in question, which means that other features are downgraded or ignored altogether. The concept of 'revolution' can be regarded as an ideal type in this sense, in that it draws attention to a process of fundamental and usually violent political change. It thus helps us make sense of, say, the 1789 French Revolution and the eastern European revolutions of 1989–91 by highlighting important parallels between them. The concept must nevertheless be used with care because it can also conceal vital differences, and thereby distort understanding, in this case, for example, about the ideological and social character of revolution. For this reason, it is better to think of concepts or ideal types not as being 'true' or 'false', but merely as more or less 'useful'.

A further problem is that political concepts are often the subject of deep ideological controversy. Politics is, in part, a struggle over the legitimate meaning of terms and concepts. Enemies may argue, fight and even go to war, all claiming to be 'defending freedom', 'upholding democracy' or 'having justice on their side'. The problem is that words such as 'freedom', 'democracy' and 'justice' have different meanings to different people. How can we establish what is 'true' democracy, 'true' freedom or 'true' justice? The simple answer is that we cannot. Just as with the attempt to define 'politics' above, we have to accept that there are competing versions of many political concepts. Such concepts are best regarded as 'essentially contested' concepts (Gallie, 1955/56), in that controversy about them runs so deep that no neutral or settled definition can ever be developed. In effect, a single term can represent a number of rival concepts, none of which can be accepted as its 'true' meaning. For example, it is equally legitimate to define politics as what concerns the state, as the conduct of public life, as debate and conciliation, and as the distribution of power and resources.

Models and theories are broader than concepts; they comprise a range of ideas rather than a single idea. A **model** is usually thought of as a representation of something, usually on a smaller scale, as in the case of a doll's house or a toy aeroplane. In this sense, the purpose of the model is to resemble the original object as faithfully as possible. However, conceptual models need not in any way resemble an object. It would be absurd, for instance, to insist that a computer model of the economy should bear a physical resemblance to the economy itself. Rather, conceptual models are analytical tools; their value is that they are devices through which meaning can be imposed upon what would otherwise be a bewildering and disorganised collection of facts. The simple point is that facts do not speak for themselves: they must be interpreted, and they must be organised. Models assist in the accomplishment of this task because they include a network of relationships which highlight the meaning and significance of relevant empirical data. The best way of understanding this is through an example. One of the most influential models in political analysis is the

Model: A theoretical representation of empirical data that aims to advance understanding by highlighting significant relationships and interactions.

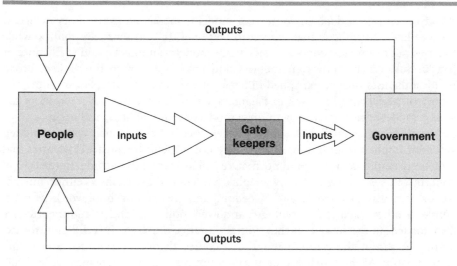

Fig. 1.3 The political system

model of the political system developed by David Easton (1979, 1981). This can be represented diagrammatically (see Figure 1.3).

This ambitious model sets out to explain the entire political process, as well as the function of major political actors, through the application of what is called systems analysis. A system is an organised or complex whole, a set of interrelated and interdependent parts that form a collective entity. In the case of the political system, a linkage exists between what Easton calls 'inputs' and 'outputs'. Inputs into the political system consist of demands and supports from the general public. Demands can range from pressure for higher living standards, improved employment prospects, and more generous welfare payments to greater protection for minority and individual rights. Supports, on the other hand, are ways in which the public contributes to the political system by paying taxes, offering compliance, and being willing to participate in public life. Outputs consist of the decisions and actions of government, including the making of policy, the passing of laws, the imposition of taxes, and the allocation of public funds. Clearly, these outputs generate 'feedback', which in turn shapes further demands and supports. The key insight offered by Easton's model is that the political system tends towards long-term equilibrium or political stability, as its survival depends on outputs being brought into line with inputs.

However, it is vital to remember that conceptual models are at best simplifications of the reality they seek to explain. They are merely devices for drawing out understanding; they are not reliable knowledge. In the case of Easton's model, for example, political parties and interest groups are portrayed as 'gatekeepers', the central function of which is to regulate the flow of inputs into the political system. Although this may be one of their significant functions, parties and interest groups also manage public perceptions, and thereby help to shape the nature of public demands. In short, these are in reality more interesting and more complex institutions than the systems model suggests. In the same way, Easton's model is more effective in explaining how and why political systems respond to popular pressures than it is in explaining why they employ repression and coercion, as, to some degree, all do.

The terms **theory** and model are often used interchangeably in politics. Theories and models are both conceptual constructs used as tools of political analysis. However, strictly speaking, a theory is a proposition. It offers a systematic explanation of

Theory: A systematic explanation of empirical data, usually (unlike a hypothesis) presented as reliable knowledge.

Paradigm

A paradigm is, in a general sense, a pattern or model that highlights relevant features of a particular phenomenon, rather in the manner of an ideal type. As used by Kuhn (1962), however, it refers to an intellectual framework comprising interrelated values, theories and assumptions, within which the search for knowledge is conducted. 'Normal' science is therefore conducted within the established intellectual framework; in 'revolutionary' science, an attempt is made to replace the old paradigm with a new one. The radical implication of this theory is that 'truth' and 'falsehood' cannot be finally established. They are only provisional judgements operating within an accepted paradigm that will, eventually, be replaced.

a body of empirical data. In contrast, a model is merely an explanatory device; it is more like a hypothesis that has yet to be tested. In that sense, in politics, while theories can be said to be more or less 'true', models can only be said to be more or less 'useful'. Clearly, however, theories and models are often interlinked: broad political theories may be explained in terms of a series of models. For example, the theory of pluralism (discussed in Chapters 4 and 5) encompasses a model of the state, a model of electoral competition, a model of group politics, and so on.

However, virtually all conceptual devices, theories and models contain hidden values or implicit assumptions. This is why it is difficult to construct theories that are purely empirical; values and normative beliefs invariably intrude. In the case of concepts, this is demonstrated by people's tendency to use terms as either 'hurrah! words' (for example 'democracy', 'freedom' and 'justice') or 'boo! words' (for example 'conflict', 'anarchy', 'ideology', and even 'politics'. Models and theories are also 'loaded' in the sense that they contain a range of biases. It is difficult, for example, to accept the claim that rational-choice theories (examined above) are value-neutral. As they are based on the assumption that human beings are basically egoistical and self-regarding, it is perhaps not surprising that they have often pointed to policy conclusions that are politically conservative. In the same way, class theories of politics, advanced by Marxists, are based on broader theories about history and society and, indeed, they ultimately rest upon the validity of an entire social philosophy.

There is therefore a sense in which analytical devices, such as models and microtheories, are constructed on the basis of broader macrotheories. These major theoretical tools of political analysis are those which address the issues of power and the role of the state: pluralism (see p. 76), elitism (see p. 78), class analysis, and so on. These theories are examined in Chapters 4 and 5. At a still deeper level, however, many of these macrotheories reflect the assumptions and beliefs of one or other of the major ideological traditions. These traditions operate rather like what Thomas Kuhn in *The Structure of Scientific Revolutions* (1962) called paradigms. A paradigm is a related set of principles, doctrines and theories that help to structure the process of intellectual enquiry. In effect, a paradigm constitutes the framework within which the search for knowledge is conducted. In economics, this can be seen in the replacement of Keynesianism by monetarism (and perhaps the subsequent shift back to neo-Keynesianism); in transport policy it is shown in the rise of Green ideas.

According to Kuhn, the natural sciences are dominated at any time by a single paradigm; science develops through a series of 'revolutions' in which an old paradigm is replaced by a new one. Political and social enquiry is, however, different, in that it is a battleground of contending and competing paradigms. These paradigms take the form of broad social philosophies, usually called political ideologies: liberalism, conservatism, socialism, fascism, feminism and so on. Each presents its own account of social existence; each offers a particular view of the world. To portray these ideologies as theoretical paradigms is not, of course, to say that most, if not all, political analysis is narrowly ideological in the sense that it advances the interests of a particular group or class. Rather, it merely acknowledges that political analysis is usually carried out on the basis of a particular ideological tradition. Much of academic political science, for example, has been constructed according to liberal–rationalist assumptions, and thus bears the imprint of its liberal heritage.

The various levels of conceptual analysis are shown diagrammatically in Figure 1.4.

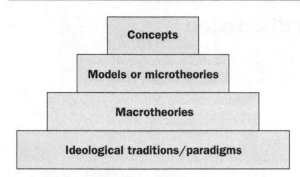

Concepts	Examples: power, social class, rights, law
Models or microtheories	Examples: systems analysis, public choice, game theory
Macrotheories	Examples: pluralism, elitism, functionalism
Ideological traditions/paradigms	Examples: liberalism, Marxism, feminism

Fig. 1.4 Levels of conceptual analysis

▨ Summary

◆ Politics is the activity through which people make, preserve and amend the general rules under which they live. As such, it is an essentially social activity, inextricably linked, on the one hand, to the existence of diversity and conflict, and on the other to a willingness to cooperate and act collectively. Politics is better seen as a search for conflict resolution than as its achievement, as not all conflicts are, or can be, resolved.

◆ Politics has been understood differently by different thinkers and within different traditions. Politics has been viewed as the art of government or as 'what concerns the state', as the conduct and management of public affairs, as the resolution of conflict through debate and compromise, and as the production, distribution and use of resources in the course of social existence.

◆ There is considerable debate about the realm of 'the political'. Conventionally, politics has narrowly been seen as embracing institutions and actors operating in a 'public' sphere concerned with the collective organisation of social existence. However, when politics is understood in terms of power-structured relationships, it may be seen to operate in the 'private' sphere as well.

◆ A variety of approaches have been adopted to the study of politics as an academic discipline. These include political philosophy or the analysis of normative theory, an empirical tradition particularly concerned with the study of institutions and structures, attempts to introduce scientific rigour through behavioural analysis, and a variety of modern approaches including the use of rational-choice theory.

◆ The study of politics is scientific to the extent that it is possible to gain objective knowledge about the political world by distinguishing between facts and values. This task is nevertheless hampered by the difficulty of gaining access to reliable data, by values that are implicit in political models and theories, and by biases that operate within all students of politics.

◆ Concepts, models and theories are the tools of political analysis, providing the building blocks of knowledge. However, they are only analytical devices. Although they help to advance understanding, they are more rounded and coherent than the unshapely and complex realities they seek to describe. Ultimately, all political and social enquiry is conducted within a particular intellectual framework or ideological paradigm.

◼ Questions for discussion

▶ If politics is essentially social, why is not all social activity political?

▶ Why has politics so often carried negative associations?

▶ How could you defend politics as a worthwhile and ennobling activity?

▶ Is politics inevitable? Could politics ever be brought to an end?

▶ Why has the idea of a science of politics been so attractive?

▶ Is it possible to study politics objectively and without bias?

◼ Further reading

Crick, B. *In Defence of Politics* (rev. ed.) (Harmondsworth and New York: Penguin, 1993). A thoughtful and stimulating attempt to justify politics (understood in a distinctively liberal sense) against its enemies.

Heywood, A. *Political Ideas and Concepts: An Introduction* (Basingstoke: Macmillan, 1994). A clear and accessible guide to the major ideas and concepts encountered in political analysis.

Leftwich, A. (ed.) *What is Politics? The Activity and Its Study* (Oxford and New York: Blackwell, 1984). A very useful collection of essays examining different concepts of politics as well as contrasting views of the discipline.

Marsh, D. and G. Stoker (eds) *Theory and Methods in Political Science.* (Basingstoke: Macmillan, 1995). An accessible, yet comprehensive and sophisticated, exploration of the nature and scope of the discipline of political science.

Governments, Systems and Regimes

CHAPTER 2

'That government is best which governs not at all.'

HENRY DAVID THOREAU *Civil Disobedience* (1849)

Contents

Classifying the various forms of government has been one of the principal concerns of political analysis through the ages. This process can be traced back to the fourth century BCE, when Aristotle made the first recorded attempt to describe the political regimes then in existence, using terms such as 'democracy', 'oligarchy', and 'tyranny' that are still commonly employed today. From the eighteenth century onwards, governments were increasingly classified as monarchies or republics, or as autocratic or constitutional regimes. During the twentieth century, these distinctions were further sharpened. The 'three worlds' classification of political systems, which was particularly fashionable during the Cold War period, created an image of world politics dominated by a struggle between democracy and totalitarianism. However, in the light of modern developments, such as the collapse of communism, the rise of East Asia, and the emergence of political Islam, all such classifications appear outdated. Nevertheless, it is not entirely clear what these shifts mean. Some interpret them as indications of the triumph of western liberal democracy; others see evidence of the modern world becoming politically more diffuse and fragmented.

The central issues addressed in this chapter are as follows:

Key issues

▶ What is the difference between governments, political systems and regimes?

▶ What is the purpose of classifying systems of government?

▶ On what basis have, and should, regimes be classified?

▶ What are the major regimes of the modern world?

▶ Has western liberal democracy triumphed worldwide?

Concept

Government

In its broadest sense, to govern means to rule or control others. Government can therefore be taken to include any mechanism through which ordered rule is maintained, its central features being the ability to make collective decisions and the capacity to enforce them. A form of government can thus be identified in almost all social institutions: families, schools, businesses, trade unions and so on. However, 'government' is more commonly understood to refer to the formal and institutional processes which operate at the national level to maintain public order and facilitate collective action. The core functions of government are thus to make law (legislation), implement law (execution) and interpret law (adjudication). In some cases, the political executive (see p. 316) alone is referred to as 'the Government', making it equivalent to 'the Administration' in presidential systems.

Political system: A network of relationships through which government generates 'outputs' (policies) in response to 'inputs' (demands or support) from the general public.

Government gridlock: Paralysis resulting from institutional rivalry within government or the attempt to respond to conflicting public demands.

■ Traditional systems of classification

Before we examine how different systems of rule have been classified, it is necessary for us to reflect on both *what* is being classified, and *why* such classifications have been undertaken. First, what is 'government', and how do governments differ from 'political systems' or 'regimes'? 'Government' refers to the institutional processes through which collective and usually binding decisions are made; its various institutions constitute the subject matter of Part 4 of this book. A **political system** or regime, on the other hand, is a broader term that encompasses not only the mechanisms of government and the institutions of the state, but also the structures and processes through which these interact with the larger society.

A political system is, in effect, a subsystem of the larger social system. It is a 'system' in that there are interrelationships within a complex whole, and 'political' in that these interrelationships relate to the distribution of power, wealth and resources in society. Political regimes can thus be characterised as effectively by the organisation of economic life as they are by the governmental processes through which they operate. A regime is therefore a 'system of rule' that endures despite the fact that governments come and go. Whereas governments can be changed by elections, through dynastic succession, as a result of *coup d'états* (see p. 369), and so on, regimes can only be changed by military intervention from without or by some kind of revolutionary upheaval from within.

Why classify political systems?

The interest in classifying political systems stems from two sources. First, classification is an essential aid to the *understanding* of politics and government. As in most social sciences, understanding in politics is largely acquired through a process of comparison, particularly as experimental methods are generally inapplicable. It is not possible, for instance, to devise experiments to test whether, say, US government would be less susceptible to institutional **government gridlock** if it abandoned the separation of powers (see p. 297), or whether communism could have survived in the USSR had reforms been instigated a generation earlier. In consequence, we look to comparison to throw into relief what we are studying. Through the highlighting of similarities and differences between what might otherwise be bewildering collections of facts, comparison helps us to distinguish between what is significant and meaningful, and what is not. In this process, we are able both to develop theories, hypotheses and concepts, and, to some extent, to test them. As Alexis de Tocqueville (see p. 201) put it, 'without comparisons to make, the mind does not know how to proceed'. The attempt to classify systems of rule is therefore merely a device for making the process of comparison more methodical and systematic.

The second purpose of classification is to facilitate *evaluation* rather than analysis. Since Aristotle (see p. 7), those who have sought to understand political regimes have often been as keen to 'improve' government as to understand it. In other words, descriptive understanding is closely tied up with normative judgements: questions about what *is* are linked to questions about what *should* be. In its extreme form, this process may involve a search for an 'ideal' system of rule, or even a utopia, and this can be seen in works such as Plato's (see p. 13) *Republic*, Thomas More's *Utopia* ([1516] 1965), and Peter Kropotkin's *Fields, Factories and Workshops* (1912). In a more modest form, this type of classification allows for qualitative judgements to be made in relation to political structures and governmental forms. Only a comparative approach, for instance, enables us to consider questions such as 'should the transition to liberal democracy in Russia and other former communist states be welcomed and encouraged?', 'should India abandon federalism in favour of either a unitary system or regional independence?', and 'should the UK adopt a "written" constitution and a bill of rights?'.

All systems of classification have their drawbacks, however. In the first place, as with all analytical devices, there is a danger of simplification. The classification of regimes under the same heading draws attention to the similarities that they share, but there is a risk that the differences that divide them will be ignored or disguised. A related problem is a possible failure to see that a phenomenon may have different meanings in different contexts. For instance, in Japan and throughout East Asia, 'the state' may be different in kind and significance from 'the state' as generally understood in the context of the West. Comparative analysis is therefore hampered by the constant danger of **ethnocentrism**. Secondly, value biases tend to intrude into the classification process. This can be seen in the tendency to classify communist and fascist regimes as 'totalitarian', implying that western liberal democracies were fighting the *same* enemy in the Cold War as they had done in the Second World War. Finally, all systems of classifications have the drawback that they are necessarily state-bound: they treat individual countries as coherent or independent entities in their own right. Although this approach is by no means invalid, it is now widely viewed as incomplete in the light of the phenomenon of globalisation (see p. 140).

Classical typologies

Without doubt, the most influential system of classification was that devised by Aristotle in the fourth century BCE, which was based on his analysis of the 158 Greek city states then in existence. This system dominated thinking on the subject for roughly the next 2500 years. Aristotle held that governments could be categorised on the basis of two questions: 'who rules?', and 'who benefits from rule?'. Government, he believed, could be placed in the hands of a single individual, a small group, or the many. In each case, however, government could be conducted either in the selfish interests of the rulers or for the benefit of the entire community. He thus identified the six forms of government shown in Figure 2.1.

Aristotle's purpose was to evaluate forms of government on normative grounds in the hope of identifying the 'ideal' constitution. In his view, tyranny, oligarchy and democracy were all debased or perverted forms of rule in which a single person, a

> ### Concept
>
> ## Utopia, utopianism
>
> A utopia (from the Greek *outopia*, meaning 'nowhere', or the Greek *eutopia*, meaning 'good place') is literally an ideal or perfect society. Although utopias of various kinds can be envisaged, most are characterised by the abolition of want, the absence of conflict, and the avoidance of violence and oppression. Utopianism is a style of political theorising that develops a critique of the existing order by constructing a model of an ideal or perfect alternative. Good examples are anarchism and Marxism. Utopian theories are usually based on assumptions about the unlimited possibilities of human self-development. Utopianism is often used as a pejorative term to imply deluded or fanciful thinking, and a belief in an unrealistic and unachievable goal.

> **Ethnocentrism:** The application of values and theories drawn from one's own culture to other groups and peoples; ethnocentrism implies bias or distortion (see p. 385).

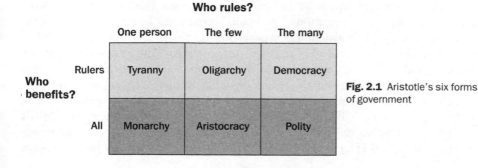

Who rules?

	One person	The few	The many
Rulers	Tyranny	Oligarchy	Democracy
All	Monarchy	Aristocracy	Polity

Who benefits?

Fig. 2.1 Aristotle's six forms of government

Concept

Absolutism

Absolutism is the theory or practice of absolute government, most commonly associated with an absolute monarchy (see p. 324). Government is 'absolute' in the sense that it possesses unfettered power: government cannot be constrained by a body external to itself. The absolutist principle nevertheless resides in the *claim* to an unlimited right to rule (as in Divine Right), rather than in the *exercise* of unchallengeable power. Rationalist theories of absolute power generally advance the belief that only absolute government can guarantee order and social stability. Absolutism should, however, be distinguished from autocracy and dictatorship (see p. 363). As it is based on a principled claim, whether religious or rational, it does not invest government with arbitrary and unlimited power.

small group and the masses, respectively, governed in their own interests and therefore at the expense of others. In contrast, monarchy, aristocracy and polity were to be preferred, because in these forms of government the individual, small group and the masses, respectively, governed in the interests of all. Aristotle declared tyranny to be the worst of all possible constitutions, as it reduced citizens to the status of slaves. Monarchy and aristocracy were, on the other hand, impractical, because they were based on a God-like willingness to place the good of the community before the rulers' own interests. Polity (rule by the many in the interests of all) was accepted as the most practicable of constitutions. Nevertheless, in a tradition that endured through to the twentieth century, Aristotle criticised popular rule on the grounds that the masses would resent the wealth of the few, and too easily fall under the sway of a **demagogue**. He therefore advocated a 'mixed' constitution that combined elements of both democracy and aristocracy, and left the government in the hands of the 'middle classes', those who were neither rich nor poor.

The Aristotelian system was later developed by thinkers such as Thomas Hobbes (see p. 285) and Jean Bodin (1530–96). Their particular concern was with the principle of sovereignty (see p. 143), viewed as the basis for all stable political regimes. Sovereignty was taken to mean the 'most high and perpetual' power, a power which alone could guarantee orderly rule. Bodin's *The Six Books of the Commonweal* ([1576] 1962) offered a wider-ranging account of the locus of sovereignty in political regimes, both contemporary and classical. He concluded that absolutism was the most defensible of regimes, as it established a sovereign who makes law but is not bound by those laws. The overriding merit of vesting sovereignty in a single individual was that it would then be indivisible: sovereignty would be expressed in a single voice that could claim final authority. Bodin nevertheless argued that absolute monarchs were constrained by the existence of higher law in the form of the will of God or natural law. On the other hand, in *Leviathan* ([1651] 1968), Hobbes portrayed sovereignty as a monopoly of coercive power, implying that the sovereign was entirely unconstrained.

These ideas were later revised by early liberals such as John Locke (see p. 43) and Montesquieu (see p. 294), who championed the cause of constitutional government. Locke, in *Two Treatises of Government* ([1690] 1965), argued that sovereignty resided with the people, not the monarch, and he advocated a system of limited government to provide protection for natural rights, notably the rights to life, liberty and property. In his epic *The Spirit of the Laws* ([1734] 1949), Montesquieu attempted to develop a 'scientific' study of human society, designed to uncover the constitutional circumstances that would best protect individual liberty. A severe critic of absolutism and an admirer of the English parliamentary tradition, he proposed a system of checks and balances in the form of a 'separation of powers' between the executive, legislative and judicial institutions. This principle was incorporated into the US constitution (1787), and it later came to be seen as one of the defining features of liberal democratic government.

The 'classical' classification of regimes, stemming from the writings of Aristotle, was rendered increasingly redundant by the development of modern constitutional systems from the late eighteenth century onwards. In their different ways, the constitutional **republicanism** established in the USA following the American War of Independence of 1775–83, the democratic radicalism unleashed in France by the 1789 French Revolution, and the form of parliamentary government that gradually emerged in the UK created political realities that were substantially more complex

Demagogue: A political leader whose control over the masses is based on the ability to whip up hysterical enthusiasm.

Republicanism: The principle that political authority stems ultimately from the consent of the people; the rejection of monarchical and dynastic principles.

than early thinkers had envisaged. Traditional systems of classification were therefore displaced by a growing emphasis on the constitutional and institutional features of political rule. In many ways, this built on Montesquieu's work in that particular attention was paid to the relationships between the various branches of government. Thus monarchies were distinguished from republics, parliamentary systems (see p. 295) were distinguished from presidential ones (see p. 320), and unitary systems were distinguished from federal ones (see p. 125).

The 'three worlds' typology

During the twentieth century, historical developments once again altered the basis of political classification. The appearance in the interwar period of new forms of authoritarianism (see p. 36), particularly in Stalinist Russia, Fascist Italy and Nazi Germany, encouraged the view that the world was divided into two kinds of regime: democratic states and totalitarian states. The stark contrast between democracy and totalitarianism dominated attempts at regime classification through much of the 1950s and 1960s, despite the fact that the fascist and Nazi regimes had collapsed at the end of the Second World War. Nevertheless, there was a growing awareness that this approach was shaped by the antagonisms of the Cold War, and that it could perhaps be seen as a species of Cold War ideology, and this stimulated the search for a more value-neutral and ideologically impartial system of classification. This led to the growing popularity of the so-called 'three worlds' approach: the belief that the political world could be divided into three distinct blocs:

- a capitalist 'first world'
- a communist 'second world'
- a developing 'third world'.

The three-worlds classification had economic, ideological, political and strategic dimensions. Industrialised western regimes were 'first' in economic terms, in that their populations enjoyed the highest levels of mass affluence. In 1983, these countries generated 63 per cent of the world's **gross domestic product** (GDP) while having only 15 per cent of the world's population (World Bank, 1985). Communist regimes were 'second', insofar as they were largely industrialised and capable of satisfying the population's basic material needs. These countries produced 19 per cent of the world's GDP with 33 per cent of the world's population. The less developed countries of Africa, Asia and Latin America were 'third' in the sense that they were economically dependent and often suffered from widespread poverty. They produced 18 per cent of the world's GDP with 52 per cent of the world's population.

The first and second worlds were further divided by fierce ideological rivalry. The first world was wedded to 'capitalist' principles, such as the desirability of private enterprise, material incentives, and the free market; the second world was committed to 'communist' values such as social equality, collective endeavour, and the need for centralised planning. Such ideological differences had clear political manifestations. First-world regimes practised liberal-democratic politics based on a competitive struggle for power at election time. Second-world regimes were one-party states, dominated by 'ruling' communist parties. Third-world regimes were typically authoritarian, and governed by traditional monarchs, dictators or simply the army. The three-worlds classification was underpinned by a bipolar world order, in which a

---

Concept

Totalitarianism

Totalitarianism is an all-encompassing system of political rule that is typically established by pervasive ideological manipulation and open terror and brutality. Totalitarianism differs from both autocracy and authoritarianism in that it seeks 'total power' through the politicisation of every aspect of social and personal existence. Autocratic and authoritarian regimes have the more modest goal of a monopoly of political power, usually achieved by excluding the masses from politics. Totalitarianism thus implies the outright abolition of **civil society**: the abolition of 'the private'. Totalitarian regimes are sometimes identified through a 'six-point syndrome' (Friedrich and Brzezinski, 1963):

- an official ideology
- a one-party state, usually led by an all-powerful leader
- a system of terroristic policing
- a monopoly of the means of mass communication
- a monopoly of the means of armed combat
- state control of all aspects of economic life.

Civil society: The realm of autonomous groups and associations; a private sphere independent from public authority (see p. 8).

Gross domestic product: The total financial value of final goods and services produced in an economy over one year.

Concept

Liberal democracy

Liberal democracy is a form of democratic rule that balances the principle of limited government against the ideal of popular consent. Its 'liberal' features are reflected in a network of internal and external checks on government that are designed to guarantee liberty and afford citizens protection against the state. Its 'democratic' character is based on a system of regular and competitive elections, conducted on the basis of universal suffrage and political equality (see p. 67). Although it may be used to describe a political principle, the term 'liberal democracy' is more commonly used to describe a particular type of regime. The defining features of this type of regime are as follows:

- constitutional government based on formal, usually legal, rules
- guarantees of civil liberties and individual rights
- institutionalised fragmentation and a system of checks and balances
- regular elections that respect the principle of 'one person, one vote; one vote, one value'
- party competition and political pluralism
- the independence of organised groups and interests from government
- a private-enterprise economy organised along market lines.

USA-dominated West confronted a USSR-dominated East. This order was sustained by the emergence of two rival military camps in the form of NATO and the Warsaw Pact. Not infrequently, the 'nonaligned' third world was the battleground upon which this geopolitical struggle was conducted, a fact that did much to ensure its continued political and economic subordination.

Since the 1970s, however, this system of classification has been increasingly difficult to sustain. New patterns of economic development have brought material affluence to parts of the third world, notably the oil-rich states of the Middle East and the newly industrialised states of East Asia, South East Asia, and, to some extent, Latin America. In contrast, poverty has, if anything, become more deeply entrenched in parts of sub-Saharan Africa, which now constitutes a kind of 'fourth world'. Moreover, the advance of **democratisation** in Asia, Latin America and Africa, especially during the 1980s, has meant that third-world regimes are no longer uniformly authoritarian. Indeed, the phrase 'third world' is widely resented as being demeaning, because it implies entrenched disadvantage. The term 'developing world' is usually seen as preferable.

Without doubt, however, the most catastrophic single blow to the three-worlds model resulted from the eastern European revolutions of 1989–91. These led to the collapse of orthodox communist regimes in the USSR and elsewhere, and unleashed a process of political liberalisation and market reform. Indeed, Francis Fukuyama went as far as to proclaim that this development amounted to the 'end of history' (Fukuyama, 1989). He meant by this that ideological debate had effectively ended with the worldwide triumph of western liberal democracy. Quite simply, second-world and third-world regimes were collapsing as a result of the recognition that only the capitalist first world offered the prospect of economic prosperity and political stability.

■ Regimes of the modern world

Since the late 1980s, the regime-classification industry has been in a limbo. Older categories, particularly the 'three worlds' division, were certainly redundant, but the political contours of the new world were far from clear. Moreover, the 'end of history' scenario was only fleetingly attractive, having been sustained by the wave of democratisation in the late 1980s and early 1990s, and drawing impetus in particular from the collapse of communism. In some senses, this liberal-democratic triumphalism reflected the persistence of a western-centric viewpoint, and it may, anyway, have been a hangover from the days of the Cold War. The image of a 'world of liberal democracies' suggested the superiority of a specifically western model of development, based perhaps especially on the USA, and it implied that values such as individualism, rights and choice are universally applicable. One result of this was a

Democratisation: The advance of liberal-democratic reform, implying, in particular, the granting of basic freedoms and the widening of popular participation and electoral choice.

Francis Fukuyama (born 1952)

US social analyst and political commentator. Fukuyama was born in Chicago, USA, the son of a Protestant preacher. He was a member of the Policy Planning Staff of the US State Department before becoming a consultant for the Rand Corporation. A staunch Republican, he came to international prominence as a result of his article 'The End of History?' (1989), which he later developed into *The*

End of History and the Last Man (1992). These claimed that the history of ideas had ended with the recognition of liberal democracy as 'the final form of human government'. In *Trust* (1996), Fukuyama argued that the economic performances of different types of capitalism are closely linked to divergence in cultural resources or 'social capital'. His ideas have had considerable impact on the New Right.

failure to recognise the significance, for instance, of Islamic and Confucian political forms, which tended to be dismissed as mere aberrations, or simply as evidence of resistance to the otherwise unchallenged advance of liberal democracy.

However, one of the difficulties of establishing a new system of classification is that there is no consensus about the criteria upon which such a system should be based. No system of classification relies on a single all-important factor. Nevertheless, particular systems have tended to prioritise different sets of criteria. Among the parameters most commonly used are the following:

- Who rules?: Is political participation confined to an elite body or privileged group, or does it encompass the entire population?
- How is compliance achieved?: Is government obeyed as a result of the exercise or threat of force, or through bargaining and compromise?
- Is government power centralised or fragmented?: What kinds of check and balance operate in the political system?
- How is government power acquired and transferred?: Is a regime open and competitive, or is it monolithic?
- What is the balance between the state and the individual?: What is the distribution of rights and responsibilities between government and citizens?
- What is the level of material development?: How materially affluent is the society, and how equally is wealth distributed?
- How is economic life organised?: Is the economy geared to the market or to planning, and what economic role does government play?
- How stable is a regime?: Has the regime survived over time, and does it have the capacity to respond to new demands and challenges?

A *constitutional–institutional* approach to classification that was influenced by 'classical' typologies was adopted in the nineteenth and early twentieth centuries. This approach highlighted, for instance, differences between codified and uncodified constitutions, parliamentary and presidential systems, and federal and unitary systems. A *structural–functional* approach, however, was developed out of systems theory, which became increasingly prominent in the 1950s and 1960s. This approach was concerned less with institutional arrangements than with how political systems work in practice, and especially with how they translate 'inputs' into 'outputs'. The 'three worlds' approach was *economic–ideological* in orientation, as it paid special

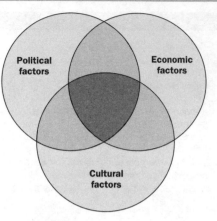

Fig. 2.2 Key regime features

attention to a systems level of material development and its broader ideological orientation. The approach adopted here, however, is in some ways different from each of these three. It attempts to take account of three key features of a regime: its political, economic and cultural aspects. The assumption in this approach is that regimes are characterised not so much by particular political, economic or cultural factors as by the way in which these interlock in practice (see Figure 2.2).

The significance of this approach is that it emphasises the degree to which formal political and economic arrangements may operate differently depending on their cultural context. For instance, multiparty elections and a market economy may have very different implications in western liberal societies than they do in non-western ones. Nevertheless, in view of the profound political upheavals of the late twentieth century, it would be foolish to suggest that any system of classification can be anything but provisional. Indeed, regimes are themselves fluid, and the regime-classification industry is constantly struggling to keep up to date with an ever-changing political reality. Nevertheless, five regime types can be identified in the modern world:

- western polyarchies
- postcommunist regimes
- East Asian regimes
- Islamic regimes
- military regimes.

Western polyarchies

Western polyarchies are broadly equivalent to regimes categorised as 'liberal democracies' or even simply 'democracies'. Their heartlands are therefore North America, western Europe and Australasia, although states ranging from India and Japan to the 'new' South Africa all exhibit strongly polyarchical features. Although polyarchies have in large part evolved through moves towards democratisation and **liberalisation**, the term 'polyarchy' is preferable to 'liberal democracy' for two reasons. First, liberal democracy is sometimes treated as a political ideal, and is thus invested with broader normative implications. Secondly, the use of 'polyarchy' acknowledges that these regimes fall short, in important ways, of the goal of democracy.

The term 'polyarchy' was first used to describe a system of rule by Dahl (p. 256) and Lindblom in *Politics, Economics, and Welfare* (1953), and it was later elaborated

Liberalisation: The introduction of internal and external checks on government power and/or shifts towards private enterprise and the market.

in Dahl's *Polyarchy: Participation and Opposition* (1971). In the view of these authors, polyarchical regimes are distinguished by the combination of two general features. In the first place, there is a relatively high tolerance of opposition that is sufficient at least to check the arbitrary inclinations of government. This is guaranteed in practice by a competitive party system, by institutionally guaranteed and protected civil liberties, and by a vigorous and healthy civil society. The second feature of polyarchy is that the opportunities for participating in politics should be sufficiently widespread to guarantee a reliable level of popular responsiveness. The crucial factor here is the existence of regular and competitive elections operating as a device through which the people can control and, if necessary, displace their rulers. In this sense, there is a close resemblance between polyarchy and the form of democratic elitism described by Joseph Schumpeter (see p. 211) in *Capitalism, Socialism and Democracy* (1942). Both Lindblom (1977) and Dahl (1985) have nevertheless acknowledged the impact on polyarchies of the disproportional power of major corporations. For this reason, they have sometimes preferred the notion of 'deformed polyarchy'.

Thus defined, the term 'polyarchy' may be used to describe a large and growing number of regimes throughout the world. All states that hold multiparty elections have polyarchical features. Nevertheless, western polyarchies have a more distinctive and particular character. They are marked not only by representative democracy and a capitalist economic organisation, but also by a cultural and ideological orientation that is largely derived from western liberalism. The most crucial aspect of this inheritance is the widespread acceptance of liberal individualism. Individualism (see p. 178), often seen as the most distinctive of western values, stresses the uniqueness of each human individual, and suggests that society should be organised so as to best meet the needs and interests of the individuals who compose it. The political culture of western polyarchies is influenced by liberal individualism in a variety of ways. It generates, for example, a heightened sensitivity to individual rights (perhaps placed above duties), the general perception that choice and competition (in both political and economic life) are healthy, and a tendency to fear government and regard the state as at least a potential threat to liberty.

Western polyarchies are not all alike, however. Some of them are biased in favour of centralisation and majority rule, and others tend towards fragmentation and pluralism. Lijphart (1984, 1990) highlighted this fact in distinguishing between 'majority' democracies and 'consensus' democracies. Majority democracies are organised along parliamentary lines according to the so-called **Westminster model**. The clearest example of this is the UK system, but the model has also, in certain respects, been adopted by New Zealand, Australia, Canada, Israel and India. Majoritarian tendencies are associated with any, or all, of the following features:

- single-party government
- a lack of separation of powers between the executive and the assembly
- an assembly that is either unicameral or weakly bicameral
- a two-party system
- a simple plurality or first-past-the-post electoral system (see p. 215)
- unitary and centralised government
- an uncodified constitution and a sovereign assembly.

Polyarchy

Polyarchy (literally 'rule by many') refers generally to the institutions and political processes of modern representative democracy. As a regime type, a polyarchy can be distinguished from all nondemocratic systems and from small-scale democratic ones based on the classical or Athenian model of direct participation. Polyarchy can be understood as a rough or crude approximation of democracy, in that it operates through institutions which force rulers to take account of the interests and wishes of the electorate. Its central features are as follows (Dahl, 1989:211):

- Government is in the hands of elected officials.
- Elections are free and fair.
- Practically all adults have the right to vote.
- The right to run for office is unrestricted.
- There is free expression and a right to criticise and protest.
- Citizens have access to alternative sources of information.
- Groups and associations enjoy at least relative independence from government.

Westminster model: A system of government in which the executive is drawn from, and (in theory) accountable to, the assembly or parliament.

In contrast, other western polyarchies are characterised by a diffusion of power throughout the governmental and party systems. The US model of pluralist democracy is very largely based on institutional fragmentation enshrined in the provisions of the constitution itself. Elsewhere, particularly in continental Europe, consensus is underpinned by the party system and a tendency towards bargaining and power sharing. In states such as the Netherlands, Belgium, Austria and Switzerland, a system of **consociational democracy** has developed that is particularly appropriate to societies that are divided by deep religious, ideological, regional, cultural or other differences. Consensual or pluralistic tendencies are often associated with the following features:

- coalition government (see p. 246)
- a separation of powers between the executive and the assembly
- an effective bicameral system
- a multiparty system
- proportional representation (see p. 220)
- federalism or devolution
- a codified constitution and a bill of rights.

On another level, of course, each polyarchical regime, and, indeed, every regime, is unique, and therefore exceptional. US **exceptionalism**, for instance, is often linked to the absence of a feudal past and the experience of settlement and frontier expansion. This may explain the USA's deeply individualist political culture, which, uniquely amongst western polyarchies, does not accommodate a socialist party or movement of any note. The USA is also the most overtly religious of western regimes, and it is the only one, for instance, in which Christian fundamentalism has developed into a major political force.

India is a still more difficult case. It is certainly not part of the West in cultural, philosophical or religious terms. In contrast to the 'developed' polyarchies of Europe and North America, it also has a largely rural population and a literacy rate of barely 50 per cent. Nevertheless, India has functioned as an effective polyarchy since it became independent in 1947, even surviving Indira Gandhi's 'state of emergency' in the late 1970s. Political stability in India was undoubtedly promoted by the crosscaste appeal of the Congress Party and the mystique of the Nehru–Gandhi dynasty. However, the decline of the former and the end of the latter has perhaps transformed the India of the 1990s into something approaching a consociational democracy.

Postcommunist regimes

The collapse of communism in the eastern European revolutions of 1989–91 undoubtedly unleashed a process of democratisation that drew heavily on the western liberal model. The central features of this process were the adoption of multiparty elections and the introduction of market-based economic reforms. In that sense, it can be argued that most (some would say all) former communist regimes are undergoing a transition that will eventually make them indistinguishable from western polyarchies. Nevertheless, for the time being at least, there are reasons for treating these systems as distinct. In the first place, the heritage of their communist past cannot be discarded overnight, especially when, as in Russia, the communist system had endured for over 70 years. Secondly, the process of transition itself has unleashed forces and generated problems quite different from those that confront western polyarchies.

One feature of postcommunist regimes is the need to deal with the politico-cultural consequences of communist rule, especially the ramifications of Stalinist totalitarianism. The ruthless censorship and suppression of opposition that underpinned the communist parties' monopoly of power guaranteed that a civic culture emphasising participation, bargaining and consensus failed to develop. In Russia this has produced a weak and fragmented party system that is apparently incapable of articulating or aggregating the major interests of Russian society. As a result, communist parties or former communist parties have often continued to provide a point of stability. In Romania and Bulgaria, for example, the institutions of the communist past have survived into the postcommunist era, while in states such as Hungary, Poland and Russia, communist parties, now embracing, if with differing degrees of conviction, the principles of social democracy, have made an electoral comeback.

> ### Concept
>
> ## Communism
>
> Communism, in its simplest sense, is the communal organisation of social existence on the basis of the collective ownership of property. As a theoretical ideal, it is most commonly associated with the writings of Marx, for whom communism meant a classless society in which wealth was owned in common, production was geared to human need, and the state had 'withered away', allowing for spontaneous harmony and self-realisation. The term is also used to describe societies founded on Marxist principles crucially adapted by Leninism and Stalinism. The key features of 'orthodox' communism as a regime type are as follows:
>
> - Marxism–Leninism is the 'official' ideology.
> - A communist party that is organised on the principles of 'democratic centralism' enjoys a monopoly of political power.
> - The communist party 'rules' in the sense that it dominates the state machine, creating a fused state–party apparatus.
> - The communist party plays a 'leading and guiding role' in society, controlling all institutions, including the economic, educational, cultural and recreational institutions.
> - Economic life is based on state collectivisation, and it is organised through a central planning system (see p. 174).

A second set of problems stem from the process of economic transition. The 'shock therapy' transition from central planning to *laissez-faire* capitalism, advocated by the International Monetary Fund, unleashed deep insecurity because of the growth of unemployment and inflation, and it significantly increased social inequality. Since the heady days of the early 1990s, the pace of economic liberalisation has sometimes been greatly reduced as a consequence of a backlash against market reforms, often expressed in growing support for communist or nationalist parties. A final set of problems result from the weakness of state power, particularly when the state is confronted by centrifugal forces effectively suppressed during the communist era. This has been most clearly demonstrated by the reemergence of ethnic and nationalist tensions. The collapse of communism in the USSR was accompanied by the breakup of the old Soviet empire and the construction of 15 new independent states, several of which (including Russia) continue to be afflicted by ethnic conflict. Czechoslovakia ceased to exist in 1992 with the creation of the Czech Republic and Slovakia. Ethnic conflict has been most dramatic in Yugoslavia, where it precipitated full-scale war between Serbia and Croatia in 1991, and led to civil war in Bosnia in 1992–96.

Important differences between postcommunist states can also be identified. The most crucial of these is that between the more industrially advanced and westernised countries of 'central' Europe, such as the Czech Republic, Hungary and Poland, and the more backward, 'eastern' states such as Romania, Bulgaria and, in certain respects, Russia. In the former group, market reform has proceeded swiftly and relatively smoothly; in the latter, it has either been grudging and incomplete or it has given rise to deep political tensions. A further distinction is between the states upon which communism was 'imposed' by the Soviet Red Army at the end of the Second World War and those that were once part of the USSR. With the exception of the

Concept

Confucianism

Confucianism is a system of ethics formulated by Confucius (551–479 BCE) and his disciples that was primarily outlined in *The Analects*. Confucian thought has concerned itself with the twin themes of human relations and the cultivation of the self. The emphasis on *ren* (humanity or love) has usually been interpreted as implying support for traditional ideas and values, notably filial piety, respect, loyalty and benevolence. The stress on *junzi* (the virtuous person) suggests a capacity for human development and potential for perfection realised in particular through education. Confucianism has been seen, with Taoism and Buddhism, as one of the three major Chinese systems of thought, although many take Confucian ideas to be coextensive with Chinese civilisation itself.

Baltic states (Estonia, Latvia and Lithuania), the former Soviet republics are marked both by their longer history of communist rule, and by the fact that they were part of the Russian empire in Tsarist times as well as the Soviet period. There is, of course, a strong argument as well for Russian exceptionalism. This may be based on Russia's imperial past and the tendency for Russian nationalism to have an authoritarian and expansionist character, or on the fact that, since the time of Peter the Great, Russia has been divided by competing western and Slavic identities, and so is unclear about both its cultural inheritance and its political destiny.

East Asian regimes

The rise of East Asia in the late twentieth century may ultimately prove to be a more important world-historical event than the collapse of communism. Certainly, the balance of the world's economy has shifted markedly from the West to the East in this period. In the final two decades of the twentieth century, economic growth rates on the western rim of the Pacific Basin have been between two and four times higher than those in the 'developed' economies of Europe and North America. However, the notion that there is a distinctively East Asian political form is a less familiar one. The widespread assumption has been that modernisation means westernisation. Translated into political terms, this means that industrial capitalism is always accompanied by liberal democracy. Those who advance this position cite, for example, the success of Japan's 1946 constitution, bequeathed by the departing USA, and the introduction of multiparty elections in countries such as Thailand, South Korea and Taiwan in the 1980s and 1990s. However, this interpretation fails to take account of the degree to which polyarchical institutions operate differently in an Asian context from the way they do in a western one. Most importantly, it ignores the difference between cultures influenced by Confucian ideas and values and ones shaped by liberal individualism.

East Asian regimes tend to have similar characteristics. First, they are orientated more around economic goals than political ones. Their overriding priority is to boost growth and deliver prosperity, rather than to enlarge individual freedom in the western sense of civil liberty. This essentially practical concern is evident in the 'tiger' economies of East and South East Asia (those of South Korea, Taiwan, Hong Kong, Singapore and Malaysia), but it has also been demonstrated in the construction of a thriving market economy in China since the late 1970s, despite the survival there of monopolistic communist rule. Secondly, there is broad support for 'strong' government. Powerful 'ruling' parties tend to be tolerated, and there is general respect for the state. Although, with low taxes and relatively low public spending (usually below 30 per cent of GDP), there is little room for the western model of the welfare state, there is nevertheless general acceptance that the state as a 'father figure' should guide the decisions of private as well as public bodies, and draw up strategies for national development. This characteristic is accompanied, thirdly, by a general disposition to respect leaders because of the Confucian stress on loyalty, discipline and duty. From a western viewpoint, this invests East Asian regimes with an implicit, and sometimes explicit, authoritarianism. Finally, great emphasis is placed on community and social cohesion, embodied in the central role accorded to the family. The resulting emphasis on what the Japanese call 'group think' tends to restrict the scope for the assimilation of ideas such as individualism and human rights, at least as these are understood in the West.

There is also differentiation between East Asian regimes. In part, this stems from cultural differences between overwhelmingly Chinese states such as Taiwan, Hong Kong and China, and Japan and ethnically mixed states such as Singapore and Malaysia. For example, plans to introduce Confucian principles in Singapore schools were dropped for fear of offending the Malay and Indian populations. Similarly, Malaysian development has been based on a deliberate attempt to reduce Chinese influence and emphasise the distinctively Islamic character of Malay culture. An additional factor is that, although China's acceptance of capitalism has blurred the distinction between it and other East Asian regimes, this has certainly not eradicated the differentiation altogether. This is demonstrated, for instance, by the stark contrast between the 'market Stalinism' that prevails in China and the entrenched and successful electoral democracy of Japan. Moreover, whereas other East Asian regimes are now industrialised and increasingly urbanised, China is still predominantly agricultural. To some extent, this also explains different modes of economic development. In Japan and 'tiger' economies such as Taiwan and Singapore, growth is now largely based on technological innovation and an emphasis on education and training, whereas China continues, in certain respects, to rely on her massive rural population to provide cheap and plentiful labour.

Islamic regimes

The rise of Islam as a political force has had a profound affect on politics in North Africa, the Middle East, and parts of Asia. In some cases, militant Islamic groups have challenged existing regimes, often articulating the interests of an urban poor since the 1970s disillusionment with Marxism–Leninism. In other cases, however, regimes have been constructed or reconstructed on Islamic lines. Since its inception in 1932, Saudi Arabia has been an Islamic state. The Iranian revolution of 1979 led to the establishment of an Islamic republic under Ayatollah Khomeini (1900–89), an example later followed in the Sudan and Pakistan. In countries such as Gaddafi's Libya, more idiosyncratic and disputed interpretations of Islam have been translated into political practice.

Islam is not, however, and never has been, simply a religion. Rather, it is a complete way of life, defining correct moral, political and economic behaviour for individuals and nations alike. The 'way of Islam' is based on the teachings of the Prophet Muhammad (570–632) as revealed in the Koran, regarded by all Moslems as the revealed word of God, and the Sunna, or 'beaten path', the traditional customs observed by a devout Moslem that are said to be based on the Prophet's own life. Political Islam thus aims at the construction of a theocracy in which political and other affairs are structured according to 'higher' religious principles. Nevertheless, political Islam has assumed clearly contrasting forms, ranging from fundamentalist to pluralist extremes.

The fundamentalist version of Islam is most commonly associated with Iran. Until his death in 1989, Khomeini presided over a system of institutionalised clerical rule, operating through the Islamic Revolutionary Council, a body of 15 senior clerics. Although a popularly elected parliament has been established in the form of the Islamic Consultative Assembly, all legislation is ratified by the Council for the Protection of the Constitution, which ensures conformity to Islamic principles. Although a more pragmatic and less ideological approach has been adopted in the 1990s under Hashemi Rafsanjani, **Shari'a** law continues to be strictly enforced throughout Iran as both a legal and a moral code. Fundamentalism (see p. 61) is no

(see p. 61)

Concept

Theocracy

Theocracy (literally 'rule by God') is the principle that religious authority should prevail over political authority. A theocracy is therefore a regime in which government posts are filled on the basis of the person's position in the religious hierarchy. This contrasts with a secular state, in which political and religious positions are kept strictly separate. Theocratic rule is illiberal in two senses. First, it violates the distinction between private and public realms, in that it takes religious rules and precepts to be the guiding principles of both personal life and political conduct. Secondly, it invests political authority with potentially unlimited power, because, as temporal power is derived from spiritual wisdom in this type of regime, it cannot be based on popular consent or be properly constrained within a constitutional framework.

Shari'a: Islamic law, believed to be based on divine revelation, and derived from the Koran, the Hadith (the teachings of Muhammad), and other sources.

Concept

Authoritarianism

Authoritarianism is a belief in, or practice of, government 'from above', in which authority is exercised regardless of popular consent. Authoritarianism thus differs from authority. The latter rests on legitimacy (see p. 193), and in that sense it arises 'from below'. Authoritarian regimes therefore emphasise the claims of authority over those of individual liberty. However, authoritarianism is usually distinguished from totalitarianism. The practice of government 'from above' associated with monarchical absolutism, traditional dictatorships, and most forms of military rule is concerned with the repression of opposition and political liberty, rather than with the more radical goal of obliterating the distinction between the state and civil society. Authoritarian regimes may thus tolerate a significant range of economic, religious and other freedoms.

Junta: Literally, a council; a (usually military) clique that seizes power through a revolution or *coup d'état*.

less significant in Saudi Arabia, where it has similarly absolutist implications, although the temper of the essentially conservative Sunni regime in Saudi Arabia differs markedly from the revolutionary populism (see p. 335) of Shi'ite Iran.

Moslems themselves, however, have often objected to the classification of any Islamic regime as 'fundamentalist', on the grounds that this perpetuates long-established western prejudices against an 'exotic' or 'repressive' East. Evidence that Islam is compatible with a form of political pluralism can be found in Malaysia. Although Islam is the official state religion of Malaysia, with the Paramount Ruler serving as both religious leader and head of state, a form of 'guided' democracy operates through the dominance of the United Malays National Organisation (UMNO), headed by Prime Minister Dr Mahathir, within a multiparty framework. Mahathir's government has, since 1981, pursued a narrowly Islamic and pro-Malay strategy fused with an explicitly Japanese model of economic development. Authoritarian tendencies have nevertheless reemerged since 1988, when the independence of the judiciary effectively collapsed following a wave of political arrests and the imposition of press censorship.

Military regimes

Whereas most regimes are shaped by a combination of political, economic, cultural and ideological factors, some survive through the exercise, above all, of military power and systematic repression. In this sense, military regimes belong to a broader category of authoritarianism. Military authoritarianism has been most common in Latin America, the Middle East, Africa and South East Asia, but it also emerged in the postwar period in Spain, Portugal and Greece. The key feature of a military regime is that the leading posts in the government are filled on the basis of the person's position within the military chain of command. Normal political and constitutional arrangements are usually suspended, and institutions through which opposition can be expressed, such as elected assemblies and a free press, are either weakened or abolished.

Although all forms of military rule are deeply repressive, this classification encompasses a number of regime types. In some military regimes, the armed forces assume direct control of government. The classical form of this is the military **junta**, most commonly found in Latin America. This operates as a form of collective military government centred on a command council of officers who usually represent the three armed services: the army, navy and air force. Junta regimes are often characterised by rivalry between the services and between leading figures, the consequence being that formal positions of power tend to change hands relatively frequently.

The second form of military regime is a military-backed personalised dictatorship (see p. 363). In these cases, a single individual gains preeminence within the junta or regime, often being bolstered by a cult of personality (see p. 333) designed to manufacture charismatic authority. Examples are Colonel Papadopoulos in Greece in 1974–80, General Pinochet in Chile after the 1973 military coup, and General Abacha in Nigeria, since 1993. In the final form of military regime, the loyalty of the armed forces is the decisive factor that upholds the regime, but the military leaders content themselves with 'pulling the strings' behind the scenes. This, for example, occurred in postwar Brazil, as the armed forces generally recognised that the legitimacy of the regime would be strengthened by the maintenance of a distinction between political and military offices and personnel. Such a distinction, however, may fuel an appetite for constitutional and representative politics, and reduce the scope for direct military intervention, thereby, over time, encouraging polyarchical tendencies. The character of military regimes is discussed at greater length in Chapter 18.

Summary

◆ Government is any mechanism through which ordered rule is maintained, its central feature being its ability to make collective decisions and enforce them. A political system, or regime, however, encompasses not only the mechanisms of government and institutions of the state, but also the structures and processes through which these interact with the larger society.

◆ The classification of political systems serves two purposes. First, it aids understanding by making comparison possible and helping to highlight similarities and differences between otherwise shapeless collections of facts. Secondly, it helps us to evaluate the effectiveness or success of different political systems.

◆ Regimes have been classified on a variety of bases. 'Classical' typologies, stemming from Aristotle, concentrated on constitutional arrangements and institutional structures, while the 'three worlds' approach highlighted material and ideological differences between the systems found in 'first world' capitalist, 'second world' communist and 'third world' developing states.

◆ The collapse of communism and advance of democratisation has made it much more difficult to identify the political contours of the modern world, making conventional systems of classification redundant. It is nevertheless still possible to distinguish between regimes on the basis of how their political, economic and cultural characteristics interlock in practice, even though all systems of classification are provisional.

◆ 'End of history' theorists have proclaimed that history has ended, or is destined to end, with the worldwide triumph of western liberal democracy. However, there is evidence that regime types have become both more complex and more diverse. The principal regime types found in the modern world are western polyarchies, post-communist regimes, East Asian regimes, Islamic regimes and military regimes.

Questions for discussion

▶ Does Aristotle's system of political classification have any relevance to the modern world?

▶ Is there any longer such a thing as the 'third world'?

▶ To what extent have postcommunist regimes discarded their communist past?

▶ Why have liberal-democratic structures proved to be so effective and successful?

▶ How democratic are western polyarchies?

▶ Do Confucianism and Islam constitute viable alternatives to western liberalism as a basis for a modern regime?

■ Further reading

Calvocoressi, P. *World Politics Since 1945* (London and New York: Longman, 1991). A lucid and comprehensive account of political developments in the postwar world.

Hague, R., M. Harrop and S. Breslin *Comparative Government and Politics: An Introduction* (3rd ed.) (Basingstoke: Macmillan, 1992) (US ed.: *Political Science: A Comparative Introduction* (New York: St Martin's Press)). A succinct and stimulating introduction to comparative politics that adopts a genuinely international approach.

Lijphart, A. *Democracies: Patterns of Majoritarian and Consensus Government in Twenty-One Countries* (New Haven, CT: Yale University Press, 1984). A classic and highly influential attempt to distinguish between forms of democratic rule.

Parry, G. and M. Moran (eds) *Democracy and Democratization* (London: Routledge, 1994). A useful examination of the idea of democracy and the process of democratisation in eastern Europe, Latin America and elsewhere.

Political Ideologies

> 'The philosophers have only interpreted the world in various ways: the point is to change it.'
>
> KARL MARX *Theses on Feuerbach* (1845)

No one sees the world as it is. All of us look at the world through a veil of theories, presuppositions and assumptions. In this sense, observation and interpretation are inextricably bound together: when we look at the world we are also engaged in imposing meaning upon it. This has important implications for the study of politics. In particular, it highlights the need to uncover the presuppositions and assumptions that we bring to political enquiry. At their deepest level, these assumptions are rooted in broad political creeds or traditions that are usually termed 'political ideologies'. Each of these 'isms' (liberalism, socialism, conservatism, feminism, fascism, and so on) constitutes a distinctive intellectual framework or paradigm, and each offers its own account of political reality, its own world view. However, there is deep disagreement both about the nature of ideology, and about the role, for good or ill, that it plays in political life.

The central issues examined in this chapter are as follows:

Key issues

▶ What is political ideology?

▶ What are the characteristic themes, theories and principles of each of the major ideologies?

▶ What rival traditions or internal tensions does each ideology encompass?

▶ How have the major ideologies changed over time?

▶ How can the rise and fall of ideologies be explained?

▶ Has ideology come to an end? Could ideology come to an end?

Contents

What is political ideology?

Ideology is one of the most controversial concepts encountered in political analysis. Although the term now tends to be used in a neutral sense, to refer to a developed social philosophy or world view, it has in the past had heavily negative or pejorative connotations. During its sometimes tortuous career, the concept of ideology has commonly been used as a political weapon to condemn or criticise rival creeds or doctrines.

The term 'ideology' was coined in 1796 by the French philosopher Destutt de Tracy (1754–1836). He used it to refer to a new 'science of ideas' (literally an idea-ology) that set out to uncover the origins of conscious thought and ideas. De Tracy's hope was that ideology would eventually enjoy the same status as established sciences such as zoology and biology. However, a more enduring meaning was assigned to the term in the nineteenth century in the writings of Karl Marx (see p. 51). For Marx, ideology amounted to the ideas of the 'ruling class', ideas that therefore uphold the class system and perpetuate exploitation. In their early work *The German Ideology*, Marx and Engels wrote the following:

The ideas of the ruling class are in every epoch the ruling ideas, i.e. the class which is the ruling *material* force in society, is at the same time the ruling *intellectual* force. The class which has the means of mental production at its disposal, has control at the same time over the means of mental production. (Marx and Engels, [1846] 1970:64)

The defining features of ideology in the Marxist sense is that it is false: it mystifies and confuses subordinate classes by concealing from them the contradictions upon which all class societies are based. As far as capitalism is concerned, the ideology of the property-owning bourgeoisie (bourgeois ideology) fosters delusion or 'false consciousness' amongst the exploited proletariat, preventing them from recognising the fact of their own exploitation. Nevertheless, Marx did not believe that all political views had an ideological character. He held that his own work, which attempted to uncover the process of class exploitation and oppression, was scientific. In his view, a clear distinction could be drawn between science and ideology, between truth and falsehood. This distinction tended, however, to be blurred in the writings of later Marxists such as Lenin (see p. 75) and Gramsci (see p. 191). These referred not only to 'bourgeois ideology' but also to 'socialist ideology' or 'proletarian ideology', terms that Marx would have considered absurd.

Alternative uses of the term have also been developed by liberals and conservatives. The emergence of totalitarian dictatorships in the interwar period encouraged writers such as Karl Popper (1902–94), J. L. Talmon and Hannah Arendt (see p. 9) to view ideology as an instrument of social control to ensure compliance and subordination. Relying heavily on the examples of fascism and communism, this Cold War liberal use of the term treated ideology as a 'closed' system of thought, which, by claiming a monopoly of truth, refuses to tolerate opposing ideas and rival beliefs. In contrast, liberalism, based as it is on a fundamental commitment to individual freedom, and doctrines such as conservatism and democratic socialism that broadly subscribe to liberal principles are clearly not ideologies. These doctrines are 'open' in the sense that they permit, and even insist upon, free debate, opposition and criticism.

A distinctively conservative use of the term 'ideology' has been developed by thinkers such as Michael Oakeshott (see p. 192). This view reflects a characteristically conservative scepticism about the value of **rationalism** that is born out of the belief

Rationalism: The belief that the world can be understood and explained through the exercise of human reason, based on assumptions about its rational structure.

that the world is largely beyond the capacity of the human mind to fathom. As Oakeshott put it, in political activity 'men sail a boundless and bottomless sea'. From this perspective, ideologies are seen as abstract 'systems of thought', that is, as sets of ideas that distort political reality because they claim to explain what is, frankly, incomprehensible. This is why conservatives have traditionally dismissed the notion that they subscribe to an ideology, preferring instead to describe conservatism as a disposition, or an 'attitude of mind', and placing their faith in **pragmatism**, tradition (see p. 195) and history.

The drawback of each of these usages, however, is that, as they are negative or pejorative, they restrict the application of the term. Certain political doctrines, in other words, are excluded from the category of 'ideologies'. Marx, for instance, insisted that his ideas were scientific, not ideological, liberals have denied that liberalism should be viewed as an ideology, and conservatives have traditionally claimed to embrace a pragmatic rather than ideological style of politics. Moreover, each of these definitions is loaded with the values and orientation of a particular political doctrine. An inclusive definition of 'ideology' (one that applies to all political traditions) must therefore be neutral: it must reject the notion that ideologies are 'good' or 'bad', true or false, or liberating or oppressive. This is the virtue of the modern, social–scientific meaning of the term, which treats ideology as an action-orientated belief system, an interrelated set of ideas that in some way guides or inspires political action.

Liberalism

Any account of political ideologies must start with liberalism. This is because liberalism is, in effect, the ideology of the industrialised West, and is sometimes portrayed as a **meta-ideology** that is capable of embracing a broad range of rival values and beliefs. Although liberalism did not emerge as a developed political creed until the early nineteenth century, distinctively liberal theories and principles had gradually been developed during the previous 300 years. Liberalism was the product of the breakdown of feudalism and the growth, in its place, of a market or capitalist society. Early liberalism certainly reflected the aspirations of a rising industrial middle class, and liberalism and capitalism have been closely linked (some have argued intrinsically linked) ever since. In its earliest form, liberalism was a political doctrine. It attacked absolutism (see p. 26) and feudal privilege, instead advocating constitutional and, later, representative government. By the early nineteenth century, a distinctively liberal economic creed had developed that extolled the virtues of *laissez-faire* capitalism (see p. 171) and condemned all forms of government intervention. This became the centrepiece of classical, or nineteenth-century, liberalism. From the late nineteenth century onwards, however, a form of social liberalism emerged which looked more favourably on welfare reform and economic intervention. Such an emphasis became the characteristic theme of modern, or twentieth-century, liberalism.

Elements of liberalism

• **Individualism:** Individualism (see p. 178) is the core principle of liberal ideology. It reflects a belief in the supreme importance of the human individual as opposed to any social group or collective body. Human beings are seen, first and foremost, as individuals. This implies both that they are of equal moral worth and

---

Con...

Ideology

From a social–scientific viewpoint, an ideology is a more or less coherent set of ideas that provides a basis for organised political action, whether this is intended to preserve, modify or overthrow the existing system of power relationships. All ideologies therefore (a) offer an account of the existing order, usually in the form of a 'world view', (b) provide a model of a desired future, a vision of the Good Society, and (c) outline how political change can and should be brought about. Ideologies are not, however, hermetically sealed systems of thought: rather, they are fluid sets of ideas which overlap with one another at a number of points. At a 'fundamental' level, ideologies resemble political philosophies; at an 'operative' level, they take the form of broad political movements (Seliger, 1976).

Pragmatism: A theory or practice that places primary emphasis on practical circumstances and goals; pragmatism implies a distrust of abstract ideas.

Meta-ideology: A higher or second-order ideology that lays down the grounds on which ideological debate can take place.

that they possess separate and unique identities. The liberal goal is therefore to construct a society within which individuals can flourish and develop, each pursuing 'the good' as he or she defines it, to the best of his or her abilities. This has contributed to the view that liberalism is morally neutral, in the sense that it lays down a set of rules which allow individuals to make their own moral decisions.

- **Freedom:** Individual freedom (see p. 282), or liberty (the two terms are interchangeable), is the core value of liberalism; it is given priority over, say, equality, justice or authority. This arises naturally from a belief in the individual and the desire to ensure that each person is able to act as he or she pleases or chooses. Nevertheless, liberals advocate 'freedom under the law', as they recognise that one person's liberty may be a threat to the liberty of others; liberty may become licence. They therefore endorse the ideal that individuals should enjoy the maximum possible liberty consistent with a like liberty for all.

- **Reason:** Liberals believe that the world has a rational structure, and that this can be uncovered through the exercise of human reason and by critical enquiry. This inclines them to place their faith in the ability of individuals to make wise judgements on their own behalf, being, in most cases, the best judges of their own interests. It also encourages liberals to believe in **progress** and the capacity of human beings to resolve their differences through debate and argument rather than bloodshed and war.

- **Equality:** Individualism implies a belief in foundational equality, that is, the belief that individuals are 'born equal', at least in terms of moral worth. This is reflected in a liberal commitment to equal rights and entitlements, notably in the form of legal equality ('equality before the law') and political equality ('one person, one vote; one vote, one value'). However, as individuals do not possess the same levels of talent or willingness to work, liberals do not endorse social equality or an equality of outcome. Rather, they favour equality of opportunity (a 'level playing field') that gives all individuals an equal chance to realise their unequal potential. Liberals therefore support the principle of **meritocracy**, with merit reflecting, crudely, talent plus hard work.

- **Toleration:** Liberals believe that toleration (that is, forbearance: the willingness of people to allow others to think, speak and act in ways of which they disapprove) is both a guarantee of individual liberty and a means of social enrichment. They believe that pluralism (see p. 76), in the form of moral, cultural and political diversity, is positively healthy: it promotes debate and intellectual progress by ensuring that all beliefs are tested in a free market of ideas. Liberals, moreover, tend to believe that there is a balance or natural harmony between rival views and interests, and thus usually discount the idea of irreconcilable conflict.

- **Consent:** In the liberal view, authority and social relationships should always be based on consent or willing agreement. Government must therefore be based on the 'consent of the governed'. This is a doctrine that encourages liberals to favour representation (see p. 206) and democracy. Similarly, social bodies and associations are formed through contracts willingly entered into by individuals intent on pursuing their own self-interest. In this sense, authority arises 'from below' and is always grounded in legitimacy (see p. 193).

- **Constitutionalism:** Although liberals see government as a vital guarantee of order and stability in society, they are constantly aware of the danger that government

Progress: Moving forwards; the belief that history is characterised by human advancement based on the accumulation of knowledge and wisdom.

Meritocracy: Rule by the talented; the principle that rewards and positions should be distributed on the basis of ability.

John Locke (1632–1704)

English philosopher and politician. Locke was born in Somerset in the UK. He studied medicine at Oxford University before becoming secretary to Anthony Ashley Cooper, First Earl of Shaftsbury, in 1661. Locke's political views were developed against the backdrop of the English Revolution, and they are often seen as providing a justification for the 'Glorious Revolution' of 1688, which ended absolutist rule and established a constitutional monarchy in Britain under William of Orange. Locke was a key thinker in the development of early liberalism, placing particular emphasis upon 'natural' or God-given rights, identified as the rights to life, liberty and property. As he was an exponent of representative government and toleration, his views had a considerable impact upon the American Revolution. Locke's most important political works are *A Letter Concerning Toleration* (1689) and *Two Treatises of Government* ([1690] 1965).

may become a tyranny against the individual ('power tends to corrupt' (Lord Acton)). They therefore believe in limited government. This goal can be attained through the fragmentation of government power, by the creation of checks and balances amongst the various institutions of government, and through the establishment of a codified or 'written' constitution embodying a bill of rights that defines the relationship between the state and the individual.

Classical liberalism

The central theme of classical liberalism is a commitment to an extreme form of individualism. Human beings are seen as egoistical, self-seeking and largely self-reliant creatures. In what C. B. Macpherson (1962) termed 'possessive individualism', they are taken to be the proprietors of their own persons and capacities, owing nothing to society or to other individuals. This view is underpinned by a belief in 'negative' liberty, meaning noninterference, or the absence of external constraints upon the individual. This implies a deeply unsympathetic attitude towards the state and all forms of government intervention.

In Tom Paine's (see p. 208) words, the state is a 'necessary evil'. It is 'necessary' in that, at the very least, it establishes order and security and ensures that contracts are enforced. However, it is 'evil' in that it imposes a collective will upon society, thus limiting the freedom and responsibilities of the individual. The classical liberal ideal is therefore the establishment of a minimal or 'nightwatchman' state, with a role that is limited to the protection of citizens from the encroachments of fellow citizens. In the form of **economic liberalism**, this position is underpinned by a deep faith in the mechanisms of the free market and the belief that the economy works best when left alone by government. *Laissez-faire* capitalism is thus seen as guaranteeing prosperity, upholding individual liberty, and, as this allows individuals to rise and fall according to merit, ensuring social justice.

Economic liberalism: A belief in the market as a self-regulating mechanism tending naturally to deliver general prosperity and opportunities for all.

Big government: Interventionist government, usually understood to imply economic management and social regulation.

Modern liberalism

Modern liberalism is characterised by a more sympathetic attitude towards state intervention. Indeed, in the USA, the term 'liberal' is invariably taken to imply support for **big government** rather than 'minimal' government. This shift was born

John Stuart Mill (1806–73)

UK philosopher, economist and politician. Mill was subject to an intense and austere regime of education by his father, the utilitarian theorist James Mill (1773–1836). This resulted in a mental collapse at the age of 20, after which he developed a more human philosophy influenced by Coleridge and the German Idealists. His major writings, including *On Liberty* (1859), *Considerations on Representative Government* (1861) and *The Subjection of Women* (1869), had a powerful influence on the development of liberal thought. In many ways, Mill's varied and complex work straddled the divide between classical and modern liberalism. His distrust of state intervention was firmly rooted in nineteenth-century principles, but his emphasis upon the quality of individual life (reflected in a commitment to 'individuality'), as well as his sympathy for causes such as female suffrage and workers' cooperatives, clearly looked forward to twentieth-century developments.

out of the recognition that industrial capitalism had merely generated new forms of injustice and left the mass of the population subject to the vagaries of the market. Influenced by the work of J. S. Mill, the so-called New Liberals (figures such as T. H. Green (1836–82), L. T. Hobhouse (1864–1929) and J. A. Hobson (1858–1940)) championed a broader, 'positive' view of freedom. From this perspective, freedom does not just mean being left alone, which might imply nothing more than the freedom to starve. Rather, it is linked to personal development and the flourishing of the individual, that is, the ability of the individual to gain fulfilment and achieve self-realisation.

This view provided the basis for social or welfare liberalism. This is characterised by the recognition that state intervention, particularly in the form of social welfare (see p. 395), can enlarge liberty by safeguarding individuals from the social evils that blight individual existence. These evils were identified in the UK by the 1942 Beveridge Report as the 'five giants': want, ignorance, idleness, squalor and disease. In the same way, modern liberals abandoned their belief in *laissez-faire* capitalism, largely as a result of J. M. Keynes' (see p. 172) insight that growth and prosperity could only be maintained through a system of managed or regulated capitalism, with key economic responsibilities being placed in the hands of the state. Nevertheless, modern liberals' support for collective provision and government intervention has always been conditional. Their concern has been with the plight of the weak and vulnerable, those who are literally not able to help themselves. Their goal is to raise individuals to the point where they are able, once again, to take responsibility for their own circumstances and make their own moral choices.

■ Conservatism

Ancien régime: (*French*) Literally, old order; usually linked with the absolutist structures that predated the French Revolution.

Conservative ideas and doctrines first emerged in the late eighteenth century and early nineteenth century. They arose as a reaction against the growing pace of economic and political change, which was in many ways symbolised by the French Revolution. In this sense, conservatism harked back to the *ancien régime*. In trying to resist the pressures unleashed by the growth of liberalism, socialism and nationalism, conservatism stood in defence of an increasingly embattled traditional social order. However, from the outset, divisions in conservative thought were apparent. In

Edmund Burke (1729–97)

Dublin-born UK statesman and political theorist who is often seen as the father of the Anglo-American conservative tradition. Burke's enduring reputation is based on a series of works, notably *Reflections on the Revolution in France* ([1790] 1968), that were critical of the French Revolution. Though sympathetic to the American Revolution, Burke was deeply critical of the attempt to recast French politics in accordance with abstract principles such as liberty, equality and fraternity, arguing that wisdom resided largely in experience, tradition and history. Nevertheless, he held that the French monarchy was in part responsible for its own fate since it had obstinately refused to 'change in order to conserve'. Burke had a gloomy view of government, recognising that it could prevent evil but rarely promote good. He regarded market forces as 'natural law'.

continental Europe, a form of conservatism emerged that was characterised by the work of thinkers such as Joseph de Maistre (1753–1821). This conservatism was starkly autocratic and reactionary, rejecting out of hand any idea of reform. A more cautious, more flexible, and ultimately more successful form of conservatism nevertheless developed in the UK and the USA that was characterised by Edmund Burke's belief in 'change in order to conserve'. This stance enabled conservatives in the nineteenth century to embrace the cause of social reform under the paternalistic banner of 'One Nation'. The high point of this tradition in the UK came in the 1950s as the Conservative Party came to accept the postwar settlement and espouse its own version of Keynesian social democracy. However, such ideas increasingly came under pressure from the 1970s onwards as a result of the emergence of the New Right. The New Right's radically antistatist and antipaternalist brand of conservatism draws heavily on classical liberal themes and values.

Elements of conservatism

• **Tradition:** The central theme of conservative thought, 'the desire to conserve', is closely linked to the perceived virtues of tradition, respect for established customs, and institutions that have endured through time. In this view, tradition reflects the accumulated wisdom of the past, and institutions and practices that have been 'tested by time', and it should be preserved for the benefit of the living and for generations yet to come. Tradition also has the virtue of promoting stability and security, giving individuals a sense of social and historical belonging.

• **Pragmatism:** Conservatives have traditionally emphasised the limitations of human rationality, which arise from the infinite complexity of the world in which we live. Abstract principles and systems of thought are therefore distrusted, and instead faith is placed in experience, history and, above all, pragmatism: the belief that action should be shaped by practical circumstances and practical goals, that is, by 'what works'. Conservatives have thus preferred to describe their own beliefs as an 'attitude of mind' or an 'approach to life', rather than as an ideology, although they reject the idea that this amounts to unprincipled opportunism.

• **Human imperfection:** The conservative view of human nature is broadly pessimistic. In this view, human beings are limited, dependent, and security-seeking creatures, drawn to the familiar and the tried and tested, and needing to live in stable and orderly communities. In addition, individuals are morally corrupt: they are tainted by selfishness, greed and the thirst for power. The roots of crime and disorder therefore reside within the human individual rather than in society. The maintenance of order (see p. 371) therefore requires a strong state, the enforcement of strict laws, and stiff penalties.

• **Organicism:** Instead of seeing society as an artefact that is a product of human ingenuity, conservatives have traditionally viewed society as an organic whole, or living entity. Society is thus structured by natural necessity, with its various institutions, or the 'fabric of society' (families, local communities, the nation and so on), contributing to the health and stability of society. The whole is more than a collection of its individual parts. Shared (often 'traditional') values and a common culture are also seen as being vital to the maintenance of the community (see p. 135) and social cohesion.

• **Hierarchy:** In the conservative view, gradations of social position and status are natural and inevitable in an organic society. These reflect the differing roles and responsibilities of, for example, employers and workers, teachers and pupils, and parents and children. Nevertheless, in this view, hierarchy and inequality do not give rise to conflict, because society is bound together by mutual obligations and reciprocal duties. Indeed, as a person's 'station in life' is largely determined by luck and the accident of birth, the prosperous and privileged acquire a particular responsibility of care for the less fortunate.

• **Authority:** Conservatives hold that, to some degree, authority is always exercised 'from above', providing leadership (see p. 330), guidance and support for those who lack the knowledge, experience or education to act wisely in their own interests (an example being the authority of parents over children). Although the idea of a **natural aristocracy** was once influential, authority and leadership are now more commonly seen as resulting from experience and training. The virtue of authority is that it is a source of social cohesion, giving people a clear sense of who they are and what is expected of them. Freedom must therefore coexist with responsibility; it therefore largely consists of a willing acceptance of obligations and duties.

• **Property:** Conservatives see property ownership as being vital because it gives people security and a measure of independence from government, and it encourages them to respect the law and the property of others. Property is also an exteriorisation of people's personalities, in that they 'see' themselves in what they own: their houses, their cars, and so on. However, property ownership involves duties as well as rights. In this view, we are, in a sense, merely custodians of property that has either been inherited from past generations ('the family silver'), or may be of value to future ones.

Paternalistic conservatism

The paternalistic strand in conservative thought is entirely consistent with principles such as organicism, hierarchy and duty, and it can therefore be seen as an outgrowth of traditional conservatism. Often traced back to the early writings of Benjamin Disraeli (1804–81), paternalism draws upon a combination of prudence and principle. In warning of the danger of the UK being divided into 'two nations: the Rich and the Poor', Disraeli articulated a widespread fear of social revolution. This warning amounted to an appeal to the self-interest of the privileged, who needed to recognise

Natural aristocracy: The idea that talent and leadership are innate or inbred qualities that cannot be acquired through effort or self-advancement.

that 'reform from above' was preferable to 'revolution from below'. This message was underpinned by an appeal to the principles of duty and social obligation rooted in neofeudal ideas such as **noblesse oblige**. In effect, in this view, duty is the price of privilege; the powerful and propertied inherit a responsibility to look after the less well-off in the broader interests of social cohesion and unity. The resulting one-nation principle, the cornerstone of what can properly be termed a **Tory** position, reflects not so much the ideal of social equality as the vision of organic balance, a cohesive and stable hierarchy.

The one-nation tradition embodies not only a disposition towards social reform, but also an essentially pragmatic attitude towards economic policy. This is clearly seen in the 'middle way' approach adopted in the 1950s by UK Conservatives such as Harold Macmillan (1894–1986), R. A. Butler (1902–82) and Iain MacLeod (1913–70). This approach eschewed the two ideological models of economic organisation: *laissez-faire* capitalism on the one hand, and state socialism and central planning on the other. The former was rejected on the grounds that it results in a free for all, which makes social cohesion impossible, and penalises the weak and vulnerable. The latter was dismissed because it produces a state monolith and crushes all forms of independence and enterprise. The solution therefore lies in a blend of market competition and government regulation ('private enterprise without selfishness' (H. Macmillan)), within which the balance between the state and the individual can be adjusted pragmatically according to 'what works'. Very similar conclusions were drawn after 1945 by continental European conservatives, who embraced the principles of Christian Democracy, most rigorously developed in the 'social market' philosophy (see p. 169) of the German Christian Democrats (the Christlich Demokratische Union (CDU)). This philosophy embraces a *market* strategy insofar as it highlights the virtues of private enterprise and competition, but it is *social* in that it believes that the prosperity so gained should be employed for the broader benefit of society.

The New Right

The New Right represents a departure in conservative thought that amounts to a kind of counter-revolution against both the postwar drift towards state intervention and the spread of liberal or progressive social values. New Right ideas can be traced back to the 1970s and the conjunction between the apparent failure of Keynesian social democracy, signalled by the end of the postwar boom, and growing concern about social breakdown and the decline of authority. Such ideas had their greatest impact in the UK and the USA, where they were articulated in the 1980s in the form of Thatcherism and Reaganism, respectively. However, the New Right does not so much constitute a coherent and systematic philosophy as attempt to marry two distinct traditions usually termed 'neoliberalism' and 'neoconservatism'. Although there is political and ideological tension between these two, they can be combined in support of the goal of a strong but minimal state, in Andrew Gamble's (1981) words, 'the free economy and the strong state'.

Neoliberalism

Neoliberalism is an updated version of classical political economy that was developed in the writings of free-market economists such as Friedrich Hayek and Milton Friedman (see p. 173), and philosophers such as Robert Nozick (see p. 94). The central pillars of neoliberalism are the market and the individual. The principle

Noblesse oblige: (*French*) Literally, the obligations of the nobility; in general terms, the responsibility to guide or protect those less fortunate or less privileged.

Toryism: An ideological stance within conservatism characterised by a belief in hierarchy, an emphasis on tradition, and support for duty and organicism.

Friedrich von Hayek (1899–1992)

Austrian economist and political philosopher. An academic who taught at the London School of Economics, and the Universities of Chicago, Freiburg and Salzburg, Hayek was awarded the Nobel Prize for Economics in 1974. As an exponent of the so-called Austrian School, he was a firm believer in individualism and market order, and an implacable critic of socialism. *The Road to Serfdom* (1948) was a pioneering work that attacked economic interventionism; later works such as *The Constitution of Liberty* (1960) and *Law, Legislation and Liberty* (1979) developed themes in political philosophy. Hayek's writings had a considerable impact on the emergent New Right.

neoliberal goal is to 'roll back the frontiers of the state', in the belief that unregulated market capitalism will deliver efficiency, growth and widespread prosperity. In this view, the 'dead hand' of the state saps initiative and discourages enterprise; government, however well intentioned, invariably has a damaging effect upon human affairs. This is reflected in the liberal New Right's concern with the politics of ownership, and its preference for private enterprise over state enterprise or nationalisation: in short, 'private, good; public, bad'. Such ideas are associated with a form of rugged individualism, expressed in Margaret Thatcher's famous assertion that 'there is no such thing as society, only individuals and their families'. The **nanny state** is seen to breed a culture of dependency and to undermine freedom, which is understood as freedom of choice in the marketplace. Instead, faith is placed in self-help, individual responsibility and entrepreneurialism.

Neoconservatism

Neoconservatism reasserts nineteenth-century conservative social principles. The conservative New Right wishes, above all, to restore authority and return to traditional values, notably those linked to the family, religion and the nation. Authority is seen as guaranteeing social stability, on the basis that it generates discipline and respect, while shared values and a common culture are believed to generate social cohesion and make civilised existence possible. The enemies of neoconservatism are therefore **permissiveness**, the cult of the self and 'doing one's own thing', thought of as the values of the 1960s. Indeed, many of those who style themselves neoconservatives in the USA are former liberals who grew disillusioned with the progressive reforms of the Kennedy–Johnson era. Another aspect of neoconservatism is the tendency to view the emergence of multicultural and multireligious societies with concern, on the basis that they are conflict-ridden and inherently unstable. This position also tends to be linked to an insular form of nationalism that is sceptical about both immigration and the growing influence of supranational bodies such as the United Nations and the European Union.

Nanny state: A state with extensive social responsibilities; the term implies that welfare programmes are unwarranted and demeaning to the individual.

Permissiveness: The willingness to allow people to make their own moral choices; permissiveness suggests that there are no authoritative values.

◼ Socialism

Although socialist ideas can be traced back to the Levellers and Diggers of the seventeenth century, or to Thomas More's *Utopia* ([1516] 1965), or even Plato's *Republic*, socialism did not take shape as a political creed until the early nineteenth century. It developed as a reaction against the emergence of industrial capitalism. Socialism first articulated the interests of artisans and craftsmen threatened by the spread of factory production, but it was soon being linked to the growing industrial working class, the 'factory fodder' of early industrialisation. In its earliest forms, socialism tended to have a fundamentalist (see p. 61), utopian and revolutionary character. Its goal was to abolish a capitalist economy based on market exchange, and replace it with a qualitatively different socialist society, usually to be constructed on the principle of common ownership. The most influential representative of this brand of socialism was Karl Marx, whose ideas provided the foundations for twentieth-century communism.

From the late nineteenth century onwards, however, a reformist socialist tradition emerged that reflected the gradual integration of the working classes into capitalist society through an improvement in working conditions and wages and the growth of trade unions and socialist political parties. This brand of socialism proclaimed the possibility of a peaceful, gradual and legal transition to socialism, brought about through the adoption of the 'parliamentary road'. Reformist socialism drew upon two sources. The first was a humanist tradition of ethical socialism, linked to thinkers such as Robert Owen (1771–1858), Charles Fourier (1772–1837) and William Morris (1854–96). The second was a form of **revisionist** Marxism developed primarily by Eduard Bernstein (see p. 55).

During much of the twentieth century, the socialist movement was thus divided into two rival camps. Revolutionary socialists, following the example of Lenin (see p. 75) and the Bolsheviks, called themselves communists, while reformist socialists, who practised a form of constitutional politics, embraced what increasingly came to be called social democracy. This rivalry focused not only on the most appropriate means of achieving socialism, but also on the nature of the socialist goal itself. Social democrats turned their backs upon fundamentalist principles such as common ownership and planning, and recast socialism in terms of welfare, redistribution and economic management. Both forms of socialism, however, experienced crises in the late twentieth century that encouraged some to proclaim the 'death of socialism' and the emergence of a postsocialist society. The most dramatic event in this process was the collapse of communism brought about by the eastern European revolutions of 1989–91, but there was also a continued retreat of social democracy from traditional principles, making it, some would argue, indistinguishable from modern liberalism.

Elements of socialism

• **Community**: The core of socialism is the vision of human beings as social creatures linked by the existence of a common humanity. As the poet John Donne put it, 'no man is an Island entire of itself; every man is a piece of the Continent, a part of the main'. This refers to the importance of community (see p. 135), and it highlights the degree to which individual identity is fashioned by social interaction and membership of social groups and collective bodies. Socialists are inclined to emphasise nurture over nature, and to explain individual behaviour mainly in terms of social factors rather than innate qualities.

• **Fraternity**: As human beings share a common humanity, they are bound together by a sense of comradeship or fraternity (literally meaning 'brotherhood', but broadened in this context to embrace all humans). This encourages socialists to prefer cooperation

Revisionism: The modification of original or established beliefs; revisionism can imply the abandonment of principle or a loss of conviction.

to competition, and to favour collectivism over individualism (see p. 178). In this view, cooperation enables people to harness their collective energies and strengthens the bonds of community, while competition pits individuals against each other, breeding resentment, conflict and hostility.

• **Social equality:** Equality (see p. 396) is the central value of socialism. Socialism is sometimes portrayed as a form of egalitarianism, the belief in the primacy of equality over other values. In particular, socialists emphasise the importance of social equality, an equality of outcome as opposed to equality of opportunity. They believe that a measure of social equality is the essential guarantee of social stability and cohesion, encouraging individuals to identify with their fellow human beings. It also provides the basis for the exercise of legal and political rights.

• **Need:** Sympathy for equality also reflects the socialist belief that material benefits should be distributed on the basis of need, rather than simply on the basis of merit or work. The classic formulation of this principle is found in Marx's communist principle of distribution: 'from each according to his ability, to each according to his need'. This reflects the belief that the satisfaction of basic needs (hunger, thirst, shelter, health, personal security and so on) is a prerequisite for a worthwhile human existence and participation in social life. Clearly, however, distribution according to need requires people to be motivated by moral incentives, rather than just material ones.

• **Social class:** Socialism has often been associated with a form of class politics. First, socialists have tended to analyse society in terms of the distribution of income or wealth, and they have thus seen class as a significant (usually the most significant) social cleavage. Second, socialism has traditionally been associated with the interests of an oppressed and exploited working class (however defined), and it has traditionally regarded the working class as an agent of social change, even social revolution (see p. 198). Nevertheless, class divisions are remediable; the socialist goal is either the eradication of economic and social inequalities or their substantial reduction.

• **Common ownership:** The relationship between socialism and common ownership has been deeply controversial. Some see it as the *end* of socialism itself, and others see it instead as simply a *means* of generating broader equality. The socialist case for common ownership (in the form of either Soviet-style state collectivisation, or selective nationalisation (a 'mixed economy')) is that it is a means of harnessing material resources to the common good, with private property being seen to promote selfishness, acquisitiveness and social division. Modern socialism, however, has moved away from this narrow concern with the politics of ownership.

Marxism

As a theoretical system, Marxism has constituted the principal alternative to the liberal rationalism that has dominated western culture and intellectual enquiry in the modern period. As a political force, in the form of the international communist movement, Marxism has also been seen as the major enemy of western capitalism, at least in the period 1917–91. This highlights a central difficulty in dealing with Marxism: the difference between Marxism as a social philosophy derived from the classic writings of Karl Marx and Friedrich Engels (1820–95), and the phenomenon of twentieth-century communism, which in many ways departed from and revised classical principles. Thus the collapse of communism at the end of the twentieth

Karl Marx (1818–83)

German philosopher, economist and political thinker, usually portrayed as the father of twentieth-century communism. After a brief career as a university teacher, Marx took up journalism and became increasingly involved with the socialist movement. He moved to Paris in 1843. He finally settled in London after being expelled from Prussia, and worked for the rest of his life as an active revolutionary and writer supported by his friend and life-long collaborator Friedrich Engels. In 1864, Marx helped to found the First International, which collapsed in 1871 because of growing antagonism between Marx's supporters and anarchists led by Bakunin. Although much of his voluminous writings remained unpublished at his death, Marx's classic work was the three-volume *Capital* ([1867, 1885, 1894] 1970). His best-known and most accessible work is the *Communist Manifesto* ([1848] 1967).

century need not betoken the death of Marxism as a political ideology; indeed, it may give Marxism, now divorced from the vestiges of Leninism and Stalinism, a fresh lease of life.

To some extent, the problem stems from the wide range and complex nature of Marx's own writings, which have allowed him to be interpreted by some as an economic determinist, but by others as a humanist socialist. A distinction has also been drawn between the character of his early writings and that of his late writings. This is often portrayed as the distinction between the 'young Marx' and the 'mature Marx'. What is clear, however, is that Marx believed that he had developed a new brand of socialism that was scientific, in the sense that it was primarily concerned with disclosing the nature of social and historical development rather than with advancing an essentially ethical critique of capitalism. Marx's ideas and theories reached a wider audience after his death, largely through the writings of his life-long collaborator Engels, the German socialist leader Karl Kautsky (1854–1938), and the Russian theoretician Georgi Plekhanov (1856–1918). A form of orthodox Marxism, usually termed **dialectical materialism** (a term coined by Plekhanov, not Marx), came into existence that was later used as the basis for Soviet communism. This 'vulgar' Marxism undoubtedly placed a heavier stress on mechanistic theories and historical determinism than did Marx's own writings.

Elements of Marxism

- **Historical materialism:** The cornerstone of Marxist philosophy is what Engels called 'the materialist conception of history'. This highlighted the importance of economic life and the conditions under which people produce and reproduce their means of subsistence. Marx held that the economic 'base', consisting essentially of the 'mode of production', or economic system, conditions or determines the ideological and political 'superstructure'. This suggests that social and historical development can be explained in terms of economic and class factors. Later Marxists portrayed this as a mechanical relationship, implying that immutable economic 'laws' drive history forwards regardless of the human agent.

- **Dialectical change:** Following Hegel (see p. 84), Marx believed that the driving force of historical change was the dialectic, a process of interaction between competing forces that results in a higher stage of development. In its materialist version, this model implies that historical change is a consequence of internal contradictions

Dialectical materialism: The crude and deterministic form of Marxism that dominated intellectual life in orthodox communist states.

within a 'mode of production' reflected in class antagonism. Orthodox Marxism ('dialectical materialism') portrayed the dialectic as an impersonal force shaping both natural and human processes.

- **Alienation:** Alienation was a central principle of Marx's early writings. It is the process whereby, under capitalism, labour is reduced to being a mere commodity, and work becomes a depersonalised activity. In this view, workers are alienated from the product of their labour, from the process of labour, from fellow workers, and, ultimately, from themselves as creative and social beings. Unalienated labour is thus an essential source of human fulfilment and self-realisation.

- **Class struggle:** The central contradiction within a capitalist society arises from the existence of private property. This creates a division between the bourgeoisie or capitalist class, the owners of the 'means of production', and the proletariat, who do not own property and thus subsist through selling their labour (literally 'wage slaves'). The bourgeoisie is a 'ruling class'. It not only has economic power through the ownership of wealth, but it also exercises political power through the agency of the state and possesses ideological power because its ideas are the 'ruling ideas' of the age.

- **Surplus value:** The relationship between the bourgeoisie and the proletariat is one of irreconcilable conflict, reflecting the fact that the proletariat is necessarily and systematically exploited under capitalism. Marx believed that all value derives from the labour expended in the production of goods. This means that the quest for profit forces capitalist enterprises to extract 'surplus value' from their workers by paying them less than the value of their labour. Capitalism is therefore inherently unstable, because the proletariat cannot be permanently reconciled to exploitation and oppression.

- **Proletarian revolution:** Marx believed that capitalism was doomed, and that the proletariat was its 'grave digger'. According to his analysis, capitalism would pass through a series of increasingly serious crises of overproduction. This would bring the proletariat to revolutionary **class consciousness**. Marx proclaimed that proletarian revolution was inevitable, and predicted that it would occur through a spontaneous uprising aimed at seizing control of the means of production. In his later years, however, he speculated about the possibility of a peaceful transition to socialism.

- **Communism:** Marx predicted that proletarian revolution would usher in a transitionary 'socialist' period during which a 'dictatorship of the proletariat' would be required to contain a counter-revolution mounted by the dispossessed bourgeoisie. However, as class antagonism faded and a fully communist society came into existence, this proletarian state would simply 'wither away'. A communist (see p. 33) society would be classless in the sense that wealth would be owned in common by all, and the system of 'commodity production' would be replaced by one of 'production for use' geared to the satisfaction of genuine human needs. With this, the 'prehistory of man' would come to an end, allowing human beings for the first time to shape their own destinies and realise their full potential ('the free development of each is the precondition for the free development of all' (Marx)).

Class consciousness: A Marxist term, denoting an accurate awareness of class interests and a willingness to pursue them; a class-conscious class is a class for-itself (see p. 199).

Orthodox communism

Marxism in practice is inextricably linked to the experience of Soviet communism, and especially to the contribution of the first two Soviet leaders, V. I. Lenin (see

Joseph Stalin (1879–1953)

USSR political leader 1924–53. Stalin (an adopted name, meaning 'man of steel') was the son of a shoemaker. He was expelled from his seminary for revolutionary activities, and joined the Bolsheviks in 1903. He became the general secretary of the Communist Party in 1922. After winning the struggle for power following Lenin's death, he established an increasingly brutal totalitarian dictatorship that was supported by an elaborate cult of personality. His ideological heritage is closely linked to the doctrine of 'Socialism in One Country', which justified industrialisation and collectivisation in terms of the need to resist capitalist encirclement, and the need to eliminate the *kulaks* (rich peasants) as a class. Stalin thus fused a quasi-Marxist notion of class war with an appeal to Russian nationalism.

p. 75) and Joseph Stalin. Indeed, twentieth-century communism is best understood as a form of Marxism–Leninism, that is, as orthodox Marxism modified by a set of Leninist theories and doctrines. Lenin's central contribution to Marxism was his theory of the revolutionary or vanguard party. This reflected Lenin's fear that the proletariat, deluded by bourgeois ideas and beliefs, would not realise its revolutionary potential because it could not develop beyond 'trade-union consciousness': a desire to improve working and living conditions rather than to overthrow capitalism. A revolutionary party, armed with Marxism, was therefore needed to serve as the 'vanguard of the working class'. This was to be a party of a new kind: not a mass party, but a tightly knit party of professional and dedicated revolutionaries capable of exercising ideological leadership. Its organisation was to be based on the principle of democratic centralism, a belief in freedom of debate married to unity of action. Thus, when Lenin's Bolsheviks seized power in Russia in 1917, they did so as a vanguard party, claiming to act in the interests of the proletarian class. The dictatorship of the proletariat therefore became, in practice, a dictatorship of the Communist Party (the Bolshevik party was renamed the Communist Party in 1918), which acted as the 'leading and guiding force' within the Soviet one-party state.

The USSR was, however, more profoundly affected by Stalin's 'second revolution' in the 1930s than it had been by the 1917 Bolshevik Revolution. In reshaping Soviet society, Stalin created a model of orthodox communism that was followed in the postwar period by states such as China, North Korea and Cuba, and throughout eastern Europe. Stalin's changes stemmed largely from his most important ideological innovation, the doctrine of 'Socialism in One Country', which proclaimed that the USSR could 'build socialism' without the need for an international revolution. What can be called economic Stalinism (see p. 53) was initiated with the launch in 1928 of the first Five Year Plan, which brought about the swift and total eradication of private enterprise. This was followed in 1929 by the collectivisation of agriculture. All resources were brought under the control of the state, and a system of central planning dominated by the State Planning Committee (Gosplan) was established.

Stalin's political changes were no less dramatic. During the 1930s, Stalin transformed the USSR into a personal dictatorship through a series of purges which eradicated all vestiges of opposition and debate from the Communist Party, the state bureaucracy and the military. In effect, Stalin turned the USSR into a totalitarian dictatorship, operating through systematic intimidation, repression and terror. Although the

Herbert Marcuse (1898–1979)

German political philosopher and social theorist, and cofounder of the Frankfurt School. A refugee from Hitler's Germany, Marcuse lived in the USA from 1934. He developed a form of neo-Marxism that drew heavily upon Hegel and Freud. Marcuse came to prominence in the 1960s as a leading thinker of the New Left and a 'guru' of the student movement. Marcuse portrayed advanced industrial society as an all-encompassing system of repression that subdued argument and debate, and absorbed opposition. His hopes rested not with the proletariat, but with marginalised groups such as students, ethnic minorities, women, and the countries of the Third World. His most important works include *Reason and Revolution* (1941), *Eros and Civilisation* (1958) and *One-Dimensional Man: Studies in the Ideology of Advanced Industrial Society* (1964).

more brutal features of orthodox communism did not survive Stalin's death in 1953, the core principles of the Leninist party (hierarchical organisation and discipline) and of economic Stalinism (state collectivisation and central planning) stubbornly resisted pressure for reform. This was highlighted by Gorbachev's **perestroika** reform process (1985–91), which merely succeeded in exposing the failings of the planning system, and releasing long-suppressed political forces. These eventually consigned Soviet communism to what Trotsky (see p. 343) had, in very different circumstances, called 'the dustbin of history'.

Modern Marxism

A more complex and subtle form of Marxism developed in western Europe. By contrast with the mechanistic and avowedly scientific notions of Soviet Marxism, western Marxism tended to be influenced by Hegelian ideas and by the stress upon 'Man the creator' found in Marx's early writings. In other words, human beings were seen as makers of history, and not simply as puppets controlled by impersonal material forces. By insisting that there was an interplay between economics and politics, between the material circumstances of life and the capacity of human beings to shape their own destinies, western Marxists were able to break free from the rigid 'base–superstructure' straightjacket. Their ideas have therefore sometimes been termed neo-Marxist (see p. 90). This indicates an unwillingness to treat the class struggle as the beginning and end of social analysis.

The Hungarian Marxist Georg Lukács (1885–1971) was one of the first to present Marxism as a humanistic philosophy. He emphasised the process of 'reification', through which capitalism dehumanises workers by reducing them to passive objects or marketable commodities. In his *Prison Notebooks*, written in 1929–35, Antonio Gramsci (see p. 191) emphasised the degree to which capitalism was maintained not merely by economic domination, but also by political and cultural factors. He called this ideological 'hegemony'. A more overtly Hegelian brand of Marxism was developed by the so-called Frankfurt School, the leading members of which were Theodor Adorno (1903–69), Max Horkheimer (1895–1973) and Herbert Marcuse. Frankfurt theorists developed what was called 'critical theory', a blend of Marxist political economy, Hegelian philosophy and Freudian psychology, which had a considerable impact upon the New Left in the 1960s. A later generation of Frankfurt members included Jurgen Habermas (see p. 197).

Perestroika: (*Russian*) Literally, restructuring; a slogan that refers to the attempt to liberalise and democratise the Soviet system within a communist framework.

Eduard Bernstein (1850–1932)

German socialist politician and theorist. An early member of the German SPD, Bernstein became one of the leading advocates of revisionism, the attempt to revise and modernise orthodox Marxism. Influenced by British Fabianism and the philosophy of Kant (see p. 141). Bernstein developed a largely empirical critique that emphasised the absence of class war, and proclaimed the possibility of a peaceful transition to socialism. This is described in *Evolutionary Socialism* ([1898] 1962). He left the SPD over his opposition to the First World War, although he subsequently returned. Bernstein is often seen as one of the founding figures of modern social democracy.

Social democracy

Social democracy lacks the theoretical coherence of, say, classical liberalism or fundamentalist socialism. Whereas the former is ideologically committed to the market, and the latter champions the cause of common ownership, social democracy stands for a balance between the market and the state, a balance between the individual and the community. At the heart of social democracy there is a compromise between, on the one hand, an acceptance of capitalism as the only reliable mechanism for generating wealth, and, on the other, a desire to distribute wealth in accordance with moral, rather than market, principles. For socialists, this conversion to the market was a difficult, and at times painful, process that was dictated more by practical circumstances and electoral advantage than by ideological conviction. In the early twentieth century, this process could be seen at work in the reformist drift of, for example, the German Social Democratic Party (Sozialdemokratische Partei Deutschlands (SPD)), especially under the influence of revisionist Marxists such as Eduard Bernstein. At its 1959 Bad Godesburg congress, the SPD formally abandoned Marxism and accepted the principle 'competition where possible, planning where necessary'. A similar process took place within ethical or 'utopian' socialist parties that had never been anchored in the certainties of Marxism. For example, the UK Labour Party, committed from the outset to a belief in 'the inevitability of gradualism', had, by the 1950s, recast its socialism in terms of equality rather than nationalisation.

The chief characteristic of modern social democratic thought is a concern for the underdog in society, the weak and vulnerable. There is a sense, however, in which social democracy cannot simply be confined to the socialist tradition. It may draw on a socialist belief in compassion and a common humanity, a liberal commitment to positive freedom and equal opportunities, or, for that matter, a conservative sense of paternal duty and care. Whatever its source, it has usually been articulated on the basis of principles such as welfarism, redistribution and social justice. In the form of Keynesian social democracy, which was widely accepted in the early period after the Second World War, it was associated with a clear desire to 'humanise' capitalism through state intervention. It was believed that Keynesian economic policies would secure full employment, a mixed economy would help government to regulate economic activity, and comprehensive welfare provision funded via progressive taxation would narrow the gap between rich and poor. However, declining economic growth and the emergence in advanced industrial societies at least of a 'contented majority' (Galbraith, 1992), has brought about a further process of revision.

John Rawls (born 1921)

US academic and political philosopher. His major work, *A Theory of Justice* (1970), is regarded as the most important work of political philosophy written in English since the Second World War. It has influenced modern liberals and social democrats alike. Rawls proposed a theory of 'justice as fairness' that is based on the belief that social inequality can only be justified if it is of benefit to the least advantaged (in that it provides them with an incentive to work). This presumption in favour of equality is rooted in Rawls's belief that most people deprived of knowledge about their own talents and abilities would choose to live in an egalitarian society, rather than an inegalitarian one. As, for most people, the fear of being poor will outweigh the desire to be rich, redistribution and welfare can be defended on grounds of fairness. The universalist presumptions of his early work were modified to a certain degree in *Political Liberalism* (1993).

To some extent, the socialist character of social democracy has long been questioned. Some socialists, for instance, use 'social democracy' as a term of abuse, implying unprincipled compromise or even betrayal. Others, such as Anthony Crosland (1918–77), have argued that socialists have had to come to terms with changing historical realities, and have thus been happy to draw on the ideas of liberal theorists such as John Rawls. In the 1980s and 1990s, however, social democracy has more obviously moved into retreat. In an attempt to distance themselves from their old 'tax and spend' image, social democrats have increasingly looked to principles such as community, social partnership, and 'stakeholder economics' (Hutton, 1995), and have adopted policy positions that more closely resemble those of Christian Democracy than those of traditionalist socialism. This is demonstrated, for example, by the growing interest in the communitarianism (see p. 136) of thinkers such as the US sociologist Amitai Etzioni (1995) who have highlighted the growing need to reestablish community in the face of the atomistic and egoistical tendencies of the market. To the extent that social democracy has been recast as a defence of community, it has assumed, its critics argue, an essentially conservative character. Instead of being a vehicle of social transformation, it has developed into a defence of duty and moral responsibility, and so serves to uphold established ways of life.

■ Other ideological traditions

Fascism

Whereas liberalism, conservatism and socialism are nineteenth-century ideologies, fascism is a child of the twentieth century. Some would say that it is specifically an interwar phenomenon. Although fascist beliefs can be traced back to the late nineteenth century, they were fused together and shaped by the First World War and its aftermath, and in particular by the potent mixture of war and revolution that characterised the period. The two principal manifestations of fascism were Mussolini's Fascist dictatorship in Italy in 1922–43, and Hitler's Nazi dictatorship in Germany in 1933–45. Forms of neofascism and neo-Nazism have also resurfaced in the final years of the twentieth century that have taken advantage of the combination of economic crisis and political instability that has followed the collapse of communism.

Adolf Hitler (1889–1945)

German Nazi dictator. Hitler was the son of an Austrian customs official. He joined the German Worker's Party (later the Nationalsozialistische Deutsche Arbeiterpartei (NSDAP), or Nazi Party) in 1919, becoming its leader in 1921. He was appointed Chancellor of Germany in 1933, and declared himself Führer (Leader) the following year, by which time he had established a one-party dictatorship. The central feature of Hitler's world view, outlined in *Mein Kampf* ([1925] 1969), was his attempt to fuse expansionist German nationalism and virulent anti-Semitism into a theory of history in which there was an endless battle between the Germans and the Jews, who represented, respectively, the forces of good and evil. Hitler's policies contributed decisively to both the outbreak of the Second World War and the Holocaust.

In many respects, fascism constituted a revolt against the ideas and values that had dominated western political thought since the French Revolution; in the words of the Italian Fascist slogan, '1789 is dead'. Values such as rationalism, progress, freedom and equality were thus overturned in the name of struggle, leadership, power, heroism and war. In this sense, fascism has an 'anticharacter'. It is defined largely by what it opposes: it is a form of anticapitalism, antiliberalism, anti-individualism, anticommunism, and so on. A core theme that nevertheless runs throughout fascism is the image of an organically unified national community. This is reflected in a belief in 'strength through unity'. The individual, in a literal sense, is nothing; individual identity must be entirely absorbed into that of the community or social group. The fascist ideal is that of the 'new man', a hero, motivated by duty, honour and self-sacrifice, prepared to dedicate his life to the glory of his nation or race, and to give unquestioning obedience to a supreme leader.

Not all fascists, however, think alike. Italian Fascism was essentially an extreme form of statism (see p. 96) that was based on unquestioning respect and absolute loyalty towards a 'totalitarian' state. As the Fascist philosopher Gentile (1875–1944) put it, 'everything for the state; nothing against the state; nothing outside the state'. German National Socialism, on the other hand, was constructed largely on the basis of racialism (see p. 114). Its two core theories were Aryanism (the belief that the German people constitute a 'master race' and are destined for world domination), and a virulent form of anti-Semitism (see p. 115) that portrayed the Jews as inherently evil and aimed at their eradication. This latter belief found expression in the 'Final Solution'.

Anarchism

Anarchism is unusual amongst political ideologies in that no anarchist party has ever succeeded in winning power, at least at national level. Nevertheless, anarchist movements were powerful in, for example, Spain, France, Russia and Mexico through to the early twentieth century, and anarchist ideas continue to fertilise political debate by challenging the conventional belief that law, government and the state are either wholesome or indispensable. The central theme within anarchism is the belief that political authority in all its forms, and especially in the form of the state, is both evil and unnecessary (anarchy literally means 'without rule'). Nevertheless, the anarchist preference for a stateless society in which free individuals manage their own affairs through voluntary agreement and cooperation has been developed on the basis of two rival traditions: liberal individualism, and socialist communitarianism. Anarchism can thus be thought of as a point of intersection between liberalism and socialism: a form of both 'ultraliberalism' and 'ultrasocialism'.

The liberal case against the state is based on individualism and the desire to maximise liberty and choice. Unlike liberals, individualist anarchists such as William Godwin (1756–1836) believed that free and rational human beings would be able to manage their affairs peacefully and spontaneously, government being merely a form of unwanted coercion. Modern individualists have usually looked to the market to explain how society would be regulated in the absence of state authority, developing a form of anarchocapitalism, an extreme form of free-market economics. The more widely recognised anarchist tradition, however, draws upon socialist ideas such as community, cooperation, equality and common ownership. Collectivist anarchists therefore stress the human capacity for social solidarity that arises from our sociable, gregarious and essentially cooperative natures. On this basis, the French anarchist Pierre-Joseph Proudhon (see p. 124), for instance, developed what he called mutualism, the belief that small communities of independent peasants, craftsmen and artisans could manage their lives using a system of fair and equitable exchange, avoiding the injustices and exploitation of capitalism. Other anarchists, such as the Russian Peter Kropotkin (1842–1921), advanced a form of anarchocommunism, the central principles of which were common ownership, decentralisation and self-management.

Feminism

Although feminist aspirations have been expressed in societies dating back to Ancient China, they were not underpinned by a developed political theory until the publication of Mary Wollstonecraft's *A Vindication of the Rights of Women* ([1792] 1985). Indeed, it was not until the emergence of the women's suffrage movement in the 1840s and 1850s that feminist ideas reached a wider audience, in the form of so-called 'first-wave feminism'. The achievement of female suffrage in most western countries in the early twentieth century deprived the women's movement of its central goal and organising principle. 'Second-wave feminism', however, emerged in the 1960s. This expressed the more radical, and sometimes revolutionary, demands of the growing Women's Liberation Movement (WLM). Feminist theories and doctrines are diverse, but their unifying feature is a common desire to enhance, through whatever means, the social role of women. The underlying themes of feminism are therefore, first, that society is characterised by sexual or gender inequality and, second, that this structure of male power can and should be overturned.

At least three contrasting feminist traditions can be identified. Liberal feminists, such as Wollstonecraft and Betty Friedan (see p. 267), have tended to understand female subordination in terms of the unequal distribution of rights and opportunities in society. This 'equal-rights feminism' is essentially reformist. It is more concerned with the reform of the 'public' sphere, that is, with enhancing the legal and political status of women and improving their educational and career prospects, than with reordering 'private' or domestic life. In contrast, socialist feminists typically highlight the links between female subordination and the capitalist mode of production, drawing attention to the economic significance of women being confined to a family or domestic life where they, for example, relieve male workers of the

Mary Wollstonecraft (1759–97)

UK social theorist and feminist. Deeply influenced by the democratic radicalism of Rousseau, Wollstonecraft developed the first systematic feminist critique some 50 years before the emergence of the female-suffrage movement. Her most important work, *A Vindication of the Rights of Women* ([1792] 1985), was influenced by Lockian liberalism, and it stressed the equal rights of women, especially the right to education, on the basis of the notion of 'personhood'.

However, the work developed a more complex analysis of womanhood itself that is relevant to the concerns of contemporary feminism. Wollstonecraft was married to the anarchist William Godwin, and she was the mother of Mary Shelley, the author of *Frankenstein*.

burden of domestic labour, rear and help to educate the next generation of capitalist workers, and act as a reserve army of labour.

However, the distinctive flavour of second-wave feminism mainly results from the emergence of a feminist critique that is not rooted in conventional political doctrines, namely radical feminism. Radical feminists believe that gender divisions are the most fundamental and politically significant cleavages in society. In their view, all societies, historical and contemporary, are characterised by patriarchy (see p. 92), the institution whereby, as Kate Millett (1969) put it, 'that half of the population which is female is controlled by that half which is male'. Radical feminists therefore proclaim the need for a sexual revolution, a revolution that will, in particular, restructure personal, domestic and family life. The characteristic slogan of radical feminism, is thus 'the personal is the political'. Only in its extreme form, however, does radical feminism portray men as 'the enemy', and proclaim the need for women to withdraw from male society, a stance sometimes expressed in the form of political lesbianism.

Environmentalism

Although environmentalism is usually seen as a new ideology that is linked to the emergence of the ecological, or Green, movement in the late twentieth century, its roots can be traced back to the nineteenth-century revolt against industrialisation. Environmentalism therefore reflects concern about the damage done to the natural world by the increasing pace of economic development (exacerbated in the second half of the twentieth century by the advent of nuclear technology, acid rain, ozone depletion, global warming and so on), and anxiety about the declining quality of human existence and, ultimately, the survival of the human species. Such concerns are sometimes expressed through the vehicle of conventional ideologies. For instance, ecosocialism explains environmental destruction in terms of capitalism's rapacious desire for profit. Ecoconservatism links the cause of conservation to the desire to preserve traditional values and established institutions. And ecofeminism locates the origins of the ecological crisis in the system of male power, reflecting the fact that men are less sensitive than women to natural processes and the natural world.

However, what gives environmentalism its radical edge is the fact that it offers an alternative to the **anthropocentric** or human-centred stance adopted by all other

Anthropocentrism: The belief that human needs and interests are of overriding moral and philosophical importance; the opposite of ecocentrism.

Concept

Ecology, ecologism

Ecology (from the Greek *oikos* and *logos*, and meaning 'study of the home') is the study of the relationship between living organisms and their environment. It thus draws attention to the network of relationships that sustain all forms of life, and highlights the inter-connectedness of nature. Ecology (a term first used by Ernst Haeckel in 1873) can be regarded as a science, a descriptive principle, or even a moral value. Ecologism is a political doctrine or ideology that is constructed on the basis of ecological assumptions, notably about the essential link between humankind and the natural world: humans are part of nature, not its 'masters'. Ecologism is sometimes distinguished from environmentalism, in that the former implies the adoption of a biocentric or ecocentric perspective, while the latter is concerned with protecting nature, ultimately for human benefit.

ideologies; it does not see the natural world simply as a convenient resource available to satisfy human needs. By highlighting the importance of ecology, environmental-ism, or, as some of its proponents would prefer to call it, ecologism, develops an ecocentric world view that portrays the human species as merely part of nature. One of the most influential theories in this field is the Gaia hypothesis, advanced by James Lovelock (1979). This portrays the planet Earth as a living organism that is primarily concerned with its own survival. Others have expressed sympathy for Eastern religions that emphasise the oneness of life, such as Taoism and Zen Buddhism (Capra, 1983). 'Shallow' ecologists, or 'light Greens', such as those in some environ-mental pressure groups, believe that an appeal to self-interest and common sense will persuade humankind to adopt ecologically sound policies and lifestyles. 'Deep' ecologists, or 'dark Greens', on the other hand, insist that nothing short of a funda-mental reordering of political priorities, and a willingness to place the interests of the ecosystem before those of any individual species, will ultimately secure planetary and human survival. Members of both groups can be found in the 'antiparty' Green parties that have sprung up in Germany, Austria and elsewhere in Europe since the 1970s.

Religious fundamentalism

Religion and politics overlap at a number of points, not least in the development of the major ideological traditions. Ethical socialism, for instance, has been grounded in a variety of religious creeds, giving rise to forms of Christian socialism, Islamic socialism and so on. Protestantism helped to shape the ideas of self-striving and individual responsibility that gained political expression in classical liberalism. Religious fundamentalism, however, is different, in that it views politics (and indeed all aspects of personal and social existence) as being secondary to the 'revealed truth' of religious doctrine. From this perspective, political and social life should be organised on the basis of what are seen as essential or original religious principles, commonly supported by a belief in the literal truth of sacred texts. As it is possible to develop such principles into a comprehensive world view, religious fundamentalism can be treated as an ideology in its own right.

Where does religious fundamentalism come from, and what explains its resurgence at the end of the twentieth century? Two contrasting explanations have been advanced. One views fundamentalism as essentially an aberration, a symptom of the adjustment that societies make as they become accustomed to a modern and secularised culture. The second suggests that fundamentalism is of enduring signifi-cance, and believes that it is a consequence of the failure of **secularism** to satisfy the abiding human desire for 'higher' or spiritual truth.

Forms of religious fundamentalism have arisen in various parts of the world. The significance of Christian fundamentalism, for example, has increased in the USA since the 1970s as a result of the emergence of the 'New Christian Right', which cam-paigns against abortion, and for the introduction of prayers in US schools and a return to traditional family values. In Israel, Jewish fundamentalism, long repre-sented by a collection of small religious parties, has grown in importance as a result of attempts to prevent parts of what are seen as the Jewish homeland being seceded to an emerging Palestinian state. Hindu fundamentalism in India has developed to resist the spread of western secularism, and to combat the influence of rival creeds such as Sikhism and Islam.

Secularism: The belief that religion should not intrude into secular (worldly) affairs, usually reflected in a desire to separate church from state.

The most politically significant of modern fundamentalisms is undoubtedly Islamic fundamentalism. This was brought to prominence by the Iranian revolution of 1979, which led to the founding of the world's first Islamic state, under Ayatollah Khomeini (1900–89). It has subsequently spread throughout the Middle East, across North Africa, and into parts of Asia. Although the Shi'ite fundamentalism of Iran has generated the fiercest commitment and devotion, Islam in general has been a vehicle for expressing antiwesternism, through both antipathy towards the neocolonialism of western powers, and attempts to resist the spread of permissiveness and materialism. Islamic fundamentalism has, in particular, succeeded in articulating the aspirations of the urban poor in developing states, who until the 1970s were more likely to be attracted to socialism, in either its Islamic or its Marxist–Leninist form.

Concept

Fundamentalism

Fundamentalism (from the Latin *fundamentum*, meaning 'base') is a style of thought in which certain principles are recognised as essential 'truths' that have unchallengeable and overriding authority, regardless of their content. Substantive fundamentalisms therefore have little or nothing in common, except that their supporters tend to evince an earnestness or fervour born out of doctrinal certainty. Although it is usually associated with religion and the literal truth of sacred texts, fundamentalism can also be found in political creeds. Even liberal scepticism can be said to incorporate the fundamental belief that all theories should be doubted (except for itself). Although the term is often used pejoratively to imply inflexibility, dogmatism and authoritarianism, fundamentalism may also give expression to selflessness and a devotion to principle.

The end of ideology?

Much of the debate about ideology in the late twentieth century has focused on predictions of its demise, or at least of its fading relevance. This has come to be known as the 'end of ideology' debate. It was initiated in the 1950s, stimulated by the collapse of fascism at the end of the Second World War and the decline of communism in the developed West. In *The End of Ideology?: On the Exhaustion of Political Ideas in the 1950s* (1960), the US sociologist Daniel Bell declared that the stock of political ideas had been exhausted. In his view, ethical and ideological questions had become irrelevant because in most western societies parties competed for power simply by promising higher levels of economic growth and material affluence. In short, economics had triumphed over politics. However, the process to which Bell drew attention was not so much an end of ideology as the emergence of a broad ideological consensus (see p. 10) amongst major parties that led to the suspension of ideological debate. The ideology that prevailed in the 1950s and 1960s was a form of welfare capitalism, which in the UK and elsewhere took the form of a Keynesian–welfarist consensus.

A more recent contribution to this debate was made by Francis Fukuyama (see p. 29) in his essay 'The End of History?' (1989). Fukuyama did not suggest that political ideology had become irrelevant, but rather that a single ideology, liberal democracy, had triumphed over all its rivals, and that this triumph was final. This essay was written against the background of the collapse of communism in eastern Europe, which Fukuyama interpreted as indicating the demise of Marxism–Leninism as an ideology of world-historical importance. An

---

Concept

Postmodernism, postmodernity

Postmodernism is a controversial and confusing term that was first used to describe experimental movements in western arts, architecture and cultural development in general. As a tool of social and political analysis, postmodernism highlights the shift away from societies structured by industrialisation and class solidarity to increasingly fragmented and pluralistic information societies (that is, to postmodernity) in which individuals are transformed from producers to consumers, and individualism replaces class, religious and ethnic loyalties. From this perspective, conventional political ideologies such as Marxism and liberalism tend to be rejected as irrelevant 'meta-narratives' that developed out of the process of modernisation. Postmodernists argue that there is no such thing as certainty; the idea of absolute and universal truth must be discarded as an arrogant pretence. Emphasis is thus placed on the importance of discourse, debate and democracy.

alternative way of interpreting these developments, however, is offered by post-modernism, which suggests that the major ideologies, or 'grand narratives', were essentially products of a period of modernisation that has now passed. On the other hand, the very assertion of an end of ideology, an end of history, or an end of modernity can be seen as ideological in itself. Rather than heralding the final demise of ideology, such assertions may merely demonstrate that ideological debate is alive and well, and that the evolution of ideology is a continuing and perhaps unending process.

■ Summary

◆ Ideology is a controversial political term that has often carried pejorative implications. In the social–scientific sense, a political ideology is a more or less coherent set of ideas that provides a basis for organised political action. Its central features are an account of existing power relationships, a model of a desired future, and an outline of how political change can and should be brought about.

◆ Ideologies link political theory with political practice. On one level, ideologies resemble political philosophies, in that they constitute a collection of values, theories and doctrines, that is, a distinctive world view. On another level, however, they take the form of broad political movements, and are articulated through the activities of political leaders, parties and groups.

◆ Every ideology can be associated with a characteristic set of principles and ideas. Although these ideas 'hang together' in the sense that they interlock in distinctive ways, they are only systematic or coherent in a relative sense. All ideologies thus embody a range of rival traditions and internal tensions. Conflict within ideologies is thus sometimes more passionate than that between ideologies.

◆ Ideologies are by no means hermetically sealed and unchanging systems of thought. They overlap with one another at a number of points, and they sometimes have shared concerns and a common vocabulary. They are also always subject to political or intellectual renewal, both because they interact with, and influence the development of, other ideologies, and because they change over time as they are applied to changing historical circumstances.

◆ The significance of particular ideologies rises and falls in relation to the ideology's relevance to political, social and economic circumstances, and its capacity for theoretical innovation. Ideological conflict in the twentieth century has forced major ideologies such as liberalism, conservatism and socialism to reexamine their traditional principles, and it has fostered the growth of new ideologies, such as feminism, ecologism and religious fundamentalism.

◆ Debate about the end of ideology has taken a number of forms. In the early post-Second-World-War period, it was linked to the declining appeal of fascism and communism and the view that economic issues had displaced ideological ones. The 'end of history' thesis suggests that liberal democracy has triumphed worldwide. Postmodernism implies that conventional ideologies are irrelevant, as they were intrinsically a product of an earlier period of modernisation.

◼ Questions for discussion

▶ Why has the concept of ideology so often carried negative associations?

▶ Is it any longer possible to distinguish between liberalism and socialism?

▶ To what extent do New Right ideas conflict with those of traditional conservatism?

▶ Has Marxism a future?

▶ What circumstances are most conducive to the rise of fascism?

▶ Do anarchists demand the impossible?

▶ Why have feminism, ecologism and fundamentalism grown in significance? Do they have the potential to displace conventional political creeds?

▶ Is it possible to dispense with ideology?

◼ Further reading

Heywood, A. *Political Ideologies: An Introduction* (2nd ed.) (Basingstoke: Macmillan; New York: St Martin's Press, 1997). An accessible, up-to-date and comprehensive guide to the major ideological traditions.

McLellan, D. *Ideology* (Milton Keynes: Open University Press; Minneapolis: University of Minnesota Press, 1986). A short and clear yet thorough discussion of this elusive concept.

Good introductions to particular ideologies include the following: (Arblaster, 1984) on liberalism, (O'Sullivan, 1976) on conservatism, (Wright, 1987) on socialism, (Marshall, P., 1991) on anarchism, (Laqueur, 1979) on fascism, (Bryson, 1992) on feminism, (Dobson, 1990) on ecologism, and (Marty and Appleby, 1993) on religious fundamentalism.

Democracy

> 'Democracy is the worst form of government except all the other forms that have been tried from time to time.'
>
> WINSTON CHURCHILL *Speech*, UK House of Commons (1947)

Contents

The mass conversion of politicians and political thinkers to the cause of democracy has been one of the most dramatic, and significant, events in political history. Even in Ancient Greece, often thought of as the cradle of the democratic idea, democracy tended to be viewed in negative terms. Thinkers such as Plato and Aristotle, for example, viewed democracy as a system of rule by the masses at the expense of wisdom and property. Well into the nineteenth century, the term continued to have pejorative implications, suggesting a system of 'mob rule'. Now, however, we are all democrats. Liberals, conservatives, socialists, communists, anarchists and even fascists are eager to proclaim the virtues of democracy and to demonstrate their own democratic credentials. Indeed, as the major ideological systems have faltered and collapsed in the late twentieth century, the flame of democracy has appeared to burn yet more strongly. As the attractions of socialism have faded, and the merits of capitalism have been called into question, democracy has emerged as perhaps the only stable and enduring principle in the postmodern political landscape.

The major issues examined in this chapter are as follows:

Key issues

▶ How has the term democracy been used?

▶ Around what issues has the debate about the nature of democracy revolved?

▶ What models of democratic rule have been advanced?

▶ What are the strengths and weaknesses of each of these models?

▶ How do democratic systems operate in practice?

▶ Does democracy actually ensure rule by the people?

▇ Defining democracy

The origins of the term democracy can be traced back to Ancient Greece. Like other words ending in 'cracy' (for example, autocracy, aristocracy and bureaucracy), democracy is derived from the Greek word *kratos*, meaning power, or rule. Democracy thus means 'rule by the *demos*' (the *demos* referring to 'the people', although the Greeks originally used this to mean 'the poor' or 'the many'). However, the simple notion of 'rule by the people' does not get us very far. The problem with democracy has been its very popularity, a popularity that has threatened the term's undoing as a meaningful political concept. In being almost universally regarded as a 'good thing', democracy has come to be used as little more than a 'hurrah! word', implying approval of a particular set of ideas or system of rule. In Bernard Crick's (1993) words, 'democracy is perhaps the most promiscuous word in the world of public affairs'. A term that can mean anything to anyone is in danger of meaning nothing at all. Amongst the meanings that have been attached to the word 'democracy' are the following:

- a system of rule by the poor and disadvantaged
- a form of government in which the people rule themselves directly and continuously, without the need for professional politicians or public officials
- a society based on equal opportunity and individual merit, rather than hierarchy and privilege
- a system of welfare and redistribution aimed at narrowing social inequalities
- a system of decision-making based on the principle of majority rule
- a system of rule that secures the rights and interests of minorities by placing checks upon the power of the majority
- a means of filling public offices through a competitive struggle for the popular vote
- a system of government that serves the interests of the people regardless of their participation in political life.

Perhaps a more helpful starting point from which to consider the nature of democracy is Abraham Lincoln's Gettysburg Address, delivered in 1864 at the height of the American Civil War. Lincoln extolled the virtues of what he called 'government of the people, by the people, and for the people'. What this makes clear is that democracy links government to the people, but that this link can be forged in a number of ways: government *of*, *by* and *for* the people. The precise nature of democratic rule has been the subject of fierce ideological and political debate. The next main section of this chapter looks at various models of democracy. This section, however, explores the terms of the 'democracy debate'. These boil down to the attempt to answer three central questions:

- Who are the people?
- In what sense should the people rule?
- How far should popular rule extend?

Who are the people?

One of the core features of democracy is the principle of political equality, the notion that political power should be distributed as widely and as evenly as possible. However, within what body or group should this power be distributed? In short, who constitutes 'the people'? On the face of it, the answer is simple: 'the *demos*', or 'the people', surely refers to *all* the people, that is, the entire population of the country. In practice, however, every democratic system has restricted political participation, sometime severely.

As noted above, early Greek writers usually used *demos* to refer to 'the many', that is, the disadvantaged and usually propertyless masses. Democracy therefore implied not political equality, but a bias towards the poor. In Greek city-states, political participation was restricted to a tiny proportion of the population, male citizens over the age of 20, thereby excluding all women, slaves and foreigners. Strict restrictions on voting also existed in most western states until well into the twentieth century, usually in the form of a property qualification or the exclusion of women. Universal suffrage was not established in the UK until 1928, when women gained full voting rights. In the USA it was not achieved until the early 1960s, when African-American people in many Southern states were able to vote for the first time, and in Switzerland it was established in 1971 when women were eventually enfranchised. Nevertheless, an important restriction continues to be practised in all democratic systems in the form of the exclusion of children from political participation, although the age of majority ranges from 21 down to as low as 15 (as in Iranian presidential elections). Technical restrictions are also often placed on, for example, the certifiably insane and imprisoned criminals.

Although 'the people' is now accepted as meaning virtually all adult citizens, the term can be construed in a number of different ways. The people, for instance, can be viewed as a single, cohesive body, bound together by a common or collective interest: in this sense, the people are one and indivisible. Such a view tends to generate a model of democracy which, like Rousseau's (see p. 73) theory, examined in the next main section, focuses upon the 'general will' or collective will, rather than the 'private will' of each individual. Alternatively, as division and disagreement exist within all communities, 'the people' may in practice be taken to mean 'the majority'. In this case, democracy comes to mean the strict application of the principle of majority rule in which the will of the majority or numerically strongest overrides the will of the minority. This can nevertheless mean that democracy degenerates into 'the tyranny of the majority'. Finally, the people can be thought of as a collection of free and equal individuals, each of whom has a right to make autonomous decisions. Not only does this view clearly contradict any form of **majoritarianism**, but it also implies that, in the final analysis, only unanimous decisions can be binding upon the *demos*, and so dramatically restricts the application of democratic principles.

How should the people rule?

Most conceptions of democracy are based on the principle of 'government *by* the people'. This implies that, in effect, people govern themselves, that they participate in making the crucial decisions that structure their lives and determine the fate of their society. This participation can take a number of forms, however. In the case of direct democracy, popular participation entails direct and continuous involvement in decision-making, through devices such as referendums, mass meetings, or even interactive television. The alternative and more common form of democratic participation is the act of voting, which is the central feature of what is usually called representative democracy. When citizens vote, they do not so much make the decisions

> **Concept**
>
> **Political equality**
>
> In broad terms, political equality means an equal distribution of political power and influence. Political equality can thus be thought of as the core principle of democracy, in that it ensures that, however 'the people' is defined, each individual member carries the same weight: all voices are equally loud. This can be understood in two ways. In liberal-democratic theory, political equality implies an equal distribution of political rights: the right to vote, the right to stand for election and so on. This is often summed up as the principle 'one person, one vote; one vote, one value'. In contrast, socialists, amongst others, link political influence to factors such as the control of economic resources and access to the means of mass communication. From this perspective, political equality implies not merely equal voting rights, but also a significant level of social equality.

Majoritarianism: A theory or practice in which priority is accorded to the will of the majority; majoritarianism implies insensitivity towards minorities and individuals.

Focus on . . .

Direct democracy and representative democracy

Direct democracy (sometimes 'participatory democracy') is based on the direct, unmediated and continuous participation of citizens in the tasks of government. Direct democracy thus obliterates the distinction between government and the governed and between the state and civil society; it is a system of popular self-government. It was achieved in ancient Athens through a form of government by mass meeting; its most common modern manifestation is the use of the referendum (see p. 209). The merits of direct democracy include the following:

- It heightens the control that citizens can exercise over their own destinies, as it is the only pure form of democracy.
- It creates a better-informed and more politically sophisticated citizenry, and thus it has educational benefits.
- It enables the public to express their own views and interests without having to rely on self-serving politicians.
- It ensures that rule is legitimate in the sense that people are more likely to accept decisions that they have made themselves.

Representative democracy is a limited and indirect form of democracy. It is limited in that popular participation in government is infrequent and brief, being restricted to the act of voting every few years. It is indirect in that the public do not exercise power themselves; they merely select those who will rule on their behalf. This form of rule is democratic only insofar as representation (see p. 206) establishes a reliable and effective link between the government and the governed. This is sometimes expressed in the notion of an electoral mandate (see p. 210). The strengths of representative democracy include the following:

- It offers a practicable form of democracy (direct popular participation is only achievable in small communities).
- It relieves ordinary citizens of the burden of decision-making, thus making possible a division of labour in politics.
- It allows government to be placed in the hands of those with better education, expert knowledge and greater experience.
- It maintains stability by distancing ordinary citizens from politics, thereby encouraging them to accept compromise.

that structure their own lives as choose who will make those decisions on their behalf. What gives voting its democratic character, however, is that, provided that the election is competitive, it empowers the public to 'kick the rascals out', and it thus makes politicians publicly accountable.

There are also models of democracy that are built on the principle of 'government *for* the people', and that allow little scope for public participation of any kind, direct or indirect. The most grotesque example of this was found in the so-called **totalitarian democracies** which developed under fascist dictators such as Mussolini and Hitler. The democratic credentials of such regimes were based on the claim that the 'leader', and the leader alone, articulated the genuine interests of the people, thus implying that a 'true' democracy can be equated with an absolute dictatorship. In such cases,

Totalitarian democracy: An absolute dictatorship that masquerades as a democracy, typically based on the leader's claim to a monopoly of ideological wisdom.

popular rule meant nothing more than ritualised submission to the will of an all-powerful leader, orchestrated through rallies, marches and demonstrations. This was sometimes portrayed as plebiscitary democracy. Although totalitarian democracies have proved to be a travesty of the conventional notion of democratic rule, they demonstrate the tension that can exist between 'government *by* the people' (or popular participation), and 'government *for* the people' (rule in the public interest). Advocates of representative democracy, for example, have wished to confine popular participation in politics to the act of voting, precisely because they fear that the general public lack the wisdom, education and experience to rule wisely on their own behalf.

How far should popular rule extend?

Now that we have decided who the people are, and how they should rule, it is necessary to consider how far their rule should extend. What is the proper realm of democracy? What issues is it right for the people to decide, and what should be left to individual citizens? In many respects, such questions reopen the debate about the proper relationship between the public realm and the private realm that was discussed in Chapter 1. Models of democracy that have been constructed on the basis of liberal individualism have usually proposed that democracy be restricted to political life, with politics being narrowly defined. From this perspective, the purpose of democracy is to establish, through some process of popular participation, a framework of laws within which individuals can conduct their own affairs and pursue their private interests. Democratic solutions, then, are only appropriate for matters that specifically relate to the community; used in other circumstances, democracy amounts to an infringement of liberty. Not uncommonly, this fear of democracy is reflected in a rejection of direct or participatory forms of democracy.

However, an alternative view of democracy is often developed by, for example, socialists and radical democrats. In **radical democracy**, democracy is not seen as a means of laying down a framework within which individuals can go about their own business, but rather as a general principle that is applicable to all areas of social existence. People are seen as having a basic right to participate in the making of *any* decisions that affect their lives, with democracy simply being the collective process through which this is done. This position is evident in socialist demands for the collectivisation of wealth and the introduction of workers' self-management, both of which are seen as ways of democratising economic life. Instead of endorsing mere political democracy, socialists have therefore called for 'social democracy' or 'industrial democracy'. Feminists, similarly, have demanded the democratisation of family life, understood as the right of all to participate in the making of decisions in the domestic or private sphere. From this perspective, democracy is regarded as a friend of liberty, not as its enemy. Only when such principles are ignored can oppression and exploitation flourish.

■ Models of democracy

All too frequently, democracy is treated as a single, unambiguous phenomenon. It is often assumed that what passes for democracy in most western societies (a system of regular and competitive elections based on a universal franchise) is the only, or the only legitimate, form of democracy. Sometimes this notion of democracy is qualified

---

Concept

Plebiscitary democracy

Plebiscitary democracy is a form of democratic rule that operates through an unmediated link between the rulers and the ruled, established by plebiscites (or referendums). These allow the public to express their views on political issues directly. This is thus a species of direct, or participatory, democracy. However, this type of democracy is often criticised because of the scope it offers for demagoguery (rule by political leaders who manipulate the masses through oratory, and appeal to their prejudices and passions). This type of democracy amounts to little more than a system of mass acclamation that gives dictatorship a populist (see p. 335) gloss. There is, nevertheless, a distinction between plebiscitary democracy and the use of referendums to supplement a system of representative democracy.

Radical democracy: A form of democracy that favours decentralisation and participation, the widest possible dispersal of political power.

by the addition of the term 'liberal', turning it into liberal democracy (see p. 28). In reality, however, there are a number of rival theories or models of democracy, each offering its own version of popular rule. This highlights not merely the variety of democratic forms and mechanisms, but also, more fundamentally, the very different grounds on which democratic rule can be justified. Even liberal democracy is a misleading term, as competing liberal views of democratic organisation can be identified. Four contrasting models of democracy can be identified as follows:

- classical democracy
- protective democracy
- developmental democracy
- people's democracy.

Classical democracy

The classical model of democracy is based on the *polis*, or city-state, of Ancient Greece, and particularly on the system of rule that developed in the largest and most powerful Greek city-state, Athens. The form of direct democracy that operated in Athens during the fourth and fifth centuries BCE is often portrayed as the only pure or ideal system of popular participation. Nevertheless, although the model had considerable impact on later thinkers such as Rousseau (see p. 73) and Marx (see p. 51), Athenian democracy developed a very particular kind of direct popular rule, one that has only a very limited application in the modern world. Athenian democracy amounted to a form of government by mass meeting. All major decisions were made by the Assembly, or *Ecclesia*, to which all citizens belonged. This met at least 40 times a year. When full-time public officials were needed, they were chosen on a basis of lot or rota to ensure that they constituted a microcosm of the larger citizenry, and terms of office were typically short to achieve the broadest possible participation. A Council consisting of 500 citizens acted as the executive or steering committee of the Assembly, and a 50-strong Committee, in turn, made proposals to the Council. The President of the Committee held office for only a single day, and no Athenian could hold this honour more than once in his lifetime. The only concession made to the need for training and experience was in the case of the ten military generals, who, unlike other public officials, were eligible for reelection.

What made Athenian democracy so remarkable was the level of political activity of its citizens. Not only did they participate in regular meetings of the Assembly but they were, in large numbers, prepared to shoulder the responsibility of public office and decision-making. The most influential contemporaneous critic of this form of democracy was the philosopher Plato (see p. 13). Plato attacked the principle of political equality on the grounds that the mass of the people possess neither the wisdom nor the experience to rule wisely on their own behalf. His solution, advanced in *The Republic*, was that government be placed in the hands of a class of philosopher kings, the Guardians, whose rule would amount to a kind of enlightened dictatorship. On a practical level, however, the principal drawback of Athenian democracy was that it could only operate by excluding the mass of the population from political activity. Participation was restricted to Athenian-born males who were over 20 years of age. Slaves (the majority of the population), women and foreigners had no political rights whatsoever. Indeed, Athenian citizens were only able to devote so much of their lives to politics because slavery relieved them of the need to engage in

Jeremy Bentham (1748–1832)

UK philosopher, legal reformer and founder of utilitarianism. Bentham developed a moral and philosophical system that was based on the idea that human beings are rationally self-interested creatures or **utility** maximisers, which he believed provided a scientific basis for legal and political reforms. Using the 'greatest happiness' principle, his followers, the Philosophic Radicals, were responsible for many of the reforms in social administration, law, government and economics in the UK in the nineteenth century. A supporter of *laissez-faire* economics, in later life Bentham also became a firm advocate of political democracy. His utilitarian creed was developed in *Fragments on Government* ([1776] 1948), and more fully in *Principles of Morals and Legislation* (1789).

arduous labour, and the confinement of women to the private realm freed them from domestic responsibilities. In this light, in fact, the Athenian *polis* could be seen as the very antithesis of the democratic ideal. Nevertheless, the classical model of direct and continuous popular participation in political life has been kept alive in certain parts of the world, notably in the township meetings of New England in the USA and in the communal assemblies which operate in the smaller Swiss cantons.

Protective democracy

When democratic ideas were revived in the seventeenth and eighteenth centuries, they appeared in a form that was very different from the classical democracy of Ancient Greece. In particular, democracy was seen less as a mechanism through which the public could participate in political life, and more as a device through which citizens could protect themselves from the encroachments of government, hence protective democracy. This view appealed particularly to early liberal thinkers whose concern was, above all, to create the widest realm of individual liberty. The desire to protect the individual from over-mighty government was expressed in perhaps the earliest of all democratic sentiments, Aristotle's response to Plato: '*quis custodiet custodes?*' ('who will guard the Guardians?').

This same concern with unchecked power was taken up in the seventeenth century by John Locke (see p. 43), who argued that the right to vote was based on the existence of **natural rights** and, in particular, on the right to property. If government, through taxation, possessed the power to expropriate property, citizens were entitled to protect themselves by controlling the composition of the tax-setting body: the legislature. In other words, democracy came to mean a system of 'government by consent' operating through a representative assembly. However, Locke himself was not a democrat by modern standards, as he believed that only property owners should vote, on the basis that only they had natural rights that could be infringed by government. The more radical notion of universal suffrage was advanced from the late eighteenth century onwards by utilitarian theorists such as Jeremy Bentham and James Mill (1773–1836). The utilitarian (see p. 383) case for democracy is also based on the need to protect or advance individual interests. Bentham came to believe that, since all individuals seek pleasure and the avoidance of pain, a universal franchise (conceived in his day as manhood suffrage) was the only way of promoting 'the greatest happiness for the greatest number'.

Utility: Use value; satisfaction derived from material consumption.

Natural rights: God-given rights that are fundamental to human beings and are therefore inalienable (they cannot be taken away).

However, to justify democracy on protective grounds is to provide only a qualified endorsement of democratic rule. In short, protective democracy is but a limited and indirect form of democracy. In practice, the **consent** of the governed is exercised through voting in regular and competitive elections. This thereby ensures the accountability of those who govern. Political equality is thus understood in strictly technical terms to mean equal voting rights. Moreover, this is above all a system of constitutional democracy that operates within a set of formal or informal rules that check the exercise of government power. If the right to vote is a means of defending individual liberty, liberty must also be guaranteed by a strictly enforced separation of powers via the creation of a separate executive, legislature and judiciary, and by the maintenance of basic rights and freedoms, such as freedom of expression, freedom of movement, and freedom from arbitrary arrest. Ultimately, protective democracy aims to give citizens the widest possible scope to live their lives as they choose. It is therefore compatible with *laissez-faire* capitalism (see p. 171) and the belief that individuals should be entirely responsible for their economic and social circumstances. Protective democracy has therefore particularly appealed to classical liberals and, in modern politics, to supporters of the New Right.

Developmental democracy

Although early democratic theory focused on the need to protect individual rights and interests, it soon developed an alternative focus: a concern with the development of the human individual and the community. This gave rise to quite new models of democratic rule which can broadly be referred to as systems of developmental democracy. The most novel, and radical, such model was developed by Jean-Jacques Rousseau. In many respects, Rousseau's ideas mark a departure from the dominant, liberal conception of democracy, and they came to have an impact on the Marxist and anarchist traditions as well as, later, on the New Left. For Rousseau, democracy was ultimately a means through which human beings could achieve freedom (see p. 282) or autonomy, in the sense of 'obedience to a law one prescribes to oneself'. In other words, citizens are only 'free' when they participate directly and continuously in shaping the life of their community. This is an idea that moves well beyond the conventional notion of electoral democracy and offers support for the more radical ideal of direct democracy. Indeed, Rousseau was a strenuous critic of the practice of elections used in England, arguing in *The Social Contract* ([1762] 1913) as follows:

The English people believes itself to be free, it is gravely mistaken; it is only free when it elects its member of parliament; as soon as they are elected, the people are enslaved; it is nothing. In the brief moment of its freedom, the English people makes such use of its freedom that it deserves to lose it.

However, what gives Rousseau's model its novel character is his insistence that freedom ultimately means obedience to the **general will**. Rousseau believed the general will to be the 'true' will of each citizen, in contrast to his or her 'private' or selfish will. By obeying the general will, citizens are therefore doing nothing more than obeying their own 'true' natures, the general will being what individuals would will if they were to act selflessly. In Rousseau's view, such a system of radical developmental democracy required not merely political equality but a relatively high level of economic equality. Although not a supporter of common ownership, Rousseau

Consent: Assent or permission; in politics, usually an agreement to be governed or ruled.

General will: The genuine interests of a collective body, equivalent to the common good; the will of all provided each person acts selflessly.

Jean-Jacques Rousseau (1712–78)

Geneva-born French moral and political philosopher, perhaps the principal intellectual influence upon the French Revolution. Rousseau was entirely self-taught. He moved to Paris in 1742, and became an intimate of leading members of the French Enlightenment, especially Diderot. His writings, ranging over education, the arts, science, literature and philosophy, reflect a deep belief in the goodness of 'natural man' and the corruption of 'social man'. Rousseau's political teaching, summarised in *Émile* (1762) and developed in *The Social Contract* ([1762] 1913), advocates a radical form of democracy which has influenced liberal, socialist, anarchist and, some would argue, fascist thought. His autobiography, *Confessions* (1770), examines his life with remarkable candour and demonstrates a willingness to expose his faults and weaknesses.

nevertheless proposed that 'no citizen shall be rich enough to buy another and none so poor as to be forced to sell himself' ([1762] 1913:96).

Rousseau's theories have helped to shape the modern idea of participatory democracy taken up by New Left thinkers in the 1960s and 1970s. This extols the virtues of a 'participatory society', a society in which each and every citizen is able to achieve self-development by participating in the decisions that shape his or her life. This goal can only be achieved through the promotion of openness, accountability (see p. 375) and decentralisation within all the key institutions of society: within the family, the workplace and the local community just as much as within 'political' institutions such as parties, interest groups and legislative bodies. At the heart of this model is the notion of 'grass-roots democracy', that is, the belief that political power should be exercised at the lowest possible level. Nevertheless, Rousseau's own theories have been criticised for distinguishing between citizens' 'true' wills and their 'felt' or subjective wills. The danger of this is that, if the general will cannot be established by simply asking citizens what they want (because they may be blinded by selfishness), there is scope for the general will to be defined from above, perhaps by a dictator claiming to act in the 'true' interests of society. Rousseau is therefore sometimes seen as the architect of so-called totalitarian democracy (Talmon, 1952).

However, a more modest form of developmental democracy has also been advanced that is compatible with the liberal model of representative government. This view of developmental democracy is rooted in the writings of John Stuart Mill (see p. 44). For Mill, the central virtue of democracy was that it promotes the 'highest and harmonious' development of individual capacities. By participating in political life, citizens enhance their understanding, strengthen their sensibilities, and achieve a higher level of personal development. In short, democracy is essentially an educational experience. As a result, Mill proposed the broadening of popular participation, arguing that the franchise should be extended to all but those who are illiterate. In the process, he suggested (radically, for his time) that suffrage should also be extended to women. In addition, he advocated strong and independent local authorities in the belief that this would broaden the opportunities available for holding public office.

On the other hand, Mill, in common with all liberals, was also aware of the dangers of democracy. Indeed, Mill's views are out of step with mainstream liberal thought in that he rejected the idea of formal political equality. Following Plato, Mill did not believe that all political opinions are of equal value. Consequently, he proposed a

Concept

Parliamentary democracy

Parliamentary democracy is a form of democratic rule that operates through a popularly elected deliberative assembly, which establishes an indirect link between government and the governed. Democracy, in this sense, essentially means responsible and representative government. Parliamentary democracy thus balances popular participation against elite rule: government is accountable not directly to the public but to the public's elected representatives. The attraction of such a system is that representatives are, by virtue of their education and the opportunities that they have to deliberate and debate, supposedly better able than citizens themselves to define the citizens' best interests. In the classical form of parliamentary democracy, associated with J. S. Mill and Burke (see p. 45), parliamentarians are required to think for themselves on behalf of their constituents. Modern party politics, however, has fused the ideas of parliamentary democracy and mandate democracy (see p. 210).

system of plural voting: unskilled workers would have a single vote, skilled workers two votes, and graduates and members of the learned professions five or six votes. However, his principal reservation about democracy was derived from the more typical liberal fear of what Alexis de Tocqueville (see p. 201) famously described as 'the tyranny of the majority'. In other words, democracy always contains the threat that individual liberty and minority rights may be crushed in the name of the people. Mill's particular concern was that democracy would undermine debate, criticism and intellectual life in general by encouraging people to accept the will of the majority, thereby promoting uniformity and dull conformism. Quite simply, the majority is not always right; wisdom cannot be determined by the simple device of a show of hands. Mill's ideas therefore support the idea of **deliberative democracy** or parliamentary democracy.

People's democracy

The term 'people's democracy' is derived from the orthodox communist regimes that sprang up on the Soviet model in the aftermath of the Second World War. It is here used, however, to refer broadly to the various democratic models that the Marxist tradition has generated. Although they differ, these models offer a clear contrast to the more familiar liberal democratic ones. Marxists have tended to be dismissive of liberal or parliamentary democracy, seeing it as a form of 'bourgeois' or 'capitalist' democracy. Nevertheless, Marxists were drawn to the concept or ideal of democracy because of its clear egalitarian implications. The term was used in particular to designate the goal of social equality brought about through the common ownership of wealth ('social democracy' in its original sense), in contrast to 'political' democracy, which establishes only a facade of equality.

Marx believed that the overthrow of capitalism would be a trigger that would allow genuine democracy to flourish. In his view, a fully communist society would only come into existence after a transitory period characterised by 'the revolutionary dictatorship of the proletariat'. In effect, a system of 'bourgeois' democracy would be replaced by a very different system of 'proletarian' democracy. Although Marx refused to describe in detail how this transitory society would be organised, its broad shape can be discerned from his admiration for the Paris Commune of 1871, which was a short-lived experiment in what approximated to direct democracy. Marx predicted, however, that, as class antagonisms faded and a fully communist society came into existence, the proletarian state would simply 'wither away'. Not only would this bring an end to the need for government, law and even politics, but it would also, effectively, make democracy redundant.

The form of democracy that was developed in twentieth-century communist states, however, owed more to the ideas of V. I. Lenin than it did to those of Marx. Although Lenin's 1917 slogan 'All power to the Soviets' (the workers' and soldiers' and sailors' councils) had kept alive the notion of commune democracy, in reality power in Soviet Russia quickly fell into the hands of the Bolshevik party (soon renamed the Communist Party). In Lenin's view, this party was nothing less than 'the vanguard of the working class'. Armed with Marxism, the party claimed that it was able to perceive the genuine interests of the proletariat and thus guide it to the realisation of its revolutionary potential. This theory became the cornerstone of 'Leninist democracy' in the USSR, and it was accepted by all other orthodox communist regimes as one of the core features of Marxism–Leninism. However, the

Deliberative democracy: A form of democracy that emphasises the need for discourse and debate to help define the public interest.

Vladimir Ilyich Lenin (1870–1924)

Russian Marxist theorist and active revolutionary. As leader of the Bolsheviks, Lenin masterminded the 1917 Russian Bolshevik Revolution, and became the first leader of the USSR. His contributions to Marxism were his theory of the revolutionary or vanguard party, outlined in *What is to be Done?* ([1902] 1968), his analysis of colonialism as an economic phenomenon, described in *Imperialism, the Highest Stage of Capitalism* ([1916] 1970), and his firm commitment to the 'insurrectionary road to socialism', developed in *State and Revolution* (1917). Lenin's reputation is inevitably tied up with the subsequent course of Soviet history; he is seen by some as the father of Stalinist oppression, but by others as a critic of bureaucracy and a defender of debate and argument.

weakness of this model is that Lenin failed to build into it any mechanism for checking the power of the Communist Party (and particularly its leaders) and for ensuring that it remained sensitive and accountable to the proletarian class. To rephrase Aristotle, 'who will guard the Communist Party?'.

Democracy in practice: rival views

Although there continues to be controversy about which is the most desirable form of democracy, much of contemporary debate revolves around how democracy works in practice. This reflects the fact that there is broad, even worldwide, acceptance of a particular model of democracy, generally termed liberal democracy. Despite the existence of competing tendencies within this broad category, certain central features are clear:

- Liberal democracy is an indirect and representative form of democracy in that political office is gained through success in regular elections that are conducted on the basis of formal political equality.

- Liberal democracy is based on competition and electoral choice. These are achieved through political pluralism, tolerance of a wide range of contending beliefs, and the existence of conflicting social philosophies and rival political movements and parties.

- In liberal democracy, there is a clear distinction between the state and civil society. This distinction is maintained through the existence of autonomous groups and interests, and the market or capitalist organisation of economic life.

Nevertheless, there is a considerable amount of disagreement about the meaning and significance of liberal democracy. Does it, for instance, ensure a genuine and healthy dispersal of political power? Do democratic processes genuinely promote long-term benefits, or are they self-defeating? Can political equality coexist with economic inequality? In short, this form of democracy is interpreted in different ways by different theorists. The most important of these interpretations are advanced by:

- pluralism
- elitism
- corporatism

• the New Right
• Marxism.

Pluralism

The term pluralism is used in two senses, one broad the other narrow. In its broader sense, pluralism is a belief in, or a commitment to, diversity or multiplicity (the existence of many things). As a descriptive term, pluralism may be used to denote the existence of party competition (political pluralism), a multiplicity of ethical values (moral pluralism), or a variety of cultural norms (cultural pluralism). As a normative term, it suggests that diversity is healthy and desirable, usually because it safeguards individual liberty and promotes debate, argument and understanding. More narrowly, pluralism is a theory of the distribution of political power. It holds that power is widely and evenly dispersed in society rather than concentrated in the hands of an elite or a ruling class. In this form, pluralism is usually seen as a theory of 'group politics' in which individuals are largely represented through their membership of organised groups, and all such groups have access to the policy process.

Bicameralism: The fragmentation of legislative power, established through the existence of two (co-equal) chambers in the assembly; a device of limited government (see p. 303).

Pluralist view

Pluralist ideas can be traced back to early liberal political philosophy, and notably to the ideas of Locke and Montesquieu (see p. 294). Their first systematic development, however, is found in the contributions of James Madison (see p. 302) to *The Federalist Papers* (Hamilton, Jay and Madison, [1787–89] 1961). In considering the transformation of America from a loose confederation of states into the federal USA, Madison's particular fear was the 'problem of factions'. In common with most liberals, Madison argued that unchecked democratic rule might simply lead to majoritarianism, to the crushing of individual rights and to the expropriation of property in the name of the people. What made Madison's work notable, however, was his stress upon the multiplicity of interests and groups in society, and his insistence that, unless each such group possessed a political voice, stability and order would be impossible. He therefore proposed a system of divided government based on the separation of powers, **bicameralism** and federalism (see p. 125), that offered a variety of access points to competing groups and interests. The resulting system of rule by multiple minorities is often referred to as 'Madisonian democracy'. Insofar as it recognises both the existence of diversity or multiplicity in society, and the fact that such multiplicity is desirable, Madison's model is the first developed statement of pluralist principles.

The most influential modern exponent of pluralist theory is Robert Dahl (see p. 256). As described in *Who Governs? Democracy and Power in an American City* (1961), Dahl carried out an empirical study of the distribution of power in New Haven, Connecticut, USA. He concluded that, although the politically privileged and economically powerful exerted greater power than ordinary citizens, no ruling or permanent elite was able to dominate the political process. His conclusion was that 'New Haven is an example of a democratic system, warts and all' (p. 311). Dahl recognised that modern democratic systems differ markedly from the classical democracies of Ancient Greece. With Charles Lindblom, he coined the term 'polyarchy' (see p. 31) to mean rule by the many, as distinct from rule by all citizens. The key feature of such a system of pluralist democracy is that competition between parties at election time, and the ability of interest or pressure groups to articulate their views freely, establishes a reliable link between the government and the governed, and creates a channel of communication between the two. While this may fall a long way short of the ideal of popular self-government, its supporters nevertheless argue that it ensures a sufficient level of accountability and popular responsiveness for it to be regarded as democratic.

However, the relationship between pluralism and democracy may not be a secure one. For instance, one of the purposes of the Madisonian system was, arguably, to constrain democracy in the hope of safeguarding property. In other words, the system of rule by multiple minorities may simply have been a device to prevent the majority (the propertyless masses) from exercising political power. A further problem is the danger of what has been called 'pluralist stagnation'. This occurs as organised groups and economic interests become so powerful that they create a log jam, resulting in the problem of government 'overload'. In such circumstances, a pluralist system may simply become ungovernable. Finally, there is the problem identified by Dahl in later works such as *A Preface to Economic Democracy* (1985), notably that the unequal ownership of economic resources tends to concentrate political power in the hands of the few, and deprive it from the many. This line of argument runs parallel to the conventional Marxist critique of pluralist democracy, and has given rise to neopluralism (see p. 88).

Elitist view

Elitism developed as a critique of egalitarian ideas such as democracy and socialism. It draws attention to the fact of elite rule, either as an inevitable and desirable feature of social existence, or as a remediable and regrettable one. Classical elitists, such as Vilfredo Pareto (1848–1923), Gaetano Mosca (1857–1941) and Robert Michels (1876–1936), tended to take the former position. For them, democracy was no more than a foolish delusion, because political power is always exercised by a privileged minority: an elite. For example, in *The Ruling Class* ([1896] 1939), Mosca proclaimed that, in all societies, 'two classes of people appear – a class that rules and a class that is ruled'. In his view, the resources or attributes that are necessary for rule are always unequally distributed, and, further, a cohesive minority will always be able to manipulate and control the masses, even in a parliamentary democracy.

Pareto suggested that the qualities needed to rule are those of one of two psychological types: 'foxes' (who rule by cunning and are able to manipulate the consent of the masses), and 'lions' (whose domination is typically achieved through coercion and violence). Michels, however, developed an alternative line of argument based on the tendency within all organisations, however democratic they might appear, for power to be concentrated in the hands of a small group of dominant figures who can organise and make decisions, rather than being in the hands of an apathetic rank and file. He termed this 'the iron law of oligarchy' (see p. 238). This notion of bureaucratic power was later developed by James Burnham, who, in *The Managerial Revolution* (1941), argued that a 'managerial class' dominated all industrial societies, both capitalist and communist, by virtue of its technical and scientific knowledge and its administrative skills.

Whereas classical elitists strove to prove that democracy was always a myth, modern elitist theorists have tended to highlight how far particular political systems fall short of the democratic ideal. An example of this can be found in C. Wright Mills' influential account of the power structure in the USA. In contrast to the pluralist notion of a wide and broadly democratic dispersal of power, Mills, in *The Power Elite* (1956), offered a portrait of a USA dominated by a nexus of leading groups. In his view, this 'power elite' comprised a triumvirate of big business (particularly defence-related industries), the US military, and political cliques surrounding the President. Drawing on a combination of economic power, bureaucratic control, and access to the highest levels of the executive branch of government, the power elite is able to shape key 'history-making' decisions, especially in the fields of defence and foreign policy, as well as strategic economic policy. The power-elite model suggests that liberal democracy in the USA is largely a sham. Electoral pressures tend to be absorbed by the 'middle levels of power' (Congress, state governments and so on), and groups such as organised labour, small businesses and consumer lobbyists are only able to exert influence at the margins of the policy process. Elitists have, moreover, argued that empirical studies have only supported pluralist conclusions because Dahl and others have ignored the importance of non-decision-making as a manifestation of power (see p. 11).

Concept

Pluralist democracy

The term pluralist democracy is sometimes used interchangeably with liberal democracy to indicate a democratic system based on electoral competition between a number of political parties. More specifically, it refers to a form of democracy that operates through the capacity of organised groups and interests to articulate popular demands and ensure government responsiveness. As such, it can be seen as an alternative to parliamentary democracy and to any form of majoritarianism. The conditions for a healthy pluralist democracy include the following:

- There is a wide dispersal of political power amongst competing groups, and, specifically, elite groups are absent.
- There is a high degree of internal responsiveness, with group leaders being accountable to members.
- There is a neutral governmental machine that is sufficiently fragmented to offer groups a number of points of access.

Elite, elitism

The term elite originally meant, and can still mean, the highest, the best, or the excellent. Used in a neutral or empirical sense, however, it refers to a minority in whose hands power, wealth or privilege is concentrated, justifiably or otherwise. Elitism is a belief in, or practice of, rule by an elite or minority. *Normative* elitism suggests that elite rule is desirable: political power should be vested in the hands of a wise or enlightened minority. *Classical* elitism (developed by Mosca, Pareto and Michels) claimed to be empirical (although normative beliefs often intruded), and it saw elite rule as being inevitable, an unchangeable fact of social existence. *Modern* elitism has also developed an empirical analysis, but it is more critical and discriminating about the causes of elite rule. Modern elitists, such as C. Wright Mills (1916–62), have often been concerned to highlight elite rule in the hope of both explaining it and challenging it.

Certain elite theorists have nevertheless argued that a measure of democratic accountability is consistent with elite rule. Whereas the power-elite model portrays the elite as a cohesive body, bound together by common or overlapping interests, competitive elitism (sometimes called democratic elitism) highlights the significance of elite rivalry (see Figure 4.1). In other words, the elite, consisting of the leading figures from a number of competing groups and interests, is fractured. This view is often associated with Joseph Schumpeter's (see p. 211) 'realistic' model of democracy outlined in *Capitalism, Socialism and Democracy* (1942:269):

The democratic method is that institutional arrangement for arriving at political decisions in which individuals acquire the power to decide by means of a competitive struggle for the people's vote.

The electorate can decide which elite rules, but cannot change the fact that power is always exercised by an elite. This model of competitive elitism was developed by Anthony Downs (1957) into the 'economic theory of democracy'. In effect, electoral competition creates a political market in which politicians act as entrepreneurs bent upon achieving government power, and individual voters behave like consumers, voting for the party with the policies that most closely reflect their own preferences. Downs argued that a system of open and competitive elections guarantees democratic rule because it placed government in the hands of the party whose philosophy, values and policies correspond most closely to the preferences of the largest group of voters. As Schumpeter put it, 'democracy is the rule of the politician'.

As a model of democratic politics, competitive elitism at least has the virtue that it corresponds closely to the workings of the liberal-democratic political system. Indeed, it emerged more as an attempt to *describe* how the democratic process works than through a desire to *prescribe* certain values and principles – political equality, popular participation, freedom or whatever. Democracy, then, is seen simply as a political method: as a means of making political decisions by reference to a competitive struggle for the popular vote. To the extent that the model is accurate, its virtue is that it allows considerable scope for political leadership by placing decision-making in the hands of the best-informed, most-skilled, and most politically committed members of society. On the other hand, although competition for power undoubtedly creates a measure of accountability, competitive elitism must at best be considered a weak form of democracy. Not only can one elite only be removed by replacing it with another, but the role allotted to the general public (that of deciding every few years which elite will rule on its behalf) is likely to engender apathy, lack of interest, and even alienation.

Corporatist view

The origins of corporatism (see p. 257) date back to the attempt in Fascist Italy to construct a so-called 'corporate state' by integrating both managers and workers into the processes of government. Corporatist theorists, however, have drawn attention to parallel developments in the world's major industrialised states. In the form of **neocorporatism**, or liberal corporatism, this gave rise to the spectre of 'tripartite government', in which government is conducted through organisations which allow state officials, employers' groups and unions to deal directly with one another. To a large extent, this tendency to integrate economic interests into government (which was common in the postwar period, and particularly prominent in, for example,

Neocorporatism: A tendency found in western polyarchies for organised interests to be granted privileged and institutionalised access to policy formulation.

Power-elite model: single, coherent elite

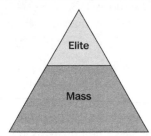

Fig. 4.1 Elite models

Competitive elite model: fractured elite

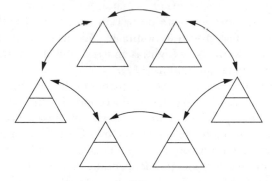

Sweden, Norway, the Netherlands and Austria) was a consequence of the drift towards economic management and intervention. As government sought to manage economic life and deliver an increasingly broad range of public services, it recognised the need for institutional arrangements designed to secure the cooperation and support of major economic interests. Where attempts have been made to shift economic policy away from state intervention and towards the free market (as in the UK since 1979), the impact of corporatism has markedly diminished.

The significance of corporatism in terms of democratic processes is clearly considerable. There are those who, like the British guild socialists, argue that corporatism makes possible a form of functional representation, in that individuals' views and interests are articulated more by the groups to which they belong than through the mechanism of competitive elections. What is called 'corporate pluralism' thus portrays tripartism as a mechanism through which the major groups and interests in society compete to shape government policy. Most commentators, however, see corporatism very much as a threat to democracy. In the first place, corporatism only advantages groups that are accorded privileged access to government. 'Insider' groups therefore possess a political voice, while 'outsider' groups are denied one. Secondly, corporatism can work to the benefit of the state rather than major economic interests, in that the **peak associations** that the government chooses to deal with can be used to exert discipline over their members and to filter out radical demands. Finally, corporatism threatens to subvert the processes of electoral or parliamentary democracy. Policy is made through negotiations between government officials and leaders of powerful economic interests rather than through the deliberations of a representative assembly. Interest-group leaders may thus exert

Peak association: A group recognised by government as representing the general or collective interests of businesses or workers.

considerable political power, even though they are in no way publicly accountable and their influence is not subject to public scrutiny.

New Right view

The emergence of the New Right from the 1970s onwards has generated a very particular critique of democratic politics. This has focused upon the danger of what has been called 'democratic overload': the paralysis of a political system that is subject to unrestrained group and electoral pressures. One aspect of this critique has highlighted the unsavoury face of corporatism. New Right theorists are keen advocates of the free market, believing that economies work best when left alone by government. The danger of corporatism from this perspective is that it empowers sectional groups and economic interests, enabling them to make demands on government for increased pay, public investment, subsidies, state protection and so on. In effect, corporatism allows well-placed interest groups to dominate and dictate to government. The result of this, according to the New Right, is an irresistible drift towards state intervention and economic stagnation (Olson, 1982).

Government 'overload' can also be seen to be a consequence of the electoral process. This was what Samuel Brittan (1977) referred to as 'the economic consequences of democracy'. In this view, electoral politics amounts to a self-defeating process in which politicians are encouraged to compete for power by offering increasingly unrealistic promises to the electorate. Both voters and politicians are held to blame here. Voters are attracted by promises of higher public spending because they calculate that the cost (an increased tax burden) will be spread over the entire population. Politicians, consumed by the desire to win power, attempt to outbid one another by making ever more generous spending pledges to the electorate. According to Brittan, the economic consequences of unrestrained democracy are high levels of inflation fuelled by public borrowing, and a tax burden that destroys enterprise and undermines growth. As characterised by David Marquand (1988), the New Right view is that 'democracy is to adults what chocolate is to children: endlessly tempting; harmless in small doses; sickening in excess'. New Right theorists therefore tend to see democracy in strictly protective terms, regarding it essentially as a defence against arbitrary government rather than a means of bringing about social transformation.

Marxist view

As pointed out in relation to people's democracy, the Marxist view of democratic politics is rooted in class analysis. In this view, political power cannot be understood narrowly in terms of electoral rights, or in terms of the ability of groups to articulate their interests by lobbying and campaigning. Rather, at a deeper level, political power reflects the distribution of economic power and, in particular, the unequal ownership of productive wealth. The Marxist critique of liberal democracy thus focuses upon the inherent tension between democracy and capitalism, that is, between the political equality which liberal democracy proclaims and the social inequality that a capitalist economy inevitably generates. Liberal democracies are thus seen as 'capitalist' or 'bourgeois' democracies that are manipulated and controlled by the entrenched power of a **ruling class**.

Marxism thus offers a distinctive critique of pluralist democracy. Power cannot be widely and evenly dispersed in society as long as class power is unequally distributed.

Ruling class: A Marxist term, denoting a class that dominates other classes and society at large by virtue of its ownership of productive wealth.

Indeed, in many respects, the Marxist view parallels the elitist critique of pluralism. Both views suggest that power is ultimately concentrated in the hands of the few, the main difference being whether the few is conceived of as a 'power elite' or as a 'ruling class'. However, significant differences can also be identified. In the first place, whereas elitists suggest that power can be derived from a variety of sources (education, social status, bureaucratic position, political connections, wealth, and so on), Marxists emphasise the decisive importance of economic factors, notably the ownership and control of the means of production. Moreover, elitists are less clear about the significance of elite rule, acknowledging, for example, that when competition exists within a fractured elite policy may, to some extent, be shaped by democratic pressures. Marxists, in contrast, tend to argue that the ruling class is bent on pursuing its own economic interests, and that it only makes concessions to other classes in order to stabilise capitalism and perpetuate a system of unequal class power.

Modern Marxists, however, have been less willing to dismiss electoral democracy as nothing more than a sham. **Eurocommunists**, for example, abandoned the idea of revolution, embracing instead the notion of a peaceful, legal and democratic 'road to socialism'. Neo-Marxists such as Jürgen Habermas (see p. 197) and Claus Offe (1984) have nevertheless drawn attention to the contradictions, and perhaps inherent instability, of capitalist democracy. In this view, on the one hand, the democratic process forces government to respond to popular demands, leading to an inexorable rise of public spending and a progressive expansion of the state's responsibilities, especially in economic and social life. On the other hand, the long-term survival of capitalism is threatened by a fiscal crisis in which high taxes become a disincentive to enterprise and ever-rising government borrowing leads to permanently high inflation. Forced either to resist democratic pressures or to risk economic collapse, capitalist democracy would, Habermas (1973) argued, find it increasingly difficult to maintain legitimacy. These issues are discussed at greater length in Chapter 10.

▌ Summary

◆ The very popularity of democracy has threatened its use as a meaningful political term, and perhaps reduced it to a mere 'hurrah!' word. The meanings of the term have ranged from a system of rule by the masses and a form of government based on direct and popular continuous popular participation, to rule by the majority and a system of party competition that operates through regular and popular elections.

◆ Debates about the nature of democracy have tended to focus on three central issues. First, who are the people, or how far should political power be distributed? Secondly, should the people in effect rule themselves, or should government be left in the hands of politicians and parties that claim to represent them? Thirdly, what matters is it appropriate to decide collectively through the use of democratic processes?

◆ There are a number of rival models of democracy, each offering its own version of popular rule. These include: classical democracy, which is based on the principle of popular self-government; protective democracy, which is rooted in the individualist assumptions of liberalism; developmental democracy, which is concerned with broadening the scope for popular participation; and people's democracy, which pays particular attention to the distribution of class power.

Eurocommunism: A form of deradicalised communism that attempted to blend Marxism with liberal-democratic principles.

◆ Classical democracy, which is based on the political system in Athens in Ancient Greece, is defended on the grounds that it alone guarantees government *by* the people. Protective democracy gives citizens the greatest scope to live their lives as they choose. Developmental democracy has the virtue that, in extending participation, it widens liberty and fosters personal growth. People's democracy aims to achieve economic emancipation, rather than merely the extension of political rights.

◆ In practice, there is broad acceptance of a particular model of democracy, generally termed liberal democracy. Its central features are that it is an indirect and representative form of democracy that is based on regular elections. It operates through party competition and electoral choice, and it observes a clear distinction between the state and civil society, thus allowing for the existence of autonomous groups and private property.

◆ There is considerable controversy about how liberal-democratic systems work in practice. Pluralists praise their capacity to guarantee popular responsiveness and public accountability. Elitists highlight the tendency for political power to be concentrated in the hands of a privileged minority. Corporatists draw attention to the incorporation of groups into government. The New Right focuses on the dangers of 'democratic overload'. And Marxists point to tensions between democracy and capitalism.

▓ Questions for discussion

▶ Why has democracy come to be so universally well regarded?

▶ Is direct democracy in any way applicable to modern circumstances?

▶ What are the principal virtues of democracy?

▶ What are the drawbacks or dangers of democracy?

▶ Which model of democracy is most attractive, and why?

▶ Do modern forms of representative democracy deserve to be described as democratic?

▶ What are the major threats to democracy in modern society?

▓ Further reading

Arblaster, A. *Democracy* (2nd ed.) (Milton Keynes: Open University Press; Minneapolis: University of Minnesota Press, 1994). A succinct and thoughtful introduction to the theory of democracy.

Dahl, R. *Democracy and its Critics* (New Haven, CT: Yale University Press, 1989) A wide-ranging and thorough discussion of the democratic ideal and democratic practices.

Held, D. *Models of Democracy* (2nd ed.) (Oxford: Polity Press; Stanford: Stanford University Press, 1996). A rigorous and stimulating examination of rival models of democracy and the present state of democratic theory.

Macpherson, C. B. *The Life and Times of Liberal Democracy* (Oxford: Oxford University Press, 1977). A short, lucid and perceptive discussion of important themes in liberal-democratic theory.

The State

> 'The purpose of the State is always the same: to limit the individual, to tame him, to subordinate him, to subjugate him.'
>
> MAX STIRNER *The Ego and His Own* (1845)

The shadow of the state falls upon almost every human activity. From education to economic management, from social welfare to sanitation, and from domestic order to external defence, the state shapes and controls, and where it does not shape or control it regulates, supervises, authorises or proscribes. Even those aspects of life usually thought of as personal or private (marriage, divorce, abortion, religious worship and so on) are ultimately subject to the authority of the state. It is not surprising, therefore, that politics is often understood as the study of the state, the analysis of its institutional organisations, the evaluation of its impact on society, and so on. Ideological debate and party politics, certainly, tend to revolve around the proper function or role of the state: what should be done by the state and what should be left to private individuals and associations? The nature of state power has thus become one of the central concerns of political analysis. This debate (the so-called 'state debate') touches on some of the deepest and most abiding divisions in political theory.

The key issues discussed in this chapter are as follows:

Key issues

▶ What is the state, and how can it be distinguished from government?

▶ How has state power been analysed and explained?

▶ Is the state a force for good or a force for evil?

▶ What roles have been assigned to the state? How have responsibilities been apportioned between the state and civil society?

▶ Is the modern state under threat, and, if so, how are its powers being usurped?

Georg Wilhelm Friedrich Hegel (1770–1831)

German philosopher. Hegel was the founder of modern idealism and developed the notion that consciousness and material objects are in fact unified. In *Phenomenology of Spirit* (1807), he sought to develop a rational system that would substitute for traditional Christianity by interpreting the entire process of human history, and indeed the universe itself, in terms of the progress of absolute Mind towards self-realisation. In his view, history is, in essence, a march of the human spirit towards a determinant endpoint. His major political work,

Philosophy of Right (1821), portrayed the state as an ethical ideal and the highest expression of human freedom. Hegel's work had considerable impact upon Marx and other so-called 'young Hegelians', and it helped to shape the development of both liberal and fascist thought.

What is the state?

The term 'state' has been used to refer to a bewildering range of things: a collection of institutions, a territorial unit, a philosophical idea, an instrument of coercion or oppression, and so on. This confusion stems, in part, from the fact that the state has been understood in three very different ways, from an idealist perspective, a functionalist perspective and an organisational perspective. The *idealist* approach to the state is most clearly reflected in the writings of G. W. F. Hegel. Hegel identified three 'moments' of social existence: the family, civil society, and the state. Within the family, he argued, a 'particular altruism' operates that encourages people to set aside their own interests for the good of their children or elderly relatives. In contrast, civil society was seen as a sphere of 'universal egoism' in which individuals place their own interests before those of others. Hegel conceived of the state as an ethical community underpinned by mutual sympathy – 'universal altruism'. The drawback of idealism, however, is that it fosters an uncritical reverence for the state and, by defining the state in ethical terms, fails to distinguish clearly between institutions that are part of the state and those that are outside the state.

Functionalist approaches to the state focus on the role or purpose of state institutions. The central function of the state is invariably seen as the maintenance of social order (see p. 371), the state being defined as that set of institutions which uphold order and deliver social stability. Such an approach has, for example, been adopted by modern Marxists, who have been inclined to see the state as a mechanism through which class conflict is ameliorated to ensure the long-term survival of the capitalist system. The weakness of the functionalist view of the state, however, is that it tends to associate *any* institution that maintains order (such as the family, mass media, trade unions and the church) with the state itself. This is why, unless there is a statement to the contrary, an organisational approach to the definition of the state (see below) is adopted throughout this book

The *organisational* view defines the state as the apparatus of government in its broadest sense, that is, as that set of institutions that are recognisably 'public' in that they are responsible for the collective organisation of social existence and are funded at the public's expense. The virtue of this definition is that it distinguishes clearly between the state and civil society (see p. 8). The state comprises the various institutions of government: the bureaucracy, the military, the police, the courts, the social-security system and so on; it can be identified with the entire 'body politic'. This makes it possible to identify the origins of the modern state in the emergence in fifteenth-century and sixteenth-century Europe of a system of centralised rule that succeeded in subordinating all other institutions and groups, spiritual and temporal. Moreover, the organisational approach allows us to talk about 'rolling forward' or 'rolling back' the state, in the sense of expanding or contracting the responsibilities of the state, and enlarging or diminishing its institutional machinery.

In this light, it is possible to identify five key features of the state:

- The state is *sovereign*. It exercises absolute and unrestricted power in that it stands above all other associations and groups in society. Thomas Hobbes (see p. 285) conveyed this idea by portraying the state as a 'leviathan', a gigantic monster, usually represented as a sea creature.

- State institutions are recognisably '*public*', in contrast to the 'private' institutions of civil society. Public bodies are responsible for making and enforcing collective decisions, while private bodies, such as families, private businesses and trade unions, exist to satisfy individual interests.

- The state is an exercise in *legitimation*. The decisions of the state are usually (although not necessarily) accepted as binding on the members of society because, it is claimed, they are made in the public interest or for common good; the state supposedly reflects the permanent interests of society.

- The state is an instrument of *domination*. State authority is backed up by coercion; the state must have the capacity to ensure that its laws are obeyed and that trans-gressors are punished. A monopoly of 'legitimate violence' (Max Weber) is there-fore the practical expression of state sovereignty.

- The state is a *territorial* association. The jurisdiction of the state is geographically defined and it encompasses all those who live within the state's borders, whether they are citizens or noncitizens. On the international stage, the state is therefore regarded (at least in theory) as an autonomous entity.

Not only is the state separate from civil society, but it is also internally differentiated, containing various branches or sections. The state apparatus thus embraces the political executive or government, in the narrow sense, possibly an assembly or parliament, the judiciary, the bureaucracy, the military, the police, local and regional institutions, and so on. The most important distinction, however, is that between the 'state' and the 'government', two terms that are often used interchangeably. This distinction is not just of academic interest. It goes to the very heart of the idea of limited and **constitutional government**. In short, government power can only be held in check when the government of the day is prevented from encroaching upon the absolute and unlimited authority of the state.

The principal differences between government and the state are the following:

- The state is more *extensive* than government. The state is an inclusive association that encompasses all the institutions of the public realm and embraces all the members of the community (in their capacity as citizens). Government is *part* of the state.

- The state is a continuing, even *permanent*, entity. Government is *temporary*: govern-ments come and go, and systems of government can be reformed and remodelled.

Constitutional government: A system of government that operates within a set of legal and institutional constraints that both limit its power and protect individual liberty.

- Government is the *means* through which the authority of the state is brought into operation. In making and implementing state policy, government is 'the brains' of the state, and it perpetuates the state's existence.

- The state exercises *impersonal* authority. The personnel of state bodies is recruited and trained in a bureaucratic manner and is (usually) expected to be politically neutral, enabling state bodies to resist the ideological enthusiasms of the government of the day.

- The state, in theory at least, represents the permanent interests of society, that is, the *common* good or general will. Government, on the other hand, represents the *partisan* sympathies of those who happen to be in power at a particular time.

Rival theories of the state

Reaching an agreement about what we mean by 'the state' provides a basis upon which to examine a deeper problem: what is the nature of state power, and what interests does the state represent? From this perspective, the state is an 'essentially contested' concept. There are a number of rival theories of the state, each of which offers a different account of its origins, development and impact on society. Indeed, controversy about the nature of state power has increasingly dominated modern political analysis and goes to the heart of ideological and theoretical disagreements in the discipline. These relate to questions about whether, for example, the state is autonomous and independent of society, or whether it is essentially a product of society, a reflection of the broader distribution of power or resources? Moreover, does the state serve the common or collective good, or is it biased in favour of privileged groups or a dominant class? Similarly, is the state a positive or constructive force, with responsibilities that should be enlarged, or is it a negative or destructive entity that must be constrained or, perhaps, smashed altogether? Four contrasting theories of the state can be identified as follows:

- the pluralist state
- the capitalist state
- the leviathan state
- the patriarchal state.

The pluralist state

The pluralist theory of the state has a very clear liberal lineage. It stems from the belief that the state acts as an 'umpire' or 'referee' in society. This view has also dominated mainstream political analysis, accounting for a tendency, at least within Anglo-American thought, to discount the state and state organisations and focus instead on 'government'. Indeed, it is not uncommon in this tradition for 'the state' to be dismissed as an abstraction, with institutions such as the courts, the civil service and the military being seen as independent actors in their own right, rather than as elements of a broader state machine. Nevertheless, this approach is only possible because it is based on underlying, and often unacknowledged, assumptions about state neutrality. The state can only be ignored because it is seen as an impartial arbiter or referee which can be bent to the will of the government of the day.

Focus on . . .

Social-contract theory

A social contract is a voluntary agreement made amongst individuals through which an organised society, or state, is brought into existence. Used as a theoretical device by thinkers such as Hobbes, Locke and Rousseau (see p. 73), the social contract has been revived by modern theorists such as John Rawls (see p. 56). The social contract is seldom regarded as a historical act. Rather, it is used as a means of demonstrating the value of government and the grounds of political obligation; social-contract theorists wish individuals to act *as if* they had concluded the contract themselves. In its classic form, social-contract theory has three elements:

- The image of a hypothetical stateless society (a 'state of nature') is established. Unconstrained freedom means that life is 'solitary, poor, nasty, brutish and short' (Hobbes).
- Individuals therefore seek to escape from the state of nature by entering into a social contract, recognising that only a sovereign power can secure order and stability.
- The social contract obliges citizens to respect and obey the state, ultimately in gratitude for the stability and security that only a system of political rule can deliver.

The origins of this theory of the state can be traced back to the writings of seventeenth-century social-contract theorists such as Thomas Hobbes and John Locke (see p. 43). The principal concern of such thinkers was to examine the grounds of **political obligation**, the grounds upon which the individual is obliged to obey and respect the state. They argued that the state had arisen out of a voluntary agreement, or social contract, made by individuals who recognised that only the establishment of a sovereign power could safeguard them from the insecurity, disorder and brutality of the **state of nature**. Without a state, individuals abuse, exploit and enslave one another; with a state, order and civilised existence are guaranteed and liberty is protected. As Locke put it, 'where there is no law there is no freedom'.

In liberal theory, the state is thus seen as a neutral arbiter amongst the competing groups and individuals in society; it is an 'umpire' or 'referee' that is capable of protecting each citizen from the encroachments of fellow citizens. The neutrality of the state reflects the fact that the state acts in the interests of *all* citizens, and therefore represents the common good or public interest. In Hobbes' view, stability and order could only be secured through the establishment of an absolute and unlimited state, with power that could neither be challenged nor questioned. In other words, he held that citizens are confronted by a stark choice between absolutism (see p. 26) and **anarchy**. Locke, on the other hand, developed a more typically liberal defence of the limited state. In his view, the purpose of the state is very specific: it is restricted to the defence of a set of 'natural' or God-given individual rights, namely 'life, liberty and property'. This establishes a clear distinction between the responsibilities of the state (essentially the maintenance of domestic order and the protection of property) and the responsibilities of individual citizens (usually seen as the realm of civil society). Moreover, since the state may threaten natural rights as easily as it may

Political obligation: The duty of the citizen towards the state; the basis of the state's right to rule.

State of nature: A society devoid of political authority and of formal (legal) checks on the individual; usually employed as a theoretical device.

Anarchy: Literally, without rule; anarchy is often used pejoratively to suggest instability or even chaos.

Concept

Neopluralism

Neopluralism is a style of social theorising that remains faithful to pluralist values whilst recognising the need to revise or update classical pluralism in the light of, for example, elite, Marxist and New Right theories. Although neopluralism embraces a broad range of perspectives and positions, certain central themes can be identified. First, it attempts to take account of modernising trends, such as the emergence of postindustrial and postcapitalist society. Secondly, while capitalism is certainly preferred to socialism, free-market economic doctrines are usually regarded as obsolete. Thirdly, western democracies are seen as 'deformed polyarchies', in which major corporations exert disproportionate influence.

uphold them, citizens must enjoy some form of protection against the state, which Locke believed could only be delivered through the mechanisms of constitutional and representative government.

These ideas were developed in the twentieth century into the pluralist theory of the state. As a theory of society, pluralism (see p. 76) asserts that, within liberal democracies, power is widely and evenly dispersed. As a theory of the state, pluralism holds that the state is neutral insofar as it is susceptible to the influence of various groups and interests and all social classes. The state is not biased in favour of any particular interest or group, and it does not have an interest of its own that is separate from those of society. As Schwarzmantel (1994:52) put it, the state is 'the servant of society and not its master'. The state can thus be portrayed as a 'pin cushion' that passively absorbs pressures and forces exerted upon it. Two key assumptions underlie this view. The first is that the state is effectively subordinate to government. Nonelected state bodies (the civil service, the judiciary, the police, the military and so on) are strictly impartial and are subject to the authority of their political masters. The state apparatus is therefore thought to conform to the principles of public service and political accountability (see p. 375). The second assumption is that the democratic process is meaningful and effective. In other words, party competition and interest-group activity ensure that the government of the day remains sensitive and responsive to public opinion. Ultimately, therefore, the state is only a weather vane that is blown in whatever direction the public at large dictates.

Modern pluralists, however, have often adopted a more critical view of the state, termed the neopluralist theory of the state. Theorists such as Robert Dahl (see p. 256), Charles Lindblom and J. K. Galbraith (see p. 181) have come to accept that modern industrialised states are both more complex and less responsive to popular pressures than classical pluralism suggested. Neopluralists, for instance, have acknowledged that business enjoys a 'privileged position' in relation to government which other groups clearly cannot rival. In *Politics and Markets* (1977), Lindblom pointed out that, as the major investor and largest employer in society, business is bound to exercise considerable sway over any government, whatever its ideological leanings or manifesto commitments. Moreover, neopluralists have accepted that the state can and does forge its own sectional interests. In this way, a state elite, composed of senior civil servants, judges, police chiefs, military leaders and so on, may be seen to pursue either the bureaucratic interests of their sector of the state or the interests of client groups. Indeed, if the state is regarded as a political actor in its own right, it can be viewed as a powerful (perhaps the most powerful) interest group in society. This line of argument encouraged Eric Nordlinger (1981) to develop a state-centred model of liberal democracy, based on 'the autonomy of the democratic state'.

The capitalist state

The Marxist notion of a capitalist state offers a clear alternative to the pluralist image of the state as a neutral arbiter or umpire. Marxists have typically argued that the state cannot be understood separately from the economic structure of society. This view has usually been understood in terms of the classic formulation that the state is nothing but an instrument of class oppression; the state emerges out of, and in a sense reflects, the class system. Nevertheless, a rich debate has taken place within Marxist theory in recent years that has moved the Marxist theory of the state a long way from this classic formulation. In many ways, the scope to revise Marxist attitudes towards the state stems from ambiguities that can be found in Marx's own writings.

Marx did not develop a systematic or coherent theory of the state. In a general sense, he believed that the state is part of a 'superstructure' that is determined or conditioned by the economic 'base', which can be seen as the real foundation of social life. However, the precise relationship between the base and the superstructure, and in this case that between the state and the capitalist mode of production, is unclear. Two theories of the state can be identified in Marx's writings. The first is expressed in his often-quoted dictum from *The Communist Manifesto* (1848:82): 'The executive of the modern state is but a committee for managing the common affairs of the whole bourgeoisie'. From this perspective, the state is clearly dependent upon society and entirely dependent upon its economically dominant class, which in capitalism is the **bourgeoisie**. Lenin thus described the state starkly as 'an instrument for the oppression of the exploited class'.

A second, more complex and subtle, theory of the state can nevertheless be found in Marx's analysis of the revolutionary events in France between 1848 and 1851, *The Eighteenth Brumaire of Louis Bonaparte* ([1852] 1963). Marx suggested that the state could enjoy what has come to be seen as 'relative autonomy' from the class system, the Napoleonic state being capable of imposing its will upon society, acting as an 'appalling parasitic body'. If the state did articulate the interests of any class, it was not those of the bourgeoisie, but those of the most populous class in French society, the smallholding peasantry. Although Marx did not develop this view in detail, it is clear that, from this perspective, the autonomy of the state is only *relative*, in that the state appears to mediate between conflicting classes, and so maintains the class system itself in existence.

Both these theories differ markedly from the liberal and, later, pluralist models of state power. In particular, they emphasise that the state cannot be understood except in a context of unequal class power, and that the state arises out of, and reflects, capitalist society, by acting either as an instrument of oppression wielded by the dominant class, or, more subtly, as a mechanism through which class antagonisms are ameliorated. Nevertheless, Marx's attitude towards the state was not entirely negative. He argued that the state could be used constructively during the transition from capitalism to communism in the form of the 'revolutionary dictatorship of the proletariat'. The overthrow of capitalism would see the destruction of the bourgeois state and the creation of an alternative, proletarian one.

In describing the state as a proletarian 'dictatorship', Marx utilised the first theory of the state, seeing the state as an instrument through which the economically dominant class (by then the proletariat) could repress and subdue other classes. All states, from this perspective, are class dictatorships. The 'dictatorship of the proletariat' was seen as a means of safeguarding the gains of the revolution by preventing counter-revolution mounted by the dispossessed bourgeoisie. Nevertheless, Marx did not see the state as a necessary or enduring social formation. He predicted that, as class antagonisms faded, the state would 'wither away', meaning that a fully communist society would also be stateless. Since the state emerged out of the class system, once the class system had been abolished, the state, quite simply, loses its reason for existence.

Bourgeoisie: A Marxist term, denoting the ruling class of a capitalist society, the owners of productive wealth.

Marx's ambivalent heritage has provided modern Marxists, or neo-Marxists, with considerable scope to further the analysis of state power. This was also encouraged

Concept

Neo-Marxism

Neo-Marxism (sometimes termed modern Marxism) refers to attempts to revise or recast the classical ideas of Marx while remaining faithful to certain Marxist principles or aspects of Marxist methodology. Neo-Marxists typically refuse to accept that Marxism enjoys a monopoly of the truth, and have thus looked to Hegelian philosophy, anarchism, liberalism, feminism, and even rational-choice theory. Two central themes can nevertheless be identified. First, neo-Marxists have tried to provide an alternative to the mechanistic and deterministic ideas of orthodox Marxism, refusing to accept the primacy of economics, or assign the proletariat a privileged role. Secondly, they have been concerned to explain the failure of Marx's predictions, looking, in particular, to the analysis of ideology and state power.

by the writings of the Italian Marxist Antonio Gramsci (see p. 191), who emphasised the degree to which the domination of the ruling class is achieved by ideological manipulation, rather than just open coercion. In this view, bourgeois domination is largely maintained through 'hegemony' (see p. 190), that is, intellectual leadership or cultural control, with the state playing an important role in the process. In the 1960s and early 1970s, Marxist theorising about the state was dominated by the rival positions adopted by Ralph Miliband and Nicos Poulantzas (1936–79). Although this debate moved through a number of phases as each author revised his position, at the heart of it lay contrasting instrumentalist and structuralist views of the state.

In *The State in Capitalist Society* (1969), Miliband portrayed the state as an agent or *instrument* of the ruling class, stressing the extent to which the state elite is disproportionately drawn from the ranks of the privileged and propertied. The bias of the state in favour of capitalism is therefore derived from the overlap of social backgrounds between, on the one hand, civil servants and other public officials, and, on the other, bankers, business leaders and captains of industry. Both groups, in other words, tend to be representatives of the capitalist class. Poulantzas, in *Political Power and Social Classes* (1968), dismissed this sociological approach, and emphasised instead the degree to which the *structure* of economic and social power exerts a constraint upon state autonomy. This view suggests that the state cannot but act to perpetuate the social system in which it operates. In the case of the capitalist state, its role is to serve the long-term interests of capitalism, even though these actions may be resisted by sections of the capitalist class itself. Examples of this are the extension of democratic rights and welfare reforms, both of which are concessions to the working class which nevertheless bind them to the capitalist system.

Developments within modern Marxism have brought about a significant convergence between pluralist and Marxist theories. Just as pluralists have increasingly recognised the importance of corporate power, neo-Marxists have been forced to abandon the idea that the state is merely a reflection of the class system. For one thing, neo-Marxists have recognised that, in modern circumstances, the classical two-class model (based on the bourgeoisie and the proletariat) is simplistic and often unhelpful. Following Poulantzas, neo-Marxists usually recognise that there are significant divisions within the ruling class (between financial and manufacturing capital, for instance) and that the emergence of electoral democracy has empowered interests and groups outside the ruling class. In addition, they have increasingly seen the state as the terrain upon which the struggle amongst interests, groups and classes is conducted. This is particularly clear in the case of Bob Jessop's (1982) 'strategic relational approach' to the state. Jessop saw the state not so much as a means of perpetuating capitalism through the dilution of class tensions, but as 'the crystallisation of political strategies', that is, as an assemblage of institutions through which competing groups and interests struggle for domination or hegemony. In this view, the state is therefore not an 'instrument' wielded by a dominant group or ruling class. Rather, it is a dynamic entity which reflects the balance of power within society at any given time, and thus reflects the outcome of an ongoing hegemonic struggle.

The leviathan state

The image of the state as a 'leviathan' (in effect, a self-serving monster intent on expansion and aggrandisement) is one associated in modern politics with the New Right. Such a view is rooted in early or classical liberalism and, in particular, a commitment to a radical form of individualism (see p. 178). The New Right, or at least its neoliberal wing, is distinguished by a strong antipathy towards state intervention in economic and social life, born out of the belief that the state is a parasitic growth which threatens both individual liberty and economic security. In this view, the state, instead of being, as pluralists suggest, an impartial umpire or arbiter, is an overbearing 'nanny', desperate to interfere or meddle in every aspect of human existence. The central feature of this view is that the state pursues interests that are separate from those of society (setting it apart from Marxism), and that those interests demand an unrelenting growth in the role or responsibilities of the state itself. New Right thinkers therefore argue that the twentieth-century tendency towards state intervention reflects not popular pressure for economic and social security, or the need to stabilise capitalism by ameliorating class tensions, but rather the internal dynamics of the state.

New Right theorists explain the expansionist dynamics of state power by reference to both demand-side and supply-side pressures. Demand-side pressures are ones that emanate from society itself, usually through the mechanism of electoral democracy. As discussed in Chapter 4, the New Right argue that electoral competition encourages politicians to 'outbid' one another by making promises of increased spending and more generous government programmes, regardless of the long-term damage that such policies inflict on the economy in the form of increased taxes, higher inflation and the 'crowding out' of investment. Supply-side pressures, on the other hand, are ones that are internal to the state. These can therefore be explained in terms of the institutions and personnel of the state apparatus. In its most influential form, this argument is known as the government oversupply thesis.

The oversupply thesis has usually been associated with public-choice theorists (see p. 258), who examine how public decisions are made on the assumption that the individuals involved act in a rationally self-interested fashion. William Niskanen (1971), for example, argued that, as budgetary control in legislatures such as the US Congress is typically weak, the task of budget making is largely shaped by the interests of government agencies and senior bureaucrats. Insofar as this implies that government is dominated by the state (the state elite being able to shape the thinking of elected politicians), there are parallels between the public-choice model and the Marxist view discussed above. Where these two views diverge, however, is in relation to the interests that the state apparatus serves. While Marxists argue that the state reflects broader class and other social interests, the New Right portrays the state as an independent or autonomous entity that pursues its own interests. In this view, bureaucratic self-interest invariably supports 'big' government and state intervention, because this leads to an enlargement of the bureaucracy itself, which helps to ensure job security, improve pay, open up promotion prospects, and enhance the status of public officials. This image of self-seeking bureaucrats is plainly at odds with the pluralist notion of a state machine imbued with an ethic of public service and firmly subject to political control.

The patriarchal state

Modern thinking about the patriarchal state must, finally, take account of the implications of feminist theory. However, this is not to say that there is a systematic feminist theory of the state. As emphasised in Chapter 3, feminist theory encompasses a range of traditions and perspectives, and has thus generated a range of very

Concept

Patriarchy

Patriarchy literally means 'rule by the father', the domination of the husband–father within the family, and the subordination of his wife and his children. However, the term is usually used in the more general sense of 'rule by men', drawing attention to the totality of oppression and exploitation to which women are subject. The use of the term patriarchy thus implies that the system of male power in society at large both reflects and stems from the dominance of the father in the family. Patriarchy is a key concept in radical feminist analysis, in that it emphasises that gender inequality is systematic, institutionalised and pervasive. Socialist feminists, in contrast, highlight links between gender inequality and private property, seeing patriarchy and capitalism as parallel systems of domination.

Radical feminism: A form of feminism that holds gender divisions to be the most politically significant of social cleavages, and believes that they are rooted in the structure of domestic life.

different attitudes towards state power. Moreover, feminists have usually not regarded the nature of state power as a central political issue, preferring instead to concentrate on the deeper structure of male power centred upon institutions such as the family and the economic system. Some feminists, indeed, may question conventional definitions of the state, arguing, for instance, that the idea that the state exercises a monopoly of legitimate violence is compromised by the routine use of violence and intimidation in family and domestic life. Nevertheless, sometimes implicitly and sometimes explicitly, feminists have helped to enrich the state debate by developing novel and challenging perspectives on state power.

Liberal feminists, who believe that sexual or gender (see p. 183) equality can be brought about through incremental reform, have tended to accept an essentially pluralist view of the state. They recognise that, if women are denied legal and political equality, and especially the right to vote, the state is biased in favour of men. However, their faith in the state's basic neutrality is reflected in the belief that any such bias can, and will, be overcome by a process of reform. In this sense, liberal feminists believe that all groups (including women) have potentially equal access to state power, and that this can be used impartially to promote justice and the common good. Liberal feminists have therefore usually viewed the state in positive terms, seeing state intervention as a means of redressing gender inequality and enhancing the role of women. This can be seen in campaigns for equal-pay legislation, the legalisation of abortion, the provision of child-care facilities, the extension of welfare benefits, and so on. Nevertheless, a more critical and negative view of the state has been developed by **radical feminists**, who argue that state power reflects a deeper structure of oppression in the form of patriarchy.

There are a number of similarities between Marxist and radical-feminist views of state power. Both groups, for example, deny that the state is an autonomous entity bent upon the pursuit of its own interests. Instead, the state is understood, and its biases are explained, by reference to a 'deep structure' of power in society at large. Whereas Marxists place the state in an economic context, radical feminists place it in a context of gender inequality, and insist that it is essentially an institution of male power. In common with Marxism, distinctive instrumentalist and structuralist versions of this feminist position have been developed. The *instrumentalist* argument views the state as little more than an 'agent' or 'tool' used by men to defend their own interests and uphold the structures of patriarchy. This line of argument draws on the core feminist belief that patriarchy is upheld by the division of society into distinct 'public' and 'private' spheres of life. The subordination of women has traditionally been accomplished through their confinement to a 'private' sphere of family and domestic responsibilities, turning them into housewives and mothers, and through their exclusion from a 'public' realm centred upon politics and the economy. Quite simply, in this view, the state is run *by* men, and it is run *for* men.

Whereas instrumentalist arguments focus upon the personnel of the state, and particularly the state elite, *structuralist* arguments tend to emphasise the degree to which state institutions are embedded in a wider patriarchal system. Modern radical feminists have paid particular attention to the emergence of the welfare state, seeing it as the expression of a new kind of patriarchal power. Welfare (see p. 395) may uphold patriarchy by bringing about a transition from private dependency (in which women as 'home makers' are dependent on men as 'breadwinners') to a system of public dependency in which women are increasingly controlled by the institutions of the extended state. For instance, women have become increasingly dependent on the state as clients or customers of state services (such as child-care institutions, nursery education and social work) and as employees, particularly in the so-called 'caring' professions (such as nursing, social work and education). Further, the extension of state responsibilities into traditionally female realms such as child rearing and caring has often merely created new forms of subordination. In particular, it has tended to reinforce the role of women as a **reserve army of labour**, with employers increasingly looking to women to provide a flexible, low-paid and usually submissive workforce.

The role of the state

Contrasting interpretations of state power have clear implications for the desirable role or responsibilities of the state. What should states do? What functions or responsibilities should the state fulfil, and which ones should be left in the hands of private individuals? In many respects, these are the questions around which electoral politics and party competition revolve. With the exception of anarchists, who dismiss the state as fundamentally evil and unnecessary, all political thinkers have regarded the state as, in some sense, worthwhile. Even revolutionary socialists, inspired by the Leninist slogan 'smash the state', have accepted the need for a temporary proletarian state to preside over the transition from capitalism to communism, in the form of the 'dictatorship of the proletariat'. Nevertheless, there is profound disagreement about the exact role the state should play, and therefore about the proper balance between the state and civil society. Among the different state forms that have developed are the following:

- the minimal state
- the developmental state
- the social-democratic state
- the collectivised state
- the totalitarian state.

Minimal states

The minimal state is the ideal of classical liberals, whose aim is to ensure that individuals enjoy the widest possible realm of freedom. This view is rooted in social-contract theory, but it nevertheless advances an essentially 'negative' view of the state. From this perspective, the value of the state is that it has the capacity to constrain human behaviour and thus to prevent individuals encroaching upon the **rights** and liberties of others. The state is merely a protective body, its core function being to provide a framework of peace and social order within which citizens can conduct their lives as they think best. In Locke's famous simile, the state acts as a nightwatchman, whose services are only called upon when orderly existence is threatened. This nevertheless leaves the 'minimal' or 'nightwatchman' state with three core functions. First and foremost, the state exists to maintain domestic order. Secondly, it ensures that contracts or voluntary agreements made between private citizens are enforced, and thirdly it provides protection against external attack. The institutional apparatus of a minimal state is thus limited to a police force, a court system and a military of some kind. Economic, social, cultural, moral and other responsibilities belong to the individual, and are therefore firmly part of civil society.

Reserve army of labour: An available supply of labour easily shed in times of recession; the 'army' enjoys no security and exercises little market power.

Rights: Legal or moral entitlements to act or be treated in a particular way; civil rights differ from human rights.

Robert Nozick (born 1938)

US academic and political philosopher. Nozick's major work *Anarchy, State and Utopia* (1974) is widely seen as one of the most important contemporary works of political philosophy, and it has had a profound influence upon New Right theories and beliefs. He developed a form of libertarianism that was close to Locke's and clearly influenced by nineteenth-century US individualists such as Spooner (1808–87) and Tucker (1854–1939). He argued that property rights should be strictly upheld, provided that wealth has been justly acquired in the first place or has been justly transferred from one person to another. This position means support for minimal government and minimal taxation, and undermines the case for welfare and redistribution. Nozick's rights-based theory of justice was developed in response to the ideas of John Rawls (see p. 56).

The cause of the minimal state has been taken up in modern political debate by the New Right. Drawing on early liberal ideas, and particularly on free-market or classical economic theories, the New Right has proclaimed the need to 'roll back the frontiers of the state'. In the writings of Robert Nozick, this amounts to a restatement of Lockean liberalism based on a defence of individual rights, especially property rights. In the case of free-market economists such as Friedrich Hayek (see p. 48) and Milton Friedman (see p. 173), state intervention is seen as a 'dead hand' that reduces competition, efficiency and productivity. From the New Right perspective, the state's economic role should be confined to two functions: the maintenance of a stable means of exchange or 'sound money' (low or zero inflation), and the promotion of competition through controls on monopoly power, price fixing and so on. Many portray Asian states such as Taiwan, Singapore and Malaysia as modern-day examples of minimal states. However, this ignores the degree to which these states engage in economic management through guiding investment and emphasising education and training.

Developmental states

The best historical examples of minimal states were those in countries such as the UK and the USA during the period of early industrialisation in the nineteenth century. As a general rule, however, the later a country industrialises, the more extensive will be its state's economic role. In Japan and Germany, for instance, the state assumed a more active 'developmental' role from the outset. A developmental state is one that intervenes in economic life with the specific purpose of promoting industrial growth and economic development. This does not amount to an attempt to replace the market with a 'socialist' system of planning (see p. 174) and control, but rather to an attempt to construct a partnership between the state and major economic interests, often underpinned by conservative and nationalist priorities.

The classic example of a developmental state is Japan. During the Meiji Period in 1868–1912, the Japanese state forged a close relationship with the *zaibutsu*, the great family-run business empires that dominated the Japanese economy up to the Second World War. Since 1945, the developmental role of the Japanese state has been assumed by the Japanese Ministry of International Trade and Industry (MITI), which, together with the Bank of Japan, helps to shape private investment decisions and steer the Japanese economy towards international competitiveness. A similar model of developmental intervention has existed in France, where governments of both left and right have tended to recognise the need for economic planning, and the state bureaucracy has seen itself as the custodian of the national interest. In countries such as Austria and, to some extent, Germany, economic development has been achieved through the construction of a 'partnership state', in which an emphasis is placed on the maintenance of a close relationship between the state and major economic interests, notably big business and organised labour. More recently, economic globalisation (see p. 140) has fostered the emergence of 'competition states', examples of which are found amongst the **tiger economies** of East Asia. Their role is to develop strategies for national prosperity in a context of intensifying transnational competition.

Social-democratic states

Whereas developmental states practise interventionism in order to stimulate economic progress, social-democratic states intervene with a view to bringing about broader social restructuring, usually in accordance with principles such as fairness, equality (see p. 396) and **social justice**. In countries such as Austria and Sweden, state intervention has been guided by both developmental and social-democratic priorities. Nevertheless, developmentalism and social democracy do not always go hand in hand. As David Marquand (1988) pointed out, although the UK state was significantly extended in the period immediately after the Second World War along social-democratic lines, it failed to evolve into a developmental state. The key to understanding the social-democratic state is that there is a shift from a 'negative' view of the state, which sees it as little more than a necessary evil, to a 'positive' view of the state, in which it is seen as means of enlarging liberty and promoting justice. The social-democratic state is thus the ideal of both modern liberals and democratic socialists.

Rather than merely laying down the conditions of orderly existence, the social-democratic state is an active participant, helping in particular to rectify the imbalances and injustices of a market economy. It therefore tends to focus less upon the generation of wealth, and more upon what is seen as the equitable or just distribution of wealth. In practice, this boils down to an attempt to eradicate poverty and reduce social inequality. The twin features of a social-democratic state are therefore Keynesianism and social welfare. The aim of Keynesian economic policies is to 'manage' or 'regulate' capitalism with a view to promoting growth and maintaining full employment. Although this may entail an element of planning, the classic Keynesian strategy involves 'demand management' through adjustments in fiscal policy, that is, in the levels of public spending and taxation. The adoption of welfare policies has led to the emergence of so-called welfare states, whose responsibilities have extended to the promotion of social well-being amongst their citizens. In this sense, the social-democratic state is an 'enabling state', dedicated to the principle of individual empowerment.

Collectivised states

While developmental and social-democratic states intervene in economic life with a view to guiding or supporting a largely private economy, collectivised states bring the entirety of economic life under state control. The best examples of such states

Tiger economies: Fast-growing and export-orientated economies modelled on Japan; for example, South Korea, Taiwan and Singapore.

Social justice: A morally justifiable distribution of material rewards; social justice is often seen to imply a bias in favour of equality.

Concept

Statism

Statism (or, in French, *étatisme*) is the belief that state intervention is the most appropriate means of resolving political problems or bringing about economic and social development. This view is underpinned by a deep and perhaps unquestioning faith in the state as a mechanism through which collective action can be organised and common goals can be achieved. The state is thus seen as an ethical ideal (Hegel), or as serving the 'general will' or public interest. Statism is most clearly reflected in government policies that regulate and control economic life. These range from selective nationalisation and economic management (sometimes called *dirigisme*, from the French *diriger*, to direct) to corporatism (see p. 257) (in both liberal and fascist forms), and Soviet-style state collectivisation.

were in orthodox communist countries such as the USSR and throughout eastern Europe. These sought to abolish private enterprise altogether, and set up centrally planned economies administered by a network of economic ministries and planning committees. So-called 'command economies' were therefore established that were organised through a system of 'directive' planning that was ultimately controlled by the highest organs of the communist party. The justification for state **collectivisation** stems from a fundamental socialist preference for common ownership over private property. However, the use of the state to attain this goal suggests a more positive attitude to state power than that outlined in the classical writings of Marx and Engels (1820–95).

Marx and Engels by no means ruled out nationalisation, and Engels in particular recognised that, during the 'dictatorship of the proletariat', state control would be extended to include factories, the banks, transportation and so on. Nevertheless, they envisaged that the proletarian state would be strictly temporary, and that it would 'wither away' as class antagonisms abated. In contrast, the collectivised state in the USSR became permanent and increasingly powerful and bureaucratic. Under Stalin (see p. 53), socialism was effectively equated with statism, the advance of socialism being reflected in the widening responsibilities and powers of the state apparatus. Indeed, after Khrushchev announced in 1962 that the dictatorship of the proletariat had ended, the state was formally identified with the interests of 'the whole Soviet peoples'.

Totalitarian states

The most extreme and extensive form of interventionism is found in totalitarian states. The essence of totalitarianism (see p. 27) is the construction of an all-embracing state, the influence of which penetrates every aspect of human existence. The state brings not only the economy but education, culture, religion, family life and so on under direct state control. The best examples of totalitarian states are Hitler's Germany and Stalin's USSR, although modern regimes such as Saddam Hussein's Iraq arguably have similar characteristics. The central pillars of such regimes are a comprehensive process of surveillance and terroristic policing, and a pervasive system of ideological manipulation and control. In this sense, totalitarian states effectively extinguish civil society and abolish the 'private' sphere of life altogether. This is a goal that only fascists, who wish to dissolve individual identity within the social whole, are prepared openly to endorse. It is sometimes argued that Mussolini's notion of a totalitarian state was derived from Hegel's belief in the state as an 'ethical community' reflecting the altruism and mutual sympathy of its members. From this perspective, the advance of human civilisation can clearly be linked to the aggrandisement of the state and the widening of its responsibilities.

■ The twilight of the state?

Although the state has traditionally been regarded as the central feature of political life, its role and significance are threatened by developments that have become increasingly pronounced in the late twentieth century. This is occurring most dramatically in certain postcommunist countries and in parts of the developing world, where fractured or disintegrating state apparatuses have confronted ethnic

Collectivisation: The abolition of private property in favour of a system of common or public ownership.

unrest or the growing menace of organised crime. The result of this has been the emergence of stateless nations, tribes and clans, notable examples being the Chechens in the Russian Federation, the ethnic Albanians in Kosovo, the Kurds, the Tamils and the Ibos in Nigeria. Elsewhere, state decline has been less striking but still significant. It has consisted of what Jessop (1990) called 'hollowing out', an insidious process through which functions that once belonged to the state have gradually been transferred to other institutions and bodies. This a process that has been brought about by three distinct developments: globalisation, **privatisation**, and localisation.

Perhaps the most significant threat to the state, or at least to the nation-state, is the process of *globalisation* (discussed in greater detail in Chapter 8). Globalisation is, broadly, the process through which events and decisions in one part of the world have come to affect people in quite another part of the world. One manifestation of this is the emergence of a global economy, in which it has become increasingly difficult, and perhaps impossible, for any country to regulate the international flow of capital. The implications of this development for states are dramatic. For example, it means that the capacity of individual states to manage economic life and deliver general prosperity is limited, because 'national' economic strategies such as Keynesianism are virtually unworkable in a global context. Further evidence of globalisation is found in the growing importance of international and supranational bodies such as the United Nations and the European Union (EU). It is clear, for instance, that membership of the EU threatens state sovereignty, because a growing range of decisions (for example, on monetary policy, agricultural and fisheries policies, defence and foreign affairs) are made by European institutions rather than by member states. On the other hand, globalisation may not so much challenge the state as bring about a transition from a world of nation-states to one dominated by a collection of supranational states or even a single global state.

The process of *privatisation*, however, shifts the responsibilities of the state not to higher supranational bodies, but to 'private' institutions within the nation itself. This process has been particularly evident in the UK in the 1980s and 1990s, where it led to the demise of the mixed economy through the 'sell off' of nationalised industries and the application of so-called market testing and contracting out to the public services. Similar policies have, however, been adopted elsewhere, perhaps most enthusiastically by the postcommunist regimes of central and eastern Europe in an attempt to dismantle their collectivised state machines. Although privatisation can be seen as a consequence of the spread of New Right priorities and beliefs, and in particular a conscious attempt to 'roll back' the frontiers of the state, it may also be dictated by broader and more irresistible forces. Amongst these are the pressures of increasing global competition and the difficulty of meeting the state's social responsibilities in a context of sluggish or unpredictable economic growth. In such circumstances, even socialist governments in the 1980s and 1990s examined ways of reducing the state's welfare commitments, and shifting the delivery of services from the public sector to the private sector.

The final challenge to the state comes from the pressure for *localism*, the tendency to transfer responsibilities from national or central bodies to a local or community level. This process is by no means universal, and indeed in countries such as the UK, the state has in recent years become markedly more centralised. Nevertheless, in many parts of the world, the growing importance of community and ethnic politics has led to demands for decentralisation and the strengthening of local and regional bodies. For example, centrifugal forces within the EU have led to the idea of a

Privatisation: The transfer of state assets from the public to the private sector, reflecting a contraction of the state's responsibilities.

'Europe of the regions', meaning that regional institutions and groups have increasingly sought direct access to EU bodies, thereby bypassing national governments. In its most dramatic form, however, localism has unleashed centrifugal pressures that have led to the reconstitution of state power or the overthrow of the state itself. Rising ethnic nationalism thus led in 1993 to the breakup of the Czechoslovakian state and the creation of separate Czech and Slovak ones, and in the early 1990s the Yugoslav state was torn apart by a civil war fuelled by a mixture of nationalist ambition and ethnic rivalry. Such forces are examined in greater depth in Chapter 7.

■ Summary

◆ The state is a political association that exercises sovereign jurisdiction within defined territorial borders. In contrast to government, which is merely one of its parts, the state encompasses all public bodies and exercises impersonal authority on the basis of the assumption that it represents the permanent interests of society rather than the partisan sympathies of any group of politicians.

◆ There are a number of rival theories of the state. Pluralists hold that the state is a neutral body that arbitrates between the competing interests of society. Marxists argue that the state maintains the class system by either oppressing subordinate classes or ameliorating class conflict. The New Right portrays the state as a self-serving monster that is intent on expansion and aggrandisement. Radical feminists point to patriarchal biases within the state that support a system of male power.

◆ Those who support the state see it either as a means of defending the individual from the encroachments of fellow citizens or as a mechanism through which collective action can be organised. Critics, however, tend to suggest that the state reflects either the interests of dominant social groups, or interests that are separate from, and antithetical to, society.

◆ States have fulfilled very different roles. Minimal states merely lay down the conditions for orderly existence. Developmental states attempt to promote growth and economic development. Social-democratic states aim to rectify the imbalances and injustices of a market economy. Collectivised states exert control over the entirety of economic life. Totalitarian states bring about all-encompassing politicisation and, in effect, extinguish civil society.

◆ The modern state is confronted by a variety of threats. Chief amongst these are: globalisation in the form of economic interdependence and the emergence of supranational bodies; privatisation through the 'hollowing out' of the state as responsibilities are transferred to private institutions; and localisation through the transfer of responsibilities from central bodies to a local or community level.

■ Questions for discussion

▶ Would life in a state of nature really be 'nasty, brutish and short'?
▶ Does government control the state, or does the state control government?
▶ Can the state be viewed as a neutral body in relation to competing social interests?

▶ Does the nature and background of the state elite inevitably breed bias?

▶ What is the proper relationship between the state and civil society?

▶ How far can the state be 'hollowed out' before it ceases to be a state altogether?

▮ Further reading

Dunleavy, P. and B. O'Leary *Theories of the State* (London: Macmillan, 1987). A carefully structured and accessible introduction to five major approaches to the state and the politics of liberal democracy.

Jessop, B. *State Theory: Putting Capitalist States in Their Place* (Oxford: Polity Press, 1990). A demanding but worthwhile collection of essays through which Jessop develops his own approach to state theory.

Poggi, G. *The State* (Cambridge: Polity Press, 1990). An analysis of the nature, development and prospects of the state that is particularly useful in relation to the 'crisis of the state'.

Schwarzmantel, J. *The State in Contemporary Society: An Introduction* (London and New York: Harvester Wheatsheaf, 1994). A clear and useful introduction to the study of politics that focuses on rival views of the liberal-democratic state.

Nations and Globalisation

Nations and Nationalism

'Nationalism is an infantile disease. It is the measles of mankind.'
ALBERT EINSTEIN *Letter* (1921)

Contents

For the last 200 years, the nation has been regarded as the most appropriate (and perhaps the only proper) unit of political rule. Indeed, international law is largely based on the assumption that nations, like individuals, have inviolable rights, notably the right to political independence and self-determination. Nowhere, however, is the importance of the nation more dramatically demonstrated than in the potency of nationalism as a political creed. In many ways, nationalism has dwarfed the more precise and systematic political ideologies examined in Chapter 3. It has contributed to the outbreak of wars and revolutions. It has caused the birth of new states, the disintegration of empires; and the redrawing of borders; and it has been used to reshape existing regimes as well as to bolster them. Nevertheless, there are reasons to believe that the age of the nation may be drawing to a close. The nation-state, the goal which generations of nationalists have strived to achieve, is increasingly beset by pressures, both internal and external.

The central issues discussed in this chapter are as follows:

Key issues

▶ What is a nation?

▶ How do cultural nationalism and political nationalism differ?

▶ How can the emergence and growth of nationalism be explained?

▶ What political forms has nationalism assumed? What causes has it articulated?

▶ What are the attractions or strengths of the nation-state?

▶ Does the nation-state have a future?

Nation

Nations (from the Latin *nasci*, meaning 'to be born') are complex phenomena that are shaped by a collection of cultural, political and psychological factors. *Culturally*, a nation is a group of people bound together by a common language, religion, history and traditions, although nations exhibit various levels of cultural heterogeneity. *Politically*, a nation is a group of people who regard themselves as a natural political community. Although this is classically expressed in the form of a desire to establish or maintain statehood, it can also take the form of civic consciousness. *Psychologically*, a nation is a group of people distinguished by a shared loyalty or affection in the form of patriotism (see p. 113). However, such an attachment is not a necessary condition for membership of a nation; even those who lack national pride may still recognise that they 'belong' to the nation.

Ethnic group: A group of people who share a common cultural and historical identity, typically linked to a belief in common dissent.

■ What is a nation?

Many of the controversies surrounding the phenomenon of nationalism can be traced back to rival views about what constitutes a nation. So widely accepted is the idea of the nation that its distinctive features are seldom examined or questioned; the nation is simply taken for granted. Nevertheless, confusion abounds. The term 'nation' tends to be used with little precision, and is often used interchangeably with terms such as state, country, ethnic group and race. The United Nations, for instance, is clearly misnamed, as it is an organisation of states, not one of national populations. What, then, are the characteristic features of the nation? What distinguishes a nation from any other social group or other sources of collective identity?

The difficulty of defining the term nation springs from the fact that all nations comprise a mixture of objective and subjective features, a blend of cultural and political characteristics. In *objective* terms, nations are cultural entities: groups of people who speak the same language, have the same religion, are bound by a shared past, and so on. Such factors undoubtedly shape the politics of nationalism. The nationalism of the Québecois in Canada, for instance, is largely based on language differences between French-speaking Quebec and the predominantly English-speaking rest of Canada. Nationalist tensions in India invariably arise from religious divisions, examples being the struggle of Sikhs in Punjab for a separate homeland (Khalistan), and the campaign by Muslims in Kashmir for the incorporation of Kashmir into Pakistan. Nevertheless, it is impossible to define a nation using objective factors alone. All nations encompass a measure of cultural, ethnic and racial diversity. The Swiss nation has proved to be enduring and viable despite the use of three major languages (French, German and Italian), as well as a variety of local dialects. Divisions between Catholics and Protestants that have given rise to rival nationalisms in Northern Ireland have been largely irrelevant in mainland UK, and of only marginal significance in countries like Germany.

This emphasises the fact that, ultimately, nations can only be defined *subjectively* by their members. In the final analysis, the nation is a psycho-political construct. What sets a nation apart from any other group or collectivity is that its members regard themselves as a nation. What does this mean? A nation, in this sense, perceives itself to be a distinctive political community. This is what distinguishes a nation from an **ethnic group**. An ethnic group undoubtedly possesses a communal identity and a sense of cultural pride, but, unlike a nation, it lacks collective political aspirations. These aspirations have traditionally taken the form of the quest for, or the desire to maintain, political independence or statehood. On a more modest level, however, they may consist of a desire to achieve a measure of autonomy, perhaps as part of a federation or confederation of states.

The complexity does not end there, however. Nationalism is a difficult political phenomenon, partly because various nationalist traditions view the concept of a nation in different ways. Two contrasting concepts have been particularly influential. One portrays the nation as primarily a cultural community, and emphasises the importance of ethnic ties and loyalties. The other sees it essentially as a political community, and highlights the significance of civil bonds and allegiances. These rival views not only offer alternative accounts of the origins of nations, but have also been linked to very different forms of nationalism.

Johann Gottfried Herder (1744–1803)

German poet, critic and philosopher, often portrayed as the 'father' of cultural nationalism. A teacher and Lutheran clergyman, Herder travelled throughout Europe before settling in 1776 in Weimar as the clerical head of the Grand Duchy. Although influenced in his early life by thinkers such as Kant (see p. 141), Rousseau (see p. 73) and Montesquieu (see p. 294), he became a leading intellectual opponent of the Enlightenment and a crucial influence on the growth in Germany of the romantic movement. Herder's emphasis on the nation as an organic group characterised by a distinctive language, culture and 'spirit' helped both to found cultural history, and to give rise to a particular form of nationalism that emphasised the intrinsic value of national culture.

Nations as cultural communities

The idea that a nation is essentially an ethnic or cultural entity has been described as the 'primary' concept of the nation (Lafont, 1968). Its roots can be traced back to late eighteenth-century Germany and the writings of figures such as Herder and Fichte (1762–1814). For Herder, the innate character of each national group was ultimately determined by its natural environment, climate and physical geography, which shaped the lifestyle, working habits, attitudes and creative propensities of a people. Above all, he emphasised the importance of language, which he believed was the embodiment of a people's distinctive traditions and historical memories. In his view, each nation thus possesses a **Volksgeist**, which reveals itself in songs, myths and legends, and provides a nation with its source of creativity. Herder's nationalism therefore amounts to a form of culturalism that emphasises an awareness and appreciation of national traditions and collective memories instead of an overtly political quest for statehood. Such ideas had a profound impact on the awakening of national consciousness in nineteenth-century Germany, reflected in the rediscovery of ancient myths and legends in, for example, the folk tales of the Grimm brothers and the operas of Richard Wagner (1813–83).

The implication of Herder's culturalism is that nations are 'natural' or organic entities that can be traced back to ancient times and will, by the same token, continue to exist as long as human society survives. A similar view has been advanced by modern social psychologists, who point to the tendency of people to form groups in order to gain a sense of security, identity and belonging. From this perspective, the division of humankind into nations reflects nothing more than the natural human propensity to draw close to people who share a culture, background and lifestyle that is similar to their own. Such psychological insights, however, do not explain nationalism as a historical phenomenon, that is, as one that arose at a particular time and place, specifically in early nineteenth-century Europe.

In *Nations and Nationalism* (1983), Ernest Gellner emphasised the degree to which nationalism is linked to modernisation and, in particular, to the process of industrialisation. Gellner stressed that, while premodern or 'agroliterate' societies were structured by a network of feudal bonds and loyalties, emerging industrial societies promoted social mobility, self-striving and competition, and so required a new source of cultural cohesion. This was provided by nationalism. Nationalism there-

Volksgeist: (*German*) Literally, the spirit of the people; the organic identity of a people reflected in their culture and particularly their language.

Concept

Cultural nationalism

Cultural nationalism is a form of nationalism that places primary emphasis on the regeneration of the nation as a distinctive civilisation, rather than as a discrete political community. Not uncommonly, cultural nationalists view the state as a peripheral, if not alien, entity. Whereas political nationalism is 'rational', and usually principled, cultural nationalism is 'mystical', in that it is based on a romantic belief in the nation as a unique, historical and organic whole, animated by its own 'spirit'. Typically, it is a 'bottom-up' form of nationalism that draws more on 'popular' rituals, traditions and legends than on elite, or 'higher', culture. Though often antimodern in character, cultural nationalism may also serve as an agent of modernisation by enabling a people to 'recreate' itself.

fore developed to meet the needs of particular social conditions and circumstances. On the other hand, Gellner's theory suggests that nationalism is now ineradicable, as a return to premodern loyalties and identities is unthinkable. However, in *The Ethnic Origins of Nations* (1986), Anthony Smith challenged the idea of a link between nationalism and modernisation by highlighting the continuity between modern nations and premodern ethnic communities, which he called 'ethnies'. In this view, nations are historically embedded: they are rooted in a common cultural heritage and language that may long predate the achievement of statehood or even the quest for national independence. Smith nevertheless acknowledged that, although ethnicity is the precursor of nationalism, modern nations only came into existence when established ethnies were linked to the emerging doctrine of political sovereignty (see p. 143). This conjunction occurred in Europe in the late eighteenth century and early nineteenth century, and in Asia and Africa in the twentieth century.

Regardless of the origins of nations, certain forms of nationalism have a distinctively cultural, rather than political, character. Cultural nationalism commonly takes the form of national self-affirmation; it is a means through which a people can acquire a clearer sense of its own identity through the heightening of national pride and self-respect. This is demonstrated by Welsh nationalism, which focuses much more on attempts to preserve the Welsh language and Welsh culture in general than on the search for political independence. Black nationalism in the USA, the West Indies and many parts of Europe also has a strong cultural character. Its emphasis is on the development of a distinctively black consciousness and sense of national pride, which, in the work of Marcus Garvey (see p. 113) and Malcolm X (1926–65), was linked to the rediscovery of Africa as a spiritual and cultural 'homeland'. A similar process can be seen at work in modern Australia and, to some extent, New Zealand. The republican movement in Australia, for example, reflects the desire to redefine the nation as a political and cultural unit separate from the UK. This is a process of self-affirmation that draws heavily upon the Anzac myth, the relationship with indigenous peoples, and the rediscovery of a settler folk culture.

The German historian Friedrich Meinecke (1907) went one step further and distinguished between 'cultural nations' and 'political nations'. 'Cultural' nations are characterised by a high level of ethnic homogeneity; in effect, national and ethnic identities overlap. Meinecke identified the Greeks, the Germans, the Russians, the English and the Irish as examples of cultural nations, but the description could equally apply to ethnic groups such as the Kurds, the Tamils and the Chechens. Such nations can be regarded as 'organic', in that they have been fashioned by natural or historical forces, rather than by political ones. The strength of cultural nations is that, bound together by a powerful and historical sense of national unity, they tend to be stable and cohesive. On the other hand, cultural nations tend to view themselves as exclusive groups. Membership of the nation is seen to derive not from a political allegiance, voluntarily undertaken, but from an ethnic identity that has somehow been inherited. Cultural nations thus tend to view themselves as extended kinship groups distinguished by common descent. In this sense, it is not possible to 'become' a German, a Russian or a Kurd simply by adopting the language and beliefs of the people. Such exclusivity has tended to breed insular and regressive forms of nationalism, and to weaken the distinction between nation and race (see p. 182).

Nations as political communities

The view that nations are essentially political entities emphasises civic loyalties and political allegiances rather than cultural identity. The nation is thus a group of people who are bound together primarily by shared citizenship, regardless of their cultural, ethnic and other loyalties. This view of the nation is often traced back to the writings of Jean-Jacques Rousseau (see p. 73), sometimes seen as the 'father' of modern nationalism. Although Rousseau did not specifically address the nation question, or discuss the phenomenon of nationalism, his stress on popular sovereignty, expressed in the idea of the 'general will' (in effect, the common good of society), was the seed from which nationalist doctrines sprang during the French Revolution of 1789. In proclaiming that government should be based upon the general will, Rousseau developed a powerful critique of monarchical power and aristocratic privilege. During the French Revolution, this principle of radical democracy was reflected in the assertion that the French people were 'citizens' possessed of inalienable rights and liberties, no longer merely 'subjects' of the crown. Sovereign power thus resided with the 'French nation'. The form of nationalism that emerged from the French Revolution therefore embodied a vision of a people or nation governing itself, and was inextricably linked to the principles of liberty, equality and fraternity.

The idea that nations are political, not ethnic, communities has been supported by a number of theories of nationalism. Eric Hobsbawm (1983), for instance, highlighted the degree to which nations are 'invented traditions'. Rather than accepting that modern nations have developed out of long-established ethnic communities, Hobsbawm argued that a belief in historical continuity and cultural purity was invariably a myth, and, what is more, a myth created by nationalism itself. In this view, nationalism creates nations, not the other way round. A widespread consciousness of nationhood (sometimes called popular nationalism) did not, for example, develop until the late nineteenth century, perhaps fashioned by the invention of national anthems and national flags, and the extension of primary education. Certainly, the idea of a 'mother tongue' passed down from generation to generation and embodying a national culture is highly questionable. In reality, languages live and grow as each generation adapts the language to its own distinctive needs and circumstances. Moreover, it can be argued that the notion of a 'national' language is an absurdity, given the fact that, until the nineteenth century, the majority of people had no knowledge of the written form of their language and usually spoke a regional dialect that had little in common with the language of the educated elite.

Benedict Anderson (1983) also portrayed the modern nation as an artefact, in his case as an 'imagined community'. Anderson pointed out that nations exist more as mental images than as genuine communities which require a level of face-to-face interaction to sustain the notion of a common identity. Within nations, individuals only ever meet a tiny proportion of those with whom they supposedly share a national identity. If nations exist, they exist as imagined artifices, constructed for us through education, the mass media and a process of political socialisation (see p. 186). Whereas in Rousseau's view a nation is animated by ideas of democracy and political freedom, the notion that nations are 'invented' or 'imagined' communities has more in common with the Marxist belief that nationalism is a species of bourgeois ideology. From the perspective of orthodox Marxism, nationalism is a device through which the ruling class counters the threat of social revolution by ensuring that national loyalty is stronger than class solidarity, thus binding the working class to the existing power structure.

Whether nations spring out of a desire for liberty and democracy or are merely cunning inventions of political elites or a ruling class, certain nations have an unmistakably political character. Following Meinecke, these nations can be classified as 'political nations'. A 'political' nation is one in which citizenship has greater political significance than ethnic identity; not uncommonly, political nations contain a number of ethnic groups, and so are marked by cultural heterogeneity. The UK, the USA and France have often been seen as classic examples of political nations. The UK is a union of what, in effect, are four 'cultural' nations: the English, the Scottish, the Welsh and the Northern Irish (although the latter may comprise two nations, the Protestant Unionists and the Catholic Republicans). Insofar as there is a distinctively British national identity, this is based on political factors such as a common allegiance to the Crown, respect for the Westminster Parliament, and a belief in the historic rights and liberties of the British people. As a 'land of immigrants', the USA has a distinctively multiethnic and multicultural character, which makes it impossible for it to construct a national identity on the basis of shared cultural and historical ties. Instead, a sense of American nationhood has been consciously developed through the educational system, and through the cultivation of respect for a set of common values, notably those outlined in the Declaration of Independence and the US Constitution. Similarly French national identity is closely linked to the traditions and principles of the 1789 French Revolution.

What such nations have in common is that, in theory, they were founded upon a voluntary acceptance of a common set of principles or goals, as opposed to an existing cultural identity. It is sometimes argued that the style of nationalism which develops in such societies is typically tolerant and democratic. If a nation is primarily a political entity, it is an inclusive group, in that membership is not restricted to those who fulfil particular language, religious, ethnic or suchlike criteria. Classic examples are the USA, with its image as a 'melting pot' nation, and the 'new' South Africa, seen as a 'rainbow society'. On the other hand, political nations may at times fail to experience the organic unity and sense of historical rootedness that is found in cultural nations. This may, for instance, account for the relative weakness of specifically British nationalism in the UK, by comparison with Scottish and Welsh nationalism and the insular form of English nationalism that is sometimes called 'little Englander' nationalism.

Developing world states have encountered particular problems in their struggle to achieve a national identity. Such nations can be described as 'political' in two senses. First, in many cases, they have achieved statehood only after a struggle against colonial rule (see p.116). In this case, the nation's national identity is deeply influenced by the unifying quest for national liberation and freedom. Third world nationalism therefore tends to have a strong anticolonial character. Secondly, these nations have often been shaped by territorial boundaries inherited from their former colonial rulers. This has particularly been the case in Africa. African 'nations' often encompass a wide range of ethnic, religious and regional groups that are bound together by little more than a shared colonial past. In contrast to the creation of classic European cultural nations, which sought statehood on the basis of a pre-existing national identity, an attempt has been made in Africa to 'build' nations on the foundations of existing states. However, the resulting mismatch of political and ethnic identities has bred recurrent tensions, as has been seen in Nigeria, Sudan,

Rwanda and Burundi, for example. However, such conflicts are by no means simply manifestations of ancient 'tribalism'. To a large extent, they are a consequence of the divide-and-rule policies used in the colonial past.

Varieties of nationalism

Immense controversy surrounds the political character of nationalism. On the one hand, nationalism can appear to be a progressive and liberating force, offering the prospect of national unity or independence. On the other, it can be an irrational and reactionary creed that allows political leaders to conduct policies of military expansion and war in the name of the nation. Indeed, nationalism shows every sign of suffering from the political equivalent of multiple-personality syndrome. As various times, nationalism has been progressive and reactionary, democratic and authoritarian, liberating and oppressive, and left-wing and right-wing. For this reason, it is perhaps better to view nationalism not as a single or coherent political phenomenon, but as a series of 'nationalisms', that is, as a complex of traditions that share but one characteristic: each, in its own particular way, acknowledges the central political importance of the nation.

This confusion derives in part from the controversies examined above about how the concept of a nation should be understood, and about whether cultural or political criteria are decisive in defining the nation. However, the character of nationalism is also moulded by the circumstances in which nationalist aspirations arise, and by the political causes to which it is attached. Thus, when nationalism is a reaction against the experience of foreign domination or colonial rule, it tends to be a liberating force linked to the goals of liberty, justice and democracy. When nationalism is a product of social dislocation and demographic change, it often has an insular and exclusive character, and can become a vehicle for racism (see p. 114) and **xenophobia**. Finally, nationalism is shaped by the political ideals of those who espouse it. In their different ways, liberals, conservatives, socialists, fascists and even communists have been attracted to nationalism (of the major ideologies, perhaps only anarchism is entirely at odds with nationalism). In this sense, nationalism is a cross-cutting ideology. The principal political manifestations of nationalism are the following:

- liberal nationalism
- conservative nationalism
- expansionist nationalism
- anticolonial nationalism.

Liberal nationalism

Liberal nationalism can be seen as the classic form of European liberalism; it dates back to the French Revolution, and embodies many of its values. Indeed, in continental Europe in the mid-nineteenth-century, to be a nationalist meant to be a liberal, and *vice versa*. The 1848 Revolutions, for example, fused the struggle for national independence and unification with the demand for limited and constitutional government. Nowhere was this more evident that in the 'Risorgimento' (rebirth) nationalism of the Italian nationalist movement, especially as expressed by the 'prophet' of Italian unification, Guiseppe Mazzini (see p. 110). Similar principles

Xenophobia: A fear or hatred of foreigners; pathological ethnocentrism.

Guiseppe Mazzini (1805–72)

Italian nationalist and apostle of liberal republicanism. Mazzini was born in Genoa, Italy, and was the son of a doctor. He came into contact with revolutionary politics as a member of the patriotic secret society, the Carbonari. This led to his arrest and exile to France and, after his expulsion from France, to Britain. He returned briefly to Italy during the 1848 Revolutions, helping to liberate Milan and becoming head of the short-lived Roman Republic. A committed republican, Mazzini's influence thereafter faded as other nationalist leaders, including Garibaldi (1807–82), looked to the House of Savoy to bring about Italian unification. Although he never officially returned to Italy, Mazzini's liberal nationalism had a profound influence throughout Europe, and on immigrant groups in the USA.

were espoused by Simon Bolivar (1783–1830), who led the Latin-American independence movement in the early nineteenth century, and helped to expel the Spanish from Hispanic America. Perhaps the clearest expression of liberal nationalism is found in US President Woodrow Wilson's 'Fourteen Points'. Drawn up in 1918, these were proposed as the basis for the reconstruction of Europe after the First World War, and provided a blueprint for the sweeping territorial changes that were implemented by the Treaty of Versailles (1919).

In common with all forms of nationalism, liberal nationalism is based on the fundamental assumption that humankind is naturally divided into a collection of nations, each possessed of a separate identity. Nations are therefore genuine or organic communities, not the artificial creation of political leaders or ruling classes. The characteristic theme of liberal nationalism, however, is that it links the idea of the nation with a belief in popular sovereignty, ultimately derived from Rousseau. This fusion was brought about because the multinational empires against which nineteenth-century European nationalists fought were also autocratic and oppressive. Mazzini, for example, wished not only to unite the Italian states, but also to throw off the influence of autocratic Austria. The central theme of this form of nationalism is therefore a commitment to the principle of **national self-determination**. Its goal is the construction of a nation-state (see p. 117), that is, a state within which the boundaries of government coincide as far as possible with those of nationality. In J. S. Mill's ([1861] 1951:392) words:

When the sentiment of nationality exists in any force, there is a *prima facie* case for uniting all members of the nationality under one government, and a government to themselves apart. This is merely saying that the question of government should be decided by the governed.

Liberal nationalism is above all a principled form of nationalism. It does not uphold the interests of one nation against other nations. Instead, it proclaims that each and every nation has a right to freedom and self-determination. In this sense, all nations are equal. The ultimate goal of liberal nationalism, then, is the construction of a world of sovereign nation-states. Mazzini thus formed the clandestine organisation Young Italy to promote the idea of a united Italy, but he also founded Young Europe in the hope of spreading nationalist ideas throughout the continent. Similarly, at the Paris Peace Conference which drew up the Treaty of Versailles, Woodrow Wilson advanced the principle of self-determination not simply because the breakup of European empires served US national interests, but because he believed that the

National self-determination:
The principle that the nation is a sovereign entity; self-determination implies both national independence and democratic rule.

Poles, the Czechs, the Yugoslavs and the Hungarians all had the same right to political independence that the Americans already enjoyed.

From this perspective, nationalism is not only a means of enlarging political freedom, but also a mechanism for securing a peaceful and stable world order. Wilson, for instance, believed that the First World War had been caused because of an 'old order' that was dominated by autocratic and militaristic empires bent on expansionism and war. In his view, democratic nation-states, however, would be essentially peaceful, because, possessing both cultural and political unity, they lacked the incentive to wage war or subjugate other nations. In this light, nationalism is not seen as a source of distrust, suspicion and rivalry. Rather, it is a force capable of promoting unity within each nation and brotherhood amongst nations on the basis of mutual respect for national rights and characteristics.

There is a sense, nevertheless, in which liberalism looks beyond the nation. This occurs for two reasons. The first is that a commitment to individualism implies that liberals believe that all human beings (regardless of factors such as race, creed, social background and nationality) are of equal moral worth. Liberalism therefore subscribes to universalism, in that it accepts that individuals everywhere have the same status and entitlements. This is commonly expressed nowadays in the notion of **human rights**. In setting the individual above the nation, liberals establish a basis for violating national sovereignty, as in the international campaign to pressurise the 'white' South African regime to abandon apartheid. The second reason is that liberals fear that a world of sovereign nation-states may degenerate into an international 'state of nature'. Just as unlimited freedom allows individuals to abuse and enslave one another, national sovereignty may be used as a cloak for expansionism and conquest. Freedom must always be subject to the law, and this applies equally to individuals and to nations. Liberals have, as a result, been in the forefront of campaigns to establish a system of international law (see p. 160) supervised by supranational bodies such as the League of Nations, the United Nations and the European Union. In this view, nationalism must therefore never be allowed to become insular and exclusive, but, instead, must be balanced against a competing emphasis upon cosmopolitanism.

Criticisms of liberal nationalism tend to fall into two categories. In the first category, liberal nationalists may be accused of being naive and romantic. They see the progressive and liberating face of nationalism; theirs is a tolerant and rational nationalism. However, they perhaps ignore the darker face of nationalism, that is, the irrational bonds or **tribalism** that distinguish 'us' from a foreign and threatening 'them'. Liberals see nationalism as a universal principle, but they have less understanding of the emotional power of nationalism, which, in time of war, can persuade people to fight, kill and die for 'their' country, almost regardless of the justice of their nation's cause. Such a stance is expressed in the assertion: 'my country, right or wrong'.

Secondly, the goal of liberal nationalism (the construction of a world of nation-states) may be fundamentally misguided. The mistake of Wilsonian nationalism, on the basis of which large parts of the map of Europe were redrawn, was that it assumed that nations live in convenient and discrete geographical areas, and that states can be constructed to coincide with these areas. In practice, all so-called 'nation-states' comprise a number of linguistic, religious, ethnic and regional groups, some of which may consider themselves to be 'nations'. This has nowhere been more clearly demonstrated than in the former Yugoslavia, a country viewed by the peacemakers at Versailles as 'the land of the Slavs'. However, it in fact consisted

Concept

Cosmopolitanism

Cosmopolitanism is literally a belief in a *cosmopolis*, or 'world state'. It thus implies the obliteration of national identities and the establishment of a common political allegiance uniting all human beings. However, the term is usually used to refer to the more modest goal of peace and harmony amongst nations, founded upon mutual understanding, toleration and, above all, interdependence. Thus the nineteenth-century 'Manchester liberals', Richard Cobden (1804–65) and John Bright (1811–89), endorsed cosmopolitanism in advocating free trade on the grounds that it would promote international understanding and economic interdependence, ultimately making war impossible. The cosmopolitan ideal is also promoted by supranational bodies that aim to foster cooperation amongst nations rather than to replace the nation-state.

Human rights: Rights to which people are entitled by virtue of being human; universal and fundamental rights (see p. 284).

Tribalism: Group behaviour characterised by insularity and exclusivity, typically fuelled by hostility towards rival groups.

of a patchwork of ethnic communities, religions, languages and differing histories. Moreover, as the disintegration of Yugoslavia in the early 1990s demonstrated, each of its constituent republics was itself an ethnic patchwork. Indeed, as the Nazis and later the Bosnian Serbs recognised, the only certain way of achieving a politically unified and culturally homogeneous nation-state is through a programme of **ethnic cleansing**.

Conservative nationalism

Historically, conservative nationalism developed rather later than liberal national-ism. Until the latter half of the nineteenth century, conservative politicians treated nationalism as a subversive, if not revolutionary, creed. As the century progressed, however, the link between conservatism and nationalism became increasingly apparent, for instance, in Disraeli's 'One Nation' ideal, in Bismarck's willingness to recruit German nationalism to the cause of Prussian aggrandisement, and in Tsar Alexander III's endorsement of pan-Slavic nationalism. In modern politics, national-ism has become an article of faith for most, if not all, conservatives. In the UK this was demonstrated most graphically by Margaret Thatcher's triumphalist reaction to victory in the Falklands War of 1982, and it is evident in the engrained 'Eurosceptic-ism' of the Conservative right, particularly in relation to its recurrent bogey: a 'federal Europe'. A similar form of nationalism was rekindled in the USA through the adoption of a more assertive foreign policy, by Reagan in the invasion of Grenada and the bombing of Libya, and by Bush in the invasion of Panama and the 1991 Gulf War.

Conservative nationalism is concerned less with the principled nationalism of universal self-determination and more with the promise of social cohesion and public order embodied in the sentiment of national patriotism. Above all, conservatives see the nation as an organic entity emerging out of a basic desire of humans to gravitate towards those who have the same views, habits, lifestyles and appearance as them-selves. In short, human beings seek security and identity through membership of a national community. From this perspective, patriotic loyalty and a consciousness of nationhood is largely rooted in the idea of a shared past, turning nationalism into a defence of values and institutions that have been endorsed by history. Nationalism thus becomes a form of traditionalism. This gives conservative nationalism a distinc-tively nostalgic and backward-looking character. In the USA, this is accomplished through an emphasis on the Pilgrim Fathers, the War of Independence, the Philadel-phia Convention and so on. In the case of British nationalism (or, more accurately, English nationalism), national patriotism draws on symbols closely associated with the institution of monarchy. The UK national anthem is *God Save the Queen*, and the Royal Family play a prominent role in national celebrations such as Armistice Day, and on state occasions such as the opening of Parliament.

Conservative nationalism tends to develop in established nation-states rather than in ones that are in the process of nation building. It is typically inspired by the perception that the nation is somehow under threat, either from within or from without. The traditional 'enemy within' has been class antagonism and the ultimate danger of social revolution. In this respect, conservatives have seen nationalism as the antidote to socialism: when patriotic loyalties are stronger than class solidarity, the working class is, effectively, integrated into the nation. Calls for national unity and the belief that unabashed patriotism is a civic virtue are therefore recurrent

Ethnic cleansing: The forcible expulsion or extermination of 'alien' peoples; often used as a euphemism for genocide.

themes in conservative thought. The 'enemies without' that threaten national identity include immigration and supranationalism.

In this view, immigration poses a threat because it tends to weaken an established
national culture and ethnic identity, thereby provoking hostility and conflict. This
fear was expressed in the UK in the 1960s by Enoch Powell, who warned that further
Commonwealth immigration would lead to racial conflict and violence. A similar
theme was taken up in 1979 by Margaret Thatcher in her reference to the danger of
the UK being 'swamped' by immigrants. Anti-immigration campaigns waged by the
British National Party, Le Pen's National Front in France, and far-right groups in
Germany such as the Republicans, also draw their inspiration from conservative
nationalism. National identity, and with it our source of security and belonging,
is threatened in the same way by the growth of supranational bodies and by the
globalisation of culture. Resistance in the UK and in other EU member states to a
single European currency reflects not merely concern about the loss of economic
sovereignty, but also a belief that a national currency is vital to the maintenance of
a distinctive national identity.

Although conservative nationalism has been linked to military adventure and
expansion, its distinctive character is that it is inward-looking and insular. If conservative governments have used foreign policy as a device to stoke up public fervour,
this is an act of political opportunism rather than because conservative nationalism
is relentlessly aggressive or inherently militaristic. This leads to the criticism that
conservative nationalism is essentially a form of elite manipulation or ruling-class
ideology. From this perspective, the 'nation' is invented and certainly defined by
political leaders and ruling elites with a view to manufacturing consent and engineering political passivity. In crude terms, when in trouble, all governments play the
'nationalism card'. A more serious criticism of conservative nationalism, however, is
that it promotes intolerance and bigotry. Insular nationalism draws upon a narrowly
cultural concept of the nation, that is, the belief that a nation is an exclusive ethnic
community, broadly similar to an extended family. A very clear line is therefore
drawn between those who are members of the nation and those who are alien to it.
By insisting upon the maintenance of cultural purity and established traditions, conservatives may portray immigrants, or foreigners in general, as a threat, and so promote, or at least legitimise, racialism and xenophobia.

Expansionist nationalism

The third form of nationalism has an aggressive, militaristic and expansionist character.
In many ways, this form of nationalism is the antithesis of the principled belief in
equal rights and self-determination that is the core of liberal nationalism. The
aggressive face of nationalism first appeared in the late nineteenth century as European powers indulged in 'the scramble for Africa' in the name of national glory and
their 'place in the sun'. Nineteenth-century European imperialism (see p. 145) differed from the colonial expansion of earlier periods in that it was fuelled by a climate
of popular nationalism in which national prestige was increasingly linked to the possession of an empire, and each colonial victory was greeted by demonstrations of
popular enthusiasm, or **jingoism**. To a large extent, both world wars of the twentieth
century resulted from this expansionist form of nationalism. When the First World
War broke out in August 1914, following a prolonged arms race and a succession of
international crises, the prospect of conquest and military glory provoked spontaneous

> **Concept**
>
> **Patriotism**
>
> Patriotism (from the Latin
> *patria*, meaning
> 'fatherland') is a sentiment,
> a psychological attachment
> to one's nation (a 'love of
> one's country'). The terms
> nationalism and patriotism
> are often confused.
> Nationalism has a doctrinal
> character and embodies the
> belief that the nation is in
> some way the central
> principle of political
> organisation. Patriotism
> provides the affective basis
> for that belief. Patriotism
> thus underpins all forms of
> nationalism; it is difficult to
> conceive of a national
> group demanding, say,
> political independence
> without possessing at least
> a measure of patriotic
> loyalty or national
> consciousness. However,
> not all patriots are
> nationalists. Not all of
> those who identify with, or
> even love, their nation see
> it as a means through
> which political demands
> can be articulated.

Jingoism: A mood of public
enthusiasm and celebration
provoked by military expansion
or imperial conquest.

Racialism, racism

The terms racialism and racism are often used interchangeably, although the latter has become more common in modern usage. Racialism includes any belief or doctrine that draws political or social conclusions from the idea that humankind is divided into biologically distinct races. Racialist theories are thus based on two assumptions. First, genetic differences justify humankind being treated as a collection of races (race effectively implying species). Secondly, cultural, intellectual and moral differences amongst humankind derive from these more fundamental genetic differences. In political terms, racialism is manifest in calls for racial segregation (apartheid), and in doctrines of 'blood' superiority and inferiority (for example, Aryanism and anti-Semitism). Racism may be used more narrowly to refer to prejudice or hostility towards people on the grounds of their racial origins, whether or not this is linked to a developed racial theory.

public rejoicing in all the major capitals of Europe. The Second World War was largely a result of the nationalist-inspired programmes of imperial expansion pursued by Japan, Italy and Germany. The most destructive modern example of this form of nationalism in Europe has been the quest by the Bosnian Serbs to construct a 'Greater Serbia'.

In its extreme form, such nationalism arises from a sentiment of intense, even hysterical nationalist enthusiasm, sometimes referred to as integral nationalism. The term integral nationalism was coined by the French nationalist Charles Maurras (1868–1952), leader of the right-wing Action Française. The centrepiece of Maurras' politics was an assertion of the overriding importance of the nation: the nation is everything and the individual is nothing. The nation thus has an existence and meaning beyond the life of any single individual, and individual existence only has meaning when it is dedicated to the unity and survival of the nation. Such fanatical patriotism has a particularly strong appeal for the alienated, isolated and powerless, for whom nationalism becomes a vehicle through which pride and self-respect can be regained. However, integral nationalism breaks the link previously established between nationalism and democracy. An 'integral' nation is an exclusive ethnic community, bound together by primordial loyalties rather than voluntary political allegiances. National unity does not demand free debate and an open and competitive struggle for power; it requires discipline and obedience to a single, supreme leader. This led Maurras to portray democracy as a source of weakness and corruption, and to call instead for the reestablishment of monarchical absolutism.

This militant and intense form of nationalism is invariably associated with chauvinistic beliefs and doctrines. Derived from the name of Nicolas Chauvin, a French soldier noted for his fanatical devotion to Napoleon and the cause of France, chauvinism is an irrational belief in the superiority or dominance of one's own group or people. National chauvinism therefore rejects the idea that all nations are equal in favour of the belief that nations have particular characteristics and qualities, and so have very different destinies. Some nations are suited to rule; others are suited to be ruled. Typically, this form of nationalism is articulated through doctrines of ethnic or racial superiority, thereby fusing nationalism and racialism. The chauvinist's own nation is seen to be unique and special, in some way a 'chosen people'. For early German nationalists such as Fichte and Jahn, only the Germans were a true *Volk* (an organic people). They alone had maintained blood purity and avoided the contamination of their language. For Maurras, France was an unequalled marvel, a repository of all Christian and classical virtues.

No less important in this type of nationalism, however, is the image of another nation or race as a threat or enemy. In the face of the enemy, the nation draws together and gains an intensified sense of its own identity and importance, achieving a kind of 'negative integration'. Chauvinistic nationalism therefore establishes a clear distinction between 'them' and 'us'. There has to be a 'them' to deride or hate in order for a sense of 'us' to be forged. The world is thus divided, usually by means of racial categories, into an 'in group' and an 'out group'. The 'out group' acts as a scapegoat for all the misfortunes and frustrations suffered by the 'in group'. This was most graphically demonstrated by the virulent anti-Semitism that was the basis of German Nazism. Hitler's *Mein Kampf* ([1925] 1969) portrayed history as a Manichean struggle between the Aryans and the Jews, respectively representing the forces of light and darkness, or good and evil.

A recurrent theme of expansionist nationalism is the idea of national rebirth or regeneration. This form of nationalism commonly draws upon myths of past greatness or national glory. Mussolini and the Italian Fascists looked back to the days of Imperial Rome. In portraying their regime as the 'Third Reich', the German Nazis harked back both to Bismarck's 'Second Reich' and Charlemagne's Holy Roman Empire, the 'First Reich'. Such myths plainly give expansionist nationalism a backward-looking character, but they also look to the future in that they mark out the nation's destiny. If nationalism is a vehicle for reestablishing greatness and regaining national glory, it invariably has a militaristic and expansionist character. In short, war is the testing ground of the nation. At the heart of integral nationalism there often lies an imperial project: a quest for expansion or a search for colonies. This can be seen in forms of **pan-nationalism.** However, Nazi Germany is again the best-known example. Hitler's writings mapped out a three-stage programme of expansion. First, the Nazis sought to establish a 'Greater Germany' by bringing ethnic Germans in Austria, Czechoslovakia and Poland within an expanded Reich. Secondly, they intended to achieve *Lebensraum* (living space) by establishing a German-dominated empire stretching into Russia. Thirdly, Hitler dreamed of ultimate Aryan world domination.

Anticolonial nationalism

The developing world has spawned various forms of nationalism, all of which have in some way drawn inspiration from the struggle against colonial rule. The irony of this form of nationalism is that it has turned doctrines and principles first developed through the process of 'nation building' in Europe against the European powers themselves. Colonialism, in other words, succeeded in turning nationalism into a political creed of global significance. In Africa and Asia, it helped to forge a sense of nationhood shaped by the desire for 'national liberation'. Indeed, during the twentieth century, the political geography of much of the world has been transformed by anticolonialism. Independence movements that sprang up in the interwar period gained new impetus after the conclusion of the Second World War. The overstretched empires of Britain, France, the Netherlands and Portugal crumbled in the face of rising nationalism.

India had been promised independence during the Second World War, which was eventually granted in 1947. China only achieved genuine unity and independence after the 1949 communist revolution, having fought an eight-year war against the occupying Japanese. A republic of Indonesia was proclaimed in 1949 after a three-year war against the Netherlands. A military uprising forced the French to withdraw from Vietnam in 1954, even though final liberation, with the unification of North and South Vietnam, was not achieved until 1975, after 14 further years of war against the USA. Nationalist struggles in South East Asia inspired similar movements in Africa, with liberation movements emerging under leaders such as Nkrumah in Ghana, Dr Azikiwe in Nigeria, Julius Nyerere in Tanganyika (later Tanzania), and Hastings Banda in Nyasaland (later Malawi). The pace of decolonisation in Africa accelerated from the late 1950s onwards. Nigeria gained independence from the UK in 1960 and, after a prolonged war fought against the French, Algeria gained independence in 1962. Kenya became independent in 1963, as did Tanzania and Malawi the next year. Africa's last remaining colony, South-West Africa, finally became independent Namibia in 1990.

Early forms of anticolonialism drew heavily on 'classical' European nationalism and were inspired by the idea of national self-determination. However, emergent

---

Concept

Anti-Semitism

Semites are by tradition the descendants of Shem, son of Noah. They include most of the peoples of the Middle East. Anti-Semitism is prejudice or hatred towards Jews. In its earliest systematic form, anti-Semitism had a *religious* character. It reflected the hostility of the Christians towards the Jews, based on the alleged complicity of the Jews in the murder of Jesus and their refusal to acknowledge him as the son of God. *Economic* anti-Semitism developed from the Middle Ages onwards, and expressed distaste for Jews in their capacity as moneylenders and traders. Jews were thus excluded from membership of craft guilds and prevented from owning land. The nineteenth century saw the birth of *racial* anti-Semitism in the work of Wagner and H. S. Chamberlain (1855–1929), which condemned the Jewish peoples as fundamentally evil and destructive. These ideas provided the ideological basis for German Nazism and found their most grotesque expression in the Holocaust.

Pan-nationalism: A style of nationalism dedicated to unifying a disparate people through either expansionism or political solidarity ('pan' means all or every).

Concept

Colonialism

Colonialism is the theory or practice of establishing control over a foreign territory and turning it into a 'colony'. Colonialism is thus a particular form of imperialism (p. 145). Colonialism is usually distinguished by settlement and by economic domination. As typically practised in Africa and South East Asia, colonial government was exercised by a settler community from a 'mother country' who were ethnically distinct from the 'native' population. In French colonialism, colonies were thought of as part of the mother country, meaning that colonial peoples were granted formal rights of citizenship. In contrast, neocolonialism is essentially an economic phenomenon based on the export of capital from an advanced country to a less developed one, as seen, for example, in so-called US 'dollar imperialism' in Latin America.

African and Asian nations were in a very different position from the newly created European states of the nineteenth century. For African and Asian nations, the quest for political independence was inextricably linked to a desire for social development and for an end to their subordination to the industrialised states of Europe and the USA. The goal of 'national liberation' therefore had an economic as well as a political dimension. This helps to explain why anticolonial movements typically looked not to liberalism but to socialism, and particularly to Marxism–Leninism, as a vehicle for expressing their nationalist ambitions. On the surface, nationalism and socialism appear to be incompatible political creeds. Socialists have traditionally preached internationalism (see p. 142), since they regard humanity as a single entity, and argue that the division of humankind into separate nations only breeds suspicion and hostility. Marxists in particular have stressed that the bonds of class solidarity are stronger and more genuine than the ties of nationality, or, as Marx put it in the *Communist Manifesto* ([1848] 1967:102): 'Working men have no country'.

The appeal of socialism to the developing world is based on the fact that the values of community and cooperation which socialism embodies are deeply established in the cultures of traditional, preindustrial societies. In this sense, nationalism and socialism are linked insofar as both emphasise social solidarity and collective action. By this standard, nationalism may simply be a weaker form of socialism, the former applying the 'social' principle to the nation, the latter extending it to cover the whole of humanity. More specifically, socialism, and especially Marxism, provide an analysis of inequality and exploitation through which the colonial experience can be understood and colonial rule challenged. In the same way as the oppressed and exploited proletariat saw that they could achieve liberation through the revolutionary overthrow of capitalism, third-world nationalists saw 'armed struggle' as a means of achieving both political and economic emancipation, thus fusing the goals of political independence and social revolution. In countries such as China, North Korea, Vietnam and Cambodia, anticolonial movements openly embraced Marxism–Leninism. On achieving power, they moved to seize foreign assets and nationalise economic resources, creating Soviet-style planned economies. African and Middle Eastern states have developed a less ideological form of nationalistic socialism, practised in Algeria, Libya, Zambia, Iraq, South Yemen and elsewhere. The 'socialism' proclaimed in these countries usually takes the form of an appeal to a unifying national cause or interest, typically proclaimed by a powerful 'charismatic' leader.

However, nationalists in the developing world have not always been content to express their nationalism in a language of socialism or Marxism borrowed from the West. Especially since the 1970s, Marxism–Leninism has often been displaced by forms of religious fundamentalism (see p. 61), and particularly Islamic fundamentalism. This has given the developing world a specifically nonwestern, indeed an antiwestern, voice. In theory at least, Islam attempts to foster a transnational political identity that unites all those who acknowledge the 'way of Islam' and the teachings of the Prophet Muhammad within an 'Islamic nation'. However, the Iranian revolution of 1979, which brought Ayatollah Khomeini (1900–89) to power, demonstrated the potency of Islamic fundamentalism as a creed of national and spiritual renewal. The establishment of an 'Islamic republic' was designed to purge Iran of the corrupting influence of western materialism in general and of the 'Great Satan' (the USA) in particular through a return to the traditional values and principles embodied in the *Shari'a*, or divine Islamic law. By no means, however, does Islamic nationalism have a unified character. In Sudan and Pakistan, for example, Islamification has essentially been used as a tool of statecraft to consolidate the power of ruling elites. Nevertheless, in Egypt and Algeria, revolutionary Islamic movements have emerged that call for moral renewal and political purification in the name of the urban poor.

▇ A future for the nation-state?

As the twentieth century progressed, claims were increasingly made that the age of nationalism was over. This was not because nationalism had been superseded by 'higher' supernational allegiances, but because its task had been completed: the world had become a world of nation-states. In effect, the nation had been accepted as the sole legitimate unit of political rule. Certainly, since 1789, the world had been fundamentally remodelled on nationalist lines. In 1910, only 15 of the 159 states recognised in 1989 as full members of the United Nations existed. Well into the twentieth century, most of the peoples of the world were still colonial subjects of one of the European empires. Only three of the current 65 states in the Middle East and Africa existed before 1910, and no fewer than 74 states have come into being since 1959. These changes have been fuelled largely by the quest for national independence, with these new states invariably assuming the mantle of the nation-state.

History undoubtedly seems to be on the side of the nation-state. The three major geopolitical upheavals of the twentieth century (the First World War, the Second World War and the collapse of communism in eastern Europe) each gave considerable impetus to the concept of the nation as a principle of political organisation. Since 1991, at least 18 new states have come into existence (14 of them as a result of the disintegration of the USSR), and all of them have claimed to be nation-states. The great strength of the nation-state is that it offers the prospect of both cultural cohesion and political unity. When a people who share a common cultural or ethnic identity gain the right to self-government, community and citizenship coincide. This is why nationalists believe that the forces that have created a world of independent nation-states are natural and irresistible, and that no other social group could constitute a meaningful political community. They believe that the nation-state is ultimately the only viable political unit. This view implies, for instance, that supranational bodies such as the European Union will never be able to rival the capacity of national governments to establish legitimacy and command popular allegiance. Clear limits should therefore be placed on the process of European integration because people with different languages, cultures and histories will never come to think of themselves as members of a united political community.

Nevertheless, just as the principle of the nation-state has achieved its widest support, other, very powerful forces have emerged that threaten to make the nation-state redundant. A combination of internal pressures and external threats has produced what is commonly referred to as a 'crisis of the nation-state'. Internally, nation-states have been subject to centrifugal pressures, generated by an upsurge in ethnic and regional politics. This heightened concern with ethnicity may, indeed, reflect the fact that, in a context of economic and cultural globalisation (see p. 140), nations are no longer able to provide a meaningful collective identity or sense of social belonging. Given that all nation-states embody a measure of cultural diversity, the politics of ethnic coherence cannot but present a challenge to the principle of the nation. Unlike nations, ethnic or regional groups are not viable political entitles in

Concept

Nation-state

The nation-state is a form of political organisation, and a political ideal. In the first case, it is an autonomous political community bound together by the overlapping bonds of citizenship and nationality. It is thus an alternative to multinational empires and city states. In the latter case, the nation-state is a principle, or ideal type (see p. 18), reflected in Mazzini's goal: 'every nation a state, only one state for the entire nation'. This acknowledges that no modern state is, or can be, culturally homogeneous. There are two contrasting views of the nation-state. For liberals and most socialists, the nation-state is largely fashioned out of civic loyalties and allegiances. For conservatives and integral nationalists, it is based on ethnic or organic unity.

their own right, and thus look to forms of federalism (see p. 125) and confederalism to provide an alternative to political nationalism. For example, within the framework provided by the European Union, the Belgian regions of Flanders and Wallonia have achieved such a degree of self-government that Belgium remains a nation-state only in a strictly formal sense. The nature of such centrifugal forces is discussed more fully in Chapter 7.

External threats to the nation-state have a variety of forms. First, advances in the technology of warfare, and especially the advent of the nuclear age, have brought about demands that world peace be policed by supranational and international bodies. This led to the creation of the League of Nations and later the United Nations. Secondly, economic life has been progressively globalised. Markets are now world markets, businesses have increasingly become transnational corporations, and capital is moved around the globe in the flick of an eyelid. Is there a future for the nation-state in a world in which no national government can control its economic destiny? Thirdly, the nation-state may be the enemy of the natural environment and a threat to the global ecological balance. Nations are primarily concerned with their own strategic and economic interests, and most pay little attention to the ecological consequences of their actions. The folly of this was demonstrated by the Chernobyl nuclear accident in the Ukraine in 1986, which released a wave of nuclear radiation across Northern Europe that will cause an estimated 2000 cancer-related deaths over 50 years in Europe.

Finally, distinctive national cultures and traditions, the source of cohesion which distinguishes nation-states from other forms of political organisation, have been weakened by the emergence of a transnational and even global culture. This has been facilitated by international tourism and the dramatic growth in communications technologies, from satellite television to the 'information superhighway'. When US films and television programmes are watched throughout the world, Indian and Chinese cuisine is as popular in Europe as native dishes, and people can communicate as easily with the other side of the world as with their neighbouring town, is the nation-state any longer a meaningful entity? These and related issues are discussed in greater depth in Chapter 8.

■ Summary

◆ Nations are defined by a combination of cultural and political factors. Culturally, they are groups of people who are bound together by a common language, religion, history and traditions. Ultimately, however, nations define themselves through the existence of a shared civic consciousness, classically expressed as the desire to achieve or maintain statehood.

◆ Distinctive cultural and political forms of nationalism can be identified. Cultural nationalism emphasises the regeneration of the nation as a distinctive civilisation on the basis of a belief in the nation as a unique, historical and organic whole. Political nationalism, on the other hand, recognises the nation as a discrete political community, and is thus linked with ideas such as sovereignty and self-determination.

◆ Some political thinkers portray nationalism as a modern phenomenon associated with industrialisation and the rise of democracy, while others trace it back to pre-modern ethnic loyalties and identities. The character of nationalism has varied considerably, and has been influenced by both the historical circumstances in which it has arisen, and the political causes to which it has been attached.

◆ There have been a number of contrasting manifestations of political nationalism. Liberal nationalism is based on a belief in a universal right to self-determination. Conservative nationalism values the capacity of national patriotism to deliver social cohesion and political unity. Expansionist nationalism is a vehicle for aggression and imperial conquest. Anticolonial nationalism is associated with the struggle for national liberation, often fused with the quest for social development.

◆ The most widely recognised form of political organisation worldwide is the nation-state, which is often seen as the sole legitimate unit of political rule. Its strength is that it offers the prospect of both cultural cohesion and political unity, thus allowing those who share a common cultural or ethnic identity to exercise the right to independence and self-government.

◆ The nation-state now confronts a number of challenges. Nation-states have been subject to centrifugal pressures generated by the growth in ethnic politics. Externally, they have confronted challenges from the growing power of supranational bodies, the advance of economic and cultural globalisation, and the need to find international solutions to the environmental crisis.

■ Questions for discussion

▶ Where do nations come from? Are they natural or artificial formations?

▶ Why have national pride and patriotic loyalty been valued?

▶ Does cultural nationalism merely imprison a nation in its past?

▶ Why has nationalism proved to be such a potent political force?

▶ Does nationalism inevitably breed insularity and conflict?

▶ Is the nation-state the sole legitimate unit of political rule?

■ Further reading

Alter, P. *Nationalism* (London: Edward Arnold, 1989). A readable and very useful introduction to the various forms of nationalism.

Gellner, E. *Nations and Nationalism* (Ithaca, NY: Cornell University Press, 1983). A highly influential account of the emergence and character of nationalism.

Hobsbawm, E. *Nations and Nationalism Since 1780* (2nd ed.) (Cambridge: Cambridge University Press, 1993). An analysis of the phenomenon of nationalism from a modern Marxist perspective.

Hutchinson, J. and A. D. Smith (eds) *Nationalism* (Oxford and New York: Oxford University Press, 1994). A comprehensive and authoritative reader that discusses recent debates on nationalism.

Subnational Politics

CHAPTER 7

'All politics is local.'

Favourite saying of former Speaker of the US House of Representatives
THOMAS (TIP) O'NEILL JR

Although nation states are treated as discrete and unified entities as far as international politics is concerned, each nation state incorporates a range of internal divisions and levels of power. Most significantly, there are territory-based divisions between central or national government and various forms of provincial, state and local government. These divisions are crucially shaped by a state's constitutional structure, that is, by whether it has a federal or unitary system of government. Each system establishes a particular territorial distribution of government power, thus providing a framework within which centre–periphery relationships can be conducted. All modern states have also been subject to contrasting pressures, if to different degrees. On the one hand, economic, international and other factors have led to a seemingly remorseless trend towards centralisation. On the other hand, especially in the late twentieth century, centrifugal tendencies have increased with the rise of ethnic, regional and community politics.

The central questions examined in this chapter are the following:

Contents

Key issues

▶ What are the respective benefits of centralisation and decentralisation?

▶ How do federal and unitary systems differ, and how successfully does each type of system reconcile territorial and other differences?

▶ Why has there been a tendency towards greater centralisation?

▶ What factors explain the rise of ethnic politics? How serious a threat does it pose to the nation state?

▶ To what extent is there scope in modern societies for community to replace the nation as the central focus of politics?

■ Centralisation or decentralisation?

All modern states are divided on a territorial basis between central (national) and peripheral (regional, provincial or local) institutions. The nature of such divisions varies enormously, however. These differences include the constitutional framework within which centre–periphery relationships are conducted, the distribution of functions and responsibilities between the levels of government, the means by which their personnels are appointed and recruited, the political, economic, administrative and other powers that the centre can use to control the periphery, and the independence that peripheral bodies enjoy. What is clear, however, is that neither central nor peripheral bodies can be dispensed with altogether.

In the absence of central government, a state would simply not be able to function as an actor on the international or world stage. It would possess no machinery for entering into strategic alliances, negotiating trade agreements, gaining representation at international summit meetings, or becoming a member of supranational bodies. This is why central government is invariably responsible for a state's external relations, as demonstrated by its control of foreign, diplomatic and defence policy. Moreover, some form of central government is necessary to mediate between peripheral bodies to ensure cooperation in areas of mutual interest. In most cases, this means that central government assumes overall control of the state's economic life, and supervises matters such as internal trade, transport and communications. There are, however, powerful reasons for further strengthening central government at the expense of peripheral institutions.

The case for **centralisation** includes the following:

• **National unity:** Central government alone articulates the interests of the whole rather than the various parts, that is, the interests of the nation rather than those of sectional, ethnic or regional groups. A strong centre ensures that the government addresses the common interests of the entire community; a weak centre leads to rivalry and disharmony.

• **Uniformity:** Central government alone can establish uniform laws and public services which help people to move more easily from one part of the country to another. Geographical mobility is likely to be restricted when there are differing tax regimes and differing legal, educational and social-security systems throughout a country.

• **Equality:** Decentralisation has the disadvantage that it forces peripheral institutions to rely on the resources available in their locality or region. Only central government can rectify inequalities that arise from the fact that the areas with the greatest social needs are invariably those with the least potential for raising revenue.

• **Prosperity:** Economic development and centralisation invariably go hand in hand. Only central government, for instance, can manage a single currency, control tax and spending policies with a view to ensuring sustainable growth, and, if necessary, provide an infrastructure in the form of roads, railways, airports and so on.

Centralisation: The concentration of political power or government authority at the national level.

On the other hand, there are limits to the amount of centralisation that is possible or desirable. Indeed, the notion of a modern state comprising tens or even hundreds of millions of citizens being entirely governed from the centre is simply absurd. For example, if all the services and functions of modern government were to be administered from the centre, the result would be hopeless inefficiency and bureaucratic chaos, reflecting what economists call the 'diseconomies of scale'. In general, the responsibilities vested in peripheral institutions are those that are 'domestic' in the sense that they primarily address the needs of the domestic population, for example, education, health, social welfare, and planning. The pressure to shift other responsibilities and decision-making power from central to peripheral bodies is, however, considerable.

The case for **decentralisation** includes the following:

- **Participation:** Local or regional government is certainly more effective than central government in providing opportunities for citizens to participate in the political life of their community. The benefits of widening the scope of political participation include the fact that it helps to create a better educated and more informed citizenry.

- **Responsiveness:** Peripheral institutions are usually 'closer' to the people and more sensitive to their needs. This both strengthens democratic accountability and ensures that government responds not merely to the overall interests of society, but also to the specific needs of particular communities.

- **Legitimacy:** Physical distance from government affects the acceptability or rightness of its decisions. Decisions made at a 'local' level are more likely to be seen as intelligible and therefore legitimate (see p. 193). In contrast, central government may appear remote, both geographically and politically.

- **Liberty:** As power tends to corrupt, centralisation threatens to turn government into a tyranny against the individual. Decentralisation protects liberty by dispersing government power, thereby creating a network of checks and balances. Peripheral bodies check central government as well as each other.

▌Centre–periphery relationships

The balance between centralisation and decentralisation within a state is shaped by a wide range of historical, cultural, geographical, economic and political factors. The most prominent of these is the constitutional structure of the state, particularly the location of sovereignty (see p. 143) in the political system. Although modified by other factors, the constitutional structure provides, as a minimum, the framework within which centre–periphery relationships are conducted. The two most common forms of territorial organisation found in the modern world are federal and the unitary systems. A third form, confederation, has generally proved to be unsustainable. As **confederations** establish only the loosest and most decentralised type of political union by vesting sovereign power in peripheral bodies, it is not surprising that their principal advocates have been anarchists such as Pierre-Joseph Proudhon (see p. 124). The confederal principle is, in fact, most commonly applied in the form of intergovernmentalism (see p. 154) as embodied in international organisations such as the North Atlantic Treaty Organisation (NATO), the United Nations (UN), the Organisation of African Unity (OAU) and the Commonwealth of Nations. Examples of confederations at the nation-state level are, however, far rarer. The USA was originally a confederation, first in the form of the Continental Congresses

Decentralisation: The expansion of local autonomy through the transfer of powers and responsibilities away from national bodies.

Confederation: A qualified union of states in which each state retains its independence, typically guaranteed by unanimous decision-making.

Pierre-Joseph Proudhon (1809–65)

French anarchist. A largely self-educated printer, Proudhon was drawn into radical politics in Lyons before settling in Paris in 1847. As a member of the 1848 Constituent Assembly, Proudhon famously voted against the constitution 'because it was a constitution'. He was later imprisoned for three years, after which, disillusioned with active politics, he concentrated on writing and theorising. His best known work, *What is Property?* ([1840] 1970), developed the first systematic argument for anarchism, based on the 'mutualist' principle; it also contained the famous dictum 'property is theft'. In *The Federal Principle* (1863), Proudhon modified his anarchism by acknowledging the need for a minimal state to 'set things in motion' (although by 'federal' he meant a political compact between self-governing communities, in effect, confederalism).

(1774–81), and then under the Articles of Confederation (1781–89). The most important modern example of a confederal state is the Commonwealth of Independent States (CIS), which in 1991 formally replaced the USSR. The CIS was established by 11 of the 15 former Soviet republics (only Georgia and the three Baltic states refused to join). However, it lacks executive authority, and therefore constitutes little more than an occasional forum for debate and arbitration. Indeed, the evidence is that, in the absence of an effective central body, confederations either, as in the USA, transform themselves into federal states, or succumb to centrifugal pressures and disintegrate altogether, as has more or less occurred in the case of the CIS.

Federal systems

Federal systems of government have been more common than confederal systems. Over a third of the world's population is governed by states that have some kind of federal structure. These states include the USA, Brazil, Pakistan, Australia, Mexico, Switzerland, Nigeria, Malaysia and Canada. Although no two federal structures are identical, the central feature of each is a sharing of sovereignty between central and peripheral institutions. This ensures, at least in theory, that neither level of government can encroach on the powers of the other. In this sense, a federation is an intermediate form of political organisation that lies somewhere between a confederation (which vests sovereign power in peripheral bodies) and a unitary state (in which power is located in central institutions). Federal systems are based upon a compromise between unity and regional diversity, between the need for an effective central power and the need for checks or constraints on that power.

Why federalism?

When a list of federal states (or states exhibiting federal-type features) is examined, certain common characteristics can be observed. This suggests that the federal principle is more applicable to some states than to others. In the first place, historical similarities can be identified. For example, federations have often been formed by the coming together of a number of established political communities which nevertheless wish to preserve their separate identities and, to some extent, their autonomy. This clearly applied in the case of the world's first federal state, the USA. Although the 13 former British colonies in America quickly recognised the inadequacy of confederal organisation, each possessed a distinctive political identity and set of traditions that it was determined to preserve within the new, more centralised, constitutional framework. Indeed, charter colonies such as Rhode Island and Connecticut had become accustomed to such a degree of independence from the British Crown that their colonial charters served, in the early years at least, as state constitutions.

The reluctance of the former colonies to establish a strong national government was demonstrated at the Philadelphia Constitutional Convention of 1787, which drafted the US constitution, and by the ensuing debate over ratification. The 'nationalist' position, which supported ratification, was advanced in the so-called *Federalist Papers*, published between 1787 and 1789. These were written by Alexander Hamilton (see p. 126), James Madison (see p. 302) and John Jay (1745–1829), who published collectively under the name Publius. They emphasised the importance of establishing a strong centralised government while at the same time preserving state and individual freedoms. Ratification was finally achieved in 1789, but only through the adoption of the Bill of Rights and, in particular, the Tenth Amendment, which guaranteed that powers not delegated to the federal government would be 'reserved to the states respectively, or to the people'. This provided a constitutional basis for US federalism. A similar process occurred in Germany. Although unification in 1871 reflected the growing might of Prussia, a federal structure helped to allay the fears of central control of the other 38 Germanic states that had long enjoyed political independence. This tradition of regional autonomy, briefly interrupted during the Nazi period, was formalised in the constitution of the Federal Republic of Germany, adopted in 1949, which granted each of the 11 *Länder* (provinces or states) its own constitution. Their number was increased to 16 as a result of the reunification of Germany in 1990.

A second factor influencing the formation of federations is the existence of an external threat or a desire to play a more effective role in international affairs. Small, strategically vulnerable states, for instance, have a powerful incentive to enter broader political unions. One of the weaknesses of the US Articles of Confederation was thus that they failed to give the newly independent US states a clear diplomatic voice, making it difficult for them to negotiate treaties, enter into alliances, and so on. The willingness of the German states in the nineteenth century to enter into a federal union and accept effective 'Prussification' owed a great deal to the intensifying rivalry of the great powers, and in particular the threat posed by both Austria and France. Similarly, the drift towards the construction of a federal Europe, which began with the establishment of the European Coal and Steel Community (ECSC) in 1952 and the European Economic Community (EEC) in 1957, was in part brought about by a fear of Soviet aggression and by a perceived loss of European influence in the emerging bipolar world order.

A third factor is geographical size. It is no coincidence that many of the territorially largest states in the world have opted to introduce federal systems. This was true of the USA, and it also applied to Canada (federated in 1867), Brazil (1891), Australia (1901), Mexico (1917) and India (1947). Geographically large states tend to be culturally diverse and often possess strong regional traditions. This creates greater pressure for decentralisation and the dispersal of power than can usually be accommodated within a unitary system. The final factor encouraging the adoption of federalism is cultural and ethnic heterogeneity. Federalism, in short, has often been an institutional response to societal divisions and diversities. Canada's ten provinces, for instance, reflect not only long-established regional traditions but also language and cultural differences between English-speaking and French-speaking

Concept

Federalism

Federalism (from the Latin *foedus*, meaning 'pact', or 'covenant') usually refers to legal and political structures that distribute power territorially within a state. Nevertheless, in accordance with its original meaning, it has been taken to imply reciprocity or mutuality (Proudhon), or, in the writings of Alexander Hamilton (see p. 126) and James Madison (see p. 302), to be part of a broader ideology of pluralism. As a political form, however, federalism requires the existence of two distinct levels of government, neither of which is legally or politically subordinate to the other. Its central feature is therefore the notion of shared sovereignty. On the basis of this definition, 'classical' federations are few in number: the USA, Switzerland, Belgium, Canada and Australia. However, many more states have federal-type features.

Alexander Hamilton (1755–1805)

US statesman, and co-author with James Madison and John Jay of the *Federalist Papers* (Hamilton, Jay and Madison, [1787–89] 1961). Hamilton was born in the West Indies. He fought in the American Revolution, becoming George Washington's aide-de-camp (1777–81). After studying law, Hamilton was returned to Congress in 1782, served as the USA's first Secretary of the Treasury (1789–95), and founded and led the Federalist Party until his death in a duel with his rival Aaron Burr. Hamilton's federalism was characterised by a deep distrust of democracy, support for an active central government, and the desire to boost manufacturing industry through national fiscal and economic policies. 'Hamiltonianism' thus came to represent the idea of a powerful national government with a strong executive authority able to support the emerging national economy.

parts of the country. India's 25 self-governing states were defined primarily by language, but in the case of states such as Punjab and Kashmir, also take religious differences into account. Nigeria's 19-state federal constitution similarly recognises major tribal and religious differences, particularly between the north and south-east of the country.

Features of federalism

Each federal system is unique in the sense that the relationship between federal (national) government and state (regional) government is determined not just by constitutional rules, but also by a complex of political, historical, geographical, cultural and social circumstances. In some respects, for example, the party system is as significant a determinant of federal-state relationships as are the constitutionally allocated powers of each level of government. Thus the federal structure of the USSR, which unlike the USA granted each of its 15 republics the right of secession, was entirely bogus given the highly centralised nature of the 'ruling' Communist Party, to say nothing of the rigidly hierarchical central-planning system. A similar situation can be found in Mexico, where the dominant Institutional Revolutionary Party (PRI) has effectively counteracted a federal system that was consciously modelled on the US example. In the USA, Canada, Australia and India, on the other hand, decentralised party systems have safeguarded the powers of state and regional governments.

There is a further contrast between federal regimes that operate a 'separation of powers' (see p. 297) between the **executive** and **legislative** branches of government (typified by the US presidential system), and parliamentary systems in which executive and legislative power is 'fused'. The former tend to ensure that government power is diffused both territorially and functionally, meaning that there are multiple points of contact between the two levels of government. This leads to the complex patterns of interpenetration between federal and state levels of government that are found in the US and Swiss systems. Parliamentary systems, however, often produce what is called 'executive federalism', most notably in Canada and Australia. In such cases the federal balance is largely determined by the relationship between the executives of each level of government.

Nevertheless, certain features are common to most, if not all, federal systems:

Executive: The branch of government that is responsible for implementing or carrying out law and policy (see p. 382).

Legislature: The branch of government that is empowered to make law through the formal enactment of legislation.

- **Two relatively autonomous levels of government:** Both central government (the federal level) and regional government (the state level) possess a range of powers which the other cannot encroach upon. These include at least a measure of legislative and executive authority and the capacity to raise revenue and thus enjoy a degree of fiscal independence. However, the specific fields of jurisdiction of each level of government and the capacity of each to influence the other varies considerably. In Germany and Austria, for instance, a system of 'administrative' federalism operates in which central government is the key policy-maker, and provincial government is charged with the responsibility for the details of policy implementation.

• **Written constitution:** The responsibilities and powers of each level of government are defined in a codified or **written constitution**. The relationship between the centre and the periphery is therefore conducted within a formal legal framework. The autonomy of each level is usually guaranteed by the fact that neither is able to amend the constitution unilaterally; for example, amendments of the US constitution require the support of two-thirds of both houses of Congress and three-quarters of the 50 state legislatures. In Australia and Switzerland, for example, amendments to the constitution must also be ratified through the use of referendums (see p. 209).

• **Constitutional arbiter:** The formal provisions of the constitution are interpreted by a supreme court, which thereby arbitrates in the case of disputes between federal and state levels of government. In determining the respective fields of jurisdiction of each level, the judiciary in a federal system is able to determine how federalism works in practice, inevitably drawing the judiciary into the policy process. The centralisation which has occurred in all federal systems in the twentieth century has invariably been sanctioned by the courts.

• **Linking institutions:** In order to foster cooperation and understanding between federal and state levels of government, the regions and provinces must be given a voice in the processes of central policy making. This is usually achieved through a bicameral legislature, in which the second chamber or upper house represents the interests of the states. The 76 members of the Australian Senate, for example, comprise 12 from each of the six states, two from the Australian Territory, and two from the Northern Territory. An exception here is the weak federal arrangements in Malaysia, which allow the majority of members of the Senate (Dewan Negara) to be appointed by the monarch.

Assessment of federalism

One of the chief strengths of federal systems is that, unlike unitary systems, they give regional and local interests a constitutionally guaranteed political voice. The states or provinces exercise a range of autonomous powers and enjoy some measure of representation in central government, usually, as pointed out above, through the second chamber of the federal legislature. On the other hand, federalism has not been able to stem the general twentieth-century tendency towards centralisation. Despite guarantees of state and provincial rights in federal systems, the powers of central government have expanded, largely as a result of the growth of economic and social intervention, and central government's own greater revenue-raising capacities.

The US system, for instance, initially operated according to the principles of 'dual federalism', in which federal and state governments occupied separate and seemingly indestructible spheres of policy power. From the late nineteenth century

Written constitution: A single authoritative document that allocates duties, powers and functions amongst the institutions of government, and so constitutes 'higher' law).

onwards, this gave way to a system of 'cooperative federalism' that was based on the growth of 'grants in aid' from the federal government to the states and localities. State and local government therefore became increasingly dependent on the flow of federal funds, especially after the upsurge in economic and social programmes that occurred under the New Deal in the 1930s. Since the mid1960s, however, co-operative federalism, based on a partnership of sorts between federal government and the states, has been replaced by what has been called 'coercive federalism'. This is a system through which federal government has increasingly brought about the compliance of the states by passing laws that preempt their powers and imposing restrictions on the states and localities in the form of mandates.

A second advantage of federalism is that, in diffusing government power, it creates a network of checks and balances that help to protect individual liberty. In James Madison's words, 'ambition must be made to counteract ambition'. Despite a worldwide tendency towards centralisation, federal systems such as those in the USA, Australia and Canada have usually been more effective in constraining national politicians than have been unitary systems. However, structures intended to create healthy tension within a system of government may also generate frustration and paralysis. One of the weaknesses of federal systems is that, by constraining central authority, they make the implementation of bold economic or social programmes more difficult. F. D. Roosevelt's New Deal in the USA, for example, was significantly weakened by Supreme Court decisions that were intended to prevent federal government from encroaching on the responsibilities of the states. In the 1980s, Ronald Reagan deliberately used federalism as a weapon against 'big' government, and specifically against the growing welfare budget. Under the slogan 'new federalism', Reagan attempted to staunch social spending by transferring responsibility for welfare from federal government to the less prosperous state governments. In contrast, the dominant pattern of cooperative federalism in Germany has facilitated, rather than thwarted, the construction of a comprehensive and well-funded welfare system.

Finally, federalism has provided an institutional mechanism through which fractured societies have maintained unity and coherence. In this respect, the federal solution may be appropriate only to a limited number of ethnically diverse and regionally divided societies, but in these cases it may be absolutely vital. The genius of US federalism, for instance, was perhaps less that it provided the basis for unity amongst the 13 original states, and more that it invested the USA with an institutional mechanism which enabled it to absorb the strains that immigration exerted from the mid-nineteenth century onwards. The danger of federalism, however, is that by breeding governmental division it may strengthen centrifugal pressures and ultimately lead to disintegration. Some have argued, as a result, that federal systems are inherently unstable, tending either towards the guaranteed unity which only a unitary system can offer, or towards greater decentralisation and ultimate collapse.

Federalism in Canada, for example, can be deemed a failure if its purpose was to construct a political union within which both French-speaking and English-speaking populations can live in harmony. In response to the growth of **separatism** in predominantly francophone Quebec, Canada has engaged since the late 1980s in a fruitless search for a constitutional formula that would reconcile Quebec to membership of the Canadian federation. The Meech Lake Accord of 1987, which attempted to meet demands for greater autonomy by granting Quebec 'special status' within the federation, failed three years later when Manitoba and Newfoundland rejected the

Separatism: The quest to secede from a political formation with a view to establishing an independent state.

principle of 'asymmetrical federalism'. The Charlottetown Agreement of 1992 offered another formula, but this was rejected in a national referendum, partly because Quebec believed that it did not go far enough in granting autonomy, and partly because many anglophone Canadians feared that it threatened the integrity of the Canadian state. Nevertheless, the option of an entirely independent Quebec, strongly backed by the separatist Parti Québecois, was also narrowly rejected by the people of Quebec in a referendum at the end of 1995.

Unitary systems

The vast majority of contemporary states have unitary systems of government. These vest sovereign power in a single, national institution. In the UK, this institution is Parliament, which possesses, at least in theory, unrivalled and unchallengeable legislative authority. Parliament can make or unmake any law it wishes; its powers are not checked by a codified or written constitution; there are no rival UK legislatures which can challenge its authority; and its laws outrank all other forms of English and Scottish law. Since constitutional supremacy is vested with the centre in a unitary system, any system of peripheral or local government exists at the pleasure of the centre. At first sight, this creates the spectre of unchecked centralisation. Local institutions can be reshaped, reorganised and even abolished at will; their powers and responsibilities can be contracted as easily as they can be expanded. However, in practice, the relationship between the centre and the periphery in unitary systems is as complex as it is in federal systems, political, cultural and historical factors being as significant as more formal constitutional ones. Two distinct institutional forms of peripheral authority nevertheless exist in unitary states: local government and devolved assemblies. Each of these give centre–periphery relationships a distinctive shape.

Local government

Local government, in its simplest sense, is government that is specific to a particular locality, for example, a village, district, town, city or county. More particularly, it is a form of government that has no share in sovereignty, and is thus entirely subordinate to central authority or, in a federal system, to state or regional authority. This level of government is in fact universal, being found in federal and confederal systems as well as in unitary ones. In the USA, for instance, there are over 86 000 units of local government that employ 11 000 000 people, compared with a total of fewer than 8 000 000 staff at federal and state levels. However, what makes local government particularly important in unitary systems is that in most cases it is the only form of government outside the centre.

It would nevertheless be a mistake to assume that the constitutional subordination of local government means that it is politically irrelevant. The very ubiquity of local government reflects the fact that it is both administratively necessary and, because it is 'close' to the people, easily intelligible. Moreover, elected local politicians have a measure of democratic legitimacy (see p. 193) that enables them to extend their formal powers and responsibilities. This often means that central–local relationships are conducted through a process of bargaining and negotiation rather than by diktat from above. The balance between the centre and the periphery is further influenced by factors such as the political culture (particularly by established traditions of local autonomy and regional diversity) and the nature of the party system. For instance, the growing tendency for local politics to be 'politicised', in the sense that national parties have increasingly dominated local politics, has usually brought with it greater centralisation. In the absence of the kind of constitutional framework that federalism provides, the preservation of local autonomy relies, to a crucial extent, on self-restraint by the centre. This tends to mean that the degree of decentralisation in unitary systems varies significantly, both over time and from country to country. This can be illustrated by the contrasting experiences of the UK and France.

The UK traditionally possessed a relatively decentralised local government system, with local authorities exercising significant discretion within a legal framework laid down by Parliament. Indeed, respect for **local democracy** was long seen as a feature of the UK's unwritten constitution. Following J. S. Mill (see p. 44), constitutional authorities usually praised local government as both a check on central power and a means through which popular participation, and thus political education, could be broadened. The expansion of the state's economic and social role in the post-1945 period, however, meant that local authorities were increasingly charged with responsibility for delivering public services on behalf of central government. This partnership approach to local–central relationships was abruptly abandoned by the Conservative governments of the 1980s and 1990s, which saw local government, in common with other intermediary agencies, as an obstacle to the implementation of their radical market-orientated policies.

The introduction in 1984 of 'rate capping' robbed local government of its most important power: the ability to control local tax levels and so determine its own spending policies. Local authorities that challenged the centre, such as the Greater London Council and the metropolitan county councils, were abolished, their functions being devolved to smaller district and borough councils and a variety of newly crated **quangos**. The responsibilities of local government were also restricted through, for example, the introduction of a national curriculum for schools and legislation that permitted schools to opt out from local authority control. The ultimate aim of these policies was fundamentally to remodel local government by creating 'enabling' councils, whose role is not to provide services themselves, but to supervise the provision of services by private bodies through a system of contracting-out and privatisation. Such policies have widely been interpreted as an attack on local democracy. On the one hand, power has been transferred from local to central government, and on the other, local authorities have been subjected to intensified market pressures from members of the local community in their new roles as 'customers' and 'clients'.

Very different policies were adopted in France during the same period. In a conscious attempt to transform the character of French society, and in particular the tradition of centralisation that the Fifth Republic inherited from the Jacobins and Napoleon, President Mitterrand embarked on a programme of political decentralisation that was implemented by the Minister for the Interior and Decentralisation, Gaston Defferre, between 1982 and 1986. Traditionally, central–local relationships in France were dominated by a system of strict administrative control that operated largely through prefects (appointed by, and directly accountable to, the Ministry of the Interior), who were the chief executives of France's 96 *départements*. The established French system therefore worked very much as a hierarchical chain of command. As well as revitalising regional government, the Defferre reforms extended both the responsibilities and the powers of local government. In particular, the executive powers of the prefects were transferred to locally elected presidents,

Local democracy: A principle that embodies both the idea of local autonomy and the goal of popular responsiveness.

Quango: An acronym for quasi-autonomous non-governmental organisation: a public body staffed by appointees rather than politicians or civil servants (see p. 350).

and the prefects were replaced by Commissaires de la République, who are concerned essentially with economic planning. In addition, local authorities were absolved of the need to seek prior approval for administrative and spending decisions, these now being subject only to *a posteriori* legal and financial control. The net result of these reforms has been to give France a more decentralised state structure than it has had at any time since the 1789 revolution.

Devolution

Devolution, at least in its legislative form, establishes the greatest possible measure of decentralisation in a unitary system of government, short, that is, of its transformation into a federal system. Devolved assemblies have usually been created in response to increasing centrifugal tensions within a state, and as an attempt, in particular, to conciliate growing regional and sometimes nationalist pressures. Despite their lack of entrenched powers, once devolved assemblies have acquired a political identity of their own, and possess a measure of democratic legitimacy, they are very difficult to weaken and, in normal circumstances, impossible to abolish. Northern Ireland's Stormont Parliament was an exception. The Stormont Parliament was suspended in 1972 and replaced by direct rule from the Westminster Parliament, but only when it became apparent that its domination by predominantly Protestant Unionist parties prevented it from stemming the rising tide of communal violence in Northern Ireland that threatened to develop into civil war.

One of the oldest traditions of devolved government in Europe is found in Spain. Although it has been a unitary state since the 1570s, Spain is divided into 50 provinces, each of which exercises a measure of regional self-government. As part of the transition to democratic government following the death of General Franco in 1975, the devolution process was extended in 1979 with the creation of 17 autonomous communities. This new tier of regional government is based on elected assemblies invested with broad control of domestic policy. Although this reform was designed to meet long-standing demands for Catalan autonomy in the Basque area, it merely provoked a fresh wave of terrorism perpetrated by the separatist movement ETA (Euskadi Ta Askatasuna). The French government has also used devolution as a means of responding to the persistence of regional identities, and, at least in Brittany and Occitania, to the emergence of forms of **ethnic nationalism**. A key element in the Defferre reforms in France was the transition from administrative devolution to legislative devolution. As part of a strategy of 'functional regionalism', 22 regional public bodies were created in 1972 to enhance the administrative coordination of local investment and planning decisions. These, however, lacked a democratic basis and enjoyed only limited powers. In 1982, they were transformed into fully-fledged regional governments, each with a directly elected council. In an attempt to stem separatism and a growing tide of terrorism, Corsica was granted the special status of a Collective Territory, which effectively made the island self-governing.

In contrast, strains within the multinational UK state have led to a devolution debate, but so far no regional tier of government. Devolution appeared on the political agenda in the UK in the late 1960s with the revival of Scottish and Welsh nationalism. By 1974, this had led to a parliamentary breakthrough for the Scottish National Party (SNP) and Plaid Cymru. In an attempt to maintain the support of nationalist parties, the minority Labour government brought forward devolution proposals in 1978 and again in 1979. In 1978, these were defeated by opposition within the Labour Party, and in 1979 by the failure of referendums in Scotland and

---

Concept

Devolution

Devolution is the transfer of power from central government to subordinate regional institutions (to 'devolve' means to pass powers or duties down from a higher authority to a lower one). Devolved bodies thus constitute an intermediate level of government between central and local governments. However, devolution differs from federalism in that, although their territorial jurisdiction may be similar, devolved bodies have no share in sovereignty; their responsibilities and powers are derived from, and are conferred by, the centre. In its weakest form, that of *administrative* devolution, devolution implies only that regional institutions implement policies decided elsewhere. In the form of *legislative* devolution (sometimes called 'home rule'), devolution involves the establishment of elected regional assemblies invested with policy-making responsibilities and a measure of fiscal independence.

Ethnic nationalism: A form of nationalism that is fuelled primarily by a keen sense of ethnic distinctiveness and the desire to preserve it.

Ethnicity

Ethnicity is the sentiment of
loyalty towards a distinctive
population, cultural group or
territorial area. The term is
complex because it has
both racial and cultural
overtones. The members of
ethnic groups are often
seen, correctly or
incorrectly, to have
descended from common
ancestors, and the groups
are thus thought of as
extended kinship groups,
united by blood. More
commonly, ethnicity is
understood as a form of
cultural identity, albeit one
that operates at a deep and
emotional level. An 'ethnic'
culture encompasses
values, traditions and
practices, but crucially, it
also gives a people a
common identity and sense
of distinctiveness, usually
by focusing on their origins
and descent. Some see
nations (see p. 104) simply
as extended ethnic groups;
others stress that, while
ethnic groups are
essentially cultural and
exclusive (you cannot 'join'
an ethnic group), nations
are more inclusive, and are,
ultimately, politically
defined.

Wales to back the proposals by the required margin. In Scotland, a narrow majority
supported devolution, but this fell short of the stipulated 40 per cent of the total electorate; in Wales, devolution was rejected by a three-to-one majority. Nevertheless,
the growing gulf in the 1980s and 1990s between the Conservative-dominated Westminster Parliament and an increasingly Labour-dominated Scotland and Wales
revived support for devolution, and the Labour Party was converted wholeheartedly
to its cause. Opposition to devolution is largely based on the fear that 'home rule' for
Scotland and Wales would merely strengthen nationalist sentiment and ultimately
lead to the breakup of the UK. Its supporters, however, believe that devolution is the
only solution to the territorial crisis of the UK state, in that it promises to restore
legitimate government and to stem the tide of rising nationalism.

Ethnic and community politics

The rise of ethnic politics

The cause of political decentralisation and, in extreme cases, the phenomenon of
state collapse have increasingly been fuelled by the emergence of a new style of politics: the politics of ethnic loyalty and regional identity. In some respects, the rise of
ethnic politics in the late twentieth century parallels the emergence of nationalist
politics in the nineteenth century, and may have similarly wide-ranging consequences. Whereas nationalism brought about a period of nation building and the
destruction of multinational empires, ethnic politics may call the long-term survival
of the nation itself into question. What accounts for the rise of this new style of politics, and what is its political character?

The growing importance of ethnic consciousness in the West is strictly a post-
Second-World-War phenomenon; indeed, it can be traced back to the 1960s. The
renewed importance of ethnicity in politics, however, came as a surprise to most
commentators. This was because it had widely been assumed that modernity would
bring about the dilution of ethnic distinctiveness, as the spread of liberal-democratic
values would mean the abandonment of atavistic rivalries and communal solidarities.
However, in the late 1960s and early 1970s, secessionist groups and forms of ethnic
nationalism sprang up in many parts of western Europe and North America. This
was most evident in Quebec in Canada, Scotland and Wales in Britain, Catalonia
and the Basque area in Spain, Corsica in France, and Flanders in Belgium. It created
pressure for political decentralisation, and sometimes precipitated major constitutional upheavals. In Italy, the process did not get under way until the 1990s, with the
rise of the Northern League in Lombardy. There have been similar manifestations of
ethnic assertiveness amongst the Native Americans in Canada and the USA, the
aboriginal peoples in Australia, and the Maoris in New Zealand. In the latter two
cases at least, this has brought about a major reassessment of national identity.

In many ways, the forerunner of, and possibly prototype for, this new style of
politics was found in the emergence of black nationalism. The origins of the black-
consciousness movement date back to the early twentieth century and the emergence of a 'back to Africa' movement inspired by activists such as Marcus Garvey.
Black politics, however, gained greater prominence in the 1960s with an upsurge in
both the reformist and revolutionary wings of the movement. In its reformist guise,
the movement took the form of a struggle for civil rights that reached national

Marcus Garvey (1887–1940)

Jamaican political thinker and activist, and an early advocate of black nationalism. Garvey was the founder in 1914 of the Universal Negro Improvement Association (UNIA). He left Jamaica for New York in 1916, where his message of black pride and economic self-sufficiency gained him a growing following, particularly in ghettos such as Harlem. Although his black business enterprises failed, and his call for a return to Africa was largely ignored, Garvey's emphasis on establishing black pride and his vision of Africa as a 'homeland' provided the basis for the later Black Power movement. Rastafarianism is also largely based on his ideas. Garvey was imprisoned for mail fraud in 1923, and was later deported, eventually dying in obscurity in London.

prominence in the USA under the leadership of Martin Luther King (1929–68) and the National Association for the Advancement of Coloured People (NAACP). The strategy of protest and nonviolent civil disobedience was nevertheless rejected by the emerging Black Power movement, which supported black separatism and, under the leadership of the Black Panther Party, founded in 1966, promoted the use of physical force and armed confrontation. Of more enduring significance in US politics, however, have been the Black Muslims, who advocate a separatist creed based on the idea that black Americans are descended from an ancient Muslim tribe. Founded in 1929, the Black Muslims were led for over 40 years by Elijah Muhammad (1897–1975), and they counted amongst their most prominent activists in the 1960s the militant black leader Malcolm X (1925–65). Renamed the Nation of Islam, the movement continues to exert influence in the USA under the leadership of Louis Farrakhan.

Black nationalism clearly highlights one of the sources of ethnic politics: the desire to challenge economic and social marginalisation, and sometimes racial oppression. In this sense, ethnic politics has been a vehicle for political liberation, its enemy being structural disadvantage and ingrained inequality. For blacks in North America and western Europe, the establishment of an ethnic identity has provided a means of confronting a dominant white culture that has traditionally emphasised their inferiority and demanded subservience. Resurgent regional loyalties have often sprung from a system of 'internal colonialism' in which 'peripheral' geographical areas are exploited by a 'core' or 'centre'. Thus nationalist sentiment in Scotland and Wales is derived in part from the economic subordination of these regions to England, and particularly south-east England. This is reflected in their traditional dependence upon 'heavy' industry, their higher unemployment levels, and their lower wage and salary levels. Very much the same can be said about areas such as Brittany in France and Catalonia and the Basque area in Spain. The tendency in such cases is for ethnic nationalism to have a left-wing character, and it is usually articulated by parties and movements that have a broadly socialist philosophy.

On the other hand, when regional loyalties have intensified in 'core' areas confronted by the growing prominence of 'peripheral' ones, ethnic politics has often assumed a more right-wing character. This has occurred, for instance, in Flanders in Belgium, when economic development in predominantly French-speaking Wallonia has precipitated growing support for neofascist movements. In the 1990s, the openly racist Flemish bloc, which calls for the mass deportation of immigrants, made

Focus on . . .

The core–periphery model

The core-periphery model is an explanatory framework that aims to demonstrate how and why regional imbalances in economic development occur. It can be applied either to regional imbalances within a state (as a theory of internal colonialism), or to imbalances in the global economy (as a theory of world order). However, it often acknowledges overlaps between the two. 'Core' areas, for instance, are ones that are better integrated into the global economy. The core–periphery model emphasises a system of unequal exchange, in which the core region prospers and develops specifically through the exploitation of the periphery, pushing it into underdevelopment. The core is thus characterised by relatively high wages, advanced technology and a diversified production mix; and the periphery is characterised by low wages, more rudimentary technology and a simple production mix.

electoral advances in industrial areas and especially in Antwerp. Similarly, the free-market philosophy of the Northern League in Lombardy in Italy in part reflects the desire of the economically advanced Italian North (so-called Padania) to disengage itself from the more rural and less prosperous South.

Nevertheless, structural inequalities and internal colonialism cannot in themselves explain the emergence of ethnic and regional politics. Why, for instance, have ethnic and regional identities become so important in the late twentieth century when the injustices that they seek to redress date back generations, if not centuries? The answer to this may lie in the phenomenon of postmodernism (see p. 61). Just as Gellner (1983) argued that nationalism arose to provide a source of cultural cohesion in modern, industrialised societies, ethnic consciousness may be a necessary integrative force in emerging postmodern ones. The problem of postmodernism is that it promotes diversity and weakens traditional social identities. For example, increased social mobility and the spread of market individualism have undermined both class solidarity and established political loyalties. At the same time, the capacity of the nation to establish a strong and stable social identity has been weakened by globalisation (see p. 140) in its economic, cultural and political forms. In such circumstances, ethnicity may replace nationality as the principal source of social integration, its virtue being that, whereas nations are bound together by 'civil' loyalties and ties, ethnic and regional groups are able to generate a deeper sense of 'organic' identity.

The rise of ethnic consciousness has by no means only occurred in the West. Although ethnic rivalry (often portrayed as 'tribalism') is sometimes seen as an endemic feature of African and Asian politics, it is better understood as a phenomenon linked to colonialism. For example, the struggle against colonial rule helped to heighten ethnic consciousness, which tended to be mobilised as a weapon of anti-colonialism. However, the divide-and-rule policies of the colonial period often bequeathed to many newly independent 'nations' a legacy of bitterness and resentment. In many cases, this was subsequently exacerbated by the attempt of majority ethnic groups to consolidate their dominance under the guise of 'nation building'. Such tensions, for instance, resulted in the Biafran War in Nigeria in the 1960s, the long-running civil war in Southern Sudan, and a resort to terrorism by the pre-dominantly Christian Tamils in Sri Lanka. The worst recent example of ethnic bloodshed,however, occurred in Rwanda in 1994, where an estimated 1 000 000 Tutsis and moderate Hutus were slaughtered in an uprising by militant Hutus.

The collapse of communism in eastern Europe has also created the spectre of ethnic rivalry and regional conflict. In the former USSR, Czechoslovakia and Yugoslavia, for example, this has led to state collapse and the creation of a series of new nation states. The causes have been complex. In the first place, although communist regimes sought to resolve the 'nationalities problem' through the construction of 'socialist man', the evidence is that they merely fossilised ethnic and national loyalties by driving them underground. Secondly, ethnic and religious nationalism were undoubtedly vehicles for expressing anticommunism or anti-Sovietism. Thirdly, the political instability and economic uncertainty that the collapse of communism precipitated were a perfect breeding ground for a form of politics that offered an 'organic' sense of collective identity. Nevertheless, these newly created nations are themselves subject to deep ethnic rivalries and tensions. This has been demonstrated by the rebellion of the Chechens in Russia, and the fragmentation of the former Yugoslav republic of Bosnia into 'ethnically pure' Muslim, Serb and Croat areas.

A politics of community?

Whereas ethnic politics has emerged from below as a populist (see p. 335) movement, community politics has usually been a concern of political elites. In other words, it has often been the preserve of politicians and academics, who have interpreted social breakdown and fragmentation as being part of a broader 'decline of community'. This theme has become increasingly prominent in western politics since the 1960s, reaching the point in the 1990s at which so-called 'communitarianism' (see p. 136) threatened to become an all-embracing political philosophy, making the old Left/Right political divide redundant. At the heart of the communitarian message is the assertion, first, that a sense of community is vital to a healthy society, and second, that in the modern period the bonds of community have been progressively weakened.

A concern with community politics and a rediscovery of 'the local' has advanced in line with the progress of globalisation, which is discussed in Chapter 8. In this sense, globalisation and localisation may be linked responses to the decline of the nation state. Insofar as the cause of community has an ideological heritage, this lies in the traditional anarchist emphasis on self-management and cooperation. Classical anarchists such as Proudhon, Peter Kropotkin (1842–1921) and Gustav Landauer (1870–1934) extolled the virtues of small, decentralised communities, or **communes**, in which human beings can organise their lives spontaneously and resolve differences through face-to-face interaction. Similar goals also inspired the establishment of the kibbutz system in Israel. In the view of contemporary anarchists such as Murray Bookchin (1989), the need for such an emphasis on community is more pressing than it was in the nineteenth century, because of the bleak and depersonalised nature of modern city life. Bookchin's stress upon 'affinity groups' as the fundamental unit of the new society has increasingly influenced town planners, who have moved away from the idea of sprawling estates and large-scale developments, and started to favour the construction of 'urban villages'. A similar message was

Concept

Community

A community, in everyday language, is a collection of people in a given location, that is, a village, town, city, or even country. As a social or political principle, however, the term community suggests a social group that possesses a strong collective identity based on the bonds of comradeship, loyalty and duty. Ferdinand Tönnies (1855–1936) distinguished between *Gemeinschaft*, or 'community', typically found in traditional societies and characterised by natural affection and mutual respect, and *Gesellschaft*, or 'association', that is, the looser, artificial and contractual relationships typically found in urban and industrialised societies. Emile Durkheim (1858–1917) emphasised the degree to which community is based on the maintenance of social and moral codes. If these are weakened, this induces 'anomie', that is, feelings of isolation, loneliness and meaninglessness.

Commune: A small-scale collective organisation based on the sharing of wealth and power, possibly also extending to personal and domestic arrangements.

Concept

Communitarianism

Communitarianism is the belief that the self or person is constituted through the community, in the sense that individuals are shaped by the communities to which they belong and thus owe them a debt of respect and consideration; there are no 'unencumbered selves'. Although it is clearly at odds with liberal individualism, communitarianism has a variety of political forms. *Left-wing* communitarianism holds that community demands unrestricted freedom and social equality (the view of anarchism). *Centrist* communitarianism holds that community is grounded in an acknowledgement of reciprocal rights and responsibilities (the perspective of Tory paternalism and social democracy). *Right-wing* communitarianism holds that community requires respect for authority and established values (the view of the New Right).

preached by the German economist and environmental theorist Fritz Schumacher (see p. 177), whose pioneering *Small is Beautiful: A Study of Economics As If People Mattered* (1973) advocated a shift towards 'human scale' economic and social organisation, based on smaller working units, communal ownership, and regional workplaces utilising local labour and resources.

The idea of community has also been taken up by academics such as Michael Sandel (1982) and Alisdair MacIntyre (1981), who have used it to highlight the failings of liberal individualism. Communitarians have argued that, in conceiving of the individual as logically prior to and 'outside' the community, liberalism has merely legitimised selfish and egoistical behaviour and downgraded the importance of the idea of the public good. Through the writings of Amitai Etzioni (1995), such views influenced the Clinton administration in the USA as well as the UK Labour and Conservative parties. Etzioni argued that social fragmentation and breakdown has largely been a result of individuals' obsession with rights and their refusal to acknowledge reciprocal duties and moral responsibilities. This is demonstrated by the so-called 'parenting deficit', that is, the abandonment of the burdens of parenthood by fathers and mothers who are more concerned about their own lifestyles and careers. However, critics point out that, in extolling duties over rights, communitarianism may represent a shift towards authority and away from individual liberty. Moreover, the concern with community commonly has conservative implications, since it tends to be associated with attempts to strengthen existing social institutions such as the family. In this form, communitarianism seeks to legitimise the *status quo* and, in the case of the family, to consolidate women's traditional role as housewives, mothers and carers.

Summary

◆ Centralisation and decentralisation both have advantages. The virtues of centralisation include the following. It allows the state to be an international actor, it enables economic life to be more efficiently organised, it helps to promote national unity, and it allows for regional inequalities to be countered. The attraction of decentralisation is that it broadens the scope of political participation, brings government 'closer' to the people, makes political decisions more intelligible, and fosters checks and balances within government.

◆ The most common forms of territorial organisation are federal and unitary systems. Federalism is based on the notion of shared sovereignty, in which power is distributed between the central and peripheral levels of government. Unitary systems, however, vest sovereign power in a single, national institution, which allows the centre to determine the territorial organisation of the state.

◆ Other factors affecting territorial divisions include the party system and political culture, the economic system and level of material development, the geographical size of the state, and the level of cultural, ethnic and religious diversity. There has been a tendency towards centralisation in most, if not all, systems. This reflects, in particular, the fact that central government alone has the resources and strategic position to manage economic life and deliver comprehensive social welfare.

◆ Political decentralisation has been fuelled by the strengthening of ethnic consciousness and regional identities. The rise of ethnic politics is linked to the capacity of ethnicity to generate a sense of 'organic' identity that is stronger than the 'civic' loyalties and ties that have been typically associated with national consciousness. To some extent, the rise of ethnic nationalism reflects the impact of globalisation.

◆ Growing concern has been expressed about the loss of community and the need to rediscover the 'local'. Communitarianism has been associated with demands for radical decentralisation and self-management, with the notion of reciprocal rights and responsibilities, and with calls for respect for authority and the strengthening of traditional values and culture.

■ Questions for discussion

▶ Where should the balance between centralisation and decentralisation lie?

▶ Is the federal principle only applicable to certain states or to all states?

▶ What are the respective merits of federalism and devolution?

▶ Is the tendency towards centralisation in modern states resistible?

▶ Does the rise of ethnic politics spell the demise of civil nationalism?

▶ Are attempts to strengthen community always implicitly conservative?

■ Further reading

Bookchin, M. *Remaking Society* (Montreal: Black Rose, 1989). A stimulating discussion from a leading modern anarchist of the need for decentralisation and sustainable communities.

Burgess, M. and A.-G. Gagnon (eds) *Comparative Federalism and Federation* (London and New York: Harvester Wheatsheaf, 1993). A useful and wide-ranging survey of federal systems.

Glazer, N. and D. Moynihan *Ethnicity: Theory and Experience* (Cambridge, MA: Harvard University Press, 1975). An introduction to the growth and significance of ethnic politics.

Meny, Y. and V. Wright (eds) *Centre–Periphery Relations in Western Europe* (London: Croom Helm, 1995). A good introduction to the various systems of territorial organisation found in European states.

Global Politics

CHAPTER 8

'War, in our scientific age, means, sooner or later, universal death.'

BERTRAND RUSSELL *Unpopular Essays*, (1950)

Contents

The late twentieth century brought with it recognition that the world had become, in Marshall McLuan's words, a 'global village'. The phenomenon of globalisation has completely altered our understanding of politics and of the nature of political interaction. The traditional view of politics was state-centric: the state was treated as the principal political actor, and attention was focused on the national level of government activity. It therefore followed that there was a clear distinction between domestic politics and foreign politics, that is, between what took place within a nation-state and what took place outside its borders. The latter, indeed, became the subject matter of a new and separate discipline, international relations. However, globalisation has weakened, and perhaps destroyed, the distinction between 'the domestic' and 'the foreign', leading, some have argued, to the emergence of a world society. Although nation-states continue to be the most significant actors on the world stage, the growing impact of supranational bodies and of transnational groups and organisations is impossible to deny.

The key themes analysed in this chapter are the following:

Key issues

▶ What is globalisation? What are its implications for the nation-state?

▶ How has international or world politics been analysed and explained?

▶ Is the new world order characterised by peace and harmony or by chaos and disorder?

▶ How is wealth and power distributed in the global economy?

▶ Why has the significance of international organisations increased?

▶ Could the idea of a world society ever become a reality?

◼ Understanding global politics

The recognition that there is an international dimension to politics is as old as the discipline itself, going back to accounts of conflict and war between the city-states of Ancient Greece. However, the modern international system did not come into existence until the emergence of centralised states in the sixteenth and seventeenth centuries. This process was completed by the Treaty of Westphalia (1648), which brought the Thirty Years War to an end with a formal recognition by the European powers of the sovereign independence of each state. The European state system was subsequently extended when the USA was recognised, after its defeat of Spain in 1898, as a great power, and when Japan was also so recognised after its victory over Russia in 1904–05. Imperialism (see p. 145), and especially the European 'scramble for colonies' in Africa and Asia in the late nineteenth century, gave the international system a truly global dimension.

The twentieth century thus witnessed the emergence of world politics in the sense that patterns of conflict and cooperation amongst states and international organisations extended across the globe. This was most chillingly seen in the First World War (1914–18), the Second World War (1939–45), and the **Cold War**. As the twentieth century has drawn to a close, however, there has been a growing recognition that the very parameters of political life have changed. This has called into question the conventional distinction between a domestic realm and an international realm of politics. These complex and multifaceted changes have increasingly been referred to as 'globalisation'.

The emergence of global interdependence has been a consequence of a variety of processes and developments. In the first place, it was one of the results of the superpower rivalry that characterised the Cold War period. Both the world wars of the twentieth century were hegemonic conflicts fought between powers seeking worldwide military dominance. However, the capabilities and resources of the post-1945 **superpowers** (the USA and the USSR) were so overwhelming that they were able to extend their influence into virtually every region of the world. Secondly, the spread of international trade and the transnational character of modern business organisations has brought a global economy into existence. As the significance of national economies has declined, the world economy has increasingly been characterised by rivalry amongst regional trading blocs. Thirdly, globalisation has been fuelled by technological innovation. This has affected almost every realm of existence, ranging from the development of nuclear weapons and the emergence of global pollution problems such as acid rain and ozone depletion to the introduction of international telephone links, satellite television, and the 'information superhighway'. Fourthly, globalisation has an

---

Concept

Globalisation

Globalisation is the emergence of a complex web of interconnectedness that means that our lives are increasingly shaped by events that occur, and decisions that are made, at a great distance from us. The central feature of globalisation is therefore that geographical distance is of declining relevance, and that territorial boundaries, such as those between nation-states, are becoming less significant. By no means, however, does globalisation imply that 'the local' and 'the national' are subordinate to 'the global'. Rather, it highlights the *deepening* as well as the *broadening* of the political process, in the sense that local, national and global events (or perhaps local, regional, national, international and global events) constantly interact. The resulting systemic interdependencies are shown in Figure 8.1.

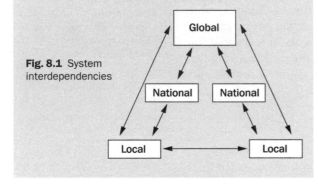

Fig. 8.1 System interdependencies

Cold War: The period of rivalry between the USA-dominated West and the USSR-dominated East that extended from 1945 to the collapse of communism in the revolutions of 1989–91 (see p. 146).

Superpower: A state with preponderant nuclear military capacity and global territorial influence; a superpower is higher than a 'great' power.

Immanuel Kant (1724–1804)

German philosopher. Kant spent his entire life in Königsberg (which was then in East Prussia), becoming professor of logic and metaphysics at the University of Königsberg in 1770. His 'critical' philosophy holds that knowledge is not merely an aggregate of sense impressions; it depends on the conceptual apparatus of human understanding. Kant's political thought was shaped by the central importance of morality. He believed that the law of reason dictated categorical imperatives, the most important of which was the obligation to treat others as 'ends', and never only as 'means'. Kant's (1970) most important works include *Critique of Pure Reason* (1781), *Critique of Practical Reason* (1788) and *Critique of Judgement* (1790).

important politico-ideological dimension. One aspect of this has been the spread of western-liberal political values, portrayed by Fukuyama (1992) as the worldwide triumph of liberal democracy. But globalisation can also be linked to the growth of Islam as a transnational political creed, and to the burgeoning interest in Green ideas and philosophies. In order to analyse these and other developments, however, it is necessary to examine the various perspectives from which international and world politics has traditionally been examined. The major theoretical 'schools' of international politics are the following:

- idealism
- realism
- pluralism
- Marxism.

Idealism

The defining characteristic of idealism is that it views international politics from the perspective of moral values and legal norms. It is concerned less with empirical analysis (that is, with how international actors behave) than with normative judgements (that is, with how they *should* behave). For this reason, idealism is sometimes seen as a species of utopianism (see p. 25). A broad range of idealist theories have been developed. In the Middle Ages, for instance, Thomas Aquinas (1224–74) discussed the nature of a 'just war', attempting to place the international actions of rulers in a moral context. He argued that war could only be justified if three conditions were met. First, it had to be declared by a ruler who had the authority to do so. Secondly, the cause that the war was fought in had to be just in the sense that it avenged a wrong. Thirdly, the intention of just belligerence had to be to achieve good or avoid evil, not to give vent to greed or cruelty. Immanuel Kant developed what amounted to an early vision of world government. In his view, morality and reason combined to dictate that there should be no war, the future of humankind being based on the prospect of 'universal and lasting peace'.

Most forms of idealism are underpinned by internationalism, that is, the belief that human affairs should be organised according to universal, and not merely national, principles. This, in turn, is usually reflected in the assumption that human affairs, on both the domestic and international levels, are characterised by harmony

Concept

Internationalism

Internationalism is the theory or practice of politics based on transnational or global cooperation. It is rooted in universalist assumptions about human nature that put it at odds with political nationalism, the latter emphasising the degree to which political identity is shaped by nationality. The major internationalist traditions are drawn from liberalism and socialism. *Liberal* internationalism is based on individualism. This is reflected, for example, in the belief that universal human rights ultimately have a 'higher' status than the sovereign authority of the nation. *Socialist* internationalism is grounded in a belief in international class solidarity (proletarian internationalism), underpinned by assumptions about a common humanity. Feminism and environmentalism have also advanced distinctive internationalist positions.

and cooperation. One of the most influential forms of idealism has been found in liberalism. Although liberals have traditionally accepted the nation as the principal unit of political organisation, they have also stressed the importance of interdependence and free trade, arguing quite simply that 'war does not pay'. Such internationalism is also reflected in a faith in collective security (see p. 159) and international law (see p. 160), which is embodied in organisations such as the League of Nations and the United Nations. President Woodrow Wilson of the USA, for example, argued that the First World War had resulted from the 'old politics' of militarism and expansionism pursued by multinational empires. In his view, the best antidote to war was the construction of a world of democratic nation-states that were prepared to cooperate in areas of common interest and had no incentive to embark upon conquest or plunder.

After years of ridicule and denigration at the hands of realist theorists, idealism has been revived in the late twentieth century. What has usually been called **neo-idealism** reflects disenchantment with the amoral power politics of the superpower era. An early example of this was the attempt by President Carter in the 1970s to restore a moral dimension to US foreign policy by emphasising that economic and military aid depended on the human-rights records of recipient regimes. The theme of international cooperation and common security was taken up more boldly in the late 1980s by the Soviet president Mikhail Gorbachev, who spoke of a 'common European house', and proclaimed that the doctrine of human rights transcended the ideological rivalry between communism and capitalism.

In many respects, the prospect of nuclear annihilation (the product of years of escalating military spending by both East and West) gave greater impetus to idealist theories. This was reflected in the emergence of the peace movement, which embraced a broadly internationalist philosophy that was often linked to pacifism, a principled rejection of war and all forms of violence as fundamentally evil. The neo-idealist position has also been advanced in relation to the notion of a 'world society', which is usually associated with the Australian diplomat and scholar John Burton (1972). The world-society perspective rejects as obsolete the notion of sovereign nation-states, emphasising instead a pattern of complexity and interdependence which Burton portrayed through the image of a cobweb. Such a view suggests that the power politics of old have largely given way to noncoercive and cooperative means of solving international conflicts.

Realism

The realist tradition, sometimes called 'political realism', can claim to be the oldest theory of international politics. It can be traced back to Thucydides' account of the Peloponnesian War (431 BCE), and to Sun Tzu's classic work on strategy, *The Art of War*, written at roughly the same time in China. Other significant figures in the realist tradition are Machiavelli (see p. 6) and Thomas Hobbes (see p. 285). However, realism only became the dominant international perspective during the twentieth century, receiving its impetus from the First World War and Second World War. Whereas idealism emphasises that international relations should be guided by morality, realism is grounded in an emphasis on **power politics** and the pursuit of national interests. Its central assumption is that the state is the principal actor on the international or world stage, and, being sovereign, is able to act as an autonomous entity. Moreover, the rise of nationalism and the emergence of modern nation-states

Neo-idealism: A perspective on international politics that emphasises the practical value of morality and, in particular, respect for human rights and national independence.

Power politics: An approach to politics based on the assumption that the pursuit of power is the principal human goal; the term is sometimes used descriptively.

(see p. 117) transformed the state into a cohesive political community, within which all other loyalties and ties are subordinate to those to the nation.

Realist scholars, such as E. H. Carr (1939) and Hans Morgenthau (1948), were particularly scathing about the idealist belief in internationalism and natural harmony. Carr, in fact, argued that a naive faith in international law and collective security in the interwar period prevented statesmen on both sides of the Atlantic from understanding, and so acting to contain, German expansion. Realists emphasise that, in contrast, as there is no higher authority than the sovereign state, international politics is conducted in a 'state of nature', and is thus characterised by anarchy, not harmony. An anarchic international system is one in which each state is forced to help itself and give priority to its own national interest, defined, most basically, as state survival and territorial defence.

> **Concept**
>
> **Sovereignty**
>
> Sovereignty, in its simplest sense, is the principle of absolute and unlimited power. However, distinctions are commonly made between legal and political sovereignty, and between internal and external notions of sovereignty. *Legal* sovereignty refers to supreme legal authority, that is, an unchallengeable right to demand compliance, as defined by law. *Political* sovereignty, in contrast, refers to unlimited political power, that is, the ability to command obedience, which is typically ensured by a monopoly of coercive force. *Internal* sovereignty is the notion of a supreme power/authority within the state, located in the body that makes decisions that are binding on all citizens, groups and institutions within the state's territorial boundaries. *External* sovereignty relates to a state's place in the international order and its capacity to act as an independent and autonomous entity.

This is why realists place such a heavy emphasis on the role of power in international affairs, and why they tend to understand power in terms of military capacity or force. By no means, however, does international anarchy mean relentless conflict and unending war. Instead, realists insist that the pattern of conflict and cooperation within the state system largely conforms to the requirements of a **balance of power**. This view recognises that, in pursuit of national security, states enter into alliances which, if balanced against one another, may ensure prolonged periods of peace and international stability. However, this type of international system is inherently dynamic, and when the balance of power breaks down, war is the probable result.

Realists have always acknowledged that the international order is not a classic 'state of nature', because power, wealth and resources are not equally distributed amongst states. Major actors have traditionally been accorded the status of **great powers** (during the Cold War, superpowers). The resulting hierarchy of states imposes a measure of order on the international system, reflecting the control that great powers exercise over subordinate ones through trading blocs, 'spheres of influence', and outright colonisation (see p. 116). During the Cold War period, this led to the creation of a bipolar world order in which rivalry between the US and Soviet power blocs extended over much of the globe. Realists have been prepared to argue, however, that bipolarity helped to maintain peace as escalating military spending led to an effective system of nuclear deterrents, especially once the condition of mutually assured destruction (MAD) was recognised in the 1960s. A stable hierarchy based on accepted rules and recognised processes thus kept anarchy at bay, and encouraged realists to adopt the modified idea of what Hedley Bull (1977) termed an 'anarchical society'.

During the 1980s, **neo-realism** (sometimes called 'new' or structural realism) developed under the influence of Waltz (1979) and others. While neo-realists continue to acknowledge the central importance of power, they tend to explain events in terms of the structure of the international system rather than the goals and make-up of individual states.

Realism and neo-realism have attracted fierce criticism, however. The central

Balance of power: A pattern of interaction amongst states that tends to curb aggression and expansionism by rendering them impracticable.

Great power: A state deemed to rank amongst the most powerful in a hierarchical state system, reflected in its influence over minor states.

Neo-realism: A perspective on international politics that modifies the power-politics model by highlighting the structural constraints of the international system.

objection is that, in divorcing politics from morality, the realist perspective legit-imises military escalation and the hegemonic ambitions of great powers. This view suggests that power politics has not so much maintained peace as kept the world on the verge of nuclear catastrophe. A second critique of realism is advanced by feminist theorists, who contend that power-seeking behaviour and an obsession with national security and military might reflect the worldwide dominance of male politicians whose priorities are essentially aggressive and competitive. The central empirical weakness of realist theories is that, in focusing attention on the state as the dominant international actor, they have ignored pluralistic tendencies that have reshaped the face of international politics in the late twentieth century. 'Classical' realism has thus largely given way to neo-realism.

Pluralism

The pluralist perspective on international politics emerged, particularly in the USA, in the 1960s and 1970s, and it built on a bedrock of liberal ideas and values. In its traditional sense, pluralism (see p. 76) is a sociopolitical theory that emphasises the diffusion of power amongst a number of competing bodies or groups. As a theory of international politics, it highlights the permeability of the state, and provides an alternative to the state-centrism of the realist model. The limitations of the state-centric approach were illustrated by John Burton's (1972) simile of the billiard table. This suggests that realism assumes that states, like billiard balls, are impermeable and self-contained units which influence each other through external pressure. Sovereign states interacting in a system of international anarchy are thus seen to behave like a collection of billiard balls moving over the table and colliding with other balls. According to pluralists, this simile distorts international politics in that it both ignores the degree to which influence is increasingly exerted by transnational actors such as multinational corporations (MNCs) and nongovernmental organ-isations (NGOs), and fails to recognise the interdependence of states, especially in relation to economic affairs.

The resulting pluralist perspective therefore offers a mixed-actors model which, while not ignoring national governments, emphasises that international politics is shaped by a much broader range of interests and groups. At the very least, the emphasis on external sovereignty that is central to realism has to be replaced, in this view, by the more modest notion of autonomy. This enables bodies such as Green-peace, the Palestine Liberation Organization, Coca-Cola, and the Papacy to be recognised as international actors in precisely the same sense as, say, the French and Argentine states. Indeed, given its emphasis on the diffusion of power, the pluralist model calls the very notion of an autonomous actor into question, emphasising that all actors (governmental and nongovernmental) operate within a framework of checks and constraints that inhibit independent movement. This view allowed, for example, Allison (1971), in analysing the 1962 Cuban Missile Crisis, to make the point that decisions are more commonly shaped by the bureaucratic–political context than by any 'rational' pursuit of national interest.

Finally, one of the important implications of the pluralist approach to inter-national politics is that it highlights a shift away from power politics and national aggrandisement. This reflects not so much an idealist faith in abstract principles as the recognition that, when power is widely distributed, competition tends to be self-defeating. As a result, pluralists tend to argue that, in an increasingly interdependent world, the tendency towards cooperation and integration (perhaps most clearly manifested in Europe) will ultimately prove to be irresistible.

Marxism

Marxism offers a perspective on international politics that contrasts sharply with conventional paradigms. What makes the Marxist approach distinctive is its stress on economic power and the role played by international capital. Although Marx (see p. 51) was primarily concerned with analysing the structures of national capitalism, and particularly the antagonistic relationship between the bourgeoisie and the proletariat, an internationalist perspective was implicit in his work. This was evident in Marx's recognition that class loyalties cut across national divisions, which enabled him to proclaim, at the end of the *Communist Manifesto* ([1848] 1967), 'workers of the world, unite!'. In other words, whereas liberal and realist theories hold that power is organised *vertically*, reflecting the division of the world into independent states, Marxism advances a theory of *horizontal* organisation based on international class. However, the implications of viewing capitalism as an international system were not fully explored until Lenin's *Imperialism: The Highest Stage of Capitalism* ([1917] 1970). Lenin (see p. 75) argued that imperial expansion reflected domestic capitalism's quest to maintain profit levels through the export of surplus capital, and that this, in turn, brought major capitalist powers into conflict with one another, the resulting war (the First World War) being essentially an imperialist war in the sense that it was fought for the control of colonies in Africa, Asia and elsewhere.

Modern Marxists or neo-Marxists (see p. 90), however, recognise the limitations of the classical Marxist–Leninist model. These include the fact that early twentieth-century imperialism did not prove to be the 'highest' (that is, the final) stage of capitalism, and the narrowness of the assumption that state policy is merely a reflection of capitalist interests. Indeed, insofar as they acknowledge the 'relative autonomy' of the state, neo-Marxists have drawn close to a pluralist belief that a variety of bodies (subnational, national and international) exert influence on the world stage. The distinctive feature of the neo-Marxist perspective, however, is that, whereas classical Marxism emphasised rivalry between separate national capitalisms, neo-Marxism focuses attention on the development, during the twentieth century, of a global capitalist system.

In neo-Marxist analysis, the central feature of this system is the organisation of class interests on an international basis through the emergence of multinational corporations. In this view, these corporations have not merely displaced sovereign states as the dominant actors on the world stage, but they also, like states themselves and international organisations, operate within structural constraints that ensure the long-term interests of global capitalism. According to neo-Marxists, this global structure of production and exchange is highly ordered in the sense that it has divided the world into 'core' and 'peripheral' areas (see p. 134). Core areas such as the developed North benefit from technological innovation and high and sustained levels of investment, while peripheral areas such as the less developed South provide a source of cheap labour, and are often dependent on cash crops. Such global inequalities mirror those found at a regional level within national economies. Whereas regional core areas are integrated into the global economy, peripheral regions are effectively marginalised, often becoming a breeding ground for ethnic nationalism. Economic globalisation thus goes hand in hand with national disintegration.

Concept

Imperialism

Imperialism is, broadly, the policy of extending the power or rule of a state beyond its boundaries. In its earliest usage, imperialism was an ideology that supported military expansion and imperial acquisition, usually by drawing on nationalist and racialist doctrines. The term is now more commonly used to describe the system of political domination or economic exploitation that the pursuit of such goals helped to establish. In the Marxist tradition, imperialism is seen as an economic phenomenon that typically results from the pressure to export capital. Neo-Marxists, however, draw attention to a more subtle form of imperialism, termed neocolonialism, through which industrialised powers control foreign territory by economic domination while respecting the territory's formal political independence. Realist theorists, however, view imperialism more as a political phenomenon, seeing it as the pursuit by states of power and strategic advantage through expansion and conquest.

Concept

Cold War

A 'cold' war (the term was coined by Walter Lippman in 1944) is a state of protracted and extreme tension between countries or rival alliances that stops short of all-out war. The term is most commonly associated with a period of political, economic, cultural and military rivalry between the 'capitalist' western bloc and the 'communist' eastern bloc, and thus between the US and Soviet superpowers. This period is usually seen as having started in 1947 with the establishment of the so-called 'Truman Doctrine', although some trace it back to the 1945 Potsdam Conference, or even to western intervention against the Bolsheviks during the 1918–21 Russian Civil War. Although the 'war' was 'cold' in the sense that the adversaries avoided direct confrontation, covert operations and proxy warfare were a feature of the period. Renewed superpower tension associated with the US military buildup under Reagan is often referred to as the Second Cold War (1981–90).

Expansionism: A policy of military aggression designed to secure territorial gains, a phenomenon closely linked to imperialism.

The changing world order

The rise and fall of the Cold War

On 9 November 1989, jubilant East German demonstrators stormed the Berlin Wall and started to dismantle what had become the chief symbol of the Cold War era. By the spring of 1990, during the Kuwait crisis which saw the construction of a broad international alliance to confront Iraqi aggression, President Bush of the USA was able to proclaim the emergence of a 'new world order'. In November 1990, representatives of the Warsaw Pact and NATO, the military faces of East–West confrontation, met in Paris formally to declare the end of hostilities, officially closing the book on the Cold War. However, how did the Cold War start in the first place? What was it that kept the Cold War 'cold' and prevented it from developing into a 'fighting war'? And what did the end of the Cold War bring: did anyone win the Cold War?

The debate about the origins of the Cold War is closely linked to the rivalries and ideological perceptions that helped to fuel the Cold War itself. The traditional, or 'orthodox', explanation lays the blame firmly at the door of the USSR. It sees the Soviet stranglehold over eastern Europe as an expression of long-standing Russian imperial ambitions, given renewed impetus by the Marxist–Leninist doctrine of worldwide class struggle. This view was articulated as early as 1947 in George Kennan's famous 'Mr X' articles (which portrayed Soviet communism as essentially aggressive), and it was revived in the 1980s in President Reagan's description of the USSR as an 'evil empire'. From this perspective, the problem was communist **expansionism**, and US policy from Truman onwards focused on its containment, initially via the economic reconstruction of Europe through the Marshall Plan (1946), and subsequently through the creation of a military alliance in the form of the North Atlantic Treaty Organisation.

A 'revisionist' interpretation of the Cold War was nevertheless developed that attracted growing support during the Vietnam War from academics such as Gabriel Kolko (1988). This view portrayed Soviet policy as defensive, rather than aggressive, motivated essentially by the desire for a buffer zone between itself and a hostile West, and a wish to see a permanently weakened Germany. It also drew attention to the expansionist policies of the USA. According to this view, the goal of US policy was to establish a *Pax Americana* that would keep the markets of the world open to US capitalism. The desire of the USA for economic domination was effectively concealed by the fanatical anti-communism of the McCarthy era. However, the weakness with both the orthodox and the revisionist accounts is that each presents a one-sided picture that reflects a wish to apportion blame for the Cold War rather than advance historical understanding. A number of 'post-revisionist' explanations have therefore developed.

Some of these acknowledge the hegemonic ambitions of both superpowers, arguing that the Cold War was the inevitable consequence of a power vacuum that was a product of the defeat of Germany and Japan as well as the exhaustion of the UK (Yergin, 1980). Alternative explanations place a heavier emphasis on misunderstanding and missed opportunities (McCauley, 1983). Early signs of hope in relation to the post-Second-World-War order were in fact evident in President Roosevelt's belief in peaceful cooperation under the auspices of the newly created United Nations, and also in Stalin's distinctly discouraging attitude towards Tito in Yugoslavia and Mao in China. Nevertheless, once a mentality of 'bombs, dollars and doctrines' took root in

Table 8.1 Chronology of the Cold War

Date	Event
1945	Potsdam Conference (July–August)
1945	Hiroshima atom-bomb attack (6 August), Nagasaki attack (9 August)
1947	Truman Doctrine (April)
1947	Marshall Plan (June)
1948	Communist takeover in Czechoslovakia
1948/49	Berlin crisis
1949	Formation of NATO (April)
1949	Soviet atom-bomb explosion (August)
1950–53	Korean War
1955	Formation of Warsaw Pact
1956	Soviet invasion of Hungary
1961	Erection of Berlin Wall
1962	Cuban Missile Crisis
1965–75	Vietnam War
1967	Strategic Arms Limitation Talks (SALT) negotiations commence
1968	Soviet invasion of Czechoslovakia
1975	Helsinki Conference, creation of the Conference on Security and Cooperation in Europe (CSCE)
1982	Strategic Arms Reduction Talks (START) negotiations commence
1989	Berlin Wall falls
1990	CSCE meeting formally ends Cold War (November)
1991	Collapse of USSR (December)

both East and West, a descent into mutual suspicion and engrained hostility became unavoidable. Table 8.1 shows the chronology of the Cold War.

The first phase of the Cold War was fought in Europe. The division of Europe that resulted from the defeat of Germany (the Soviet Red Army having advanced from the east and the USA, the UK and their allies having pushed forward from the west) quickly became permanent: in Winston Churchill's words, an 'iron curtain' descended between East and West. This process was completed in 1949 with the creation of the 'two Germanies' and the establishment of rival military alliances, consisting of NATO and, in 1955, the Warsaw Pact. Thereafter, the Cold War became global. The Korean War (1950–53) marked the spread of the Cold War to Asia following the Chinese Revolution of 1949. During the 1960s and 1970s, international crises throughout the world, from the Middle East to Latin America and from Africa to Indo-China, were incorporated into the struggle between the USSR and the USA, which represented the broader clash between communism and capitalism. The **bipolar** model of the Cold War, however, became increasingly less accurate from the 1960s onwards. This was due, first, to the growing fragmentation of the communist world (notably, the deepening enmity between Moscow and Beijing), and secondly to the resurgence of Japan and Germany as 'economic superpowers'. One of the consequences of this emerging multipolarism was *détente* between East and West. This was reflected in President Nixon's historic visit to China in 1972 and the Strategic Arms Limitation Talks between 1967 and 1979 that produced the SALT I and SALT II agreements.

Bipolarity: The tendency of the international system to revolve around two poles (major power blocs); bipolarity implies equilibrium and stability.

Détente: (*French*) Literally, loosening; the relaxation of tension between previously antagonistic states.

Debate about the end of the Cold War is mired in as much ideological controversy as is debate about its origins. One version credits Ronald Reagan with having brought the Cold War to an end by instigating a renewed US military buildup in the early 1980s, particularly in the form of the Strategic Defense Initiative (SDI) (the 'star wars' initiative) of 1983, thereby sparking off the 'Second Cold War'. The result of this was that the USSR was drawn into an arms race that its already fragile economy could not sustain. In a broader form, this explanation has been elaborated, by Fukuyama (1992) amongst others, into the triumphalist 'end of history' thesis. This thesis suggests that the West 'won' the Cold War ultimately because only US-style liberal democracy offered a viable economic and political system. Other versions, however, place heavier stress on the structural weaknesses of the Soviet economy and the catastrophic mishandling of the reform process by Mikhail Gorbachev.

From this perspective, the inefficiency of the central-planning system, and the failure to introduce reforms at an earlier stage, undermined the legitimacy of the Soviet and eastern European communist regimes, which could not satisfy the growing demand for western-style consumer goods and western-style political freedoms. The Gorbachev reforms, initiated in 1985, merely brought about the collapse of an inefficient yet still functioning economic system, and, in relaxing the grip of the Communist Party, unleashed centrifugal forces that by the end of 1991 had brought about the destruction of the USSR itself. Some even suggest that the Cold War, and particularly renewed hostilities under Reagan, helped to prolong the life of the USSR. In keeping alive the idea of an external 'capitalist' threat, the Cold War at least brought about a measure of internal consolidation.

It is doubtful, however, whether such momentous historical events as the rise and fall of the Cold War can ever have a monocausal explanation. It is clear, for instance, that the events of the 1980s to some extent built on a process established by *détente* in the 1970s. *Détente* was significant in initiating on both sides a re-examination of strategic priorities that helped to question whether continued hostility was necessary or desirable. For that matter, the resurgence of the peace movement in the early 1980s also helped to weaken domestic support for continued superpower conflict. In broader terms, however, the end of the Cold War can be seen to reflect a shift in the global balance of power. Just as the superpower era was born out of a power vacuum that left the USA and USSR as the dominant actors on the world stage, its end perhaps reflected the relative decline of both powers as a result of 'imperial over-reach' (Kennedy, 1989). The decline of the USSR was acute and unmistakable, but, in the USA, relative economic decline was effectively masked by continued demonstrations of military supremacy.

A new world order?

The birth of the post-Cold-War world was accompanied by a wave of optimism and idealism. The superpower era had been marked by East–West rivalry that extended across the globe and led to a nuclear buildup that threatened to destroy the planet. As communism collapsed in eastern Europe, and Soviet power was in retreat both domestically and internationally, 'one world' speaking with 'one voice' appeared to have come into existence. The 'new world order', at least as envisaged by President George Bush, was going to be based not on ideological conflict and a balance of terror, but on a common recognition of international norms and standards of morality. Central to this emerging world order was the recognition of the need to settle

Noam Chomsky (born 1928)

US linguistic theorist and radical intellectual. Chomsky was born in Philadelphia, the son of eastern European immigrant parents. He first achieved distinction as a scholar in the field of linguistic studies. His *Syntactic Structures* (1957) revolutionised the discipline with the theory of 'transformational grammar', which proposed that humans have an innate capacity to acquire language. Radicalised during the Vietnam War, Chomsky subsequently became the leading radical critic of US foreign policy, developing his views in works such as *American Power and the New Mandarins* (1969) and (with Edward Herman) *Manufacturing Consent* (1988). The latter examined how popular support for imperialist aggression is mobilised.

disputes peacefully, to resist aggression and expansionism, to control and reduce military arsenals, and to ensure the just treatment of domestic populations through respect for human rights. What is more, the post-Cold-War world order appeared to pass its first series of major tests with ease.

Iraq's annexation of Kuwait in August 1990 led to the construction of a broad western and Islamic alliance which, through the Gulf War of 1991, brought about the expulsion of Iraqi forces. The disintegration of Yugoslavia in 1991, which precipitated war between Serbia and Croatia, saw the first use of the Conference on Security and Cooperation in Europe (CSCE) (renamed the Organisation for Security and Cooperation in Europe (OSCE) in December 1994) as a mechanism for tackling international crises, leading to hopes that it would eventually replace both the Warsaw Pact and NATO. Although the CSCE had been effectively sidelined by superpower hostility since its creation at the Helsinki Conference of 1975, it was the CSCE Heads of Government meeting in Paris in November 1990 that produced the treaty which brought a formal end to the Cold War. However, the early promise of international harmony and cooperation quickly proved to be illusory as new forms of unrest and instability rose to the surface.

In many ways, the linchpin of the hoped-for new world order was the USA. A bipolar world order had given way to a unipolar one, with the USA, the only power with the military capacity and political authority to intervene effectively, playing the role of the 'world's police force'. This was demonstrated by Desert Storm, the military expulsion of Iraq from Kuwait, and by US intervention in Somalia in 1992, which was designed to curb warlord-initiated conflict and restore aid supplies. Moreover, the USA, unlike earlier hegemonic powers, was wedded to the principles of liberal democracy, and so was more concerned with the spread of political freedom and market capitalism than it was with plunder and conquest. A trend towards democratisation, encouraged by the USA, in parts of the world such as Latin America and Asia where authoritarianism had previously reigned, supported this view.

There are several reasons, however, for questioning this image of USA-sponsored international fraternity and world peace. In the first place, there are those who, like Noam Chomsky (1994), challenge the idea that the USA is a disinterested world power, and doubt that there is anything 'new' about the new world order. For example, the anti-Iraq coalition of 1990–91 perhaps only reflected the fact that US and broader western concerns about oil supplies coincided with regional anxieties amongst Islamic powers such as Syria and Saudi Arabia about a 'Greater Iraq'. In other words, rhetoric about international law and national sovereignty merely camouflaged power politics and the pursuit of national interest. The very idea of a new world order might, indeed, be a piece of historical engineering aimed at safeguarding US interests and maintaining the USA's mastery of the global economy.

There are also doubts about the capacity of the USA to play the role of the world's police force, even if this were thought to be desirable. In the first place, preponderant nuclear power does not always translate into effective military capacity, as was demonstrated by the USA's failure in Vietnam in the 1970s and its embarrassed withdrawal from Somalia in 1995. At a deeper level, however, it is questionable whether the USA has the economic resources to sustain its global role, particularly in a context of relative decline highlighted by the economic resurgence of Japan and Germany. As discussed below, this may be evidence of the USA succumbing to a tendency, common amongst earlier great powers, to 'imperial over-reach', that is, an expansion of military responsibilities that outstrips the growth of the domestic economy. One manifestation of this has been an upsurge in **isolationism**. How long will Americans be prepared to pay the price of the USA being 'number one'? In the same way as after the First World War, the idea of the USA disengaging itself from international affairs ('leaving the world to sort itself out') has come to have a potent appeal in the USA, and this may grow still stronger.

Further stresses within the new world order have been generated by the releasing of tensions and conflicts that the Cold War had helped to keep under control. The existence of an external threat (be it international communism or capitalist encirclement) promotes internal cohesion and gives societies a sense of purpose and identity. To some extent, for instance, the West defined itself through antagonism towards the East, and *vice versa*. There is evidence that, in many states, the collapse of the external threat has helped to unleash centrifugal pressures, usually in the form of racial, ethnic and regional tensions. This has occurred in many parts of the world, but in particular in eastern Europe, as demonstrated by the prolonged bloodshed amongst Serbs, Croats and Moslems in the former Yugoslavia, and by the war between Russia and the secessionist republic of Chechnya which broke out in 1994. Such conflicts create the prospect of an increasingly dangerous world characterised by ethnic nationalism and regional strife. Far from establishing a world order based on respect for justice and human rights, the international community stood by in former Yugoslavia and allowed Serbia to wage a war of expansion and perpetrate genocidal policies reminiscent of those used in the Second World War.

As opposed to the world being policed and orderly, the emerging international scene seems to be typified by lawlessness and inaction; it appears to resemble more a new world *dis*order. This may, indeed, be the natural condition of a multipolar world order. Whereas bipolarism is structured, albeit by mutual hostility, multipolarism creates more fluid and less predictable conditions in which major actors are unclear about their roles and responsibilities. Thus the USA, a German-led Europe, Russia, Japan and South East Asian 'tigers', China, and possibly the Islamic world are all engaged in redefining themselves as international actors freed from the straightjacket that superpower rivalry imposed. However, the very instability of post-Cold-War politics illustrates its transitionary character. The USA–USSR superpower period may have passed, but a new and stable world order has yet to come into existence. The central question is whether this order will come about through cooperation, engineered by international bodies such as the UN and the EU, or whether it will be imposed through economic domination and military force.

Isolationism: The policy of withdrawal from international affairs and, in particular, avoiding political or military commitments to other states.

The changing balance of the global economy

Whatever the emerging world order will look like, it is certain to be shaped in crucial respects by the global distribution of economic power. Economics influences politics at virtually every level, and there can be no doubt that a nation's 'weight' in world affairs is linked to its productive capacity and economic influence. Nevertheless, the precise nature of the relationship between economics and politics, and the way in which the global economy structures international politics, are matters of deep political and academic controversy. No one questions, however, that national economies have increasingly been integrated into a single, global economy, largely through the development of an international trading system. As trade no longer respects national boundaries (a tendency encouraged by the ending of the Cold War), economies can no longer be thought of as separate islands; they are interdependent elements within a global whole.

From the perspective of liberal pluralism, the emergence of a global economy is to be welcomed on the grounds that it promotes international harmony and will, over a period, reduce material inequality. Liberals have long emphasised the virtues of **free trade** and economic interdependence. Trade amongst countries allows each country to specialise in the production of those goods and services that it is best suited to produce. This leads to international specialisation and mutual benefits. In addition, free trade has been praised for promoting interdependence, making conflict and war less likely. In this light, the true significance of the passing of the superpower era was that, for the first time, the international economy could become global. In extending into the former communist 'second world', as well as into the 'third world', the global economy promises to promote worldwide development and bring about a harmonisation of interests. Unfortunately, however, the notion that economic globalisation will bring about 'one world' may prove to be hopelessly optimistic.

One of the most important features of economic globalisation is the growing importance of multinational corporations (sometimes called transnational corporations). These are business organisations that produce output in more than one state. MNCs now dominate most of the world's markets. Notable examples are General Motors and Ford in the automotive industry, Esso, Shell and BP in the oil industry, the McDonald's fast-food chain, AT&T (American Telephone & Telegraph) and the International News Corporation in the communications sector, and the major Japanese banks (23 of which are among the largest 50 banks in the world). The significance of MNCs is that they represent a concentration of economic power in the hands of nonstate actors. Major corporations such as General Motors and Ford control $100 000 000 000 empires that dwarf the economies of many poorer states.

Moreover, the transnational organisation of MNCs has markedly shifted the balance of economic power away from national governments and local communities. While nationally based corporations are forced to acknowledge the bargaining power of their workforces and operate within a political framework that they have only a limited ability to influence, MNCs have the option of relocating elsewhere. Neo-Marxist commentators therefore argue that economic globalisation often means subordination to the market power of 'the multinationals', and that this ultimately serves the class interests of international capital. This has made developing countries particularly vulnerable, as they provide MNCs with a source of cheap labour and low production costs without being able to oblige them to make long-term investments or to shift decision-making power from the 'home' country to the 'host' one.

Free trade: A system of trading between states not restricted by tariffs or other forms of protectionism.

Focus on . . .

The North–South divide

The idea of a 'North–South divide' was popularised through the work of the so-called Brandt Reports: *North–South: A Programme for Survival* (1980) and *Common Crisis: North–South Cooperation for World Recovery* (1983). Although the division of the world into a 'North' and a 'South' is based on the tendency for industrial development to be concentrated in the northern hemisphere, and for poverty and disadvantage to be concentrated in the southern hemisphere (apart from Australasia), the terms are essentially conceptual rather than geographical. The concept of the North–South divide drew attention to the way in which aid, third-world debt and the practices of MNCs help to perpetuate structural inequalities between the high-wage, high-investment industrialised North and the low-wage, low-investment, predominantly rural South. The Brandt Reports also highlighted the interdependence of the North and the South, emphasing that the long-term prosperity of the North is dependent on the development of the South.

The idea that the global economy is biased in favour of cooperation and harmony is also questionable. International trade, for instance, is always likely to generate tension and conflict; although countries always wish to penetrate the markets of other countries, they have an equally strong incentive to protect their own markets from foreign competition. Historically, the cause of free trade has been embraced by economically dominant powers (the UK in the nineteenth century, and the USA in the twentieth century) which wished to encourage weaker states to open up their markets while they themselves had little fear of foreign competition. In a multipolar global economy, the danger of rival trading blocs being formed is always acute. Tendencies in this direction have already been apparent in the form of pressures to turn the EU into 'fortress Europe', the establishment of the North American Free Trade Agreement (NAFTA), which encompasses the USA, Canada and Mexico, and moves by Japan to consolidate her relationship with China with a view, perhaps, to creating an extended East Asian trading bloc that would dwarf those of both North America and Europe.

In 1993, the Uruguay round of the General Agreement on Tariffs and Trade (GATT) negotiations was successfully completed (GATT was replaced by the World Trade Organization in 1995). This has helped to keep the 'war of the worlds' scenario at bay, but there is little doubt that the balance of the global economy has shifted, and shifted decisively. While economic growth has stagnated amongst the rich industrial countries of the West, the newly industrialising countries (NICs) of the developing world, notably the Asian 'tigers' on the eastern rim of the Pacific Basin, have experienced strong and sustained growth. One of the consequences of this is that, in order to compete in world markets, industrialised countries are increasingly being forced to find ways of promoting labour flexibility and cutting production costs. Meanwhile, endemic poverty and sometimes declining living standards afflict peripheral regions of the global economy, particularly sub-Saharan Africa. Global tensions have come to be seen less in terms of East versus West, and more in terms of a 'North–South divide'. Ironically, this global economic imbalance has, in part, been sustained by the flow of foreign aid. Aid budgets have at times, for instance, been used by industrialised states to promote trading relationships and economic dependence ('aid as trade'), or to exert political or ideological influence ('aid as imperialism').

It would be a mistake, nevertheless, to assume that globalisation necessarily means the eclipse of the nation-state as an economic actor. Certainly, the idea of economic sovereignty can now be consigned to the dustbin of history (if it was ever plausible), but globalisation has tended to alter the importance of economic policy rather than making it redundant. When capital can be transferred across the globe in the flick of a computer screen, and financial markets react to crises on the other side of the world, national governments are forced to work harder to make their societies more internationally competitive. This lesson has perhaps been learned best by Germany, Japan, and the 'tiger' economies of East and South East Asia. These states have recognised that success in the global marketplace requires heavy investment, particularly in infrastructure and in education and training, as well as state support to build up export industries and acquire modern technology. National governments, in other words, can still make a difference. National-level processes may increasingly have been superseded by global ones, but the result is an economy in which local, national and global factors interact, and where governments that understand the dynamics of globalisation have some capacity to shape its direction.

■ Towards world government?

International organisations

One of the most significant features of twentieth-century politics has been the growing importance of international organisations. These are organisations that are transnational in that they exercise jurisdiction not within a single state, but within an international area comprising several states. In this sense, there is nothing new about international organisations; indeed, these long predate the modern nation-state, and can be regarded, historically, as the most traditional form of political organisation. The most common form of international body has been the empire. These have ranged from the ancient empires of Sumeria, Egypt, China, Persia and Rome to the modern European empires of the UK, France, Spain, Portugal and the Netherlands. Empires are structures of political domination that comprise a diverse collection of cultures, ethnic groups and nationalities that are held together by force or the threat of force. Although colonies continue to exist (Tibet's enforced subordination to China and Indonesia's domination of East Timor are examples), the collapse of the USSR in 1991 brought to an end the last of the world's major empires, the Russian empire. On the other hand, modern international organisations have quite different origins and a very different character. Typically, they have been set up by a number of sovereign states to facilitate international cooperation. International organisations thus now reflect a growing recognition of national interdependence in an increasingly shrinking world.

Political communities have always recognised the need for diplomatic contact with other communities, usually involving the despatch of emissaries or ambassadors. The earliest permanent diplomatic missions were located in the Italian city-states of the fifteenth century. However, the first attempt to estalish a standing body to facilitate international negotiations did not develop until the nineteenth century, in the form of the Concert of Europe. Established by the Congress of Vienna (1815), the concert constituted a system of *ad hoc* conferences through which the great powers (the UK, Russia, Austria, Prussia and France) attempted to maintain a

Intergovernmentalism, supranationalism

Intergovernmentalism is any form of interaction between states which takes place on the basis of sovereign independence. This includes treaties and alliances as well as leagues and confederations, such as the League of Nations and the EEC. Sovereignty is preserved through a process of unanimous decision-making that gives each state a veto, at least over matters of vital national importance.

Supranationalism is the existence of an authority that is 'higher' than that of the nation-state and capable of imposing its will on it. It can therefore be found in international federations, where sovereignty is shared between central and peripheral bodies. The European Union thus encompasses a mixture of both intergovernmental and supranational elements.

balance of power in post-Napoleonic Europe, and to resolve disputes that threatened international stability. The concert system finally collapsed as a result of the Crimean War (1854–56) with the outbreak of hostilities between the UK and France, on the one hand, and Russia on the other.

The twentieth century, however, saw a burgeoning of international organisations. The League of Nations, formed in 1919, was the world's first international body that was intended to establish universal jurisdiction. It was succeeded in 1945 by the United Nations and a plethora of other organisations, for example, NATO, the European Economic Community (EEC), the World Bank, the International Monetary Fund (IMF), the Organisation for Economic Cooperation and Development (OECD), the Organisation of Petroleum Exporting Countries (OPEC) and the Organisation of African Unity (OAU). What all such organisations have in common is that they provide a framework for intergovernmental relations that enables states, at least in theory, to take concerted action without sacrificing sovereign power.

The principal reason for the growth in the number and importance of international organisations is the recognition by states that, in a number of areas, they provide a more effective means of pursuing national interests. This applies particularly to national security and economic development. Quite simply, an anarchic international order in which states refuse to acknowledge an authority higher than themselves is inevitably biased towards conflict, **protectionism** and war. Whereas splendid isolation was a luxury that states could afford in the nineteenth or early twentieth century, this option is no longer available in a world of nuclear weapons and economic globalisation. State survival is now dependent on collective security, and economic development requires guaranteed access to international and global markets. Both these goals can only be achieved through cooperation under the auspices of international organisations such as NATO and the OSCE on the one hand, and the World Trade Organization (WTO) and the IMF on the other. Growing awareness of ecological problems, such as global warming and acid rain, make the need to construct effective international and supranational bodies all the more pressing.

In addition to providing a way of tackling problems that are beyond the power of national governments to solve, international organisations have also managed to acquire a momentum and identity of their own. Once seen as peripheral and untested, many international bodies have become established and seemingly indispensable features of world politics. This is clearly illustrated by the contrasting histories of the League of Nations and the UN. The League of Nations unfortunately never lived up to its name. Despite the efforts of President Wilson of the USA, Congress blocked US membership of the league. Germany, defeated in the First World War, was admitted only in 1926, and resigned once Hitler assumed power in 1933. Japan walked out of the League in 1932 after criticisms of its invasion of Manchuria. The USSR, shunned at first, only became a member in 1934, after Germany and Japan had departed. The UN, on the other hand, was created in 1945 with a membership of 51 that included the so-called 'Big Five': the USA, the USSR,

Protectionism: Import restrictions such as quotas and tariffs, designed to protect domestic producers.

Jean Monnet (1888–1979)

French economist and administrator. Monnet was largely self taught. He found employment during the First World War coordinating Franco-British war supplies, and he was later appointed Deputy Secretary-General of the League of Nations. He was the originator of Winston Churchill's offer of union between the UK and France in 1940, which was abandoned once Pétain's Vichy regime had been installed. Monnet took charge of the French modernisation programme under de Gaulle in 1945, and in 1950 he produced the Schuman Plan, from which the European Coal and Steel Community and the European Economic Community were subsequently developed. Although Monnet rejected intergovernmentalism in favour of supranational government, he was not a formal advocate of European federalism.

the UK, France and China. Of these, only China subsequently left when it was expelled in 1949 following the communist revolution; however, it returned in 1971. By 1992, the UN's membership had grown to 179, leaving no significant power outside its compass.

It is not possible, however, to explain the drift towards supranational organisations simply in terms of convenience and the pursuit of national self-interest. To some extent, the growing number and importance of international organisations reflects an idealist commitment to internationalism and the belief that such institutions embody a moral authority that is higher than that commanded by nation-states. This was certainly the case with the 'Wilsonianism' that helped to inspire both the League of Nations and the UN, and it was also evident in the 'federalist' dream of an integrated Europe that was espoused by, for example, Jean Monnet and Robert Schuman (1886–1963). In this respect, international organisation has given renewed impetus to the notion of a global state or world government, an idea that can be traced back to Imperial Rome. To examine how viable such a project is in modern circumstances, it is instructive to look at the experience of European integration, and the progress that has been made by the UN.

European integration

The 'European idea' (broadly, the belief that, regardless of historical, cultural and linguistic differences, Europe constitutes a single political community) was born long before 1945. Before the Reformation in the sixteenth century, common allegiance to Rome invested the Papacy with supranational authority over much of Europe. Even after the European state system came into existence, thinkers as different as Rousseau (see p. 73), Saint-Simon (1760–1825) and Mazzini (see p. 110) championed the cause of European cooperation, and in some cases advocated the establishment of Europe-wide political institutions. However, until the second half of the twentieth century, such aspirations proved to be hopelessly utopian. Since the Second World War, Europe has undergone a historically unprecedented process of integration, aimed, some argue, at the creation of what Winston Churchill in 1946 called a 'United States of Europe'. Indeed, it is sometimes suggested that European integration provides a model of political organisation that will eventually be accepted worldwide as the deficiencies of the nation-state become increasingly apparent.

It is clear that this process was precipitated by a set of powerful, and possibly irresistible, historical circumstances in post-1945 Europe. The most significant of these were the following:

- the need for economic reconstruction in war-torn Europe through cooperation and the creation of a larger market, thus preventing any return to protectionism and economic nationalism
- the desire to preserve peace by permanently resolving the bitter Franco-German rivalry that stemmed from the creation of a united Germany in 1871 after the Franco-Prussian War (1870–71), and led to war in 1914 and 1939
- the recognition that the 'German problem' (the structural instability in the European state system caused by the emergence of the powerful and ambitious central European power) could only be tackled by integrating Germany into a wider Europe
- the desire to safeguard Europe from the threat of Soviet expansionism and to mark out for Europe an independent role and identity in a bipolar world order
- the wish of the USA to establish a prosperous and united Europe, both as a market for US goods and as a bulwark against the spread of communism and Soviet influence
- the widespread acceptance, especially in continental Europe, that the sovereign nation-state was the enemy of peace and prosperity, and that it had therefore to be superseded by supranational structures.

Early dreams of a 'federal' Europe in which the sovereignty of the European nations would be 'pooled' came to nothing, however. For instance, plans in 1948 for the construction of a European parliament only led to the creation of the Council of Europe. This has developed into little more than a debating society and is composed not of elected members, but of ones appointed by national governments. Instead, a 'functionalist' road to unity was followed which allowed for incremental steps to be taken towards European integration, but only within specific areas of policy making and at a pace controlled by the states themselves. This is why the European project tended to focus on the means of promoting economic cooperation, seen by states as the least controversial but most necessary form of integration. The European Coal and Steel Community (ECSC) was founded in 1952 on the initiative of Jean Monnet, adviser to the French foreign minister, Robert Schuman. Under the Treaty of Rome (1957), the European Economic Community came into existence. This was committed to the establishment of a common European market and the broader goal of an 'ever closer union among the peoples of Europe'.

The ECSC, EEC and Euratom were formally merged in 1967, forming what became known as the European Community (EC). Although the community of the original 'Six' (France, Germany, Italy, the Netherlands, Belgium and Luxembourg) was expanded in 1973 with the inclusion of the UK, Ireland and Denmark, the 1970s was a period of stagnation. The integration process was relaunched, however, as a result of the signing in 1986 of the Single European Act (SEA), which envisaged an unrestricted flow of goods, services and people throughout Europe (a 'single market'), to be introduced by 1993. The Maastricht Treaty (or more correctly the Treaty on European Union (TEU)), which was negotiated in 1991 and ratified in 1993, marked the creation of the European Union (EU). This committed the EU's 15 members (Greece had joined the EC in 1981, Portugal and Spain had joined in 1986,

Focus on . . .

How the European Union works

▶ **European Commission**: This is the bureaucratic arm of the EU. It is headed by 19 commissioners (two from each of the large states and one from each small one) and a president (Jacques Santer's term of office as president began in 1995). It proposes legislation, is a watchdog that ensures that EU treaties are respected, and is broadly responsible for policy implementation.

▶ **Council of Ministers**: This is the legislature of the EU, and it comprises ministers from the 15 states who are accountable to their own assemblies and governments. The presidency of the Council of Ministers rotates amongst member states every six months. Important decisions are made by unanimous agreement, and others are reached through qualified majority voting or by a simple majority.

▶ **European Council**: This is a forum in which heads of government, accompanied by foreign ministers and two commissioners, meet to discuss the overall direction of the Union's work. The council usually meets twice a year.

▶ **European Parliament**: The EP is composed of 567 Members of the European Parliament (MEPs) (81 from the UK), who are directly elected every five years. The European Parliament is a scrutinising assembly, not a legislature. Its major powers (to reject the European Union's budget and dismiss the European Commission) are too far-reaching to exercise.

▶ **European Court of Justice**: The ECJ interprets, and adjudicates on, European Union law. There are 15 judges, one from each member state, and six advocates general, who advise the court. As EU law has primacy over the national law of EU member states, the court can 'disapply' domestic laws. A Court of First Instance handles certain cases brought by individuals and companies.

and Austria, Finland and Sweden joined in 1995) to both political union and monetary union. The centrepiece of this proposal was for the establishment of a single European currency, due to take place, according to the TEU, in 1999.

The EU is a very difficult political organisation to categorise. In strict terms, it is no longer a confederation of independent states (as the EEC and EC were at their inception). The sovereignty of member states was enshrined in the so-called 'Luxembourg compromise' of 1966. This accepted the general practice of unanimous voting in the Council of Ministers, and granted each member state an outright **veto** on matters threatening vital national interests. As a result of the SEA and the TEU, however, the practice of qualified majority voting, which allows even the largest state to be outvoted, was applied to a wider range of policy areas, thereby narrowing the scope of the national veto. The result is a political body that has both intergovernmental and supranational features, the former evident in the Council of Ministers and the latter primarily in the Court of Justice. The EU may not yet have created a federal Europe, but because of the superiority of European law over the national law of the member states, it is perhaps accurate to talk of a federalising Europe.

The difficulty of defining the EU is compounded by the fact that there are two starkly contrasting visions of what a united Europe should look like. The first is

Veto: The formal power to block a decision or action through the refusal of consent.

Concept

Subsidiarity

Subsidiarity (from the Latin *subsidiarii*, meaning a contingent of supplementary troops) is, broadly, the devolution of decision-making from the centre to lower levels. However, it is understood in two crucially different ways. In federal states such as Germany, subsidiarity is understood as a *political* principle that implies decentralisation and popular participation, with local and provincial institutions thus being supported. This is expressed in the TEU in the form of the commitment that decisions should be 'taken as closely as possible to the citizen'. However, subsidiarity is also interpreted, usually by anti-federalists, as a *constitutional* principle that defends national sovereignty against the encroachment of EU institutions. This is expressed in the TEU in the commitment that the competence of the European Union should be restricted to those actions that 'cannot be sufficiently achieved by the member states'.

rooted in the vision of President Charles de Gaulle of France of a '*Europe des patries*', that is, a Europe of sovereign and independent states. Adopted most assertively by Margaret Thatcher in the 1980s, this view sees Europe as essentially a market, in other words, as a liberal trading bloc that should impinge as little as possible on the political autonomy of member states. This position places heavy emphasis on the principle of subsidiarity, and is usually at odds with the idea of monetary union, its supporters fearing that this will inevitably bring closer political union in its wake. The alternative model, outlined most clearly in the plans of the then president of the European Commission Jacques Delors for monetary union, is of a union of states, a fully-fledged federal Europe. Central to this vision is the progressive 'deepening' of the integration process through an increase in the powers of EU institutions. Typically, this position favours the strengthening of European social policy through the Social Chapter (sometimes called the Social Charter), and the extension of collective decision-making into areas such as immigration policy, defence and foreign affairs. The loss of national sovereignty that this would inevitably bring about would be more than compensated for, federalists argue, by the greater influence that Europe would be able to exert on the world stage.

Whichever model of European integration ultimately prevails, the EU will undoubtedly be confronted by a number of testing problems. Perhaps the oldest of these is the Common Agricultural Policy (CAP), which ensures that the bulk of EU funds are still used to subsidise uncompetitive farming. Although the need to reform the CAP is widely accepted, this entails tackling powerful farming lobbies in states such as France and Germany, and throughout southern Europe. A second problem is the so-called 'democratic deficit'. This is usually understood to mean the EU's lack of democratic accountability, which is reflected in the weakness of its only directly elected body, the European Parliament. While lack of accountability is a common criticism of the European Union, anti-federalists are also reluctant to grant the European Parliament greater powers for fear that this might accelerate the integration process. Thirdly, the collapse of communism and the end of the division of Europe has created pressure for the eastward expansion of the European Union. Not only does this raise serious difficulties related to the incorporation of former communist states still in the process of transition, but it also raises questions about how far the EU can be 'deepened' at the same time as it is 'widened'. Finally, there are serious doubts about the ability of the EU to be an effective international actor in any capacity other than as a trading bloc. This was underlined by its paralysis in relation to the collapse of the former Yugoslavia and the ensuing ethnic carnage.

The United Nations

The United Nations, constructed at the San Francisco Conference (April–June 1945) in the dying days of the Second World War, is the most advanced experiment in world government to date. It has attempted to avoid the manifest failures of the League of Nations, which stood by powerless as Germany, Japan and Italy pursued their expansionist ambitions in the 1930s. The UN was born out of a mixture of realism and idealism. On the one hand, there were clear advantages to extending the anti-Axis alliance of the USA, the USSR and the UK into the postwar period. On the other, there were high expectations, expressed most clearly by Franklin D. Roosevelt, that this period would be marked by a rejection of the power politics of the past, paving the way for an era of peace and international cooperation.

The UN charter laid down the highest standards of international conduct for nations wishing to join the organisation. These included the renunciation of the use of force (except in self defence), the settlement of international disputes by peaceful means, cooperation to ensure respect for human rights and fundamental freedoms, and the recognition of national sovereignty and the right to self-determination. At the heart of this approach lies a commitment to the principle of collective security and the belief that collective action can provide an alternative to the 'old politics', which were based on the pursuit of national interest and the maintenance of a balance of power. Nevertheless, although the UN has undoubtedly established itself as a genuinely world body, and is regarded by most as an indispensable part of the international political scene, it is difficult to argue that it has, or perhaps could ever, live up to the expectations of its founders.

The structure of the UN centres around the General Assembly, which consists of all the member states, each of which has a single vote. The General Assembly can debate and pass resolutions on any matter covered by the charter. Important decisions must be carried by a two-thirds majority, but these decisions are recommendations rather than being enforceable international law (see p. 160). The UN is a propaganda arena as opposed to an effective parliament, and it tends to be dominated by the large numbers of developing states. The most significant UN body is the Security Council, which is charged with the maintenance of international peace and security, and is thus responsible for the UN's role as negotiator, observer, peace keeper, and, ultimately, peace enforcer. The council has 15 members. The 'Big Five' are permanent 'veto powers', meaning that they can cancel decisions made by other members of the council. The other ten members are nonpermanent members that are elected for two years by the General Assembly. The makeup of the Security Council has attracted growing criticism, however. In particular, the right of the UK and France to permanent places has been challenged by the growing stature of Japan and Germany, and developing states have pushed for permanent representation, usually in the form of the inclusion of India or Brazil.

The World Court (formerly the International Court of Justice) is the judicial arm of the UN. It consists of a panel of 15 judges elected for nine-year terms by a majority of the members of both the Security Council and General Assembly. Its weaknesses are that it can only arbitrate when states choose to refer their disputes to the court, and only about a third of UN member states are prepared to acknowledge its jurisdiction in any area. The Secretariat is the executive branch of the UN, and it is headed by the UN Secretary General (since December 1996, Kofi Annan). In security matters, the Secretary General works closely with the Security Council. As the closest thing to a 'president of the world', he or she can do much to influence the status and direction of the organisation. Although the UN is best known for its high-profile peacekeeping operations, its reputation is shaped by the work of a number of specialist agencies coordinated by the Economic and Social Council of the General Assembly. These include the World Health Organisation (WHO), the United Nations Children's Fund (UNICEF), the United Nations Educational, Scientific and Cultural Organisation (UNESCO), and the United Nations Higher Commission for Refugees (UNHCR).

The capacity of the UN to develop into a form of world government is severely limited by the fact that it is essentially a creature of its members; it can do no more than its member states, and particularly the permanent members of the Security Council, permit. As a result, its role has essentially been confined to providing mech-

Concept

Collective security

The idea of collective security, simply stated, is that aggression can best be resisted by united action taken by a number of states. The theory of collective security is based on the assumption that war and international conflict are rooted in the insecurity and uncertainty of power politics. It suggests that states, as long as they pledge themselves to defend one another, have the capacity either to deter aggression in the first place, or to punish the transgressor if international order has been breached. Successful collective security depends on three conditions. First, the states must be roughly equal, or at least there must be no preponderant power. Second, *all* states must be willing to bear the cost and responsibility of defending one another. Third, there must be an international body that has the moral authority and military capacity to take effective action.

Concept

International law

International law is a
system of rules that are
binding on states, and thus
define the relationships
between states. (Law (see
p. 284) is a set of public
and enforceable rules.) In
the absence of a world
legislature, international law
draws on a number of
sources: treaties, custom,
general principles (such as
respect for territorial
integrity), and legal
scholarship accumulated by
the international courts.
Idealists have traditionally
placed heavy emphasis on
international law, seeing it
as a means of establishing
order through respect for
moral principles, which thus
makes possible the
peaceful resolution of
international conflicts.
Realists, on the other hand,
have questioned the status
of international law, arguing
that, as it is not
enforceable, it constitutes
not 'law', but merely a set
of moral principles.

anisms that facilitate the peaceful resolution of international conflicts. Even in this respect, however, its record has been patchy. There have been undoubted successes, for example, in negotiating a ceasefire between India and Pakistan in 1959, maintaining peace in 1960 in the Belgian Congo (now Zaire) following the attempted breakaway by Katanga, and mediating between the Dutch and the Indonesians over West Irian (New Guinea) in 1962. However, for much of its history, the UN has been virtually paralysed by superpower rivalry. The Cold War ensured that, on most issues, the USA and the USSR adopted opposing positions, which prevented the Security Council from taking decisive action.

The UN's intervention in Korea in 1950 was only possible because the USSR temporarily withdrew from the council (in protest against the exclusion of communist China), and in any case this merely fuelled fears that the UN was western-dominated. As the world drew close to nuclear war during the Cuban Missile Crisis of 1962, the UN was a powerless spectator. It was unable to prevent the Soviet invasions of Hungary (1956), Czechoslovakia (1968) and Afghanistan (1979), and it had only a very limited influence on the succession of Arab–Israeli wars in 1948, 1956, 1967 and 1973. Nevertheless, it cannot be denied that, regardless of its practical impact on world affairs, the UN has accumulated considerable moral authority as the principal vehicle through which international law can be established. This was clearly demonstrated by the UK's anxiety during the 1982 Falklands War to ensure that it was acting in accordance with UN resolutions, and by the USA's decision during the 1991 Gulf War not to pursue fleeing Iraqi troops into Iraq for fear of acting outside the authority of the UN.

The ending of the Cold War was the beginning of a new chapter for the UN. For so long marginalised by superpower antagonism, the UN suddenly assumed a new prominence as the instrument through which 'one world' could be brought about. The UN's intervention in 1990–91 to expel Iraq from Kuwait seemed to demonstrate a renewed capacity to fulfil its obligation of deterring aggression and maintaining peace. However, these early hopes were quickly disappointed. UN peace keepers were little more than spectators during the genocidal slaughter in Rwanda in 1994. UN-backed US intervention in Somalia led to humiliation and withdrawal in 1995, with warlord conflict continuing unabated. Recurrent fighting in the former Yugoslavia demonstrated the ineffectiveness of UN-negotiated ceasefires and UN-backed sanctions against Serbia. Why did this happen?

Quite simply, the UN has been one of the casualties of the insecurity and shifting balances that the breakdown of the 'old' world order has precipitated. Instead of stepping into centre stage as a proto-world-government, the UN has been forced to confront a range of new problems and conflicts. These include the reluctance of states whose security is no longer threatened by East–West rivalry to commit resources to the cause of collective security or for the defence of states on the other side of the globe. This 'new isolationism' helped to prevent EU member states from taking concerted action in Bosnia, and it also discouraged the USA from getting involved at an earlier stage. Moreover, there are serious problems related to the distribution of responsibilities and burdens within the new international system. For example, while relative economic decline is damaging the ability of the USA to fulfil the role of the world's police force, the current economic superpowers, Japan and Germany, are unwilling to take on this role for fear of damaging their prosperity and reducing growth rates. Finally, the international political focus has itself shifted. The UN's role used to be to keep the peace in a world dominated by the conflict between communism and capitalism. Now it is being forced to find a new role in a world structured by the dynamics of global capitalism, in which conflict increasingly arises from imbalances in the distribution of wealth and resources.

Summary

◆ Globalisation is a complex web of interconnectedness that means that our lives are increasingly shaped by decisions and actions taken at a distance from ourselves. It implies that nation-states can no longer be viewed as independent actors on the world stage. However, it may mean not that the state is irrelevant, but that its role has changed and now largely relates to the promotion of international competitiveness.

◆ International politics has been analysed in a number of ways. Idealism adopts a perspective that is based on moral values and legal norms. Realism emphasises the importance of power politics. Neo-realism highlights the structural constraints of the international system. Pluralism advances a mixed-actor model, and it stresses a growing diffusion of power. Marxism draws attention to economic inequalities within the global capitalist system.

◆ The 'new' world order has been interpreted in various ways. Some observers argue that the passing of the bipolar world order allows for a transition from the entrenched antagonism of the Cold War to broader cooperation based on inter-dependence. Others warn that bipolarism was at least stable, whereas multipolarism may merely generate new and unpredictable forms of international conflict.

◆ The balance of the global economy has shifted. The growth of multinational cor-porations means that states are no longer the only, or perhaps no longer the most significant, economic actors. Moreover, the emergence of rival trading blocs sug-gests a 'war of the worlds' scenario, and global inequality has increased through the economic decline of sub-Saharan Africa and the advance, in particular, of the states of the Asian Pacific region.

◆ The significance of international organisations has grown as states have recog-nised that these bodies provide the most effective means of guaranteeing national security and economic development. On the other hand, their success has been hampered because they remain, in most cases, devices that are used by states to pursue self-interest, and they have yet to rival nation-states in terms of their capacity to elicit political allegiance.

◆ The argument for world government is basically that, if there is no global state, the international system will operate as a 'state of nature'. However, the capacity of the United Nations to play this role is restricted because of the unwillingness of states to commit resources to the cause of collective security, the unequal distribu-tion of responsibilities in the new international system, and the difficulty of finding a new role for the UN in a world that is no longer structured by East–West rivalry.

Questions for discussion

▶ Is globalisation a reality or a myth?
▶ Which perspective on international politics offers the greatest insight into con-temporary developments?

▶ Is a multipolar world order necessarily unstable?

▶ Does a globalised economy mean opportunity for all or greater insecurity and deeper inequality?

▶ Is the process of European integration unstoppable?

▶ What role could, or should, the United Nations adopt in the new international system?

▶ Is world government an attractive prospect?

Further reading

Bretherton, C. and G. Ponton (eds) *Global Politics: An Introduction* (Oxford: Blackwell, 1996). A lucid and wide-ranging examination of issues and problems related to globalisation.

Burchill, S. and A. Linklater *Theories of International Relations* (Basingstoke: Macmillan, 1996). A concise and informative introduction to the range of theoretical traditions in the field of international relations.

Chomsky, N. *World Order, Old and New* (London: Pluto Press, 1994). A trenchant examination of the new world order that highlights the hegemonic ambitions of the USA.

Gill, S. and D. Law *The Global Political Economy: Perspectives, Problems and Policies* (Brighton: Harvester Wheatsheaf, 1988). A useful analysis of the dynamics and implications of the global economy.

Kennedy, P. *The Rise and Fall of the Great Powers* (London: Fontana, 1989). An influential, accessible and stimulating discussion of general trends and regional developments in the new world order.

PART
3

Political Interaction

• • • • • • • • •

The Economy and Society

'It's the Economy, Stupid.'

> Reminder on the wall of Bill Clinton's office during the 1992 US presidential election campaign

At almost every level, politics is intertwined with the economy and with society. Ideological argument and debate has traditionally revolved around the battle between two rival economic philosophies: capitalism and socialism. Voting behaviour and party systems are largely shaped by social divisions and cleavages. Parties compete for power by promising to increase economic growth, reduce inflation, tackle poverty and so on. As President Clinton recognised, election results are often determined by the state of the economy: governments win elections when the economy booms, but are likely to be defeated during recessions or slumps. Indeed, orthodox Marxists go further and suggest that politics is merely a part of a 'superstructure' determined or conditioned by the economic 'base', the political process being nothing more than a *reflection* of the class system. Although few people (including Marxists) now hold such a simplistic view, no one would deny that socio-economic factors are critical in political analysis. Quite simply, politics cannot be understood except within an economic and social context.

The central themes addressed in this chapter are as follows:

Key issues

► How, and to what extent, does the economy condition politics?

► What are the major economic systems in the world today? What are their respective strengths and weaknesses?

► How far can, and should, government control the economy?

► What are the key economic and social cleavages in modern societies?

► To what extent do class, race and gender structure political life?

■ Economic systems

An economic system is a form of organisation through which goods and services are produced, distributed and exchanged. Marxists refer to economic systems as 'modes of production'. A recurrent difficulty, however, is confusion between such systems of economic organisation and the ideas and doctrines through which they have been defended. Capitalism, for instance, is sometimes treated not merely as an economic system, but also as an ideology in its own right, specifically one that defends private property, emphasises the virtues of competition, and suggests that general prosperity will result from the pursuit of self-interest. This confusion is yet more marked in the case of socialism. The term socialism is used to refer both to a distinctive set of values, theories and beliefs, and to a system of economic organisation through which these values will supposedly be realised. Although this chapter considers some of the strengths and weaknesses of economic systems (how they have been defended and why they have been criticised), its central concern is with socio-economic organisation rather than normative political theory. A fuller account of relevant ideological disputes is found in Chapter 3.

For almost 200 years, debate about economic organisation has revolved around a clash between two rival systems: capitalism and socialism. So fundamental did the choice appear that it structured the political spectrum itself, reducing political views to the question of where one stood on economic organisation. Left-wing beliefs were thought to favour socialism, right-wing ones reflected sympathy for capitalism. The fact that the rival systems appeared to be so fundamentally divergent helped to underpin this dichotomy.

The central features that were usually associated with a capitalist economy were the following:

- There is generalised commodity production, a commodity being a good or service produced for *exchange* – it has a market value.
- Productive wealth (the 'means of production') is predominantly held in *private* hands.
- Economic life is organised according to *market* principles: the forces of demand and supply.
- Material *self-interest* and profit maximisation provide the motivation for enterprise and hard work.

In contrast, socialist economies were thought to be based on the following principles:

- There is a system of production for *use*, geared, at least in theory, to the satisfaction of human needs.
- There is predominantly *public* or common ownership of productive wealth, certainly including the 'commanding heights' of the economy.
- Economic organisation is based on *planning*, a supposedly rational process of resource allocation.
- Work is based on *cooperative* effort that results from a desire for general well-being.

In practice, however, economic systems were always more complex and difficult to categorise. In the first place, it was a mistake to suggest that there was ever a single,

universally accepted model of either capitalism or
socialism. In practice, societies constructed their own
models of capitalism and socialism depending upon
their particular economic and political circumstances,
and their cultural and historical inheritance. It thus
makes more sense to discuss capitalisms and socialisms. Further, the simplistic 'capitalism versus socialism' model of economic organisation distorted the
truth by overemphasising (often as a result of Cold War
rivalry) the differences between the two models.

The abrupt abandonment of central planning following the eastern European revolutions of 1989–91
not only brought an end to the system of **state socialism**, but also destroyed the illusion that there was ever a
'pure' socialist system or a 'pure' capitalist one. No
capitalist system is entirely free of 'socialist' impurities
such as labour laws and at least a safety-net level of welfare, and there has never been a socialist system that did
not have 'capitalist' impurities such as a market in
labour and some form of 'black' economy. There have,
moreover, been attempts to construct economic
systems that conform to neither capitalist nor socialist
models; these are usually referred to as 'third ways'.
Corporatism in Fascist Italy, Perónism in Argentina,
and Swedish social democracy have all been described
in this way. Environmentalists, for their part, have
developed their own critique, arguing that capitalism
and socialism are essentially similar, both being production-orientated and growth-
obsessed economic systems. A Green economy would require a radical shift in
economic priorities towards ones rooted in sustainability and ecological balance.

> **Concept**
>
> ## Market
>
> A market is a system of commercial exchange which brings
> buyers wishing to acquire a good or service into contact with
> sellers offering the same for purchase. In all but the most
> simple markets, money is used as a convenient means of
> exchange, rather than barter. Markets are impersonal
> mechanisms in that they are regulated by price fluctuations
> that reflect the balance of supply and demand, so-called
> market forces.
>
> Supporters of the market argue that it has the following
> advantages:
>
> - It promotes efficiency through the discipline of the profit
>   motive.
> - It encourages innovation in the form of new products and
>   better production processes.
> - It allows producers and consumers to pursue their own
>   interests and enjoy freedom of choice.
> - It tends towards equilibrium through the coordination of an
>   almost infinite number of individual preferences and
>   decisions.
>
> Critics, however, point out that the market has serious
> disadvantages:
>
> - It generates insecurity because people's lives are shaped
>   by forces they cannot control.
> - It widens material inequality and generates poverty.
> - It increases the level of greed and selfishness, and ignores
>   the broader needs of society.
> - It promotes instability through periodic booms and slumps.

Capitalisms of the world

Capitalist economic forms first emerged in sixteenth-century and seventeenth-
century Europe, developing from within predominantly feudal societies. Feudalism
was characterised by agrarian-based production geared to the needs of landed
estates, fixed social hierarchies, and a rigid pattern of obligations and duties. Capitalist practices initially took root in the form of commercial agriculture that was
orientated towards the market, and relied increasingly on waged labour instead of
bonded serfs. The market mechanism, the heart of the emerging capitalist system,
certainly intensified pressure for technological innovation and brought about a
substantial expansion in productive capacity.

The pressure to expand output and increase productivity was reflected in the so-
called 'agricultural revolution', which saw the enclosure of overgrazed common land
and the increased use of fertilisers and scientific methods of production. By the mid-
eighteenth-century, first in the UK but soon in the USA and across Europe, an
industrial revolution was beginning. Industrialisation entirely transformed society
through the advent of machine-based factory production and the gradual shift of
populations from the land to the expanding towns and cities. Indeed, so closely were

State socialism: A form of
socialism in which the state
controls and directs economic
life, acting, in theory, in the
interests of the people.

Adam Smith (1723–90)

Scottish economist and philosopher, usually seen as the founder of the 'Dismal Science'. After holding the chair of logic and then moral philosophy at Glasgow University, Smith became tutor to the Duke of Buccleuch, which enabled him to visit France and Geneva and to develop his economic theories. *The Theory of Moral Sentiments* (1759) developed a theory of motivation that tried to reconcile human self-interestedness with an unregulated social order. Smith's most famous work, *The Wealth of Nations* ([1776] 1930), was the first systematic attempt to explain the workings of the economy in market terms, emphasising the importance of the division of labour. Though he is often seen as a free-market theorist, Smith was nevertheless also aware of the limitations of the market.

capitalism and industrialisation linked that industrial capitalism is generally taken to be capitalism's classical form. However, three types of capitalist system can be identified in the modern world:

- enterprise capitalism
- social capitalism
- collective capitalism.

Enterprise capitalism

Enterprise capitalism is widely seen, particularly in the Anglo-American world, as 'pure' capitalism, that is, as an ideal towards which other capitalisms are inevitably drawn. It is nevertheless apparent that this model has been rejected in most parts of the world except for the USA (the home of enterprise capitalism) and, despite its early postwar flirtation with Keynesian social democracy, the UK. Enterprise capitalism is based on the ideas of classical economists such as Adam Smith and David Ricardo (1772–1823) updated by modern theorists like Milton Friedman (see p. 173) and Friedrich Hayek (see p. 48). Its central feature is faith in the untrammelled workings of market competition, born out of the belief that the market is a self-regulating mechanism (or, as Adam Smith put it, an 'invisible hand'). This idea is expressed in Adam Smith's famous words: 'it is not from the benevolence of the butcher, the brewer, or the baker, that we expect our dinner, but from their regard to their own interest'. In the USA, such free-market principles have helped to keep public ownership to a minimum, and ensure that welfare provision operates as little more than a safety net. US businesses are typically profit-driven, and a premium is placed on high productivity and labour flexibility. Trade unions are usually weak, reflecting the fear that strong labour organisations are an obstacle to profit maximisation. The emphasis on growth and enterprise of this form of capitalism stems, in part, from the fact that productive wealth is largely owned by financial institutions, such as insurance companies and pension funds, that demand a high rate of return on their investments.

The undoubted economic power of the USA bears testament to the vigour of enterprise capitalism. Despite clear evidence of relative decline (whereas the USA accounted for half of the world's manufacturing output in 1945, this had fallen to one-fifth by 1990), the average productivity of the USA is still higher than Germany's and Japan's. The USA undoubtedly enjoys natural advantages that enable it to benefit from the application of market principles, notably a continent-wide domestic market, a wealth of natural resources, and a ruggedly individualist popular culture, seen as a 'frontier ideology'. However, its success cannot be put down to the market alone. For instance, the USA possesses, in the main, a strong and clear sense of national purpose, and it has a network of regulatory bodies that constrain the worst excesses of competitive behaviour.

Enterprise capitalism also has serious disadvantages, however. Perhaps the most significant of these is a tendency towards wide material inequalities and social fragmentation. This is demonstrated in the USA by levels of absolute poverty that are not found, for example, in Europe, and in the growth of a poorly educated and welfare-dependent underclass. The tensions that such problems generate may be contained by growth levels that keep alive the prospect of social mobility. In societies such as that in the UK, however, which lack the cultural and economic resources of the USA, enterprise capitalism may generate such deep social tensions as to be unsustainable in the long run.

Social capitalism

Social capitalism refers to the form of capitalism that has developed in much of central and western Europe. Germany is its natural home, but the principles of social capitalism have been adopted in various forms in Austria, the Benelux countries, Sweden, France and much of Scandinavia. This economic form has drawn more heavily on the flexible and pragmatic ideas of economists such as Friedrich List (1789–1846) than on the strict market principles of classical political economy as formulated by Smith and Ricardo. A leading advocate of the *Zollverein* (the German customs union), List nevertheless emphasised the economic importance of politics and political power, arguing, for instance, that state intervention should be used to protect infant industries from the rigours of foreign competition. The central theme of this model is the idea of a social market, that is, an attempt to marry the disciplines of market competition with the need for social cohesion and solidarity.

In Germany, this system is founded on a link between industrial and financial capital in the form of a close relationship between business corporations and regionally based banks, which are often also major shareholders in the corporations. This has been the pivot around which Germany's postwar economy has revolved, and it has orientated the economy towards long-term investment rather than short-term profitability. Business organisation in what has been called Rhine–Alpine capitalism also differs from Anglo-American capitalism in that it is based on social partnership. Trade unions enjoy representation through works councils and participate in annual rounds of wage negotiation that are usually industry-wide. This relationship is underpinned by comprehensive and well-funded welfare provisions which provide workers and other vulnerable groups with social guarantees. In this way, a form of 'stakeholder capitalism' has developed which takes into account the interests of workers and those of the wider community. This contrasts with the 'shareholder capitalism' found in the USA and the UK (Hutton, 1995).

The strengths of social capitalism are clearly demonstrated by the 'economic miracle' that transformed war-torn Germany into Europe's leading economic power by the 1960s. High and stable levels of capital investment, together with a strong emphasis on education and training, particularly in vocational and craft skills, enabled Germany to achieve the highest productivity levels in Europe. However, the virtues of

Concept

Social market

The idea of a 'social-market economy' emerged in Germany in the 1950s. It was advanced by economists such as Alfred Muller-Armack and taken up by Christian Democrat politicians, notably Ludwig Erhard. A social market is an economy that is structured by market principles and largely free from government interference, operating in a society in which cohesion is maintained through a comprehensive welfare system and effective public services. The market is thus not an end in itself so much as a means of generating wealth in order to achieve broader social ends. A stress on partnership, cooperation and subsidiarity (see p. 158) distinguishes a social market from a free market. The social-market strategy allows Germany to achieve a policy consensus that binds together conservative and socialist opinion, and has been imitated by many EU member states.

the social-market model are by no means universally accepted. One of its drawbacks is that, because it places such a heavy stress on consultation, negotiation and consensus, it tends to encourage inflexibility and make it difficult for businesses to adapt to changing market conditions (for example, economic globalisation and intensified competition from East Asia). Further strain is imposed by the relatively high levels of social expenditure required to maintain high-quality welfare provision. These push up taxes and so burden both employers and employees. Whereas the supporters of the social market insist that the social and the market are intrinsically linked, its critics argue that social capitalism is nothing more than a contradiction in terms. In their view, the price of financing ever-expanding social programmes is a decline in international competitiveness and a weakening of the wealth-creating base of the economy.

Collective capitalism

The third form of capitalism is based on the example of postwar Japan. It is a model that the East Asian 'tigers' (South Korea, Taiwan, Singapore, and so on) have eagerly adopted, and, more recently, it has influenced emergent Chinese capitalism. The distinctive character of collective capitalism is its emphasis on cooperative long-term relationships. This allows the economy to be directed not by an impersonal price mechanism, but through what have been called 'relational markets'. An example of this is the pattern of interlocking share ownership that ensures that there is a close relationship between industry and finance in Japan. Some 40 per cent of the shares traded on the Tokyo stock exchange are held by industrial groups that create a nexus of sister firms, the *kigyo shudan*. The *keiretsu*, networks of cross-shareholdings that bind industrial concerns to their various subcontractors, make up a further 30 per cent of the Tokyo stock market's shares. This stability of ownership provides Japanese firms with an abundance of capital, which enables them to adopt strategies based on long-term investment rather than short-term or medium-term profit.

The firms themselves provide the social core of Japanese life. Workers (particularly male workers in larger businesses) are 'members' of firms in a way that does not occur in the USA or even social-market Europe. In return for their loyalty, commitment and hard work, workers have traditionally expected lifetime employment, pensions, social protection, and access to leisure and recreational opportunities. Particular stress is placed on teamwork and the building up of a collective identity, which is underpinned by relatively narrow income differentials between managers and workers. This emphasis on labour and the importance of collaborative effort has led to the Japanese system being dubbed 'peoplism'. The final element in this economic mix is the government. Although East Asian levels of public spending and taxation are relatively low by international standards (often below 30 per cent of GNP), the state plays a vital role in 'guiding' investment, research and trading decisions. The model here is undoubtedly the Ministry of International Tradeand Industry (MITI), which (if less overtly than in the 1950s and 1960s) continues to oversee the Japanese economy through a system of 'indicative' planning (see p. 174).

In many respects, the pre-Second-World-War Japanese economy exhibited many of the features of enterprise capitalism, including an obsession with profit maximisation and a tendency towards short-termism. Economic restructuring, however, which had commenced before the war and was stepped up afterwards, proved to be spectacularly successful. The Japanese 'economic miracle' has created an industrial power that, if current investment rates are maintained, will become the largest economy in the world by 2005. However, Japanese success may soon be eclipsed by the rising might of China, the growth rates of which exceed even those of the East Asian 'tigers'. Nevertheless, a price has had to be paid for this success. Behind the public face of cooperation and collaboration, the Japanese economic model places heavy demands on workers and their families. Long hours and highly disciplined working conditions can mean that individualism is stifled and work becomes the centrepiece of human existence. Similarly, the dominance of the 'community' firm in Japanese society has kept alive a neofeudal sense of obligation, with the recognition of duty being placed above respect for rights. Critics therefore argue that collective capitalism is invariably underpinned by authoritarianism (see p. 36), the most obvious example of authoritarian capitalism being found in China's blend of burgeoning capitalism and entrenched one-party communist rule.

Managed or unmanaged capitalism?

As this review of the world's capitalisms makes clear, the central issue in economic policy is the proper balance between politics and economics, and thus between the state and the market. Does a capitalist economy work best when it is left alone by government, or can stable growth and general prosperity only be achieved through a system of economic management? In practice, this question boils down to an evaluation of two rival economic strategies: Keynesianism and monetarism. The centrepiece of Keynes' (see p. 172) challenge to classical political economy, advanced in *The General Theory of Employment, Interest and Money* ([1936] 1965), was the rejection of the idea of a natural economic order based on a self-regulating market. He argued that *laissez-faire* policies that established a strict distinction between government and the economy had merely resulted in instability and unemployment, most clearly demonstrated by the Great Depression of the 1930s.

In Keynes' view, capitalist economies had spiralled downwards into deepening depression during the 1930s because, as unemployment grew, market forces brought about cuts in wages which further reduced the demand for goods and services. Keynes argued against free-market orthodoxy by stating that the level of economic activity is geared to 'aggregate demand', that is, the total level of demand in the economy, which government has the capacity to manage through its tax and spending policies. When unemployment rises, government should 'reflate' the economy either by increasing public spending or by cutting taxes. The resulting budget deficit, Keynes suggested, would be sustainable because the growth thus brought about would boost tax revenues and reduce the need for government borrowing. Moreover, any such stimulus to the economy would be magnified by the **multiplier** effect.

The advent of Keynesian demand management in the early post-Second-World-War period revolutionised economic policy and appeared to provide governments with a reliable means of delivering sustained growth and ever-widening prosperity. For many, Keynesianism was the key to the 'long boom' of the 1950s and 1960s, the most sustained period of economic growth the world has ever seen. The intellectual credibility of Keynesianism, however, was damaged by the emergence in the 1970s of 'stagflation' (a simultaneous rise in both unemployment and inflation), a condition that Keynes's theories had not anticipated and could not explain. Politically, Keynesian ideas were undermined by their association with the 'tax and spend' policies that, free-market economists claimed, had sapped enterprise and initiative and undermined growth by creating permanently high inflation (a general increase in the price level). In such circumstances, pre-Keynesian monetarist ideas gained a new lease of life, particularly on the political right.

Concept

Laissez-faire

Laissez-faire (in French meaning literally 'leave to do') is the principle of nonintervention of government in economic affairs. It is the heart of the doctrine that the economy works best when left alone by government. The phrase originated with the Physiocrats of eighteenth-century France, who devised the maxim '*laissez faire est laissez passer*' (leave the individual alone, and let commodities circulate freely). Classical economists such as David Ricardo and Alfred Marshall (1842–1924) took up the theme from Adam Smith. The central assumption of *laissez-faire* is that an unregulated market economy tends naturally towards equilibrium. This is usually explained by the theory of 'perfect competition'. From this perspective, government intervention is seen as damaging unless it is restricted to actions that promote market competition, such as checks on monopolies and the maintenance of stable prices.

Multiplier: The mechanism through which a change in aggregate demand has an increased effect on national income as it circulates through the economy.

John Maynard Keynes (1883–1946)

UK economist. Keynes' reputation was established by his critique of the Treaty of Versailles, outlined in *The Economic Consequences of the Peace* (1919). His major work, *The General Theory of Employment, Interest and Money* ([1936] 1965), departed significantly from neoclassical economic theories, and went a long way towards establishing the discipline now known as macroeconomics. By challenging *laissez-faire* principles, he provided the theoretical basis for the policy of demand management, which was widely adopted by western governments in the early post-Second-World-War period. Keynesian theories have had a profound effect upon both modern liberalism and social democracy.

The rise of **monetarism**, particularly as a result of the work of economists such as Friedrich Hayek (see p. 48) and Milton Friedman, signalled a shift in economic priorities away from the reduction of unemployment, and towards the control of inflation. In a move led in the 1980s by the Thatcher government in the UK and the Reagan administration in the USA, the principal economic responsibility of government came to be seen as ensuring 'sound money'. The job of government was to squeeze inflation out of the system and leave matters such as growth, employment and productivity to the natural vigour of the market. Monetarism suggests that, in Friedman's words, 'inflation is always and everywhere a monetary phenomenon'. The implication of monetarism is that Keynesian policies designed to boost output and reduce unemployment merely fuel inflation by encouraging the government to borrow, and so 'print money'. The alternative is to shift attention away from demand-side policies that encourage consumers to consume, and towards supply-side ones that encourage producers to produce. For monetarists, this invariably means deregulation and tax cuts.

To a large extent, however, modern economics has moved beyond the simplistic nostrums of Keynesianism and monetarism, and developed more sophisticated economic strategies, even a 'new' political economy. Monetarism, at the very least, succeeded in convincing Keynesians of the importance of inflation and of the significance of the economy's supply side. 'Crude' Keynesianism has been superseded as a result of economic globalisation, 1950s-style and 1960s-style economic management having been based on the existence of discrete national economies. On the other hand, the idea of an unregulated market economy has also been difficult to sustain, particularly in the light of the tendency for this type of economy to bring about low investment, short-termism, and social fragmentation or breakdown. As Francis Fukuyama (1996) pointed out, wealth creation of any kind depends on **social capital** in the form of trust, and not just on impersonal market forces. A 'new Keynesianism' has therefore emerged that rejects top-down economic management but also acknowledges the fact that the workings of the market are hampered by uncertainty, inequality and differential levels of knowledge.

Monetarism: The theory that inflation is caused by an increase in the supply of money; 'too much money chases too few goods'.

Social capital: Cultural and moral resources that help to promote social cohesion, political stability and prosperity.

Varieties of socialism

Modern socialists have increasingly been prepared to accept that capitalism is the only reliable means of generating wealth. They have, as a result, looked not to

Milton Friedman (born 1912)

US academic and economist. Professor of economics at the University of Chicago from 1948 and founder of the so-called Chicago School, Friedman has also worked as a *Newsweek* columnist and a US presidential advisor. He was awarded the Nobel prize for economics in 1976. A leading exponent of monetarism and free-market economics, Friedman is a powerful critic of Keynesian theory and 'tax and spend' government policies. His major works, *Capitalism and Freedom* (1962) and, with his wife Rose, *Free to Choose* (1980), have had a considerable impact on the economic thinking of the New Right.

abolish capitalism, but to reform or 'humanise' it. This has usually entailed embracing Keynesian or social-market ideas. Traditionally, however, socialists have looked to construct an alternative to market capitalism, seeing socialism as a qualitatively different economic formation from capitalism. Such attempts have been based on the assumption that socialism is superior to capitalism, both morally and productively. Although socialist literature abounds with economic models (ranging from the technocratic industrialism of Saint-Simon (1760–1825) to the decentralised self-management of Peter Kropotkin (1842–1921)), the most influential of these have been developed within the Marxist tradition. What socialist models have in common, however, is the belief that the market mechanism can and should be replaced by some form of economic planning.

Unfortunately, Marx (see p. 51) did not lay down a blueprint for the economic organisation of the future socialist society, restricting himself instead to a number of broad principles. Certainly, he envisaged that private property would be abolished and replaced by a system of collective or social ownership, which would allow the economy to serve the material needs of society rather than the dictates of an all-powerful market. Nevertheless, in supporting broad popular participation at every level in society, and in predicting that the state would 'wither away' as full communism was established, Marx set himself apart from the state collectivisation and central planning that was to characterise Soviet economics in the twentieth century.

Two very different models of a socialist economy have been developed:

- state socialism
- market socialism.

State socialism

Following the Bolshevik Revolution of 1917, the USSR became the first society to adopt an explicitly socialist model of economic organisation. This model was not fully developed until Stalin's (see p. 53) so-called 'second revolution' in the 1930s, significant aspects of market organisation having continued under Lenin's New Economic Policy in the 1920s. The model that was later exported to eastern Europe and that dominated orthodox communism in the period after the Second World War can therefore be dubbed economic Stalinism. This system was based on state collectivisation, which brought all economic resources under the control of the

Concept

Planning

Planning is a system of economic organisation which relies on a rational allocation of resources in accordance with clearly defined goals that are realised through the partial or complete coordination of production, distribution and exchange. However, in practice, planning systems differ markedly. State socialist regimes developed a system of *directive* planning orientated around output targets set for all economic enterprises, and administered centrally through a hierarchy of party–state institutions. So-called *indicative* planning has been used in, for example, France, the Netherlands and Japan to supplement or guide the workings of the capitalist economy using the tools of economic management rather than state direction.

The strengths of planning include the following:

- It places the economy in human hands, rather than leaving it to the impersonal and sometimes capricious whims of the market.
- It gears the economy towards the satisfaction of human needs rather than the maximisation of private profit.
- It is less susceptible than the market is to instability and crises.
- It can ensure a high level of material equality.

Opponents nevertheless point out the following:

- Planning cannot cope with the complexity of a modern industrialised economy.
- It is implicitly or explicitly authoritarian in that it allows central agencies to control the economy.
- It imposes elite opinions upon the masses instead of responding to consumer demand.
- It fails to reward or encourage enterprise, and tends towards bureaucratic stagnation.

party–state apparatus. In the USSR, a system of 'directive planning' placed overall control of economic policy in the hands of the highest organs of the Communist Party, which supervised the drawing up of output targets (in the form of Five Year Plans) by a network of planning agencies and committees. The key organ was Gosplan, the State Planning Committee, which set production targets for the entire economy, and in the process allocated resources to each enterprise, controlled trade, and fixed prices, wage levels, taxes and subsidies. The execution of these plans was the responsibility of powerful economic ministries, which controlled particular sectors of the economy, and directed the work of Soviet enterprises such as banks, factories, shops, and state and collective farms (see Figure 9.1).

The spectacular collapse of the state socialist model in eastern Europe and the USSR in the revolutions of 1989–91 has been widely used to demonstrate the inherent flaws of central planning, and has gone a long way towards discrediting the very idea of planning. However, this is to ignore the undoubted achievements of Soviet-style planning. For example, the central-planning system was remarkably successful in building up 'heavy' industries, and provided the USSR by 1941 with a sufficiently strong industrial base to enable it to withstand the Nazi invasion. Moreover, although planning failed dismally in its attempt to produce western-style consumer goods, it nevertheless helped the USSR and much of eastern Europe to eradicate homelessness, unemployment and absolute poverty, problems that continue to blight the inner cities in some advanced capitalist countries. Despite chronic economic backwardness, Cuba, for instance, achieved a literacy race of over 98 per cent and a system of primary healthcare that compares favourably with those in many western countries.

However, the drawbacks of central planning are difficult to disguise. Perhaps the most fundamental of these is its inherent inefficiency, which results from the fact that, however competent and committed the planners may be, they are confronted by a range and complexity of information that is simply beyond their capacity to handle (Hayek, 1948). It is estimated, for example, that planners in even a relatively small central-planning system are confronted by a range of options which exceed the number of atoms in the universe. A further explanation of the poor economic performance of the communist system is that the social safeguards built into central planning, together with its relatively egalitarian system of distribution, did little to encourage enterprise or promote efficiency. Quite simply, although all Soviet workers had a job, it was more difficult to ensure that they actually worked. Finally, central planning was associated with the emergence of new social divisions based on political or bureaucratic position. In Milovan Djilas' (1957) phrase, a 'new class' of party–state bureaucrats emerged who enjoyed a status and privileges equivalent to

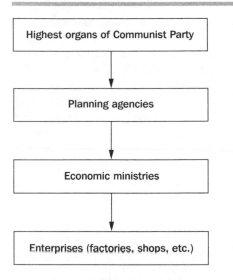

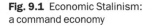

Fig. 9.1 Economic Stalinism: a command economy

those of the capitalist class in western societies. In the eyes of its left-wing critics, Soviet planning amounted to little more than a system of **state capitalism**.

Market socialism

As an alternative to the heavily centralised Soviet economic model, attempts were made to reconcile the principles of socialism with the dynamics of market competition. Such a model was introduced in Yugoslavia following the split between President Tito of Yugoslavia and Stalin in 1949, and it was also taken up in Hungary after the USSR suppressed the political uprising of 1956. Similar ideas were applied in the USSR during Mikhail Gorbachev's *perestroika* programme of 'economic restructuring' in 1985–90. *Perestroika* developed as a rolling programme which initially permitted the development of cooperatives and single-proprietor businesses to supplement the central-planning system, but eventually allowed Soviet enterprises to disengage themselves from the planning system altogether and become self-financing and self-managing. The central feature of a socialist market economy is thus the attempt to balance self-management against market competition. This does not amount to the re-introduction of capitalism, because, as economic enterprises are owned and controlled by their workers, there is no market in labour, and therefore no exploitation. What sets such a system firmly apart from the Soviet model, however, is that self-managing enterprises operate not according to 'the tyranny of the planners', but within a market environment shaped by competition, incentives and profit.

The attraction of market socialism is that it appears to compensate for many of the most serious defects of central planning. Not only does a market environment provide a guarantee of consumer responsiveness and efficiency, but the dangers of bureaucratic power are also kept at bay. However, this is not to say that a socialist market is entirely unplanned and unregulated. Indeed, most attempts to propose a 'feasible' or 'viable' form of socialism (Nove, 1983; Breitenbach, Burden and Coates, 1990), acknowledge the continuing need for a framework of planning, albeit one that uses collaborative and interactive procedures. At the same time, although self-management encourages cooperation and ensures a high level of material equality, it cannot be denied that the market imposes harsh disciplines. Failed businesses

State capitalism: A system of state ownership which replicates capitalist class relationships by concentrating economic power in the hands of a party–state elite.

collapse and unprofitable industries decline, but this, in the long run, is the price that has to be paid for a vibrant and prosperous economy.

Neither the Yugoslav nor Hungarian economies, however, despite their early promise, proved to be more successful or enduring than the Soviet central-planning system. Certainly, *perestroika* was distinguished more by its role in uprooting an existing, if inefficient, economic system than by its capacity to provide the USSR with a viable alternative. One of the chief weaknesses of market socialism is that self-management conflicts with market disciplines, as it dictates that enterprises respond first and foremost to the interests of their workforces. Free-market economists have therefore usually argued that only hierarchically organised private businesses can achieve optimal efficiency, because only they are capable of responding consistently to the dictates of the market, in that they place profit maximisation above all other considerations.

Is there a 'third way'?

The idea of an economic 'third way' that provides an alternative to both capitalism and socialism has attracted political thinkers from various traditions. For instance, this has been a recurrent theme in fascist thought, first outlined by Mussolini in relation to corporatism (see p. 257), and later embraced by, for example, Moseley in the UK and Perón in Argentina. Fascist corporatism, in contrast to its liberal variant, is based on the belief that business and labour are bound together in an organic and spiritually unified whole. In practice, however, corporatism in Italy amounted to little more than an instrument through which the fascist state smashed independent trade unions and tried to intimidate major business interests. A very different 'third way', Keynesian social democracy, is found in its most developed form in Sweden. The Swedish economic model attempts to combine elements of both socialism and capitalism. Productive wealth is largely concentrated in private hands, but social justice is maintained through the most comprehensive welfare system and highest tax regime found anywhere in the world. In this sense, the social-democratic 'third way' can be seen as a left-wing version of social capitalism. As in the case of the social-market model, however, doubts have been raised about the viability of continued high levels of social expenditure in an increasingly competitive global economy. This has been reflected in Sweden in the 1980s and 1990s in growing sensitivity to the pressure of international competition and a tendency to retreat from welfarist priorities.

An entirely different approach to economic organisation has been advanced by environmental theorists. From their perspective, capitalism and socialism are merely different manifestations of the same 'super-ideology' of **industrialism**. In other words, they are seen, essentially, as alternative ways of exploiting nature in order to satisfy the material interests of humankind. Environmentalists argue not only that this obsession with economic growth has led to the despoiling of the natural environment, but that it has also, by damaging the fragile ecosystem on which all life depends, threatened the survival of the human species itself. The Green alternative is to recast economic priorities on the basis of sustainability, that is, the capacity of a system (in this case the planet Earth) to maintain its health and continue in existence. Although ecosocialists have held capitalism's relentless pursuit of profit to be responsible for environmental destruction, the record of state socialist regimes in achieving 'sustainable growth' is hardly inspiring. The principle of sustainability

Industrialism: An economic theory or system based on large-scale factory production and the relentless accumulation of capital.

E. F. Schumacher (1911–77)

German-born UK economist and environmental theorist. 'Fritz' Schumacher moved to the UK in 1930 as an Oxford Rhodes scholar. He went on to gain practical experience in business, farming and journalism before re-entering academic life. He was an economic advisor to the British Control Commission in Germany (1946–50) and the UK National Coal Board (1950–70). His seminal *Small is Beautiful:*

A Study of Economics As If People Mattered (1973) championed the cause of human-scale production, and advanced a 'Buddhist' economic philosophy (economics 'as if people mattered') that stresses the importance of morality and 'right livelihood'. Schumacher founded the Intermediate Technology Development Group to help spread his ideas.

perhaps suggests that questions about the ownership and organisation of wealth are secondary to the more fundamental issue of the relationship between humankind and the natural world. In order to abandon the view that nature is essentially a resource available to satisfy human needs, it is necessary for an entirely different value system to be constructed, placing ecology before economics and morality before materialism. Such ideas were developed by E. F. Schumacher (1973) into the notion of 'Buddhist economics'.

■ Social structure and divisions

To suggest, as textbooks tend to do, that politics takes place in a social context fails to convey just how intimately politics and social life are related. Politics is by its very nature a social activity, and it is viewed by some as nothing more than the process through which the conflicts of society are articulated and perhaps resolved. In this sense, society is no mere ' context', but the very stuff and substance of politics itself. However, the concepts of 'the social' and 'the political' also mark out distinct (if intrinsically connected) spheres of activity. What do we mean by 'society'? In its most general sense, a society is a collection of people who occupy the same territorial area. However, not every group of people constitutes a society. Societies are characterised by regular patterns of social interaction. This suggests the existence of some kind of social *structure*, that is, a usually stable set of interrelationships amongst a number of elements. Moreover, 'social' relationships involve mutual awareness and at least a measure of cooperation. For instance, strictly speaking, warring tribes do not constitute a 'society', even though they may live in close proximity to one another and interact regularly. Societies are also usually characterised by social *divisions*, in which groups and individuals occupy very different positions, reflecting an unequal distribution of status, wealth and/or power within the society. The nature of these divisions or cleavages, and the political significance of particular divisions (class, race, gender, age, religion and so on), of course, differ from society to society.

In all cases, though, society can be seen to shape politics in a number of important ways:

• The distribution of wealth and other resources in society conditions the nature of state power (as discussed in Chapter 5).

Individualism, collectivism

Individualism is a belief in the primacy of the individual over any social group or collective body, which suggests that the individual is central to any political theory or social explanation. This view has been closely associated with classical liberalism and, in the modern period, the New Right. From this perspective, all statements about society should be made in relation to the individuals who compose it; strictly speaking, 'there is no such thing as society' (Margaret Thatcher). This view is usually underpinned by the belief that human beings are naturally self-interested and largely self-reliant, owing nothing to society for their talents and skills.

Collectivism stresses the capacity of human beings for collective action, highlighting their willingness and ability to achieve goals by working together rather than through self-striving. It draws from the belief that there is a social core to human nature, implying that social groups (including 'society' itself) are meaningful political entities. This view can be seen, for instance, in the socialist stress on class analysis and the feminist use of gender categories, as well as in all nationalist and racialist doctrines. Collectivism is sometimes linked to statism (see p. 96), although this relationship is by no means essential.

- Society influences public opinion and the political culture (as discussed in Chapter 10).
- Social divisions and conflicts help to bring about political change in the form of reforms and revolutions (also as discussed in Chapter 10).
- The social structure shapes political behaviour, that is, who votes, how they vote, who joins parties, and so on (as discussed in Chapters 11–13).

The nature of society, however, is one of the most contentious areas of political and ideological debate, being no less controversial, in fact, than the attempt to define the content of human nature. For example, whereas Marxists and others hold that society is characterised by irreconcilable conflict, liberals tend to emphasise that harmony exists amongst competing interests and groups. Similarly, while liberals are inclined to view society as an artefact fashioned by individuals to satisfy their various needs, conservatives have traditionally portrayed it as organic, ultimately shaped by the forces of natural necessity. Perhaps the most important debate, however, concerns the relationship between the individual and society, and whether or not there is such an entity as 'society'. At the heart of this question lies the rivalry between two contrasting modes of social understanding: individualism and collectivism.

Social class

Since the advent of modern industrial societies, class has generally been viewed as the deepest and most politically significant of social divisions. Only in more traditional societies have fixed social hierarchies and preindustrial systems of stratification continued to have an impact. For example, although the caste system in India has declined in importance, the Harijan (known in the past, in English, as the 'untouchables') remain a significant political force. Class divisions reflect economic and social differences in society, and are thus based on an unequal distribution of wealth, income and/or social status. A social class is therefore a group of people who have similar economic and social positions, and are united by a common economic interest. However, any analysis of the relationship between class and politics is bedevilled by a number of problems. These include the difficulty of identifying class divisions and of establishing the relationships between or among classes. Also, has the influence of class declined, and if so, why? Underlying these questions, though, is disagreement about precisely how social class should be defined.

The rise and fall of class politics

The leading proponents of the theory of class politics have come from the Marxist tradition. Marxists regard class as the most fundamental, and politically the most significant, social division. As Marx put it at the beginning of the *Communist Manifesto* ([1848] 1967), 'the history of all hitherto existing societies is the history of class struggle'. This reflected his belief that politics, together with aspects of life such as the law, culture, the arts, and religion, is part of a 'superstructure' that is determined or conditioned by the economic 'base'. Crudely, this implied that the political process is nothing more than the working out of class tensions or conflicts. These, in turn, are rooted in the mode of production and, in the final analysis, in the institution of private property.

In this view, in a capitalist system, a 'ruling' class of property owners (the bourgeoisie) dominates and exploits a class of wage slaves (the proletariat). This gave rise to a two-class model of industrial capitalism that emphasised conflict and progressive polarisation. In Marx's view, classes were the key actors on the political stage, and they had the ability to make history. The proletariat, he argued, was destined to be the 'grave digger' of capitalism. It would fulfil this destiny once it had achieved 'class consciousness' (see p. 199) and become aware of its genuine class interests, thus specifically recognising the fact of its own exploitation. The proletariat would therefore be transformed from a 'class *in*-itself' (an economically defined category) to a 'class *for*-itself' (a revolutionary force). This, Marx, believed, would be a consequence of the deepening crises of capitalism and the declining material conditions, or immiseration, of the working class.

The Marxist two-class model has, however, been discredited by the failure of Marx's predictions to materialise, and by declining evidence of class struggle, at least in advanced capitalist societies. Even by the end of the nineteenth century, it was becoming clear that the class structure of industrial societies was becoming increasingly complex, and that it varies from system to system, as well as over time. Max Weber (see p. 194) was one of the first to take stock of this shift, developing a theory of stratification that acknowledged economic or class differences but also took account of the importance of political parties and social status. In drawing attention to status as a 'social estimation of honour' expressed in the lifestyle of a group, Weber helped to prepare the ground for the modern notion of occupational class, widely used by social and political scientists. Modern Marxists have also attempted to refine the crude two-class model. Whilst still emphasising the importance of wealth ownership, they have been prepared to accept that an 'intermediate' class of managers and technicians has emerged, and that there are internal divisions within both the bourgeoisie and the proletariat. Rivalry, for instance, exists between finance and industrial capital, between big business and small employers, and between workers with supervisory responsibilities and ones who are merely supervised.

For some, however, the late twentieth century has been characterised by the final eclipse of class politics. By the 1960s, neo-Marxists such as Herbert Marcuse

Concept

Social class

A class is, broadly, a group of people who share a similar social and economic position. For Marxists, class is linked to economic power, which is defined by the individual's relationship to the means of production. From this perspective, class divisions are thus divisions between 'capital' and 'labour', that is, between the owners of productive wealth (the bourgeoisie) and those who live off the sale of their labour power (the proletariat). Non-Marxist definitions of class are usually based on income and status (see p. 179) differences between occupational groups. An example is the distinction between 'middle' class, white-collar (or nonmanual) workers and 'working' class, blue-collar (or manual) workers. A more sophisticated marketing-based distinction is sometimes made between professionals (class A), managers (B), clerical workers (C1), skilled manual workers (C2), semiskilled and unskilled workers (D), and those who are unemployed, unavailable for work, or unable to work (E).

Concept

Status

Status is a person's position within a hierarchical order. It is characterised by the person's role, rights and duties in relation to the other members of that order. As status is a compound of factors such as honour, prestige, standing and power, it is more difficult to determine than an essentially economic category such as class. Also, because it is a measure of social respect (that is, a measure of whether someone is 'higher' or 'lower' on a social scale), it is more subjective. While traditional societies typically possess clear and fixed status hierarchies, these are more fluid in modern industrial societies in which status often correlates, if imprecisely, with wealth and occupation. Status hierarchies nevertheless continue to operate in relation to factors such as family background, education, gender, and race and ethnicity.

(see p. 54) were lamenting the deradicalisation of the urban proletariat, and looked instead to the revolutionary potential of students, women, ethnic minorities and the third world. The traditional link between socialism and the working class was formally abandoned in works such as André Gorz's *Farewell to the Working Class* (1982). In the same period, studies of electoral behaviour drew attention to the process of class dealignment (see p. 226), a weakening of the relationship between social class and party support. It appeared that voting was becoming an increasingly issue-based activity that reflects an individual's calculation of his or her material self-interest rather than any sense of class solidarity.

Most commentators agree that behind the declining political significance of class lies the phenomenon of deindustrialisation. **Deindustrialisation** is the decline of traditional labour-intensive industries such as the coal, steel and shipbuilding industries. These tended to be characterised by a solidaristic culture rooted in clear political loyalties and, usually, strong union organisation. In contrast, the expanding service sectors of economies foster more individualistic and instrumentalist attitudes. In *The Second Industrial Divide: Possibilities for Prosperity* (1984), Piore and Sabel suggested that these changes are part of a transition from a 'Fordist' to a 'post-Fordist' era. The eclipse of the system of mass production and mass consumption, the chief characteristics of Fordism, has produced more pluralised class formations. In the political realm, this has been reflected in the decline of class-based political parties, and in the emergence of new social movements that articulate concern about, for example, feminism, world peace, animal rights and environmental protection.

Who are the underclass?

Reports of the death of class have nevertheless been exaggerated. When issued by socialists, they reflect bitter disillusionment, but when issued by liberals and conservatives, they are little more than wishful thinking. Modern industrial, or even post-Fordist, societies are classless neither in the Marxist sense of collectively owned wealth, nor in the liberal sense of genuine equality of opportunity. For example, in the UK in 1990, the richest 10 per cent of the population owned 51 per cent of the wealth, and 12 000 000 people (22 per cent of the population) lived in households with a total income of less than 50 per cent of the national average (*Social Trends*, 1993). What has happened, however, is that new patterns of deprivation and disadvantage have emerged in place of the class divisions of old.

One of the most influential attempts to discuss this shift and its political implications is found in J. K. Galbraith's *The Culture of Contentment* (1992). Galbraith pointed to the emergence in modern societies, at least amongst the politically active, of a 'contented majority' whose material affluence and economic security encourages them to be politically conservative. This contented majority, for instance, provides an electoral base for the anti-welfarist and tax-cutting policies that have become fashionable since the 1970s. The concentration of poverty and disadvantage amongst a minority of the population is reflected in the development of a so-called 'two-thirds, one-third' society, or, as refined by Will Hutton (1995) for the UK, a 'three-fifths, two-fifths' society. Debate about the nature of social inequality has therefore increasingly focused on what is fashionably called the 'underclass'.

The term underclass is both poorly defined and politically controversial. In its broadest sense, it refers to those who suffer from multiple deprivation (unemployment or low pay, poor housing, inadequate education and so on) and are socially marginalised: 'the excluded'. Right-wing commentators such as Charles Murray

---

Concept

Fordism, post-Fordism

Fordism and post-Fordism are terms that are used to explain the economic, political and cultural transformation of modern society by reference to the changing form and organisation of production. Fordism refers to the large-scale mass-production methods pioneered by Henry Ford in Detroit in the USA. Using techniques widely imitated until the 1960s, Ford relied on mechanisation and highly regimented production-line labour processes to produce standardised, relatively cheap products. Fordist societies were largely structured by solidaristic class loyalties. Post-Fordism emerged as the result of the introduction of more flexible microelectronics-based machinery that gave individual workers greater autonomy and made possible innovations such as subcontracting and batch production. Post-Fordism has been linked to decentralisation in the workplace, social and political fragmentation, and a greater emphasis on choice and individuality.

Deindustrialisation: A contraction of the economy's manufacturing base, reflected in the decline of 'heavy' industries.

John Kenneth Galbraith (born 1908)

Canadian economist and social theorist. Following wartime service as the Director of the US Strategic Bombing Survey, Galbraith became a professor of economics at Harvard University. He served as the American Ambassador to India in 1961–63. Galbraith is closely identified with the Democratic Party, and he is perhaps the leading modern exponent of Keynesian economics (he is certainly its most innovative advocate). He has become one of the USA's most eminent social commentators. His major works include *The Affluent Society* (1958), *The New Industrial State* (1967), and *The Culture of Contentment* (1992).

(1984), however, explain the emergence of the underclass largely in terms of welfare dependency and personal inadequacy. From this perspective, welfare is seen as the cause of disadvantage, not its cure. In this view, a 'culture of dependency' has developed amongst those classified as unemployed, disadvantaged or handicapped, weakening individual initiative and robbing them of self-respect and personal responsibility. Murray further argued that, as welfare relieves women of dependence upon 'breadwinning' men, it is a major cause of family breakdown, producing an underclass increasingly made up of single mothers and fatherless children. In *The Bell Curve: Intelligence and Class Structure in American Life* (1995), written with Richard Herrnstein, Murray went further still, linking social deprivation to what he alleged to be the innate inferiority of American blacks in particular.

Left-wing commentators, on the other hand, tend to define the underclass in terms of structural disadvantage and the changing balance of the global economy. From their point of view, the chief problem is long-term unemployment, and the apparent incapacity of many modern economies, faced by technological change and stiffer international competition, to provide jobs for large numbers of their citizens. For Galbraith, the underclass is a 'functional underclass', which results from the need in all industrial countries for a pool of low-paid workers to do the jobs that the more fortunate reject as distasteful or demeaning. As this need is often met by ethnic minorities and immigrant labour, the underclass is not uncommonly doubly disadvantaged, suffering from both social exclusion and racial prejudice.

Race

Racial and ethnic divisions are a significant feature of many modern societies. There is nothing new, however, in the link between race and politics. The first explicitly racialist (see p. 114) political theories were developed in the nineteenth century against the background of European imperialism. Works such as Gobineau's *Essay on the Inequality of Human Races* (Gobineau, [1855] 1970) and H. S. Chamberlain's *The Foundations of the Nineteenth Century* ([1899] 1913) attempted to provide a pseudoscientific justification for the dominance of the 'white' races of Europe and North America over the 'black', 'brown' and 'yellow' peoples of Africa and Asia. Anti-Semitic (see p. 115) political parties and movements emerged in countries such as Germany, Austria and Russia in the late nineteenth century. The most grotesque twentieth-century manifestation of such racialism was found in German Nazism,

Concept

Race

Race refers to physical or genetic differences amongst humankind that supposedly distinguish one group of people from another on biological grounds such as skin and hair colour, physique, and facial features. A race is thus a group of people who share a common ancestry and 'one blood'. The term is, however, controversial, both scientifically and politically. Scientific evidence suggests that there is no such thing as 'race' in the sense of a species-type difference between peoples. Politically, racial categorisation is commonly based on cultural stereotypes, and is simplistic at best and pernicious at worst. The term ethnicity (see p. 132) is sometimes preferred because it refers to cultural and social differences that are not necessarily rooted in biology.

which, through the so-called 'Final Solution', attempted to carry out the extermination of European Jewry. Apartheid (Afrikaans for 'apartness') in South Africa consisted of the strict segregation of whites and nonwhites between the election of the Nationalist party in 1948 and the establishment of a nonracial democracy under the leadership of the African National Congress (ANC) in 1994. Elsewhere, racialism has been kept alive through campaigns against immigration, organised, for example, by the British National Party (BNP) and Le Pen's National Front (FN) in France.

Very different forms of racial or ethnic politics have developed out of the struggle against colonialism in particular, and as a result of racial discrimination and disadvantage in general. Ethnic minorities in many western societies are poorly represented within political elites and suffer from higher levels of unemployment and social deprivation than do indigenous or white populations. For instance, 31.9 per cent of black Americans live below the government's poverty line, compared with 8.8 per cent of American whites (Peele *et al.*, 1994:260). This conjunction of racial and social disadvantage has generated various styles of political activism.

The 1960s witnessed the emergence in the USA of both a civil-rights movement which, under the leadership of Martin Luther King (1929–68), practised nonviolent protest, and a militant Black Power movement which advocated revolutionary struggle and, in the case of Malcolm X (1926–65) and the Black Muslims, preached racial segregation. Other organisations have attempted to mobilise anti-racism and counter the rise of fascist movements through marches, protests and other demonstrations. In the UK, this task has been undertaken by the Anti-Nazi League, which was formed in the 1970s to combat the National Front and was reformed in the 1990s to confront the BNP. SOS Racisme emerged in France in the 1980s to offer similar resistance against the FN. Such action is commonly undertaken by organisations outside the conventional party system, because mainstream parties have generally feared that, by openly confronting racism, they risk weakening their electoral base.

Gender

Social divisions based on gender or sex have traditionally attracted less attention than those rooted in, for example, social class. Researchers and academics, who were overwhelmingly male, either failed to recognise the underrepresentation of women within their own ranks and in all dominant positions in society, or merely assumed that this was natural and inevitable. The rise of 'second wave' feminism in the 1960s did much to redress this oversight, and to establish a clearer awareness of the political significance of gender. Despite the steps taken since the 1960s to reduce gender-based inequality, it is estimated by the United Nations that women worldwide contribute 66 per cent of the hours worked, earn about 10 per cent of the world's income, and own only 1 per cent of the world's property. In the UK, fewer than 4 per cent of the members of the boards of major companies are women. Even though women gained the right to vote in 1918, only 9 per cent (around 60) of Members of Parliament were women in 1996.

In more traditional societies, such as Japan, still-powerful informal (and sometimes formal) rules mean that women have to leave employment and return to the home on getting married, becoming pregnant, or reaching the age of 30. In Islamic states, women are required to wear the veil and conform to other dress codes. They are sometimes subject to enforced seclusion in the home, and may be excluded altogether from political life. Even in progressive Scandinavia, where women have made the most significant breakthroughs in political representation, women constitute only one-quarter to one-third of the members of the national assemblies.

In the eyes of radical feminists, such as Kate Millett (1970) and Mary Daly (1978), gender divisions are the deepest and most politically significant of all social cleavages. All contemporary and historical societies are seen to be characterised by patriarchy (see p. 92), that is, the dominance of men and subordination of women, usually rooted in the rule of the husband–father within the family. From this perspective, nothing short of a 'sexual revolution' that would fundamentally transform cultural and personal relationships as well as economic and political structures could bring an end to gender inequality.

Most women's political organisations, however, have adopted a liberal or reformist stance. They have set out to tackle eradicable inequalities in public life, such as the under-representation of women in senior political, managerial and professional posts, and the injustices that flow from anti-abortion legislation and inadequate childcare and welfare support for women. This reflects their belief that such goals can be achieved through a gradual process of incremental reform rather than through a 'sex war' between women and men. The most advanced such organisations have developed in the USA: the National Organisation for Women (NOW) (founded in 1966), the National Women's Political Caucus (NWPC), and Emily's List. Their tactics have included an attempt to exploit the so-called gender gap (the difference in voting behaviour between women and men) to get more women elected to Congress and the state legislatures. Although their record in this respect has been modest, they have nevertheless increased the prominence of women's rights issues. For example, they have succeeded in the 1980s and 1990s in resisting a shift towards a pro-life position by the Supreme Court.

■ Summary

◆ Economics influences politics at almost every level. Parties compete for power by outbidding each other with promises to increase growth, reduce inflation and so on. Voting behaviour is largely shaped by class divisions and social cleavages. Election results are invariably influenced by the state of the economy. Ideological divisions have also traditionally revolved around questions about ownership and economic organisation.

◆ Traditionally, capitalism and socialism were seen as clearly distinct economic forms. Capitalism was characterised by general commodity production, the private ownership of wealth, and the market organisation of economic life. Socialism featured a system of public or common ownership that was based on planning, and it was supposedly geared to the satisfaction of human needs rather than market demand.

◆ Neither capitalism nor socialism has ever existed in its 'pure' form, however. The capitalist systems of the world include those that emphasise enterprise and market individualism, those that recognise the importance of social justice, and those that are based on collaborative long-term relationships. Socialist systems have either practised state collectivism or attempted to find an accommodation with the market in the form of managed or regulated capitalism.

Concept

Gender

Although the terms gender and sex are often used interchangeably in everyday language, the distinction between them is crucial to social and political theory. In this context, the term gender is used to refer to social and cultural distinctions between males and females, while the term sex is used to highlight biological, and therefore ineradicable, differences between men and women. Gender is therefore a social construct, usually based on stereotypes of 'feminine' and 'masculine' behaviour. Feminist theories typically highlight the distinction in order to demonstrate that physical or biological differences (sexual differences) need not mean that women and men must have different social roles and positions (gender differences). In short, the quest for gender equality reflects the belief that sexual differences have no social or political significance. Antifeminist positions are often rooted in a denial of the distinction between gender and sex, implying, quite simply, that 'biology is destiny'.

◆ All market systems are regulated to some extent. Supporters of regulation argue that economic management is essential to counter an inevitable tendency towards market instability, which can lead to slumps and soaring unemployment. Opponents, however, warn that economic management can upset the fragile balance of the market, undermine competition and efficiency, and result in uncontrollable inflation.

◆ The structure of society, and particularly its divisions, influences politics in a number of ways. The distribution of wealth conditions the nature of state power. Society influences public opinion and the political culture. Social conflict helps to generate change through either reform or revolution. The social structure shapes all forms of political behaviour and participation.

◆ Class, race and gender divisions are the most politically significant of the social cleavages in modern society. Class politics may have been diluted by the emergence of post-Fordism, but still persist, in particular because of the influence of the 'underclass'. The growth of the civil-rights and women's movements has ensured that once-ignored race and gender divisions are now recognised as being as significant as class-based ones.

▌ Questions for discussion

▶ Why do political questions so often boil down to economic issues? Is this healthy?

▶ What type of capitalist system is likely to be the most viable in the twenty-first century?

▶ Are socialist economic models any longer of relevance?

▶ What would be the features of an ecologically sustainable economy?

▶ Has class conflict in modern societies been resolved or merely suppressed?

▶ To what extent has the recognition of racial and gender divisions produced meaningful political change?

▌ Further reading

Brown, M. B. *Models in Political Economy: A Guide to the Arguments* (2nd ed.) (Harmondsworth: Penguin, 1995). An accessible and comprehensive account of the various economic systems and the economic factors that lie behind social and political problems.

Hampden-Turner, C. and F. Trompenaars, *The Seven Cultures of Capitalism* (New York: Doubleday, 1993). A fascinating and authoritative overview of the diverse range of capitalist forms.

Rush, M. *Politics and Society: An Introduction to Political Sociology* (Hemel Hempstead: Harvester Wheatsheaf, 1992). A comprehensive introduction to the relationship between political and social institutions, and between social and political behaviour.

For references on societal divisions, see the following: (Saunders, 1990) on social class, (Rex and Mason, 1992) on race and ethnicity, and (McDowell and Pringle, 1992) on gender divisions.

Political Culture and Legitimacy

> 'The strongest is never strong enough unless he turns right into might and obedience into duty.'
>
> JEAN-JACQUES ROUSSEAU *Social Contract* (1862)

Much of politics takes place in our heads, that is, it is shaped by our ideas, values and assumptions about how society should be organised, and our expectations, hopes and fears about government. At the end of the day, what we believe about the society in which we live may be more important than the reality of its power structure and the actual distribution of resources and opportunities within it. Perception may not only be more important than reality; in practical terms, perception may *be* reality. This highlights the vital role played by what is called political culture. People's beliefs, symbols and values structure both their attitude to the political process, and, crucially, their view of the regime in which they live, most particularly, whether or not they regard their regime as rightful or legitimate. Legitimacy is thus the key to political stability, and it is nothing less than the source of a regime's survival and success.

The principal issues addressed in this chapter are the following:

Contents

Key issues

▶ How do individuals and groups acquire their political attitudes and values?

▶ Do democratic regimes depend on the existence of a distinctive 'civic culture'?

▶ Are modern societies characterised by free competition between values and ideas, or by a 'dominant' culture?

▶ How do regimes maintain legitimacy?

▶ Are modern societies facing a crisis of legitimation?

▶ What happens when legitimacy collapses? Why do revolutions occur?

Political culture

Culture, in its broadest sense, is the way of life of a people. Sociologists and anthropologists tend to distinguish between 'culture' and 'nature', the former encompassing that which is passed on from one generation to the next by learning, rather than through biological inheritance. Political scientists, however, use the term in a narrower sense to refer to a people's psychological orientation, political culture being the 'pattern of orientations' to political objects such as parties, government, the constitution, expressed in beliefs, symbols and values. Political culture differs from public opinion in that it is fashioned out of long-term values rather than simply people's reactions to specific policies and problems.

Political socialisation: The process through which individuals acquire political beliefs and values, and by which these are transmitted from generation to generation.

■ Political culture: politics in the mind

Political thinkers through the ages have acknowledged the importance of attitudes, values and beliefs. However, these past thinkers did not see them as part of a 'political culture'. Burke (see p. 45), for instance, wrote about custom and tradition, Marx (see p. 51) about ideology, and Herder (see p. 105) about national spirit. All of them nevertheless agreed about the vital role that values and beliefs play in promoting the stability and survival of a regime. Interest amongst political scientists in the idea of political culture emerged in the 1950s and 1960s as new techniques of behavioural analysis displaced more traditional, institutional approaches to the subject. The classic work in this respect was Almond and Verba's *The Civic Culture* (1963), which used opinion surveys to analyse political attitudes and democracy in five countries: the USA, the UK, West Germany, Italy and Mexico. This work was stimulated in part by a desire to explain the collapse of representative government in interwar Italy, Germany and elsewhere, and the failure of democracy in many newly independent developing states after 1945. Although interest in political culture faded in the 1970s and 1980s, the debate was revitalised in the 1990s as a result of efforts in eastern Europe to construct democracy out of the ashes of communism, and growing anxiety in mature democracies, such as the USA, about the apparent decline of social capital and civic engagement.

Political socialisation

Political attitudes and beliefs clearly do not drop from the sky like rain; they are 'acquired' through learning and social experience. The process through which this happens is usually called **political socialisation**. However, the idea of political socialisation has been subject to much dispute and criticism. Although everyone accepts that political attitudes and behaviour are in some way shaped by learning and by the broader social environment, there is fierce disagreement about how this process occurs and what its political significance might be.

Interest in the socialisation process arises from two very different sources. Radicals and Marxists have long emphasised the degree to which the ideas of a 'ruling' or economically dominant class pervade society, encouraging subordinate classes to accept the existing distribution of wealth and resources. This is political socialisation as ideological domination. In this view, the socialisation process is seen as essentially conscious or deliberate. It amounts, in its crudest form, to a process of indoctrination that takes place throughout a person's life and is carried out by institutions such as the media and the state. Conventional political scientists, however, tend to understand socialisation in the light of the behavioural revolution of the 1950s and 1960s. Influenced by the picture of human nature as essentially malleable, they look to the social environment to explain individual and group behaviour. Socialisation, from this perspective, is typically unplanned and informal; it operates largely through the agency of the family, and shapes individuals during childhood when the human organism is a 'black box' waiting to be filled. Political socialisation is therefore portrayed as the transmission of values and beliefs from one generation to the next in the interests of social cohesion and political stability, rather than in the cause of economic subordination.

Enthusiasm about political socialisation has dimmed since the 1960s, in part because it has proved frustratingly difficult to demonstrate empirically how the process works. Whether socialisation is formal or informal, deliberate or unplanned, it operates through a linkage between social factors on the one hand, and attitudes and behaviour on the other. Empirical political scientists have, at best, been able to establish *correlations* between particular social factors and specific forms of political behaviour, for instance, between social class and voting behaviour. Although this may enable predictions to be made (in this case about the outcome of elections), it does not amount to an *explanation*. To note that a particular social factor is statistically 'significant' is not to explain how or why it exerts an influence. The limitation of theories of political socialisation is therefore that, in common with behaviouralism itself, they fail to take account of personality and individual experience. For good or ill, human beings are not simply robots programmed by their social environment to behave as instructed.

A further problem is that there is no reason to assume that the various social agents (family, school, peer group, work group, media and so on) are part of an interlinked process that tends to produce a homogeneous political culture. While one agent may reinforce values and attitudes acquired through another, it may just as easily stimulate conflict, the result being a political culture that is fragmented or pluralistic. Moreover, the impact of the various agents of socialisation, as well as the attitudes and values they impart, vary from society to society and over time. The influence of these agents is notoriously difficult to quantify because the context they provide is often as important as the content of the message they transmit. For instance, what schools teach about authority, discipline and obedience is perhaps less significant than the ways in which lessons are organised and the teachers behave (the so-called 'hidden curriculum'). This is what Marshall McLuhan (1911–80) meant when he pointed out in relation to modern mass communications that 'the medium is the message'. The agents of political socialisation that have been most widely discussed are the following:

- the family
- education
- religion
- the mass media
- government.

The family is often seen as the agent that accomplishes 'primary' socialisation, providing individuals, in late childhood and adolescence in particular, with a framework of political sympathies and leanings that adult experience may modify or deepen, but seldom radically transform. In the past, this was certainly demonstrated by habitual patterns of voting behaviour linked to family background (Butler and Stokes, 1969), but the link has been weakened with the growth of instrumental voting, shaped by the pursuit of self-interest. The significance of education results from the susceptibility of the young, unformed and impressionable, to external influences and pressures. Education is, after all, a process of formal tuition, but it may also involve important informal learning processes. Social thinkers such as Paul Goodman (1911–72) and Ivan Illich (born 1926), for instance, have argued that formal schooling routinised unthinking obedience, which encouraged them to call for the 'deschooling' of society. Religion may have declined in significance with the advance of secularisation, but, in certain parts of the world, has acquired renewed

Focus on . . .

The impact of the mass media

The media comprise those societal institutions that are concerned with the production and distribution of all forms of knowledge, information and entertainment. The 'mass' character of the mass media is derived from the fact that the media channel communication towards a large and undifferentiated audience using relatively advanced technology. Grammatically and politically, the mass media are plural. Different messages may be put out by the 'broadcast' media (television and radio) and the 'print' media (newspapers and magazines). Similarly, tabloid and broadsheet newspapers may exhibit different sympathies. Models of the political influence of the mass media include the following:

- **Pluralist model:** The media is a forum that allows all political views to be debated and discussed, thus promoting democracy and checking government power.
- **Market model:** The media does not impose its views, but merely reflects those of its audience, perhaps pandering to the appetites and prejudices of the masses.
- **Elite-values model:** The media articulates the values of groups disproportionately represented amongst its senior professionals, be they liberal intellectuals, middle class conservatives, or men.
- **Dominant-ideology model:** The media propagates bourgeois ideas and maintains capitalist hegemony, in line with the interests of major corporations and media moguls.

importance through the emergence of fundamentalist sects and movements. This has been especially evident in the case of political Islam. Even when religion no longer lays down the organisational principles of society, it may nevertheless keep alive subcultures that conflict with more widely held values and attitudes, as occurs with the Mormons, the Jehovah's Witnesses and Islam in the West.

As most political information is now disseminated by television, radio, newspapers and magazines, much of the modern debate about socialisation focuses on the role of the mass media. When the communications system is subject to formal political control, as in state socialist, fascist or authoritarian regimes, the media becomes little more than a **propaganda** machine. Nevertheless, despite their formal independence from government and the existence of pluralism and debate, both left-wing and right-wing critics have argued that the liberal–democratic media convey a more subtle but no less effective political message. Government is inevitably an agent of political socialisation. Some governments explicitly acknowledge this as a key task. Fascist and Nazi regimes, for instance, set out to create 'fascist' or 'new' man, while the USSR aimed to construct 'socialist' man. Although in democratic states such ambitions are constrained by constitutional devices and party competition, all governments recognise that their capacity to remain in power depends, in part, on their ability to construct a value system that commands broad popular support. Conservative dominance in the UK in the 1980s and 1990s was thus linked to the spread of 'Thatcherite' values such as freedom of choice, individual responsibility and self-reliance.

Propaganda: Information disseminated in a deliberate attempt to shape opinions and, possibly, stimulate political action; communication as manipulation.

The civic culture

Debate about the nature of political culture has often focused on the idea of civic culture, usually associated with the writings of Almond and Verba (1963, 1980). Almond and Verba set out to identify the political culture that most effectively upheld democratic politics. They identified three general types of political culture: participant culture, subject culture and parochial culture.

A *participant* political culture is one in which citizens pay close attention to politics and regard popular participation as both desirable and effective. A *subject* political culture is characterised by more passivity amongst citizens, and the recognition that they have only a very limited capacity to influence government. A *parochial* political culture is marked by the absence of a sense of citizenship, with people identifying with their locality rather than the nation, and having neither the desire nor the ability to participate in politics. Although Almond and Verba accepted that a participant culture came closest to the democratic ideal, they argued that the 'civic culture' is a blend of all three in that it reconciles the participation of citizens in the political process with the vital necessity for government to govern. Democratic stability, in their view, is underpinned by a political culture that is characterised by a blend of activity and passivity on the part of citizens, and a balance between obligation and performance on the part of government.

In their initial study (1963), Almond and Verba concluded that the UK came closest to the civic culture, exhibiting both participant and subject features. In other words, while the British thought that they could influence government, they were also willing to obey authority. The USA also scored highly, its relative weakness being that, as participant attitudes predominated over subject ones, Americans were not particularly law-abiding. The difficulty of building or rebuilding a civic culture was underlined by the examples of both West Germany and Italy. A decade and a half after the collapse of fascism, neither country appeared to have a strong participant culture; while the subject culture was dominant in Germany, parochial attitudes remained firmly entrenched in Italy. Almond and Verba's later study (1980) highlighted a number of shifts, notably declining national pride and confidence in the UK and the USA, which contrasted with a rise in civic propensities in Germany.

Robert Putnam (1996) discussed such trends in terms of the USA's declining 'social capital', understood in terms of networks, norms and trust, and highlighted the emergence of a 'post-civic' generation. This was demonstrated by a 25–50 per cent drop in the number of voluntary clubs and associations since 1965, and by sharp declines in attendance at public, town and school meetings, as well as membership of, and work done for, political parties. He dismissed geographical mobility and changing family structures as explanations of the passing of the 'long civic generation'. Instead, he identified television as the culprit. In particular, he blamed television for privatising leisure time, misshaping social perceptions and reducing achievement levels in children.

The civic-culture approach to the study of political attitudes and values has, however, been widely criticised. In the first place, its model of the psychological dispositions that make for a stable democracy is highly questionable. In particular, the emphasis on passivity and the recognition that deference to authority is healthy has been criticised by those who argue that political participation is the very stuff of democratic government. Almond and Verba suggested a 'sleeping dogs' theory of democratic culture that implies that low participation indicates broad satisfaction

Hegemony

Hegemony (from the Greek *hegemonia*, meaning 'leader') is, in its simplest sense, the ascendancy or domination of one element of a system over others (an example being the predominance of a state within a league or confederation). In Marxist theory, the term is used in a more technical and specific sense. In the writings of Antonio Gramsci (see p. 191), hegemony refers to the ability of a dominant class to exercise power by winning the *consent* of those it subjugates, as an alternative to the use of *coercion*. As a noncoercive form of class rule, hegemony is typically understood as a cultural or ideological process that operates through the dissemination of bourgeois values and beliefs throughout society. However, it also has a political and economic dimension: consent can be manipulated by pay increases or by political or social reform.

Bourgeois ideology: A Marxist term, denoting ideas and theories that serve the interests of the bourgeoisie by disguising the contradictions of capitalist society.

with government, which politicians, in turn, will be anxious to maintain. On the other hand, when less than half the adult population bothers to vote, as regularly occurs in the USA, this could simply reflect widespread alienation and ingrained disadvantage.

Secondly, the civic-culture thesis rests on the unproven assumption that political attitudes and values shape behaviour, and not the other way round. In short, a civic culture may be more a consequence of democracy than its cause. If this is the case, political culture may provide an index of the health of democracy, but it cannot be seen as a means of promoting stable democratic rule. Finally, Almond and Verba's approach tends to treat political culture as homogenous, that is, as little more than a cipher for national culture or national character. In so doing, it pays little attention to political subcultures and tends to disguise fragmentation and social conflict. In contrast, radical approaches to political culture tend to highlight the significance of social divisions, such as those based on class, race and gender (see Chapter 9).

Ideological hegemony

A very different view of the role and nature of political culture has been developed within the Marxist tradition. Although Marx portrayed capitalism as a system of class exploitation and oppression operating through the ownership of the means of production, he also acknowledged the power of ideas, values and beliefs. As Marx and Engels put it in *The German Ideology* ([1846]1970:64), 'the ideas of the ruling class are in every epoch the ruling ideas, i.e. the class which is the ruling *material* force of society, is at the same time the ruling *intellectual* force'. In Marx's view, ideas and culture are part of a 'superstructure' that is conditioned or determined by the economic 'base', the mode of production.

These ideas have provided Marxism with two theories of culture. The first suggests that culture is essentially class-specific: as members of a class share the same experiences and have a common economic position and interests, they are likely to have broadly similar ideas, values and beliefs. In Marx's words, 'it is not the consciousness of men that determines their existence, but their social existence that determines their consciousness'. Proletarian culture and ideas can therefore be expected to differ markedly from bourgeois ones. The second theory of culture emphasises the degree to which the ideas of the ruling class (what Marx referred to as 'ideology') pervade society and become the 'ruling ideas' of the age. In this view, political culture, or even civic culture, is thus nothing more than **bourgeois ideology**. What is important about this view is that it sees culture, values and beliefs as a form of power. From the Marxist perspective, the function of ideology is to reconcile subordinate classes to their exploitation and oppression by propagating myths, delusions and falsehoods (in Engels' words, 'false consciousness'). Later Marxists have understood this process in terms of bourgeois 'hegemony'.

Modern Marxists have been quick to acknowledge that in no sense do the 'ruling ideas' of the bourgeoisie monopolise intellectual and cultural life in a capitalist society, excluding all rival views. Rather, they accept that cultural, ideological and political competition does exist, but stress that this competition is unequal. Quite simply, ideas and values that uphold the capitalist order have an overwhelming advantage over ideas and values that question or challenge it. Such ideological hegemony may, in fact, be successful precisely because it operates behind the illusion of free speech, open competition and political pluralism, what Herbert Marcuse (see p. 54) termed 'repressive tolerance'.

Antonio Gramsci (1891–1937)

Italian Marxist and social theorist. The son of a minor public official. Gramsci joined the Socialist Party in 1913, becoming in 1921 the General Secretary of the newly formed Italian Communist Party. Although an elected member of parliament, he was imprisoned by Mussolini in 1926. He remained in prison until his death. His *Prison Notebooks* (Gramsci, 1971), written in 1929–35, tried to counterbalance the emphasis within orthodox Marxism on 'scientific' determinism by stressing the importance of the political and intellectual struggle. Although proponents of Eurocommunism have claimed him as an influence, he remained throughout his life a Leninist and a revolutionary.

The most influential twentieth-century exponent of this view was Antonio Gramsci. Gramsci drew attention to the degree to which the class system is upheld not simply by unequal economic and political power, but also by bourgeois hegemony. This consists of the spiritual and cultural supremacy of the ruling class, brought about through the spread of bourgeois values and beliefs via 'civil society': the media, the churches, youth movements, trade unions and so forth. What makes this process so insidious is that it extends beyond formal learning and education into the very common sense of the age. The significance of Gramsci's analysis is that, in order for socialism to be achieved, a 'battle of ideas' has to be waged through which proletarian principles, values and theories displace, or at least challenge, bourgeois ideas.

The Marxist view of culture as ideological power rests on the distinction between subjective or *felt* interests (what people think they want) and objective or *real* interests (what people would want if they could make independent and informed choices). This draws attention to what Stephen Lukes (1974:27) called a radical view of power (see p. 11): 'A exercises power over B when A affects B in a manner contrary to B's interests'. Such a view of political culture has, however, attracted considerable criticism. Some have argued that it is unwarrantedly patronising to suggest that the values and beliefs of ordinary people have been foisted upon them by manipulation and indoctrination. The acceptance of capitalist values and beliefs by the working classes may, for instance, merely reflect their perception that capitalism works.

The dominant-ideology model of political culture may also overstate the degree of homogeneity in the values and beliefs of modern societies. Whilst a 'ruling' ideology may provide a dominant class with self-belief and a sense of purpose, it is less clear, as Abercrombie, Hill and Turner (1980) argued, that subordinate classes have been successfully integrated into this value system. Finally, the Marxist view, which purports to establish a link between unequal class power and cultural and ideological bias, may do nothing more than describe a tendency found in all societies for powerful groups to propagate self-serving ideas. Whether this constitutes a dominant value *system*, in which a coherent and consistent message is disseminated through the mass media, schools, the churches and so on, is rather more questionable.

Traditional values or a postmaterial culture?

One of the most enduring debates about political culture concerns the importance of what are usually portrayed as 'traditional values'. These are values and beliefs that

Michael Oakeshott (1901–90)

UK political philosopher. Oakeshott was a professor of political science at the London School of Economics from 1951 until his retirement in 1968. His collection of essays *Rationalism in Politics and Other Essays* (1962) and his more systematic work of political philosophy *On Human Conduct* (1975) are often seen as major contributions to conservative traditionalism. By highlighting the importance of civil association and insisting upon the limited province of politics, he also developed themes closely associated with liberal thought. Though often seen as an advocate of a non-ideological style of politics, Oakeshott influenced many of the thinkers of the New Right.

have supposedly been passed down from earlier generations and so constitute a kind of cultural bedrock. Conservative politicians regularly call for such values to be 'strengthened' or 'defended', believing that they are the key to social cohesion and political stability. In the UK in the 1980s, for example, Margaret Thatcher called for the resurrection of what she called 'Victorian values', while John Major's ill-starred 'Back to Basics' initiative attempted much the same in the 1990s. In the USA, Ronald Reagan embraced the notion of the 'frontier ideology', harking back to the conquest of the American West and the virtues of self-reliance, hard work and adventurousness which he believed it exemplified. Not uncommonly, such values are linked to the family, the church and the nation, that is, to long-established institutions that supposedly embody the virtues of continuity and endurance.

Such a stance is supported by an important tradition of conservative social thought. Conservative thinkers have traditionally portrayed society as 'organic', that is, as a living entity within which each element is linked to every other element in a delicate balance. The 'social whole' is therefore more than simply a collection of its individual parts, and if any part is damaged the whole is threatened. Edmund Burke (see p. 45) referred to society as a partnership 'between those who are living, those who are dead and those who are to be born'. Tradition (see p. 195) thus reflects the accumulated wisdom of the past, in other words, beliefs and practices that have been 'tested by time' and have been proved to have worked.

In his essay 'Rationalism in Politics' (Oakeshott, 1962), Michael Oakeshott developed a further defence of continuity and tradition. Oakeshott argued that traditional values and established customs should be upheld and respected on account of their familiarity, which engenders a sense of reassurance, stability and security. This suggests that there is a general human disposition to favour tradition over innovation, the established over the new. To be a conservative, Oakeshott suggested, is 'to prefer the familiar to the unknown, to prefer the tried to the untried, fact to mystery, the actual to the possible, the limited to the unbound, the near to the distant, the sufficient to the super abundant, the convenient to the perfect, present laughter to utopian bliss' (Oakeshott, 1962:169).

The defence of traditional values and established beliefs has been one of the central themes of neoconservatism, advanced in the USA by social theorists such as Daniel Bell (1976) and Irving Kristol (1983), who have warned against the destruction of spiritual values brought about by both market pressures and the spread of permissiveness. The problem with this position, however, is that it assumes there is an authoritative moral system upon which order and stability can be based. The simple fact is that in modern multicultural and multireligious societies, it is doubtful whether any set of values can be regarded as authoritative. To define certain values as 'traditional', 'established' or 'majority' values may simply be an attempt to impose a particular moral system on the rest of society. Indeed, empirical evidence appears to support the view that political culture is becoming increasingly fragmented, and that modern societies are characterised by growing moral and cultural diversity.

According to Inglehart (1977, 1990), this shift is closely linked to the spread of affluence and to the growth, particularly amongst young people, of 'postmaterial' values. As new generations have grown up since the 1960s accustomed, in advanced industrial countries at least, to economic security and material well-being, 'traditional' ideas about subjects such as sex, marriage and personal conduct have been displaced by more 'liberal' or 'permissive' ones. At the same time, traditional political attitudes and allegiances have been weakened and sometimes replaced by growing interest in issues such as feminism, nuclear disarmament, animal rights and environmental protection. Post-Fordist (see p. 180) theorists argue that such cultural changes are irresistible, because they are linked to a wholesale shift in economic and political organisation that is bringing about a decline in deference and a rise of individualism.

> ### Concept
>
> ## Postmaterialism
>
> Postmaterialism is a theory that explains the nature of political concerns and values in terms of levels of economic development. It is loosely based on Abraham Maslow's (1908–70) 'hierarchy of needs', which places esteem and self-actualization above material or economic needs. Postmaterialism assumes that conditions of material scarcity breed egoistical and acquisitive values, meaning that politics is dominated by economic issues. However, in conditions of widespread prosperity, individuals express more interest in 'postmaterial' or 'quality of life' issues. These are typically concerned with morality, political justice and personal fulfilment, and include feminism, world peace, racial harmony, ecology and animal rights. Postmaterialism has been used to explain developments such as class dealignment (see p. 226) and the rise of new social movements.

Legitimacy and political stability

The issue of legitimacy, the rightfulness of a regime or system of rule, is linked to the oldest and one of the most fundamental of political debates, the problem of political obligation. Why should citizens feel obliged to acknowledge the authority of government? Do they have a duty to respect the state and obey its laws? In modern political debate, however, legitimacy is usually understood less in terms of moral obligations and more in terms of political behaviour and beliefs. In other words, it addresses not the question of why people *should* obey the state, in an abstract sense, but the question of why they *do* obey a particular state or system of rule. What are the conditions or processes that encourage them to see authority as rightful, and therefore underpin the stability of a regime? This reflects a shift from philosophy to sociology, but it also highlights the contested nature of the concept of legitimacy.

> ### Concept
>
> ## Legitimacy
>
> The term legitimacy (from the Latin *legitimare*, meaning 'to declare lawful') broadly means rightfulness. Legitimacy therefore confers on an order or command an authoritative or binding character, thus transforming power into authority (see p. 6). It differs from legality in that the latter does not necessarily guarantee that a government is respected or that its citizens acknowledge a duty of obedience. Political philosophers treat legitimacy as a moral or rational principle, the grounds on which governments may demand obedience from citizens. The *claim* to legitimacy is thus more important than the *fact* of obedience. Political scientists, however, usually see legitimacy in sociological terms, that is, as a willingness to comply with a system of rule regardless of how this is achieved. Following Weber, this view takes legitimacy to mean a *belief* in legitimacy, that is, a belief in the 'right to rule'.

Legitimising power

The classic contribution to the understanding of legitimacy as a sociological phenomenon was provided by Max Weber (see p. 194). Weber was concerned to

Max Weber (1864–1920)

German political economist and sociologist. Following a breakdown in 1898, Weber withdrew from academic teaching, but he continued to write and research until the end of his life. He was one of the founders of modern sociology, and he championed a scientific and value-free approach to scholarship. He also highlighted the importance to social action of meaning and consciousness. Weber's interests ranged from social stratification, law, power and organisation to religion. His most influential works include *The Protestant Ethic and the Spirit of Capitalism* (1902), *The Sociology of Religion* (1920) and *Economy and Society* (1922).

categorise particular 'systems of domination', and to identify in each case the basis on which legitimacy was established. He did this by constructing three ideal types (see p. 18) or conceptual models, which he hoped would help to make sense of the highly complex nature of political rule. These ideal types amount to three kinds of authority: traditional authority, charismatic authority and legal–rational authority. Each of these is characterised by a particular source of political legitimacy and thus different reasons that people may have for obeying a regime. In the process, Weber sought to understand the transformation of society itself, contrasting the systems of domination found in relatively simple traditional societies with those typically found in industrial and highly bureaucratic ones.

Weber's first type of political legitimacy is based on long-established customs and traditions. In effect, traditional authority is regarded as legitimate because it has 'always existed'; it has been sanctified by history because earlier generations had accepted it. Typically, it operates according to a body of concrete rules, that is, fixed and unquestioned customs, that do not need to be justified because they reflect the way things have always been. The most obvious examples of traditional authority are found amongst tribes or small groups in the form of patriarchalism (the domination of the father within the family or the 'master' over his servants) and gerontocracy (the rule of the aged, normally reflected in the authority of village 'elders'). Traditional authority is closely linked to hereditary systems of power and privilege, as reflected, for example, in the survival of dynastic rule in Saudi Arabia, Kuwait and Morocco. Although it is of marginal significance in advanced industrial societies, the survival of monarchy (see p. 324), albeit in a constitutional form, in the UK, Belgium, the Netherlands and Spain, for example, helps to shape political culture by keeping alive values such as deference, respect and duty.

Weber's second form of legitimate domination is charismatic authority. This form of authority is based on the power of an individual's personality, that is, on his or her 'charisma'. Owing nothing to a person's status, social position or office, charismatic authority operates entirely through the capacity of a leader to make a direct and personal appeal to followers as a kind of hero or saint. Although modern political leaders such as de Gaulle, Kennedy and Thatcher undoubtedly extended their authority through their personal qualities and capacity to inspire loyalty, this did not amount to charismatic legitimacy, because their authority was essentially based on the formal powers of the offices they held. Napoleon, Mussolini, Hitler,

Ayatollah Khomeini, Fidel Castro and Colonel Gaddafi are more appropriate examples.

However, charismatic authority is not simply a gift or a natural propensity; systems of personal rule are invariably underpinned by 'cults of personality' (see p. 333), the undoubted purpose of which is to 'manufacture' charisma. Nevertheless, when legitimacy is constructed largely or entirely through the power of a leader's personality, there are usually two consequences. The first is that, as charismatic authority is not based on formal rules or procedures, it often has no limits. The leader is a Messiah, who is infallible and unquestionable; the masses become followers or disciples, who are required only to submit and obey. Secondly, so closely is authority linked to a specific individual, that it is difficult for a system of personal rule to outlive its founding figure. This certainly applied in the case of the regimes of Napoleon, Mussolini and Hitler.

Weber's third type of political legitimacy, legal–rational, links authority to a clearly and legally defined set of rules. In Weber's view, legal–rational authority is the typical form of authority operating in most modern states. The power of a president, prime minister or government official is determined in the final analysis by formal, constitutional rules, which constrain or limit what an office holder is able to do. The advantage of this form of authority over both traditional and charismatic authority is that, as it is attached to an office rather than a person, it is far less likely to be abused or to give rise to injustice. Legal–rational authority therefore maintains limited government and, in addition, promotes efficiency through a rational division of labour. However, Weber also recognised a darker side to this type of political legitimacy. The price of greater efficiency would, he feared, be a more depersonalised and inhuman social environment typified by the relentless spread of bureaucratic (see p. 341) forms of organisation.

Although Weber's classification of types of legitimacy is still seen as relevant, it also has its limitations. One of these is that, in focusing on the legitimacy of a political regime or system of rule, it tells us little about the circumstances in which political authority is challenged as a result of unpopular policies or a discredited leader or government. For example, the anti-poll-tax campaign in the UK in 1990 undoubtedly indicated widespread popular hostility to the policy and contributed to the downfall of Prime Minister Margaret Thatcher in the November of that year. However, it did not amount to a loss of legitimacy, in the sense that it did not call the rightfulness of the political system into question. More significantly, as Beetham (1991) pointed out, to see legitimacy, as Weber did, as nothing more than a 'belief in legitimacy' is to ignore how it is brought about. This may leave the determination of legitimacy largely in the hands of the powerful,

---

Concept

Tradition

The term tradition encompasses anything handed down or transmitted from the past to the present (long-standing customs and practices, institutions, social or political systems, values and beliefs, and so on). Strictly speaking, tradition differs from reaction in that it denotes continuity with the past, rather than an attempt to 'turn the clock back' and re-establish the past. This continuity is usually understood to link the generations, although the line between the traditional and the merely fashionable is often indistinct. The term tradition has also been used to contrast 'traditional' societies and 'modern' societies, the former generally being seen to be structured on the basis of status (see p. 179) and by supposedly organic hierarchies, and the latter on the basis of contractual agreement and by democratic processes.

Concept

Charisma

Charisma was originally a theological term meaning the 'gift of grace'. This was the source of the power that Jesus exerted over his disciples, and the power attributed to saints in Catholic theology. As a sociopolitical phenomenon, however, charisma refers to charm or personal power: the capacity to establish leadership (see p. 330) through psychological control over others. Charismatic authority therefore has a near-mystical character and includes the ability to inspire loyalty, emotional dependence and even devotion. Although it is usually seen as a 'natural' capacity, all political leaders cultivate their charismatic qualities through propaganda, practised oratory, presentational skills and so on. Weber distinguished between *individual* charisma (linked to a person) and the charisma of *office* (linked to a position).

who may be able to 'manufacture' rightfulness through public-relations campaigns and the like.

Beetham suggested that power can only be said to be legitimate if three conditions are fulfilled. First, power must be exercised according to established rules, whether these are embodied in formal legal codes or informal conventions. Secondly, these rules must be justified in terms of the shared beliefs of the government and the governed. Thirdly, legitimacy must be demonstrated by an expression of consent on the part of the governed. For instance, the legitimacy of the UK system in 1990 was maintained through the recognition on the part of the public that, however unpopular policies and leaders might become, governments are elected to power, and can be elected out of it. This highlights two key features of the legitimation process. The first is the existence of elections and party competition, a system through which popular consent can be exercised (which is discussed in Chapters 11 and 12). The second is the existence of constitutional rules that broadly reflect how people feel they should be governed (which are examined in Chapter 14).

Legitimation crises

An alternative to the Weberian approach to legitimacy has been developed by neo-Marxist (see p. 90) theorists. While orthodox Marxists were inclined to dismiss legitimacy as bogus, seeing it as nothing more than a bourgeois myth, modern Marxists, following Gramsci, having acknowledged that capitalism is in part upheld by its ability to secure political support. Neo-Marxists such as Jürgen Habermas and Claus Offe (1984) have therefore focused attention not merely on the class system, but also on the machinery through which legitimacy is maintained (the democratic process, party competition, welfare and social reform, and so on). Nevertheless, they have also highlighted what they see as the inherent difficulty of legitimising a political system that is based on unequal class power. In *Legitimation Crisis* (1973), Habermas identified a series of 'crisis tendencies' within capitalist societies that make it difficult for them to maintain political stability through consent alone. At the heart of this tension, he argued, lie contradictions and conflicts between the logic of capitalist accumulation on the one hand, and the popular pressures which democratic politics unleashes on the other.

From this perspective, capitalist economies are seen to be bent on remorseless expansion, dictated by the pursuit of profit. However, the extension of political and social rights in an attempt to build legitimacy within such systems has stimulated countervailing pressures. In particular, the democratic process has led to escalating demands for social welfare as well as for increased popular participation and social equality. The resulting expansion of the state's responsibilities into economic and social life, and the inexorable rise of taxation and public spending, nevertheless constrain capitalist accumulation by restricting profit levels and discouraging enterprise. In Habermas's view, capitalist democracies cannot permanently satisfy both popular demands for social security and welfare rights and the requirements of a market economy based on private profit. Forced either to resist popular pressures or to risk economic collapse, such societies would find it increasingly difficult, and eventually impossible, to maintain legitimacy.

A very similar problem was identified in the 1970s in the form of what was called government 'overload'. Writers such as Anthony King (1975) and Richard Rose

Jürgen Habermas (born 1929)

German philosopher and social theorist. After growing up during the Nazi period, Habermas was politicised by the Nuremburg trials and the growing awareness after the war of the concentration and death camps. Drawn to study with Adorno (1903–69) and Horkheimer (1895–1973), he became the leading exponent of the 'second generation' of the Frankfurt School of critical theory. Habermas's work ranges over epistemology, the dynamics of advanced capitalism, the nature of rationality, and the relationship between social science and philosophy. During the 1970s, he moved further away from orthodox Marxism, developing critical theory into what became a theory of 'communicative action'. His main works include *Theory and Practice* (1974), *Towards a Rational Society* (1970), and *The Theory of Communicative Competence* (1984, 1988).

(1980) argued that governments were finding it increasingly difficult to govern because they were subject to over-demand. This had come about both because politicians and political parties were encouraged to outbid one another in the attempt to get into power and because pressure groups were able to besiege government with unrelenting and incompatible demands. Government's capacity to deliver was further undermined by a general drift towards corporatism (see p. 257) that created growing interdependence between government agencies and organised groups. However, whereas neo-Marxists believed that the 'crisis tendencies' identified in the 1970s were beyond the capacity of capitalist democracies to control, overload theorists tended to call for a significant shift of political and ideological priorities in the form of the abandonment of a 'big' government approach.

In many ways, the politics of the 1980s and 1990s can be seen as a response to this legitimation or overload crisis. The call for a change in priorities came most loudly from the New Right. Theorists such as Samuel Brittan (1977) highlighted the **fiscal crisis of the welfare state** and spoke about the 'economic contradictions of democracy'. In the 1990s, governments such as Reagan's in the USA and Thatcher's in the UK sought to lower popular expectations of government. They did this by trying to shift responsibilities from the state to the individual. Welfare, for instance, was portrayed as largely a matter of individual responsibility, individuals being encouraged to provide for themselves by hard work, savings, private pensions, medical insurance and so on. Unemployment was no longer seen by the government as the responsibility of government; there was a 'natural rate' of unemployment which could only be pushed up by greedy workers 'pricing themselves out of jobs'.

More radically, the New Right attempted to challenge and eventually displace the theories and values that had previously legitimised the progressive expansion of the state's responsibilities. In this sense, the New Right amounted to a 'hegemonic project' that tried to establish a rival set of pro-individual and pro-market values and theories. This constituted a public philosophy that extolled rugged individualism, and denigrated the 'nanny state'. The success of this project is demonstrated by the fact that socialist parties in states as different as the UK, France, Spain, Australia and New Zealand have accommodated themselves to broadly similar goals and values. As this has happened, a political culture that once emphasised social justice, welfare rights and public responsibilities has given way to one in which choice, enterprise, competition and individual responsibility have become more prominent.

Fiscal crisis of the welfare state: The crisis in state finances that occurs when expanding social expenditure coincides with recession and declining tax revenues.

Concept

Revolution

The term revolution, in its earliest usage, meant cyclical change (from the verb 'revolve'), as in the restoration of 'proper' political order in the so-called 'Glorious Revolution' (1688) in England. The French Revolution (1789), however, established the modern concept of revolution as a process of dramatic and far-reaching change, involving the destruction and replacement of an old order. Revolutions are popular uprisings involving extra-legal mass action; they are often, although not necessarily, violent in character. This distinguishes a revolution from a *coup d'état* (see p. 369), a seizure of power by a small band. Revolutions differ from rebellions and revolts in that they bring about fundamental change (a change in the political system itself), as opposed to merely a change of policy or the displacement of a governing elite.

Why do revolutions occur?

If legitimacy helps to ensure political stability and the survival of a regime, when legitimacy collapses, the result is likely to be either a resort to repression (see p. 369), or far-reaching political change. Change is one of the most important features of political life. Many of those engaged in politics would certainly agree with Marx's assertion in *Theses on Feuerbach* ([1845] 1968) that 'The philosophers have only *interpreted* the world, in various ways; the point, however, is to *change* it'. However, attitudes to change amongst political thinkers have differed enormously. While conservatives have usually evinced a 'desire to conserve' and resisted change in the name of continuity and tradition, liberals and socialists have typically welcomed change as a manifestation of progress. Deeply embodied in the belief in progress is a faith in human reason and the capacity of people to move history forwards and create a better society through the accumulation of wisdom and knowledge.

Whether change marks progress or decay, growth or decline, it is the product of one of two processes: evolution or revolution. Evolutionary change is usually thought of as reform, gradual and incremental improvements *within* a social or political system. Reform therefore represents change within continuity, the reorganisation or restructuring of, for instance, an institution, rather than its abolition or replacement. Revolution, on the other hand, is root-and-branch change. Revolutions entirely recast the political order, typically bringing about an abrupt and often violent break with the past. There has been considerable debate both about the nature of revolution and about the historical, social and political circumstances in which revolutions are most likely to occur.

Marxist theories of revolution

Marxists have used the term 'revolution' in a very specific way. Although they recognise that revolutions are crucial political events that involve the replacement of a government or the establishment of an entirely new regime, they interpret these changes as a reflection of a deeper social transformation. From this point of view, the essence of revolution is a fundamental *social* change, that is, the destruction of one economic system or 'mode of production' and its replacement by another. A Marxist may therefore reject the idea that the American Revolution (1776) brought about revolutionary change, because, although it brought independence to the former British colonies and led to the creation of a constitutional republic, it left the system of ownership and the social structure intact. Most Marxists nevertheless interpret the English, American and French Revolutions as 'bourgeois' revolutions, in that they marked a more gradual transition from a feudal mode of production to a capitalist one. Revolutions, from this perspective, are not simply abrupt and dramatic periods of political upheaval, but longer and more profound periods of social transformation. There is a sense, for example, in which the Russian Revolution started in 1917, but continued until the collapse of the USSR in 1991, its goal of 'building communism' still not having been completed.

In Marxist theory, revolution emerges out of contradictions which exist at a socioeconomic level. Revolution reflects, at heart, the conflict between the oppressor and the oppressed, the exploiter and the exploited. All class societies are thus doomed. Marx believed that revolution would mark the point at which the class struggle would develop into open conflict, leading one class to overthrow and displace another. Just as the French Revolution was interpreted as a 'bourgeois' revolution, the Russian Revolution was later seen as a 'proletarian' revolution that set in motion a process that would culminate in the establishment of socialism and eventually full communism. In Marx's view, the epoch of social revolution began when the class system, the 'relations of production', became a 'fetter' upon the further development of productive techniques and innovation, the so-called 'forces of production'. He believed that this would heighten class antagonism, bringing the exploited class (in capitalism, the proletariat) to 'class consciousness'. As the proletariat achieves class consciousness, it would become a revolutionary force and would rise spontaneously in revolt.

For Marx, revolutionary change was part of an inevitable process that would drive history through a series of epochs to the eventual achievement of a classless society, a society in which there are no internal contradictions. However, revolutions have not come about as Marx forecast. Revolution has not occurred, as he predicted it would, in the advanced capitalist countries of western and central Europe. Instead of the class system becoming a fetter constraining the further development of productive forces, capitalism has exhibited a seemingly endless appetite for technological innovation, generating continual, if at times erratic, improvements in living standards. The proletariat has, in consequence, been rendered politically passive. Where Marxist revolutions have occurred in the twentieth century they have conformed to a very different pattern.

The 1917 Bolshevik Russian Revolution, led by Lenin (see p. 75), advanced the Marxist theory of revolution in two important senses. First, while classical Marxists portrayed revolution as an inevitable breakdown of class society that would occur when objective conditions were ripe, Lenin grasped the point that revolutions have to be *made*. The Bolsheviks seized power in October 1917 even though the supposed 'bourgeois' revolution had only occurred in February 1917, and the proletariat was still small and politically unsophisticated. Secondly, Lenin recognised the need for political leadership in the form of a 'vanguard party', a role was taken by the Bolsheviks (later renamed the Communist Party). In a strict sense, therefore, the Russian Revolution was more a *coup d'état* than a popular revolution. In October 1917, unlike in the February Revolution which led to the fall of the Tsar, power was seized not by the masses but by a tightly-knit band of revolutionaries acting in their name. Many have therefore argued that the communist regimes set up in the twentieth century under the banner of Marxism–Leninism were perversions of the Marxist revolutionary ideal.

A further important shift in Marxist theory was the displacement of the proletariat by the peasantry as the 'revolutionary class'. Lenin had hinted at this in 1917 in talking about an alliance between the urban proletariat and the peasantry, but it was more clearly established by the Chinese Revolution (1949) under the leadership of Mao Zedong (see p. 200). In a pattern later adopted by Marxists in Latin America, Africa and elsewhere in Asia, the Chinese Revolution was a peasant revolution carried out in the countryside rather than in large urban areas. Rather than serving as a philosophy of social revolution, Marxism–Leninism tended in practice to be employed more as an ideology of modernisation and industrialisation that was particularly attractive to developing countries.

Non-Marxist theories of revolution

A variety of non-Marxist theories of revolution have been advanced. These each agree with the Marxist view in highlighting the importance of social conflict, but

---

Concept

Class consciousness

Class consciousness is a subjective awareness of a class's objective situation and interests. It thus highlights the crucial Marxist distinction between a 'class *in*-itself' and a 'class *for*-itself'. The latter supposedly exemplifies the solidarity of a class actively engaged in pursuing its common (and genuine) interests. Class consciousness is therefore the opposite of 'false consciousness', deluded understanding that conceals the fact of exploitation from subordinate classes, thus breeding political passivity. Marx believed that class consciousness would develop inevitably as a result of intensifying class conflict; Lenin argued that the proletariat needed to be brought to class consciousness through the leadership and guidance of a 'vanguard' or revolutionary party.

Mao Zedong (Mao Tse-tung) (1893–1976)

Chinese Marxist theorist and leader of the People's Republic of China, 1949–76. Mao was the son of a peasant farmer in Hunan. He initially worked as a librarian and teacher. In 1921, he helped to found the Chinese Communist Party, and in 1935 became its leader. As a political theorist, Mao adapted Marxism–Leninism to the needs of an overwhelmingly agricultural and still traditional society. His legacy is often associated with the Cultural Revolution (1966–70), a radical egalitarian movement that denounced elitism and 'capitalist roaders', and resulted in widespread social disruption, repression and death. Maoism is usually understood as an anti-bureaucratic form of Marxism that places its faith in the radical zeal of the masses.

they disagree with Marxism in two crucial respects. First, they are not prepared to interpret political events as merely a reflection of deeper economic or social developments. Revolution is understood more as a transformation of the *political* system than as a transformation of the *social* system. Secondly, revolution is seen not as an inevitable process (that is, as the working out of the logic of history), but rather as a consequence of a particular set of political and social circumstances. However, there is considerable debate about what circumstances and which set of sociopolitical factors help to bring revolutions about.

One of the most influential theories of revolution has been developed on the basis of the **systems theory** approach to politics. This approach implies that a political system will tend towards long-term stability as the 'outputs' of government are brought into line with the 'inputs' or pressures placed upon it. In this light, revolutions can be understood as a form of 'disequilibrium' in the political system that is brought about by economic, social, cultural or international changes to which the system itself is incapable of responding. For example, in *Revolutionary Change* (1966), Chalmers Johnson argued that revolutions occur in conditions of 'multiple disfunction', when the political system breaks down under the pressure of competing demands for change. The autocratic Tsarist regime in Russia, for example, proved to be incapable of responding to the mixture of pressures created by early industrialisation and the dislocation and demoralisation caused by the First World War. Similarly, it can be argued that, in the late twentieth century, orthodox communist regimes in the USSR and eastern Europe were unable to deal with the strains generated by the growth of an urbanised, better educated and more politically sophisticated population. However, systems analysis tends to ignore the important subjective or psychological factors that help precipitate revolution.

A second theory of revolution has been developed out of the lessons of social psychology, but was perhaps first used by Alexis de Tocqueville in an attempt to explain the outbreak of the 1789 French Revolution. These ideas have been developed into a model of a 'revolution of rising expectations'. In *The Old Regime and the French Revolution* ([1856] 1947), de Tocqueville pointed out that revolution rarely results from absolute poverty and gross deprivation, conditions that are more commonly associated with despair, resignation and political inertia. Rather, revolutions tend to break out when a government relaxes its grip after a long period of oppressive rule. As de Tocqueville put it, 'the most perilous moment for a bad government is when it seeks to mend its ways' (p. 177). This occurred, for instance,

Systems theory: The theory that treats the political system as a self-regulating mechanism responding to 'inputs' (demands and support) by issuing authoritative decisions or 'outputs' (policies).

Alexis de Tocqueville (1805–59)

French politician, political theorist and historian. Following the July Revolution of 1830 in France, Tocqueville visited the USA, ostensibly to study its penal system. This resulted in his epic *Democracy in America* (1835–40). His political career was ended by Louis Napoleon's coup in 1849, leaving him free to devote his time to historical work such as *The Old Regime and the French Revolution* ([1856] 1947). A friend and correspondent of J. S. Mill, de

Tocqueville's writings reflect a highly ambiguous attitude to the advance of political democracy. His ideas have influenced both liberal and conservative theorists, as well as academic sociologists.

in France when Louis XVI summoned the Estates General in 1788, and, arguably, also occurred throughout eastern Europe as a result of the Gorbachev reforms in the late 1980s. Instead of satisfying the demand for political change, reform can heighten popular expectations and generate revolutionary fervour.

The classic statement of this theory of revolution is found in Ted Gurr's *Why Men Rebel* (1970). In Gurr's view, rebellion is the result of 'relative deprivation', brought about by the gap between what people expect to receive (their 'value expectations') and what they actually get (their 'value capability'). The greatest likelihood of revolution therefore occurs when a period of economic and social development that has produced rising expectations is abruptly reversed. This creates a gap between expectations and capabilities that can lead to revolution. In *When Men Revolt and Why* (1971), James Davies explained this in terms of the J-curve theory of revolutions. The shape of the letter 'J' represents a period of rising expectations which is suddenly brought to a halt. The notion of relative deprivation is significant, because it draws attention to the fact that people's perception of their position is more important than their objective circumstances. What is crucial is how people evaluate their condition relative either to the recent past, or to what other people have. For example, popular discontent and instability in eastern Europe in the late 1980s was undoubtedly fuelled, in part, by the perceived affluence and political liberty enjoyed by populations in the capitalist West.

A third theory of revolution focuses not on pressures operating within the political system, but on the strengths and weaknesses of the state itself. There is a sense in which a state can withstand any amount of internal pressure as long as it possesses the coercive power to maintain control and the political will to employ it. In this sense, the consequence of a loss of legitimacy is either revolution or repression. Certainly, regimes such as Hitler's Germany, Stalin's USSR and Saddam Hussein's Iraq each survived as long as they did through their ability to crush internal opposition by the use of terror and repression. In such regimes, political change is more likely to result from a rebellion within the political or military elite than a popular revolution.

In a comparative analysis of the French Revolution, Russian Revolution and Chinese Revolution, Theda Skocpol (1979) advanced a social–structural explanation of revolutions, which highlights the international weakness and domestic ineffectiveness of regimes that succumb to breakdown. War and invasion, for instance, have often been decisive in precipitating revolutionary situations; this occurred in China in 1911 and 1949, and in Russia in 1905 and 1917. In domestic politics, states become vulnerable to revolution when they are no longer able to count upon the loyalty of their armed forces, or no longer possess the resolve and determination to exercise widespread repression. This is demonstrated by the comparison between the brutal but successful suppression of the Chinese student rebellion in Tiananmen Square in June 1989 and the swift and largely bloodless collapse of communist regimes in eastern Europe in the autumn and winter of the same year. A decisive factor in the latter case was the unwillingness of the USSR under Gorbachev either to sanction repression or to step in and suppress nascent revolutions, as it had earlier done in East Germany (1949), Hungary (1956) and Czechoslovakia (1968).

■ Summary

◆ A political culture is a people's psychological orientation in relation to political objects such as parties, government and the constitution, expressed in their political attitudes, beliefs, symbols and values. Political culture differs from public opinion in that it is fashioned out of long-term values rather than reactions to specific policies, problems or personalities.

◆ Individuals and groups acquire their political attitudes and values through a process of political socialisation. This may be seen either as a process of indoctrination that takes place throughout a person's life, or as the transmission of values from one generation to the next, largely accomplished during childhood. The major agents of socialisation are the family, education, religion, the mass media and government.

◆ Considerable debate has surrounded the idea of civic culture. It has been used to identify psychological orientations, such as participation and respect for government, that help to sustain stable democratic rule. A civic culture may, however, be a consequence rather than a cause of democracy. It may overstate the value of deference, and underestimate the extent of cultural heterogeneity.

◆ The nature of the political culture of modern societies has been hotly disputed. Pluralists emphasise the existence of free competition between values and ideas, while radicals and Marxists claim that a 'dominant' culture is imposed from above in the interests of privileged groups. Conservatives highlight the value of tradition and authority in the face of growing cultural diversity, stimulated, in part, by the spread of postmaterialism.

◆ Legitimacy maintains political stability because it establishes a regime's right to rule, and so underpins the regime's authority over its people. Legitimacy may be based on traditional, charismatic or legal–rational authority. Legal–rational authority is the most common basis of legitimacy in modern societies, being linked to the establishment of rule-governed behaviour through constitutionalism and electoral democracy.

◆ Structural imbalances in modern society may make it increasingly difficult to maintain legitimacy. Legitimation crises may arise from the conflict between the pressure for social and economic interventionism generated by democracy on the one hand, and the market economy's need for incentives, enterprise and price stability on the other.

◆ Revolutions are popular uprisings that consist of extra-legal mass action aimed at changing the political system. Revolutions have been explained in a variety of ways. They have been portrayed as a symptom of a supposedly deeper social transformation, as a sign of disequilibrium in the political system, as a consequence of the thwarting of rising expectations, and as a result of the declining effectiveness of the state.

Questions for discussion

▶ What are the most important agents of political socialisation? At what age are people most susceptible to political influences?

▶ Do the mass media reflect public opinion or shape it?

▶ What values and beliefs are most likely to sustain a democratic political system?

▶ What conditions are required for the maintenance of legitimacy in modern societies?

▶ Are capitalist systems inevitably prone to legitimation crises?

▶ Are revolutions best thought of as social phenomena or political phenomena?

Further reading

Almond, G. A. and S. Verba (eds) *The Civic Culture Revisited* (Boston, MA: Little, Brown, 1980). An updated version of the author's classic 1963 analysis of the conditions required for democratic stability.

Beetham, D. *The Legitimation of Power* (Basingstoke: Macmillan, 1991). An original and thought-provoking examination of the nature of power relations and legitimacy.

Cohen, A. *Theories of Revolution: An Introduction* (London: Nelson, 1975). A clear and accessible analysis of various approaches to the understanding of revolution.

Gibbins, J. (ed.) *Contemporary Political Culture: Politics in a Post-Modern Age* (London: Sage, 1989). A useful and wide-ranging collection of essays on various aspects of political culture.

Representation, Elections and Voting

If Voting Changed Anything They'd Abolish It
Title of book by KEN LIVINGSTONE (1987)

Elections are often thought of as the heart of the political process. Perhaps no questions in politics are as crucial as do we elect the politicians who rule over us, and under what rules are these elections held? Elections are seen as nothing less than democracy in practice. They are a means through which the people can control their government, ultimately by 'kicking the rascals out'. Central to this notion is the principle of representation. Put simply, this portrays politicians as servants of the people, and invests them with a responsibility to act for or on behalf of those who elect them. When democracy, in the classical sense of direct and continuous popular participation, is regarded as hopelessly impractical, representation may be the closest we can come to achieving government by the people. There is nevertheless considerable disagreement about how representation can be achieved in practice, and about how politicians should be elected and what election results actually mean.

The key questions examined in this chapter are as follows:

Contents

Key issues

► What is representation? How can one person 'represent' another?

► How can representation be achieved in practice?

► What do elections do? What are their functions?

► How do electoral systems differ? What are their strengths and weaknesses?

► What do election results mean?

► Why do people vote as they do? How can electoral behaviour be explained?

Representation

The term represent means, in everyday language, to 'portray' or 'make present', as when a picture is said to represent a scene or a person. As a political principle, representation Is a relationship through which an individual or group stands for, or acts on behalf of, a larger body of people. Representation differs from democracy in that, while the former acknowledges a distinction between government and the governed, the latter, at least in its classical form, aspires to abolish this distinction and establish popular *self*government. Representative democracy (see p. 68) may nevertheless constitute a limited and indirect form of democratic rule, provided that the representation links government and the governed in such a way that the people's views are articulated or their interests are secured.

Representation

The issue of representation has generated deep and recurrent political controversy. Even the absolute monarchs of old were expected to rule by seeking the advice of the 'estates of the realm' (the major landed interests, the clergy, and so on). In this sense, the English Civil War of the seventeenth century, fought between King and Parliament, broke out as a result of an attempt to deny representation to key groups and interests. Similarly, debate about the spread of democracy in the nineteenth and twentieth centuries has largely centred upon the question of who should be represented. Should representation be restricted to those who have the competence, education and perhaps leisure to act wisely and think seriously about politics (variously seen as men, the propertied, or particular racial or ethnic groups), or should representation be extended to all adult citizens?

Such questions have now largely been resolved through the widespread acceptance of the principle of political equality (see p. 67), at least in the formal sense of universal suffrage and 'one person, one vote'. Plural voting, for example, was abolished in the UK in 1949, women were enfranchised in Switzerland in 1971, and racial criteria for voting were swept away in South Africa in 1994. However, this approach to representation is simplistic in that it equates representation with elections and voting, politicians being seen as 'representatives' merely because they have been elected. This ignores more difficult questions about *how* one person can be said to represent another, and *what* it is that he or she represents. Is it the views of the represented, their best interests, the groups from which they come, or what?

Theories of representation

There is no single, agreed theory of representation. Rather, there are a number of competing theories, each of which is based on particular ideological and political assumptions. For example, does representative government imply that government 'knows better' than the people, that government has somehow 'been instructed' by the people what to do and how to behave, or that the government 'looks like' the people in that it broadly reflects their characteristics or features? Such questions are not of academic interest alone. Particular models of representation dictate very different behaviour on the part of representatives. For instance, should elected politicians be bound by policies and positions outlined during an election and endorsed by the voters, or is it their job to lead public opinion and thereby help to define the public interest? Moreover, it is not uncommon for more than one principle of representation to operate within the same political system, suggesting, perhaps, that no single model is sufficient in itself to secure representative government.

Four principal models of representation have been advanced:

- trusteeship
- delegation
- the mandate
- resemblance.

Trustee model

A trustee is a person who is vested with formal responsibility for another's property or affairs. The classic expression of representation as trusteeship is found in Edmund Burke's (see p. 45) speech to the electors of Bristol in 1774:

You choose a member indeed; but when you have chosen him he is *not* member of Bristol, but he is a member of parliament . . . Your representative owes you, not his industry only, but his judgement; and he betrays, instead of serving you, if he sacrifices it to your opinion (Burke, 1975, p. 157).

For Burke, the essence of representation was to serve one's constituents by the exercise of 'mature judgement' and 'enlightened conscience'. In short, representation is a moral duty: those with the good fortune to possess education and understanding should act in the interests of those who are less fortunate. This view had strongly elitist implications, since it stresses that, once elected, representatives should think for themselves and exercise independent judgement on the grounds that the mass of people do not know their own best interests. A similar view was advanced by J. S. Mill (see p. 44) in the form of the liberal theory of representation. This was based on the assumption that, although all individuals have a right to be represented, not all political opinions are of equal value. Mill therefore proposed a system of plural voting in which four or five votes would be allocated to holders of learned diplomas or degrees, two or three to skilled or managerial workers, and a single vote to ordinary workers. He also argued that rational voters would support politicians who could act wisely on their behalf, rather than ones who merely reflected the voters' own views. Trustee representation thus portrays professional politicians as representatives insofar as they are members of an educated elite. It is based on the belief that knowledge and understanding are unequally distributed in society, in the sense that not all citizens know what is best for them.

This Burkian notion of representation has also attracted severe criticism, however. For instance, it appears to have clearly anti-democratic implications. If politicians should think for themselves because the public is ignorant, poorly educated or deluded, then surely it is a mistake to allow the public to elect their representatives in the first place. Secondly, the link between representation and education is questionable. Whereas education may certainly be of value in aiding the understanding of intricate political and economic problems, it is far less clear that it helps politicians to make correct moral judgements about the interests of others. There is little evidence, for example, to support Burke's and Mill's belief that education breeds **altruism** and gives people a broader sense of social responsibility. Finally, there is the fear traditionally expressed by radical democrats such as Thomas Paine (see p. 208) that, if politicians are allowed to exercise their own judgement, they will simply use that latitude to pursue their own selfish interests. In this way, representation could simply become a substitute for democracy. In his pamphlet *Common Sense* ([1776] 1987:68), Paine came close to the rival ideal of delegate representation in insisting that 'the elected should never form to themselves an interest separate from the electors'.

Delegate model

A delegate is a person who is chosen to act for another on the basis of clear guidance or instructions. In other words, a delegate is expected to act as a conduit conveying the views of others, while having little or no capacity to exercise his or her own judgement or preferences. Examples include sales representatives and ambassadors,

Altruism: A concern for the welfare of others, based on either enlightened self-interest or a recognition of a common humanity.

Thomas Paine (1737–1809)

UK-born writer and revolutionary. Paine was brought up in a Quaker family. He went to America in 1774 and fought for the colonists in the War of Independence. He returned to England in 1789, but, after being indicted for treason, fled to France as a supporter of the republican cause, where he narrowly escaped the guillotine during the Terror. Paine's radicalism fused a commitment to political liberty with a deep faith in popular sovereignty, providing inspiration for both liberal republicanism and socialist egalitarianism. His most important writings include *Common Sense* ([1776] 1987), *The Rights of Man* (1791/92) and *The Age of Reason* (1794).

Focus on . . .

Referendums: for and against

A referendum is a vote in which the electorate can express a view on a particular issue of public policy. It differs from an election in that the latter is essentially a means of filling a public office and does not provide a direct or reliable method of influencing the content of policy. The referendum is therefore a device of direct democracy (see p. 68). It is typically used not to replace representative institutions, but to supplement them. Referendums may be either advisory or binding; they may also raise issues for discussion (initiatives), or be used to decide policy questions (propositions or plebiscites).

Amongst the advantages of referendums are the following:

- They check the power of elected governments, ensuring that they stay in line with public opinion.
- They promote political participation, thus helping to create a more educated and better informed electorate.
- They strengthen legitimacy by providing the public with a way of expressing their views about specific issues.
- They provide either a means of settling major constitutional questions, or of gauging public opinion on issues not raised in elections because major parties agree on them.

The disadvantages of referendums include the following:

- They leave political decisions in the hands of those who have the least education and experience, and are most susceptible to media and other influences.
- They provide, at best, only a snapshot of public opinion at one point in time.
- They allow politicians to manipulate the political agenda and absolve themselves of responsibility for making difficult decisions.
- They tend to simplify and distort political issues, reducing them to questions that have a yes/no answer.

neither of which are, strictly speaking, authorised to think for themselves. Similarly, a trade-union official who attends a conference with instructions on how to vote and what to say is acting as a delegate, not as a Burkian representative. Those who favour this model of representation as delegation usually support mechanisms that ensure that politicians are bound as closely as possible to the views of the represented. These include what Paine referred to as 'frequent interchange' between representatives and their constituents in the form of regular elections and short terms in office. In addition, radical democrats have advocated the use of **initiatives** and the right of **recall** as means of giving the public more control over politicians. Although delegation stops short of direct democracy, its supporters nevertheless usually favour the use of referendums to supplement the representative process.

The virtue of what has been called 'delegated representation' is that it provides broader opportunities for popular participation and serves to check the self-serving inclinations of professional politicians. It thus comes as close as is possible in representative government to realising the ideal of **popular sovereignty**. Its disadvantages are nevertheless also clear. In the first place, in ensuring that representatives are bound to the interests of their constituents, it tends to breed narrowness and foster conflict. This is precisely what Burke feared would occur if members of the legislature acted as ambassadors who took instructions from their constituents rather than as representatives of the nation. As he put it, 'Parliament is a deliberative assembly of one nation, with one interest, that of the whole'. A second drawback is that, because professional politicians are not trusted to exercise their own judgement, delegation limits the scope for leadership (see p. 330) and statesmanship. Politicians are forced to reflect the views of their constituents or even pander to them, and are thus not able to mobilise the people by providing vision and inspiration.

Mandate model

Both the trustee model and the delegate model were developed before the emergence of modern political parties, and therefore view representatives as essentially independent actors. However, individual candidates are now rarely elected on the basis of their personal qualities and talents; more commonly, they are seen as foot soldiers for a party, and are supported because of its public image or programme of policies. New theories of representation have therefore emerged. The most influential of these is the so-called doctrine of the mandate. This is based on the idea that, in winning an election, a party gains a popular mandate that authorises it to carry out whatever policies or programmes it outlined during the election campaign. As it is the party, rather than individual politicians, that is the agency of representation, the mandate model provides a clear justification for party unity and party discipline. In effect, politicians serve their constituents not by thinking for themselves or acting as a channel to convey their views, but by remaining loyal to their party and its policies.

The strength of the mandate doctrine is that it takes account of the undoubted practical importance of party labels and party policies. Moreover, it provides a means of imposing some kind of meaning on election results, as well as a way of keeping politicians to their word. Nevertheless, the doctrine has also stimulated fierce criticism. First, it is based on a highly questionable model of voting behaviour, insofar as it suggests that voters select parties on the grounds of policies and issues. Voters are not always the rational and well informed creatures that this model suggests. They can be influenced by a range of 'irrational' factors, such as the personalities of leaders, the images of parties, habitual allegiances and social conditioning.

Initiative: A type of referendum through which the public is able to raise legislative proposals.

Recall: A process whereby the electorate can call unsatisfactory public officials to account and ultimately remove them.

Popular sovereignty: The principle that there is no higher authority than the will of the people (the basis of the classical concept of democracy).

Secondly, even if voters are influenced by policies, it is likely that they will be attracted by certain **manifesto** commitments, but be less interested in, or perhaps opposed to, others. A vote for a party cannot therefore be taken to be an endorsement of its entire manifesto, or indeed of any single election promise. Thirdly, the doctrine imposes a straightjacket. It limits government policies to those positions and proposals that the party took up during the election, and leaves no scope to adjust policies in the light of changing circumstances. What guidance do mandates offer in the event of, say, international or economic crises? Finally (as will be discussed in the next main section of this chapter) the doctrine of the mandate can only be applied in the case of majoritarian electoral systems, and its use even there may appear absurd if the winning party fails to gain 50 per cent of the popular vote.

Resemblance model

The final theory of representation is based less on the manner in which representatives are selected than on whether they typify or resemble the group they claim to represent. This notion is embodied in the idea of a 'representative cross-section', as used by market researchers and opinion pollsters. By this standard, a representative government would constitute a microcosm of the larger society, containing members drawn from all groups and sections in society (in terms of social class, gender, religion, ethnicity, age and so on), and in numbers that are proportional to the size of the groups in society at large. The idea of characteristic representation, or as it has been called 'microcosmic representation', has traditionally been endorsed by socialist and radical thinkers. They argue that the 'under-representation' of groups such as the working class, women and racial minorities at senior levels in key institutions ensures that their interests are marginalised or ignored altogether.

The resemblance model suggests that only people who come from a particular group, and have shared the experiences of that group, can fully identify with its interests. This is the difference between 'putting oneself in the shoes of another' and having direct and personal experience of what other people go through. A 'New Man' or a 'pro-feminist' male may, for instance, sympathise with women's interests and support the principle of sexual equality, but will never take women's problems as seriously as women do themselves, because they are not *his* problems. On the other hand, the idea that representatives should resemble the represented undoubtedly causes a number of difficulties.

One of these is that this model portrays representation in exclusive or narrow terms, believing that only a woman can represent women, only a black person can represent other black people, only a member of the working class can represent the working classes, and so on. If all representatives simply advance the interests of the groups from which they come, the result would be social division and conflict, with no one being able to defend the common good or advance a broader public interest. Moreover, a government that is a microcosm of society would reflect that society's weaknesses as well as its strengths. What would be the advantage, for example, of government resembling society if the majority of the population are apathetic, ill informed and poorly educated? Finally, the microcosmic ideal can only be achieved by imposing powerful constraints upon electoral choice and individual freedom. In the name of representation, political parties may be forced to select quotas of female and minority candidates, constituencies may be set aside for candidates from particular backgrounds, or, more dramatically, the electorate might have to be classified

Joseph Schumpeter (1883–1950)

Moravian-born US economist and sociologist. Following an early academic career and a brief spell as Minister of Finance in post-First-World-War Austria, Schumpeter became professor of economics at Harvard University in 1932. His economic thought, developed in *Theory of Economic Development* (1912) and *Business Cycles* (1939), centred on the long-term dynamics of the capitalist system and in particular the role of 'risk-loving' entrepreneurs. In *Capitalism, Socialism and Democracy* (1942), Schumpeter drew on economic, sociological and political theories to advance the famous contention that western capitalism was, impelled by its very success, evolving into a form of socialism.

on the basis of class, gender, race and so on, and only be allowed to vote for candidates from their own group.

 # Elections

Although controversy continues to rage about the nature of representation, there is one point of universal agreement: the representative process is intrinsically linked to elections and voting. **Elections** may not in themselves be a sufficient condition for political representation, but there is little doubt that they are a necessary condition. Indeed, some thinkers have gone further and portrayed elections as the very heart of democracy. This was the view developed by Joseph Schumpeter in *Capitalism, Socialism and Democracy* (1942), which portrayed democracy as an 'institutional arrangement', as a means of filling public office by a competitive struggle for the people's vote. As he put it, 'democracy means only that the people have the opportunity of accepting or refusing the men [*sic*] who are to rule them'. In interpreting democracy as nothing more than a political method, Schumpeter in effect identified it with elections, and specifically with competitive elections. While few modern democratic theorists are prepared to reduce democracy simply to competitive elections, most nevertheless follow Schumpeter in understanding democratic government in terms of the rules and mechanisms that guide the conduct of elections. This focuses attention on the very different forms that elections can take.

First, which offices or posts are subject to the elective principle? Although elections are widely used to fill those public offices whose holders have policy making responsibilities (the legislature and executive in particular), key political institutions are sometimes treated as exceptions. This applies, for instance, to the second chambers of legislature in states like the UK and Canada, and where constitutional monarchs still serve as heads of state. Secondly, who is entitled to vote, how widely is the franchise drawn? As pointed out above, restrictions on the right to vote based on factors such as property ownership, education, gender and racial origin have been abandoned in most countries. Nevertheless, there may be informal restrictions, as in the practice in most US states of leaving electoral registration entirely in the hands of the citizen, with the result that non-registration and non-voting are widespread. On the other hand, in Australia, Belgium and Italy, for instance, voting is compulsory.

Thirdly, how are votes cast? Although public voting was the norm in the USSR

Election: A device for filling an office or post through choices made by a designated body of people: the electorate.

until 1989, and it is still widely practised in small organisations in the form of a show of hands, modern political elections are generally held on the basis of a secret ballot (sometimes called an 'Australian ballot', as it was first used in South Australia in 1856). The secret ballot is usually seen as the guarantee of a 'fair' election, in that it keeps the dangers of corruption and intimidation at bay. Nevertheless, electoral fairness cannot simply be reduced to the issue of how people vote. It is also affected by the voters' access to reliable and balanced information, the range of choice they are offered, the circumstances under which campaigning is carried out, and, finally, how scrupulously the vote is counted.

Fourthly, are elections competitive or non-competitive? This is usually seen as the most crucial of distinctions, as only about half of the countries that use elections offer their electorates a genuine choice of both candidates and parties. Single-candidate elections, for example, were the rule in orthodox communist states. This meant that public office was effectively filled through a nomination process dominated by the communist party. Electoral competition is a highly complex and often controversial issue. It concerns not merely the right of people to stand for election and the ability of political parties to nominate candidates and campaign legally, but also broader factors that affect party performance, such as their sources of funding and their access to the media. From this point of view, the nature of the party system may be as crucial to the maintenance of genuine competition as are rules about who can stand and who can vote. Finally, how is the election conducted? As will be discussed later, there are a bewildering variety of electoral systems, each of which has its own particular political and constitutional implications.

Functions of elections

Because of the different kinds of elections, and the variety of electoral systems, generalisation about the roles or functions of elections is always difficult. Nevertheless, the advance of democratisation in the 1980s and 1990s, stimulated in part by the collapse of communism, has usually been associated with the adoption of liberal-democratic electoral systems, characterised by universal suffrage, the secret ballot and electoral competition. The significance of such systems is, however, more difficult to determine. As Harrop and Miller (1987) explained, there are two contrasting views of the function of competitive elections.

The conventional view is that elections are a mechanism through which politicians can be called to account and forced to introduce policies that somehow reflect public opinion. This emphasises the *bottom-up* functions of elections: political recruitment, representation, making government, influencing policy and so on. On the other hand, a radical view of elections, developed by theorists such as Ginsberg (1982), portrays them as a means through which governments and political elites can exercise control over their populations, making them more quiescent, malleable, and, ultimately, governable. This view emphasises *top-down* functions: building legitimacy, shaping public opinion and strengthening elites. In reality, however, elections have no single character; they are neither simply mechanisms of public accountability nor a means of ensuring political control. Like all channels of political communication, elections are a 'two-way street' that provide the government and the people, the elite and the masses, with the opportunity to influence one another. The central functions of elections include the following:

- **Recruiting politicians:** In democratic states, elections are the principal source of political recruitment, taking account also of the processes through which parties nominate candidates. Politicians thus tend to possess talents and skills that are related to electioneering, such as charisma (see p. 195), oratorical skills and good looks, not necessarily those that suit them to carrying out constituency duties, serving on committees, running government departments and so on. Elections are typically not used to fill posts that require specialist knowledge or experience, such as those in the civil service or judiciary.

- **Making governments:** Elections only make governments directly in states such as the USA, France and Venezuela in which the political executive is directly elected. In the more common parliamentary systems, elections influence the formation of governments, most strongly when the electoral system tends to give a single party a clear parliamentary majority. The use of proportional representation (see p. 220) may mean that governments are formed through post-election deals, and that governments can be made and unmade without the need for an election.

- **Providing representation:** When they are fair and competitive, elections are a means through which demands are channelled from the public to the government. Short of the use of initiatives and the recall, however, the electorate has no effective means of ensuring that mandates are carried out, apart from its capacity to inflict punishment at the next election. Moreover, elected governments nowhere constitute a microcosm of the larger society.

- **Influencing policy:** Elections certainly deter governments from pursuing radical and deeply unpopular policies, but only in exceptional cases, when a single issue dominates the election campaign, can they be said to influence policy directly. It can also be argued that the range of policy options outlined in elections is typically so narrow that the result can only be of marginal policy significance. Others suggest that government policy is in any case shaped more by practical dictates such as the state of the economy than it is by electoral considerations.

- **Educating voters:** The process of campaigning provides the electorate with an abundance of information, about parties, candidates, policies, the current government's record, the political system, and so on. However, this only leads to education if the information that is provided, and the way it is provided, engages public interest and stimulates debate, as opposed to apathy and alienation. As candidates and parties seek to persuade rather than to educate, they also have a strong incentive to provide incomplete and distorted information.

- **Building legitimacy:** One reason why even authoritarian regimes bother to hold elections, even if they are non-competitive, is that elections help to foster legitimacy (see p. 193) by providing justification for a system of rule. This happens because the ritual involved in campaigning somehow confers on an election a ceremonial status and importance. Most importantly, by encouraging citizens to participate in politics, even in the limited form of voting, elections mobilise active consent.

- **Strengthening elites:** Elections can also be a vehicle through which elites can manipulate and control the masses. This possibility encouraged Proudhon (see p. 124) to warn that 'universal suffrage is counter-revolution'. Political discontent and opposition can be neutralised by elections that channel them in a constitutional direction, and allow governments to come and go while the regime itself survives. Elections are particularly effective in this respect because, at the same time, they give citizens the impression that they are exercising power over the government.

Electoral systems: debates and controversies

An electoral system is a set of rules that governs the conduct of elections. Not only do these rules vary across the world, but they are also, in many countries, the subject of fierce political debate and argument. These rules vary in a number of ways:

- Voters may be asked to choose between candidates or between parties.

- Voters may either select a single candidate, or vote preferentially, ranking the candidates they wish to support in order.

- The electorate may or may not be grouped into electoral units or constituencies.

- Constituencies may return a single member or a number of members.

- The level of support needed to elect a candidate varies from a plurality (the largest single number of votes or a 'relative' majority) to an overall or 'absolute' majority or a quota of some kind.

For general purposes, however, the systems available can be divided into two broad categories on the basis of how they convert votes into seats. On the one hand, there are *majoritarian* systems, in which larger parties typically win a higher proportion of seats than the proportion of votes they gain in the election. This increases the chances of a single party gaining a parliamentary majority and being able to govern on its own. In the UK in 1983, for example, the Conservatives gained 61 per cent of the seats in the House of Commons with only 43 per cent of the vote. On the other hand, there are *proportional* systems, which guarantee an equal, or at least more equal, relationship between the seats won by a party and the votes gained in the election. In a pure system of proportional representation (PR) (see p. 222), a party that gains 45 per cent of the votes would win exactly 45 per cent of the seats. PR systems therefore make single-party majority rule less likely, and are commonly associated with multiparty systems and coalition government. The electoral systems described in the following Focus boxes range from the most majoritarian type of system to the purest type of proportional system.

Although in some countries the electoral system provokes little debate or interest, in others it is an issue of pressing political and constitutional significance. France, for instance, has changed its electoral system so many times that any statement about it runs the risk of being out of date. The second ballot was abandoned for parliamentary elections in 1985, when France switched to a regional-list system, but it was reintroduced for the 1993 election. Electoral reform has been a major issue in UK politics since the decline of the Conservative–Labour two-party system in the 1970s, its staunchest advocates being 'third' parties such as the Liberals (and in successive incarnations, the Social-Democrat/Liberal Alliance and the Liberal Democrats). The confusing thing about the electoral reform debate is that the shifts that have occurred reflect no consistent pattern. In 1994, while New Zealand adopted proportional representation in place of the FPTP system, Italy moved in the opposite direction, replacing the party list with the less proportional additional member system (75 per cent of members of the Chamber of Deputies are elected by the FPTP system).

Electoral systems attract attention in part because they have a crucial impact on party performance, and particularly on their prospects of winning (or at least sharing) power. It would be foolish, then, to deny that attitudes towards the electoral system are largely shaped by party advantage. President Mitterrand's twists and

Focus on . . .

Electoral systems: simple plurality system ('first past the post' system)

Used: The UK, the USA, Canada and India, for example. **Type**: Majoritarian.
Features:

- The country is divided into single-member constituencies, usually of equal size.
- Voters select a single candidate, usually marking his or her name with a cross on the ballot paper.
- The winning candidate needs only to achieve a plurality of votes (the 'first past the post' rule).

Advantages:

- The system establishes a clear link between representatives and constituents, ensuring that constituency duties are carried out.
- It offers the electorate a clear choice of potential parties of government.
- It allows governments to be formed that have a clear mandate from the electorate, albeit often on the basis of plurality support amongst the electorate.
- It keeps extremism at bay by making it more difficult for small radical parties to gain seats and credibility.
- It makes for strong and effective government in that a single party usually has majority control of the assembly.
- It produces stable government in that single-party governments rarely collapse as a result of disunity and internal friction.

Disadvantages:

- The system 'wastes' many (perhaps most) votes, those cast for losing candidates and those cast for winning ones over the plurality mark.
- It distorts electoral preferences by 'under-representing' small parties and ones with geographically evenly distributed support (the 'third-party effect').
- It offers only limited choice because of its duopolistic (two-major-parties) tendencies.
- It undermines the legitimacy of government in that governments often enjoy only minority support, producing a system of plurality rule.
- It creates instability because a change in government can lead to a radical shift of policies and direction.
- It leads to unaccountable government in that the legislature is usually subordinate to the executive, because the majority of its members are supporters of the governing party.
- It discourages the selection of a socially broad spread of candidates in favour of those who are attractive to a large body of voters.

turns in France in the 1980s and 1990s were dictated mainly by his desire to strengthen Socialist representation in the National Assembly. Similarly, the UK Labour Party's interest in PR in the 1980s and 1990s waxed and waned according to whether it appeared that the party could win under FPTP rules. However, other less cynical and more substantial considerations need to be taken into account. The problem, though, is that there is no such thing as a 'best electoral system'.

The electoral reform debate is, at heart, a debate about the desirable nature of government and the principles that underpin 'good' government. Is representative government, for instance, more important than effective government? Is a bias in favour of compromise and consensus preferable to one that favours conviction and principle? These are normative questions that do not permit objective answers. Moreover, in view of the complex role they play, elections can be judged according to a diverse range of criteria, which not uncommonly contradict one another. Electoral systems therefore merit only a qualified endorsement, reflecting a balance of advantages over disadvantages and their strength relative to other systems. These criteria fall into two general categories: those related to the quality of representation, and those linked to the effectiveness of government.

Majoritarian systems are usually thought to be at their weakest when they are evaluated in terms of their representative functions. To a greater or lesser extent, each

Focus on . . .

Electoral systems: second ballot system

Used: Traditionally in France (although changes in France's electoral system have been common). **Type**: Majoritarian. **Features**:

- There are single-candidate constituencies and single-choice voting, as in the first-past-the-post (FPTP) system.
- To win on the first ballot, a candidate needs an overall majority of the votes cast.
- If no candidate gains a first-ballot majority, a second, run-off ballot is held between the leading two candidates.

Advantages:

- The system broadens electoral choice: voters can vote with their hearts for their preferred candidate in the first ballot, and with their heads for the least-bad candidate in the second.
- As candidates can only win with majority support, they are encouraged to make their appeal as broad as possible.
- Strong and stable government is possible, as with FPTP systems.

Disadvantages:

- As the system is little more proportional than the FPTP system, it distorts preferences and is unfair to 'third' parties.
- Run-off candidates are encouraged to abandon their principles in search of short-term popularity or as a result of deals with defeated candidates.
- The holding of a second ballot may strain the electorate's patience and interest in politics.

Focus on . . .

Electoral systems: alternative vote system (AVS)

Used: Australia (House of Representatives). **Type**: Majoritarian. **Features**:

- There are single-member constituencies.
- There is preferential voting. Voters rank the candidates in order of preference: 1 for their first preference, 2 for their second preference, and so on.
- Winning candidates must gain 50 per cent of all the votes cast.
- Votes are counted according to the first preferences. If no candidate reaches 50 per cent, the bottom candidate is eliminated and his or her votes are redistributed according to the second (or subsequent) preferences. This continues until one candidate has a majority.

Advantages:

- Fewer votes are 'wasted' than in the FPTP system.
- Unlike the second-ballot system, the outcome cannot be influenced by deals made between candidates.
- Although winning candidates must secure at least 50 per cent support, single-party majority government is not ruled out.

Disadvantages:

- The system is not much more proportional than the FPTP system, and so is still biased in favour of large parties.
- The outcome may be determined by the preferences of those who support small, possibly extremist, parties.
- Winning candidates may enjoy little first-preference support, and have only the virtue of being the least unpopular candidate available.

majoritarian system distorts popular preferences in the sense that party representation is not commensurate with electoral strength. This is most glaringly apparent in their 'unfairness' to small parties and parties with evenly distributed geographical support, and their 'over-fairness' in relation to large parties and ones with geographically concentrated support. For example, in 1992 in the UK, the Conservatives gained 52 per cent of the parliamentary seats with 42 per cent of the vote, the Labour Party won 42 per cent of the seats with 35 per cent of the vote, and the Liberal Democrats gained merely 3.1 per cent representation with 18 per cent of the vote. Such biases are impossible to justify in representative terms, especially since the unfortunate 'third' parties are often centrist parties, and not the extremist parties of popular image.

Two-party systems and single-party government are thus 'manufactured' by the majoritarian bias of the electoral system, and do not reflect the distribution of popular preferences. Moreover, the fact that parties can come to power with barely two-fifths of the popular vote (in October 1974 in the UK, for example, the Labour Party gained a House of Commons majority with 39.2 per cent of the vote) strains the legitimacy of the entire political system, and creates circumstances in which radical, ideologically driven parties can remain in power for prolonged periods under little pressure to broaden their appeal. The Conservatives in the UK were thus able to implement a programme of market-orientated reforms in the 1980s and 1990s while never gaining more than 43 per cent of support in elections. When the majority of voters oppose the party in power, it is difficult to claim that that party has a popular mandate for anything.

Looked at in this light, proportional electoral systems seem to be manifestly more representative (see p. 220). Nevertheless, it may be naive simply to equate electoral fairness with proportionality. For instance, much of the criticism of PR systems stems from the fact that they make coalition government (see p. 246) much more likely. Although it can be argued that, unlike single-party governments, coalitions enjoy the support of at least 50 per cent of the electors, their policies are typically thrashed out in postelection deals, and thus are not endorsed by *any* set of electors. An additional danger is that parties within a coalition government may not exert influence in line with their electoral strength. The classic example of this is when small centre parties (such as the Free Democrats in Germany) can dictate to larger parties (for example, the CDU or the SPD in Germany) by threatening to switch their support to another party. Then, in effect, 'the tail wags the dog'.

The defence of majoritarian systems is more commonly based on government functions, and specifically on the capacity of such systems to deliver stable and effective rule. In other words, a lack of proportionality may simply be the price that is paid for strong government. In these systems, the bias in favour of single-party rule means that the electorate can usually choose between two parties, each of which has the capacity to deliver on its election promises by translating its manifesto commit-

Focus on . . .

Electoral systems: limited vote system

Used: Japan (House of Representatives). **Type**: Proportional. **Features**:

- There are multi-member constituencies, each returning 3–5 members.
- Electors cast only a single non-transferable vote.
- The 3–5 winning candidates are returned on a simple plurality basis.

Advantages:

- The system is fairer to small parties, which can improve their chances of victory by putting up only a single candidate, so concentrating their support.
- Competition amongst candidates from the same party broadens electoral choice and provides a strong incentive for candidates to develop a personal appeal.
- Constituents have a number of members to go to if they have grievances they wish to redress.

Disadvantages:

- Although this system is more proportional than the majoritarian systems, it is still only a semi-proportional system, and thus does not satisfy many PR supporters.
- Intra-party competition breeds factionalism and conflict.
- Members may more easily escape their constituency responsibilities because other members are always available.

ments into a programme of government. Supported by a cohesive majority in the assembly, such governments are usually able to survive for a full term in office. In contrast, coalition governments are weak and unstable, in the sense that they are endlessly engaged in a process of reconciling opposing views, and are always liable to collapse as a result of internal splits and divisions. The classic example here is post-war Italy, which up to 1996, had had no fewer than 55 governments

Supporters of PR argue, on the other hand, that having a strong government, in the sense of a government that is able to push through policies, is by no means an unqualified virtue, tending as it does to restrict scrutiny and parliamentary account-ability. Instead, they suggest that 'strong' government should be understood in

Focus on . . .

Electoral systems: additional member system (AMS)

Used: Germany, and favoured by the Royal Commission in New Zealand. **Type**: Proportional. **Features**:

- A proportion of seats (50 per cent in Germany) are filled by the FPTP system using single-member constituencies.
- The remaining seats are filled using a party list (as explained in the party-list system box).
- Electors cast two votes: one for a candidate in the constituency election, and the other for a party.

Advantages:

- The hybrid nature of this system balances the need for constituency representation against the need for electoral fairness. The party-list process ensures that the whole assembly is proportionally representative.
- Although the system is broadly proportional in terms of its outcome, it keeps alive the possibility of single-party government.
- It allows electors to choose a constituency representative from one party and yet support another party to form a government.
- It takes account of the fact that representing constituents and holding ministerial office are very different jobs that require very different talents and experience.

Disadvantages:

- The retention of single-member constituencies prevents the achievement of high levels of proportionality.
- The system creates two classes of representative, one burdened by insecurity and constituency duties, the other having higher status and the prospect of holding ministerial office.
- Constituency representation suffers because of the size of constituencies (generally twice as large as in FPTP systems).
- Parties become more centralised and powerful under this system, as they not only decide who has the security of being on the list and who has to fight constituencies, but also where on the list candidates are placed.

Proportional representation

The principle of proportional representation is the principle that parties should be represented in an assembly or parliament in direct proportion to their overall electoral strength, their percentage of seats equalling their percentage of votes. The term is generally used to refer not to a single method of election, but to a variety of electoral mechanisms, those able to secure proportional outcomes, or at least a high and reliable degree of proportionality. The best known PR systems are the party list system, the single transferable-vote system and the additional member system, although the dividing line between proportional and majoritarian systems is sometimes unclear. Commonly used in continental Europe, PR systems are concerned with the representation of parties, not individual candidates, and may be particularly suitable for divided or plural societies.

terms of popular support and the willingness of citizens to obey and respect the government. Broadly-based coalitions may possess these qualities in greater abundance than do single-party governments. By the same token, 'stable' government could mean a consistent development of government policies over a number of governments, rather than a government with the ability to survive for a single electoral term. This is more likely to be achieved by coalition governments (in which one or more parties may remain in power over a number of governments, albeit reshuffled) than by single-party governments, in which more sweeping changes in personnel and priorities are unavoidable when power changes hands.

The electoral reform debate, however, constantly risks overestimating the importance of electoral systems. In practice, elections are only one amongst a variety of factors

Focus on . . .

Electoral systems: single-transferable-vote system (STVS)

Used: Ireland, and supported for adoption in the UK by the Liberal Democrats.
Type: Proportional. **Features**:

- There are multimember constituencies, each of which returns up to five members.
- Parties may put forward as many candidates as there are seats to fill.
- Electors vote preferentially, as in the alternative vote system.
- Candidates are elected if they achieve a quota. This is the minimum number of votes needed to elect the stipulated number of candidates, calculated according to the Droop formula:

$$\text{quota} = \frac{\text{total number of votes cast}}{(\text{number of seats to be filled} + 1)} + 1$$

For example, if 100 000 votes are cast in a constituency that elects four members, the quota is $100\,000/(4 + 1) + 1 = 20\,001$.

- The votes are counted according to first preferences. If not all the seats are filled, the bottom candidate is eliminated. His or her votes are redistributed according to second preferences, and so on, until all the seats have been filled.

Advantages:

- The system is capable of achieving highly proportional outcomes.
- Competition amongst candidates from the same party means that they can be judged on their records and on where they stand on issues that cut across party lines.
- The availability of several members means that constituents can choose who to take their grievances to.

Disadvantages:

- The degree of proportionality achieved varies, largely on the basis of the party system.
- Strong and stable single-party government is unlikely.
- Intra-party competition may be divisive, and may allow members to evade their constituency responsibilities.

that shape the political process, and may not be the most crucial. Indeed, the impact of particular electoral systems is largely conditioned by other circumstances, namely the political culture, the nature of the party system, and the economic and social context within which politics is conducted. Generalisations about the nature of coalition government are always highly suspect, for instance. Whereas coalitions in Italy have typically been weak and short-lived, in Germany they have usually produced stable and effective government. Similarly, although majoritarian systems can produce significant shifts in policy as one government follows another, board policy consensuses are also not uncommon. In the 1950s and 1960s, despite an alternation in power between the Conservative and the Labour parties, UK government policy displayed a remarkable consistency of policy direction, rooted in a cross-party commitment to Keynesian social democracy. Furthermore, it is far from clear what dam-

Focus on . . .

Electoral systems: party list system

Used: Israel, and in countries throughout Europe, including Belgium, Luxembourg and Switzerland. **Type**: Proportional. **Features**:

- Either the entire country is treated as a single constituency, or, in the case of regional party lists, there are a number of large multimember constituencies.
- Parties compile lists of candidates to place before the electorate, in descending order of preference.
- Electors vote for parties, not for candidates.
- Parties are allocated seats in direct proportion to the votes they gain in the election. They fill these seats from their party list.
- A 'threshold' may be imposed (5 per cent in Germany) to exclude small, possibly extremist, parties from representation.

Advantages:

- This is the only potentially pure system of proportional representation, and is therefore fair to all parties.
- The system promotes unity by encouraging electors to identify with their nation or region rather than a constituency.
- The system makes it easier for women and minority candidates to be elected, provided, of course, they feature on the party list.
- The representation of a large number of small parties ensures that there is an emphasis upon negotiation, bargaining and consensus.

Disadvantages:

- The existence of many small parties can lead to weak and unstable government.
- The link between representatives and constituencies is entirely broken.
- Unpopular candidates who are well placed on a party list cannot be removed from office.
- Parties become heavily centralised, because leaders draw up party lists, and junior members have an incentive to be loyal in the hope of moving up the list.

Concept

Public interest

The public interest consists of the general or collective interests of a community, that is, that which is good for society as a whole. Two contrasting notions of the public interest can be identified. *Strong* versions distinguish clearly between public and private interests, between the interests of the public as a collective body and the selfish or personal interests of each individual. In the view of Rousseau and many socialists, the interests of the public are 'higher' than, or morally superior to, those of the individual. *Weak* versions recognise only private interests, and therefore see the public interest as nothing more than a collection of private interests, those which all individuals recognise as good for themselves. Liberal individualists often dismissed the very idea of a 'public' interest as absurd.

age electoral systems can cause. Despite Italy's famed political instability, often blamed on its now-abandoned party-list electoral system, in the post-Second-World-War period, the north of the country at least experienced steady economic growth, making Italy, by the 1990s, the third most prosperous state in the EU.

What do elections mean?

The importance of elections cannot be doubted. At the very least, they provide the public with its clearest formal opportunity to influence the political process, and also help, directly or indirectly, to determine who will hold government power. From this perspective, elections are about results, in other words, who wins and who loses. This view is encouraged by media coverage, which, with the aid of opinion polls, increasingly turns elections into horse races. Nevertheless, politicians are not backward in claiming that elections have a broader and more profound meaning. Elections are, in this sense, seen as nothing less than a visible manifestation of the public interest; in short, 'the public has spoken'. Political commentators also express their opinions, proclaiming, for instance, that elections reflect a 'shift in the popular mood'. The problem, however, is that all such claims and interpretations have a strongly arbitrary character; any attempt to invest an election with 'meaning' is fraught with dangers. The people may have spoken, but it is frustratingly difficult to know what they have said.

Many of these problems stem from the difficult notion of the 'public interest'. If such a thing as a 'public' interest exists, it surely reflects the common or collective interests of *all* citizens. This is precisely what J.-J. Rousseau (see p. 73) implied in the idea of the 'general will', which he understood to mean the will of all citizens, provided each of them acts selflessly. The difficulty with this view is obvious. Quite simply, individuals do not in practice act selflessly in accordance with a general or collective will; there is no such thing as an indivisible public interest. All generalisations about 'the public' or 'the electorate' must therefore be treated with grave suspicion. There is no electorate as such, only a collection of electors who each possess particular interests, sympathies, allegiances and so on. At best, election results reflect the preferences of a majority, or perhaps a plurality, of voters. However, even then there are perhaps insuperable problems in deciding what these votes 'mean'.

The difficulty in interpreting election results lies in the perhaps impossible task of knowing why voters vote as they do. As is made clear in the next section, generations of political scientists have grappled with the question of electoral behaviour but have failed to develop a universally accepted theory of voting. Voting, on the surface a very simple act, is shaped by a complex of factors, conscious and unconscious, rational and irrational, selfish and selfless. All theories are therefore partial and must be qualified by a range of other considerations. This can be seen in relation to the so-called economic theory of democracy, advanced by Anthony Downs (1957). This theory suggests that the act of voting reflects an expression of self-interest on the part of voters, who select parties in much the same way as consumers select goods or services for purchase. On this basis, the winning party in an election can reasonably claim that its policies most closely correspond to the interests of the largest group of voters.

On the other hand, it can be argued that, rather than 'buying' policies, voters are typically poorly informed about political issues and are influenced by a range of 'irrational' factors such as habit, social conditioning, the image of the parties, and the personalities of their leaders. Moreover, the ability of parties to attract votes may have less to do with the 'goods' they put up for purchase than with the way those goods are 'sold' through advertising, political campaigning, propaganda and so on. To the extent that this is true, election results may reflect not so much the interests of the mass of voters as the resources and finances available to the competing parties.

A further, and some would argue more intractable, problem is that no elective mechanism may be able reliably to give expression to the multifarious preferences of voters. This is a problem that the US economist Kenneth Arrow described in terms of his 'impossibility theorem'. In *Social Choice and Individual Values* (1951), Arrow drew attention to the problem of 'transitivity' that occurs when voters are allowed to express a range of preferences for candidates or policy options rather than merely cast a single vote. The drawback of casting but a single vote is not only that it is a crude all-or-nothing device, but also that no single candidate or option may gain majority support. For instance, candidate A may gain 40 per cent of the vote, candidate B 34 per cent, and candidate C 26 per cent. The situation could nevertheless become more confused if second preferences were taken into account.

Let us assume, for the sake of argument, that the second preference of all candidate A's supporters go to candidate C, the second preferences of candidate B favour candidate A, and the second preferences of candidate C go to candidate B. This creates a situation in which each candidate can claim to be preferred by a majority of voters. The first and second preferences for candidate A add up to 74 per cent (40 per cent plus B's 34 per cent). Candidate B can claim 60 per cent support (34 per cent plus C's 26 per cent), and candidate C can claim 66 per cent support (26 per cent plus A's 40 per cent). This problem of 'cyclical majorities' draws attention to the fact that it may not be possible to establish a reliable link between individual preferences and collective choices. In other words, election results cannot speak for themselves, and politicians and political commentators who claim to find meaning in them are, to some extent, acting arbitrarily. Nevertheless, the latitude that this allows politicians is not unlimited, because they know that they will be called to account at the next election. In this light, perhaps the most significant function of elections is to set limits to arbitrary government by ensuring that politicians who claim to speak *for* the public must ultimately be judged *by* the public.

Voting behaviour

The growth of academic interest in voting behaviour coincided with the rise of behavioural political science. As the most widespread and quantifiable form of political behaviour, voting quickly became the focus for new techniques of sample surveying and statistical analysis. *The American Voter* (Campbell *et al.*, 1960), the product of painstaking research by the University of Michigan, became the leading work in the field and stimulated a wealth of similar studies, such as Butler and Stokes' *Political Change in Britain* (1969). At the high point of the behavioural revolution, it was thought that voting held the key to disclosing all the mysteries of the political system, perhaps allowing for laws of mass political psychology to be developed. Even though these lofty hopes have not been fulfilled, psephology (the scientific study of voting behaviour) still commands a central position in political analysis. This is because voting provides one of the richest sources of information about the interaction between individuals, society and politics. By investigating the mysteries of voting behaviour, we are thus able to learn important lessons about the nature of the political system, and gain insight into the process of social and political change.

Voting behaviour is clearly shaped by short-term and long-term influences. Short-term influences are specific to a particular election and do not allow conclusions to be drawn about voting patterns in general. The chief short-term influence is the state of the economy, which reflects the fact that there is usually a link between a government's popularity and economic variables such as unemployment, inflation and disposable income. Optimism about one's own material circumstances (the so-called 'feel-good' factor) appears to be particularly crucial here. Indeed, it is often alleged that governments attempt to create pre-election booms in the hope of improving their chances of gaining reelection. The chances that political and business cycles can be brought into conjunction are clearly strengthened by flexible-term elections that allow the government to choose when to 'go to the country'.

Another short-term influence on voting is the personality and public standing of party leaders. This is particularly important, because media exposure portrays leaders as the brand image of their party. This means that a party may try to rekindle popular support by replacing a leader who is perceived to be an electoral liability, as the Conservatives in the UK did with Margaret Thatcher in 1990, and the Australian Labor Party did with Bob Hawke in 1991. Another factor is the style and effectiveness of the parties' electoral campaigning. The length of the campaign can vary from about three weeks for flexible-term elections to up to two years in the case of fixed-term elections, such as those for the US president. Opinion polls are usually thought to be significant in this respect, either giving a candidate's or party's campaign momentum, or instilling disillusionment or even complacency amongst voters.

A final short-term influence, the mass media (see p. 188), may also be of long-term significance if biased or partisan coverage reflects structural, and therefore continuing, factors such as press ownership. However, the pattern of media coverage may change from election to election. Neil Kinnock highlighted this by claiming that a campaign of personal vilification against him by the UK tabloid press explained the Labour Party's defeat in the 1992 UK general election. All such considerations, however, operate within a context of psychological, sociological, economic and ideological influences upon voting. These are best examined in relation to rival models of voting. The most significant of these are the following:

- the party-identification model
- the sociological model
- the rational-choice model
- the dominant-ideology model.

Theories of voting

Party-identification model

The earliest theory of voting behaviour, the party-identification model, is based on the sense of psychological attachment that people have to parties. Electors are seen as people who *identify* with a party, in the sense of being long-term supporters who regard the party as 'their' party. Voting is therefore a manifestation of partisanship, not a product of calculation influenced by factors such as policies, personalities, campaigning and media coverage. This model places heavy stress on early political socialisation, seeing the family as the principal means through which political loyalties are forged. These are then, in most cases, reinforced by group membership and later social experiences.

In this model, attitudes towards policies and leaders, as well as perceptions about group and personal interests, tend to be developed on the basis of party identification. Events are thus interpreted to fit with pre-existing loyalties and attachments. This partisan alignment tends to create stability and continuity, especially in terms of habitual patterns of voting behaviour, often sustained over a lifetime. From this point of view, it should be possible to calculate the 'normal' vote of a party by reference to partisanship levels. Deviations from this 'normal' level presumably reflect the impact of short-term factors. One of the weaknesses of this model is the growing evidence from a number of countries of partisan dealignment. This indicates a general fall in party identification and a decline in habitual voting patterns. In the USA, partisan dealignment is reflected in a decline in the number of registered Democrats and Republicans and a rise in the number of Independents (up from 9 per cent in 1920 to around 30 per cent in the 1980s). In the UK, it is demonstrated by a decline in the strength of allegiance to the Conservative Party and the Labour Party, 'very strong' identification with either party having fallen from 82 per cent in 1964 to 35 per cent in 1987.

Sociological model

The sociological model links voting behaviour to group membership, suggesting that electors tend to adopt a voting pattern that reflects the economic and social position of the group to which they belong. Rather than developing a psychological attachment to a party on the basis of family influence, this model highlights the importance of a social alignment, reflecting the various divisions and tensions within society. The most significant of these divisions are class, gender, ethnicity, religion and region. Although the impact of socialisation is not irrelevant to this model, social-base explanations allow for rationality insofar as group interests may help to shape party allegiances. This has perhaps been clearest in relation to social class.

Not uncommonly, party systems have been seen to reflect the class system, with the middle classes providing the electoral base for right-wing parties, and the working classes providing the electoral base for left-wing parties. The Labour–Conservative two-party system in the UK was traditionally understood in precisely this light. Peter Pulzer (1967:98) was able to declare, famously, 'class is the basis of British party politics; all else is embellishment and detail'. The sociological model, however, has been attacked on the grounds that, in focusing on social groups, it ignores the individual and the role of personal self-interest. Moreover, there is growing empirical evidence that the link between sociological factors and party support has weakened in modern societies. In particular, attention has been paid to the phenomenon of class dealignment (see p. 226). Evidence of class dealignment can be found in most western societies. For example, absolute class voting (the proportion of voters who support their 'natural' class party) fell in the UK from 66 per cent in 1966 to 47 per cent in 1983.

Rational-choice model

Rational-choice models of voting shift attention onto the individual and away from socialisation and the behaviour of social groups. In this view, voting is seen as a rational act, in the sense that individual electors are believed to decide their party

Concept

Partisan dealignment

Partisan dealignment is a decline in the extent to which people align themselves with a party by identifying with it. As party loyalties weaken, electoral behaviour is likely to become more volatile, leading to greater uncertainty and perhaps the rise of new parties or the decline of old ones. What is seen as the 'normal' support of parties falls, and a growing number of electors become 'floating' or 'swing' voters. The principal reasons for partisan dealignment are the expansion of education, an increase in geographical and social mobility, and growing reliance on television as a source of political information. Some argue that partisan dealignment reflects growing disenchantment with conventional politics, and the failure of the party system to respond to the needs of a postindustrial society.

Concept

Class dealignment

Class dealignment is the weakening of the relationship between social class and party support. Social class (see p. 179) may nevertheless remain a significant (perhaps the most significant) factor influencing electoral choice. The impact of dealignment has been to undermine traditional class-based parties, notably working class parties of the left, often bringing about a realignment of the party system. Explanations of class dealignment usually focus on changes in the social structure that have weakened the solidaristic character of class identity. These include the embourgeoisement of the working class brought about by growing affluence, the shift from manufacturing to service industries, and the growing importance of sectoral cleavages based on the public-sector/private-sector divide.

preference on the basis of personal self-interest. Rather than being habitual, a manifestation of broader attachments and allegiances, voting is seen as essentially instrumental, that is, as a means to an end. Rational-choice models differ in that some, like V. O. Key (1966), see voting as a retrospective comment on the party in power and how its performance has influenced citizen's choice, while others, such as Himmelveit, Humphreys and Jaeger (1985), portray voters as active in the sense that they behave like consumers expressing a choice amongst the available policy options.

The latter view stresses the importance of what is called 'issue voting', and suggests that parties can significantly influence their electoral performance by revising and reshaping their policies. It is generally accepted that one of the consequences of partisan and class dealignment has been the spread of issue voting. This has also been encouraged by the pluralism and individualism that postmodernism (see p. 61) has fostered. The weakness of rational-choice theories is that they abstract the individual voter from his or her social and cultural context. In other words, to some extent, the ability to evaluate issues and calculate self-interest (the essence of instrumental voting) is structured by broader party attachments and group loyalties.

Dominant-ideology model

Radical theories of voting tend to highlight the degree to which individual choices are shaped by a process of ideological manipulation and control. In some respects, such theories resemble the sociological model in that voting is seen to reflect a person's position in a social hierarchy. Where these theories differ from the sociological model, however, is in emphasising that how groups and individuals interpret their position depends on how it has been presented to them through education, by the government, and, above all, by the mass media. Dunleavy and Husbands (1985), for instance, argued that, as the impact of class on UK voting declines, party competition and political debate are increasingly influenced by the media.

In contrast to the earlier view that the mass media merely reinforce pre-existing preferences, this suggests that the media are able to distort the flow of political communications, both by setting the agenda for debate and structuring preferences and sympathies. The consequence of this is that, if voters' attitudes conform to the tenets of a dominant ideology, parties will not be able to afford to develop policies that fall outside that ideology. In this way, far from challenging the existing distribution of power and resources in society, the electoral process tends to uphold it. The weakness of the dominant-ideology model is that, by overstating the process of social conditioning, it takes individual calculation and personal autonomy out of the picture altogether.

■ Summary

◆ Representation is a relationship in which an individual or group stands for, or acts on behalf of, a larger body of people. This may be achieved through the exercise of wisdom by an educated elite, through guidance or instructions given to a delegate, through the winning of a popular mandate, or through representatives being drawn from the groups they represent.

◆ In modern politics, representation is invariably linked with elections. Elections may not be a sufficient condition for political representation, but are certainly a necessary condition. For elections to serve representative purposes, however, they must be competitive, free and fair, and conducted on the basis of universal adult suffrage.

◆ Elections have a variety of functions. On the one hand, they have 'bottom-up' functions, such as political recruitment, representation, making government and influencing policy. On the other hand, radical theorists emphasise their 'top-down' functions, which include that they build legitimacy, shape public opinion, and help to strengthen elites.

◆ Electoral systems are often classified as either majoritarian systems or proportional systems. In majoritarian systems, large parties typically win a higher proportion of seats than votes, thereby increasing the chances of single-party government. In proportional systems, there is an equal, or at least more equal, relationship between the percentages of seats and votes won, increasing the likelihood of coalition government.

◆ Majoritarian systems are usually defended on the grounds that they offer the electorate a clear choice of potential governments, invest winning parties with a policy mandate, and help to promote strong and stable government. In contrast, proportional systems are defended on the grounds that they usually give government a broader electoral base, promote consensus and cooperation amongst a number of parties, and establish a healthy balance between the executive and the assembly.

◆ The meaning of elections is closely linked to the factors that shape voting behaviour. Amongst the various theories of voting are models that highlight the importance of party identification and habitual attachments, ones that emphasise the importance of group membership and social alignment, ones that are based on rational choice and calculations of self-interest, and ones that suggest that individual choices are shaped by ideological manipulation and control.

▊ Questions for discussion

▶ Is representation merely a substitute for democracy?

▶ What conditions best promote representative government?

▶ Are elections more significant in calling politicians to account, or in ensuring the survival of a regime?

▶ Is there inevitably a trade-off between electoral fairness and strong and stable government?

▶ How successful are elections in defining the public interest?

▶ To what extent is voting behaviour a rational and issue-based activity?

▊ Further reading

Birch, A. H. *Representation* (London: Macmillan; New York: Praeger, 1972). A clear and thorough discussion of the concept of representation and the conditions of representative government.

Bogdanor, V. and D. Butler (eds) *Democracy and Elections* (Cambridge: Cambridge University Press, 1983). A useful collection of essays that survey how electoral systems work in various countries.

Harrop, M. and W. L. Miller *Elections and Voters: A Comparative Introduction* (Basingstoke: Macmillan, 1987). An accessible and very informative analysis of the role of elections and debates about voting behaviour.

LeDuc, L., R. Niemi and P. Norris (eds) *Comparing Democracies: Elections and Voting in Global Perspective* (London: Sage, 1996). A good examination of the nature and health of electoral democracy and the significance of electoral systems.

CHAPTER 12

Parties and Party Systems

'In politics, shared hatreds are almost always the basis of friendships.'

ALEXIS DE TOCQUEVILLE *Democracy in America* (1835)

So fundamental are political parties to the operation of modern politics that their role and significance is often taken for granted. It is forgotten, for instance, that parties are a relatively recent invention. As political machines organised to win elections and wield government power, parties only came into existence in the early nineteenth century. Now, however, they are virtually ubiquitous. The only parts of the world in which they do not exist are those where they are suppressed by dictatorship or military rule. Quite simply, the political party is the major organising principle of modern politics. Whether they are the great tools of democracy or sources of tyranny and repression, political parties are the vital link between the state and civil society, between the institutions of government and the groups and interests that operate within society. Nevertheless, parties and party systems have increasingly come under attack. They have been blamed for failing to articulate the new and more diverse aspirations that have emerged in modern societies, and for failing to solve, or perhaps even address, many of their most serious problems.

The principal issues discussed in this chapter are the following:

Contents

Key issues

▶ What is a political party? How can parties be classified?

▶ What are the major functions of political parties?

▶ How are parties organised, and where is power located within them?

▶ What kinds of party system are there?

▶ How does the party system shape the broader political process?

▶ Are parties in decline, and is this decline terminal?

■ Party politics

Political parties are found in the vast majority of countries and in most political systems. Parties may be authoritarian or democratic; they may seek power through elections or through revolution; and they may espouse ideologies of the left, right or centre, or, indeed, disavow political ideas altogether. However, parties of some kind exist from Brazil to Burundi and from Norway to New Zealand. The development of political parties and the acquisition of a party system came to be recognised as a mark of political modernisation. By the late 1950s, some 80 per cent of the world's states were ruled by political parties. During the 1960s and early 1970s, however, a decline set in with the spread of military rule in the developing world. Political parties were accused of being divisive, and of failing to solve overriding problems of poverty and ethnic and tribal rivalry. They also proved to be inconvenient for economic and military elites. The upsurge of 'democratisation' in the 1980s and 1990s nevertheless led to a renewed flourishing of parties. In Asia, Africa and Latin America, the relaxation or collapse of military rule was invariably accompanied by the re-emergence of parties. In former communist states, one-party rule was replaced by the establishment of competitive party systems.

It would be a mistake, however, to assume that parties have always been with us. Political parties are part of the structures of mass politics, ushered in by the advent of representative government and the progressive extension of the franchise during the nineteenth century. Until then, what were called 'factions' or 'parties' were little more than groups of like-minded politicians, usually formed around a key leader or family. So-called 'court' parties, for instance, often developed within autocratic monarchies as a result of the struggle for influence amongst notables and advisers. Thus, when Edmund Burke (see p. 45) in the late eighteenth century described a party as 'a body of men united . . . upon some particular principle upon which they all agree', he was thinking about fluid and informal groupings such as the Whigs and the Tories, not about the organised and increasingly disciplined machines into which they were to develop.

Parties of the modern kind first emerged in the USA. Despite the abhorrence of parties felt by the 'founding fathers' who created the US constitution, the Federalist Party (later the Whigs and, from 1860, the Republican Party) appeared as a mass-based party during the US presidential election of 1800. Many conservative and liberal parties started life as legislative factions. Only later, forced to appeal to an ever-widening electorate,

---

Concept

Political party

A political party is a group of people that is organised for the purpose of winning government power, by electoral or other means. Parties are often confused with interest groups (see p. 254) or political movements.

Four characteristics usually distinguish parties from other groups:

- Parties aim to exercise government power by winning political office (small parties may nevertheless use elections more to gain a platform than to win power).
- Parties are organised bodies with a formal 'card carrying' membership. This distinguishes them from broader and more diffuse political movements.
- Parties typically adopt a broad issue focus, addressing each of the major areas of government policy (small parties, however, may have a single-issue focus, thus resembling interest groups).
- To varying degrees, parties are united by shared political preferences and a general ideological identity.

Concept

Faction, factionalism

Originally, the terms faction and party were used interchangeably. Faction is now more commonly used to mean a section or group within a larger formation, usually a political party. Although factions may be stable and enduring, and may possess formal organisation and membership, their aims and organisational status are compatible with those of their host party. If they are not, the group is seen as a 'party within a party'. A distinction is sometimes drawn between factions and tendencies, the latter being looser and more informal groups, distinguished only by a common policy or ideological disposition. Factionalism refers either to the proliferation of factions or to the bitterness of factional rivalry. The term faction is often used pejoratively; the term factionalism is always pejorative, implying debilitating infighting.

did they develop an extraparliamentary machinery of constituency branches, local agents and so on. In contrast, socialist parties and parties representing religious, ethnic and language groups were invariably born as social movements or interest groups operating outside government. Subsequently, they developed into fully fledged parliamentary parties in the hope of winning formal representation and shaping public policy. By the beginning of the twentieth century, parties and party systems had, in effect, become the political manifestation of the social and other cleavages that animated society at large. However, the resulting party forms varied considerably.

Types of party

A variety of classifications have been used for political parties. The most important of these are the following:

- cadre and mass parties
- representative and integrative parties
- constitutional and revolutionary parties
- left-wing and right-wing parties.

The most common distinction is that between cadre parties and mass parties. The term cadre party originally meant a 'party of notables', dominated by an informal group of leaders who saw little point in building up a mass organisation. Such parties invariably developed out of parliamentary factions or cliques at a time when the franchise was limited. However, the term cadre is now more commonly used (as in communist parties) to denote trained and professional party members who are expected to exhibit a high level of political commitment and doctrinal discipline. In this sense, the Communist Party of the Soviet Union (CPSU), the Nazi Party in Germany, and the Fascist Party in Italy were cadre parties, as are the Chinese Communist Party (CCP) and, in certain respects, the Indian Congress Party in the modern period. The distinguishing feature of cadre parties is their reliance on a politically active elite (usually subject to quasi-military discipline) which is capable of offering ideological leadership to the masses. Although strict political criteria are laid down for party membership, careerism and simple convenience are often powerful motives for joining such parties, as both the CPSU and the Nazis found out.

A mass party, on the other hand, places a heavy emphasis on broadening membership and constructing a wide electoral base. Although the extension of the franchise forced liberal and conservative parties to seek a mass appeal, the earliest examples of mass parties were European socialist parties, such as the German Social Democratic Party (SPD) and the UK Labour Party, which constructed organisations specifically designed to mobilise working-class support. The key feature of such parties is that they place heavier stress on recruitment and organisation than on ideology and political conviction. Although such parties often have formally democratic organisations, except for a minority of activists, membership usually entails little in the way of participation and only general agreement about principles and goals.

Most modern parties fall into the category of what Otto Kirchheimer (1966) termed 'catch-all parties'. These are parties that drastically reduce their ideological baggage in order to appeal to the largest possible number of voters. Kirchheimer particularly had in mind the Christian Democratic Union (CDU) in Germany, but the best examples of catch-all parties are found in the USA in the form of the Republicans and the Democrats. Modern de-ideologised socialist parties such as the German Social Democrats and the Labour Party in the UK also fit this description. These parties differ from the classic model of a mass party in that they emphasise leadership and unity, and downgrade the role of individual party members in trying to build up broad coalitions of support rather than relying on a particular social class or sectional group.

The second party distinction, advanced by Sigmund Neumann (1956), is that between so-called parties of representation and parties of integration. Representative parties see their primary function as being the securing of votes in elections. They thus attempt to reflect, rather than shape, public opinion. In this respect, representative parties adopt a catch-all strategy and therefore place pragmatism before principle and market research before popular mobilisation. The prevalence of such parties in modern politics gave considerable force to arguments based on **rational choice** models of political behaviour, like those of Joseph Schumpeter (see p. 211) and Anthony Downs, which portray politicians as power-seeking creatures who are willing to adopt whatever policies are likely to bring them electoral success.

Parties of integration, in contrast, adopt pro-active, rather than reactive, political strategies; they wish to mobilise, educate and inspire the masses, rather than merely respond to their concerns. Although Neumann saw the typical mobilising party as an ideologically-disciplined cadre party, mass parties may also exhibit mobilising tendencies. For example, until they became discouraged by electoral failure, socialist parties set out to 'win over' the electorate to a belief in the benefits of public ownership, full employment, redistribution, social welfare and so on. This approach was also, rather ironically, adopted by the UK Conservatives under Margaret Thatcher in the 1980s. Abandoning the party's traditional distaste for ideology (see p. 41) and abstract principle, Thatcher embraced 'conviction politics' in pursuing a mobilising strategy based on firm support for cutting taxes, encouraging enterprise, promoting individual responsibility, tackling trade-union power and so forth.

The third type of classification distinguishes between constitutional parties and revolutionary parties. Constitutional parties acknowledge the rights and entitlements of other parties and thus operate within a framework of rules and constraints. In particular, they acknowledge that there is a division between the party and the state, between the party in power (the government of the day) and state institutions (the bureaucracy, judiciary, police and so on) that enjoy formal independence and political neutrality. Above all, constitutional parties acknowledge and respect the rules of electoral competition. They recognise that they can be voted out of power as easily as they can be voted into it. Mainstream parties in liberal democracies all have such a constitutional character.

Revolutionary parties, on the other hand, are anti-system or anticonstitutional parties, either of the left or of the right. Such parties aim to seize power and overthrow the existing constitutional structure using tactics that range from outright insurrection and popular revolution to the quasi-legalism practised by the Nazis and the Fascists. In some cases, revolutionary parties are formally banned by being classified as 'extremist' or 'antidemocratic', as has been the case in postwar Germany. When such parties win power, however, they invariably become 'ruling' or regime parties, suppressing rival parties and establishing a permanent relationship with the state machinery. In one-party systems, whether established under the banner of communism, fascism, nationalism or whatever, the distinction between the party and the

Rational choice: An approach to politics based on the assumption that individuals are rationally self-interested actors; an 'economic' theory of politics.

state has been so weakened that the 'ruling' party has in effect substituted itself for the government, creating a fused 'party–state' apparatus. It was common in the USSR, for instance, for the General Secretary of the CPSU to act as the chief executive or head of government without bothering to assume a formal state post.

The final way of distinguishing between parties is on the basis of ideological orientation, specifically between those parties labelled left-wing and those labelled right-wing (see p. 234). Parties seen as part of 'the Left' (progressive, socialist and communist parties) are characterised by a commitment to change, in the form of either social reform or wholesale economic transformation. These have traditionally drawn their support from the ranks of the poor and disadvantaged (in urban societies, the working classes). Parties thought to constitute 'the Right' (conservative and fascist parties in particular) generally uphold the existing social order and are, in that sense, a force for continuity. Their supporters usually include business interests and the materially contented middle classes. However, this notion of a neat left–right party divide is at best simplistic and at worst deeply misleading. Not only are both the left and the right often divided along reformist/revolutionary and constitutional/insurrectionary lines, but also all parties, especially constitutional ones, tend to be 'broad churches' in the sense that they encompass their own left and right wings. Moreover, electoral competition has the effect of blurring ideological identities, once-cherished principles commonly being discarded in the search for votes. Finally, the shift away from old class polarities and the emergence of new political issues such as environment, animal rights and feminism has perhaps rendered the conventional ideas of left and right redundant (Giddens, 1994).

Functions of parties

Although political parties are defined by a central function (the filling of political office and the wielding of government power), their impact on the political system is substantially broader and more complex. It goes without saying that there are dangers in generalising about the functions of parties. Constitutional parties operating in a context of electoral competition tend to be portrayed as bastions of democracy; indeed, the existence of such parties is often seen as the litmus test of a healthy democratic system. On the other hand, regime parties that enjoy a monopoly of political power are more commonly portrayed as instruments of manipulation and political control. A number of general functions of parties can nevertheless be identified. The main functions are as follows:

- representation
- elite formation and recruitment
- goal formulation
- interest articulation and aggregation
- socialisation and mobilisation
- organisation of government.

Representation

Representation (see p. 206) is often seen as the primary function of parties. It refers to the capacity of parties to respond to and articulate the views of both members and the voters. In the language of systems theory, political parties are major 'inputting'

Focus on . . .

The political spectrum

The left–right political spectrum is a shorthand method of describing political ideas and beliefs, summarising the ideological positions of politicians, parties and movements. Its origins date back to the French Revolution and the positions groups adopted at the first meeting of the French Estates-General in 1789. The terms left and right do not have exact meanings, however. In a narrow sense, the *linear* political spectrum (see Figure 12.1) summarises different attitudes to the economy and the role of the state: left-wing views support intervention and collectivism, right-wing ones favour the market and individualism. This supposedly reflects deeper ideological or value differences, as follows:

Left	Right
Liberty	Authority
Equality	Hierarchy
Fraternity	Order
Rights	Duties
Progress	Tradition
Reform	Reaction
Internationalism	Nationalism

An alternative, *horseshoe-shaped* political spectrum (see Figure 12.2) was devised in the postwar period to highlight the totalitarian and monistic (anti-pluralist) tendencies of both fascism and communism, by contrast with the alleged tolerance and openness of mainstream creeds. Those, like Hans Eysenck (1964), who have developed a *two-dimensional* political spectrum (see Figure 12.3) have tried to compensate for the crudeness and inconsistencies of the conventional left–right spectrum by adding a vertical authoritarian–libertarian one. This enables positions on economic organisation to be disentangled from those related to civil liberty.

devices that ensure that government heeds the needs and wishes of the larger society. Clearly, this is a function that is best carried out, some would say only carried out, in an open and competitive system that forces parties to respond to popular preferences. Rational-choice theorists, such as Anthony Downs (1957), explain this process by suggesting that the political market parallels the economic market, in that politicians act essentially as entrepreneurs seeking votes, meaning that parties behave very much like businesses. Power thus ultimately resides with the consumers, the voters. This 'economic model' can, however, be criticised on the grounds that parties seek to 'shape' or mobilise public opinion as well as respond to it, that the image of voters as well informed, rational and issue-orientated consumers is questionable, and that the range of consumer (or electoral) choice is often narrow.

Elite formation and recruitment

Parties of all kinds are responsible for providing states with their political leaders. One of the rare exceptions to this rule was General de Gaulle, who offered himself to France in 1944 as a 'saviour figure' standing above party divisions. Parties such as the Union for the New Republic (UNR) were his creation, as opposed to him being

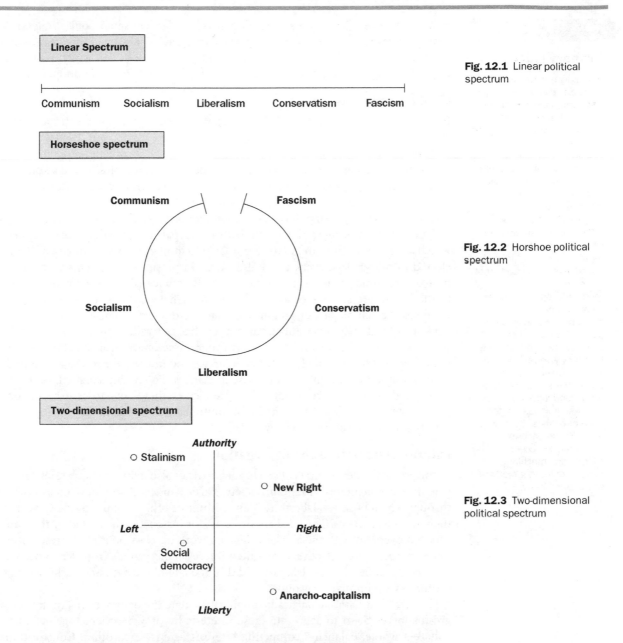

Linear Spectrum

Communism   Socialism   Liberalism   Conservatism   Fascism

Fig. 12.1 Linear political spectrum

Horseshoe spectrum

Communism   Fascism

Socialism   Conservatism

Liberalism

Fig. 12.2 Horshoe political spectrum

Two-dimensional spectrum

Authority

○ Stalinism

○ **New Right**

Left ———————————— *Right*

○
Social
democracy

○ **Anarcho-capitalism**

Liberty

Fig. 12.3 Two-dimensional political spectrum

theirs. Much more commonly, politicians achieve office by virtue of their party post; contestants in a presidential election are usually party leaders, while in parliamentary systems the leader of the largest party in the assembly normally becomes prime minister. Cabinet and other ministerial posts are usually filled by senior party figures, though exceptions are found in presidential systems like the USA's, which allow non-party ministers to be appointed.

In most cases, parties therefore provide a training ground for politicians, equipping them with skills, knowledge and experience, and offering them some form of career structure, albeit one that depends on the fortunes of the party. On the other hand, the stranglehold that parties exert over government offices can be criticised for

Concept

Primary election

A primary election is an intraparty election in which candidates are selected to contest a subsequent 'official' election. During the twentieth century, primaries became the principal nominating device used in the USA, also being used to choose convention delegates and party leaders. Most US states hold 'closed' primaries in which participation is restricted to registered supporters of the party (not the same as a party member); 'open' primaries allow all voters to participate regardless of party affiliation. The significance of primaries is that they give rank-and-file voters more of a voice in party affairs and lead to a more candidate-orientated and less party-orientated style of politics. Success in the primaries allows a candidate to seize control of the party machine, instead of leaving matters to the party itself.

ensuring that political leaders are drawn from a relatively small pool of talent: the senior figures in a handful of major parties. In the USA, however, this stranglehold has been weakened by the widespread use of primary elections, which reduce the control that a party has over the process of candidate selection and nomination.

Goal formulation

Political parties have traditionally been one of the means through which societies set collective goals and, in some cases, ensure that they are carried out. Parties play this role because, in the process of seeking power, they formulate programmes of government (through conferences, conventions, election manifestos and so on) with a view to attracting popular support. Not only does this mean that parties are a major source of policy initiation, but it also encourages them to formulate coherent sets of policy options that give the electorate a choice amongst realistic and achievable goals.

This function is most clearly carried out by parties in parliamentary systems which are able to claim a mandate (see p. 210) to implement their policies if they are elected to power. However, it can also occur in presidential systems with usually non-programmic parties, as in the case of the Republicans' 'Contract with America' in the US congressional elections of 1994. Nevertheless, the tendency towards de-ideologised catch-all parties, and the fact that electoral campaigns increasingly stress personality and image over policies and issues, has generally reduced the impact that parties have on policy formulation. Party programmes, moreover, are almost certain to be modified by pressure from the civil service and interest groups, as well as in the light of domestic and international circumstances. Policy implementation, on the other hand, is usually carried out by bureaucracies rather than parties, except in one-party systems like those in orthodox communist states, where the 'ruling' party supervises the state apparatus at every level.

Interest articulation and aggregation

In the process of developing collective goals, parties also help to articulate and aggregate the various interests found in society. Parties, indeed, often develop as vehicles through which business, labour, religious, ethnic or other groups advance or defend their various interests. The UK Labour Party, for instance, was created by the trade-union movement with the aim of achieving working-class political representation. Other parties have, effectively, recruited interests and groups in order to broaden their electoral base, as the US parties did in the late nineteenth and early twentieth centuries with immigrant groups.

The fact that national parties invariably articulate the demands of a multitude of groups forces them to aggregate these interests by drawing them together into a coherent whole, balancing competing interests against each other. Constitutional parties are clearly forced to do this by the pressures of electoral competition, but even monopolistic parties articulate and aggregate interests through their close relationship with the state and the economy, especially in centrally planned systems. However, not even in competitive party systems are all interests articulated, those of small groups, the relatively poor and the politically unorganised being the most vulnerable to exclusion.

Socialisation and mobilisation

Through internal debate and discussion, as well as campaigning and electoral competition, parties are important agents of political education and socialisation. The issues parties choose to focus on helps to set the political agenda, and the values and attitudes that they articulate become part of the larger political culture (see p. 186). In the case of monopolistic parties, the propagation of an 'official' ideology (be it Marxism–Leninism, National Socialism, or simply the ideas of a charismatic leader) is consciously acknowledged to be a central, if not its supreme, function.

Mainstream parties in competitive systems play no less significant a role in encouraging groups to play by the rules of the democratic game, thus mobilising support for the regime itself. For example, the emergence of socialist parties in the late nineteenth and early twentieth centuries was an important means of integrating the working class into industrial society. Nevertheless, the capacity of parties to mobilise and socialise has been brought into doubt by evidence in many countries of partisan dealignment (see p. 225) and growing disenchantment with conventional pro-system parties. The problem that parties have is that, to some extent, they themselves are socialised (some would say corrupted) by the experience of government, making them, it appears, less effective in engaging partisan sympathies and attracting emotional attachments.

Organisation of government

It is often argued that complex modern societies would be ungovernable in the absence of political parties. In the first place, parties help with the formation of governments, in parliamentary systems to the extent that it is possible to talk of 'party government' (see p. 243). Parties also give governments a degree of stability and coherence, especially if the members of the government are drawn from a single party and are therefore united by common sympathies and attachments. Even governments that are formed from a coalition of parties are more likely to foster unity and agreement than ones that consist of separate individuals each with his or her own priorities.

Parties, furthermore, facilitate cooperation between the two major branches of government, the assembly and the executive. In parliamentary systems, this is effectively guaranteed by the fact the government is formed from the party or parties that have majority control of the assembly. However, even in presidential systems the chief executive can wield some influence, if not control, through an appeal to party unity. Finally, parties provide, in competitive systems at least, a vital source of opposition and criticism, both inside and outside of government. As well as broadening political debate and educating the electorate, this helps to ensure that government policy is more thoroughly scrutinised and therefore more likely to be workable.

Party organisation: where does power lie?

Because of the crucial role that political parties play, considerable attention has been focused on where power lies within parties. The organisation and structure of parties thus provides vital clues about the distribution of power within society as a whole. Can parties function as democratic bodies that broaden participation and access to power? Or do they simply entrench the dominance of leaders and elites?

One of the earliest attempts to investigate internal party democracy was undertaken in Mosei Ostrogorski's *Democracy and the Organisation of Political Parties* (1902), which argued that the representation of individual interests had lost out to the growing influence of the party machine and control exerted by a caucus of senior

Focus on . . .

The iron law of oligarchy

Oligarchy is government or domination by the few. The iron law of oligarchy, formulated by Michels ([1911] 1962), suggests that there is an inevitable tendency for political organisations, and by implication all organisations, to be oligarchic. Participatory or democratic structures cannot check oligarchic tendencies; they can only disguise them.

Michels advanced a number of arguments in support of his law:

- Elite groups result from the need for specialisation. Elite members have greater *expertise* and better organisational skills than those possessed by ordinary members.
- Leaders form *cohesive* groups because they recognise that this improves their chances of remaining in power.
- Rank-and-file members of an organisation tend to be *apathetic*, and are therefore generally disposed to accept subordination and venerate leaders.

party figures. This view was more memorably expressed by Robert Michel in *Poltiical Parties* ([1911] 1962) in the form of the 'iron law of oligarchy', or, as Michels put it, 'he who says organisation says oligarchy'. Michels (1876–1936), a prominent elite theorist, wished to analyse the power structure of the German SPD; he argued that, despite the party's formally democratic organisation, power was concentrated in the hands of a small group of party leaders.

For Michels, the 'law' explained the inevitable failure of democratic socialism and, indeed, exploded the myth of political democracy. Critics, however, point out that Michels' observations are generalisations made on the basis of a single political party at a particular moment in time, and also rest on questionable psychological theories. In practice, party elites have often proved to be more faction-ridden, and mass memberships less deferential and quiescent, than Michels suggested. A more modern version of the same theory was developed in *British Political Parties* (1955) by Robert McKenzie. McKenzie challenged the established view that the Conservative Party was elitist and leader-dominated, while the Labour Party was characterised by a high measure of internal democracy. Despite the parties' different structures and value systems, McKenzie concluded that the distribution of power within the two parties was essentially the same: both were dominated by a nexus of parliamentary leaders.

Attempts have been made to strengthen the democratic and participatory features of parties through reform. One of the clearest examples of this occurred in the USA in the 1970s and 1980s. US parties differ in many respects from their European counterparts. Being loose coalitions of sometimes conflicting interests held together by little more than the need to contest presidential elections, they are highly decentralised and generally non-programmic. Traditionally, state-based or city-based party bosses (a legacy of the **machine politics** of the early twentieth century) acted as power brokers and exercised a decisive influence at nominating conventions. Following protests and clashes at the 1968 Democratic national convention in Chicago, however, a reform movement sprang up aimed at weakening the power of local party leaders and strengthening the role of rank-and-file members.

This was largely accomplished through the wider use of nominating primaries

Machine politics: A style of politics in which party 'bosses' control a mass organisation through patronage and the distribution of favours.

and **caucuses**. These, first with the Democrats and later the Republicans, attracted a growing number of issue and candidate activists into party politics, leading to the nomination of more ideological candidates such as George McGovern for the Democrats in 1972 and Ronald Reagan for the Republicans in 1980. Such tendencies have nevertheless generated concern, particularly amongst Democrats, who feared that more open and participatory structures simply result in the nomination of unelectable 'outsider' candidates. Both the main US parties have responded to this by modernising and strengthening their committee structures, especially at national, congressional and senatorial levels. Although this has been portrayed as a process of 'party renewal', it is evidence of the parties' desire to provide better electoral support for individual candidates, rather than of the emergence of European-style, party-focused elections.

Similar moves towards democratisation were also apparent in the UK Labour Party in the early 1980s. Growing resentment amongst constituency activists about the 'betrayal of socialism' by parliamentary leaders broke out into open conflict after the party's 1979 election defeat. Reformers, spearheaded by Tony Benn, succeeded in strengthening the extraparliamentary party by introducing the mandatory reselection of Members of Parliament (MPs) and an **electoral college** to elect the leader and deputy leader. This, for the first time, allowed members of constituency parties and affiliated trade unions to participate in leadership elections. The strengthening of internal democracy, however, merely deepened divisions within the party, and this contributed to the split that led to the formation of the Social Democratic Party (SDP) in 1981, and encumbered the party with its incoherent 1983 election manifesto.

The Labour Party's response to successive election defeats was to shift back towards centralised leadership. The re-emergence of a top-down authority structure could be seen in the 1987–89 policy review, initiated by the then Labour leader Neil Kinnock, the weakening of trade-union influence by the introduction of 'one member, one vote' (OMOV) under the leadership of John Smith in 1993, and in Tony Blair's success in scrapping Clause 4 (which committed the party to public ownership) in 1995. The transition from the hegemony of left-wing activists in the early 1980s to the reassertion of leadership domination has encouraged many to resurrect Robert McKenzie's oligarchic thesis of the 1950s, which suggested that Labour and Conservative power structures are basically similar. What is interesting about this process, however, is that the oligarchic tendencies appeared to stem not from the dynamics of organisation, but from the party's need for unity and the restoration of electoral credibility.

The existence of factions and tendencies is as important as formal organisation in determining the location of power within a party. While all parties, even those with an apparently monolithic character, embrace some measure of political and ideological rivalry, the degree to which this rivalry is reflected in conflict between organised and coherent groups is crucial in determining the degree of authority of party leaders. In some cases, factions can break away from parties in the manner that in Europe communist parties often emerged out of socialist parties in the years following the 1917 Russian Revolution. Factionalism is often linked to the weight parties place on political ideas and ideological direction. Whereas pragmatic right-wing parties usually merely have to balance or conciliate rival tendencies, more ideological parties of the left often have to deal with open disagreement and institutionalised rivalry. Together with their inclination to endorse internal democracy, this has generally made socialist parties more difficult to lead than liberal or conservative ones.

Concept

Party democracy

Party democracy is a form of popular rule that operates through the agency of a party as a democratic institution. There are two views about how this can be achieved. In the first (intraparty democracy) parties are democratic agents in that power within them is dispersed widely and evenly. This implies, for instance, that there should be broad participation in the election of leaders and selection of candidates, and a prominent role for conferences and conventions in policy formulation. In the second model, democracy dictates that policy making power should be concentrated in the hands of party members who are elected and therefore publicly accountable. In this view, a wide and even dispersal of power within the party may lead to the tyranny of non-elected constituency activists.

Caucus: A meeting of party members held to nominate election candidates or to discuss legislative proposals in advance of formal proceedings.

Electoral college: An indirect electoral mechanism; a body of electors charged with responsibility for filling a party or public office.

Perhaps a more significant consideration, however, is the extent to which parties have a secure hold on power. Factionalism is, in a sense, a luxury that only long-time parties of government can afford. This is why monopolistic communist parties were only able to keep factionalism at bay by exercising ruthless discipline enforced through the strictures of **democratic centralism**. It also explains the deeply factional nature of 'dominant' parties such as the Liberal Democratic Party (LDP) in Japan and the Italian Christian Democratic Party (Democrazia Christiana (DC)). The UK Conservative Party is an example of a party with an ethos that once stressed, above all, deference and loyalty, but which became increasingly factionalised in the 1980s and 1990s through a combination of its more ideological character and prolonged electoral success after 1979. Bottom-up pressures thus gave the party a more democratic character than its formal leader-dominated structure suggested was possible. The most conspicuous casualty of this process was Margaret Thatcher, who was rejected as party leader in 1990 despite having won three successive general elections. The same phenomenon is also apparent in John Major's embattled leadership in the 1990s.

◼ Party systems

Political parties are important not only because of the range of functions they carry out (representation, elite recruitment, aggregation of interests, and so on), but also because the complex interrelationships between and among parties are crucial in structuring how political systems work in practice. This network of relationships is called a party system. The most familiar way of distinguishing between different types of party system is by reference to the number of parties competing for power. On this basis, Duverger (1954) distinguished between 'one-party', 'two-party' and 'multiparty' systems. Although such a typology is commonly used, party systems cannot simply be reduced to a 'numbers game'.

As important as the number of parties competing for power is their relative size, as reflected in their electoral and legislative strength. As Sartori (1976) pointed out, what is vital is to establish the 'relevance' of parties in relation to the formation of governments, and in particular whether their size gives them the prospect of winning, or at least sharing, government power. This approach is often reflected in the distinction made between 'major', or government-orientated, parties and more peripheral, 'minor' ones (although neither category can be defined with mathematical accuracy). A third consideration is how these 'relevant' parties relate to one another. Is the party system characterised by cooperation and consensus, by conflict and polarisation? This is closely linked to the ideological complexion of the party system and the traditions and history of the parties that compose it.

The mere presence of parties does not, however, guarantee the existence of a party system. The pattern of relationships amongst parties only constitutes a system if it is characterised by stability and a degree of orderliness. Where neither stability nor order exists, a party system may be in the process of emerging, or a transition from one type of party system to another may be occurring. For instance, this can be said of postcommunist Russia. The collapse of communist rule in 1991 and the initial banning of the CPSU was always going to make the emergence of a competitive party system a difficult, perhaps tortuous, business. Russia's problem has been a proliferation of parties and political groupings, none of which has come close to establishing a mass membership or a nationwide organisation. No fewer than 43

Democratic centralism: The Leninist principle of party organisation, based on a supposed balance between freedom of discussion and strict unity of action.

parties contested the December 1995 parliamentary elections, with the largest of these, the Russian Communist Party, gaining just 22 per cent of the vote.

The major party systems found in modern politics are as follows:

- one-party systems
- two-party systems
- dominant-party systems
- multiparty systems

One-party systems

Strictly speaking, the term one-party system is contradictory since 'system' implies interaction amongst a number of entities. The term is nevertheless helpful in distinguishing between political systems in which a single party enjoys a monopoly of power through the exclusion of all other parties (by political or constitutional means) and ones characterised by a competitive struggle amongst a number of parties. Because monopolistic parties effectively function as permanent governments, with no mechanism (short of a coup or revolution) through which they can be removed from power, they invariably develop an entrenched relationship with the state machine. This allows such states to be classified as 'one-party states', their machinery being seen as a fused 'party–state' apparatus. Two rather different types of one-party system can be identified, however.

The first type has been found in state socialist regimes where 'ruling' communist parties have directed and controlled virtually all the institutions and aspects of society. Such parties are subject to strict ideological discipline, in accordance with the tenets of Marxism–Leninism, and they have highly structured internal organisations in line with the principles of democratic centralism. These are cadre parties in the sense that membership is restricted on political and ideological grounds. Some 4 per cent of the Chinese population are members of the Chinese Communist Party, and around 9 per cent of the Soviet population belonged to the CPSU. In this type of party, the party core consists of well paid full-time officials, the *apparatchiki*, who run the party *apparat*, or apparatus, and exercise supervision over both the state machine and social institutions.

A central device through which communist parties control the state, economy and society, and ensure the subordination of 'lower' organs to 'higher' ones, is the *nomenklatura* system. This is a system of vetted appointments in which, effectively, all senior posts are filled by party-approved candidates. The justification for both the party's monopoly of power and its supervision of state and social institutions lies in the Leninist claim that the party acts as the 'vanguard of the proletariat' in providing the working masses with the ideological leadership and guidance needed to ensure that they fulfil their revolutionary destiny. Vanguardism (the belief in the need for a leading or revolutionary party) has, however, been criticised for being deeply elitist and providing the seed from which Stalinism later grew. Trotsky (1937), on the other hand, offered an alternative interpretation by suggesting that, far from the 'ruling' party dominating Soviet development, its formal monopoly of power merely concealed the burgeoning influence of the state bureaucracy.

The second type of one-party system is associated with anticolonial nationalism and state consolidation in the developing world. In Ghana, Tanzania and Zimbawe, for example, the 'ruling' party developed out of an independence movement that proclaimed the overriding need for nation building and economic development. In Zimbabwe, one-party rule only developed in 1986 (six years after independence) through the merger of the two major parties, ZANU and ZAPU, both former guerrilla groups. In other cases, such parties have developed as little more than vehicles through which a national leader has tried to consolidate power, as with General Ershad's People's Party in Bangladesh and President Mobutu's Popular Movement of the Revolution in Zaire.

One-party systems in Africa and Asia have usually been built around the dominant role of a charismatic leader and drawn whatever ideological identity they have possessed from the views of that leader. Kwame Nkrumah, the leader of the Convention People's Party (CPP) in Ghana until his overthrow in 1966 is often seen as the model such leader, but other examples are Julius Nyerere in Tanzania and Robert Mugabe in Zimbabwe. Not uncommonly, these parties are weakly organised (very different from the tight discipline found in communist one-party states), and they play, at best, only a peripheral role in the process of policy making. Their monopolistic position nevertheless helps to entrench authoritarianism (see p. 36) and to keep alive the danger of corruption.

Two-party systems

A two-party system is duopolistic in that it is dominated by two 'major' parties that have a roughly equal prospect of winning government power. In its classical form, a two-party system can be identified by three criteria:

- Although a number of 'minor' parties may exist, only two parties enjoy sufficient electoral and legislative strength to have a realistic prospect of winning government power.

- The larger party is able to rule alone (usually on the basis of a legislative majority); the other provides the opposition.

- Power alternates between these parties; both are 'electable', the opposition serving as a 'government in the wings'.

The UK and the USA are the most frequently cited examples of states with two-party systems, though others have included Canada, Australia and New Zealand. Archetypal examples of two-party politics are nevertheless rare. The UK, for instance, often portrayed as the model two-party system, has only conformed to its three defining criteria for particular (and, some would argue, untypical) periods of its history. Even the apparent Labour–Conservative two-partyism of the early post-Second-World-War period (power alternating four times between 1945 and 1970) was punctuated by 13 years of continuous Conservative rule (1951–64), a period during which time Labour's electability was called into question. Moreover, despite persistent major party domination of the House of Commons in the UK, it is more doubtful that a two-party system has existed 'in the country' since 1974. This is suggested by the decline of combined Labour–Conservative support (down from over 95 per cent in the early 1950s to a postwar low of 70 per cent in 1983), as well as by prolonged Conservative rule after 1979.

Even the seemingly incontrovertible two-partyism of the US, which, for instance, sees the Republicans and Democrats holding between them all the seats in the House of Representatives and the Senate, can be questioned. On the one hand, the presidential system allows one party to capture the White House (the presidency) while the other controls Capitol Hill (Congress), as has occurred since 1984, meaning that it may not be possible to identify a clear government–opposition divide. On the other hand, 'third' party candidates are sometimes of significance. Ross Perot's 16 per cent of the vote in the 1992 presidential election not only highlighted the decline of the Republican and Democratic parties, but also, arguably, proved decisive in securing victory for Clinton.

Two-party politics was once portrayed as the surest way of reconciling responsiveness with order, representative government with effective government. Its key advantage is that it makes possible a system of party government, supposedly characterised by stability, choice and accountability. The two major parties are able to offer the electorate a straightforward choice between rival programmes and alternative governments. Voters can support a party knowing that, if it wins the election, it will have the capacity to carry out its manifesto promises without having to negotiate or compromise with coalition partners. This is sometimes seen as one of the attractions of majoritarian electoral systems that exaggerate support for large parties. Two-party systems have also been praised for delivering strong but accountable government based on relentless competition between the governing and opposition parties. Although government can govern, it can never relax or become complacent because it is constantly confronted by an opposition that acts as a government in waiting. Two-partyism, moreover, creates a bias in favour of moderation, as the two contenders for power have to battle for 'floating' votes in the centre ground. This was, for example, reflected in the so-called social-democratic consensus that prevailed in the UK in the 1950s and 1960s.

However two-party politics and party government have not been so well regarded since the 1970s. Instead of guaranteeing moderation, two-party systems such as the UK's have displayed a periodic tendency towards adversary politics (see p. 308). This is reflected in ideological polarisation and an emphasis on conflict and argument rather than consensus and compromise. In the UK in the early 1980s, this was best demonstrated by the movement to the right by a 'Thatcherised' Conservative Party and the movement to the left by a radicalised Labour Party, although a new, post-Thatcherite consensus soon emerged. Adversarial two-partyism has often been explained by reference to the class nature of party support (party conflict being seen, ultimately, as a reflection of the class struggle), or as a consequence of party democratisation and the influence of ideologically committed grass-roots activists.

A further problem with the two-party system is that two evenly matched parties are encouraged to compete for votes by outdoing each other's electoral promises, perhaps causing spiralling public spending and fuelling inflation. This amounts to irresponsible party government, in that parties come to power on the basis of election manifestos that they have no capacity to fulfil. A final weakness of two-party systems is the obvious restrictions they impose in terms of electoral and ideological choice. While a choice between just two programmes of government was perhaps sufficient in an era of partisan alignment and class solidarity, it has become quite inadequate in a period of greater individualism and social diversity.

Dominant-party systems

Dominant-party systems should not be confused with one-party systems, although they may at times exhibit similar characteristics. A dominant-party system is

Concept

Party government

Party government is a system through which single parties are able to form governments and carry through policy programmes. In competitive systems, party government exists nowhere in pristine form; it is therefore sensible to talk about *more* party government or *less* party government, but not about whether it exists.

The key features of party government are the following:

- The major parties possess a clear programmic character and thus offer the electorate a meaningful choice between potential governments.
- The governing party is able to claim a popular mandate and enjoys sufficient ideological cohesion and organisational unity to delivery on its manifesto commitments.
- Responsibility is maintained by the government's accountability to the electorate through its mandate, and by the existence of a credible opposition acting as a balancing force.

competitive in the sense that a number of parties compete for power in regular and popular elections, but is dominated by a single major party that consequently enjoys prolonged periods in power. This apparently neat definition, however, runs into problems, notably in relation to determining how 'prolonged' a governing period must be for a party to be considered 'dominant'. Japan is usually cited as the classic example of a dominant-party system. Until its fall in 1993, the Liberal Democratic Party had been in power continuously for 38 years, having only failed to gain an overall majority in the House of Representatives (the lower chamber of the Japanese Diet) in 1976, 1979 and 1983. LDP dominance was underpinned by the Japanese 'economic miracle'. It also reflected the powerful appeal of the party's neo-Confucian principles of duty and obligation in the still-traditional Japanese countryside, and the strong links that the party had forged with business elites.

The Congress Party in India enjoyed an unbroken spell of 30 years in power commencing with the achievement of independence in 1947. Until 1989, it had only endured three years in opposition, following Indiri Gandhi's 1975–77 state of emergency. The best European examples of a dominant-party system are Sweden, where the Social Democratic Labour Party (SAP) remained in power from 1951 to 1993 for all but two years (either alone or as the senior partner in a coalition), and Italy, where the Christian Democratic Party dominated every one of the country's 52 post-Second-World-War governments until the party's effective collapse amidst mounting allegations of corruption in 1993.

The most prominent feature of a dominant-party system is the tendency for the political focus to shift from competition between parties to factional conflict within the dominant party itself. The DC in Italy, for example, functioned as little more than a coalition of privileged groups and interests in Italian society, the party acting as a broker to these various factions. The most powerful of these groups were the Catholic Church (which exercised influence through organisations such as Catholic Action), the farming community and industrial interests. Each of these were able to cultivate voting loyalty and exert influence upon DC's members in the Italian parliament.

Factions are also an integral institution in the Japanese political process. A perennial struggle for power has taken place within the LDP as various subgroups have coalesced around rising or powerful individuals. Such factionalism is maintained at the local level by the ability of faction leaders to provide political favours for their followers, and at the parliamentary level through the allocation of senior government and party offices. Although the resulting infighting may be seen as a means of guaranteeing argument and debate in a system in which small parties are usually marginalised, in Japan, factionalism tends to revolve more around personal differences than it does around policy or ideological divisions. One example of this was the conflict between the Fukuda and Tanaka factions during the 1970s and 1980s, which continued long after the two principals had left the scene.

Whereas other competitive party systems have their supporters, or at least apologists, few are prepared to come to the defence of the dominant-party system. Apart from a tendency towards stability and predictability, dominant-partyism is usually seen as a regrettable and unhealthy phenomenon. In the first place, it tends to erode the important constitutional distinction between the state and the party in power. When governments cease to come and go, an insidious process of politicisation takes place through which state officials and institutions adjust to the ideological and political priorities of the dominant party. For example, about one-quarter of the

LDP's Diet members are former civil servants; this creates the kind of party-state nexus that is usually associated with one-party systems.

Secondly, an extended period in power can engender complacency, arrogance and even corruption in the dominant party. The course of Italian and Japanese politics has, for example, regularly been interrupted by scandals, usually involving allegations of financial corruption. Indeed, the decline of both the LDP and the DC in the 1990s was closely linked to such allegations. When parties cease to 'fear the ballot box', they are likely to become unresponsive and ideologically entrenched. Prolonged Conservative rule in the UK since 1979, for instance, has resulted in a party seemingly incapable of breaking loose from its Thatcherite heritage, and, in particular, unable to criticise or question the dogma of the market.

Thirdly, a dominant-party system is characterised by weak and ineffective opposition. Criticism and protest can more easily be ignored if they stem from parties that are no longer regarded as genuine rivals for power. Finally, the existence of a 'permanent' party of government may corrode the democratic spirit by encouraging the electorate to fear change and to stick with the 'natural' party of government. Dominant-party systems may, then, be psychologically self-perpetuating. A genuinely democratic political culture arguably requires a general public that has a healthy distrust of all parties, and most importantly, a willingness to remove governments that have failed.

Multiparty systems

A multiparty system is characterised by competition amongst more than two parties reducing the chances of single-party government and increasing the likelihood of coalitions. However, it is difficult to define multiparty systems in terms of the number of major parties, as such systems sometimes operate through coalitions including smaller parties that are specifically designed to exclude larger parties from government. This is precisely what happened to the French Communist Party (Parti Communiste Français or PCF) in the 1950s, and to the Italian Communist Party (PCI) throughout its existence. If the likelihood of coalition government is the index of multipartyism, this classification contains a number of sub-categories.

Germany, for example, appears to have a 'two-and-a-half-party' system, in that the CDU and SDP have electoral strengths roughly equivalent to those of the Conservative and Labour parties in the UK. However, they are forced into coalitions with the small Free Democrat Party (which usually receives less than 10 per cent of the vote) by the workings of the additional member electoral system (see p. 219). In contrast, Italian multipartyism involves a larger number of relatively small parties. Thus, even the DC rarely came close to achieving 40 per cent of the vote. Sartori (1976) distinguished between two types of multiparty system, which he termed the moderate and polarised pluralist systems. In this categorisation, moderate pluralism exists in countries such as Belgium, the Netherlands and Norway where ideological differences between major parties are slight, and there is a general inclination to form coalitions and move towards the middle ground. Polarised pluralism, on the other hand, exists when more marked ideological differences separate major parties, some of which adopt an anti-system stance. The existence of electorally strong communist parties, as in France, Italy and Spain, or of significant fascist movements, such as the Movimento Sociale Italiano (MSI) (reborn in 1995 as the 'post-Fascist' Alleanza Nazionale), provides evidence of polarised pluralism.

Coalition

A coalition is a grouping of rival political actors brought together either through the perception of a common threat, or the recognition that their goals cannot be achieved by working separately. Electoral coalitions are alliances through which parties agree not to compete against one another with a view to maximising their representation. Legislative coalitions are agreements between two or more parties to support a particular bill or programme. Coalition governments are formal agreements between two or more parties that involve a cross-party distribution of ministerial portfolios. They are usually motivated by the need to ensure majority control of the assembly. A 'grand coalition' or 'national government' comprises all the major parties, but are usually only formed at times of national crisis or economic emergency.

The strength of multiparty systems is that they create internal checks and balances within government and exhibit a bias in favour of debate, conciliation and compromise. The process of coalition formation and the dynamics of coalition maintenance ensure a broad responsiveness that cannot but take account of competing views and contending interests. Thus, in Germany, the liberal Free Democrats act as a moderating influence upon both the conservative CDU and the socialist SPD. Where SPD–Green coalitions have been formed in the *Länder* (provinces), the Green presence has helped to push environmental issues up the political agenda. Similarly, the multiparty features of the Swedish system, which make coalition government more common than not, have encouraged the SAP to build a broad welfare consensus, and to pursue moderate policies that do not alienate business interests. The conviction politics and ideological radicalism that was, for example, exemplified by Thatcherism in the UK in the 1980s and 1990s would therefore be quite unthinkable in a multiparty system.

The principle criticisms of multiparty systems relate to the pitfalls and difficulties of coalition formation. The post-election negotiations and horse trading that take place when no single party is strong enough to govern alone can take weeks, or (as in Israel and Italy) sometimes months, to complete. More seriously, coalition governments may be fractured and unstable, paying greater attention to squabbles amongst coalition partners than to the tasks of government. Italy is usually cited as the classic example of this, its postwar governments having lasted on average only ten months. It would nevertheless be a mistake to suggest that coalitions are always associated with instability, as the record of stable and effective coalition government in Germany and Sweden clearly demonstrates. In some respects, in fact, the Italian experience is peculiar, owing as much to the country's political culture and the ideological complexion of its party system as to the dynamics of multipartyism.

A final problem is that the tendency towards moderation and compromise may mean that multiparty systems are so dominated by the political centre that they are unable to offer clear ideological alternatives. Coalition politics tends, naturally, to be characterised by negotiation and conciliation, a search for common ground, rather than by conviction and the politics of principle. This process can be criticised as being implicitly corrupt, in that parties are encouraged to abandon policies and principles in their quest for power. It can also lead to the over-representation of centrist parties and centrist interests, especially when, as in Germany, a small centre party is the only viable coalition partner for larger conservative and socialist ones. Indeed, this is sometimes seen as one of the drawbacks of proportional representation electoral systems, which, by ensuring that the legislative size of parties reflects their electoral strength, are biased in favour of multiparty politics and coalition government.

The decline of parties?

Criticism of political parties is certainly not new. Indeed, the emergence of political parties was usually greeted with grave suspicion and distrust. For instance, in common with other 'founding fathers' who wrote the US constitution, Thomas Jefferson was fiercely critical of parties and factions, believing that they would promote conflict and destroy the underlying unity of society. The view that there is an indivisible public or national interest has also been used in the modern period by one-party

Thomas Jefferson (1743–1826)

US political philosopher and statesman. A wealthy Virginian planter who was Governor of Virginia 1779–81, Jefferson served as the first US Secretary of State, 1789–94. He was the third president of the USA, 1801–90. Jefferson was the principal author of the Declaration of Independence, and wrote a vast number of addresses and letters. He developed a democratic form of agrarianism that sought to blend a belief in rule by a natural aristocracy with a commitment to limited government and *laissez-faire*. He also demonstrated sympathy for social reform, favouring the extension of public education, the abolition of slavery, and greater economic equality.

systems to justify the suppression of rival parties, and by military rulers to explain the suppression of all political parties. A further concern, expressed by liberals such as J. S. Mill (see p. 44), was that, as collective bodies, parties necessarily suppress freedom of thought and the politics of individual conscience. Modern concern about parties, however, stems from evidence of their decline as agents of representation and as an effective link between government and the people.

Evidence of a 'crisis of party politics' can be found in a decline of both party membership and partisanship, reflected in partisan dealignment. For example, since the high point of party membership in the UK in the early 1950s, the Labour Party has lost approximately two-thirds of its members, and the Conservatives over half. A seemingly inexorable rise in the age of party members is as significant, the average age of Conservative Party members in 1995 being 62. Dramatic electoral swings against governing parties have intensified such concerns. Notable examples of this include the slump of the French Socialists in 1993 from 282 seats to just 70, and the virtual annihilation the same year of the Canadian Progressive Conservatives, who were swept out of office retaining only two seats.

Alongside these changes, there is evidence of what has been called 'antipolitics', that is, the rise of political movements and organisations the only common feature of which appears to be antipathy towards conventional centres of power and opposition to established parties of government. This has been reflected in the emergence of new political movements the principle attraction of which is that they are untainted by having held power. Good examples have been the 19 per cent support that billionaire Ross Perot gained in his independent bid for the US presidency in 1992, and the dramatic success of media mogul Silvio Berlesconi's newly created Forza Italia in 1994. The rise of new social movements (see p. 265), such as the women's movement, peace movement and environmental movement, is also part of the same phenomenon. Even when they articulate their views through party organisation, as in the case of Green parties, these movements tend to assume the mantle of **antiparty parties**.

How can the decline of parties be explained? One of the problems that parties suffer from is their real or perceived oligarchical character. Parties are seen as bureaucratised political machines, whose grass-roots members are either inactive or engaged in dull and routine tasks (attending meetings, sitting on committees, and so on). In contrast, single-issue protest groups have been more successful in attracting mem-

Antiparty parties: Parties that set out to subvert traditional party politics by rejecting parliamentary compromise and emphasising popular mobilisation.

bership and support, particularly from amongst the young, partly because they are more loosely organised and locally based, and partly because they place a heavier emphasis on participation and activism. The public image of parties has been further tarnished by their links to government and to professional politicians. As political 'insiders', parties are tainted by the power, ambition and corruption that is often associated with high office. In other words, parties are not seen as being '*of* the people'; too often, they appear to be consumed by political infighting and the scramble for power, so becoming divorced from the concerns of ordinary people.

An alternative way of explaining party decline is to see it as a symptom of the fact that complex, modern societies are increasingly difficult to govern. Disillusionment and cynicism grow as parties seek power by proclaiming their capacity to solve problems and improve conditions, but fail to deliver once in government. This reflects the mounting difficulties that confront any party of government in the form of the expanding power of interest groups and an increasingly globalised economy. A final explanation is that parties may be declining because the social identities and traditional loyalties that gave rise to them in the first place have started to fade. This can certainly be seen in the decline of class politics, linked to the phenomenon of post-Fordism (see p. 180). In addition, with the decline of old social, religious and other solidarities, new aspirations and sensibilities have come onto the political agenda, notably those associated with postmaterialism (see p. 193). Whereas broad, programmic parties once succeeded in articulating the goals of major sections of the electorate, issues such as gender equality, nuclear power, animal rights and pollution may require new and different political formations to articulate them. Single-issue groups and social movements may thus be in the process of replacing parties as the crucial link between government and society.

■ Summary

◆ A political party is a group of people organised for the purpose of winning government power, and usually displays some measure of ideological cohesion. The principal classifications of parties have distinguished between cadre and mass or, later, catch-all parties, parties of representation and parties of integration, constitutional or 'mainstream' parties and revolutionary or anti-system ones, and left-wing parties and right-wing parties.

◆ Parties have a number of functions in the political system. These include their role as a mechanism of representation, the formation of political elites and recruitment into politics, the formulation of social goals and government policy, the articulation and aggregation of interests, the mobilisation and socialisation of the electorate, and the organisation of governmental processes and institutional relationships.

◆ The organisation and structure of parties crucially influences the distribution of power within society at large. Party democracy can be promoted by either a wide dispersal of power within the party, or the concentration of power in the hands of the party's elected and publicly accountable members. Oligarchic tendencies may be an inevitable consequence of organisation, or they may arise from the need for party unity and electoral credibility.

◆ A party system is a network of relationships through which parties interact and influence the political process. In one-party systems, a 'ruling' party effectively functions as a permanent government. In two-party systems, power alternates between two 'major' parties. In dominant-party systems, a single 'major' party retains power for a prolonged period. In multiparty systems, no party is large enough to rule alone, leading to a system of coalition government.

◆ Party systems shape the broader political process in various ways. They influence the range and nature of choice available to the electorate, and affect the cohesion and stability of governments. They structure the relationship between the executive and the assembly, establish a bias in favour of either conflict or consensus, and shape the general character of the political culture.

◆ Evidence of a crisis in party politics can be found in the decline in party membership and partisanship, as well as in the rise of 'antiparty' groups and movements. This can be explained by the perception that parties are tainted by power, ambition and corruption, and that they have suffered as a result of general disillusionment caused by the growing inability of governments to deliver on their promises. They are also seen to have failed to articulate the aspirations and sensibilities associated with postmaterialism or generated by postmodernism.

Questions for discussion

▶ Are all modern political parties essentially catch-all parties?

▶ Could government function in contemporary circumstances without political parties?

▶ In what ways, and to what extent, do parties promote democracy?

▶ Why do political parties so often tend to be leader-dominated?

▶ By what criteria should party systems be judged?

▶ How have modern parties adjusted to the decline of class politics and the weakening of traditional loyalties?

Further Reading

Castles, F. and R. Wildmann (eds) *The Future of Party Government – Vol. 1* (Berlin: Gruyter, 1986). An analysis of the conditions of party government and the problems associated with it.

Graham, B. D. *Representation and Party Politics: A Comparative Perspective* (Oxford: Blackwell, 1993). An up-to-date discussion of the relationship between parties, representation and democracy.

Mair, P. *The West European Party System* (Oxford: Oxford University Press, 1990). A comprehensive account of parties and party systems in western Europe.

Sartori, G. *Parties and Party Systems: A Framework for Analysis* (Cambridge: Cambridge University Press, 1976). A classic if challenging analysis of the role of parties and the nature of party systems.

Groups, Interests and Movements

> 'Ten persons who speak make more noise than ten thousand who are silent.'
>
> NAPOLEON 1 *Maxims*

Patterns of political interaction were transformed in the twentieth century by the growing prominence of organised groups and interests. Indeed, in the 1950s and 1960s, at the high point of enthusiasm about 'group politics', it was widely asserted that business interests, trade unions, farm lobbies and the like had displaced assemblies and parties as the key political actors. The interest-group universe was further expanded, particularly from the 1960s onwards, by the growth of single-issue protest groups taking up causes ranging from consumer protection to animal rights and from sexual equality to environmental protection. Such groups were often associated with broader social movements (the women's movement, the civil-rights movement, the Green movement, and so on) and were characterised by the adoption of new styles of activism and campaigning, sometimes termed 'new politics'. Considerable debate nevertheless surrounds the nature and significance of groups, interests and movements, especially in relation to their impact on the democratic process.

The principal issues addressed in this chapter are the following:

Key issues

▶ What are interest groups, and what different forms do they take?

▶ What have been the major theories of group politics?

▶ Do groups help or hinder democracy and effective government?

▶ How do interest groups exert influence?

▶ What determines the success or failure of interest groups?

▶ Why have new social movements emerged, and what is their broader significance?

◼ Group politics

Interest groups, like political parties, constitute one of the major linkages between government and the governed in modern societies. In some respects, their origins parallel those of parties. They were the children of a new age of representative government and came into existence to articulate the increasingly complex divisions and cleavages of an emerging industrial society. While political parties, concerned with winning elections, sought to build coalitions of support and broaden their appeal, interest groups usually staked out a more distinct and clear-cut position, in accordance with the particular aspirations or values of the people they represented.

It is difficult to identify the earliest such group. Some groups predated the age of representative government, for example, the Abolition Society, which was founded in Britain in 1787 to oppose the slave trade. The Anti-Corn Law League, established in 1839, is often seen as the model for later UK groups, in that it was set up with the specific purpose of exerting pressure on government. After visiting the USA in the 1830s, Alexis de Tocqueville (see p. 201) reported that what he called **association** had already become a 'powerful instrument of action'. Young Italy, set up in 1831 by the Italian patriot Guiseppe Mazzini (see p. 110), became the model for sister nationalist organisations that later sprang up throughout Europe. Similarly, the Society for Women's Rights, founded in France in 1866, stimulated the formation of a worldwide women's suffrage movement. By the end of the nineteenth century, powerful farming and business interests operated in most industrial societies, along-side a growing trade-union movement. However, most of the interest groups currently in existence are of much more recent origin. They are, in the main, a product of the explosion in pressure and protest politics that has occurred since the 1960s. As such, they may be part of a broader process that has seen the decline of political parties and a growing emphasis on organised groups and social movements (see p. 266) as agents of mobilisation and representation.

Types of group

The task of defining and classifying groups is fraught with danger, given the imprecise nature of groups and their multiplicity of forms. Are we, for instance, concerned with groups or with **interests**? In other words, do we only recognise groups as associations which have a certain level of cohesion and organisation, or merely as collections of people who happen to share the same interest but may lack consciousness of the fact? Similarly, are interest groups only concerned with selfish and material interests, or may they also pursue broader causes or public goals? There is also the difficult issue of the relationship between interest groups and government. Are interest groups always autonomous, exerting influence from outside, or may they operate in and through government, perhaps even being part of the government machine itself?

This confusion is compounded by the lack of agreed terminology amongst political scientists active in this field. For instance, whereas the term 'interest group' is used in the USA and elsewhere to describe all organised groups, it tends to be used in the UK to refer only to those groups that advance or defend the interests of their members. The term 'pressure group' is therefore usually preferred in the UK, 'interest group' tending to be used as a sub-category of the broader classification.

Association: A group formed by voluntary action, reflecting a recognition of shared interests or common concerns.

Interest: That which benefits an individual or group; interests (unlike wants or preferences) are usually understood to be objective or 'real'.

Groups can nevertheless be classified into three types:

* communal groups
* institutional groups
* associational groups.

Communal groups

The chief characteristic of communal groups is that they are embedded in the social fabric, in the sense that membership is based on birth, rather than recruitment. Examples of such groups are families, tribes, castes and ethnic groups. Unlike conventional interest groups, to which members *choose* to belong, and which possess a formal structure and organisation, communal groups are founded on the basis of a shared heritage and traditional bonds and loyalties. Such groups still play a major role in the politics of developing states. In Africa, for instance, ethnic, tribal and kinship ties are often the most important basis of interest articulation. Communal groups also continue to survive and exert influence in advanced industrial states, as the resurgence of ethnic nationalism and the significance of Catholic groups in countries like Italy and Ireland demonstrate.

Institutional groups

Institutional groups are groups that are part of the machinery of government and attempt to exert influence in and through that machinery. They differ from interest groups in that they enjoy no measure of autonomy or independence. Bureaucracies and the military are the clearest examples of institutional groups, and, not uncommonly, each of these contains a number of competing interests. In the case of authoritarian or totalitarian states, which typically suppress autonomous groups and movements, rivalry amongst institutional groups may become the principal form of interest articulation. The highly centralised Stalinist system in the USSR, for instance, was largely driven by entrenched bureaucratic and economic interests, in particular those centred around heavy industry. Similarly, the apparently monolithic character of the Hitler state in Germany, 1933–45, concealed a reality of bureaucratic infighting as Nazi leaders built up sprawling empires in an endless struggle for power.

Institutional groups are not only of significance in non-democratic regimes. Some go so far as to argue that the bureaucratic elites and vested interests that develop in the ministries, departments and agencies of democratic systems in effect shape the policy process; they serve to constrain, some would say dictate to, elected politicians and elected governments. Such groups certainly also form alliances with conventional interest groups, as in the case of the celebrated 'military–industrial complex'. The significance of the bureaucracy and the military, and the importance of the interests that operate in and through them, are discussed in Chapters 17 and 18.

Associational groups

Associational groups are ones that are formed by people who come together to pursue shared, but limited, goals. Groups as associations are characterised by voluntary action and the existence of common interests, aspirations or attitudes. The most obvious examples of associational groups are thus what are usually thought of as interest groups or pressure groups. However, the distinction between these and

◆ **Concept**

Interest group

An interest group (or pressure group) is an organised association which aims to influence the policies or actions of government. Interest groups differ from political parties (see p. 230) in that they seek to exert influence from outside, rather than to win or exercise government power. Further, interest groups typically have a narrow issue focus, in that they are usually concerned with a specific cause or the interests of a particular group, and seldom have the broader programmic or ideological features that are generally associated with political parties. Interest groups are distinguished from social movements by their greater degree of formal organisation. Nevertheless, not all interest groups have members in the formal sense, hence the preference of some commentators for the looser term 'organised interests'.

Direct action: Political action taken outside the constitutional and legal framework; direct action may range from passive resistance to terrorism.

communal groups may sometimes be blurred. For example, when class loyalties are strong and solidaristic, membership of an associational group such as a trade union may be more an expression of social identity than an instrumental act aimed at furthering a particular goal. Although associational groups are becoming increasingly important in developing states, they are usually seen as a feature of industrial societies. Industrialisation both generates social differentiation, in the form of a complex web of competing interests, and, in a capitalist setting at least, encourages the growth of self-seeking and individualised patterns of behaviour in place of ones shaped by custom and tradition. When their primary function is to deal with government and other public bodies, such groups are usually called interest groups.

Interest groups appear in a variety of shapes and sizes. They are concerned with an enormous array of issues and causes, and use tactics that range from serving on public bodies and helping to administer government programmes to organising campaigns of civil disobedience (see p. 265) and popular protest. However, anti-constitutional and paramilitary groups are excluded from this classification. Groups such as the Black Panthers and the Irish Republican Army (IRA) cannot be categorised as interest groups because they seek fundamentally to restructure the political system, not merely to influence it, and use the tactics of **direct action** instead of pressure politics. Structure must, however, be imposed on the apparently shapeless interest-group universe by the attempt to identify the different types of group. The two most common classifications are:

- sectional and promotional groups
- insider and outsider groups.

Sectional groups (sometimes called protective or functional groups) exist to advance or protect the (usually material) interests of their members. Trade unions, business corporations, trade associations and professional bodies are the prime examples of this type of group. Their 'sectional' character is derived from the fact that they represent a section of society: workers, employers, consumers, an ethnic or religious group, and so on. Strictly speaking, however, only groups engaged in the production, distribution and exchange of goods and services can be seen as 'functional' groups. In the USA, sectional groups are often classified as '*private* interest groups', to stress that their principal concern is the betterment and well-being of their members, not of society in general.

In contrast, promotional groups (sometimes termed cause or attitude groups) are set up to advance shared values, ideals or principles. These causes are many. They include 'pro-choice' and 'pro-life' lobbies on abortion, campaigns in favour of civil liberties or against sex and violence on television, protests about pollution and animal cruelty or in defence of traditional or religious values. In the USA, promotional groups are dubbed '*public* interest groups', to emphasise that they promote collective, rather than selective, benefits. These groups are therefore defined by the fact that they aim to help groups other than their own members. Save the Whale, for instance, is an organisation *for* whales, not one *of* whales. Some organisations, of course, have both sectional and promotional features. The National Association for the Advancement of Coloured People (NAACP) addresses the sectional interests of American black people (by opposing discrimination and promoting employment opportunities), but is also concerned with causes such as social justice and racial harmony.

The alternative system of classification is based on the status that groups have in relation to government and the strategies they adopt in order to exert pressure. Insider groups enjoy privileged and usually institutionalised access to government through routine consultation or representation on government bodies. In many cases, there is an overlap between sectional and insider classifications. This reflects the ability of key economic interests, such as business groups and trade unions, to exert powerful sanctions if their views are ignored by government. Government may also be inclined to consult groups that possess specialist knowledge and information that assists in the formulation of workable policy. Insider status, however, is not always an advantage, since it is only conferred upon groups with objectives that are broadly compatible with those of the government and which have a demonstrable capacity to ensure that their members abide by agreed decisions.

Outsider groups, on the other hand, are either not consulted by government or only consulted irregularly and not usually by a senior level. In many cases, outsider status is an indication of weakness, in that, lacking formal access to government, these groups are forced to 'go public' in the hope of exercising indirect influence on the policy process. Ironically, then, there is often an inverse relationship between the public profile of an interest group and the political influence it exerts. Radical protest groups in fields like environmental protection and animal rights may have little choice about being outsiders. Not only are their goals frequently out of step with the priorities of government, but their members and supporters are often attracted by the fact that such groups are untainted by close links with government.

Models of group politics

Some commentators believe that the pattern and significance of group politics are entirely derived from factors that are specific to each political system. The role of groups thus reflects a particular political culture, party system, set of institutional arrangements, and so on. This means that general conclusions cannot be drawn about the nature of group politics. On the other hand, the understanding of group politics is often shaped by broader assumptions about both the nature of the political process and the distribution of power in society. These assumptions are closely linked to the rival theories of the state examined in Chapter 5. The most influential of these as models of interest-group politics are the following:

- pluralism
- corporatism
- the New Right.

Pluralist model

Pluralist theories offer the most positive image of group politics. They stress the capacity of groups to both defend the individual from government and promote democratic responsiveness. The core theme of pluralism (see p. 76) is that political power is fragmented and widely dispersed. Decisions are made through a complex process of bargaining and interaction that ensures that the views and interests of a large number of groups are taken into account. One of the earliest and most influential attempts to develop a pluralist 'group theory' was undertaken by Arthur Bentley in *The Process of Government* ([1908] 1948). Bentley's emphasis on organised groups as the fundamental building blocks of the political process is neatly summed up in his famous dictum: 'when the groups are adequately stated, everything is stated'

Robert Dahl (born 1915)

US political scientist. Appointed professor of political science at Yale University in 1946, Dahl subsequently became one of the USA's most eminent political analysts. In 1953 (with Charles Lindblom) he coined the term 'polyarchy' (rule by the many) to distinguish modern societies from classical democracy. Dahl's early writings reflect the impact of positivist and behaviouralist doctrines, and he developed in the 1950s and early 1960s a conventional pluralist position. From the late 1960s, however, together with Lindblom and Galbraith (see p. 181), he developed a radicalised form of liberalism, neo-pluralism, that revealed an increasing concern with the power of major capitalist corporations. His major works include *A Preface to Democratic Theory* (1956), *Who Governs?* (1961) and *Dilemmas of Pluralist Democracy* (1982).

(p. 208). David Truman's *The Governmental Process* (1951) is usually seen to have continued this tradition, even if his conclusions were more narrowly focused on the US political process.

Enthusiasm for groups as agents of interest articulation and aggregation was strengthened by the spread of behaviouralism in the 1950s and early 1960s. Systems analysis, for example, portrayed interest groups as 'gatekeepers' that filtered the multiple demands made of government into manageable sets of claims. At the same time, community power studies carried out by analysts such as Robert Dahl (1961) and Nelson Polsby (1963) claimed to find empirical support for the pluralist assertion that no single local elite is able to dominate community decision-making.

From the pluralist perspective, group politics is the very stuff of the democratic process. Indeed, it became common in the 1960s to argue that a form of pluralist democracy (see p. 77) had superseded more conventional electoral democracy, in that groups and organised interests had replaced political parties as the principal link between government and the governed. The central assumptions of this theory are that all groups and interests have the potential to organise and gain access to government, that they are internally responsive in the sense that leaders broadly articulated the interests or values of their members, and that their political influence is roughly in line with their size and the intensity of their support. One way in which this was demonstrated was by evidence that political power is fragmented in such a way that no group or interest can achieve dominance for any period of time. As Dahl (1956:145) put it, 'all the active and legitimate groups in the population can make themselves heard at some crucial stage in the process of decision'. The alternative idea of 'countervailing powers', developed in Galbraith's early writings, suggests that a dynamic equilibrium naturally emerges amongst competing groups, as the success of, say, business merely encourages opponents, such as labour or consumers, to organise to counter that success. Group politics is thus characterised by a rough balance of power.

This highly optimistic view of group politics has been heavily criticised by elitists and Marxists. Elitists challenge the empirical claims of pluralism by suggesting that they recognise only one 'face' of power: the ability to influence decision-making (see p. 11). In contrast to the notion that power is widely and evenly distributed, elite theorists draw attention to the existence of a 'power elite', comprising the heads of business corporations, political leaders and military chiefs (Mills, 1956). Marxists, for their part, have traditionally emphasised that political power is closely linked to the ownership of productive wealth, which suggests the existence of a capitalist 'ruling class'. For neo-Marxists such as Ralph Miliband (1969), this is reflected in 'unequal competition' between business and labour groups, the former enjoying a control of economic resources, a public status, and a level of access to government that the latter can not match. In the face of such criticism, a more critical or qualified form of pluralism, neo-pluralism (see p. 88), emerged. This has perhaps been most clearly expressed in Charles Lindblom's *Politics and Markets* (1977), which highlighted the privileged position that business groups enjoy in western polyarchies, while acknowledging that this seriously compromises the claim that such societies are democratic.

Corporatist model

Corporatist models of group politics differ from pluralism in that they attempt to trace the implications of the closer links that have developed in industrialised societies between groups and the state. Corporatism is a social theory that emphasises the privileged position that certain groups enjoy in relation to government, enabling them to influence the formulation and implementation of public policy. Some commentators regard corporatism as a state-specific phenomenon, shaped by particular historical and political circumstances. They thus associate it with countries such as Austria, Sweden, the Netherlands and, to some extent, Germany and Japan in which the government has customarily practised a form of economic management.

Others, however, see corporatism as a general phenomenon that stems from tendencies implicit in economic and social development, and thus believe that it is manifest, in some form or other, in all advanced industrial states. Even the USA, usually portrayed as the model of pluralist democracy, has invested its regulatory agencies with quasi-legislative powers, thereby fostering the development of formal bonds between government and major interests. From this perspective, corporatist tendencies may merely reflect the symbiotic relationship that exists between groups and government. Groups seek 'insider' status because it gives them access to policy formulation, which enables them better to defend the interests of their members. Government, on the other hand, needs groups, both as a source of knowledge and information, and because the compliance of major interests is essential if policy is to be workable. In increasingly differentiated and complex industrial societies, the need for consultation and bargaining continues to grow, with the result that, perhaps inevitably, institutional mechanisms emerge to facilitate it.

The drift towards corporatism in advanced capitalist states, particularly pronounced in the 1960s and 1970s, provoked deep misgivings about the role and power of interest groups. In the first place, corporatism considerably cut down the number and range of groups that enjoyed access to government. Corporatism invariably privileges economic or functional groups, because it leads to a form of **tripartitism** that binds government to business and organised labour. However, it may leave consumer or promotional groups out in the cold, and institutionalised access is likely to be restricted to so-called 'peak' associations that speak on behalf of a range of organisations and groups. In Austria this role is carried out by the Chamber of Commerce and the Trade Union Federation, in the UK by the Confederation of British Industry (CBI) and the Trade Union Congress (TUC), and in the USA by the National Association of Manufacturers and the American Federation of Labor–Congress of Industrial Organisations (AFL–CIO).

Concept

Corporatism

Corporatism, in its broadest sense, is a means of incorporating organised interests into the processes of government. There are two faces of corporatism. First, *authoritarian* corporatism is an ideology or economic form closely associated with Italian Fascism. It was characterised by the political intimidation of industry and the destruction of independent trade unions. Secondly, *liberal* corporatism ('societal' corporatism or 'neo-corporatism') refers to the tendency found in mature liberal democracies for organised interests to be granted privileged and institutional access to policy formulation. The mechanisms through which this is achieved vary considerably, as does the degree of group integration. In contrast with its authoritarian variant, liberal corporatism strengthens groups in relation to government, not the other way round.

Tripartitism: The construction of bodies that represent government, business and the unions, designed to institutionalise group consultation.

Public choice

Public-choice theory is a subfield of rational-choice theory, based on the assumptions of neo-classical economics. Its central assertion is that political issues are best analysed by examining the behaviour of individuals understood as rationally self-interested actors. The 'public' character of public-choice theory stems from its concern with the provision of so-called public goods, goods that are delivered by government rather than the market, because (as with clean air) their benefit cannot be withheld from individuals who choose not to contribute to their provision. Public-choice theorists have generally highlighted the failures and defects of government in this respect, focusing on issues such as the impact of the bureaucracy on the policy process and the consequences of lobbying and interest-group politics.

A second problem is that, in contrast to the pluralist model, corporatism portrays interest groups as hierarchically ordered and dominated by leaders who are not directly accountable to members. Indeed, it is sometimes argued that the price that group leaders pay for privileged access to government is a willingness to deliver the compliance of their members. From this point of view, 'government by consultation' may simply be a sham concealing the fact that corporatism acts as a mechanism of social control. Thirdly, concern has been expressed about the threat that corporatism poses to representative democracy. Whereas pluralism suggests that group politics supplements the representative process, corporatism creates the spectre of decisions being made outside the reach of democratic control and through a process of bargaining in no way subject to public scrutiny. Finally, corporatism has been linked to the problem of government 'overload', in which government may effectively be 'captured' by consulted groups and thus be unable to resist their demands. This critique has been advanced most systematically by the New Right.

New Right model

The antipathy of the New Right towards interest groups is derived, ideologically, from the individualism that lies at the heart of neoliberal economics. Social groups and collective bodies of all kinds are therefore viewed with suspicion. This is clearly reflected in the New Right's preference for a market economy driven by self-reliance and entrepreneuralism. However, the New Right has expressed particular concern about the alleged link between corporatism and escalating public spending and the associated problems of over-government. New Right anti-corporatism has been influenced by public-choice theory, notably Mancur Olson's *The Logic of Collective Action: Public Goods and the Theory of Groups* (1968). Olson argued that people join interest groups only to secure 'public goods', that is, goods which are to some extent indivisible in that individuals who do not contribute to their provision cannot be prevented from enjoying them.

A pay increase is thus a public good in that workers who are not union members, or who choose not to strike in furtherance of the pay claim, benefit equally with union members and those who did strike. This creates opportunities for individuals to become 'free riders', reaping benefits without incurring the various costs that group membership may entail. This analysis is significant because it implies that there is no guarantee that the existence of a common interest will lead to the formation of an organisation to advance or defend that interest. The pluralist assumption that all groups have some kind of political voice therefore becomes highly questionable. Olson also argued that group politics may often empower small groups at the expense of large ones. A larger membership encourages free riding because individuals may calculate that the group's effectiveness will be little impaired by their failure to participate.

This analysis was further developed in Olson's later work, *The Rise and Decline of Nations* (1982), which advanced a trenchant critique of interest-group activity, seeing it as a major determinant of the prosperity or economic failure of particular states. The UK and Australia, for example, were seen as suffering from 'institutional sclerosis'. This occurred as strong networks of interest groups emerged that were typically dominated by coalitions of narrow, sectional interests, including trade unions, business organisations and professional associations. The message that there is an inverse relationship between strong and well organised interest groups, on the one hand, and economic growth and national prosperity on the other, had a powerful impact on

Focus on . . .

Interest groups: for and against

Arguments in favour of interest groups include the following:

- They strengthen *representation* by articulating interests and advancing views that are ignored by political parties, and by providing a means of influencing government between elections.

- They promote *debate* and discussion, thus creating a better informed and more educated electorate, and improving the quality of public policy.

- They broaden the scope of political *participation,* both by providing an alternative to conventional party politics and by offering opportunities for grass-roots activism.

- They *check* government power and, in the process, defend liberty by ensuring that the state is balanced against a vigorous and healthy civil society.

- They help to maintain political *stability* by providing a channel of communication between government and the people, bringing outputs into line with inputs.

The arguments against interest groups include the following:

- They entrench political *inequality* by strengthening the voice of the wealthy and privileged, those who have access to financial, educational, organisational or other resources.

- They are socially and politically *divisive*, in that they are concerned with the particular, not the general, and advance minority interests against those of society as a whole.

- They exercise *non-legitimate* power, in that their leaders, unlike politicians, are not publicly accountable and their influence bypasses the representative process.

- They tend to make the policy process *closed* and more secretive by exerting influence through negotiations and deals that are in no way subject to public scrutiny.

- They make societies *ungovernable*, in that they create an array of vested interests that are able to block government initiatives and make policy unworkable.

New Right policies and priorities. The clearest demonstration of this was the backlash against corporatism in the 1980s, spearheaded in the USA by Reagan and in the UK by Thatcher. In the USA, this took the form of an attempt to deregulate the economy by weakening regulatory agencies; in the UK, it was evident in the marginalisation and later abolition of corporatist bodies such as the National Economic Development Council (NEDC or Neddy) and a determined assault on trade union power.

Patterns of group politics

How important are interest groups?

It is widely accepted that interest group activity is closely linked to economic and social development. Whereas agrarian or traditional societies tend to be dominated by a small number of interests, advanced industrial ones are complex and highly differentiated. Interest groups thus come to assume a central importance in mediating between the state and a more fragmented society, especially as the spread of education extends political awareness and organisational skills. This occurred, for example, in the USSR, where, by the 1970s, despite the persistence of formal political monolithicism, most commentators had come to accept the existence of what was seen as 'institutional pluralism'. However, the roles and significance of organised interests vary from system to system, from state to state, and over time. The principal factors determining group influence are the following:

- the political culture
- the institutional structure
- the nature of the party system
- the nature and style of public policy.

The political culture is crucial for two reasons. First, it determines whether interest groups are viewed as legitimate or non-legitimate actors, whether their formation and influence is permitted and encouraged, or otherwise. Secondly, it affects the willingness of people to form or join organised interests or to engage in group politics. At one extreme, regimes can practise **monism**, suppressing all forms of voluntary associational activity in order to ensure a single, unchallengeable centre of state power. This typically occurs in military regimes and one-party states. Although no contemporary or historical state has succeeded in stamping out all forms of group or factional activity, monistic regimes at least push group activity underground or ensure that it is expressed through the party–state apparatus and is thus entangled with the political and ideological goals of the regime.

Pluralist regimes, on the other hand, not only permit group politics, but encourage and even, in some cases, require it. Groups may be asked to participate in policy formulation or to be represented on public bodies or quangos (see p. 350). One of the reasons for the generally high level of group activity found in the USA, for instance, is the recognition in US political culture of the right of private groups to be heard. This is enshrined in constitutional guarantees of free speech, freedom of the press, freedom of assembly, and so forth. In Japan, the absence of clear distinctions between the public and private realms has created a political culture in which, in pre-democratic and democratic periods alike, a close relationship between government and business has been taken for granted.

In contrast, in some European states, organised interests are regarded with suspicion. This has traditionally been the case in France, where, influenced of Jacobin ideology, groups have been seen to both undermine the 'general will' of the people and challenge the strength and unity of the French state. At its high point in 1975, for instance, only 24 per cent of the French workforce belonged to a union, a figure that had fallen to 13 per cent by 1989. However, French political culture also embodies a tradition of direct action, demonstrated by the use by French farmers of road blocks and even lorry hijacks, and by the rebellion of students and trade unionists during the political troubles of May 1968.

The institutional structure of government is clearly significant in terms of interest-group activity in that it establishes points of access to the policy process. Unitary and centralised political systems, such as the UK's, tend to narrow the scope of group politics and concentrate it around the executive branch of government. Although this does not condemn groups to a marginal existence, it places heavy emphasis on

Monism: A belief in only one theory or value; monism is reflected politically in enforced obedience to a unitary power and is thus implicitly totalitarian.

'insider' status and broadens the capacity of the government of the day to choose whether or not to respond to group pressure. This was most clearly demonstrated in the UK under Thatcher in the 1980s in the downgrading of corporatist bodies and the consigning of trade unions to the political wilderness. Interest-group activity in France is similarly focused on direct consultation with the administration, particularly since the strengthening of presidential government and the weakening of the National Assembly in the Fifth Republic of 1958.

US government, on the other hand, is fragmented and decentralised. This reflects the impact of bicameralism, the separation of powers, federalism and judicial review. The range of 'access points' that this offers interest groups makes the US system peculiarly vulnerable to group pressures. Groups know, for instance, that battles lost in Congress can be refought in the courts, at the state or local level, and so on. Although this undoubtedly acts as a stimulus to group formation, and enlarges the number of influential groups, it may also be self-defeating, in that the activities of groups can end up cancelling each other out. Organised interests may thus act only as 'veto groups'.

The relationship between political parties and interest groups is always complex. In some senses, they are clearly rivals. While parties seek to aggregate interests and form political programmes typically based on broad ideological goals, interest groups are concerned with a narrower and more specific range of issues and objectives. Nevertheless, interest groups often seek to exert influence in and through parties, in some cases even spawning parties in an attempt to gain direct access to power. Many socialist parties, such as the UK Labour Party, were effectively created by the trade unions, and institutional and financial links, albeit modified, endure to this day.

The pattern of interest-group politics is also influenced by the party system. Dominant-party systems tend, quite naturally, to narrow the focus of group politics, concentrating it on the governing party. Major industrial and commercial interests in Italy and Japan therefore tried to exert pressure through 'ruling' parties such as the Christian Democrats and the Liberal-Democratic Party, which, in the process, did much to entrench the factional tendencies within these parties. Multiparty systems, on the other hand, are fertile ground for interest-group activity, because they broaden the scope of access. The legislative influence of interest groups is perhaps greatest in party systems like the USA's, in which political parties are weak in terms of both organisation and discipline. This was demonstrated in the late 1970s by the capacity of business interests effectively to destroy President Carter's energy programme, despite the existence of Democrat majorities in both the House of Representatives and the Senate.

Finally, the level of group activity fluctuates in relation to shifts in public policy, particularly the degree to which the state intervenes in economic and social life. As a general rule, **interventionism** goes hand in hand with corporatism, although there is a debate about which is the cause and which is the effect. Do interventionist policies force government into a closer relationship with organised interests in the hope of gaining information, advice and cooperation? Or do groups exploit their access to government to extract subsidies, supports and other benefits for their members? Whatever the answer is, it is clear that, amongst western states, the integration of organised interests, particularly functional interests, into public life has been taken furthest where social-democratic policies have been pursued.

The Swedish system is the classic example of this. Interest groups constitute an integral part of the Swedish political scene at every level. There are close, if not

Interventionism: Government policies designed to regulate or manage economic life; more broadly, a policy of engagement or involvement.

institutional, links between the trade unions and the Social Democratic Labour Party (SAP). The legislative process in the Riksdag is geared to wide consultation with affected interests, and state officials recognise 'peak' associations such as the Swedish Trade Union Confederation and the Employers' Confederation as 'social partners'. A similar pattern of corporate representation has developed in the Austrian 'chamber' system, which provides statutory representation for major interests such as commerce, agriculture and labour. In Germany, key economic groups such as the Federation of German Employers' Associations, the Federation of German Industry and the German Trades Union Federation are so closely involved in policy formulation that the system has been described as one of 'polyarchic elitism'.

How do groups exert influence?

Interest groups have at their disposal a broad range of tactics and political strategies. Indeed, it is almost unthinkable that a group should confine itself to a single strategy or try to exert influence through just one channel of influence. The methods that groups use vary according to a number of factors. These include the issue with which the group is concerned and how policy in that area is shaped. For instance, in the UK, since most policies relating to civil liberties and political rights are developed by the Home Office, a group such as Liberty (formerly the National Council for Civil Liberties) is compelled to seek 'insider' status, which it does by emphasising its specialist knowledge and political respectability. Similarly, the nature of the group and the resources at its disposal are crucial determinants of its political strategy. These resources include the following:

- public sympathy for the group and its goals
- the size of its membership or activist base
- its financial strength and organisational capabilities
- its ability to use sanctions that in some way inconvenience or disrupt government
- personal or institutional links it may have to political parties or government bodies.

Business groups are more likely than, say, trade unions or consumer groups to employ professional lobbyists or mount expensive public-relations campaigns, because, quite simply, they have the financial capacity to do so. The methods used by interest groups are shaped by the channel of access through which influence is exerted. The principal channels of access available are:

- the bureaucracy
- the assembly
- the courts
- political parties
- the mass media
- supranational bodies.

In all states, interest-group activity tends to centre on the bureaucracy as the key institution in the process of policy formulation. Access via this channel is largely confined to major economic and functional groups, such as large corporations, employers' associations, trade unions, farming interests and key professions. In Austria, the Netherlands and the Scandinavian states, for example, corporatist institutions have been developed specifically to facilitate group consultation, usually giving 'peak' employers' and employees' associations a measure of formal representation. More commonly, the consultative process is informal yet institutionalised, taking place through meetings and regular contacts that are rarely publicised and are beyond the scope of public scrutiny.

The crucial relationship here is usually that between senior bureaucrats and leading business or industrial interests. The advantages that business groups enjoy in this respect include the key role they play in the economy as producers, investors and employers, the overlap in social background and political outlets between business leaders and ministers and senior officials, and the widely held public belief that business interests coincide with the national interest ('what is good for General Motors is good for America'). This relationship is often consolidated by a 'revolving door', through which bureaucrats, on retirement, move into well paid jobs in private business. In Japan, this practice is so clearly established that it is known as *amakudari*, literally meaning 'descent from heaven'.

Influence exerted through the assembly, often called lobbying, is another important form of interest-group activity. One manifestation of this is the growth in the number of professional lobbyists, over 11 000 of whom were registered in Washington DC in 1990. The significance of the assembly or legislature in this respect depends on two factors: first, the role it plays in the political system and the degree to which it can shape policy, and secondly, the strength and discipline of the party system. Interest-group activity surrounding the US Congress is usually seen as the most intense in the world. This reflects the strength of Congress in terms of its constitutional independence and powerful committee system, and the fact that its decentralised party system allows individual representatives to be easily recruited by groups and causes. Much of this influence is exerted through financial contributions made to election campaigns by political action committees (PACs). In 1990, over 4000 PACs dispensed some $1.5 billion to candidates in Senate and House of Representatives races.

Policy networks (see p. 388) have also developed through institutionalised contacts between legislators (particularly key figures on legislative committees) and 'affected' groups and interests. In the USA, these form two 'legs' (executive agencies being the third leg) of the so-called 'iron triangles' that dominate much of domestic policy making. Lobbying activities focused on the assembly are less extensive and less significant in states like Canada and the UK in which party discipline is strong and parliaments are usually subject to executive control. Nevertheless, a US-style lobbying industry developed in the UK in the 1980s, with a trebling of the amount of money spent on professional lobbying, usually by parliamentary consultancies. This was in part a consequence of the dismantling of corporatism in the UK. However, it created growing concern about a decline in standards in public life in general, and especially amongst MPs, which resulted in the creation of the Nolan Committee on standards in public life in 1995.

In systems in which the courts are unable to challenge legislation and rarely check executive actions, interest-group activity focused on the judiciary is of only limited significance. This applies in states like the UK and New Zealand, despite a general tendency in the 1980s and 1990s towards judicial activism, which encouraged civil liberties and environmentalist groups in particular to fight campaigns through the courts. Where codified constitutions invest judges with the formal power of judicial review, however, as in Australia and the USA, the court system attracts far greater

Concept

Lobby

The term lobby is derived from the areas in parliaments or assemblies where the public may petition legislators, or politicians meet to discuss political business. In modern usage, the term is both a verb and a noun. The verb to lobby means to make direct representations to a policy maker, using argument or persuasion. Broadly, a lobby (noun) is equivalent to an interest group, in that both aim to influence public policy, as with the farm lobby, the environmental lobby and the roads lobby. Narrowly, following US practice, a lobbyist is a 'professional persuader', that is, a person hired to represent the arguments of interest-group clients. Professional lobbying has been criticised for amounting to the 'buying' of political influence.

attention from interest groups. The classic example of this in the US was the landmark *Brown* v. *Board of Education* Supreme Court ruling in 1954, which rejected the constitutionality of segregation laws. The NAACP had lobbied the US legal community for several years in an attempt to shift attitudes on issues such as race and segregation, and helped to sponsor the case. Similarly, in the 1980s and 1990s, the energies of the US pro-life (anti-abortion) lobby were largely directed at the Supreme Court, specifically in an attempt to overturn the 1974 *Roe* v. *Wade* judgement, which established the constitutionality of abortion.

Interest-group pressure is often also exerted through political parties. In some cases, parties and groups are so closely linked by historical, ideological and even institutional ties that they are best thought of as simply two wings of the same social movement. The UK and Australian Labour parties began in this way, and still function, if to a lesser extent, as part of a broader labour movement. Agrarian parties such as the Centre parties in Sweden and Norway are still part of a broad farmers' movement, and even Christian Democratic parties in central Europe can be seen as part of a broad Catholic movement. In other cases, however, the relationship between parties and groups is more pragmatic and instrumental.

The principal means through which groups influence parties is via campaign finance, and the benefits they hope to achieve are clear: 'he who pays the piper plays the tune'. Throughout the world, conservative or right-wing parties are largely funded by business contributions, while support for socialist or left-wing parties comes mainly from organised labour. However, groups may also have good reasons for avoiding too close an association with parties. For one thing, if 'their' party is in opposition, the government of the day may be less sympathetic to their interests; for another, open partisanship may restrict their ability to recruit members from amongst supporters of other parties. As a result, groups such as Shelter and the Child Poverty Action Group in the UK have assiduously guarded their nonpartisan status. There are, in addition, examples of political parties that have sought to 'divorce' themselves from interest groups. In the 1990s, the UK Labour Party thus reduced the influence of affiliated trade unions at every level in the party in an attempt to destroy the image that the Labour Party is merely a puppet of the union movement.

Very different methods are employed by groups that seek to influence government indirectly via the mass media (see p. 188) and public opinion campaigns. Tactics here range from petitions, protests and demonstrations to civil disobedience and even the tactical use of violence. Interest groups use such methods for one of two reasons. They may either reflect the group's outsider status and its inability to gain direct access to policy makers, or they may follow from the nature of the group's activist base or the character of its ideological goals. The traditional practitioners of this form of politics were trade unions, which utilised their 'industrial muscle' in the form of strikes, pickets and marches.

However, the spectacular rise of promotional and cause groups since the 1960s has seen the emergence of new styles of activist politics practised by peace campaigners, environmental lobbyists, animal rights groups, anti-roads protesters, and so on. A common aim of these groups is to attract media attention and stimulate public awareness and sympathy. Greenpeace and Friends of the Earth, for example, have been particularly imaginative in devising protests against nuclear testing, air and water pollution, deforestation, and the use of non-renewable energy sources. The nature and significance of such activities in relation to new social movements are examined in the next main section of the unit.

Finally, in the closing decades of the twentieth century, interest-group activity has increasingly adjusted to the impact of globalisation (see p. 140) and the strengthening of supranational bodies. Amongst the groups best suited to take advantage of such shifts are charities and environmental campaigners (such as Greenpeace and Friends of the Earth) which already possess transnational structures and an international membership. Since its creation in 1971, Greenpeace, for example, has established offices in over 30 countries and built up an annual income of $50 000 000. Many of these organisations gained formal representation as non-governmental organisations (NGOs) at the 1992 UN Conference on Environment and Development (commonly known as the Earth Summit) in Brazil. The better-funded NGOs now have permanent offices in Washington DC and Brussels which monitor the work of the UN and EU respectively, and conduct regular lobbying campaigns.

Sectional interest groups in EU member states have also adjusted to the fact that, in a number of policy areas, key decisions are increasingly made by EU institutions rather than national ones. This particularly applies in relation to agriculture, trade agreements, competition policy and social and workers' rights. The most financially powerful and best organised groups operating at the EU level are undoubtedly business interests. Their influence is exerted in various ways: through direct lobbying by large corporations, national trade bodies and 'peak' associations, and through the activities of a new range of EU 'peak' associations such as the European Round Table of Industrialists and the Union of Industrial and Employers' Confederations of Europe (UNICE). To some extent, however, the UK trade-union movement, and the Trades Union Congress (TUC) in particular, has been able to compensate for its marginalisation at the national level by conducting its campaigns in favour of workers' and social rights through EU institutions.

Social movements

Interest in social movements has been revived by the emergence of so-called 'new' social movements since the 1960s: the women's movement, the environmental or Green movement, the peace movement, and so on. However, social movements can be traced back to the early nineteenth century. The earliest were the labour movement, which campaigned for improved conditions for the growing working class, various national movements, usually struggling for independence from multinational European empires, and, in central Europe in particular, a Catholic movement that fought for emancipation through the granting of legal and political rights to Catholics. In the twentieth century, it was also common for fascist and right-wing authoritarian groups to be seen as movements rather than as conventional political parties.

New social movements

What is 'new' about the social movements that emerged in the final decades of the twentieth century? In the first place, whereas their more traditional counterparts were movements of the oppressed or disadvantaged, contemporary social movements have more commonly attracted the young, the better-educated and the relatively affluent. This is linked to the second difference: new movements typically

---

Concept

Civil disobedience

Civil disobedience is law breaking that is justified by reference to 'higher' religious, moral or political principles. Civil disobedience is an overt and public act; it aims to break a law in order to 'make a point', not to get away with it. Indeed, its moral force is largely based on the willing acceptance of the penalties that follow from law breaking. This both emphasises the conscientious or principled nature of the act and provides evidence of the depth of feeling or commitment that lies behind it. The moral character of civil disobedience is normally demonstrated by the strict avoidance of violence, as exemplified by Gandhi's (1869–1948) notion of *satyagraha* (literally 'insistence on truth'), non-violent resistance. Other advocates of civil disobedience have included D. H. Thoreau (1817–62) and Martin Luther King (1929–68).

Social movement

A social movement is a particular form of collective behaviour in which the motive to act springs largely from the attitudes and aspirations of members, typically acting within a loose organisational framework. Being part of a social movement requires a level of commitment and political activism rather than formal or card-carrying membership; above all, movements move. A movement is different from spontaneous mass action (such as an uprising or rebellion) in that it implies a level of intended and planned action in pursuit of a recognised social goal. Not uncommonly, social movements embrace interest groups and may even spawn political parties; trade unions and socialist parties, for instance, can be seen as part of a broader labour movement.

New Left

The New Left comprises the thinkers and intellectual movements (prominent in the 1960s and early 1970s) that sought to revitalise socialist thought by developing a radical critique of advanced industrial society. The New Left rejected both 'old' left alternatives: Soviet-style state socialism and de-radicalised western social democracy. Influenced by the humanist writings of the 'young' Marx, anarchism and radical forms of phenomenology and existentalism, New Left theories were often diffuse. Common themes nevertheless included a fundamental rejection of conventional society ('the system') as oppressive, a commitment to personal autonomy and self-fulfilment in the form of 'liberation', disillusionment with the role of the working class as the revolutionary agent, and a preference for decentralisation and participatory democracy.

Mass society: A society characterised by atomism and cultural and political rootlessness; the concept highlights pessimistic trends in modern societies.

Postindustrial society: A society no longer dependent on manufacturing industry, but more reliant on knowledge and communication; an 'information society'.

have a postmaterial (see p. 193) orientation, being more concerned with 'quality of life' issues than with social advancement. Although the women's movement, for example, addresses material concerns such as equal pay and equal opportunities, it draws from a broader set of values associated with gender equality and opposition to patriarchy. Thirdly, while traditional movements had little in common and seldom worked in tandem, new social movements subscribe to a common, if not always clearly defined, ideology.

In broad terms, their ideological stance is linked to the New Left; it challenges prevailing social goals and political styles, and embraces libertarian aspirations such as personal fulfilment and self-expression. It is therefore not surprising that there is a significant membership overlap, as well as mutual sympathy, amongst the women's, environmental, animal rights, peace, anti-roads and other movements.

A final difference between traditional and new social movements is that the latter tend to have organisational structures that stress decentralisation and participatory decision-making and have also developed new forms of political activism. They thus practise what is sometimes called the 'new politics', which turns away from 'established' parties, interest groups and representative processes towards a more innovative and theatrical form of protest politics.

The emergence of a new generation of social movements practising new styles of activism has significantly shifted views about the nature and significance of movements themselves. The experience of totalitarianism (see p. 27) in the period between the two world wars encouraged **mass society** theorists such as Erich Fromm (1900–80) and Hannah Arendt (see p. 9) to see movements in distinctly negative terms. From the mass society perspective, social movements reflect a 'flight from freedom' (Fromm, 1941), an attempt by alienated individuals to achieve security and identity through fanatical commitment to a cause and obedience to a (usually fascist) leader. In contrast, new social movements are usually interpreted as rational and instrumental actors, whose use of informal and unconventional means merely reflects the resources available to them (McCarthy and Zald, 1973). The emergence of new social movements is widely seen as evidence of the fact that power in **postindustrial societies** is increasingly dispersed and fragmented. The class-based politics of old has thus been replaced by a new politics based on what Laclau and Mouffe (1985) called 'democratic pluralism'. Not only do new movements offer new and rival centres of power, but they also diffuse power more effectively by resisting bureaucratisation and developing more spontaneous, affective and decentralised forms of organisation.

Nevertheless, the impact of social movements is more difficult to assess than that of political parties or interest groups. This is because of the broader nature of their

Betty Friedan (born 1921)

US feminist and political activist, sometimes seen as the 'mother' of women's liberation. Betty Friedan's *The Feminine Mystique* (1963) is often credited with having stimulated the emergence of 'second wave' feminism. In it, she examined 'the problem with no name': the sense of frustration and despair afflicting suburban American women. In 1966, she helped to found the National Organisation of Women (NOW), becoming its first president. In *The Second Stage* (1983), Friedan drew attention to the danger that the pursuit of 'personhood' might encourage women to deny the importance of children, the home, and the family. Her later writings include *The Fountain of Age* (1993).

goals, and because, to some extent, they exert influence through less tangible cultural strategies. However, it is clear that in cases like the women's movement and the environmental movement profound political changes have been achieved through shifts in cultural values and moral attitudes brought about over a number of years. For example, the Women's Liberation Movement (WLM) emerged in the 1960s as a collection of groups and organisations mobilised by the emerging ideas of 'second wave' feminism, as expressed in the writings of such as Betty Friedan, Germaine Greer (born 1939) and Kate Millett (born 1934). Despite the achievement by the women's movement of advances in specific areas, such as equal pay and the legalisation of abortion, perhaps its most significant achievement is an increasing general awareness of gender issues and the eroding of support for patriarchal attitudes and institutions. This is a cultural change that has had a deep, if unquantifiable, impact on public policy at many levels.

The environmental movement has brought about similar politico-cultural shifts. Not only have governments been confronted by interest-group campaigns mounted by the likes of Greenpeace, Friends of the Earth and the Worldwide Fund for Nature, but they have also been influenced by broader anxieties about the environment that extend well beyond those expressed by the formal membership of such organisations. Since the 1970s, these concerns have also been articulated by Green parties. Typically, these parties have embraced the idea of 'new politics', styling themselves as 'anti-system' parties, and placing a heavy emphasis on decentralisation and popular activism. The impact of the environmental movement has also extended to conventional or 'grey' parties, many of which have responded to new popular sensibilities by trying to establish their Green credentials.

■ Summary

◆ An interest or pressure group is an organised association which aims to influence the policies or actions of government. Sectional groups advance or protect the (usually material) interests of their members, while promotional ones are concerned with shared values, ideals or principles. Whereas insider groups enjoy privileged access to policy formulation, outsider groups lack access to government and so are forced to 'go public'.

◆ Group politics has been understood in a number of ways. Pluralism emphasises the dispersal of power and the ability of groups to guarantee democratic accountability. Corporatism highlights the privileged position that certain groups enjoy in relation to government. The New Right draws attention to the threat that groups pose in terms of over-government and economic inefficiency.

◆ Organised groups benefit the political system by strengthening representation, promoting debate and discussion, broadening political participation, and acting as a check on government power. They may nevertheless pose a threat in that they entrench political inequality, are socially and politically divisive, exercise non-legitimate and unaccountable power, and make the policy process more closed and secretive.

◆ Interest groups exert influence through a variety of channels, including the bureaucracy, the assembly, the courts, the mass media, the parties and international bodies. The level of influence that groups have in a particular system, however, relates to how accommodating that system is to group activity in general, and to what access points it offers groups in terms of the distribution of policy making power.

◆ Interest groups have at their disposal a wide range of tactics and political strategies. Their resources may include public sympathy for the group and its goals, the size of its membership or activist base, its financial strength and organisational capabilities, its ability to use sanctions against government, and its personal or institutional links with political parties or government bodies.

◆ A social movement is a collective body in which there is a high level of commitment and political activism not necessarily based on a formal organisation. New social movements are distinguished by their capacity to attract the young, better-educated and relatively affluent, their generally postmaterial orientation, and their commitment to new forms of political activism, sometimes called the 'new politics'.

■ Questions for discussion

▶ Why is it sometimes difficult to distinguish between interest groups and political parties?

▶ Are organised groups the principal means through which interests are articulated in modern societies?

▶ Does corporatism work more to the benefit of groups, or more to the benefit of government?

▶ Do interest groups help to promote democracy or to undermine it?

▶ Why are some interest groups more powerful than others?

▶ To what extent have new social movements had an impact on public policy?

■ Further reading

Ball, A. and F. Millward *Pressure Politics in Industrial Societies* (London: Macmillan, 1986). A comprehensive and accessible analysis of the power of groups and their significance in the political system.

Cigler, C. and B. Loomis (eds) *Interest Group Politics* (Washington DC: Congressional Quarterly Press, 1985). An examination of various aspects of group politics in the USA.

Pakulski, J. *Social Movements: The Politics of Protest* (Melbourne: Longman, 1990). A useful introduction to the study of contemporary social movements.

Wilson, G. *Interest Groups* (Oxford: Blackwell, 1990). A clear and concise discussion of the role of groups in liberal democracies.

PART
4

Machinery of Government

Constitutions, the Law and Judiciaries

CHAPTER 14

'Government without a Constitution is Power without Right.'

THOMAS PAINE *The Rights of Man* (1795)

In the 1950s and 1960s the study of constitutions and constitutional issues became distinctly unfashionable. Political analysts turned instead to what were seen as deeper political realities, such as political culture and the distribution of economic and social power. To be interested in constitutions was to perpetuate an outdated, legalistic and, frankly, boring approach to politics, to focus on how a political system portrays itself, rather than on how it actually works. Since the 1970s, however, constitutional questions have moved to the centre of the political stage. Developed and developing states have adopted new constitutions, and political conflict has increasingly been expressed in terms of calls for constitutional reform. This, in turn, has had major implications for the role of law and the position of judges. Although in theory the courts and the judiciary are strictly separate from politics, in practice, in many parts of the world, they have developed into key political institutions that have a growing capacity to shape public policy.

The central issues addressed in this chapter are the following:

Key issues

▶ What is a constitution, and what forms can it take?

▶ What is the purpose of a constitution?

▶ To what extent do constitutions shape political practice?

▶ What is the relationship between law and politics?

▶ What is the political significance of the courts?

▶ Can judges keep out of politics? Should judges keep out of politics?

Constitutions

Traditionally, constitutions were seen as important for two reason. First, they were believed to provide a description of government itself, a neat introduction to key institutions and their roles. Secondly, they were regarded as the linchpin of liberal democracy, even its defining feature. Sadly, neither view is correct. While constitutions may *aim* to lay down a framework in which government and political activity is conducted, none have been entirely successful in this respect. Inaccuracies, distortions and omissions can be found in all constitutions. Similarly, although the idea of constitutionalism (see p. 279) is closely linked to liberal values and aspirations, there is nothing to prevent a constitution being undemocratic or authoritarian. In the case of communist states and some developing states, constitutions have indeed been profoundly illiberal. Why then bother with constitutions? Why begin an account of the machinery of government with a discussion of constitutions? The reason is that the objective of constitutions is to lay down certain meta-rules for the political system. In effect, these are rules that govern the government itself. Just as government establishes ordered rule in society at large, the purpose of a constitution is to bring stability, predictability and order to the actions of government.

The idea of a code of rules providing guidance for the conduct of government has an ancient lineage. These codes traditionally drew on the idea of a higher moral power, usually religious in character, to which worldly affairs were supposed to conform. Egyptian pharaohs acknowledged the authority of *Ma'at* or 'justice', Chinese emperors were subject to *Ti'en* or 'heaven', Jewish kings conformed to the Mosaic Law, and Islamic caliphs paid respect to *Shari'a* law. Not uncommonly, 'higher' principles were also enacted in ordinary law, as seen, for example, in the distinction in the Athenian constitution between the *nomos* (laws that could only be changed by a special procedure) and the *psephismata* (decrees that could be passed by a resolution of the assembly). However, such ancient codes did not amount to constitutions in the modern sense, in that they generally failed to lay down specific provisions relating to the authority and responsibilities of the various institutions, and rarely established authoritative mechanisms through which provisions could be enforced and breaches of the fundamental law punished.

Constitutions are thus best thought of as a relatively recent development. Although the evolution of the British constitution is sometimes traced back to the Bill of Rights of 1689 and the Act of Settlement of 1701, or even to the Magna Carta (1215), it is more helpful to think of constitutions as late eighteenth-century creations. The 'age of constitutions' was initiated by the enactment of the first 'written' constitutions: the US constitution in 1787 and the French Declaration of the Rights of Man and the Citizen in 1789. The examples of the USA and revolutionary France not only provided in form and substance a model for later constitution makers to follow, but also shed light on why and how constitutions come about.

The enactment of a constitution marks a major breach in political continuity, usually resulting from an upheaval such as a war, revolution or national independence. Constitutions are above all a means of establishing a new political order following the rejection, collapse or failure of an old order. In this light, the revival of interests in constitutions since the 1970s (with new constitutions being adopted in countries like Portugal, Spain, Canada, Sweden and the Netherlands, and the issue of constitutional reform becoming more prominent in, for example, the UK, India and

Australia) indicates growing disenchantment, even disillusionment, with existing political systems. In general, it can be said that political conflicts assume a constitutional dimension only when those demanding change seek to redraw, and not merely readjust, the rules of the political game. Constitutional change is therefore about the reapportionment of both power and political authority.

Classifying constitutions

Constitutions can be classified in many different ways. These include the following:

- the form of the constitution and *status* of its rules (whether the constitution is written or unwritten, or codified or uncodified)
- the ease with which the constitution can be *changed* (whether it is rigid or flexible)
- the degree to which the constitution is *observed* in practice (whether it is an effective, nominal or a facade constitution)
- the *content* of the constitution and the institutional structure that it establishes (whether it is, for example, monarchical or republican, federal or unitary, or presidential or parliamentary).

Traditionally, considerable emphasis has been placed on the distinction between written and unwritten constitutions. This was thought to draw a divide between constitutions that are enshrined in law and ones that are embodied in custom and tradition (see p. 195). The former are human artifacts in the sense that they have been 'created', while the latter have been seen as organic entities that have evolved through history. This system of classification, however, has now been largely abandoned. In the first place, an overwhelming majority of states now possess basic written documents that lay down major constitutional provisions. Only three liberal democracies (Israel, New Zealand and the UK) continue to have unwritten constitutions, together with a handful of non-democratic states such as Bhutan, Saudi Arabia and Oman. Moreover, the classification has always been misleading. No constitution is entirely written in the sense that all its rules are formal and legally enforceable. Few constitutions, for instance, specify the roles of, or even mention, political parties and interest groups. Similarly, no constitution is entirely unwritten in the sense that none of its provisions have any legal substance, all of them being conventions, customs or traditions.

Every constitution, then, is a blend of written and unwritten rules, although the balance between these varies significantly. In countries such as France and Germany in which constitutional documents act as state codes, specifying in considerable detail the powers and responsibilities of political institutions, the emphasis is clearly on written rules. The US constitution (the world's first written constitution) is, however, a document of only 7000 words which confines itself, in the main, to broad principles and so only lays down a loose framework for government. US institutions of undoubted constitutional significance, such as congressional committees, primary elections (see p. 236) and the bureaucracy, have simply evolved over time. Other constitutions, although not entirely unwritten, place considerable stress on conventions. For example, the ability of UK ministers to exercise the powers of the Royal Prerogative (technically, the monarch's powers) and their responsibility, individually and collectively, to Parliament is based entirely on convention.

The worldwide trend, however, is to favour the adoption of written and formal

Convention

A convention, in everyday language, is either a formal political meeting or an agreement reached through debate and negotiation. A constitutional convention, however, is a rule of conduct or behaviour that is based not on law but on custom and precedent. These nonlegal rules are upheld either by a sense of constitutional propriety (what is 'correct') or by practical circumstances (what is 'workable'). Conventions of this sort exist in all constitutional systems, and they usually provide guidance where formal rules are unclear or incomplete. In 'unwritten' constitutions, they are particularly significant, because they define the procedures, powers and duties of the major institutions, thus compensating for the absence of a codified document. Typically, they modify the effect of powers laid down in strict law.

Bill of rights: A constitutional document that specifies the rights and freedoms of the individual, and so defines the legal extent of civil liberty.

Common law: Law based on custom and precedent; law that is supposedly 'common' to all.

rules. Not only has the number of unwritten constitutions diminished, but also, within them, there has been a growing reliance on legal rules. Although respect for the Torah, the Jewish book of holy law, encouraged the Israelis to establish an independent state in 1948 without an authoritative constitutional document, within two years the Knesset had voted to adopt such a constitution by evolution over an unspecified period of time. The publication in the UK of documents such as Questions on Procedure for Ministers has given detailed formal substance to practices that were previously covered by ill defined conventions. The passage in New Zealand of the Constitution Act 1986 (which consolidated previously scattered laws and principles), and the adoption in 1990 of a **bill of rights**, has been interpreted by many commentators as indicating that New Zealand should no longer be classified amongst the ranks of states with unwritten constitutions.

More helpful (and more accurate) than the written/unwritten distinction is the contrast between codified and uncodified constitutions. A codified constitution is one in which key constitutional provisions are collected together within a single legal document, popularly known as a 'written constitution' or 'the constitution'. As pointed out above, most constitutions can be so classified, even though they may differ in the degree to which constitutional detail is specified and the extent to which other provisions are unwritten. The significance of codification is, nevertheless, considerable.

First, in a codified constitution, the document itself is authoritative in the sense that it constitutes 'higher' law, indeed, the highest law of the land. The constitution binds all political institutions, including those that enact ordinary law. The existence of a codified constitution thus establishes a hierarchy of laws. In unitary states, a two-tier legal system exists, in which the constitution stands above statute law made by the national legislature. In federal states, there is a third tier in the form of 'lower' state or provincial laws. Secondly, the status of the codified document is ensured by the fact that at least certain of its provisions are entrenched, in the sense that it is difficult to amend or abolish them. The procedure for establishing the constitution and for subsequently revising it must therefore be in some way more complex and difficult than the procedure for enacting ordinary statute laws. Finally, the logic of codification dictates that, as the constitution sets out the duties, powers and functions of government institutions in terms of 'higher' law, it must be justiciable, meaning that all political bodies must be subject to the authority of the courts, and in particular a supreme or constitutional court. This substantially enhances the importance of judges, or at least senior judges, who become, in effect, the final arbiters of the constitution, and thereby acquire the power of judicial review (see p. 288).

Uncodified constitutions, although few in number, have very different characteristics. The British constitution, which is properly thought of as an uncodified but partly written constitution, draws on a variety of sources. Chief amongst these are statute law, which is made by Parliament, **common law**, conventions, and various works of authority that clarify and explain the constitution's unwritten elements. The absence of a codified document implies, most importantly, that the legislature enjoys sovereign or unchallengeable authority. It has the right to make or unmake any law whatsoever, no body having the right to override or set aside its laws. By virtue of their legislative supremacy, bodies such as the UK Parliament and the Knesset in Israel are able to function as the ultimate arbiters of the constitution: the constitution means what they say it means.

Focus on . . .

A codified constitution: strengths and weaknesses

The strengths of a codified or written constitution include the following:

- Major principles and key constitutional provisions are *entrenched*, safeguarding them from interference by the government of the day.
- The power of the legislature is *constrained*, cutting its sovereignty down to size.
- Nonpolitical judges are able to *police* the constitution to ensure that its provisions are upheld by other public bodies.
- Individual *liberty* is more securely protected, and authoritarianism is kept at bay.
- The codified document has an *educational* value, in that it highlights the central values and overall goals of the political system.

The drawbacks or weaknesses of codification include the following:

- A codified constitution is more *rigid*, and may therefore be less responsive and adaptable than an uncodified one.
- Government power may be more effectively *constrained* by regular elections than by a constitutional document.
- With a codified constitution, constitutional supremacy resides with *nonelected* judges rather than publicly accountable politicians.
- Constitutional provisions enshrined in custom and convention may be more widely *respected* because they have been endorsed by history and not 'invented'.
- Constitutional documents are inevitably *biased*, because they endorse one set of values or principles in preference to others, meaning that they may precipitate more conflicts than they resolve.

In the UK in particular, this has stimulated deep controversy and mounting criticism. Parliamentary sovereignty (see p. 283) has been held responsible for what Lord Hailsham (1976) termed **elective dictatorship**, that is, the ability of a government to act in any way it pleases as long as it maintains majority control of the House of Commons. The concentration of power in the hands of the executive to which this leads, and the consequent threat that it poses to individual rights and liberties, has encouraged some to argue that the UK has no constitution at all. If governments can, once elected, act in whatever way they wish, they are surely at liberty to enlarge their own powers at will, and are thereby unconstrained by constitutional rules of any kind. In Griffith's (1991) phrase, the constitution in the UK is 'what happens'. This analysis clearly adds fuel to the campaign in the UK for constitutional reform, either in the form of a revision of the constitutional structure to ensure a wider dispersal of government power (for example, through electoral reform, an elected second chamber, devolution or freedom of information), or in the form of a codified constitution embodying an entrenched bill of rights.

An alternative form of classification distinguishes between rigid and flexible constitutions. What procedures exist for amending a constitution? How easily does the constitution adapt to changing circumstances? On the face of it, codified constitu-

Elective dictatorship: A constitutional imbalance in which executive power is checked only by the need to win subsequent elections.

tions are likely to be relatively inflexible because their provisions are in some way entrenched in 'higher' law. By the same token, uncodified ones appear to be flexible and adaptable, because laws of constitutional significance can be changed through the ordinary legislative process and conventions are, by their nature, based on conduct and practice. However, there is no simple relationship between written constitutions and rigidity, or unwritten ones and flexibility.

Various degrees of flexibility are possible, and, surprisingly, the flexibility of a constitution is not directly proportional to the formality of its procedures and rules. Whereas the US constitution has endured, albeit with amendments, since 1787, France has had, over the same period, no fewer than 17 constitutions. Similarly, amendment procedures may be more or less complex or difficult. In Australia, Denmark, Ireland and Spain, for example, referendums (see p. 209) are used to obtain the public's approval for constitutional amendments or ratify ones endorsed by the legislature. In other cases, special majorities must be achieved in the legislature, as in the requirement in Germany's Basic Law that amendments must have two-thirds support in both the Bundestag and the Bundesrat. In the USA, in addition to two-thirds majorities in both houses of Congress, constitutional amendments must be ratified by three-quarters of the states. This requirement has meant that a mere 26 constitutional amendments have been passed, with ten of these (the so-called Bill of Rights) having been introduced in the first two years of the constitution's existence.

The seeming rigidity this produces is, however, misleading. Although the words of the US constitution and other codified documents may change little, their meanings are subject to constant revision and updating through the process of judicial interpretation and reinterpretation. The role of the judiciary in this respect is examined in the final main section of this chapter. Just as written provisions can allow for flexibility, unwritten ones can, at times, be rigid. While in the UK the conventions of ministerial responsibility have proved to be so adaptable they can almost be reshaped at the convenience of the government of the day, other conventions are so deeply engrained in the political culture and in popular expectations that their abandonment or modification is virtually unthinkable. This certainly applies in the case of conventions that restrict the political role of the monarchy and prevent monarchs challenging the authority of Parliament.

A third system of classification takes account of the relationship between constitutional rules and principles, on the one hand, and the practice of government (the 'working' constitution) on the other. As early as 1867, Walter Bagehot in *The English Constitution* ([1867] 1963) distinguished between the 'dignified' parts of the constitution (the monarchy and the House of the Lords), which promoted popular allegiance but exercised little effective power, and its 'efficient' parts (the cabinet and the House of Commons). An effective constitution is one that fulfils two criteria. First, in major respects at least, the practical affairs of government correspond to the provisions of the constitution. Secondly, this occurs because the constitution has the capacity, through whatever means, to limit governmental behaviour.

An effective constitution therefore requires not merely the existence of constitutional rules, but also the capacity of those rules to constrain government and establish constitutionalism. As we shall see below, however, all constitutions are violated to a greater or lesser extent; the real issue is thus the significance and regularity of such violations. Some constitutions can be classified as nominal, in that their texts or principles may accurately describe governmental behaviour but fail to limit it. For instance, communist states such as the USSR had constitutions that, amongst other things, acknowledged the monopoly of power of the country's communist party, but the constitutions were politically irrelevant because the judiciary, charged with interpreting the constitution, was kept under firm party control. Other states have sham or facade constitutions. These differ substantially from political practice and tend to fulfil, at best, only a propaganda role. This is particularly the case in dictatorial or authoritarian states, where the commitment to individual rights and liberties extends little further than the content of the state's constitutional documents.

Constitutions have also been classified in terms of their content and, specifically, by the institutional structure they underpin. This enables a number of distinctions to be made. For example, constitutions have traditionally been categorised as either monarchical or republican. In theory, the former invest constitutional supremacy in a dynastic ruler, while in the latter political authority is derived from the people. However, the emergence of constitutional monarchies (see p. 324), in which power has effectively been transferred to representative institutions, has meant that, apart from in the surviving absolute monarchies in states like Nepal and Saudi Arabia, this distinction is no longer of central importance. More widely used, though, is the distinction between unitary and federal constitutions (discussed more fully in Chapter 7), that is, the difference between constitutions that concentrate sovereignty in a single national body and ones that divide it between two levels of government.

Yet another approach is to differentiate between what are seen as parliamentary constitutions and presidential constitutions. The key here is the relationship between the executive and the assembly. In parliamentary systems, the executive is derived from and accountable to the assembly, while in presidential ones the two branches of government function independently on the basis of a separation of powers (see p. 297). These different systems are examined in Chapters 15 and 16. Finally, pluralist constitutions can be contrasted with monopolistic ones. The former are characteristic of liberal democracies in that they ensure that political power is dispersed, usually through guarantees of participatory rights and party competition. The latter are more commonly found in communist or authoritarian states where the unquestionable authority of a 'ruling' party or supreme leader is formally entrenched, thus demonstrating that a constitution and liberal constitutionalism do not necessarily go hand in hand.

The purpose of a constitution

Not only do the vast majority of states have constitutions, but also most institutions and organised groups have rules that have some kind of constitutional effect. This applies in the case of international bodies such as the United Nations and the European Union, and is also true of regional and provincial government, political parties, interest groups, corporations, churches, clubs and so on. The popularity of these constitutional rules draws attention to the fact that constitutions somehow play a vital role in the running of organisations. Why is it difficult, and perhaps impossible, for states and other organised bodies to function without a constitution? The difficulty with answering this question is that constitutions do not have a single or simple purpose. Rather, they have a number of functions and are used in a variety of ways. The most important of these are the following:

• to empower states
• to establish unifying values and goals

Concept

Constitutionalism

Constitutionalism, in a narrow sense, is the practice of limited government ensured by the existence of a constitution. Thus constitutionalism can, in this sense, be said to exist when government institutions and political processes are effectively constrained by constitutional rules. More broadly, constitutionalism is a set of political values and aspirations that reflect the desire to protect liberty through the establishment of internal and external checks on government power. In this sense, constitutionalism is a species of political liberalism. It is typically expressed in the form of support for constitutional provisions that achieve this goal, for example, a codified constitution, a bill of rights, a separation of powers, bicameralism, and federalism or decentralisation.

- to provide government stability
- to protect freedom
- to legitimise regimes.

Empowering states

Although the popular image of constitutions is that they limit government power, a more basic function is that they mark out the existence of states and make claims concerning their sphere of independent authority. The creation of new states (whether through the overthrow of colonialism, the fragmentation of larger states, or an amalgamation of smaller ones) is invariably accompanied by the enactment of a constitution. Indeed, it can be argued that such states only exist once they have a constitition, since without one they lack formal jurisdiction over a particular territory or a governing apparatus that can effectively exercise that jurisdiction.

The state of India can thus be said to have come into existence in the period between the granting of independence in 1947 and the adoption of its federal constitution in 1950; during this time, a UK-appointed Governor General continued to exercise supervision. In the same way, the American Declaration of Independence in 1776 initiated the process through which the USA achieved statehood, but this was not completed until the US constitution was ratified in 1789. The need for empowerment also applies to subnational and supranational bodies. In federal systems, for example, constituent provinces or states have their own constitutions in order to guarantee their sphere of authority relative to that of central government. The 'constitution' of the EU, which comprises treaties and agreements such as the Treaty of Rome (1957), the Single European Act (1986) and the Treaty on European Union (or Maastricht Treaty) (1991), authorises EU bodies to intervene in various ways in the affairs of EU member states.

Establishing values and goals

In addition to laying down a framework for government, constitutions invariably embody a broader set of political values, ideals and goals. This why constitutions cannot be neutral; they are always entangled, more or less explicitly, with ideological priorities. The creators of constitutions therefore seek to invest their regime with a set of unifying values, a sense of ideological purpose, and a vocabulary that can be used in the conduct of politics. In many cases, these aims are accomplished explicitly in preambles to constitutional documents which often function as statements of national ideals. These ideals can vary from a commitment to democracy, freedom or the welfare state to a belief in socialism, federalism or Islam. The 1977 Soviet constitution thus proclaimed the USSR to be a 'developed socialist society', while Germany's Basic Law states a determination to 'serve the peace of the world'.

In other cases, however, these values and ideological priorities are largely implicit. Charles Beard (1913), for example, argued that the provisions of the US constitution were essentially shaped by economic interests, in particular the desire to defend property against the rising power of the propertyless masses. Similarly, it can be argued that, while the Fourteenth Amendment and Fifteenth Amendment to the US constitution acknowledge the significance of racial divisions, the constitution effectively conceals divisions that arise from social class or gender. In the case of the British constitution, the doctrine of parliamentary sovereignty has been interpreted as a means of discouraging, or even discrediting, forms of extraparliamentary political action.

Providing government stability

In allocating duties, powers and functions amongst the various institutions of government, constitutions act as 'organisational charts', 'definitional guides', or 'institutional blueprints'. As such, they formalise and regulate the relationships between political bodies and provide a mechanism through which conflicts can be adjudicated and resolved. The Indian constitution, for instance, contains a highly detailed description of institutional powers and relationships in a lengthy document containing almost 400 articles. Despite varying in their degree of specificity and their effectiveness, all constitutions fulfil the vital function of introducing a measure of stability, order and predictability to the workings of government. From this point of view, the opposite of constitutional government is random, capricious or arbitrary government. This is precisely why constitutions go hand in hand with organisation. Complex patterns of social interaction can only be maintained if all concerned know the 'rules of the game' and therefore who can be expected to do what.

Protecting freedom

In liberal democracies it is often taken for granted that the central purpose of a constitution is to constrain government with a view to protecting individual liberty. This is why constitutions tend to be viewed as devices for establishing and maintaining **limited government**. Certainly, constitutions lay down the relationship between the state and the individual, marking out the respective spheres of government authority and personal freedom (see p. 282). They do this largely by defining civil rights and liberties, often through the means of a bill of rights. The impact of liberal constitutionalism has ensured that in many cases 'classic' or traditional civil liberties (see p. 365), such as freedom of expression, freedom of religious worship, freedom of assembly and freedom of movement, are recognised as 'fundamental' in that they are constitutionally guaranteed. These so-called **negative rights** have a liberal character in that, because the state is thus prevented from encroaching upon the individual, they mark out a sphere of government *in*activity.

A growing number of states have, in addition, entrenched a range of economic, social and cultural rights, such as the right to healthcare, the right to education and even the right to work. These **positive rights**, however, have caused controversy, because they are linked to the expansion, not contraction, of government, and because their provision is dependent upon the economic and social resources available to the state in question. Can these rights and freedoms be thought of as 'fundamental' when there is no practical way of guaranteeing their delivery? In the Indian constitution this is acknowledged through the qualification that the right to work, for example, is secured 'within the limits of economic capacity and development'.

Legitimising regimes

The final function of a constitution is to help build legitimacy (see p. 193). This explains the widespread use of constitutions, even by states with constitutions that are merely nominal or a complete facade. This legitimation process has two dimensions. In the first place, the existence of a constitution is almost a prerequisite for a state's membership of the international community and for its recognition by other states. More significant, however, is the ability to use a constitution to build legitimacy within a state through the promotion of respect and compliance

Limited government:
Government operating within constraints, usually imposed by law, a constitution or institutional checks and balances.

Negative rights: Rights that mark out a realm of unconstrained action, and thus check the responsibilities of government.

Positive rights: Rights that make demands of government in terms of the provision of resources and support, and thus extend its responsibilities.

Concept

Freedom

The term freedom (or liberty) means, in its broadest sense, the ability to think or act as one wishes. A distinction is nevertheless often made between 'negative' and 'positive' liberty, that is, between being free *from* something and being free *to* do something (Berlin, 1958). *Negative* freedom means noninterference: the absence of external constraints on the individual. The individual is thus 'at liberty' to act as he or she wishes. *Positive* freedom is linked to the achievement of some identifiable goal or benefit, usually personal development, self-realisation or self-mastery. The 'freedom from' and 'freedom to' distinction is misleading, however, because every example of freedom can be described in both ways. For instance, being free *from* ignorance means being free *to* gain an education.

amongst the domestic population. This is possible because a constitution both symbolises and disseminates the values of the ruling elite, and invests the governmental system with a cloak of legality. To make the constitution more effective in this respect, attempts are often made to promote veneration for the constitution itself, either as a document of historical importance or as a symbol of national purpose and identity.

Do constitutions matter?

The value of a constitution is often taken for granted. The existence of a constitution, so the assumption goes, provides benefits such as political stability, limited government and guaranteed rights and liberties. Nowhere is this faith in a constitution more developed than in the USA, where it amounts, in Louis Hartz's (1955) words, to 'the cult of constitution worship'. Of course this faith has been severely tested, not least by allegations during the Watergate crisis that President Richard Nixon had helped to cover up illegal acts by senior White House officials during the 1972 election campaign. Nevertheless, Nixon's resignation in 1974 enabled his successor, Gerald Ford, to declare that 'our constitution works', reiterating the classic sentiment of constitutionalism: 'we have a government of laws, not of men'. However, the mere existence of a constitution does not ensure that a government is constitutional. Indeed, there is little evidence that a constitution is a major guarantee against tyranny, still less that it offers a 'ticket to Utopia'.

Constitutions 'work' in certain circumstances. In other words, they only serve their various purposes when they are supported by a range of other cultural, political, economic and social conditions. In particular, constitutions must correspond to and be supported by the political culture; successful constitutions are as much a product of the political culture as they are its creator. This is why so many of the model liberal-democratic constitutions bequeathed to developing states by departing colonial rulers failed to take root. Constitutional rules guaranteeing individual rights and political competition may be entirely irrelevant in societies with deeply entrenched collectivist values and traditions, especially when such societies are struggling to achieve basic economic and social development.

In the same way, the various Soviet constitutions not only enshrined 'socialist' values that were foreign to the mass of the people, but also failed to develop popular support for such values during the 74 years of the USSR's existence. In the USA, as a result of widespread and institutionalised racism, the constitutional guarantees of civil and voting rights for American black people enacted after the Civil War were often not upheld in Southern states until the 1960s. On the other hand, the 1947 Japanese constitution, despite the fact that it was imposed by the occupying USA and emphasised individual rights in place of the more traditional Japanese stress on duty, has proved to be remarkably successful, providing a stable framework for postwar reconstruction and political development. As in postwar Germany, however, the Japanese constitution has had the advantage of being sustained by a 'economic miracle'.

A second key factor is whether or not a constitution is respected by rulers and accords with the interests and values of dominant groups. Germany's Weimar constitution, for example, despite the fact that it enshrined an impressive array of rights and liberties, was easily set aside in the 1930s as Hitler constructed his Nazi dictatorship. Not only did the competitive democracy of the Weimar regime conflict with the ambitions of the Nazis and conservative elites in business and the military, but it was also poorly supported by a population facing economic crisis and little accustomed to representative government. In India under Indira Gandhi during 1975–77, and in Pakistan under General Zia ul-Haq during 1977–81, major provisions of the constitutions were abrogated by the declaration of 'states of emergency'. In these cases, the support of the military leadership proved to be far more crucial than respect for constitutional niceties. The UK's uncodified constitution is often said to provide unusual scope for abuse because it relies so heavily on the self-restraint of the government of the day. This became particularly apparent as the Conservative governments of the 1980s and 1990s exploited the flexibility inherent in parliamentary sovereignty to alter the constitutional roles of institutions such as the civil service, local government and the trade unions, and, some have argued, substantially undermined civil liberties (Graham and Prosser, 1988).

The final factor is the adaptability of a constitution and its ability to *remain* relevant despite changing political circumstances. No constitution reflects political realities, and few set out specifically to do so. Generally, successful constitutions are sufficiently flexible to accommodate change within a broad and enduringly relevant framework; those that are infinitely flexible are, strictly speaking, not constitutions at all. The US constitution is particularly interesting in this respect. Its 'genius' has been its concentration on broad principles and the scope it therefore provides to rectify its own deficiencies. US government has thus been able to evolve in response to new challenges and new demands. The formal amendment process, for example, allowed US institutions to be democratised, and in the twentieth century judicial interpretation made possible the growth of presidential powers, a shift of authority from state to federal government, and, in certain respects, a widening of individual rights.

Such changes, however, can be said to have occurred *within* the constitution, in that core principles such as the separation of powers, federalism and individual liberty have continued to be respected, albeit in renewed form. In contrast, the constitution of the Fourth French Republic proved to be unworkable, because the emphasis it placed upon the National Assembly tended to produce a succession of weak and unstable governments. As the constitution offered no solution to this impasse, the result was a new constitution in 1958, inaugurating the Fifth Republic, which broadened presidential power according to a blueprint devised by General de Gaulle.

The law

Law, morality and politics

The relationship between **law** and morality is one of the thorniest problems in political theory. On the surface, law and morality are very different things. Law is a distinctive form of social control, backed up by the means of enforcement; it defines what *can* and what *cannot* be done. Morality, on the other hand, is concerned with ethical questions and the difference between 'right' and 'wrong'; it prescribes what *should* and what *should not* be done. Moreover, while law has an objective character, in that it is a social fact, morality is usually treated as a subjective entity, that is, as a matter of opinion or personal judgement. Nevertheless, natural law theories

> **Concept**
>
> **Parliamentary sovereignty**
>
> Parliamentary sovereignty refers to the absolute and unlimited authority of a parliament or legislature, reflected in its ability to make, amend or repeal any law it wishes. Parliamentary sovereignty is usually seen as the central principle of the British constitution, and results from the absence of a codified constitution, the supremacy of statute law over other forms of law, the absence of rival legislatures, and the convention that no parliament can bind its successors. Supporters commended the principle for investing constitutional supremacy in a representative institution rather than an artificial body of rules or a nonelected body of judges. Critics point out that the principle is implicitly authoritarian, leading to 'elective dictatorship' when the parliament is executive-dominated.

> **Law:** A set of public and enforceable rules that apply throughout a political community; law is usually recognised as binding.

Human rights

Human rights are rights to which people are entitled by virtue of being human; they are a modern and secular version of natural rights. Human rights are 'universal' in the sense that they belong to all humans rather than to members of any particular state, race, religion, gender or other group. They are also 'fundamental', in that they are inalienable; unlike civil rights, they do not depend on the freedoms and status accorded citizens in particular societies. Supporters of the doctrine of human rights portray them as universally applicable moral principles that stand above the traditional ideological divide. Opponents, on the other hand, argue that it is nonsense to suggest that individuals have rights that are separate from the traditions, cultures and societies to which they belong.

that date back to Plato (see p. 13) and Aristotle (see p. 7) suggest that law is, or should be, rooted in a moral system of some kind. In the early modern period, such theories were often based on the idea of God-given 'natural rights'. This assertion of a link between law and morality became fashionable again as the twentieth century progressed, and it was usually associated with the ideas of civil liberties or human rights.

However, the rise in the nineteenth century of the 'science of positive law' offered a very different view of the relationship between law and morality. Its purpose was quite simply to free the understanding of law from moral, religious and mystical assumptions. John Austin (1890–1859) developed the theory of 'legal positivism', which defined law not in terms of its conformity to higher moral or religious principles, but in terms of the fact that it was established and enforced: the law is the law because it is obeyed. This approach was refined by H. L. A. Hart in *The Concept of Law* (1961). Hart suggested that law stemmed from the union of 'primary' and 'secondary' rules, each of which had a particular function. Primary rules regulate social behaviour and can be thought of as the 'content' of the legal system; criminal law is an example. Secondary rules, on the other hand, are rules that confer powers upon the institutions of government. They lay down how primary rules are made, enforced and adjudicated, thus determining their validity.

In view of the crucial role that law plays in regulating social behaviour, no one can doubt that it has immense political significance. Nevertheless, questions about the actual and desirable relationship between law and politics – reflecting on the nature of law, and its function and proper extent – have provoked deep controversy. Much of our understanding of law derives from liberal theory. This portrays law as the essential guarantee of civilised and orderly existence, drawing heavily on social-contract theory (see p. 87). In the absence of the state and a system of law, that is, in the 'state of nature', each individual is at liberty to abuse or threaten every other individual. The role of law, then, is to protect each member of society from his or her fellow members, thereby preventing their rights and liberties being encroached upon.

Rule of law

The rule of law is the principle that the law should 'rule' in the sense that it establishes a framework to which all conduct and behaviour conform, applying equally to all the members of society, be they private citizens or government officials. The rule of law is thus a core liberal-democratic principle, embodying ideas like constitutionalism and limited government. In continental Europe, it has often been enshrined in the German concept of the *Rechtsstaat*, a state based on law. In the USA, the rule of law is closely linked to the status of the constitution as 'higher' law and to the doctrine of 'due process'. In the UK, it is seen to be rooted in common law and to provide an alternative to a codified constitution (Dicey, [1885] 1939).

As this protection extends throughout society and to every one of its members, law has, liberals insist, a neutral character. Law is therefore 'above' politics, and a strict separation between law and politics must be maintained to prevent the law favouring the state over the individual, the rich over the poor, men over women, whites over blacks, and so on. This is why liberals place such a heavy emphasis on the universal authority of law, embodied in the principle of the rule of law. This view of law also has significant implications for the judiciary, whose task it is to interpret law and adjudicate between parties to a dispute. Notably, judges

Thomas Hobbes (1588–1679)

English political philosopher. Hobbes was the son of a minor clergyman who subsequently abandoned his family. He became tutor to the exiled Prince of Wales Charles Stewart, and lived under the patronage of the Cavendish family. Writing at a time of uncertainty and civil strife, precipitated by the English Revolution, Hobbes developed the first comprehensive theory of nature and human behaviour since Aristotle. His classic work, *Leviathan*

(1651), discussed the grounds of political obligation and undoubtedly reflected the impact of the Civil War. It provided a defence for absolutist government but, by appealing to reasoned argument in the form of the social contract, also disappointed advocates of **divine right**.

must be independent, in the sense that they are 'above' or 'outside' the machinery of government and not subject to political influence.

However, if the central purpose of law is to protect liberty, this also implies that the proper sphere of law should be limited. In other words, law should only be endorsed as long as it enlarges, rather than contracts, freedom. One of the clearest liberal statements of this principle was made by John Stuart Mill (see p. 44), who, in *On Liberty* ([1859] 1982:73), asserted that, 'Over himself, over his own body and mind the individual is sovereign'. Mill was only prepared to accept the legitimacy of law when it was designed 'to prevent harm to others'. This is understood by moral philosophers as the 'harm principle'. By this standard, paternalistic laws aimed at preventing self-harm, like those prohibiting addictive drugs or enforcing the use of seat belts in cars, or ones that supposedly promote moral behaviour, such as laws against suicide or prostitution, are entirely unfounded.

An alternative view of law has been developed by conservative theorists. This draws more heavily on the idea that law is linked to order, even to the extent that 'law and order' become a single, fused concept. This position draws from two sources. The first is a deeply pessimistic, even Hobbesian, view of human nature. In *Leviathan* ([1651] 1968:49), Thomas Hobbes described the principle human inclination as 'a perpetual and restless desire for power after power, that ceaseth only in death'. In this light, the roots of social disorder can be seen to reside in the individual human being, a view sometimes linked to the Christian doctrine of 'original sin'. Order can therefore only be maintained by strict laws, firm enforcement and harsh penalties. For Hobbes, law was the only means of preventing a descent into chaos and barbarity.

The second source of this conservative view of the importance of law is the belief that social stability depends on the existence of shared values and a common culture. A classic statement of this position was advanced in Patrick Devlin's *The Enforcement of Morals* (1968), which argued that society has the right to enforce 'public morality' through the instrument of law. This position goes clearly beyond Mill's **libertarianism** in implying, for example, that society has the right to protect itself against what have been seen as 'nonconsensus' practices, such as homosexuality and drug taking. In the 1980s and 1990s, the New Right took up a very similar position in extolling the virtues of 'traditional morality' and 'family values', believing also that these should be upheld through the authority of law.

Divine right: The doctrine that earthly rulers are chosen by God and thus wield unchallengeable authority; a defence for monarchical absolutism.

Libertarianism: The belief that the realm of individual liberty should be maximised, usually associated with attempts to minimise the scope of public authority.

■ The judiciary

The judiciary is the branch of government that is empowered to decide legal disputes. The central function of judges is therefore to adjudicate on the meaning of law, in the sense that they interpret or 'construct' law. The significance of this role varies from state to state and from system to system. However, it is particularly important in states with codified constitutions, where it extends to the interpretation of the constitution itself, and so allows judges to arbitrate in disputes between major institutions of government or in ones between the state and the individual. In the case of supranational bodies such as the World Court or the European Court of Justice, judges interpret international treaties and agreements and thus lay down international law (see p. 160).

One of the chief characteristics of the judiciary – in liberal-democratic systems, its defining characteristic – is that judges are strictly independent and nonpolitical actors. Indeed, the ability of judges to be 'above' politics is normally seen as the vital guarantee of a separation between law and politics. However, this image of the judiciary is always misleading. The judiciary is best thought of as a political, not merely a legal, institution. As central figures in the legal process, judges play a vital role in such undeniably political activities as conflict resolution and the maintenance of state authority. Although judges are clearly political in the sense that their judgements have an undeniable political impact, debate about the political significance of the judiciary revolves around two more controversial questions. First, are judges political in that their actions are shaped by political considerations or pressures? Secondly, do judges make policy in the sense that they encroach upon the proper responsibilities of politicians.

Are judges political?

Certain political systems make no pretence of judicial neutrality or impartiality. For example, in orthodox communist regimes, the principle of 'socialist legality' dictated that judges interpret law in accordance with Marxism–Leninism, subject to the ideological authority of the state's communist party. Judges thus became mere functionaries who carried out the political and ideological objectives of the regime itself. This was most graphically demonstrated by the 'show trials' of the 1930s in the USSR. The German courts during the Nazi period were similarly used as instruments of ideological repression and political persecution. In other states, however, judges have been expected to observe strict political neutrality. In states that subscribe to any form of liberal constitutionalism, the authority of law is linked to its nonpolitical character, which, in turn, is based on the assumption that the law is interpreted by independent and impartial judges.

Judges may be political in two senses: they may be subject to external bias or internal bias. External bias is derived from the influence that political bodies, such as parties, the assembly and government, are able to exert on the judiciary. Internal bias stems from the prejudices and sympathies of judges themselves, particularly from those that intrude into the process of judicial decision-making. External bias is supposedly kept at bay by respect for the principle of **judicial independence**. In most liberal democracies, the independence of the judiciary is protected by their security of tenure (the fact that they cannot be sacked), and through restrictions on the

Judicial independence: The constitutional principle that there should be a strict separation between the judiciary and other branches of government; an application of the separation of powers.

criticism of judges and court decisions. However, in practice, the independence of judges may be compromised because of the close involvement of political bodies in the process of judicial recruitment and promotion.

Judges in the USA supposedly hold office for life on condition of 'good behaviour'. Supreme Court judges, however, are appointed by the US president, and these appointments are subject to confirmation by the Senate. This process has, since F. D. Roosevelt's battles with the court in the 1930s, led to a pattern of overt political appointment. Presidents select justices on the basis of party affiliation and ideological disposition, and, as occurred to Robert Bork in the 1980s, the Senate may reject them on the same grounds. The liberal tendencies of the Warren Court (1954–69), and the more conservative inclinations of the Burger Court (1969–86) and subsequently the Rehnquist Court, were thus largely brought about through external political pressure. UK judges are also appointed by the government of the day, senior judges being appointed by the prime minister on the advice of the Lord Chancellor. Despite conventions stipulating that such appointments should be impartial, political considerations often intrude, as in the 1980 appointment to Master of the Rolls of Lord Donaldson, a former Conservative councillor and a known supporter of legal restrictions on trade union activity.

The Conseil Constitutionnel (Constitutional Court) in France, which is empowered to examine the constitutionality of laws and can thus restrain both the assembly and the executive, is subject to particularly marked political influence. Its members have, in the main, been politicians with long experience rather than professional judges. The French president and the presidents of the National Assembly and the Senate each select one-third of the members of the court, party affiliation often being a significant factor. In Japan, the Supreme Court is effectively appointed by the cabinet, with the high judges being selected by the emperor on the nomination of the cabinet. Prolonged Liberal-Democratic Party domination in the post-Second-World-War period meant, however, that the LDP packed the court with its own supporters, ensuring that it remained firmly subordinate to the Diet. One of the consequences of this was that, despite widespread **gerrymandering** in favour of the LDP in rural districts, the Supreme Court was never prepared to nullify election results, even when, as in 1983, elections were declared to be unconstitutional because of the disproportionate allocation of seats (Eccleston, 1989).

Judicial independence is not the only issue; bias may creep in through the values and culture of the judiciary as easily as through external pressure. From this perspective, the key factor is not so much *how* judges are recruited, but *who* is recruited. A long-standing socialist critique of the judiciary holds that it articulates the dominant values of society, and so acts to defend the existing political and social order. This tendency is underpinned by the social exclusivity of judges and by the peculiar status and respect that the judicial profession is normally accorded. Griffith (1991) argued that this conservative bias is particularly prominent in the British higher judiciary, and that it stems from the remarkable homogeneity of senior judges, who are overwhelmingly male, white, upper-middle-class, and public-school and 'Oxbridge' educated. Similar arguments have been used to suggest that judges are biased against women, racial minorities, and, indeed, any group poorly represented within its ranks.

Although the US Supreme Court has included a nominal black judge since the 1950s and now contains two female judges, its membership has generally been dominated by white Anglo-Saxon Protestants drawn from the USA's middle and

Concept

Neutrality

Neutrality is the absence of any form of partisanship or commitment; it consists of a refusal to 'take sides'. In international relations, neutrality is a legal condition through which a state declares its noninvolvement in a conflict or war, and indicates its intention to refrain from supporting or aiding either side. As a principle of individual conduct, applied to the likes of judges, civil servants, the military and other public officials, it implies, strictly speaking, the absence of political sympathies and ideological leanings. Neutral actors are thus political eunuchs. In practice, the less exacting requirement of impartiality is usually applied. This allows that political sympathies may be held as long as these do not intrude into, or conflict with, professional or public responsibilities.

Gerrymandering: The manipulation of electoral boundaries so as to achieve political advantage for a party or candidate.

Concept

Judicial review

The power of judicial review is the power of the judiciary to 'review' and possibly invalidate laws, decrees and the actions of other branches of government, notably the legislature and the executive. In its classical sense, the principle of judicial review stems from the existence of a codified constitution and allows the courts to strike down as 'unconstitutional' actions that are deemed to be incompatible with the constitution. A more modest form of judicial review, found in uncodified systems, is restricted to the review of executive actions in the light of ordinary law using the principle of *ultra vires* (beyond the powers) to determine whether the executive has acted outside its powers. Seen by many as a cornerstone institution of liberal constitutionalism, as it ensures a 'government of laws', judicial review also goes beyond the separation of powers in establishing, for better or worse, the supremacy of the judiciary.

upper middle classes. On the other hand, in states such as Australia attempts have been made to counter such tendencies by making the judiciary more socially representative. For instance, since the 1980s, Australian judges have been recruited from the ranks of academics as well as lawyers. Nevertheless, even critics of the judiciary recognise that there is a limit to the extent to which judges can be made socially representative. To achieve a judiciary that is a microcosm of the larger society, it would be necessary for criteria such as experience and professional competence to be entirely ignored in the appointment of judges.

Do judges make policy?

The images of judges as simple appliers of law has always been a myth. Judges cannot apply the so-called 'letter of the law', because no law, legal term or principle has a single, self-evident meaning. In practice, judges *impose* meaning on law through a process of 'construction' that forces them to choose amongst a number of possible meanings or interpretations. In this sense, *all* law is judge-made law. Clearly, however, the range of discretion available to judges in this respect, and the significance of the laws that they invest with meaning, vary considerably. Two factors are crucial here. The first is the clarity and detail with which law is specified. Generally, broadly framed laws or constitutional principles allow greater scope for judicial interpretation. The second factor is the existence of a codified or 'written' constitution. The existence of such a document significantly enhances the status of the judiciary, investing it with the power of judicial review.

Although sometimes seen to have arisen from English law as early as *Dr. Bonham's Case* in 1610, judicial review is best understood as a US development that resulted from the establishment of the world's first written constitution. The US constitution makes no mention of judicial review, but, arguably, embodies the logic that made its emergence inevitable. As the constitution laid down legal standards for the behaviour of government institutions, these clearly needed to be supervised or policed, and the judiciary (more specifically, the Supreme Court) was the only institution equipped for this purpose. The power of judicial review was first exercised in Chief Justice John Marshall's decision in *Marbury* v. *Madison* (1803). In this, the Supreme Court declared that the Judiciary Act of 1789 was incompatible with the 'superior paramount law' of the US constitution. This made the Supreme Court, as Robert Dahl (1956) put it, 'a political institution, an institution, that is to say, for arriving at decisions on controversial questions of national policy'.

The Supreme Court's significance as a policy maker has been evident throughout US history. In the late nineteenth century and early twentieth century, for example, Supreme Courts wedded to *laissez-faire* principles used the doctrine of 'due process' to strike down welfare and social legislation; in particular, the court blocked much of Roosevelt's New Deal programme in the early 1930s. It was only after the so-called 'court revolution' of 1937, following the appointment of pro-New-Deal judges such as Hugo Black and William O'Douglas, that the shift to economic and social intervention gained judicial endorsement. During the 1950s and 1960s the court, under Chief Justice Earl Warren, made landmark liberal decisions such as *Brown* v. *Board of Education* (1954), which rejected segregation in schools as unconstitutional, and *Baker* v. *Carr* (1962), which required that legislative constituencies in the USA be of uniform size.

In many cases, the Supreme Court was ahead of Congress and the presidency, often paving the way for later legislation, as in the case of the civil rights reforms of the mid 1960s. Similarly, the Supreme Court upheld the constitutionality of abortion in *Roe* v. *Wade* (1973), at a time when elective institutions refused to address such a deeply controversial issue. Although the **judicial activism** of this period has since subsided, reflecting conservative appointments of Republican presidents like Nixon, Reagan and Bush, the court has continued to exert influence, for instance, in allowing the gradual reintroduction of capital punishment and growing restrictions on the right to abortion.

However, it would be a mistake to imply that US-style constitutional judicial review guarantees the supremacy of the judiciary. In the first place, judicial review is only effective as long as judges remain scrupulously independent from other institutions of government. As pointed out above, this is seldom the case in practice. Moreover, although judges can interpret laws and even the constitution, they do not decide or influence their wording. Court rulings can thus be superseded by constitutional amendments, as when the Sixteenth Amendment of the US constitution reversed an earlier Supreme Court ruling declaring federal income tax to be unconstitutional. Perhaps the greatest weakness of judges and courts, however, is their lack of the means of enforcement and thus their reliance on other branches of government. This was demonstrated in 1958 when President Eisenhower had to despatch federal troops to Little Rock, Arkansas, to force its schools to comply with the court's 1954 desegregation ruling, which had until that point been disregarded.

If judges are policy makers, they must therefore operate as part of the broader machinery of government and within constraints established by the political culture and public opinion. The difficulties the judiciary may encounter in fulfilling its role as guardian of the constitution were demonstrated by the battle between Indira Gandhi and the Indian courts in the 1970s. Despite its written constitution, the balance between US-style judicial review and Westminster-style parliamentary sovereignty in India has never been fully resolved. Amid mounting criticism of Prime Minister Gandhi's autocratic leadership style, the Indian High Court in June 1975 declared her guilty of electoral malpractice and disqualified her from political office for five years. Although the Indian Supreme Court suspended the disqualification pending an appeal, within days Gandhi declared a 'state of emergency', allowing for the arrest of hundreds of her political opponents and for the introduction of stiff censorship. Even though the judiciary was able to restore its authority after the lifting of the emergency in March 1977, it has subsequently practised greater self-restraint and been reluctant to challenge the government of the day so openly again.

The view that judges are policy makers is less persuasive in the absence of a codified constitution. Where the constitution is unwritten, judges lack a legal standard against which to measure the constitutionality of political acts and government decisions. The UK Parliament is therefore sovereign, and the judiciary is firmly subordinate to it. Before the Glorious Revolution of 1688 in the UK, judges were prepared to set aside acts of Parliament when they violated common law principles, as occurred in *Dr. Bonham's Case* (1610). The revolution, however, established the supremacy of statute law (law made by Parliament), a principle that has never subsequently been challenged by the courts.

The power of judicial review can nevertheless be applied in a narrower sense in the case of executive powers that are derived from enabling legislation. In such cases, the principle of *ultra vires* can be used to declare actions of ministers, for instance, unlawful. Indeed, the 1980s and 1990s witnessed a marked upsurge in judicial activism in

Judicial activism: The willingness of judges to arbitrate in political disputes, as opposed to merely saying what the law means.

the UK, highlighting the growing political significance of judges. In 1984, for example, the House of Lords upheld a judgement of the Court of Appeal that declared the Greater London Council's system of subsidies to London Transport (the 'fares fair' scheme) to be illegal. Similarly, in 1995, the then UK Foreign Secretary, Douglas Hurd, was censored for the illegal use of the overseas-aid budget in relation to the construction of the Pergau Dam in Malaysia. Between 1992 and 1996, the UK Home Secretary Michael Howard was defeated by the courts on no fewer than ten occasions. This growing activism reflects both the spread of a 'human rights culture' within the UK judiciary and growing anxiety about the misuse of executive power that flows from the absence of effective constitutional checks and balances in the UK.

■ Summary

◆ A constitution is a set of rules that seek to establish the duties, powers and functions of the institutions of government and define the relationship between the state and the individual. Constitutions can be classified on the basis of the status of their rules, how easily their rules can be changed, the degree to which their rules are observed in practice, and the content of their rules and the institutional structure that they establish.

◆ Constitutions do not serve a single or simple purpose. Amongst their functions are that they empower states by defining a sphere of independent authority, establish a set of values, ideals and goals for a society, bring stability, order and predictability to the workings of government, protect individuals from the state, and legitimise regimes in the eyes of other states and their people.

◆ There is an imperfect relationship between the content of a constitution and political practice. Constitutions 'work' in certain conditions, notably when they correspond to, and are supported by, the political culture, when they are respected by rulers and accord with the interests and values of dominant groups, and when they are adaptable and can remain relevant in changing political circumstances.

◆ Questions about the actual and desirable relationship between law and politics are deeply controversial. Liberal theory, sensitive to civil liberties and human rights, tends to emphasise the limited province of law operating simply as a means of guaranteeing orderly existence. The conservative view, however, emphasises the link between law and social stability, acknowledging that law has an important role to play in enforcing public morality.

◆ The separation of law from politics is accomplished through attempts to make the judiciary independent and impartial. Judicial independence, however, is threatened by the close involvement of political bodies in the process of judicial recruitment and promotion. Judicial impartiality is compromised by the fact that nowhere are judges representatives of the larger society. In western polyarchies, for instance, they are overwhelmingly male, white, materially privileged and relatively old.

◆ As judges impose meaning on law, they cannot but be involved in the policy process. The extent of their influence varies according to the clarity and detail with which the law is specified and the scope available for judicial interpretation, and according to the existence or otherwise of a codified or written constitution, which invests in judges the power of judicial review.

■ Questions for discussion

▶ How useful is a constitution as a guide to political practice?

▶ What factors determine the level of respect that rulers show for their constitution?

▶ On what grounds (if any) is it justifiable to break the law?

▶ Is it desirable that law be separate from politics, and if so, why?

▶ How scrupulously is judicial independence maintained in practice?

▶ Does it matter that the social composition of the judiciary does not reflect that of society at large?

■ Further reading

Bogdanor, V. (ed.) *Constitutions in Democratic Politics* (Aldershot: Gower, 1988). A good collection of essays that considers the nature of constitutionalism and the issue of constitutional reform.

Griffiths, J. A. G. *The Politics of the Judiciary* (4th ed.) (London: Fontana, 1991). A critical analysis of the political role of judges from a UK standpoint.

Lane, J.-E. *Constitutions and Political Theory* (Manchester: Manchester University Press, 1996). A thorough and coherent discussion of key debates related to constitutions and constitutionalism.

Waltman, J. and K. Holland, (eds) *The Political Role of Law Courts in Modern Democracies* (New York: St Martin's Press, 1988). An interesting book that examines the broader impact of the courts and judiciary from a comparative perspective.

Assemblies

CHAPTER 15

'A Parliament is nothing less than a big meeting of more or less idle people.'

WALTER BAGEHOT *The English Constitution* (1867)

Assemblies (sometimes called parliaments or legislatures) occupy a key position in the machinery of government. Traditionally, they have been treated with special respect and status as the public, even democratic, face of government. In written constitutions, for instance, they are usually accorded pride of place, being described before executives and judiciaries. Assemblies are respected because they are composed of lay politicians who claim to represent the people rather than by trained or expert government officials. Moreover, they act as national debating chambers, public forums in which government policies and the major issues of the day can be openly discussed and analysed. In most cases, they are also invested with formal law-making power, giving them some capacity to shape or at least influence public policy. Nevertheless, it is widely alleged that the twentieth century has witnessed a progressive weakening of parliamentary power in the form of a decline of assemblies. Although some may still play an important role in the policy process, many assemblies have been reduced to mere 'talking shops' that do little more than rubber stamp decisions that have effectively been made elsewhere.

The principal issues discussed in this chapter are the following:

Contents

Key issues

▶ What is an assembly?

▶ How do parliamentary systems of government differ from presidential ones?

▶ What are the main functions of assemblies?

▶ How are assemblies organised, and how do their internal structures differ?

▶ What are the principal determinants of parliamentary power?

▶ Why have assemblies declined? Does this decline matter?

Charles-Louis de Secondat Montesquieu (1689–1775)

French political philosopher. Montesquieu came from an aristocratic family and became an advocate before establishing his literary reputation with the publication of *Persian Letters* (1721). After settling in Paris in 1726, he travelled throughout Europe studying political and social institutions. Montesquieu's masterpiece, *The Spirit of the Laws* ([1748] 1949), is a long and rambling comparative examination of political and legal issues. He championed a form of parliamentary liberalism that was based on the writings of Locke (see p. 43) and, to some extent, a misreading of English political experience. Montesquieu emphasised the need to resist tyranny by fragmenting government power, particularly through the device of the separation of powers.

■ Role of assemblies

In practice, a bewildering variety of terms are used to describe political bodies with very similar functions: congress (USA), national assembly (France), house of representatives (Japan), parliament (Singapore), congress of deputies (Spain), and so on. Students of comparative politics usually classify such bodies as assemblies, legislatures or parliaments. An assembly, in its simplest sense, is a collection or gathering of people, as in, for example, a school assembly. As a political term, assembly has come to be associated with representation and popular government, an assembly, certainly in the French tradition, being viewed as a surrogate for the people. For this reason, the term is sometimes reserved for the lower, popularly elected chamber in a bicameral system (as in, for instance, Pakistan and France), or for the single chamber in a unicameral system (as in Egypt and Turkey). In this book, however, the term assembly is used to refer to both houses or chambers, and is used interchangeably with the terms legislature and parliament.

To see these bodies as legislatures is to classify them according to their primary function as law-making bodies. From this point of view, three distinct branches of government can be identified:

- Legislatures *make* law; they enact legislation.
- Executives *implement* law; they execute the law.
- Judiciaries *interpret* law; they adjudicate on the meaning of the law.

This division of government into legislative, executive and judicial institutions has been sustained by the doctrine of the separation of powers (see p. 297), and has been the traditional basis on which to analyse government since the time of Montesquieu. This view is seriously misleading, however. Institutions that are formally classified as legislatures rarely monopolise law-making power. For instance, executives (see p. 316) possess some ability to make law, through devices such as decrees or orders, and usually also have the capacity to influence, if not shape, the formal legislative process. Furthermore, the enactment of law is only one of the functions of legislatures, and not necessarily their most important one.

The term parliament (from the French *parler*, meaning 'to speak') is sometimes preferred because it avoids the limitations of the term assembly and the confusion of the term legislature. It nevertheless suggests that these bodies have a very particular character. It implies that their defining feature is that they are consultative or deliberative bodies. Regardless of their legislative powers and representative features, parliaments are above all debating chambers, that is, forums in which policies and political issues can be openly discussed and scrutinised.

Parliamentary systems and presidential systems

One of the key features of any political system is the relationship between the assembly and the government, that is, the relationship between legislative and executive authority. In exceptional cases, a form of 'assembly government' may develop in which executive and legislative power is vested in the assembly, there being no separate executive body. Such a system, for example, briefly emerged under Robespierre and the Jacobins during the French Revolution, influenced by the radical democracy of Rousseau (see p. 73). In other cases, notably in orthodox communist regimes, both the legislative and the executive bodies have been subordinate to the unchallengeable authority of a 'ruling' party. However, assembly–executive relations more commonly conform to one of two institutional arrangements: parliamentary and presidential systems of government.

Most liberal democracies have adopted some form of parliamentary government. These are often Westminster-style systems, in that they are based on the model of the UK Parliament. Often portrayed as the 'mother of parliaments', the origins of the Westminster Parliament can be traced back to the thirteenth century, when knights and burgesses were incorporated into the king's court. During the fourteenth century, separate chambers (the House of Commons and the House of Lords) were created to represent the knights and burgesses on the one hand, and the barons and churchmen on the other. Parliament's supremacy over the king was nevertheless not established until the Glorious Revolution of 1688, and its capacity to call government to account not recognised until the gradual emergence of a democratic franchise during the nineteenth century.

Similar parliamentary systems came into existence in states like Germany, Sweden, India, Japan, New Zealand and Australia. The central feature of these systems is a fusion of legislative and executive power: government is parliamentary in that it is drawn from and accountable to the assembly or parliament. The strength of this system is that it supposedly delivers effective but **responsible government**. Government is effective in that it rests on the confidence of the assembly and so can, in most cases, ensure that its legislative programme is passed. In short, governments can get things done. However, responsible government is maintained because the government can only govern as long as it retains the confidence of the assembly. In

Concept

Parliamentary government

A parliamentary system of government is one in which the government governs in and through the assembly or parliament, thereby 'fusing' the legislative and executive branches. Although they are formally distinct, the assembly and the executive (usually seen as the government) are bound together in a way that violates the doctrine of the separation of powers, setting parliamentary systems clearly apart from presidential ones (see p. 320).

The chief features of a parliamentary system are as follows:

- Governments are formed as a result of assembly elections, based on the strength of party representation; there is no separately elected executive.
- The personnel of government are drawn from the assembly, usually from the leaders of the party or parties that have majority control.
- The government is responsible to the assembly in the sense that it rests on the assembly's confidence and can be removed (generally by the lower chamber) if it loses that confidence.
- The government can, in most cases, 'dissolve' the assembly, meaning that electoral terms are usually flexible within a maximum limit.
- As the head of government (usually a prime minister) is a parliamentary officer, there is a separate head of state: a constitutional monarch or a non-executive president.

Responsible government: A government that is answerable or accountable to an elected assembly and, through it, to the people.

theory, the assembly has the upper hand because it has the ultimate power: the ability to remove the government.

Unfortunately, however, parliamentary systems often fail to live up to these high expectations. Certainly, there are examples such as Sweden in which, supported by strong norms of consultation and partnership, the assembly (the Riksdag) exerts a strong policy influence without threatening to immobilise the workings of government. However, parliamentary government is often associated with the problem of executive domination. This is the case in the UK, where a combination of strict party discipline and a disproportional electoral system (the simple plurality system) normally allows government to control Parliament through a cohesive and reliable majority in the House of Commons. This encouraged Lord Hailsham (1976) to dub UK government an 'elective dictatorship'. Ironically, therefore, parliamentary systems may allow parliaments to become little more than 'talking shops', and may reduce their members to mere 'lobby fodder'.

Parliamentary systems have also been linked with weak government and political instability. This usually occurs when the party system is fractured, and it is often associated with highly proportional electoral systems. In the French Fourth Republic during 1945–58, for instance, 25 governments came and went in little over 12 years. During this period, no French government could command a stable majority in the National Assembly, in which both the Communists on the left and the Gaullists on the right were implacably opposed to the regime itself. Similar problems have afflicted post-Second-World-War Italian politics. A polarised multiparty system led to the establishment of no fewer than 52 governments between 1945 and 1996. Such apparent **immobilism** may, however, be misleading. In Italy, for example, changes in government typically involve a reshuffling of ministerial personnel, not a political upheaval, and only occasionally result in general elections.

The principal alternative to a parliamentary system is a presidential system of government. Presidential systems are based on the strict application of the doctrine of the separation of powers. This ensures that the assemblies and executives are formally independent from one another and separately elected. The classic example of this is found in the USA, where the so-called 'founding fathers' were particularly anxious to prevent the emergence of an over-strong executive, fearing that the presidency might assume the mantle of the British monarchy. The resulting system therefore incorporated a network of **checks and balances**. Congress, the US presidency and the Supreme Court are separate institutions, in the sense that no overlap of personnel is permitted, but nevertheless possess the ability to constrain one another's power. Thus, while Congress has the ability to make law, the president can veto it, but Congress can, in turn, override this veto with a two-thirds majority in both houses. In the same way, although the president has the power to make senior executive and judicial appointments, these are subject to confirmation by the upper house, the Senate.

Outside the USA, US-style presidential systems have largely been confined to Latin America. However, a 'hybrid' or semi-presidential system was established in France during the Fifth Republic. In this system, there is a 'dual executive' in which a separately elected president works in conjunction with a prime minister and cabinet drawn from and responsible to the National Assembly. How such a system works in practice depends on a delicate balance between, on the one hand, the personal authority and popularity of the president and, on the other, the political complexion of the National Assembly. A similar semi-presidential system operates in Finland in

Immobilism: Political paralysis stemming from the absence of a strong executive, caused by multiple divisions in the assembly and (probably) society.

Checks and balances: Internal tensions within the governmental system that result from institutional fragmentation.

which the president is largely concerned with foreign affairs and leaves the burden of domestic responsibilities in the hands of the cabinet.

The principal virtue of presidential systems is that, by separating legislative power from executive power, they create internal tensions that help to protect individual rights and liberties. As Hobbes (see p. 285) put it, 'liberty is power cut into pieces'. In the USA, for instance, the danger of executive domination is protected against by the range of powers vested in the Congress. For instance, Congress has the right to declare war and raise taxes, the Senate must ratify treaties and confirm presidential appointments, and the two houses can combine to charge and impeach the president. Such fragmentation, however, may also have drawbacks.

In particular, presidential systems may be ineffective and cumbersome because they offer an 'invitation to struggle' to the executive and legislative branches of government. Critics of the US system, for example, argue that, since it allows the president to propose and Congress to dispose, it is nothing more than a recipe for institutional deadlock, or 'government gridlock'. This may be more likely when the White House (the presidency) and Capitol Hill (Congress) are controlled by rival parties, but can also occur, as the Carter administration of 1977–81 demonstrated, when both branches are controlled by the same party. A similar problem occurs in France in the form of **cohabitation** when the president is forced to work with a hostile prime minister and National Assembly, as occurred twice under Mitterrand, in 1986–88 and 1993–95.

Functions of assemblies

To simply classify assemblies as legislatures, debating chambers or representative bodies obscures their true significance. Although the role of the assembly varies from state to state and from system to system, in every case it fulfils a complex of functions. Above all, assemblies provide a link between government and the people, a channel of communication that can both support government and help to uphold the regime, and force government to respond to public demands and anxieties. The principal functions of assemblies are:

- legislation
- representation
- scrutiny
- political recruitment
- legitimacy.

Legislation

Legislation is often seen as the key function of assemblies, as is clearly implied by their common classification as legislatures. Assemblies or parliaments are typically vested with legislative power in the hope that the laws thus made will be seen to be authoritative and binding. This applies for two reasons. First, an assembly is a forum in which proposed laws can be openly discussed and debated. Secondly, assemblies are constituted so as to suggest that the people (or in pre-democratic days, the major interests in society) make the laws themselves. However, the idea that assemblies possess the formal legislative authority is often deeply misleading. As pointed out above, assemblies rarely monopolise legislative authority. Constitutional law is

Concept

Separation of powers

The doctrine of the separation of powers proposes that each of the three functions of government (legislation, execution and adjudication) should be entrusted to a separate branch of government (the legislature, the executive and the judiciary, respectively). Its purpose is to fragment government power in such a way as to defend liberty and keep tyranny at bay. In its formal sense, it demands *independence*, in that there should be no overlap of personnel between the branches. However, it also implies *interdependence*, in the form of shared powers to ensure that there are checks and balances. The separation of powers is applied most strictly in the USA, where it is the basis of the constitution, but the principle is respected in some form in all liberal democracies, notably in the principle of judicial independence.

Cohabitation: An arrangement in a semi-presidential system in which the president works with a government and assembly controlled by a rival party or parties.

usually placed beyond the competence of the assembly. In Ireland, for example, the constitution is amended by referendums, and in Belgium by special constitutional conventions. Executive officers, such as the French president, are often able to make law by decree, or, like the US president, can veto laws when they have been passed. The European Parliament is not a legislature at all, European law being enacted largely by the Council of Ministers. Even in the UK, where Parliament is invested with legal sovereignty (see p. 283), ministers routinely make law through statutory instruments that are subject to little effective parliamentary scrutiny.

More significantly, parliaments exercise little *positive* legislative power. Legislative proposals and programmes emanate, in the main, from the executive, which has the organisational coherence and access to specialist advice and information necessary for policy formulation. British MPs, for instance, still have a residual capacity to initiate legislation in the form of private member's bills, but these are only debated if the government is prepared to make time for them alongside its own legislative programme. Approximately 80 per cent of the legislation considered by the US Congress, the most independent and strongest assembly in the developed world, now stems from presidential initiatives. The *negative* legislative power of assemblies, that is, their ability to reject or amend proposed laws, is also limited. In cases like the First Chamber of the Dutch States-General, up to half of all legislative measures are significantly redrafted as a result of parliamentary consultations. However, in the UK, government defeats in the House of Commons are rare, even exceptional events, examples being the rejection of the Shop Bill in 1986, and the defeat of the second increase in value added tax (VAT) on domestic fuel in 1995. All too often, legislation is passed *through* assemblies, rather than *by* assemblies.

Representation

Assemblies play an important representative role in providing a link between government and the people. In the eighteenth century, this was expressed by the slogan adopted by the 13 American colonies that rebelled against British rule: 'no taxation without representation'. The extension of the franchise and the eventual achievement of universal adult suffrage turned assemblies into popular forums, bodies that 'stood for' the people themselves. For this reason, the power of an assembly within the political system is usually seen as an important index of democratic government. However, it is less clear how this representative function is carried out in practice.

Representation (see p. 206) is a complex principle that has a number of contrasting implications. For example, Westminster-style parliamentary systems based on British traditions have often portrayed representatives as trustees whose prime responsibility is to exercise their own judgement and wisdom on behalf of their constituents. However, this Burkian notion of representatives as independent actors conflicts sharply with the strict party discipline now found in most assemblies, particularly those in parliamentary systems. The alternative theory of representation, the doctrine of the mandate (see p. 210), views parties, not assemblies, as the central mechanism through which representation takes place.

In other states, the idea of constituency representation takes pride of place. This applies particularly to the US Congress, as a result of its relatively weak party system and the unusually short, two-year terms of Representatives. The primary concern of both Representatives and Senators is to 'bring home the bacon'. Congress is therefore commonly dominated by what is called 'pork barrel' politics, a style of politics characterised by measures designed to bring benefits to particular constituencies that are pushed through by a form of cooperation amongst individual legislators known as 'log rolling'. However, it is the very effectiveness of Congress in its representative function that makes it an unsuitable policy maker; it is better able to block the president's programme than to propose a coherent alternative of its own.

In the USSR and other communist states, in the absence of electoral choice and party competition, representation was often based on the degree to which assemblies resembled the larger society. The Supreme Soviet thus came far closer to being a microcosm of Soviet society (in terms of gender, nationality, occupation and so on) than assemblies in the developed West have ever done. Finally, assemblies are often mechanisms of interest representation. This is particularly the case when they are seen to exert a significant degree of policy influence, and party systems are sufficiently relaxed to offer interest groups a point of access. Once again, the USA provides the prime example, approximately one-quarter of congressional election expenses being currently provided by political action committees (PACs). The upsurge in professional lobbying in the UK in the 1980s and 1990s also raised anxiety about MPs' traditional loyalty to constituents being compromised by the growing influence of business interests (Leigh and Vulliamy, 1997).

Scrutiny and oversight

While the legislative and representative roles of assemblies have declined in significance, greater emphasis has been placed on the ability of assemblies to constrain or check executive power. Assemblies have increasingly become scrutinising bodies, the principal role of which is to deliver responsible or accountable government (see p. 300). Most assemblies have developed institutional mechanisms designed to facilitate this role. Parliamentary systems, for example, usually subject ministers to regular oral or written questioning, the classic example being Question Time in the UK House of Commons. This allows the prime minister to be cross-examined twice a week, and subjects other senior ministers to similar scrutiny about once every two weeks. Germany and Finland use the practice of 'interpellation', a process of oral questioning followed by a vote to establish the confidence of the assembly in the answers given. Since questioning and debate on the floor of a chamber inevitably tends to be generalised, much of the scrutinising work of assemblies is carried out by committees set up for this purpose. The powerful standing committees of the US Congress have served as a model for many other assemblies in this respect.

However, assemblies are not always effective in calling executives to account. In the National People's Congress in China, for example, control by a monopolistic party has turned the assembly into a mere propaganda weapon, with government policy nearly always being approved by unanimous votes. Party discipline also constrains parliamentary scrutiny elsewhere. For instance, it can be argued that, in Westminster-style systems, the principal function of the assembly is to uphold and support government, since the majority of the members of the assembly belong to the governing party. The job of scrutiny thus passes to the opposition parties, which, as long as the government retains majority control, have no power to remove it.

A further key factor is the ability of the assembly to extract information from the executive. Knowledge is power; without full and accurate information, meaningful scrutiny is impossible. In the USA, France, the Netherlands, Canada and Australia, for instance, formal freedom of information acts have been passed to establish a general right of public access to government information and records. Finally, oversight of

Concept

Responsibility

Responsibility can be understood in two contrasting ways. First, it means to act in a sensible, reasonable or morally correct fashion, often in the face of pressure to behave otherwise. A government may thus claim to be 'responsible' when it resists electoral pressures and risks unpopularity by pursuing policies designed to meet long-term public interests. Secondly, responsibility means accountability (see p. 375) or answerability. This implies the existence of a higher authority to which an individual or body is subject, and by which it can be controlled. Government is 'responsible' in this sense if its actions are open to scrutiny and criticism by an assembly that has the ability to remove it from power. This sense of the term also has an important moral dimension: it implies that the government is willing to accept blame and bear an appropriate penalty.

the executive requires that parliamentary representatives be well resourced and have access to research services and expert advice. Here the contrast is dramatic, ranging from the lavish funding and large personal staffs provided for the members of the US Congress to the less well paid, inadequately resourced and sometimes overworked UK MPs.

Recruitment and training

Assemblies often act as major channels of recruitment, providing a pool of talent from which leading decision-makers emerge. This applies less in authoritarian states, where rubber-stamp assemblies seldom attract serious politicians, and less in presidential systems, in which a separation of powers prevents executive office from being filled by current members of the assembly. However, although the trend of late has been for US presidents to have been former state governors, presidents like Kennedy and Nixon first cut their teeth as members of Congress. In parliamentary systems, however, service in the assembly is a required career path for ministers and prime ministers, who then continue to hold their assembly seats alongside their executive offices. In many developed and developing states, assemblies recruit and train the next generation of political leaders, thus giving them experience of political debate and policy analysis.

On the other hand, assemblies can also be inadequate in this respect. Parliamentarians certainly gain experience of politics as **rhetoric**, of what is derogatorily known as 'speechifying', but they have few opportunities to acquire the bureaucratic and managerial skills required to run government departments and oversee the process of policy formulation. Moreover, it is sometimes argued that assemblies 'corrupt' politicians by socialising them into norms and values that distance them from the needs of their constituents and the instincts of grass-roots party workers. Parliamentary socialists, for example, may thus come to subscribe more passionately to the ideals of parliamentarianism than they do to the principles of socialism (Miliband, 1972).

Legitimacy

The final function of assemblies is to promote the legitimacy (see p. 193) of a regime by encouraging the public to see the system of rule as 'rightful'. This is why most authoritarian and even totalitarian states tolerate assemblies, though, of course, ones that have no legislative independence or policy making power. The ability of assemblies to mobilise consent depends largely on their ability to function as popular conventions, endorsing laws and policies in the name of the public as well as in their interest. In addition to having propaganda value, assemblies may also perform more creditable educational functions. Parliamentary debates can help to inform and instruct citizens about the affairs of government and the major issues of the day. Thus reactions in the UK to the Argentine invasion of the Falklands in 1982 were clearly influenced by the rare Saturday sitting of the House of Commons, and what the US public knew of the Iran–Contra affair in 1988 was largely based on the hearings of the Senate Committee on Intelligence.

To a growing extent, however, the propaganda/educational role of assemblies has been taken over by the mass media (see p. 188). The rise of the electronic media in the form of radio and particularly television has given government direct access to literally millions of voters instead of it having, as before, to rely on the reporting of parliamentary debates and discussions. As a result, the status that assemblies enjoy increasingly depends less on their constitutional position and more on the media

Rhetoric: The art of using language to persuade or influence; rhetoric can imply high-sounding but essentially vacuous speech.

attention they receive. This helps to explain why assemblies have been increasingly anxious for their proceedings to receive television coverage. The public impact of US congressional committees has long been enhanced by the televising of their hearings. In the case of the UK, television cameras were not allowed into the House of Commons until 1989, shortly after they were first introduced in the Soviet parliament.

Structure of assemblies

Assemblies differ in a number of respects. For example, their members may be elected, appointed or even selected by inheritance, or any combination of these methods. When members are elected, this may be on the basis of population (in the form of equal-sized constituencies), or through regions or states. The franchise may be restricted or universal, and various electoral systems may be used (see pp. 215–221). The sizes of assemblies also vary considerably. The tiny republic of Nauru, in the West Central Pacific, has an assembly of 18 members, each of whom represents approximately 440 people. At the other extreme, there is the 2000 member National Peoples' Congress in China, in which one member represents over 350 000 people. However, the principal structural differences between assemblies are whether they comprise one chamber or two, and the nature and role of their committee systems.

One chamber or two?

Although Yugoslavia once experimented with a five-chamber assembly, and from 1984 to 1994 South Africa had a three-chamber assembly, the vast majority of assemblies have either one or two chambers. Single-chamber, or unicameral, assemblies have been common in much of Africa, in communist states such as China, and in postcommunist states that have maintained an earlier tradition of unicameralism. Indeed, there was a clear trend towards unicameralism in the post-Second-World-War period. For instance, in 1948, Israel established a single-chamber parliament (the Knesset), and second chambers were abolished in New Zealand in 1950, Denmark in 1954, and Sweden in 1970. Such developments support the view that unicameral assemblies are more streamlined and effective than bicameral ones, especially in terms of responding to the needs of small and relatively cohesive societies. In the famous remark of the Abbé Siéyès in 1789: 'if the second Chamber agrees with the first it is unnecessary; if it disagrees it is pernicious'. Nevertheless, about half the world's states retain two-chamber, or bicameral, assemblies.

In terms of strengthening checks and balances within assemblies and between executives and assemblies, bicameralism has usually been seen as a central principal of liberal constitutionalism (see p. 279). This was the case in the debates amongst the 'founding fathers' who drew up the US constitution in 1787. Whereas earlier second chambers, such as the British House of Lords, had developed as vehicles through which powerful economic and social interests could be represented in government, delegates such as James Madison (see p. 302) saw the US Senate as a means of fragmenting legislative power and as a safeguard against executive domination.

The representative advantages of bicameralism are particularly important in federal states (see p. 125), where the sharing of sovereignty creates a constant danger of irreconcilable conflict between the centre and the periphery. All of the world's 16

James Madison (1751–1836)

US statesman and political philosopher. A Virginian delegate to the Constitutional Convention of 1787, Madison was a strong proponent of US nationalism and a keen advocate of ratification. He later served as Jefferson's Secretary of State (1801–89) and was the fourth president of the USA (1809–17). Usually regarded as a leading supporter of pluralism and divided government, Madison urged the adoption of federalism, bicameralism and the separation of powers. However, when in government, he was prepared to strengthen the power of national government. His best known political writings are his contributions, with Alexander Hamilton (see p. 126) and John Jay, to *The Federalist Papers* (Hamilton, Jay and Madison, [1787–89] 1961).

federal states thus have bicameral legislatures, and in 14 of them the second chamber represents the provinces or component states. These may enjoy equal represent-ation, as in Australia, Switzerland and the USA, or they may be represented according to the size of their populations, as in Austria and Germany. Second chambers in some nonfederal states are also used to resolve regional differences. In France most members of the second chamber, and in the Netherlands all members, are elected indirectly via local government.

Most second chambers are constitutionally and politically subordinate to first chambers, which are usually seen as the locus of popular authority. This is particu-larly the case in parliamentary systems, in which government is generally responsible to and drawn, largely or wholly, from the lower house. In Norway, the Netherlands and Fiji all **bills**, and in India, Canada and the UK money bills, must be introduced in the first chamber. Second chambers may also be denied veto powers. The Japanese first chamber, the House of Representatives, is thus able, by a two-thirds majority, to override the House of Counsellors. The UK House of Lords only has the power to delay non-financial legislation for a single year, although it can still veto the sacking of judges and the postponement of parliamentary elections.

Not uncommonly, such weaker versions of bicameralism reflect the restricted representative basis of the upper house. Indirect elections are used in Germany, Austria and India, for example, and a combination of election and appointment is used in Belgium, Malaysia and Ireland. The Canadian Senate is wholly nominated, and the majority of the members of the UK House of Lords are still hereditary peers. A stronger version of bicameralism is found in assemblies with two chambers that have broadly equal powers. The Italian Chamber of Deputies and the Italian Senate, for example, are both elected by universal adult suffrage, and are legislatively co-equal. An electoral college representing both chambers elects the president, and the prime minister and council of ministers are collectively responsible to the whole assembly. The US Congress is perhaps the only example of an assembly that has a dominant upper chamber. Although all tax legislation must be introduced in the House of Representatives, the Senate alone exercises ratification and confirmation powers.

One of the greatest drawbacks of legislative fragmentation is the possibility of conflict between the two chambers. When the houses have broadly equal powers, a device is needed to resolve differences and prevent institutional immobilism. The most common mechanism is that used in the US congress, in which a special

Bill: Proposed legislation in the form of a draft statute; if passed, a bill becomes an act.

Focus on . . .

Bicameralism: strengths and weaknesses

The chief benefits of bicameralism are the following:

- Second chambers check the power of first chambers and prevent majoritarian rule.
- Bicameral assemblies more effectively check the power of the executive, because there are two chambers to expose the failings of government.
- Two-chamber assemblies widen the basis of representation, allowing each house to articulate a different range of interests and respond to different groups of voters.
- The existence of a second chamber can ensure that legislation is more thoroughly scrutinised, as it can relieve the legislative burden of the first chamber and rectify its mistakes and oversights.
- Second chambers can act as a constitutional safeguard, delaying the passage of controversial legislation and allowing time for discussion and public debate.

The drawbacks of bicameralism include the following:

- Unicameral assemblies are more efficient, because the existence of a second chamber can make the legislative process unnecessarily complex and difficult.
- Second chambers often act as a check on democratic rule, particularly when their members are non-elected or indirectly elected.
- Bicameral assemblies are a recipe for institutional conflict in the legislature, as well as for government gridlock.
- Bicameral assemblies may narrow access to policy making by placing final legislative decisions in the hands of joint committees.
- Second chambers introduce a conservative political bias by upholding existing constitutional arrangements and, sometimes, the interests of social elites.

joint congressional committee, composed of senior figures from both chambers, is authorised to produce a compromise agreement. In Germany, although the lower chamber (the Bundestag) is in most cases legislatively dominant, the upper chamber (the Bundesrat) enjoys considerable veto powers in relation to constitutional questions and matters related to the *Länder*. When disputes occur, they are referred to a joint Bundestag–Bundesrat conciliation committee, the members of which are drawn from the two chambers in equal proportions. A further criticism of bicameralism is that it tends to entrench a conservative political bias. To the extent that second chambers defend the constitutional structure by making it more difficult to pass radical or controversial measures, this tendency is usually seen as laudable. However, when second chambers are able to block or delay legislation approved by democratically elected first chambers, they may merely help to insulate political and social elites from popular pressure. Ironically, the opposite can also be the case. The US Senate is now as liberal, or more liberal, than the House of Representatives, and in the UK in the 1980s the House of Lords was a more effective check on the Thatcher government than was the House of Commons.

Focus on . . .

Committees: advantages and disadvantages

A committee is a small work group composed of members drawn from a larger body and charged with specific responsibilities. Whereas *ad hoc* committees are set up for a particular purpose and disbanded when that task is complete, permanent or standing committees have enduring responsibilities and an institutionalised role. Committee structures have become increasingly prominent in legislative and executive branches of government, as deliberative and consultative forums and also as decision-making bodies.

Amongst the advantages of committees are the following:

- They allow a range of views, opinions and interests to be represented.
- They provide the opportunity for fuller, longer and more detailed debate.
- They encourage decisions to be made more efficiently and speedily by restricting the range of opposing opinions.
- They make possible a division of labour that encourages the accumulation of expertise and specialist knowledge.

However, committees have been criticised for the following reasons:

- They can easily be manipulated by those who set up and staff them.
- They encourage centralisation by allowing a chairperson to dominate proceedings behind a mask of consultation.
- They narrow the range of views and interests that are taken into account in decision-making.
- They divorce their members from the larger body, creating a form of sham representation.

Committee systems

Almost all assemblies have a committee system of some sort. Indeed, the trend towards the use of committees, in assemblies and elsewhere, is often seen as one of the distinctive features of modern politics. Committee systems have increasingly been portrayed as the power houses of assemblies, the very hub of the legislative process; whereas parliamentary chambers are for talking, committees are for working. As Woodrow Wilson ([1885] 1961) put it: 'Congressional government is committee government. Congress in session is Congress on public exhibition. Congress in its committee-rooms is Congress at work'. It is therefore not surprising that assemblies are often classified according to their committees. In crude terms, strong assemblies have strong committees, and weak assemblies have weak committees.

Assembly committees usually have one of three functions. First, they may carry out detailed consideration of legislative measures and financial proposals. They thus not only help to relieve the legislative burden on chambers, but also engage in more thorough and exacting examination than is possible on the floor of a house. This task is usually carried out by standing committees, which may be broad and flexible, as in the UK and France, or permanent and highly specialised, as in Germany and the USA. Secondly, committees may be set up to scrutinise government administration and oversee the exercise of executive power. Such committees must be permanent and specialised, because, to be effective, they have to rival the executive in terms of detailed knowledge and expertise. In the US Congress, for example, legislative and scrutinising responsibilities are vested in standing committees, whereas, in the UK Parliament and the French National Assembly, separate select or supervisory committees are set up. Thirdly, *ad hoc* committees may investigate matters of public concern. Some of the most important examples of investigatory committees have been found in the USA, notably the Irvin Committee on Watergate, and the House Un-American Activities Committee, which became a vehicle for **McCarthyism** in the 1950s.

If powerful committees mean a powerful assembly, what makes committees powerful? It is generally agreed that the US Congress has the most powerful committees found anywhere in the world, and these provide a model which many other assemblies have tried to adopt. Their power certainly stems from their specialist responsibilities, permanent membership and lavish support in terms of funding and access to advice. This allows them to match the expertise of the bureaucracy. Moreover, their role in the legislative process is crucial. Whereas in the UK, France and Japan bills reach committees having been debated and approved in principle by the floor of the house, in Congress committee scrutiny comes first. This means that many bills are completely redrafted, and others never see the light of day.

Most importantly, however, Congress has a relatively weak party system, which allows its committees considerable independence from the presidency. Where stricter party discipline operates, as in Australia, New Zealand and the UK, committees are effectively neutered by the fact that the majority of their members owe an overriding loyalty to the government of the day. Germany is an exception in this respect. Although Germany has an effective party system, it also possesses strong legislative committees, largely as a consequence of the need for coalition governments to conciliate the assembly in order to maintain the support of two or more parties.

In an attempt to strengthen Parliament in the UK against the executive, a system of departmental select committees was established in 1979. These were consciously modelled on the US example, and the system sought to promote open government (see p. 392) by allowing for the examination of government papers and the cross-examination of ministers and senior civil servants. It was hoped that these committees would become effective watchdogs that would be capable of influencing government policy. However, the experiment has proved disappointing for a number of reasons. First, the hoped-for less partisan character of committees has failed to materialise, as the government has ensured that party disciplines intrude into the work of committees. Secondly, the select committees are inadequately resourced and have limited powers. Although they can send for 'persons, papers and records', they cannot force particular civil servants or ministers to attend, neither can they ensure that their questions are fully answered. Thirdly, no alternative career structure has developed around the committees; MPs still look to advance their careers through jobs in government, and so tend to be more sensitive to party pressures than parliamentary ones. In fact, some critics have argued that, far from strengthening the House of Commons, select committees have weakened it, in that they draw attention away from the activity on the floor of the house, which alone has the capacity to ensure responsible government.

McCarthyism: The use of witch hunts and unscrupulous investigations, as practised in the 1950s against 'communists' by US Senator Joseph McCarthy.

■ Performance of assemblies

Do assemblies make policy?

The difficulty with assessing the performance of assemblies is that they carry out such a wide range of functions. Should they be judged on the quality of the legislation they pass, their effectiveness in mobilising consent, the degree to which they represent public opinion, or what? The greatest political concern, however, relates to the policy impact of assemblies, that is, their capacity to shape or at least influence what governments actually do. Do assemblies have power in the sense that they affect the content of public policy, or are they merely talking shops that draw attention away from where the real business of government happens? The key issue here is the nature of assembly–executive relations and the distribution of power between the two major branches of government. On this basis, the assemblies of the world can be classified into three broad categories:

- policy making assemblies, which enjoy significant autonomy and have an active impact on policy
- policy-influencing assemblies, which can transform policy but only by reacting to executive initiatives
- executive-dominated assemblies, which exert marginal influence or merely rubber-stamp executive decisions.

Policy making assemblies are rare. To exert a positive influence on the policy process, an assembly has to fulfil three criteria. First, it must command significant constitutional authority and respect. Secondly, it must enjoy meaningful political independence from the executive, and, thirdly, it must possess sufficient organisational coherence to undertake concerted action. As far as the UK Parliament is concerned, these conditions were perhaps only fulfilled during its so-called 'golden age', the period between the Great Reform Act of 1832 and the Second Reform Act of 1867. In this period, Parliament, its authority enhanced by the extension of the franchise but not yet hampered by the emergence of effective party discipline, changed governments, forced the removal of individual ministers, rejected government legislation, and initiated significant measures.

In the modern period, the best (and, some would argue, the only) example of a policy making assembly is the US Congress. Congress is perhaps unique in that it enjoys an unusual combination of advantages. The separation of powers invests Congress with constitutional independence and an impressive range of autonomous powers. Relatively weak party cohesion deprives the president of the usual means of exerting legislative control. A powerful committee system guarantees the organisational effectiveness of Congress. Finally, particularly since the Legislative Reorganisation Act (1946), Congress has had the staffing and informational resources to operate without depending on the executive branch for assistance.

Nevertheless, despite these advantages, Congress has lost some of its influence during the twentieth century. Since the time of the New Deal, the US public, and for that matter Congress itself, has increasingly looked to the White House (the presidency) for political leadership (see p. 330). The main burden of Congress's work is therefore to examine the president's legislative programme. This has weakened Congress's role as a policy initiator, and has led to a situation in which 'the president proposes and Congress disposes'. Indeed, growing anxiety about the subordination of Congress was expressed in the 1960s in fears about the emergence of a so-called 'imperial presidency'. In the aftermath of Watergate, however, a resurgent Congress adopted a more assertive attitude towards presidential power, and initiated a series of reforms in the committee and seniority systems. These reforms have fragmented congressional power by reducing the influence of committee chairs, and strengthened party cohesion by widening party influence over appointments. The most striking example of Congress seizing control of public policy occurred after the 1994 elections, when the Republican Congress, led by the Speaker of the House Newt Gingrich, pushed through a radical programme of tax and spending cuts under the slogan 'Contract with America'.

The collapse of communism in the USSR and the emergence of a postcommunist regime also underlined, albeit briefly, the importance of parliamentary power. As part of his political reforms in the late 1980s, President Gorbachev replaced the docile Supreme Soviet with a two-tier parliament, in which a competitively elected Congress of People's Deputies elected a permanent assembly, still referred to as the Supreme Soviet. Although it was still overwhelmingly communist in orientation, liberal and reformist views could also be expressed. Following the CPSU's abandonment of its monopoly of power in 1990, similar parliaments were elected in the 15 Soviet republics, for the first time under conditions of **political pluralism**. When conservatives in August 1991 staged a military coup to overthrow Gorbachev, Boris Yeltsin took up residence in the Russian parliament (the White House), which immediately became the focal point of resistance to the military takeover.

The failure of the coup and the collapse in the December of the USSR, however, meant that President Yeltsin was confronted by a parliament largely unsympathetic to the liberal reforms that his administration attempted to advance. Nationalists, anti-Semites and erstwhile communists in the parliament combined to force Yeltsin to sack key ministers and to slow down and even reverse major economic reforms. However, this period of genuine parliamentary government came to a spectacular end when hardliners rebelled against Yeltsin's decision to dissolve parliament. This led in October 1993 to the military seizure of the White House and the imposition of presidential rule.

In parliamentary systems, assemblies have generally played a policy-influencing, rather than a policy making, role. Where exceptions have occurred, as in the Italian assembly and the National Assembly of the Fourth French Republic, this has usually been a consequence of weak coalition government (see p. 246) and a fragmented party system. More commonly, assembly–executive relations are structured by party divisions. This is most clearly the case when majoritarian or weakly proportional electoral systems invest a single party with majority control of the assembly, as has traditionally occurred in the UK, New Zealand and Australia. In such cases, the central dynamic of the parliamentary system is an antagonistic relationship between the government and the opposition, usually termed 'adversary politics' (see p. 308). Government governs in the sense that it is responsible for formulating and later implementing a legislative programme, while the assembly plays an essentially reactive role.

The scope that the assembly has to influence policy in these circumstances largely depends on two factors: the strength in the assembly of the governing party, and the party's ability to maintain internal unity. The Thatcher government dominated the UK House of Commons in the 1980s by virtue of parliamentary majorities that were

Political pluralism: The existence of a range of political values, philosophies and movements; in particular, a competitive party system.

Focus on . . .

Adversary politics: for and against

Adversary politics is a style of politics characterised by an antagonistic relationship between major parties that turns political life into an on-going electoral battle. Parliamentary debate thus becomes a 'continuous polemic' before what is seen as the 'bar of public opinion'.
  Adversarialism has been defended on the following grounds:

- It offers voters clear alternatives, thus promoting electoral choice and democratic accountability.
- It checks government power by ensuring that there is opposition and scrutiny.

Its dangers nevertheless include the following:

- It discourages sober and rational debate, and precludes compromise.
- It fosters polarisation, which, as governments change, gives rise to political instability.

large enough to insulate it from backbench pressure, and the divided and demoralised state of the Labour opposition. Nevertheless, governments in parliamentary systems must remain constantly sensitive to the morale of their backbenchers. Margaret Thatcher discovered this to her cost in November 1990 when she was abruptly removed as Conservative party leader.

The resurgence of parliamentary power in the UK was demonstrated in the 1990s by the adoption of an increasingly 'Eurosceptical' stance by the Major government following the reduction of its majority in the 1992 election and the spread of anti-European sentiments among backbench Conservatives. According to Norton (1993), such developments are part of a trend dating back to about 1970 which has seen the transformative role of Parliament strengthened by a progressive decline in party unity. Other assemblies that exert a strong influence on policy are the German Bundestag and the Swedish Riksdag. However, in both these cases, parliamentary influence stems less from adversary politics than from ingrained habits of negotiation and compromise fostered both by the political culture and by long experience of coalition government.

Parliamentary systems that have become accustomed to prolonged domination by a single party often have assemblies that are weak or executive-dominated. A deliberate attempt was made in the Fifth French Republic to weaken parliamentary power so as to avoid the conflict and obstructionism that had undermined the Fourth Republic. A system of rationalised parliamentarianism came into existence. This allowed the French president to dominate government largely through party control, but also through his power to dissolve the National Assembly in order to gain a new majority, as de Gaulle did in 1962 and 1968, and Mitterrand did in 1981 and 1988. De Gaulle also reduced the National Assembly's powers of political control, and limited its legislative competence by creating the Conseil Constitutionnel to ensure that its laws conform to the constitution. However, the end of Gaullist domination in 1981 created opportunities for a greater degree of parliamentary influence, particularly when the Socialists lost control of the assembly and Mitterrand was forced into cohabitation with a Gaullist government under Jacques Chirac.

The Japanese Diet (Kokkai) is another example of a traditionally subordinate assembly. Until the 1980s the Diet was required to do little more than ratify the decisions of the executive; this was a consequence of the unbroken domination of the Liberal Democratic Party after 1955. Rival parties were eternal outsiders, and factional divisions within the LDP were generally played out away from the Diet. However, the progressive decline in the sizes of LDP majorities led by the 1970s to a less adversarial and more conciliatory attitude towards parliamentary opposition. For instance, the membership of standing committees was broadened to include minority parties as the LDP started to relax its grip on the parliamentary process. A full system of parliamentary scrutiny and oversight finally emerged in Japan following the LDP's defeat in the 1993 election.

Less ambiguous examples of marginal assemblies have been found in communist regimes and developing states. In the former, tight control by 'ruling' communist parties and the practice of noncompetitive elections ensured that assemblies did little more than provide formal approval for the government's programme. When this control was relaxed, the consequences were often devastating for the regime. The sweeping victories for Solidarity in the 1989 parliamentary elections in Poland, for example, led directly to the fall of a communist government that had been in power since 1945. In the developing states of Africa and Asia, assemblies have played a largely integrative, rather than policy-influencing, role. Their central function has been to strengthen legitimacy and so assist in the process of nation building. It is a backhanded compliment to assemblies that the establishment of military rule has usually been accompanied by their suspension or abolition. This occurred in Chile, Pakistan and the Philippines in the 1970s, and in Turkey and Nigeria in the 1980s.

Why are assemblies in decline?

There is nothing new about the 'decline of assemblies' debate. Since the late nineteenth century, anxiety has been expressed about the strengthening of executives, and particularly bureaucracies, at the expense of assemblies. This anxiety has been heightened by the fact that, since the days of Locke and Montesquieu, assemblies have been seen as the principal vehicles for delivering responsible and representative government. The notion that good government requires a strong assembly is questionable, however. Assembly power can certainly become 'excessive', especially when it leads to immobilism and policy stalemate. The model of the US Congress, for instance, has as many critics as it has admirers. There is nevertheless general agreement that, during the twentieth century, the power and status of assemblies has changed, and usually for the worse. Whether this amounts to a general 'decline of assemblies', or rather a shift in their purpose or function, is another matter. The principal factors that have brought about these changes are the following:

* the emergence of disciplined political parties
* the growth in the role of government
* the organisational weaknesses of assemblies
* the rise of interest-group power.

Disciplined political parties

The emergence from the late nineteenth century onwards of mass-membership parties weakened assemblies in a number of respects. In the first place, the transition from loose factions (see p. 230) to disciplined party groupings undermined the ability of individual members to represent constituents as trustees by exercising their own judgement and conscience. Parties rather than assemblies thus became the principal agents of representation, operating through the doctrine of the mandate. Party loyalty also weakened assemblies in terms of their function as debating chambers. However articulate, impassioned or persuasive parliamentary oratory may be, it has little or no impact on voting in party-dominated assemblies, which means that debate becomes sterile or ritualised. As Richard Cobden (1804–65) commented about the UK House of Commons, 'In this House I have heard many a speech that moved men to tears – but never one that turned a vote'. More important, however, is the tendency of party unity to facilitate executive domination. In parliamentary systems in particular, loyalty to party means, for the majority of parliamentarians, loyalty to the government of the day, which comprises, after all, the leading members of their own party. Far from checking or even embarrassing the executive, many assemblies have therefore come to function as its willing accomplices or doughty defenders.

Big government

The growth in the role of government, especially in the areas of social welfare and economic management, has usually been associated with a redistribution of power from assemblies to executives. This occurs for three reasons. First, it leads to an increase in the size and status of bureaucracies, which are responsible for administering government policy and overseeing an ever-widening range of public services. Secondly, it places greater emphasis on the process of policy initiation and formulation. Although individual assembly members can initiate policy in specific areas, the task of developing broad and coherent government programmes is quite beyond them. During the twentieth century, most assemblies therefore adjusted to the loss of positive legislative power by accepting that their central role was to scrutinise and criticise, rather than to make policy. Thirdly, 'big' government has meant that government policy is increasingly complex and intricate. This, in turn, has placed a higher premium on expertise, a quality more abundantly possessed by 'professional' bureaucrats than by 'amateur' politicians.

Lack of leadership

By virtue of their function as representative forums and debating chambers, assemblies suffer from a number of organisational weaknesses. In particular, they usually comprise several hundred members, who enjoy formal equality in the sense that they can all vote and contribute to debates. Although advantageous in other respects, the egalitarian and fragmented character of assemblies weakens their capacity to provide leadership and take concerted action. This problem has become more acute in an age in which the public looks to government to solve social problems and deliver sustained prosperity, and in which states have no choice but to participate in international affairs and global politics. Party-organised assemblies are certainly better able to adopt clear and coherent domestic and foreign policies, but in these cases leadership tends to be provided *by* parties and only *through* assemblies. In general, it has been political executives rather than assemblies that have been able to respond to this need for leadership, by virtue of their greater organisational coherence and the fact that they are headed by a single individual, usually a president or prime minister.

Interest group power

Not only have power and public attention shifted from assemblies to executives, but they have also been lost to interests and groups external to government. The rise of interest groups has threatened assemblies in two important respects. The first is that the groups have provided the public with an alternative mechanism of representation. Often set up specifically for this purpose, interest groups tend to be more effective than assemblies in taking up popular grievances and giving expression to the concerns and aspirations of particular groups. Single-issue groups, for instance, now engage in, and promote, the kind of public debate that previously only took place in parliamentary chambers. The second factor is that, while assemblies have increasingly been excluded from the process of policy formulation, organised interests have become more prominent both as representatives of 'affected groups' and as sources of expert advice and information. Policy analysis and discussion in assemblies is therefore often little more than a formality, meaningful debate taking place elsewhere.

The rise of assemblies?

Many argue that the above analysis paints an over-gloomy picture. To some extent, the 'decline of assemblies' is too sweeping a notion, since it conceals the perhaps more important fact that the role of assemblies in the political process has fundamentally changed. Whereas their decline as legislatures and as policy-shaping bodies can hardly be doubted, many agree with Blondel (1973) that, if anything, they have become more important as 'communicating mechanisms'. The willingness of a growing number of assemblies to open up their proceedings to television cameras has certainly helped to raise their public profiles and strengthen them as arenas of debate and agencies of oversight. Similarly, there is a trend towards the professionalisation of assembly work. Following the example of the US Congress, this has seen the adoption and strengthening of specialised committees and an improvement in the staff and resources available to individual assembly members.

More broadly, there is evidence in the UK and elsewhere of assemblies becoming more critical and independent as a result of the decline of parties as tightly disciplined blocs. Not only may better-informed voters expect more of individual assembly members, but also better-educated and better-resourced members may be less willing to defer to a party line and act as 'lobby fodder'. If nothing else, general recognition that the legitimacy and stability of a political system is linked to the perceived effectiveness of its assembly guarantees that, whenever assembly power is weakened, voices will be raised in protest. Ultimately, however, the desirable balance between the assembly and the executive boils down to a normative judgement about the need for representation and accountability on the one hand, and for leadership and strong government on the other.

■ Summary

◆ The terms assembly, legislature and parliament are usually used interchangeably. The term assembly suggests that the body is a surrogate for the people as it is composed of lay politicians who claim to represent the people rather than of trained or expert government officials. The term legislature is misleading, because assemblies never monopolise law-making power. The term parliament draws attention to the importance within assemblies of debate and deliberation.

◆ A parliamentary system is one in which government governs in and through the assembly or parliament, the executive being drawn from, and accountable to, the assembly. A presidential system is based on a separation of powers between the assembly and the executive. This establishes a relationship characterised by a combination of independence and interdependence between the two branches.

◆ Assemblies provide a link between government and the people, that is, a channel of communication that can support government and uphold the regime, and force government to respond to popular demands. The chief functions of an assembly are to enact legislation, act as a representative body, oversee and scrutinise the executive, recruit and train politicians, and assist in maintaining the political system's legitimacy.

◆ Assemblies generally comprise either one or two chambers. The attraction of bicameralism is that it strengthens checks and balances and broadens representation, which is particularly useful in federal systems. Its disadvantage is that, in this type of system, there is a tendency towards immobilism and government gridlock. Committee systems are increasingly important in the legislative process; strong assemblies usually have strong committees, weak ones have weak committees.

◆ Assemblies rarely make policy. More usually, they influence policy or are executive-dominated. The amount of power an assembly has is determined by a variety of factors. These include the extent of the assembly's constitutional authority, its degree of political independence from the executive, the nature of the party system, and the assembly's level of organisational coherence.

◆ The decline of assemblies provokes anxiety because it is linked to the health of responsible and representative government. Assemblies have declined because of the emergence of disciplined political parties, the growth in the role of government, the executive's greater capacity to formulate policy and provide leadership, and the increasing strength of interest groups and the mass media.

▉ Questions for discussion

▶ Does the widespread adoption of parliamentary government reflect the system's success and efficiency?

▶ Why is the separation of powers considered to be such an important liberal-democratic principle?

▶ What conditions are most conducive for the promotion of responsible government?

▶ Are two chambers always better than one?

▶ In complex modern societies, are assemblies doomed to lose out to executives?

▶ Does the decline of assemblies necessarily weaken representation and accountability?

Further reading

Davidson, R. H. (ed.) *The Post-Reform Congress* (New York: St Martin's Press, 1992). A useful discussion of the role of the US Congress and shifts in congressional power.

Lijphart, A. (ed.) *Parliamentary Versus Presidential Government* (Oxford: Oxford University Press, 1992). A wide-ranging collection of essays that reflect on the merits of parliamentarianism and presidentialism.

Mezey, M. *Comparative Legislatures* (Durham, NC: Duke University Press, 1979). A good and accessible comparative introduction to assemblies.

Norton, P. (ed.) *Parliaments in Western Europe* (London: Frank Cass, 1990b). A thorough analysis of the performance of assemblies in western Europe.

Political Executives

'A ruler must learn to be other than good.'

NICCOLO MACHIAVELLI *The Prince* (1513)

The executive is the irreducible core of government. Political systems can operate without constitutions, assemblies, judiciaries, and even parties, but they cannot survive without an executive branch to formulate government policy and ensure that it is implemented. Such is the potential power of executives that much of political development has taken the form of attempts to check or constrain them, either by forcing them to operate within a constitutional framework, or by making them accountable to a popular assembly or democratic electorate. Political executives, and particularly chief executives, are certainly the face of politics with which the general public is most familiar. This is because the executive is the source of political leadership. This role has been greatly enhanced by the widening responsibilities of the state in both the domestic and international realms, and the media's tendency to portray politics in terms of personalities. However, the hopes and expectations focused on executives may also prove to be their undoing. In many political systems, leaders are finding it increasingly difficult to 'deliver the goods'. This problem is linked to growing disenchantment with politics in general and with politicians in particular.

The key issues discussed in this chapter are the following:

Key issues

► What is the executive branch of government? Who does it comprise?

► What are the principal functions of political executives?

► How do presidential executives differ from parliamentary executives?

► Where does power lie in political executives?

► How should political leadership be understood and explained?

► Is there a crisis of leadership in modern politics?

Executive

In its broadest sense, the executive is the branch of government responsible for the implementation of laws and policies made by the legislature. The executive branch extends from the head of government to the members of enforcement agencies such as the police and the military, and includes both ministers and civil servants. More commonly, the term is now used in a narrower sense to describe the smaller body of decision-makers who take overall responsibility for the direction and coordination of government policy. This core of senior figures is often called the *political* executive (roughly equivalent to 'the government of the day', or, in presidential systems, 'the administration'), as opposed to the *official* executive, or bureaucracy (p. 341).

■ Role of the executive

Who's who in the executive?

The executive is, technically, the branch of government that is responsible for the execution or implementation of policy. In practice, however, its responsibilities tend to be substantially broader as well as more complex. This complexity also extends to the composition of the executive. Members of executives have been categorised in one of two ways. First, a distinction is often drawn between the 'political' executive and the 'bureaucratic' executive. This highlights the differences between politicians and civil servants, and, more broadly, between politics and administration (see p. 345). Secondly, various levels of status and responsibility have been identified within executives. Whereas assemblies tend to respect at least the formal equality of their members, executive branches are typically pyramidal, organised according to a clear leadership structure.

The distinction between political and bureaucratic or official posts is most clear-cut in the case of parliamentary executives, where differences in recruitment, responsibility, status and political orientation can be identified. In parliamentary systems, the political executive comprises elected politicians, ministers drawn from and accountable to the assembly; their job is to make policy, in accordance with the political and ideological priorities of their party, and to oversee its implementation. The official executive comprises appointed and professional civil servants whose job it is to offer advice and administer policy, subject to the requirements of political neutrality (see p. 287) and loyalty to their ministers.

Nevertheless, in parliamentary systems such as those in Australia, Canada, India and the UK, the political/bureaucratic distinction is blurred by the fact that senior civil servants often make a substantial contribution to policy making and because use is commonly made of temporary, politically committed advisers. The overlap is usually even greater in presidential executives. In the USA, for example, the president is the only elected politician in the executive. Cabinet members are, in effect, appointed officials, and all the senior and many middle-ranking civil servants are politically partisan and temporary. In communist executives, for example, in China and the USSR of old, the distinction is rendered virtually redundant by the all-pervasive reach of the 'ruling' communist party. Chinese bureaucrats are thus 'political' in the sense that they are in all cases ideologically committed supporters, and usually members, of the Chinese Communist Party.

In comparison with political/bureaucratic distinctions, hierarchial divisions within executive branches are easier to identify. In the first place, executives tend to be centralised around the leadership of a single individual. As Montesquieu (see p. 294) put it, 'this branch of government, having need of dispatch, is better administered by one than by many'. Two separate posts can nevertheless be identified, although they may be held by the same person. On the one hand, there is the head of state, an office of formal authority and largely symbolic importance. On the other, there is the head of government, or the chief executive, a post that carries policy making and political responsibilities. Whereas executive presidents, as in the USA, Russia and France, 'wear two hats', the posts in parliamentary systems are usually separate. A prime minister serves as the chief executive, and the post of head of state is usually held by a non-partisan figurehead.

Focus on . . .

Heads of state

The head of state is the personal embodiment of the state's power and authority. As the leading representative of the state, the head of state enjoys the highest status in the land. However, he or she is often a figure of essentially symbolic or formal significance, with real power residing in the hands of the head of government (a post that may or may not be held by the same person). Heads of state exercise a range of ceremonial powers and responsibilities, such as awarding honours, assenting to legislation and treaties, and receiving visiting heads of state. Their power to appoint the head of government (which is significant in parliamentary systems) may nevertheless allow some scope for residual political influence. The head of state is usually either a president or monarch (see p. 324).

Beneath the chief executive, a range of ministers or secretaries have responsibility for developing or implementing policy in specific areas. There is often a hierarchy amongst these departmental bosses, imposed either by the importance of their policy areas (economics and foreign ministers generally hold leading positions) or by their entitlement to sit in the **cabinet** or in senior committees. As discussed further below, cabinets have responsibilities that range from the sharing of policy making power in a form of collective leadership to the offering of advice and the broader coordination of executive policy. At a lower level are the massed ranks of bureaucrats and administrators (discussed in Chapter 17) who, at least in theory, are less concerned with policy formulation than with policy implementation. Finally, there are enforcement agencies, such as the police force and armed forces (examined in Chapter 18), and an array of quasi-governmental bodies, popularly known as quangos (see p. 350). These are part of the executive insofar as they help to put government policy into effect, but they are staffed by personnel who enjoy at least formal independence from the government itself.

Functions of political executives

At its most simple, the task of the political executive is to provide leadership (see p. 330). In this sense, the executive functions as the 'commanding heights' of the state apparatus, the core of the state itself. This role extends over a variety of areas, and this means that the members of the political executive have to carry out several functions, sometimes simultaneously. The most important of the areas are the following:

- ceremonial duties
- control of policy making
- popular political leadership
- bureaucratic management
- crisis response.

Cabinet: A group of senior ministers that meets formally and regularly, and is chaired by the chief executive; cabinets may make policy or be consultative.

Ceremonial leadership

Heads of state, chief executives and, to a lesser extent, senior ministers or secretaries 'stand for' the state. In giving state authority personal form, they represent the larger society and symbolise, accurately or otherwise, its unity. This role is largely formal and ceremonial, and covers, for example, state occasions, foreign visits, international conferences, and the ratification of treaties and legislation. Nonexecutive presidents and constitutional monarchs are sometimes charged with these essentially ceremonial responsibilities, allowing other executive officers to get on with the day-to-day business of government. The role is nevertheless of broader significance for two reasons. First, it provides a focus for unity and political loyalty, and so helps to build legitimacy (see p. 193). Secondly, it allows those at the top of the executive to portray themselves as 'national leaders', which is vital to the maintenance of public support and electoral credibility.

Policy making leadership

The key function of the political executive is to direct and control the policy process. In short, the executive is expected to 'govern'. This role has been substantially expanded during the twentieth century in response to the broadening responsibilities of government. The political executive is looked to, in particular, to develop coherent economic and social programmes that meet the needs of more complex and politically sophisticated societies, and to control the state's various external relationships in an increasingly interdependent world. One important consequence of this has been the growth of the executive's legislative powers, and its encroachment on the traditional responsibilities of the assembly.

Not only do political executives usually initiate legislative programmes and help, by persuasion or direction, to make the legislative process work, but, in many cases, they also exercise a wide range of law-making powers, using decrees, orders and other instruments. However, it is misleading to imply that the political executive always dominates the policy process. Much policy, for instance, is initiated by political parties and interest groups. Moreover, by virtue of their expertise and specialist knowledge, bureaucrats or civil servants may play a crucial role in policy formulation, at best leaving the political executive to establish the overall direction of government policy.

Popular leadership

The popularity of the political executive, more than any other part of the political system, is crucial to the character and stability of the regime as a whole. At a policy level, it is the ability of the executive to mobilise support that ensures the compliance and cooperation of the general public. Quite simply, without support from the public, or from key groups in society, policy implementation becomes difficult, perhaps impossible. More importantly, the political executive's popularity is linked to the legitimacy of the broader regime. The unpopularity of a particular government or administration does not in itself weaken support for the political system, but it may do so in the absence of a mechanism for removing and replacing that government. This goes some way towards explaining the widespread use of regular and competitive elections. Of course, this is not to say that unpopular and immovable executives always spell systemic breakdown. Such regimes can survive, but only by resorting to authoritarianism (see p. 36), meaning that popular compliance is brought about through repression and ideological manipulation.

Bureaucratic leadership

Its task of overseeing the implementation of policy means that the political executive has major bureaucratic and administrative responsibilities. In this sense, chief executives, ministers and secretaries constitute a 'top management' charged with running the machinery of government. This work is largely organised along departmental lines, senior ministers having responsibility for particular policy areas and for the bureaucrats engaged to administer those areas. At a higher level, there is a need for policy coordination, which is usually accomplished through some kind of cabinet system.

However, doubts have been expressed about the effectiveness of this bureaucratic leadership. First, as political executives are staffed by politicians, they often lack the competence, managerial experience and administrative knowledge to control a sprawling bureaucratic machine effectively. Secondly, particular government departments can develop their own interests, especially when they forge alliances with powerful client groups. Thirdly, the bureaucracy as a whole can develop interests that are separate from those of the political executive, encouraging it to resist the control of its notional political masters. These issues are examined in greater detail in Chapter 17 in relation to bureaucratic power.

Crisis leadership

A crucial advantage that the political executive has over the assembly is its ability to take swift and decisive action. When crises break out in either domestic or international politics, it is invariably the executive that responds, by virtue of its hierarchical structure and the scope it provides for personal leadership. It is therefore common for assemblies to grant political executives near-dictatorial powers in times of war, and for executives to seize 'emergency powers' when confronted by domestic crises such as natural disasters, terrorist threats, industrial unrest and civil disorder. Clearly, however, the power to declare 'states of emergency' and to impose effective executive rule is subject to abuse. Not uncommonly, governments have used these powers to weaken or eradicate political opposition under the guise of constitutionalism.

Power in the executive: who leads?

As already noted, the roles and responsibilities of the political executive have been substantially enhanced by the emergence of democratic politics, growing government intervention, and political and economic globalisation. During the twentieth century, political executives have acquired ever wider policy making and legislative responsibilities, taken command of sprawling bureaucratic machines, and increasingly become the focus of popular politics and media attention. These developments have, in turn, profoundly affected the internal organisation of the executive branch of government, and the distribution of power within it. By common consent, the main beneficiary of this process has been the chief executive. Heads of government now commonly have institutional responsibilities, a political status, and a public profile that sets them clearly apart from their cabinet or ministerial colleagues. Nevertheless, this image of growing centralisation and the rise of personal power

Concept

Presidential government

A presidential system of government is characterised by a constitutional and political separation of powers between the legislative and executive branches of government. Executive power is thus vested in an independently elected president who is not directly accountable to or removable by the assembly.

The principal features of a presidential system are the following:

- The executive and the legislature are separately elected, and each is invested with a range of independent constitutional powers.
- The roles of head of state and head of government (the chief executive) are combined in the office of the presidency.
- Executive authority is concentrated in the hands of the president, the cabinet and ministers being merely advisers responsible to the president.
- There is a formal separation of the personnel of the legislative and the executive branches (except in semi-presidential systems).
- Electoral terms are fixed. The president can neither 'dissolve' the legislature nor be dismissed by it (except through **impeachment**).

Impeachment: A formal process for the removal of a public official in the event of personal or professional wrongdoing.

Semi-presidential system: A system of government in which a separately elected president presides over a government drawn from, and accountable to, the assembly.

conflicts sharply with evidence of leadership failure, and the growing incapacity of chief executives to carry out what people have elected them to do. The complex dynamics of executive power can be examined more closely by looking at the roles of presidents, prime ministers and cabinets.

In each of these three cases, however, three dimensions of power must be borne in mind:

- the *formal* dimension of power: the constitutional roles and responsibilities of executive officers and the institutional frameworks in which they operate
- the *informal* dimension of power: the role of personality, political skills and experience, and the impact of factors such as parties and the mass media
- the *external* dimension of power: the political, economic and diplomatic context of government, and the broader pressures that bear on the executive branch.

Presidents

A president is a formal head of state, a title which is held in other states by a monarch or emperor. An important distinction, however, must be made between constitutional presidents and executive presidents. Constitutional or nonexecutive presidents, found in India, Israel and Germany, for example, are a feature of parliamentary systems and have responsibilities largely confined to ceremonial duties. In these circumstances, the president is a mere figurehead, and executive power is wielded by a prime minister and/or a cabinet. This section is concerned with executive presidents, who combine the formal responsibilities of a head of state with the political power of a chief executive. Presidencies of this kind constitute the basis of what is called presidential government, as opposed to parliamentary government (see p. 295).

Presidential executives may be either limited or unlimited. Limited presidential executives operate within constraints imposed by a constitution, political democracy, party competition, and some form of separation of powers (see p. 297). Above all, the powers of the president are counterbalanced by those of a popularly accountable assembly. The best-known example of limited presidentialism is found in the USA, but **semi-presidential systems** like those in France and Finland also conform to this model. In unlimited presidential executives, on the other hand, the president is invested with near-unchecked powers, meaning that these regimes are effectively dictatorships (see p. 363). They are commonly found in one-party states that rest heavily on the support of the military. Unlimited executives can be found, for example, in Libya, Iraq and Indonesia.

US-style presidential government has spawned imitations throughout the world, mainly in Latin America and, more recently, in postcommunist states such as Poland, the Czech Republic and Russia. In investing executive power in a presidency, the architects of the US constitution were aware that they were, in effect, creating an 'elective kingship'. Wishing to avoid the abuse of power they believed had occurred under the British Crown, they established an intricate separation of powers between the legislative, executive and judicial branches. This was more accurately described by Richard Neustadt ([1964] 1980) as 'separated institutions sharing powers'. Thus, although the president was designated head of state, chief executive, commander-in-chief of the armed forces and chief diplomat, and was granted wide-ranging powers of patronage and the right to veto legislation, Congress was invested with strong counterbalancing powers. In particular, Congress could declare war and override presidential vetoes, and the Senate was empowered to approve appointments and ratify treaties. Indeed, until the early twentieth century, the presidency remained a generally secondary institution; such policy leadership as was required was provided by Congress.

The status of the US presidency was then transformed by two key developments. First, a national economy developed that required the government to abandon its traditional *laissez-faire* policies and adopt a more interventionist approach to economic and social life. Secondly, the USA was forced to drop its policy if isolationism and accept a world role, assuming after the Second World War a superpower status in a bipolar (and now, arguably, unipolar) world system. Since President Franklin Roosevelt's New Deal in the 1930s, US presidents have played the role of chief legislator, and since 1945 have worn the mantle of the leader of the 'free world'. Alarmed by the ease with which President Johnson and President Nixon escalated the Vietnam War without war being formally declared by Congress, Arthur Schlesinger (1974) went so far as to proclaim the emergence of an 'imperial presidency', a presidency that had broken free from its constitutional bounds and threatened to dominate the two other branches of government.

Presidential power is nevertheless often fragile and insubstantial. Neustadt's classic text *Presidential Power* ([1964] 1980) remains correct: the chief power of the US president is the 'power to persuade', that is, the ability to bargain, encourage, and even cajole, but not dictate. The ability of US presidents to get their way depends on four crucial relationships, specifically those with:

- Congress
- the federal bureaucracy
- the Supreme Court
- the mass media.

The president's relationship with Congress is undoubtedly the most crucial. The success of particular presidents, for instance, is often quantified in terms of their 'success rate' with Congress, that is, the proportion of their legislative programme that survives congressional scrutiny. Following the Vietnam War and the Watergate scandal, however, presidents have had to confront more assertive Congresses, intent on reclaiming some of their lost powers. An early example of this was the passage of the War Powers Act 1974, which meant that congressional support was required for the dispatching of US troops abroad. More significantly, the USA's relatively weak party system deprives the president of the major lever of legislative control available to parliamentary executives: an appeal to party unity. This means, as President Jimmy Carter discovered in the 1970s, that presidents can be rebuffed by Congress even when both houses are dominated by their own party.

Presidents may be weaker still when they are confronted by a Congress that is controlled by the opposition party. This was the problem that President Clinton experienced after the election of a Republican Congress in 1994. The difficulty confronting the president is that, regardless of party affiliation, both Representatives and Senators are primarily concerned with the 'folks back home'. Indeed, the interest that this forces them to take in domestic affairs has encouraged commentators to speak of the 'two presidencies'. These are the 'domestic' presidency, which is typically characterised by policy failure and gridlock, and from which most presidents retreat, and the 'foreign' presidency, to which they gravitate in the hope of demonstrating their leadership credentials. Even President Clinton, elected to office on a promise to focus 'like a laser beam' on the economy, could not avoid, in Rose's (1987) words, 'going international'.

In theory, the federal bureaucracy exists to serve the president, but in practice it often acts as an embarrassing constraint. Although presidents make, directly or indirectly, about 3000 appointments at senior and middle-ranking levels in their administrations, this is tiny in proportion to the total number of professional bureaucrats in the US, who number over 2 000 000. Moreover, it is widely argued that these bureaucrats frequently respond to interests at odds with the priorities of the administration. As Secretary of the Navy under Woodrow Wilson, F. D. Roosevelt described influencing the Navy Department as like punching a feather mattress: 'you punch and punch but it remains the same'. In his famous comment on his successor, General Eisenhower, President Truman referred to a similar problem:

He'll sit here and he'll say 'Do this! Do that!' and nothing will happen. Poor Ike – it won't be a bit like the Army.

Similar difficulties exist in relation to the Supreme Court. Since the 1950s, the court has played a significant role in US political life, forcing presidents to shape the political agenda, in part, by exercising influence over it. Although presidents appoint justices to the Supreme Court, these appointments may be rejected by the Senate (as Nixon discovered twice and Reagan once), and, once they have been appointed, judges cannot be controlled because of their security of tenure. Much of the New Deal programme in the 1930s was blocked by the Supreme Court, until F. D. Roosevelt was able to shift its ideological balance through the 'court revolution' of 1937. Eisenhower, in turn, appointed Earl Warren as Chief Justice, only later discovering his taste for judicial activism and his liberal interpretation of the constitution.

The final key relationship is that between the US president and the mass media. The media are vital to presidents who need to appeal directly to the US public 'over the heads of Congress'. In this respect, presidents like Ronald Reagan, a former actor and journalist, have been remarkably successful in 'managing' media coverage and ensuring favourable comment. Nevertheless, presidents who live by the media may also die by it. The mass media is often portrayed as the USA's fourth branch of government, and prizes both its political independence and its reputation for seeking truth. *The Washington Post*'s exposure of the Watergate scandal eventually led to the resignation of President Nixon in 1974, and relentless coverage of the Whitewater affair seriously weakened the Clinton administration in the early 1990s.

To some extent, the example of the US presidency influenced Mikhail Gorbachev's political reforms in the USSR and his decision to construct an executive presidency in 1990. Executive power in the USSR had previously been invested in the highest organs of the CPSU, notably the Central Committee and the Politburo, with the general secretary of the Communist Party serving as the nearest thing to a chief executive. The attraction of a presidential system loosely based on US practice was that it promised to emancipate Gorbachev from the clutches of a Communist Party that was increasingly perceived to be hostile to the reform process. However, there was a fatal weakness in President Gorbachev's position. Since he had only been elected indirectly, via the newly established Congress of People's Deputies, he lacked an electoral base and a popular mandate. This proved to be crucial at the time of the August 1991 coup, when opposition forces coalesced around the democratically elected Russian president, Boris Yeltsin, as he was barricaded in his parliament building in Moscow.

In the early postcommunist period in Russia, President Yeltsin's political authority was undoubtedly bolstered by his reputation as a critic of the CPSU and an opponent of corruption and bureaucracy. The potential within presidential systems for institutional conflict was nevertheless realised as the Russian parliament came increasingly under the control of hardliners intent on resisting Yeltsin's 'shock therapy' reform package. Ultimately, Yeltsin's presidency only survived because of the support of the military in crushing the parliament's rebellion in October 1993, which led to the imposition of presidential rule. The possibility of the emergence in Russia of an unlimited presidential executive was, however, off-set by Yeltsin's need to balance the volatile and conflicting pressures within the Russian political system. Caught between radical reformers, conservative hardliners and die-hard nationalists, Yeltsin struggled to hold on to electoral credibility and maintain the effectiveness of his government.

A different form of presidential government is found in semi-presidential systems, such as those in France, Austria, Finland and Portugal. These are hybrid systems. They comprise, as in presidential systems, a separately elected president invested with a range of executive powers and, as in parliamentary systems, a government, usually featuring a prime minister and a cabinet, drawn from and accountable to the assembly. In Finland and Austria, for example, such systems operate largely through a division of executive responsibilities, allowing the president to concentrate on foreign affairs and broader constitutional issues, while the prime minister and cabinet take charge of domestic policy.

However, the system constructed in the Fifth French Republic, and completed with the introduction of a separately elected president in 1962, is significantly more complex. On the one hand, in addition to carrying out the roles that the US president plays as head of state, chief executive and dispenser of appointments, French presidents enjoy a fixed seven-year term in office, and can also bring the legislature to heel by using their power to dissolve the National Assembly. On the other hand, they are seriously constrained by the need for their governments to maintain parliamentary and public support. Thus presidents like de Gaulle in 1958–69, Pompidou in 1969–74, and Giscard d'Estaing in 1974–81 derived their strength largely from the control Gaullist forces exercised in the National Assembly. However, the right to call a general election does not necessarily guarantee party control of the National Assembly, as the Socialist President Mitterrand discovered in 1986, and again in 1993, when he was forced into cohabitation with Gaullist governments, led first by Chirac and then Balladur. Similarly, despite the fact that he possessed the formal powers of an elected monarch, de Gaulle's presidency ended in resignation in 1969 after the student riots of May 1968 and a financial crisis. The fragility of presidential power was also demonstrated by the pressures on President Chirac after 1995 that arose from the wide-ranging and sometimes conflicting expectations that his election campaign had stimulated.

Focus on . . .

The monarchy debate

A monarchy is a system of the rule dominated by one person (it literally means 'rule by one person'). In general usage, however, it is the institution through which the post of head of state is filled through inheritance or dynastic succession. In absolute monarchies, the monarch claims, if seldom exercises, a monopoly of political power (examples being Saudi Arabia, Nepal and Morocco). In constitutional monarchies, the monarch fulfils an essentially ceremonial function largely devoid of political significance (for example, in Spain, the Netherlands and the UK).

The advantages of a constitutional monarchy are as follows:

- It provides a solution to the need for a nonpartisan head of state who is 'above' party politics.
- The monarch embodies traditional authority and so serves as a symbol of patriotic loyalty and national unity.
- The monarch constitutes a repository of experience and wisdom, especially in relation to constitutional matters, available to elected governments.

The disadvantages of a constitutional monarchy include the following:

- It violates democratic principles in that political authority is not based on popular consent and is in no way publicly accountable.
- The monarch symbolises (and possibly supports) conservative values such as hierarchy, deference and respect for inherited wealth and social position.
- The monarchy binds nations to outmoded ways and symbols of the past, thus impeding progress.

Prime ministers

Most of the political executives in the modern world can be classified as parliamentary executives. The structure and form of executive power found in parliamentary systems differs significantly from that in presidential ones. Parliamentary executives have three essential features. First, since executive power is derived from the assembly and closely linked to party politics, a separate head of state, in the form of a constitutional monarch or nonexecutive president, is required to fulfil ceremonial duties and act as a focus of patriotic loyalty. Secondly, the political executive is drawn from the assembly, which means that the separation of the personnel between the legislature and executive found in presidential systems does not occur in parliamentary systems. Thirdly, the executive is directly responsible to the assembly, or at least to its lower chamber, in the sense that it survives in government only as long as it retains the confidence of the assembly.

The external dynamics of executive power in parliamentary systems thus contrast sharply with those found in presidential ones. In short, parliamentary executives are forced to govern in and through assemblies, while presidential executives tend to rely on a personal mandate and an independent set of constitutional powers. This undoubtedly also affects the internal dynamics of power. In particular, it creates a greater pressure in parliamentary executives for collective decision-making and collaboration, often reflected in the higher status of the cabinet in these systems.

However, many commentators have interpreted the growth of prime-ministerial power in terms of the emergence of a form of 'presidentialism' in parliamentary systems.

Prime ministers (sometimes seen as chancellors, as in Germany, minister-presidents as in the Netherlands, or referred to by a local title like the Irish Taoiseach) are heads of government whose power is derived from their leadership of the majority party, or coalition of parties, in the assembly. The range of formal powers with which the office of prime minister is invested are typically modest in comparison with those of executive presidents. The most important of these is the control of patronage – the ability to hire and fire, promote and demote, ministers. In the Netherlands and Australia, for example, even this power is exercised by the assembly or the majority party. As the job of prime minister can only have a loose constitutional description, it is no exaggeration to say that the post is what its holder chooses to make of it or, more accurately, is able to make of it.

In practice, this boils down to two key sets of prime-ministerial relationships. The first set are with the cabinet, individual ministers and government departments; the second with his or her party and, through it, the assembly and the public. The support of the cabinet is particularly crucial to prime ministers who are designated *primus inter pares* (first among equals), such as those in the UK, India and Australia. This status forces prime ministers to operate through a system of collective cabinet government (see p. 328). Their power is therefore a reflection of the degree to which, by patronage, cabinet management and the control of the machinery of government, they can ensure that ministers serve *under* them. In contrast, German chancellors are personally empowered by Article 65 of the Basic Law to decide the general lines of government policy. However, the same article also constrains their power by stipulating that ministers enjoy autonomy in relation to their departments.

There is no doubt that the key to prime-ministerial power and influence lies in his or her position as party leader. Indeed, the modern premiership is largely a product of the emergence of disciplined political parties. Not only is the post of prime minister allocated on the basis of party leadership, but it also provides its holder with a means of controlling the assembly and a base from which the image of a national leader can be constructed. The degree of party unity, the parliamentary strength of the prime minister's party (in particular, whether it rules alone or as a member of a coalition), and the authority vested in the assembly or at least its first chamber, are therefore important determinants of prime-ministerial power. Factional rivalry within the LDP, for instance, ensured that, for much of the postwar period, the tenure of Japanese prime ministers was short (five prime ministers came and went between 1974 and 1982) and cabinets were frequently reconstructed. Similarly, Italy's fragmented party system usually forces prime ministers to play the role of a broker within what tend to be fragile coalition governments. German chancellors, for their part, are restricted by the independence of the *Länder*, the power of the second chamber (the Bundesrat), and the authority of the Constitutional Court, as well as by the autonomy of the Bundesbank.

There is nevertheless agreement that, despite their differing constitutional and political positions, prime-ministerial power has grown in recent years. This results in part from the tendency of the broadcast media in particular to focus on personalities, meaning that prime ministers become a kind of 'brand image' of their parties. The growth of international summitry and foreign visits also provides prime ministers with opportunities to cultivate an image of statesmanship, and gives them

Focus on . . .

Prime-ministerial government: virtues and vices

Prime-ministerial government has two key features. First, the office of prime minister is the central link between the legislative and executive branches of government, its holder being drawn from and accountable to the assembly, and also serving as chief executive and head of the bureaucracy. Secondly, prime-ministerial government reflects the centralisation of executive power in the hands of the prime minister and the effective subordination of both the cabinet and departmental ministers. In this, it parallels presidentialism.

Prime-ministerial government has been criticised for the following reasons:

- It strengthens centralisation by weakening the constraints formerly exerted by the cabinet and government departments.
- It narrows policy debate and weakens scrutiny by excluding criticisms and alternative viewpoints.

However, it can be defended on the following grounds:

- It reflects the personal mandate that prime ministers acquire in general elections.
- It gives government policy clearer direction by checking the centrifugal pressures embodied in departmentalism (see p. 348) and the 'nudge and fudge' of collective decision-making.

scope to portray themselves as national leaders. In some cases, this has led to the allegation that prime ministers have effectively emancipated themselves from cabinet constraints and established a form of prime-ministerial government. For instance, in India, an imperial style of premiership developed under Indira Gandhi and her son Rajiv that reached its peak during the state of emergency, 1975–77. This was possible because of the secure majorities that the Congress party enjoyed in parliament, the ruthless control exerted over the apparatus of central government, and the sway that the Gandhi dynasty continued to exert over important sections of the Indian public.

Allegations of prime-ministerial government have often been made in the UK, associated with commentators such as Crossman (1963) and Mackintosh (1977). The unusual level of power wielded by UK prime ministers stems from various sources, including the following:

- the level and range of their patronage
- their control of the cabinet system, especially their ability to set up and staff cabinet committees
- their ability to dominate Parliament by virtue of single-party majorities and a weak second chamber
- their position as head of the civil service, and the control this gives them over the bureaucratic machine
- their direct access to the media, which enables them to make personalised appeals to the voters.

In Crossman's view, these advantages gave prime ministers 'near presidential powers', turning the cabinet into a US-style advisory body that no longer exercised policy making responsibility. The prime-ministerial government thesis appeared to have become a reality during the 1980s as Margaret Thatcher effectively recast the nature and authority of the office.

What distinguished Thatcher's premiership was the fact that she saw herself as a 'conviction prime minister', her role being to provide ideological leadership and policy coherence, orientated around ideas that came to be called **Thatcherism**. For Michael Foley (1993), this development merely exposed the degree to which an 'authentically British presidency' had come into existence. By this he meant that the structural dynamics of the UK's parliamentary system had come to demand that prime ministers dissociate themselves from the broader cabinet and bureaucratic machines, cultivating the image of 'outsiders'. This strengthened their appeal to ordinary voters and enabled them to practise a form of leadership based on the popular resonance of their personalities, aspirations and personal vision. In these respects, UK prime ministers, like their counterparts in Canada, Australia and New Zealand, have come to adopt a leadership style more commonly associated with US presidents.

Although prime ministers who command cohesive parliamentary majorities can wield power that would be the envy of many a president, they are also subject to important constraints. By no means, for instance, do prime ministers have a free hand in terms of hiring and firing. The need to maintain party unity by ensuring that the various factions and ideological wings of the party are represented in the cabinet, and the pressure in countries such as Canada to maintain regional and linguistic representation, act as important checks on prime-ministerial power. Ultimately, prime ministers are only as powerful as their cabinets, parties and broader political circumstances allow them to be. This can be seen in India, where, following the excesses of the emergency in the 1970s, prime ministers such as Desai, Singh and Rao, leading coalition or minority governments, reduced the size of the prime minister's staff, were willing to respect the autonomy of government departments, and interfered less in the affairs of state governments.

It is also interesting that the power wielded by Margaret Thatcher in the UK may have been less a consequence of her indomitable character and ideological resolution than a reflection of the unusually favourable circumstances that confronted her. Chief amongst these were the weak and divided nature of the Labour opposition, the Falklands victory of 1982, the revival of the world economy in the mid1980s, and, partly as a result of these, the ability of the Conservatives to win three successive elections under her leadership. However, the fragility of prime-ministerial power was underlined by her removal as leader in November 1990.

Support for Thatcher in the 1980s amongst Conservative backbenchers and cabinet colleagues had largely been based on her ability to deliver continued electoral success. Once she was perceived to be an electoral liability, particularly in the light of the need to scrap the poll tax and adopt a less divisive European policy, support slipped away to such an extent that she was unable, when challenged for the leadership by Michael Heseltine, to gain re-election. Similarly, the relative weakness of John Major's premiership in the 1990s stemmed less from his personal inadequacies and more from the greater difficulties his government had to face. These included the UK's slow recovery from the recession of the early 1990s, the diminishing Conservative parliamentary majority after 1992, the party's deepening rift over Europe, and

Thatcherism: The free-market/strong-state ideological stance adopted by Margaret Thatcher; the UK version of the New Right political project.

the fact that the government had to confront a more electorally credible and more effectively led Labour opposition.

Cabinets

Virtually all political executives feature a cabinet of some sort. In France the cabinet is known as the Council of Ministers, and in the USSR it was called the Politburo. A cabinet is a committee of senior ministers who represent the various government departments or ministries. This term is not to be confused with *cabinet*, as used in France and the EU to denote small groups of policy advisers who support individual ministers. The widespread use of cabinets reflects the political and administrative need for collective procedures within the political executive. In the first place, cabinets enable government to present a collective face to assemblies and the public. Without a cabinet, government could appear to be a personal tool wielded by a single individual. Secondly, cabinets are an administrative device designed to ensure the effective coordination of government policy. In short, in the absence of a cabinet, government would consist of rival bureaucratic empires each bent on self-aggrandisement, rather as occurred in the Hitler state in Nazi Germany.

The precise role and political importance of cabinets varies from system to system and state to state. In presidential systems such as the USA's, the cabinet exists to serve the president by acting as a policy adviser rather than a policy maker. Indeed, in the second half of the twentieth century, executive growth in the USA has largely occurred at a non-cabinet level, in the form of the construction of the Executive

Focus on . . .

Cabinet government: advantages and disadvantages

Cabinet government is characterised by two central features. First, the cabinet constitutes the principal link between the legislative and executive branches of government; its members are drawn from and accountable to the parliament, but also serve as the political heads of the various government departments. Secondly, the cabinet is the senior executive organ and policy making responsibility is shared within it, the prime minister being 'first' in name only. This system is usually underpinned by collective responsibility – all the cabinet ministers are required to 'sing the same song' and support official government policy.

The virtues of cabinet government are the following:

- It encourages full and frank policy debate within the democracy of cabinet meetings, subjecting proposals to effective scrutiny.
- It guarantees the unity and cohesion of government, since the cabinet makes decisions collectively and collectively stands by them.

However, cabinet government has been criticised for the following reasons:

- It acts as a cloak for prime-ministerial power because it forces dissenting ministers to support agreed government policy in public.
- It means that government policy becomes incoherent and inconsistent, as decisions are based on compromises between competing ministers and departmental interests.

Office of the President (discussed in Chapter 17). In contrast, the cabinet, in theory at least, is the apex of the executive in states that respect the principle of cabinet government, such as the UK, most Commonwealth countries, and several European ones, including Italy, Sweden and Norway.

It is nevertheless difficult in practice to find examples of collective executives that operate through a cabinet or equivalent body. In theory, a form of collective leadership operated in the USSR, reflecting the Marxist–Leninist belief that the Communist Party, rather than a single leader, was the leading and guiding force in Soviet society. In practice, Communist Party general secretaries from Stalin onwards so dominated the Politburo and its equivalent state body, the Presidium of the Council of Ministers, that all general secretaries were able to remain in office until they died, with the exception of Khrushchev, the victim of a party coup in 1964, and Gorbachev. In Germany, and commonly throughout continental Europe, a tradition of departmental specialisation discourages ministers from seeing themselves as 'team players' and so counters any tendency towards cabinet government. Even in the UK system, supposedly the archetypal example of cabinet government, it is difficult to see the cabinet as a decision-making body, and still less as a democratic forum.

Not only has the rise of prime-ministerial power subverted the collective nature of UK government, but the growth in the range and complexity of government policy has also ensured that most decisions are effectively made elsewhere, and thus reach the cabinet in a prepackaged form. This highlights the important contribution that government departments make to policy formulation, as well as the impact of cabinet committees and, indeed, subcommittees. In the UK and elsewhere, the full cabinet is merely the hub of a cabinet *system*, comprising committees of subject specialists able to examine policy proposals in greater detail and depth than is possible in the cabinet itself. This system weakens the cabinet both because it strengthens the levers of control that are available to the prime minister, who sets up and staffs committees, and because full cabinets usually lack the time and expertise to challenge proposals that emanate from committees.

On the other hand, it would be a mistake to dismiss cabinets as merely 'dignified' institutions. Many prime ministers, for example, have paid a high price for ignoring the collective element within modern government. German chancellors are generally considered to be even stronger than UK prime ministers because they can only be removed by a vote of 'constructive no confidence'. This means that the Bundestag can only remove a government by approving an alternative one, not merely by withdrawing support from the existing one (as occurs in the UK). Nevertheless, Chancellor Schmidt was forced to resign in 1982 when the small Free Democratic Party withdrew from his Social-Democrat-led coalition cabinet to join forces with the Christian Democrats, led by Helmut Kohl. Coalitions certainly add to the difficulties of cabinet management, as Italian prime ministers have regularly discovered, but a single-party cabinet can also cause problems for chief executives.

Margaret Thatcher's resignation in 1990 was, to a significant degree, a consequence of her declining support within the cabinet. The resignations of senior ministers such as Heseltine in 1986, Lawson in 1989, and eventually Howe in October 1990 undoubtedly weakened her authority and damaged her public standing. Indeed, in her own version of the events of November 1990, Thatcher claimed to have been ousted by a cabinet coup through the withdrawal of ministerial support once she had failed to secure re-election as party leader on the first ballot (Thatcher, 1993). Bob Hawke's removal as Australian prime minister in 1991 reinforces the lesson that parliamentary leaders cannot long survive without cabinet support. Having resisted a leadership bid by his deputy, Paul Keating, in the early summer, Hawke tried to rebuild his authority by sacking his federal treasurer, John Kerin, in the December, only to be toppled by Keating's second challenge.

■ The politics of leadership

In some respects, the subject of political leadership appears to be outdated. The division of society into leaders and followers is rooted in a predemocratic culture of deference and respect in which leaders 'knew best' and the public needed to be led, mobilised or guided. Democratic politics may not have removed the need for leaders, but it has certainly placed powerful constraints on leadership, notably by making leaders publicly accountable and establishing an institutional mechanism through which they can be removed. In other respects, however, the politics of leadership has become increasingly significant, helping to contribute to the establishment of a separate discipline of political psychology, whose major concerns include a study of the psychological makeup and motivations of political leaders (Kressel, 1993).

This growing focus on leadership has occurred for a number of reasons. For instance, to some extent, democracy itself has enhanced the importance of personality by forcing political leaders, in effect, to 'project themselves' in the hope of gaining electoral support. This tendency has undoubtedly been strengthened by modern means of mass communication (especially television), which tend to emphasise personalities rather than policies, and provide leaders with powerful weapons with which to manipulate their public images. Furthermore, as society becomes more complex and fragmented, people may increasingly look to the personal vision of individual leaders to give coherence and meaning to the world in which they live.

Theories of leadership

The question of political leadership is surrounded by controversy. To what extent is leadership compatible with freedom and democracy? Does leadership inspire and motivate, or does it subdue and repress? Are strong leaders to be admired or feared? At the heart of these disagreements lie differing views about the nature of political leadership. What does the phenomenon of leadership consist of? Where does leadership come from? Four contrasting theories of leadership can be identified:

- leadership as a *personal* gift
- leadership as a *sociological* phenomenon
- leadership as an *organisational* necessity
- leadership as a *political* skill.

Concept

Leadership

Leadership can either be understood as a pattern of behaviour or as a personal quality. As a pattern of behaviour, leadership is the influence exerted by an individual or group over a larger body to organise or direct its efforts towards the achievement of desired goals. As a personal attribute, leadership refers to the character traits which enable the leader to exert influence over others; leadership is thus effectively equated with charisma (see p. 195).

Among the virtues of leadership are the following:

- It mobilises and inspires people who would otherwise be inert and directionless.
- It promotes unity and encourages members of a group to pull in the same direction.
- It strengthens organisations by establishing a hierarchy of responsibilities and roles.

The dangers of leadership include the following:

- It concentrates power, and can thus lead to corruption and tyranny, hence the democratic demand that leadership be checked by accountability.
- It engenders subservience and deference, thereby discouraging people from taking responsibility for their own lives.
- It narrows debate and argument, because of its emphasis on ideas flowing down from the top, rather than up from the bottom.

Friedrich Nietzsche (1844–1900)

German philosopher. Nietzsche was a professor of Greek at Basel by the age of 25. He abandoned theology for philology, and became increasingly interested in the ideas of Schopenhauer (1788–1860) and the music of Wagner (1813–83). Growing illness and insanity after 1889 brought him under the control of his sister Elizabeth, who edited and distorted his writings. Nietzsche's complex and ambitious work stressed the importance of will, especially the 'will to power', and it anticipated modern existentialism in emphasising that people create their own worlds and make their own values. His best known writings include *Thus Spake Zarathustra* (1883/84), *Beyond Good and Evil* (1886) and *On the Genealogy of Morals* (1887).

The traditional view of leadership sees it as a rare but natural gift. As Aristotle (see p. 7) put it, 'men are marked out from the moment of birth to rule or be ruled'. From this perspective, leadership is strictly an individual quality, manifest in the personalities of what were traditionally thought of as 'men of destiny'. The most extreme version of this theory is found in the fascist 'leader principle' (*Führerprinzip*). This is based on the idea of a single, supreme leader (always male), who alone is capable of leading the masses to their destiny. Such an idea was in part derived from Friedrich Nietzsche's notion of the *Übermensch* ('superman'), who rises above the 'herd instinct' of conventional morality and so achieves self-mastery. In a more modest form, this theory of leadership is embodied in the idea of charisma, generally understood to mean the power of personality. The classic examples of charismatic leaders are usually seen as forceful personalities (such as Hitler, Castro, Nasser and Thatcher), although the more modest, but no less effective, 'fireside chats' of F. D. Roosevelt and the practised televisual skills of almost all modern leaders also exemplify charismatic qualities. However, unfortunately, leaders who exhibit genuine moral authority, such as Nelson Mandela and the Dalai Lama (see Figure 16.1), are rare.

Modern political psychology adopts a similar view of leadership, in that it analyses it in terms of human personality. One of the earliest attempts to do this was the collaboration in the late 1920s between Sigmund Freud (1856–1939) and William C. Bullitt on a controversial psychological study of President Woodrow Wilson (Freud and Bullitt, 1967). Harold Lasswell's ground-breaking *Psychopathology and Politics* (1930) suggested that leaders are largely motivated by private, almost pathological, conflicts, which are then rationalised in terms of actions taken in the public interest. A widely discussed modern analysis of political leadership has been advanced by James Barber (1988). Focusing on what he called 'presidential character', Barber categorised US presidents according to two key variables: first, whether they were 'active' or 'passive' in terms of the energy they put into their jobs, and, secondly, whether they were 'positive' or 'negative' in terms of how they felt about political office. He therefore identified four character types:

- active–positive (for example, Kennedy, Bush and Clinton)
- active–negative (for example, Harding and Reagan)

Fig. 16.1 President Nelson Mandela and the Dalai Lama in Cape Town, South Africa, in 1996

- passive–positive (for example, Johnson and Nixon)
- passive–negative (for example, Coolidge and Eisenhower).

An alternative view of leadership sees it as a sociological, rather than psychological, phenomenon. From this perspective, in other words, leaders are 'created' by particular socio-historical forces. They do not so much impose their will on the world as act as a vehicle through which historical forces are exerted. This is certainly the approach adopted by Marxists, who believe that historical development is largely structured by economic factors, reflected in a process of class struggle. The personalities of individual leaders are thus less important than the broader class interests they articulate. Marx nevertheless acknowledged that **Bonapartism** was an exception. This was a phenomenon based on Louis Bonaparte's *coup d'état* in France in 1851, through which a personal dictatorship was established in conditions in which the bourgeoisie had lost power, but the proletariat was not sufficiently developed to seize it. Even in this case, however, Marx insisted that the Bonapartist dictatorship reflected the interests of the numerically strongest class in France, the smallholding peasantry. Similarly, in analysing Stalinism in the USSR, Trotsky (see p. 343) emphasised the degree to which Stalin's power was rooted in the dominance of the

Bonapartism: A style of government that fuses personal leadership with conservative nationalism; for Marxists, it reflects the relative autonomy of the state.

state bureaucracy (Trotsky, 1937). Sociological factors have also provided the basis for the very different idea that political leadership is largely a product of collective behaviour. In his seminal *The Crowd* ([1895] 1960), Gustav Le Bon analysed the dynamics of crowd psychology, arguing that leaders are impelled by the collective behaviour of the masses, not the other way round.

The third theory of leadership sees it in largely technical terms as a rational or bureaucratic device. In this view, leadership is essentially an organisational necessity that arises from the need for coherence, unity and direction within any complex institution. Leadership therefore goes hand in hand with bureaucracy (see p. 341). Modern large-scale organisations require specialisation and a division of labour, which, in turn, give rise to a hierarchy of offices and responsibilities. This bureaucratic leadership conforms to what Weber (see p. 194) called legal–rational authority, in that it is essentially impersonal and based on formal, usually written, rules. The rise of constitutional government has undoubtedly invested political leadership with a strongly bureaucratic character by ensuring that power is vested in a political office rather than the individual office holder. This nevertheless conflicts with democratic pressures that force political leaders to cultivate charisma and emphasise personal qualities in order to win and retain power.

The final theory of leadership portrays it very much as an artefact, that is, as a political skill that can be learned and practised. Political leadership in this sense is akin to the art of manipulation, a perhaps inevitable feature of democratic politics in an age of mass communications. This can be seen most graphically in the cults of personality that have been constructed to support the dictatorial leaderships of figures such as Mao Zedong, Colonel Gaddafi and Saddam Hussein. Indeed, many of the classic examples of charismatic leadership can in practice be seen as forms of manufactured leadership. Stalin, for example, bolstered his own popularity by building up an elaborate cult of Lenin in the 1920s; he erected statues, renamed streets and towns, and placed Lenin's embalmed body in a mausoleum in Red Square. During the 1930s, having carefully linked himself to Lenin's heritage, Stalin transferred this cult to himself.

Similarly, Hitler's performances at the Nuremburg rallies were carefully stage managed by Albert Speer. His every word and gesture were carefully rehearsed and choreographed; the whole event was designed to build up emotional tension that would be released by Hitler's appearance. Modern democratic politicians have no less strong a need to project themselves and their personal vision, though the skills appropriate to the television age are modest and refined compared with those suitable for mass rallies and public demonstrations. Leadership nevertheless remains an artefact; its emphasis has simply shifted towards televisual skills, the use of 'sound bites', and a reliance upon media advisers or 'spin doctors'.

Styles of leadership

A style of leadership refers to the strategies and behavioural patterns through which a leader seeks to achieve his or her goals. Quite simply, leaders are not all alike: leadership can be exercised in a number of different ways. The factors that shape the adoption of a particular leadership strategy or style are, of course, numerous. Amongst the most obvious are the personality and goals of the leader, the institutional framework within which he or she operates, the political mechanisms by which power is won and retained, the means of mass communication available, and

Concept

Cult of personality

A cult of personality (or cult of leadership) is a propaganda device through which a political leader is portrayed as a heroic or God-like figure. By treating the leader as the source of all political wisdom and an unfailing judge of the national interest, the cult implies that any form of criticism or opposition amounts to treachery or lunacy. Cults of personality have typically been developed in totalitarian regimes (first by Stalin) through the exploitation of the possibilities of modern means of mass communication, and the use of state repression to cultivate a form of ritualised idolatrisation. However, the point at which routine propaganda (found in all systems) becomes a fully fledged 'cult' may be unclear in practice.

the nature of the broader political culture. Three distinctive styles of leadership have been identified (Burns, 1978):

- *laissez-faire* leadership
- transactional leadership
- transformational leadership.

The chief feature of *laissez-faire* leadership is the reluctance of the leader to interfere in matters outside his or her personal responsibility. Such leaders have a 'hands off' approach to cabinet and departmental management. An example of such leadership could be found in the Reagan White House, and the relatively slight interest Reagan took in the day-to-day workings of his administration. A *laissez-faire* style is not irreconcilable with ideological leadership, but it certainly requires that ideological goals constitute only a broadly-stated strategic vision. The strengths of this approach to leadership are that, because subordinates are given greater responsibility, it can foster harmony and teamwork, and it can allow leaders to concentrate on political and electoral matters by relieving them of their managerial burdens. On the other hand, it can also lead to the weak coordination of government policy, with ministers and officials being allowed too much scope to pursue their own interests and initiatives. The Iran–Contra affair, for example, demonstrated how little President Reagan knew about the activities of the Central Intelligence Agency officers and White House officials for whom he was supposedly responsible.

In contrast, transactional leadership is a more 'hands-on' style of leadership. Transactional leaders adopt a positive role in relation to policy making and government management, but are motivated by essentially pragmatic goals and considerations. Prominent amongst these are likely to be the maintenance of party unity and government cohesion, and the strengthening of public support and electoral credibility. Such leaders act as brokers who are concerned to uphold the collegiate face of government by negotiating compromises and balancing rival individuals, factions and interests against one another. In the USA, Lyndon Johnson and George Bush could be seen as transactional leaders, as could Harold Wilson and John Major in the UK. This is above all a managerial, even technocratic, style of leadership, its advantage being that it is fiercely practical and allows scope for tactical flexibility. Its central drawback, however, is that such leaders may be seen as opportunistic wheeler-dealers who are devoid of firm principles or deep convictions. This was illustrated by George Bush's damaging admission during the 1992 US presidential election that he did not understand what he called 'the vision thing'.

In the third style of leadership, transformational leadership, the leader is not so much a coordinator or manager as an inspirer or visionary. Not only are such leaders motivated by strong ideological convictions, but they also have the personal resolution and political will to put them into practice. Instead of seeking compromise and consensus, transformational leaders attempt to mobilise support from within government, their parties and the general public for the realisation of their personal vision. Howard Gardner (1996) suggested that a leader is 'an individual who creates a story'. The effectiveness of such a leader hinges on the degree to which the leader in question 'embodies' the story, and the extent to which the story resonates with the broader public.

General de Gaulle, for instance, recast the nature of political leadership in France as much by presenting himself as a 'father figure' and 'national leader' as by establishing a presidential system in the form of the Fifth Republic. A very similar style was adopted in the UK by Margaret Thatcher, whose avowed aim when coming into office was to run a 'conviction government'. The continued use of terms such as Gaullism and Thatcherism bears witness to the enduring impact of these leaders' ideological visions. Not uncommonly, transformational leadership is linked to populism, reflecting the desire of such leaders to demonstrate that they are articulating the concerns and interests of 'the people'. Although the strength of transformational leadership is that it provides a basis for pushing through radical programmes of social, economic or political reform, it may also encourage a drift towards authoritarianism and lead to ideological rigidity. It is thus possible to see Thatcher herself as one of the casualties of Thatcherism, in that in 1990 she paid the price for her domineering leadership style and her unwillingness to change policy priorities even when these had become electorally unpopular.

Regardless of the leadership style they adopt, there are reasons to believe that modern political leaders face greater challenges than their predecessors did. This is important, because attitudes towards leaders, and the perceived effectiveness of leadership, does much to influence people's general view of the political process. The first difficulty that leaders face is that modern societies have perhaps become so complex and enmeshed with global influences that politicians find it almost impossible to get things done. Leaders are therefore doomed to disappoint, to fail to live up to expectations. Secondly, leaders suffer because old ideological and moral certainties are breaking down, and this makes it more difficult to construct compelling narratives that have wide popular resonance.

Thirdly, modern societies are becoming more diverse and fragmented. Political leaders are therefore finding it increasingly difficult to construct a political appeal based on a common culture and a set of shared values. Fourthly and finally, a cultural gap has perhaps developed between the political and the nonpolitical worlds. Political leaders are increasingly career politicians whose lifestyles, sensibilities and even language are remote from the concerns of private citizens. Far from being seen as providing inspiration and articulating popular hopes and aspirations, modern leaders tend to be viewed as self-serving and out of touch. To the extent that this is true, people become alienated from conventional politics, and perhaps look elsewhere for a source of political leadership.

Concept

Populism

Populism (from the Latin *populus*, meaning 'the people') has been used to describe both distinctive political movements and a particular tradition of political thought. Movements or parties described as populist have been characterised by their claim to support the common people in the face of 'corrupt' economic or political elites. As a political tradition, populism reflects the belief that the instincts and wishes of the people provide the principal legitimate guide to political action. Populist politicians therefore make a direct appeal to the people and claim to give expression to their deepest hopes and fears, all intermediary institutions being distrusted. Although populism may be linked with any cause or ideology, it is often seen to be implicitly authoritarian, 'populist' democracy being the enemy of 'pluralist' democracy (see p. 77).

■ Summary

◆ The executive branch of government is responsible for the execution or implementation of policy. The political executive comprises a core of senior figures and is roughly equivalent to 'the government of the day' or 'the administration'. The bureaucratic executive consists of public officials or civil servants. However, the political/bureaucratic distinction is often blurred by the complexities of the policy making process.

◆ Political executives act as the 'commanding heights' of the state apparatus and carry out a number of leadership roles. These include representing the state on ceremonial occasions, offering policy making leadership in relation to strategic priorities, mobilising popular support for the government or administration, overseeing the bureaucratic machine, and taking the initiative in the event of domestic or international crises.

◆ Presidential executives concentrate executive power in the hands of a president who combines the roles of head of state and head of government, but confronts an assembly that enjoys constitutional and political independence. Prime ministers in parliamentary systems operate through two key sets of relationships: the first is with their cabinets, ministers and departments, and the second is with their parties and the assembly from which their power stems.

◆ The power of chief executives has been enhanced by the tendency of the media and electoral politics to focus on personality and image, by the opportunities to display statesmanship provided by international affairs and summitry, and by the need for political and ideological leadership within an increasingly large and complex executive branch. Their power is nevertheless checked by the importance of government and party unity, the need to maintain support in the assembly, and the difficulty of controlling the sprawling bureaucratic machine.

◆ Political leadership has been understood in various ways. It has been interpreted as a personal gift based on individual qualities such as charisma, as a sociological phenomenon in which leaders express particular socio-historical forces, as an organisational necessity rooted in the need for coherence and unity of direction, and as a political skill that can be learned by leaders intent on manipulating their colleagues and the masses.

◆ Leaders have adopted very different strategies to achieve their goals. *Laissez-faire* leadership attempts to foster harmony and teamwork by broadening the responsibilities of subordinates. Transactional leadership allows leaders to act as brokers and balance rival factions and interests against each other. Transformational leadership places a heavy emphasis on the mobilisation of support through the leader's capacity to inspire and to advance a personal vision.

▮ Questions for discussion

▶ In what circumstances may heads of state play a significant political role?

▶ Is the only power that a chief executive possesses the power to persuade?

▶ Are presidents or prime ministers more powerful?

▶ Is collective cabinet government a principle worth preserving?

▶ Should strong leaders be admired or feared?

▶ Are cults of personality a feature of all political systems, not just dictatorial ones?

▶ Do we get the political leaders we deserve?

▮ Further reading

Elgie, R. *Political Leadership in Liberal Democracies* (Basingstoke: Macmillan, 1995). A good and accessible analysis of the dynamics of political leadership.

Gardner, H. *Leading Minds* (London: Harper Collins, 1996). A fascinating exploration of the nature of leadership and the skills and strategies deployed by leaders.

Rose, R. *The Postmodern Presidency: The White House Meets the World* (2nd ed.) (New York: Chartham House, 1991). A stimulating analysis that examines the 'no win' theory of presidential power.

Weller, P. *First Among Equals: Prime Ministers in Westminster Systems* (Sydney: Allen & Unwin, 1985). A useful discussion of parliamentary executives in Australia, the UK, Canada and New Zealand.

Bureaucracies

CHAPTER 17

> 'Bureaucracy is a giant mechanism operated by pygmies.'
>
> HONORÉ DE BALZAC *Epigrams*

To many, the term bureaucracy suggests inefficiency and pointless and time-consuming formalities: in short, 'red tape'. In the field of politics, bureaucracy refers to the administrative machinery of the state, that is, the massed ranks of civil servants and public officials who are charged with the execution of government business. Others follow Max Weber in seeing bureaucracy as a distinctive form of organisation found not just in government but in all spheres of modern society. What cannot be doubted, however, is that, as government has grown and the breadth of its responsibilities expanded, bureaucracy has come to play an increasingly important role in political life. No longer can civil servants be dismissed as mere administrators or policy implementors; instead, they are key figures in the policy process, and even sometimes *run* their countries. A reality of 'rule by the officials' may lie behind the facade of representation and democratic accountability. The organisation and control of bureaucratic power is therefore one of the most pressing problems in modern politics, and one that no political system has found easy to solve.

The central issues addressed in this chapter are as follows:

Key issues

▶ What is bureaucracy?

▶ What are the major theories of bureaucracy?

▶ What are the functions of bureaucracies?

▶ How are bureaucracies organised? How should they be organised?

▶ Why are bureaucrats so powerful, and why has bureaucratic power expanded?

▶ How, and how successfully, are bureaucracies controlled?

■ Theories of bureaucracy

The question of bureaucracy engenders deep political passions. In the modern period, these have invariably been negative. Liberals criticise bureaucracy for its lack of openness and accountability. Socialists, particularly Marxists, condemn it as an instrument of class subordination; and the New Right, for its part, portrays bureaucrats as self-serving and inherently inefficient. Underlying these contrasting views is deeper disagreement about the very nature of bureaucracy. Quite simply, the term bureaucracy has been used in so many different ways that the attempt to develop an overall definition may have to be abandoned altogether. Albrow (1970:84–105) identified no fewer than seven modern concepts of bureaucracy:

- bureaucracy as rational organisation
- bureaucracy as organisational inefficiency
- bureaucracy as rule by officials
- bureaucracy as public administration
- bureaucracy as administration by officials
- bureaucracy as organisation
- bureaucracy as modern society.

To some extent, these contrasting concepts and usages reflect the fact that bureaucracy has been viewed differently by different academic disciplines. Students of government, for example, traditionally understood bureaucracy in a literal sense to mean 'rule by the bureau', that is, rule by appointed officials. In *Considerations on Representative Government* ([1861] 1951), J. S. Mill (see p. 44) therefore contrasted bureaucracy with representative forms of government, in other words, rule by elected and accountable politicians. In the field of sociology, bureaucracy has typically been understood as a particular type of organisation, as a system of administration rather than a system of government. Bureaucracy in this sense can be found not only in democratic and authoritarian states, but also in business corporations, trade unions, political parties and so on. Economists, on the other hand, sometimes view bureaucracies as specifically 'public' organisations. They are thus characterised by the fact that being funded through the tax system they are neither disciplined by the profit motive nor responsive to market pressures. In order to make sense of these various usages, three contrasting theories of bureaucracy will be examined:

- bureaucracy as a rational–administrative machine
- bureaucracy as a conservative power bloc
- bureaucracy as a source of government oversupply.

Rational–administrative model

The academic study of bureaucracy has been dominated by the work of Max Weber (see p. 194). For Weber, bureaucracy was an 'ideal type' (see p. 18) of rule based on a system of rational rules, as opposed to either tradition or charisma. He identified a set of principles that supposedly characterise bureaucratic organisation. The most important of these are the following:

- Jurisdictional areas are fixed and official, and ordered by laws or rules.

- There is a firmly ordered hierarchy, which ensures that lower offices are supervised by specified higher ones within a chain of command.

- Business is managed on the basis of written documents and a filing system.

- The authority of officials is impersonal and stems entirely from the post they hold, not from personal status.

- Bureaucratic rules are strict enough to minimise the scope of personal discretion.

- Appointment and advancement within a bureaucracy is based on professional criteria, such as training, expertise and administrative competence.

The central feature of bureaucracy from the Weberian perspective is its rationality, because bureaucratisation reflects the advance of a reliable, predictable and, above all, efficient means of social organisation. For Weber, bureaucracy was nothing less than the characteristic form of organisation found in modern society, and, in his view, its expansion was irreversible. Not only was this a result of the technical superiority of bureaucracy over other forms of administration, but it was also a consequence of significant economic, political and cultural developments. The development of bureaucratisation was closely linked to the emergence of capitalist economies, in particular, to the greater pressure for economic efficiency and the emergence of larger-scale business units. The development of the modern state, and the extension of its responsibilities into the social and economic spheres, also led to the growth of powerful government bureaucracies.

In Weber's view, the growth of bureaucratisation was further stimulated by the pressures of democratisation, which weakened ideas such as tradition (see p. 195), privilege and duty, and replaced them with a belief in open competition and meritocracy. He believed that the process of 'rationalisation' would ensure that all industrial societies, whether nominally capitalist or communist, would increasingly resemble each other as they adopted bureaucratic forms of administration. This version of what is called the **convergence thesis** was subsequently developed by James Burnham (1905–87) in *The Managerial Revolution* (1941). This seminal text of **managerialism** suggested that, regardless of their ideological differences, all industrial societies are governed by a class of managers, technocrats and state officials whose power is vested in their technical and administrative skills.

Weber was nevertheless aware that bureaucracy was a mixed blessing. In the first place, organisational efficiency would be purchased at the expense of democratic participation. Bureaucratisation would strengthen hierarchical tendencies, albeit ones based on merit, meaning that command would be exercised from above by senior officials rather than from below by the masses. This would destroy the socialist dream of a dictatorship of the proletariat, which, Weber (accurately, as it turned out) predicted, would develop into a 'dictatorship of the official'. In this respect, Weber drew conclusions similar to those of his friend Robert Michels (1878–1936), who developed the iron law of oligarchy (see p. 238) on the basis of his study of political parties.

However, Weber was less pessimistic than Michels about the prospects for liberal democracy. Although he recognised the tendency of bureaucrats to seek the perpetuation of bureaucracy and to exceed its administrative function, he believed that this could at least be resisted through the use of liberal devices such as electoral competition and institutional fragmentation. The other potential danger that Weber highlighted was that the domination of the bureaucratic ideal could bring about a

Concept

Bureaucracy

Bureaucracy (literally 'rule by officials') is, in everyday language, a pejorative term meaning pointless administrative routine, or 'red tape'. In the social sciences, the concept of bureaucracy is used in a more specific and neutral sense, but refers to phenomena as different as rule by nonelected officials, the administrative machinery of government, and a rational mode of organisation. Despite disagreement about its location and character, it is generally accepted that abstract organisation and rule-governed professional administration are features of bureaucracy. There are fewer difficulties with the use of the term bureaucracy in the field of comparative government. Here, it refers to the administrative machinery of the state, bureaucrats being nonelected state officials or civil servants.

Convergence thesis: The theory that politico-economic factors dictate that capitalist and socialist states will become increasingly similar.

Managerialism: The theory that in modern society class divisions have been replaced by ones based on managerial position and bureaucratic power; technocracy (rule by experts or specialists).

'pigeon-holing of the spirit' as the social environment became increasingly depersonalised and mechanical. Reason and bureaucracy could therefore become an 'iron cage' confining human passions and individual freedom.

Power-bloc model

The view of bureaucracy as a power block stems largely from socialist analysis, and particularly from Marxism. Although Marx (see p. 51) developed no systematic theory of bureaucracy in the manner of Weber, the outlines of a theory are discernible in his writings. Rather than seeing bureaucracy as a consequence of the emergence of a complex industrial society, Marx linked it to the specific requirements of capitalism. He was thus concerned less with bureaucratisation as a broader social phenomenon, and more with the class role played by the state bureaucracy. In particular, he saw the bureaucracy as a mechanism through which bourgeois interests are upheld and the capitalist system defended.

This analysis of class biases running through the state bureaucracy has been extended by neo-Marxists such as Ralph Miliband (1969). Particular attention has been paid to the capacity of senior civil servants to act as a conservative veto group that dilutes, even blocks, the radical initiatives of socialist ministers and socialist governments. As Miliband put it, top civil servants 'are conservative in the sense that they are, within their allotted sphere, the conscious or unconscious allies of existing economic and social elites' (p. 123). This happens for a number of reasons. Most obviously, despite the formal requirements of political neutrality (see p. 287), top civil servants share the same educational and social background as industrialists and business managers, and are therefore likely to share their ideas, prejudices and general outlook. The possibility that rising civil servants may harbour radical or socialist sympathies is also countered by recruitment and promotion procedures designed to ensure their ideological 'soundness'.

Miliband believed that the most important factor reinforcing the conservative outlook of higher civil servants is their ever-increasing closeness to the world of corporate capitalism. This has been a consequence of growing state intervention in economic life, ensuring an ongoing relationship between business groups and civil servants, who invariably come to define the 'national interest' in terms of the long-term interests of private capitalism. In turn, this relationship is reinforced by the interchange of personnel between government and business (often seen as a 'revolving door'), through which the state bureaucracy recruits from the private sector, and civil servants are offered lucrative employment opportunities when they retire. The implication of this analysis is that, if senior bureaucrats are wedded to the interests of capitalism, a major obstacle stands in the way of any attempt to achieve socialism through constitutional means.

One of the flaws of the Marxist theory of bureaucracy is that it pays little attention to the problem of bureaucratisation in socialist systems. For Marx and Engels, this problem was effectively discounted by the assumption that the bureaucracy, with the state, would 'wither away' as a classless, communist society came into existence. This left Marxism open to criticism by social scientists such as Weber and Michels, who argued that bureaucracy is a broader social phenomenon, and one that the socialist emphasis on common ownership and planning could only strengthen. The experience of twentieth-century communism made it impossible for Marxist thinkers to continue ignoring this problem.

Leon Trotsky (1879–1940)

Russian Marxist political thinker and revolutionary. An early critic of Lenin's theory of the party and leader of the 1905 St Petersburg Soviet, Trotsky joined the Bolsheviks in 1917, becoming Commissar for Foreign Affairs and later Commissar for War. Isolated and out-manoeuvred after Lenin's death in 1924, he was banished from the USSR in 1929, and assassinated in Mexico in 1940 on the instructions of Stalin. Trotsky's theoretical contribution to Marxism consists of his theory of 'permanent revolution', his consistent support for internationalism, and his analysis of Stalinism as a form of 'bureaucratic degeneration'.

The most influential Marxist analysis of postcapitalist bureaucracy was developed by Leon Trotsky. In *The Revolution Betrayed* (1937), Trotsky highlighted the problem of 'bureaucratic degeneration'. In his view, a combination of Russian backwardness and the proletariat's lack of political sophistication had created conditions in which the state bureaucracy could expand and block further advances towards socialism. The Stalinist dictatorship was thus merely the political expression of these dominant bureaucratic interests, entirely cut off from those of the masses. While Trotsky saw the bureaucracy as a social stratum that could be removed by a political revolution, the Yugoslav dissident (and former colleague of Marshal Tito) Milovan Djilas (1911–95) portrayed it as a 'new class'. For Djilas (1957), the power of the bureaucracy in orthodox communist regimes stemmed from its control of productive wealth, and this meant that communist social systems increasingly resembled a form of state capitalism.

Bureaucratic oversupply model

The idea that critics of bureaucracy come exclusively from the left has been overturned by the emergence of rational choice and public choice (see p. 258) theories. These have had considerable impact on the New Right, and in particular have helped to shape its views about the nature of the state and the emergence of 'big' government. Central to this model of bureaucracy is a concern with the interests and motivations of bureaucrats themselves. Rational choice theory is based on the same assumptions about human nature as those in neoclassical economics, that is, that individuals are rationally self-seeking creatures or utility maximisers. Public choice theory, particularly prominent in the USA and associated with the Virginia school of political analysis, applies this economic model of decision-making to the public sector.

In *Bureaucracy and Representative Government* (1971), William Niskanen argued that senior bureaucrats, regardless of their image as public servants, are primarily motivated by career self-interest and thus seek an expansion of the agency in which they work and an increase in its budget. This is because bureaucratic growth guarantees job security, expands promotion prospects, improves salaries, and brings top officials greater power, patronage and prestige. Bureaucracies thus contain a powerful inner dynamic, leading to the growth of government itself and the expansion of public responsibilities. For the New Right, the ability of appointed officials to dictate policy priorities to elected politicians goes a long way towards explaining how state growth has occurred under governments of very different ideological complexions. Similarly, the image of bureaucrats as nature's social democrats has important implications for New Right governments intent on rolling back the frontiers of the state. They believe that, quite simply, unless bureaucratic power can be checked or circumvented, any attempt to pursue free-market policies is doomed to failure.

This New Right critique also focuses attention on the non-market character of state bureaucracies, and draws an unflattering comparison between private-sector and public-sector bodies. In this view, private-sector bodies such as business corporations are structured by a combination of internal and external factors. The principal internal influence on a business is the quest for profit maximisation, which impels the firm towards greater efficiency through the exertion of a constant downward pressure on costs. Externally, businesses operate in a competitive market environment, which forces them to respond to consumer pressures through product innovation and price adjustments.

In contrast, bureaucracies are not disciplined by the profit motive. If costs exceed revenue, the tax payer is always there to pick up the bill. Similarly, state bureaucracies are usually monopolies, and are therefore in no way forced to respond to market pressures. The result is that bureaucracies (in common with all public-sector bodies) are inherently wasteful and inefficient. Moreover, the service they provide is invariably of poor quality and does not meet consumer needs or wishes. This 'private, good; public, bad' philosophy of the New Right not only dictates that state bureaucracies should be scaled down, but also that, when this is not possible, private-sector management techniques should be introduced.

Critics of public choice theory usually argue that it is flawed because it abstracts the individual from his or her social environment. A conservative value bias, so the argument goes, is built into the theory by the assumption that human beings are always rationally self-interested. Others, however, have used a public choice approach but reached very different conclusions. Dunleavy (1991), for example, argued that, if individual bureaucrats are rational actors, they are more likely to favour bureau-shaping strategies than, as conventional public-choice theory suggests, budget-maximising ones.

Budget-maximising priorities certainly go hand in hand with state growth, especially in the absence of market disciplines. However, it is difficult to undertake collective action to achieve this end, and senior officials tend to be more interested in work-related benefits than narrowly financial benefits. Dunleavy suggested that bureaucrats are likely to assign their highest priority to providing themselves with congenial work and an amenable and attractive working environment. This is both because senior civil servants are especially concerned with the interest and importance of their work tasks, and because public-sector employment provides them with relatively modest opportunities to improve their salaries, job security and promotion prospects. Clearly, top officials concerned about bureau shaping would operate in a very different way from the empire builders of New Right demonology.

▉ Role of bureaucracies

Functions of bureaucracies

On the face of it, bureaucracies fulfil a single, but vital, function. Their primary concern is with the execution and enforcement of the laws made by the legislature and the policies decided by the political executive. Indeed, while other functions of government (such as representation, policy making and interest articulation) are carried out by a variety of institutions, policy implementation is solely the responsibility of civil servants, albeit working under their political masters. Moreover, the Weberian model of bureaucracies as rational and objective machines appears to divorce the administrative world from the political world. In this view, bureaucrats are seen simply as cogs in a machine, as reliable and efficient administrators operating within a fixed hierarchy and according to clearly defined rules. The reality is very different. Despite their formal subordination and impartiality, bureaucrats exert considerable influence on the policy process, and thus fulfil a number of key functions in any political system. The most important of these functions are the following:

- carrying out administration
- offering policy advice
- articulating and aggregating interests
- maintaining political stability.

Administration

The core function of the bureaucracy is to implement or execute law and policy; it is thus charged with administering government business. This is why the bureaucracy is sometimes referred to as 'the administration', while the political executive is termed 'the government'. This distinction implies that a clear line can be drawn between the policy making role of politicians and the policy-implementing role of bureaucrats. Certainly, the vast majority of the world's civil servants are almost exclusively engaged in administrative responsibilities that range from the implementation of welfare and social-security programmes to the regulation of the economy, the granting of licences, and the provision of information and advice to citizens at home and abroad. The sizes of bureaucracies are therefore closely linked to the broader responsibilities of government. Civil service employment in the UK expanded in proportion to the role of government throughout the twentieth century. It reached a peak of 735 000 in the 1970s, but then contracted to 499 000 by 1996 owing to the pursuit of neoliberal policies from the 1980s onwards. The federal bureaucracy in the USA expanded significantly as a result of the New Deal and has now grown to over 2.5 million strong; and the USSR's central planning system eventually required 20 million state officials to administer it.

Nevertheless, the image of bureaucrats as mere functionaries who apply rules and carry out orders issued by others can be misleading. In the first place, since much administrative details is of necessity left to officials, civil servants may be allowed significant discretion in deciding precisely how to implement policy. Secondly, the degree of political control exercised over the bureaucracy varies greatly from state to state. Whereas state officials in China are subject to strict and continuous party supervision, in France and Japan their high status and reputation for expertise guarantees them a considerable degree of autonomy. Thirdly, in their capacity as policy advisers, senior civil servants at least have the ability to shape the policies that they are later required to administer.

Policy advice

The political significance of the bureaucracy largely stems from its role as the chief source of the policy information and advice available to government. This policy role helps to distinguish top-level civil servants, who have daily contact with politicians and are expected to act as policy advisers, from middle-ranking and junior-ranking civil servants, who deal with more routine administrative matters. Debate about the political significance of bureaucracies therefore tends to concentrate on this elite group of senior officials. In theory, a strict distinction can be drawn between the policy responsibilities of bureaucrats and politicians. Policy (see p. 382) is supposedly *made* by politicians; bureaucrats simply offer *advice*. The policy role of civil servants therefore boils down to two functions: outlining the policy options available to ministers, and reviewing policy proposals in terms of their likely impact and consequences. The policy influence of senior officials is further restricted by the fact that they are either required to be politically neutral, as in the UK, Japan and Australia, or are subject to a system of political appointment, as in the USA.

However, there are reasons to believe that the policy role of civil servants is politically more significant than is suggested above. For instance, there is no clear distinction between making policy and offering policy advice. Quite simply, decisions are made on the basis of the information available, and this means that the content of decisions is invariably structured by the advice offered. Moreover, as the principal source of the advice available to politicians, bureaucrats effectively control the flow of information: politicians know what civil servants tell them. Information can thus be concealed or at least 'shaped' to reflect the preferences of the civil service. The principal source of bureaucratic power is nevertheless the expertise and specialist knowledge that accumulates within the bureaucracy. As the responsibilities of government expand and policy becomes more complex, 'amateur' politicians almost inevitably come to depend on their 'professional' bureaucratic advisers.

Articulating interests

Although by no means one of their formal functions, bureaucracies often help to articulate and sometimes aggregate interests. Bureaucracies are brought into contact with interest groups through their task of policy implementation and their involvement in policy formulation and advice. This has increased as a result of corporatist (see p. 257) tendencies that have blurred the divisions between organised interests and government agencies. Groups such as doctors, teachers, farmers and business corporations thus become 'client groups', serviced by their respective agencies, and also serve as an invaluable source of information and advice. This **clientelism** may benefit the political system insofar as it helps to maintain consensus. By virtue of having access to policy formulation, it is more likely that organised interests will cooperate with government policy. On the other hand, clientelism may also interfere with the public responsibilities and duties of civil servants. This, for instance, occurs when US regulatory agencies end up being controlled by the industries they supposedly regulate. When group interests coincide with those of the bureaucracy, a policy nexus may develop that democratic politicians find impossible to break down.

Political stability

The final function of bureaucracies is to provide a focus of stability and continuity within political systems. This is sometimes seen as particularly important in developing states, where the existence of a body of trained career officials may provide the only guarantee that government is conducted in an orderly and reliable fashion. This stability very largely depends on the status of bureaucrats as permanent and professional public servants; while ministers and governments come and go, the

Clientelism: A relationship through which government agencies come to serve the interests of the client groups they are responsible for regulating or supervising.

bureaucracy is always there. The Northcote–Trevelyan reforms of 1870 that created the modern UK civil service were based on the principles of impartial selection, political neutrality, permanence and anonymity. Even in the USA, where senior officials are appointed politically through a so-called 'spoils system', the mass of federal bureaucrats are career civil servants.

However, continuity can also have its disadvantages. In the absence of effective public scrutiny and accountability, it can undoubtedly lead to corruption, a problem that is found in many developing states, where it is compounded by widespread poverty and disadvantage. In other cases, permanence may breed in civil servants either a tendency towards arrogance and insularity, or a bias in favour of conservatism. Career civil servants can come to believe that they are more capable of defining the common good or general will than are elected politicians. They may therefore feel justified in resisting radical or reformist political tendencies, seeing themselves as custodians of the state's interest.

Organisation of bureaucracies

One of the limitations of Weber's theory of bureaucracy is that it suggests that the drive for efficiency and rationality will lead to the adoption of essentially similar bureaucratic structures the world over. Weber's 'ideal type' thus ignores the various ways in which bureaucracies can be organised, as well as differences that arise from the political, social and cultural contexts in which bureaucracies operate. The organisation of bureaucracies is important for two reasons. It influences the administrative efficiency of government, and affects the degree to which public accountability and political control can be achieved. The issue of organisation has, however, assumed a deeper significance as pressure has built up, especially from the 1980s onwards, to reduce public spending. This partly reflects the spread of New Right ideas but is also one of the consequences of economic globalisation. Many states have therefore looked to rationalise their administrative machinery, a process that has sometimes been portrayed as 'reinventing government'. This process nevertheless has major political, and even constitutional, implications.

All state bureaucracies are in some way organized on the basis of purpose or function. This is achieved through the construction of departments, ministries and agencies charged with responsibility for particular policy areas: education, housing, defence, drug control, taxation and so forth. Of course, the number of such departments and agencies varies over time and from state to state, as do the ways in which functional responsibilities are divided or combined. For example, the broadening responsibilities of the US government were reflected in the creation of the Department of Health and Human Services in 1953, and the Department of Housing and Urban Development in 1965. In the UK, the Department of Employment was abolished in 1995, allowing the establishment of the Department for Education and Employment.

The most significant feature of these functionally defined bureaucracies is the degree of centralisation or decentralisation within them. The systems found in the remaining communist regimes, such as China, which are subject to strict party control and supervision at every level, are amongst the most centralised bureaucratic systems in the world. Nevertheless, the sizes and complexity of communist bureaucracies has also provided considerable scope for bureau and departmental independence. Despite the formal 'leadership' of the CPSU, the Soviet bureaucracy, for example,

Departmentalism

Departmentalism refers to centrifugal pressures within a bureaucratic structure that strengthen the identity of individual departments and agencies. Agencies are thus able to pursue their own separate interests and resist both political control and broader administrative disciplines. The distinctive culture of a government agency is shaped by factors such as its policy responsibilities, the collective interests of its body of officials, and the interests of the client groups that it serves. Attempts to counter departmentalism by transferring officials from agency to agency, or by imposing stricter political control, risk diminishing levels of expertise and specialisation. Such attempts may also be undermined by the tendency of ministers and senior officials to 'go native', that is, be absorbed into the culture of their department.

functioned as a labyrinthine mechanism for interest articulation and aggregation, amounting to a form of 'institutional pluralism' (Hough, 1977). The UK civil service has traditionally been centralised. It has a common recruitment and promotion policy, and a single career and salary structure. In some ways, the Fulton Report of 1966 furthered the ideal of a unified civil service by abolishing the division between the clerical, executive and administrative grades, which had amounted to a form of class system. However, by shifting emphasis away from 'generalists' in senior positions, it placed greater stress on subject expertise and specialist knowledge, so strengthening 'departmentalism'. Moreover, in establishing the Civil Service Department (subsequently abolished) to take responsibility for recruitment, promotions and conditions of work, it also facilitated bureaucratic autonomy.

The most centralised liberal-democratic bureaucracy has traditionally been that in France. Whereas bureaucracies in states like the UK and Germany have developed through a process of reform and adaptation, the French system was constructed on the basis of the Napoleonic model of administration. This emphasised the importance of a highly centralised and hierarchically structured body of technical experts, wedded to the long-term interests of the French state. The Conseil d'Etat (Council of State) is the supreme administrative body in France; it advises on legislative and administrative matters and acts as the highest administrative court. The École Nationale d'Administration and the École Polytechnique function as training schools for civil servants, giving the so-called *grands corps* (senior administrators and technical experts) unrivalled prestige. To some extent, however, the Napoleonic model of strict discipline and uniformity has never been fully realised. Divisions tend to exist between generalists and specialists, between the *grand corps* and junior civil servants, and between rival bureaux and departments, particularly between the finance ministry and the major spending ministries.

The USA, in contrast, is an example of a decentralised bureaucracy. The federal bureaucracy operates under the formal authority of the president as chief administrator. However, it is so diffuse and unwieldy that all presidents struggle to coordinate and direct its activities. One reason for this fragmentation is that the responsibilities of the federal government overlap with those of state and local governments, whose cooperation is required to ensure effective implementation. A second reason is the impact of the separation of powers (see p. 297). While executive departments and agencies operate under presidential authority via their cabinet secretaries or directors, a bewildering array of independent regulatory commissions have been created, and are funded, by Congress. Although presidents appoint the members of these commissions, they cannot dismiss them or interfere with their responsibilities as laid down by Congress. A third reason is that there is tension between permanent civil servants, who are appointed through competitive public examination and placed on one of the General Schedule grades, and the much smaller number of political appointees in so-called Schedule C posts. While the latter can be expected to make loyalty to the administration their priority, the former may be more committed to the growth of their bureaux or the continuance of their services and programmes.

The conventional structure of government bureaucracies has come under particular scrutiny and pressure since the 1970s. In extreme cases, this has led to attempts to restructure the administrative state. The Clinton administration, for instance, was deeply impressed by the ideas developed in Osborne and Gaebler's *Reinventing Government* (1992). This suggested that the job of government is to 'steer' not to 'row'; in other words, government works best when it concerns itself with policy making and leaves the delivery of services or policy implementation to other bodies acting as agents of the state. In theory, such an approach need not necessarily be linked to the contraction of state responsibilities, but its most enthusiastic advocates have undoubtedly come from the New Right, which has embraced this analysis as part of its broader attack on 'big' government.

These ideas have been influential in the USA and a number of other western countries, but the construction of an 'enabling state', even a 'skeletal state', has been taken furthest in the UK, through the civil service reforms introduced by Thatcher and Major. These ideas have provided the basis for the 'new public administration', which stands broadly for the use of private-sector management techniques in government and for the transfer of government functions to private bodies via 'market testing' and 'contracting out'. A significant step down this road was taken in 1988 with the launching of the Next Steps initiative, which began dismantling a unified national administration by restricting ministries to their 'core' policy functions and handing over responsibility for implementation to executive agencies, as occurs in Sweden. By 1996, 70 per cent of the UK's civil servants were working in these Next Steps agencies, with a growing body of work being contracted-out to private bodies.

The Citizen's Charter initiative, launched in the UK in 1991, attempted to compensate for inefficiency and unresponsiveness in public administration through the use of performance targets and quality measurement. Such innovations have also been accompanied by a substantial increase in the role of quangos (see p. 350) in the administration of services such as health, education, urban development and regulation. In 1993, there were some 1389 quasi-governmental bodies in the UK, spending over £15 billion a year and employing 111 300 staff. However, the most radical attempt to 'roll back the state' in the UK has been made through the policy of privatisation, which has seen industries such as telecommunications, electricity, gas, water and local transport transferred from public to private ownership. The creation of Next Steps agencies may, indeed, be a prelude to full privatisation.

As governments struggle to keep public spending under control, such developments, especially the divorce between policy advice and policy implementation, are likely to become more common. However, the drive to streamline administration, promote efficiency and cut costs carries political costs. The most obvious of these is the weakening of public accountability and the emergence of a 'democratic deficit'. One of the strengths of a unified civil service is that it supports the doctrine of ministerial responsibility (see p. 300), which ensures that appointed officials are ultimately answerable to elected politicians, and through them, to the public. The creation of semi-independent executive agencies and, above all, quangos tends to mean that ministers no longer take responsibility for day-to-day administrative or operational matters. Supporters of reorganisation, on the other hand, argue that this can be counterbalanced by the improvement of delivery standards through the use of charters and other performance targets.

A second problem is that the introduction of management techniques, structures and, increasingly, personnel from the private sector may weaken the public-service ethos which state bureaucracies have striven over the years to develop. The civil-service culture in states as different as Japan, India, France and the UK may be criticised for its aloofness, even arrogance, but it is at least linked to ideas like public service and the national interest, rather than private gain and entrepreneurialism. Amongst other things, public service culture has helped to keep corruption at bay in most of the world's pluralist democracies. A final disadvantage is that, although this

Quangos: advantages and disadvantages

Quango is an acronym for quasi-autonomous nongovernmental organisation. This is a notoriously loose and confusing term. In its most general sense, quango refers to any body carrying out government functions that is staffed by appointees rather than ministers or civil servants. Quangos thus include bodies with executive functions of various kinds, as well as advisory committees and tribunals. The quasi-autonomous status of quangos means that they are part of 'arms-length' government; their nongovernmental character means that they are part of the 'nonelected state'.

The benefits of quangos include the following:

- They allow government to call on the experience, expertise and specialist knowledge of outside advisers.
- They reduce the burden of work of 'official' government departments and agencies.

Quangos have been criticised for the following reasons:

- They expand the range of ministerial patronage and so contribute to the centralisation of political power.
- They weaken democratic accountability by reducing the ability of representative institutions to oversee the workings of government.
- They foster **balkanisation** by making public administration more disjointed and less systematic.

type of reorganisation tends to be associated with the rolling back of the state, it may in practice lead to greater centralisation and government control. This occurs because, as government relinquishes direct responsibility for the delivery of services, it is forced to set up a range of bodies to carry out funding and regulatory functions. This, in turn, allows politicians to exert influence through patronage and the setting of performance targets, powers that formerly came within the jurisdiction of professional bureaucrats (Jenkins, 1995).

■ Bureaucratic power: out of control?

Sources of bureaucratic power

Balkanisation: The fragmentation of a political unit into a patchwork of antagonistic entities (as has often occurred in the Balkans).

Despite their constitutional image as loyal and supportive public servants, bureaucrats have widely been seen as powerful and influential figures who collectively constitute a 'fourth branch of government'. Theorists as different as Weber, Burnham and Trotsky have drawn attention to the phenomenon of bureaucratic power and the degree to which politicians are subordinate to it. Japanese civil servants, especially those in the prestigious Japanese Ministry of International Trade and Industry, are generally viewed as the 'permanent politicians' who masterminded the Japanese 'economic miracle' of the 1950s and 1960s. Kellner and Crowther-Hunt (1980) dubbed the UK's civil service 'Britain's ruling class'. This view was reinforced in the memoirs of former ministers such as Richard Crossman (1979), Barbara Castle (1980) and Brian Sedgemore (1980). Similarly, there is a perception that the driving force in the EU behind monetary and political union is the Brussels-based administrative staff of the European Commission, the so-called Eurocrats.

Concern about bureaucratic power has been particularly acute amongst those on the political left and the political right who have dismissed the conventional notion of civil service neutrality. As pointed out above, Marxists have traditionally argued that class interests operate through the bureaucracy, tending, in particular, to dilute radical policy initiatives by socialist governments. The New Right insists that self-interested public officials foster state growth and are thus inclined to resist neoliberal or free-market policies. However, it is important to remember that the nature of bureaucratic power is, perhaps inevitably, shrouded in mystery and conjecture. This is both because, if civil servants exert power, they do so through private dealings with ministers which are not subject to public scrutiny, and because, in view of the myriad other pressures bearing on ministers, the influence of the civil service cannot be quantified. Nevertheless, three key sources of bureaucratic power can be identified:

- the strategic position of bureaucrats in the policy process
- the logistical relationship between bureaucrats and ministers
- the status and expertise of bureaucrats.

The policy process in all modern states is structured in a way that offers considerable scope for civil service influence. Most crucially, in their capacity as policy advisers, civil servants have access to information and are able to control its flow to their ministerial bosses. In government departments, knowledge is undoubtedly power, and it is officials who decide what ministers know and what they do not know. Policy options can thus be selected, evaluated and presented in such a way as to achieve a desired decision. This need not, of course, imply that bureaucrats are deliberately manipulative or openly political, but merely that their preferences – conscious or unconscious – significantly structure policy debate and so can influence the content of decisions made.

Links that develop between the bureaucracy and organised interests further strengthen their position. As the major interface between government and business, labour, professional and other groups, the bureaucracy can build up powerful alliances and play a crucial role in formulating and reviewing policy options. This has led to the emergence of 'policy networks' (see p. 388), that is, complex relationships between senior bureaucrats and representatives of interest groups that tend to be relatively impervious to influence from the public or elected politicians. Needless to say, bureaucratic power does not cease to play a role once policy decisions have been made. Whereas politicians can seek alternative sources of policy advice, they are compelled to leave policy implementation in the hands of the bureaucracy, whether organised as a unified entity or as a series of quasi-independent agencies. Control of implementation gives civil servants the opportunity to reinterpret the content of policy, as well as to delay or even thwart its introduction.

The second source of bureaucratic power is the operational relationship and distribution of advantage between ministers and civil servants. Ostensibly, ministers are political masters and appointed bureaucrats are loyal subordinates. However, there are reasons to believe that this relationship may be different, even reversed, in practice. The first of these is that politicians are heavily outnumbered by leading bureaucrats. For example, in the USA, even if only top-level political appointees (those who require Senate approval) are considered, US presidents, aided by a cabinet of fewer than 20 secretaries, confront more than 600 senior officials. In the UK, the ratio of ministers to civil servants of the rank of under secretary and above is 2:13. Politicians' spans of control are therefore very limited, meaning that civil servants are necessarily allowed considerable discretion in carrying out their policy and administrative responsibilities.

A second factor is the different career structures of civil servants and elected politicians. Except where 'spoils systems' operate, as in the USA, civil servants are permanent in the sense that they remain in office while governments come and go. In contrast, ministers are only temporary, and in parliamentary systems like the UK's where reshuffles are frequent, may only remain in office for about two years on average. In-coming ministers may therefore be particularly susceptible to official influence while they acquire the administrative experience and specialist knowledge required to run their departments effectively, and they may well be moved to another department once this task has been accomplished. Civil servants, for their part, have the confidence of knowing that they are likely to outlive an unsympathetic political master.

The third advantage enjoyed by civil servants is that they are full-time policy advisers, while ministers are only part-time departmental bosses. At the same time as ministerial workloads have increased, owing to the growing scale and complexity of government business, ministers have also been faced by an expanding range of demands on their time and energy. These include cabinet and cabinet-committee duties, sometimes parliamentary responsibilities and constituency work, media appearances, attendance at ceremonial and public functions, and foreign visits and summitry. In short, however dedicated, tenacious and resourceful ministers may be, their role is restricted to the offering of strategic guidance, knowing that much of the detail of policy and operational matters must be left to appointed officials.

The final source of bureaucratic power is the status and respect that is often accorded to civil servants. This principally stems from their expertise and specialist knowledge. In many systems, senior bureaucrats are regarded as a meritocratic elite, and are invested with responsibility for the national interest. This is certainly reflected in an emphasis on merit and achievement in the recruitment and training of civil servants. Top German civil servants, for instance, are recruited by competitive examination from the ranks of university graduates, usually in law, and then endure a rigorous three-year training programme followed by a second state examination. In France, the École Nationale d'Administration was set up specifically to recruit and train the nation's top generalist civil servants, thus supplementing the work of schools like the École Polytechnique, which turn out technical experts. The elite status of Japanese bureaucrats is maintained by an examination system that recruits only one candidate in 40, and by the preponderance of Tokyo University entrants, who provide 70 per cent of senior civil servants, two-thirds of whom have law degrees. Their status was heightened by the responsibility the relatively unpurged Japanese bureaucracy shouldered in the process of postwar reconstruction, especially in the establishment of a planned market economy. The status of the UK civil service has similarly been linked with a reliance on Oxbridge candidates and the rigours of the fast-stream entrance procedure.

In comparison, governments and ministers often come into office ill prepared and in need of advice and support. Although governments are formed on the basis of party programmes and manifestos, they depend on civil servants to translate broad policy goals into practical and workable legislative programmes. This problem is particularly acute because of the mismatch between the skills and attributes required to win elective office and those needed to run an effective administration. In parliamentary systems in particular, ministers are appointed from an unusually small pool of talent (the members of the majority party or parties in the assembly), and it is rare for them to have either specialist knowledge of their departmental remit or previous experience of administering a large-scale organisation.

How can bureaucrats be controlled?

The perceived need to control the bureaucracy reflects a wide range of concerns. Most importantly, unchecked bureaucratic power spells the demise of representative and responsible government. For political democracy to be meaningful, appointed officials must in some way be accountable to politicians who, in turn, are accountable to the general public. Indeed, one of the long-standing criticisms of liberal democracy is that behind the facade of party competition and public accountability lies the entrenched power of bureaucrats who are responsible to no one. Guarantees against corruption, **maladministration** and the arbitrary exercise of government power must therefore be established.

Political control is also required because of the need to promote efficiency in a bureaucracy that may be bent on maintaining its professional comforts and material security, and because of the need for administrative coordination to resist the centrifugal pressures of departmentalism. Bureaucrats themselves may argue that external control is unnecessary in view of the self-discipline imposed by strict professional standards and a deeply ingrained public-service ethos, especially in permanent civil services like those found in Germany, France, India and the UK. On the other hand, such a civil service culture may be part of the problem rather than part of the solution; it may entrench a lofty arrogance based on the belief that 'bureaucrats know best'. The principal forms of control over bureaucracies can be classified as follows:

- the creation of mechanisms of political accountability
- the politicisation of the civil service
- the construction of counter-bureaucracies.

Political accountability

State bureaucracies can be made accountable (see p. 375) to the political executive, the assembly, the judiciary, or the public. The political executive is easily the most important of these bodies, because of its overall responsibility for government administration and its close working relationship with the civil service. The most elaborate system of executive control has been found in state socialist regimes such as those in China and the USSR, where a hierarchically structured network of party organs was constructed to run parallel to, and exercise supervision over, the state administration. However, so complex and extensive was the machinery of government in these regimes that even the pervasive influence of a 'leading' party failed to prevent communist bureaucracies from developing interests of their own or acting as conduits through which economic, social and regional interests could be expressed.

Maladministration: Bad administration; the improper use of powers, biased application of rules, failure to follow procedures, or simple incompetence.

◤ **Concept**

Ministerial responsibility

The doctrine of ministerial responsibility ('individual' responsibility) defines the relationship between ministers and their departments and ostensibly guarantees that the civil service is publicly accountable. This doctrine is observed in most parliamentary systems, most clearly in the UK, and has two key features. First, ministers are responsible for the acts and omissions of their departments, maintaining the fiction that ministers themselves make all the decisions taken in their name: 'the buck stops' with the minister. Secondly, ministers are accountable to the assembly, in the sense that they are answerable for anything that goes on in their departments, and are removable in the event of wrongdoing or incompetence by their civil servants. In theory, ministerial responsibility establishes a chain of accountability that links civil servants to the public via ministers and assemblies. In practice, it is often bent to the will of the government of the day.

In liberal democracies, especially ones with parliamentary executives, political control largely depends on respect for the doctrine of ministerial responsibility. This holds that ministers alone are responsible *to* the assembly *for* the actions of their officials and the policies pursued by their departments. Ministerial responsibility has been developed in its most extreme form in the UK, where it is taken to imply that civil servants have an exclusive responsibility to their minister and, therefore, to the government of the day. The ability of this doctrine to deliver political control is nevertheless hampered by three factors. First, as discussed above, the expertise, size and complexity of modern bureaucracies makes effective ministerial oversight virtually impossible. Secondly, ministers have been unwilling to sacrifice their political careers by resigning as a result of blunders made by officials (or themselves), and prime ministers have been reluctant to encourage resignations that will attract adverse publicity. Thirdly, assemblies usually lack the expertise and political will to subject either ministers or civil servants to effective scrutiny.

Legislative oversight may also help to ensure that bureaucrats are politically accountable. The decision in the UK in 1979 to allow the newly created departmental select committees to cross-examine senior civil servants as well as ministers was an implicit acknowledgement of the failings of the system of ministerial responsibility. Effective legislative control is tied up with the supply of money, however. The US Congress scrutinises the presidential budget and has the constitutional authority to provide funds for the various executive departments and agencies. This gives congressional committees the opportunity to probe and investigate the workings of each department, scrutinise their estimates, and expose cases of maladministration and misappropriation. Congressional oversight may nevertheless allow powerful alliances to form, as in the so-called 'iron triangles', policy networks that comprise an executive agency, its relevant congressional committee and the interest groups with which both deal.

Judicial scrutiny of the bureaucracy is in particular found in systems in which administrative law, which defines the powers and functions of the executive organs of the state, is established as a separate branch of public law. In many continental European states, this leads to the creation of a network of administrative courts and tribunals empowered to resolve disputes between the government bureaucracy and private citizens. In France, the Conseil d'État is the supreme administrative court. It exercises general supervision over all forms of French administration, but may also weaken political control by protecting civil servants from unwarranted interference by their political masters.

Bureaucrats can be made accountable to the public in a number of ways, formal and informal. One method, Scandinavian in origin but later extended in different variations to countries like New Zealand, Australia, the UK and France, is the ombudsman system. Although the ombudsman system offers a means through which individual grievances can be redressed, ombudsmen rarely operate with the force of law, and generally lack direct means of enforcing their decisions. The UK Parliamentary Commissioner for Administration is particularly ineffective, since complaints cannot be made directly by the public, but only on referral from an MP, and because there is widespread public ignorance about the office and its function.

Amongst the informal pressures on the bureaucracy are those exercised by the mass media and well organised interest groups. Bureaucrats recognise that, regardless of the mechanisms of formal accountability, their status and public standing can be damaged by the exposure of scandals, corruption and administrative ineptitude. The publicity given to the Watergate affair in the USA in the 1970s thus led to tighter oversight of US government agencies such as the Central Intelligence Agency (CIA) and the Federal Bureau of Investigation (FBI). Similarly, the French newspaper *Le Monde* played a significant role in exposing the sinking in 1985 of the Greenpeace ship the *Rainbow Warrior*, thus contributing to the resignation of the defence minister. On the other hand, such investigations can be severely hampered by the culture of secrecy that usually pervades state administration, and by the absence of open government (see p. 292).

Politicisation

One of the most common ways of exercising political control is to recruit the senior bureaucracy into the ideological enthusiasms of the government of the day. This effectively blurs the distinctions between politics and administration, and between politicians and public officials. Control is overtly accomplished through a system of political appointments. A spoils system, as it became known, was institutionalised in the USA by Andrew Jackson in the nineteenth century, when he replaced about 20 per cent of the federal civil service with his own men. When there is a new US president, the administration changes. Some 3000 top posts are filled by political appointees, mostly in a rush between the election in November and the inauguration of the new president in January. Fewer than 200 of these appointments are likely to be made by the president personally; the others are made by senior executive officers subject to presidential approval.

In Germany, although the formal scope for making ministerial appointments is limited, the *Berufsverbot* (literally, the 'denial of access to a profession') system allows incoming ministers and governments to discard unwanted officials by retiring them on full pay and appoint more sympathetic ones in their place. However, covert politicisation is more widespread. In the UK, the abolition of the Civil Service Department in 1981 led to allegations that the senior personnel of the civil service were being 'Thatcherised'. Criticism stemmed from the close interest that Margaret Thatcher was able to take in the new senior appointments system, and her well publicised criteria for preferment: are they 'one of us'? Creeping politicisation has also become a feature of French administration. Approximately 500 senior posts are now filled at the discretion of leading government figures, and, since the 1980s, those appointed have usually had a highly partisan profile or been linked personally or politically with senior politicians. The French higher civil service therefore now resembles a patchwork of politicised clans, rather than a unified body standing above party politics.

The attraction of a politicised senior bureaucracy is plainly that it ensures that there is a higher level of loyalty and commitment in such a group than would be likely amongst politically impartial civil servants. Moreover, those observers who believe that neutrality is always a myth, arguing that some kind of political bias is inevitable in the state bureaucracy, generally hold that a system of overt politicisation is preferable to one of covert politicisation. However, political commitment also brings serious disadvantages. In the first place, politicisation strikes at the very heart of the idea of a professional and permanent civil service. Once bureaucrats are selected on political grounds by the government of the day, or encouraged to share their ideological sympathies, their appointments become as temporary as those of their political masters. This, in turn, means that knowledge and experience

Concept

Ombudsman

Ombudsman is a Scandinavian word that has no exact English equivalent. An ombudsman is an officer of the state who is appointed to safeguard citizens' rights in a particular sector and investigate allegations of maladministration, ranging from the improper use of powers to the failure to follow procedures and simple incompetence. The role of an ombudsman is to supplement, not replace, normal avenues of complaints such as administrative courts or elected representatives. However, as ombudsmen are concerned with wider administrative morality, their investigations and findings seldom have the force of law. While the ombudsman system may strengthen the exercise of oversight and redress, it has been criticised as tokenistic (ombudsmen lack executive power), and because it relies too heavily on the qualities of the incumbent (who is usually an 'insider').

are not accumulated over a number of governments, and, as in the USA, that a change in administration brings about a major breach in the continuity of government.

Furthermore, it is difficult to have both political commitment and meritocracy within the civil service. In a politicised service, not only are appointments made on the basis of political affiliation and personal loyalty, rather than ability and training, but it may be more difficult to attract high-calibre staff to work in temporary positions that offer no form of job security. A more insidious danger is that ideological enthusiasm may blind civil servants to the drawbacks and disadvantages of policy proposals. From this point of view, the virtue of neutrality is that it establishes an 'arm's length' relationship between bureaucrats and politicians, allowing the former to see the weaknesses, as well as the strengths, of the policy options they are required to examine. For instance, perhaps the ease with which the disastrous 'poll tax' was devised in the UK in the late 1980s bears witness to the degree to which civil servants under Margaret Thatcher had ceased to interject, 'But minister. . .'.

Counter-bureaucracies

The final mechanism of political control is through structures designed to support or assist politicians or to act as a counterweight to the official bureaucracy. The simplest such system is the use of political advisers or 'outsiders', which is now a feature of almost all modern states. More significantly, institutions of various kinds have been established to share ministers' workloads and provide them with personal advisory staff. In the UK, this has occurred on an *ad hoc* basis. Edward Heath set up the Central Policy Review Staff (CPRS) in 1970, Harold Wilson created the Policy Unit in 1974, and Margaret Thatcher in the 1980s expanded the role of the Private Office and also sought advice from right-wing 'think tanks' such as the Centre for Policy Studies and the Adam Smith Institute. Of more general application is the device of the *cabinet ministériel*. These have long been established in France and been taken up in states like Italy and Austria, as well as by the EU. *Cabinets* are ministers' personal teams of advisers (in France, usually 15–20 strong) that help to formulate policy, assist in supervising departmental activities, and help ministers to carry out their various other responsibilities.

The idea of a counter-bureaucracy has been most elaborately developed in the USA, in the form of the Executive Office of the President (EOP). This was established by President Roosevelt following the Brownlow Committee's declaration that 'the President needs help'. The EOP is the president's personal bureaucracy. It consists of a growing number of councils and offices and employs about 1400 staff. Its key agencies are the White House Office, which comprises the president's closest political advisers, the Office of Management and Budget, which assists in the preparation of budgetary and legislative proposals, the National Security Council (NSC), which advises on defence and foreign-affairs issues, and the Council of Economic Advisers, which provides the president with professional advice on economic policy.

The purpose of counter-bureaucracies is to compensate for the imbalance in the relationship between amateur, temporary and outnumbered politicians and their expert, permanent and professional officials. However, this form of political control has its drawbacks. In the case of the EOP, it leads to the duplication of government agencies and so causes jurisdictional conflicts and a measure of bureaucratic infighting. This has been particularly evident in the often fraught relationship between the National Security Council and the State Department.

A further difficulty is that counter-bureaucracies may compound, rather than solve, the problem of political control. Margaret Thatcher, for instance, abolished the CPRS in 1983, believing it to be the source of damaging leaks during that year's election campaign. Similarly, NSC staff, including Lieutenant-Colonel Oliver North, were at the centre of the Iran–Contra affair that rocked the Reagan administration in the 1980s. Lastly, allowing politicians to surround themselves with hand-picked advisers creates the danger that they will cut themselves off from political reality and be told only what they want to hear. This problem was highlighted by both the Watergate and the Iran–Contra affairs, when the respective presidents, Nixon and Reagan, became overdependent on EOP advisers, partly because they believed that they could neither trust nor control an essentially hostile federal bureaucracy.

■ Summary

◆ The term bureaucracy has been used in a number of ways. Originally, it meant rule by officials as opposed to elected politicians. In the social sciences, it is usually understood as a mode of organisation. Modern political analysts, however, use the term bureaucracy to mean the administrative machinery of the state, bureaucrats being nonelected state officials or civil servants, who may or may not be subject to political control.

◆ Three major theories of bureaucracy have been advanced. The Weberian mode suggests that bureaucracy is a rational–administrative machine, the characteristic form of organisation in modern society. The conservative power-bloc model emphasises the degree to which the bureaucracy reflects broader class interests and can resist political control. The bureaucratic oversupply model emphasises a tendency towards 'big' government caused by the pursuit of career self-interest on the part of civil servants.

◆ The core function of the bureaucracy is to implement or execute law and policy through the administration of government business. However, civil servants also play a significant role in offering policy advice to ministers, in articulating and aggregating interests (especially through links to client groups), and in maintaining political stability and continuity when there is a change of government or administration.

◆ Bureaucracies have traditionally been organised on the basis of purpose or function, hence their division into departments, ministries and agencies. The degree of centralisation or decentralisation within them varies considerably. Modern trends, however, are towards the divorce of policy making from policy implementation, and the incorporation of private-sector management techniques, if not outright privatisation.

◆ There is concern about bureaucratic power because of the threat it poses to democratic accountability. The principal sources of bureaucratic power include the ability of civil servants to control the flow of information and thus determine what their political masters know, the logistical advantages that they enjoy as permanent and full-time public officials, and their status as experts and custodians of the national interest.

◆ Control is exerted over bureaucracies in a number of ways. Mechanisms of public accountability to ministers, assemblies, the courts or ombudsmen can be established. The civil service can be politicised so that it shares the ideological enthusiasms of the government of the day. Counter-bureaucracies can be constructed to provide an alternative source of advice and to strengthen the hands of elected politicians.

◼ Questions for discussion

▶ Do bureaucrats really 'run' their countries?

▶ Can a clear distinction be drawn between making policy and offering policy advice?

▶ Can civil servants ever be politically neutral?

▶ Are public bureaucracies inherently inefficient?

▶ Do the benefits of a politically committed civil service outweigh the costs?

▶ What are the most effective mechanisms for controlling bureaucratic power?

◼ Further reading

Beetham, D. *Bureaucracy* (Milton Keynes: Open University Press, 1987). A clear and concise discussion of models of bureaucracy and theories of bureaucratic power.

Blau, P. and M. Meyer (eds) *Bureaucracy in Modern Society* (3rd ed.) (New York: Random House, 1987). A useful introduction to the phenomenon of bureaucracy and the impact of bureaucracies.

Rowat, D. (ed.) *Public Administration in Developed Democracies: A Comparative Study* (New York: Marcel Dekker, 1988). A wide-ranging and thorough study of public administration in a number of states.

Self, P. *Government by the Market? The Politics of Public Choice* (Basingstoke: Macmillan, 1994). A perceptive discussion of the remodelling of government according to the principles of market competition and efficiency.

Militaries and Police Forces

CHAPTER 18

> 'Political power grows out of the barrel of a gun.'
>
> MAO ZEDONG *Problems of War and Strategy* (1938)

No regime remains in power on the basis of political legitimacy or administrative efficiency alone. All systems of rule are underpinned, to a greater or lesser extent, by the exercise of coercive power through the institutions of the military and the police. However, the coercive power of the military and the police can be put to a wide variety of political uses. Militaries may function simply as instruments of foreign policy, or they may play a decisive domestic role, perhaps by quelling civil unrest or even propping up unpopular regimes. They may operate as powerful interest groups, or may, through the construction of military regimes, provide an alternative to civilian rule. In the same way, the police can act as a means of maintaining public order and civil liberty, or as a mechanism of political repression which may, in extreme cases, lead to the establishment of a police state. So great is the potential power of these institutions that questions about how they can be controlled or be made publicly accountable are of enduring political significance.

The major issues addressed in this chapter are as follows:

Contents

Key issues

▶ What are the distinctive features of the military as a political institution?

▶ How, and in what ways, can the military intervene in politics?

▶ How can military power be brought under political control?

▶ In what ways does civil policing differ from political policing?

▶ What mechanisms are used to make police forces publicly accountable?

■ The military and politics

The development of modern armed forces can be traced back to the period following the Middle Ages when European powers started to develop a standardized form of military organisation, usually based on a standing army. During the nineteenth century, the military became a specialised institution with a professional leadership separate from the rest of society. European colonialism, in turn, ensured that this military model was adopted all over the world, turning the military into a near-universal component of state organisation. Puerto Rico is sometimes identified as the classic exception to this rule, but its lack of armed forces is only possible because of the security provided by the US military.

The military is a political institution of a very particular kind. Four factors distinguish the military from other institutions and give it a distinct, and at times overwhelming, advantage over civilian organisations. First, as an instrument of war, the military enjoys a virtual monopoly of weaponry and substantial coercive power. As the military has the capacity to prop up or topple a regime, its loyalty is essential to state survival. Secondly, armed forces are tightly organised and highly disciplined bodies, characterised by a hierarchy of ranks and a culture of strict obedience. They are thus an extreme example of bureaucracy (see p. 341) in the Weberian sense. This gives the military an unusual degree of organisational effectiveness, although it can also breed inflexibility and discourage initiative and innovation. Thirdly, the military is invariably characterised by a distinctive culture and set of values, and an *esprit de corps* that prepare its personnel to fight, kill and possibly die. Sometimes portrayed as implicitly right-wing and deeply authoritarian (by virtue of its traditional emphasis on leadership, duty and honour), military culture can also be grounded in creeds such as revolutionary socialism (as in China) or Islamic fundamentalism (as in Iran). Fourthly, the armed forces are often seen, and generally regard themselves, as being 'above' politics, in the sense that, because they guarantee the security and integrity of the state, they are the repository of the national interest. This secures for most militaries a special status and respect, but it may also incline the military to intervene in politics, particularly when, in its view, vital national interests are under threat.

On the other hand, it is a mistake to view the military as a single, cohesive institution with common political features in all societies. Divisions within the military may stem from various sources. For example, conflicts may develop between broadly conservative senior officers, often recruited from elite backgrounds, and more junior officers, who may be either impatient for promotion or more open to progressive or radical ideas. Similarly, there is likely to be tension between an officer core that is privileged both socially and professionally, and conscripts or enlisted personnel, who are usually drawn from the working class or peasantry. Rivalry and competition for prestige and scarce resources may also divide the various services and units within the military, while regional or ethnic divisions can also be significant.

The character of particular armed forces is shaped by internal and external factors. These include the history and traditions of the military and specific regiments or units, and the nature of the broader political system, the political culture and the values of the regime itself. For example, the political orientation of the People's Liberation Army (PLA) in China is deeply influenced by the decisive role it played in establishing the communist regime in 1949 and by strict party control at every level of the Chinese military. In West Germany, the armed forces were subjected to a systematic process of political indoctrination to root out Nazi sympathies and values and to build support for the principles of political democracy. Finally, it is difficult to generalise about the nature and significance of the military because of the very different roles that the military can play in political life. The most important of these are the following:

- an instrument of war
- a guarantee of political order and stability
- an interest group
- an alternative to civilian rule.

Role of the military

Instrument of war

The central purpose of the military is to serve as an instrument of war that can be directed against other political societies if necessary. This is why the development of the military as a separate and permanent institution coincided with the emergence of the state system in early modern Europe. Crucially, however, the armed forces can be put to either defensive or offensive uses. It is the capacity of the military to defend a country against external aggression that ensures that practically all countries have armed forces, the military being seen as no less essential to the modern state than a police force, the courts or a postal service. However, this defensive role has conflicting implications for the size and nature of the military.

On the one hand, the armed forces must be powerful enough to at least match the might of likely aggressors and, preferably, to deter aggression in the first place. Not uncommonly, such calculations have led to arms races and resulted in war, as defensive buildups have created international tension by appearing to neighbouring states to constitute an offensive threat. This certainly happened in the case of the naval race between the UK and imperial Germany in the years leading up to the outbreak of the First World War. However, an arms race that maintains an effective balance of power can also discourage military aggression, as was demonstrated by the Cold War.

On the other hand, if the military has an exclusively defensive role, this can restrict it to long periods of inactivity, during which it must maintain a state of readiness that is never utilised. Moreover, success in deterring aggression may actually weaken public support for military spending, as support is usually linked to the existence of a perceived threat. The end of the Cold War has thus led to a 'peace dividend' in the form of the transfer of resources, in both the former communist East and the capitalist West, from military to domestic purposes. In Switzerland, with its long history of nonintervention and neutrality, the army has been reduced to a mere symbol of national integrity.

When armed forces are used to pursue offensive or expansionist ends, the military becomes substantially more important. To wage war against other states requires both that the military is able and willing to act as an agent of aggression and that its offensive actions enjoy a significant measure of public support. Expansionist states are therefore usually characterised by a high level of military spending, the recruit-

> ### Concept
>
> **War**
>
> War is a condition of open armed conflict between two or more parties (usually states). The term is also used metaphorically, as in 'class war', 'trade war' and 'cold war' (see p. 146). The emergence of war as an organised and goal-directed activity stems from the development of the European state system in the early modern period. War has a formal or quasi-legal character in that the declaration of a 'state of war' need not necessarily be accompanied by an outbreak of hostilities. The notion that war legitimises unchecked barbarity is challenged by the sometimes controversial concept of war crimes. A civil war is an armed conflict between politically organised groups *within* a state, usually fought to gain (or retain) control of the state or to establish a new state.

◆ Concept

Militarism

The term militarism can be used in two ways. First, it refers to the achievement of ends by the use of military force. Any attempt to solve problems by military means can be described as militarism in this sense. Secondly, and more commonly, militarism is a cultural or ideological phenomenon in which military priorities, ideals and values come to pervade the larger society. This typically includes a glorification of the armed forces, a heightened sense of national patriotism, the recognition of war as a legitimate instrument of policy, and an atavistic belief in heroism and self-sacrifice. In some cases, but not all, militarism is characterised by the abuse by the military of its legitimate functions, and its usurpation of responsibilities normally ascribed to civilian politicians.

ment of military leaders into the process of policy making, and the growth of militarism, in the sense that ideas and values usually associated with the military are spread throughout civilian society. The classic example of a militaristic regime was Hitler's Third Reich in Germany.

Nazi totalitarianism (see p. 27) operated in part through the collapse of the distinction between military and civilian institutions, bringing about the militarisation of political life. The Nazi Party was organised along military lines. Its senior figures wore uniforms, and a military-style culture and a hierarchy of ranks were adopted. Armed organisations also developed within it, notably, the SA (Sturmabteilung) and the SS (Schutzstaffel). Hitler's assumption of power in 1933 was followed by a process of military expansion and the construction of an alliance with army leaders; this was cemented by the purge of the SA in June 1934, in the so-called 'night of the long knives'. Moreover, constant agitation and propaganda highlighting the alleged injustices of the Treaty of Versailles (1919) helped to prepare the German people for the programme of military aggression that led to the outbreak of the Second World War in 1939. However, militarism should not be equated with the prioritisation of military interests and the dominance of military leaders over civilian ones. To some extent, German militarism in the 1930s was a means of subordinating the army and turning it into an instrument for the achievement of Nazi ideological goals. Hostility between Hitler and key generals, who believed that he had drawn Germany into a war that would ultimately destroy both Germany and the army, led to the abortive attempt on Hitler's life in the bomb plot of 1943.

Guarantee of domestic order

Needless to say, the military's coercive power and operational efficiency is not only of significance in international politics. Although military force is usually directed against other political societies, it may also be a decisive factor in domestic politics. However, the circumstances in which militaries are deployed, and the uses to which they are put, vary from system to system and from state to state. One of the least controversial nonmilitary tasks that armed forces may be called upon to undertake is to act as an emergency service in the event of natural and other disasters. This type of involvement in domestic affairs is exceptional and is usually devoid of political significance. However, the same cannot be said of circumstances in which the armed forces are used to police domestic civil disturbances or disputes.

US troops, for instance, were deployed to implement federal racial desegregation orders during the civil rights struggles of the 1950s and 1960s. Similarly, in the UK in the 1970s and 1980s, the army was brought in during industrial disputes to provide emergency fire and ambulance services. Such actions provoke criticism, not only because the military is used in ways that encroach on responsibilities that usually belong to the police, but also because they compromise the traditional neutrality (see p. 287) of the armed forces. This highlights the difficulty of distinguishing between the domestic use of the military as a 'public' instrument serving the national interest and its use as a 'political' weapon furthering the partisan goals of the government of the day. This distinction becomes still more blurred when the military is used to quell civil unrest or counter popular insurrection.

Certain states confront levels of political tension and unrest that are quite beyond the capacity of the civilian police to contain. This particularly occurs in the case of serious religious, ethnic or national conflict. In such circumstances, the military can become the only guarantee of the integrity of the state, and may even be drawn in to what may amount to a civil war to achieve this end. In 1969, UK troops were despatched to Northern Ireland, initially to defend the beleaguered minority Catholic community, but increasingly to contain a campaign of sectarian terror waged by the Irish Republican Army (IRA) and opposing 'loyalist' groups such as the Ulster Defence Association (UDA) and the Ulster Defence Force (UDF). The Indian army has been used on a number of occasions to counter civil unrest and restore political order (see p. 371). These have included the eviction of Sikh separatists from the Golden Temple at Amritsar in 1984 at the cost of 1000 lives, and the seizure of Ayodhya from Hindu fundamentalists in 1992 following the destruction of the ancient Babri Masjid mosque. Russian troops were despatched to the republic of Chechnya in 1994 to thwart its bid for independence in an operation that turned into a full-scale war, later developing into an ongoing guerilla struggle.

In cases in which political legitimacy has collapsed altogether, the military may become the only prop of the regime, safeguarding it from popular **rebellion** or revolution. When this occurs, however, all semblance of constitutionalism (see p. 279) and consent is abandoned as the government becomes an outright dictatorship. Thus, in May 1989, the survival of the Chinese communist regime was only maintained by the military assault on Tiananmen Square, which effectively neutralised the growing democracy movement. Such circumstances place a heavy strain on the loyalty of officers and the obedience of troops required to inflict violence on civilian demonstrators. Trouble was taken to deploy in Beijing only PLA divisions brought in from the countryside whose political loyalty could be counted on. In contrast, in Romania in December 1989, soldiers ordered to quell popular unrest went over to the demonstrators, effectively bringing about the collapse of the Ceauşescu regime.

Interest group

The military has been seen above largely as an instrument of policy, that is, as a device through which governments can achieve their foreign or domestic ends. However, armed forces are not neutral bodies that have no interest in the policy uses to which they are put. Rather, like bureaucracies, militaries can act as interest groups that seek to shape or influence the content of policy itself. In this respect, the military has a number of clear advantages. First, it possesses considerable technical knowledge and expertise. Although armed forces are usually constrained by formal subordination to civilian politicians and the requirements of political neutrality, it is difficult for governments not to listen to, and often heed, the advice of senior members of the military on strategic, defence and broader foreign policy matters.

Secondly, the military is an 'insider' group in the sense that it is represented on key policy making bodies and so possesses an institutional power base. The US military, for instance, is able to exert influence through the Department of Defense ('the Pentagon') and the National Security Council, as well as through appearances before the congressional Armed Services Committees. Thirdly, the military benefits from its status as the guarantor of national security and state integrity, and from the significance the public normally attaches to the issue of defence. Governments may thus calculate that there are votes in strengthening military capacity and increasing defence spending.

Just as public choice theorists (see p. 258) claim that civil servants are essentially concerned with career self-interest, it is possible to argue that the senior military is likely to 'push' policies that enhance the size and status of the armed forces, or

> ### Concept
> **Dictatorship**
>
> A dictatorship is, strictly, a form of rule in which absolute power is vested in one individual; in this sense, dictatorship is synonymous with autocracy. Originally, the term was associated with the unrestricted emergency powers granted to a supreme magistrate in the early Roman Republic, which created a form of constitutional dictatorship. In the modern usage of the term, however, dictators are seen as being above the law and as acting beyond constitutional constraints. Early examples of dictators were Sulla, Julius Caesar and Augustus Caesar in Rome, more recent ones are Hitler, Mussolini and Saddam Hussein. More generally, dictatorship is characterised by the arbitrary and unchecked exercise of power, as in 'class dictatorship', 'party dictatorship', 'military dictatorship' and 'personal dictatorship'.

Rebellion: A popular uprising against the established order, usually (unlike a revolution) aimed at replacing rulers rather than the political system itself.

guarantee their independence. This view sees the military as a lobby group that campaigns mainly for an increase in the military budget, or as a series of rival services or units that struggle for the largest possible cut of the defence cake. The armed forces are aided in this by a number of powerful allies in the form of what President Eisenhower, in his farewell address in 1961, referred to as the **military–industrial complex**. It is widely accepted, for example, that the Cold War was partly sustained by the vested interests of the US and Soviet military–industrial complexes, both of which had a strong incentive to exaggerate the strategic threat and offensive capabilities of the other. Some estimates of Soviet military and defence-related expenditure in the 1980s put it as high as 40 per cent of gross national product (GNP), Soviet military industry (in Khrushchev's words, 'the metal eaters') being the only efficient sector of a declining economy. While US defence spending in the same period accounted for only about 6 per cent of GNP, this represented, in real terms, an amount probably less than 10 per cent smaller than total Soviet defence spending.

Similarly, it has been suggested that one of the forces behind the outbreak of the 1991 Gulf War was the desire of the senior military and leading defence contractors in the USA to justify high levels of military investment by demonstrating the effectiveness of new technology such as the Stealth bomber and Cruise and Patriot missiles. On the other hand, it would be misleading always to characterise the military as warmongers. Following the humiliations of the Vietnam War, Colin Powell, President Bush's most senior military adviser, was amongst the most reluctant to support a military solution to the Gulf crisis, fearing the damage to the armed forces that would be caused by an operation that lacked clear and achievable political objectives.

To some extent, the Russian military has played a greater role in Russian foreign policy and security policy since the collapse of communism in 1991. During the Soviet period, military interests, although always powerful, were generally constrained because of the leading role of the CPSU. However, a combination of political insecurity and strategic uncertainty in postcommunist Russia has created conditions that allow the armed forces greater influence and independence. The assault on the Russian parliament building by elite paratroops that ended the hardline rebellion in October 1993 merely emphasised that President Yeltsin had become, in a sense, a captive of the military. This was compounded by the electoral weakness of the reformers and Yeltsin's failure to gain support from a Duma (parliament) dominated by nationalists and communists. The Russian military, operating through the Defence Ministry, thus came to play a decisive role in shaping policy in relation to both the 'near abroad' and the 'far abroad'.

Although Russian military leaders were prepared to withdraw troops from the Baltic states, they succeeded in persuading Yeltsin to adopt a general policy of treating the borders of the Commonwealth of Independent States (CIS) as an extension of the Russian frontier. This led to a closer military association between Moscow and former Soviet republics like Georgia and Tajikistan that border Islamic Central Asia. A shift in Russian policy towards the 'far' abroad was evident in 1995 in the adoption of a more assertively pro-Serbian stance in the Bosnian crisis, which effectively thwarted NATO moves to resolve the conflict through military pressure. The war in Chechnya, however, provided the clearest demonstration to date of the influence of the Russian military and its desire to maintain the integrity of the Russian Federation, following the abandonment of eastern Europe in 1989 and the breakaway of the non-Russian Soviet republics in 1991.

Military–industrial complex: A symbiotic relationship between the armed forces and defence industries, based on a common desire to increase military spending.

Alternative to civilian rule

Of course, the military is not always content to act as an interest group exerting pressure on and through civilian politicians. The control of weaponry and coercive power gives it the capacity to intervene directly in political life, leading in extreme cases to the establishment of military rule. Just as the military can prop up an unpopular government or regime, it can also remove and replace the governing elite or topple the regime itself. The precise circumstances in which armed forces seize power are examined later in this chapter; however, the form of rule they establish has a number of distinguishing characteristics. The defining feature of military rule is that members of the armed forces displace civilian politicians, meaning that the leading posts in government are filled on the basis of the person's position within the military chain of command.

One version of military rule is the military junta (from the Spanish *junta*, meaning council or board). Most commonly found in Latin America, the military junta is a form of collective military government centred on a command council of officers whose members usually represent the three services (the army, navy and air force). In its classic form, for example, in Argentina in 1978–83, civilians are excluded from the governing elite, and trade union and broader political activity is banned. However, rivalry between the services and between leading figures usually ensures that formal positions of power change hands relatively frequently. In other cases, a form of military dictatorship emerges as a single individual gains preeminence within the junta, as with Colonel Papadopoulos in Greece in 1974–80, General Pinochet in Chile after the 1973 coup, and General Abacha in Nigeria from 1993. In Africa especially, it has not been unknown for noncommissioned or junior officers to seize power. This occurred in Ghana in 1979, when power was seized by Flight Lieutenant Jerry Rawlings, and in Sergeant Samuel Doe's *coup d'état* in Liberia in 1980.

It is difficult, however, for military rule to exist in a stable and enduring political form. While military leaders may highlight the chronic weakness, intractable divisions and endemic corruption (see p. 347) of civilian government, it is unlikely that military rule will provide a solution to these problems or that it will be perceived as legitimate, except during temporary periods of national crisis or political emergency. This is why military regimes are typically characterised by the suspension of civil liberties and the suppression of all potential sources of popular involvement in politics. Protest and demonstrations are curtailed, opposition political parties and trade unions are banned, and the media are subjected to strict **censorship**. As a result, the military often prefers to rule behind the scenes and exercise power covertly through a civilianised leadership. This occurred in Zaire under Mobutu, who came to power in a military coup in 1965, but later allowed the army to withdraw progressively from active politics by ruling through the Popular Movement of the Revolution, founded in 1967. In the 1960s and 1970s, Egypt's transition from military government to authoritarian civilian rule was achieved under Gamal Nasser and Anwar Sadat, both military figures. The appointment of civilian cabinets and the emergence of parties and interest group politics not only strengthened the regime's legitimacy, but also gave Nasser and Sadat a greater measure of freedom from their own militaries.

Military regimes may come to a more dramatic end by collapsing or being overthrown when the authority of the armed forces is fatally compromised, usually by military defeat. This may also happen when military rulers are confronted by levels of popular opposition that can no longer be contained through repression (see p. 369)

Concept

Civil liberty

Civil liberty refers to a private sphere of existence that belongs to the citizen, not the state. Civil liberty therefore encompasses a range of 'negative' rights, usually rooted in the doctrine of human rights (see p. 284), which demand noninterference on the part of government. The classic civil liberties are usually thought to include the right to freedom of speech, freedom of the press, freedom of religion and conscience, freedom of movement, and freedom of association. These key freedoms are generally seen as vital to the functioning of liberal-democratic societies, since they provide the individual with protection against arbitrary government. In many cases, the principle of civil liberty is given constitutional expression through documents such as a bill of rights.

Censorship: The control or suppression of publications, expressions of opinion, or other public acts; censorship may be formal or informal.

alone. Examples of the first situation include the fall of the Greek generals in 1974 following the Turkish seizure of northern Cyprus, and the collapse of the Argentine military junta in 1983, a year after its failure to win the Falklands (Malvinas) War. On the other hand, the overthrow in 1986 of the army-backed Marcos dictatorship in the Philippines resulted from a combination of internal pressures for democratic reform, articulated by Cory Aquino, and diplomatic pressure from the USA. However, once the military has had experience of direct intervention in politics, it may be reluctant to return to barracks permanently. This has been demonstrated in the Philippines by a series of abortive coups against President Aquino.

Controlling the military

The undoubted power of the armed forces might suggest that the military is always a crucial, if not decisive, factor in politics. The reality is very different, however. Direct military intervention in politics, certainly when it is intended to displace civilian government, is in fact rare in many parts of the world, largely being confined to Latin America, Africa and parts of Asia. Both western liberal democracies and orthodox communist states have been comparatively free of military coups, attempted or successful. Since 1945, the only exceptions to this in western Europe have been in France in 1958 and 1961 (the first brought about the collapse of the Fourth Republic, and the latter was unsuccessful), in Portugal in 1974, when the army seized power to 'save the nation from government', and in Spain in 1981, when the army staged an abortive uprising. Exceptions in the communist world include the failed coup in China in 1971 associated with Lin Biao's leadership bid, General Jaruzelski's takeover in Poland in 1981, and the August 1991 hardline coup in Russia that briefly removed Gorbachev from power.

How is civilian control over the military achieved in other circumstances? The mechanisms and methods through which political control is exerted have been classified, broadly, into two types. Samuel Huntington (1957) described these as 'objective' and 'subjective' methods, while Eric Nordlinger (1977) used the terms 'liberal' and 'penetration'. The liberal, or objective, model of civil–military relations is best exemplified by western polyarchies. The chief feature of this form of control is that there is a clear division between political and military roles and responsibilities; quite simply, the military is kept out of politics. This is achieved in a number of ways.

First of all, the military is formally subordinate to civilian leaders, who are usually accountable to an assembly or the public. Secondly, policy making, even in defence and military realms, is the responsibility of civilian politicians, the military being required merely to offer advice and to take charge of implementation. Although the military may be able to exert considerable policy influence in practice, it is only one interest group amongst many and is restricted by the recognition that it does not have the authority to *challenge* decisions made by civilian leaders. This, in turn, is underpinned by a third requirement: strict political neutrality within the armed forces, ensuring that they will remain loyal regardless of the party or government that is in power.

The USA offers a good example of the political subordination of the armed forces, although this is perhaps surprising in view of the role that military force played in the birth of the republic in the American War of Independence of 1775–83. This subordination was secured through the establishment of the US president as commander-in-chief of the armed forces, and the refusal of George Washington (first as the leader of the American troops fighting for independence, and later as the first president of the USA) to countenance military intervention in civilian affairs. This liberal pattern of civil–military relations later successfully withstood the pressures of the bloody American Civil War (1861–65), as well as the tests of the First World War and Second World War, despite the politically contentious nature of US involvement on both occasions. Even when the US president has been a former military leader and war hero, as in the case of President Eisenhower, 1953–61, the US armed forces have acknowledged the ascendancy of civilian politicians. However, civilian control does mean that the military is politically impotent. While the US armed forces have never attempted to intervene directly in the political process, their routine interference as well-placed and influential lobbyists has had a significant impact on US defence and foreign policy.

A similar model of civil–military relations can be found in the UK. The UK armed forces are ultimately responsible to the Crown, which in practice means the prime minister and cabinet, via the Ministry of Defence. Not since the English Civil War of the seventeenth century and the rule of soldier–statesman Oliver Cromwell has the army exerted a direct influence on British political life. Indeed, in common with most other liberal democracies, the professionalism of the military in the UK is largely founded on its determination to keep out of politics. Only on very rare occasions has this self-restraint been tested. During the First World War, for instance, the soldier and administrator Lord Kitchener used his appointment as Secretary of State for War to instigate the raising of a vast volunteer army. Sir Douglas Haig, Commander-in-Chief of the British Expeditionary Force, had a crucial influence on the decision to use costly and exhausting trench-warfare tactics on the Western Front. He was able to exert this influence because the prime minister, H. H. Asquith, believed that it was the generals' job to run the war, and because King George V sometimes backed the military in its struggle against civilian politicians. No similar problems occurred under Churchill during the Second World War. Indeed, the general rule has been that developed western states with a history of constitutional stability and an entrenched democratic culture have experienced little difficulty in maintaining a liberal model of civil–military relations.

A very different form of civilian control has been employed in dictatorial or one-party states. Instead of relying on 'objective' mechanisms to establish the supremacy of civilian authority, the military is controlled by 'subjective' methods which bind it to the civilian leadership by imbuing it with the leadership's values and ideals. Whereas the liberal model operates through the exclusion of the armed forces from politics, the penetration model uses the opposite approach of systematic and thoroughgoing politicisation. This has been achieved in various ways, and with differing degrees of success. Hitler attempted to turn the German army into 'political soldiers' through the personal oath of allegiance sworn to him as Führer in August 1934. At the same time, he declared himself Head of the Armed Forces, and in 1941 he assumed the post of Supreme Commander. However, the army's loyalty was based more on the overlap between its authoritarian nationalism and the expansionist goals of the Hitler regime, than on its penetration by Nazi dogma. This was reflected in Hitler's growing reliance on the Waffen SS as a politically reliable elite army. Before committing suicide in April 1945, Hitler declared Admiral Dönitz the next Führer, because he believed that, of the various armed services, only the German navy had not abandoned him.

A substantially more brutal approach was adopted by Stalin in the USSR in the 1930s. Moves towards greater professionalisation in the Soviet armed forces, reflecting rising concern about the expansionist intentions of Nazi Germany, were abruptly ended in 1937 with the inauguration of a series of bloody purges. These led to the execution of three out of every five Soviet marshals and 13 out of 15 army commanders. In total, 90 per cent of all generals, 80 per cent of all colonels, and an estimated 30 000 officers of lower rank lost their posts, and often their lives. This effectively robbed the Red Army of its military expertise and threw it into almost total disarray, just at the time when it was being used to wage war against Finland, 1939–40, and was supposedly being prepared to defend the USSR against a possible German invasion.

In most instances, however, the penetration model entails not so much the culling of politically 'unreliable' members of the military as the promotion of politically 'correct' views and values through constant propaganda and agitation. For example, the Iraqi army, especially since Saddam Hussein assumed power in 1979, has been infused by the pan-Arab nationalism of the Ba'ath party. Ba'athism is committed to the unification of the Arab nation and to freeing it from western imperialism and **Zionism**. These goals provided an ideological justification for the invasion of Iran in 1980 and the annexation of Kuwait in 1990.

The institutional penetration of the armed forces has been developed in its highest form in communist states. In China, an elaborate network of party bodies parallels the structure of the military, offering leadership and guidance in areas of political and ideological significance. Civilian control is thus maintained through a level of interpenetration between the party and the armed forces that virtually obliterates any distinction between civil and military responsibilities. Party affiliation and a record of political commitment and loyalty to the communist regime is a precondition for the appointment and promotion of officers in the PLA. To the extent that the party operates in and through the military, however, the military also gains a voice in the policy process and is able to exert influence through an integrated party–state–military elite. In the USSR, this approach sometimes allowed the senior military to play a decisive political role, as it did in 1957 in backing Khrushchev and helping him to foil an attempted coup by the so-called anti-party group, and again in 1964 when, in the aftermath of the Cuban Missile Crisis, it withdrew its support from Khrushchev, so contributing to his fall.

When does the military seize power?

The most dramatic political manifestation of the power of the armed forces is, of course, the removal of a civilian government through a military *coup d'état*. The military can seize power either to displace the civilian leadership and establish a form of direct military rule, or to replace one set of civilian leaders by another through whom it is able to rule indirectly. In other cases, effective military government can be established without a formal bid for power on the part of the armed forces, as occurred in the Philippines under President Marcos, especially after the declaration of martial law in 1972. In certain parts of the world, military intervention in politics has become a normal occurrence, and military regimes have achieved such a degree of stability that they can no longer be classified as exceptional or transitory phenomena. The military coup thus becomes the principal device for bringing about the transition of government power from one group of leaders to the next.

Zionism: The movement for the establishment of a Jewish homeland, now linked to the defence of the interests and territorial integrity of Israel.

This regularly happened in the nineteenth century in Latin America (particularly in Mexico, Peru and Chile), in Spain, and in the Balkan states. In the twentieth century, military intervention has largely been confined to developing states in Africa, Latin America and parts of Asia. Military coups appear to be associated with particular circumstances. The most significant of these are the following:

- economic backwardness
- loss of legitimacy by civilian rulers
- conflict between the military and the government
- a favourable international context.

There is a clear link between the incidence of military coups and economic underdevelopment. Pinkney (1990) pointed out that, of the 56 countries that have experienced military government since 1960, the vast majority are in the third world. Moreover, particular coups can be linked to economic downturns. The overthrow of four years of civilian rule in Nigeria in 1983, for example, occurred after a deterioration in the economy caused by falling oil prices. By the same token, growing prosperity appears to be an antidote to military intervention, as demonstrated by the tendency in Latin America since the 1970s for the military to return to the barracks. Widespread poverty and deep social inequality are clearly of significance in that they weaken support for the incumbent government and provide the military with a pretext for stepping in with a promise to deliver economic development. However, economic factors alone cannot explain military takeovers. India, for instance, suffers from serious levels of material deprivation, but its armed forces have maintained strict political neutrality and have never openly challenged the authority of civilian governments.

Part of the answer to the question why do military coups occur is surely that they occur because they *can* occur. In other words, the military is likely to intervene in politics only when it senses that the legitimacy (see p. 193) of existing institutions and the ruling elite is challenged, and when it calculates that its intervention is going to be successful. The armed forces thus rarely interfere directly in politics when a stable democratic culture has been successfully established. This is because military rule can only operate through a level of systematic repression, which, in turn, may be difficult to sustain because it strains the unity and discipline of the military itself. It is therefore not surprising that the most of the successful military regimes have been established in parts of the world that have had a long history of colonial rule: Latin America, the Middle East, Africa and South East Asia. The political weakness and instability on which the military attempts to capitalise is certainly most acute in relatively new states. This stems not merely from an unfamiliarity with democratic politics, but is also linked to

Concept

Coup d'état

A *coup d'état* (from the French, a 'stroke of state') is a sudden and forcible seizure of government power through illegal and unconstitutional action. Coups are usually carried out by, or with the help of, the military; violence is often involved, although it may be limited and bloodless coups are not unheard of. *Coups d'état* differ from revolutions (see p. 198) in two respects. First, they are typically carried out by relatively small groups, usually from key institutions within the state (for example, the bureaucracy, the police or the armed forces), and thus do not involve mass political action. Secondly, they typically seek to replace the government or ruling group without necessarily changing the regime or bringing about broader social change.

Concept

Repression

Repression, in the political sense, is a state of subjugation brought about through systematic intimidation or open violence. Similar in kind to suppression, it differs in degree, being typically pro-active rather than reactive (its aim is to 'root out' opposition rather than merely contain it). The purpose of repression is to uphold a regime or ruling elite by keeping the masses out of politics and depriving them of the means of expression. This is accomplished through both political and psychological means. Repressive regimes weaken or abolish the machinery of representative politics (elections, parties, trade unions, a free press and so on), and establish a climate of fear through routine surveillance and the exercise of force.

the heightened expectations that independence brings, the poorly embedded nature of new political institutions and, sometimes, regional and ethnic tensions that have been inherited from the colonial past.

A good example is Nigeria, which has enjoyed only two brief periods of civilian government since gaining independence from the UK in 1960. The colonial government had attempted to weaken and split the nationalist movement by politicising national and ethnic divisions, particularly those between the Hausa in the north, the Yoruba in the west, and the Ibo in the east. This left Nigeria with a fractured and regionalised political elite and no ability to achieve the social consensus necessary for political stability. Growing civil disorder, a consequence of heightened ethnic tensions, led to an army takeover in 1966. However, intensified regional rivalry led to the outbreak of civil war the following year, as the eastern region, renamed Biafra, attempted to break away from the federal government. Rather than being the solution to Nigeria's problems, the military has merely perpetuated them. This is because the same ethnic, religious and regional conflicts that bedevil Nigerian society at large now permeate the military itself, and the army invariably exploits these conflicts in order to strengthen its hold on the country.

The third factor associated with military intervention is the degree to which the values, goals and interests of the armed forces differ from those of the broader regime. For example, despite widespread poverty and deep religious, linguistic and regional divisions, the Indian army has been prepared to leave politics to the politicians because of its engrained respect for the principles of liberal constitutionalism. When militaries move against governments, they do so either because they believe that their interests or values are threatened, or because they think that their actions are justified. In many newly-independent developing states, the military has taken over to 'save the nation', seeing itself as a 'westernising' or 'modernising' force confronting a traditionalist, rural, hierarchical and frequently divided political elite. This has occurred in Nigeria, Indonesia and Pakistan.

In other cases an authoritarian conservative military elite, often working in alliance with big business and enjoying support amongst the middle classes, has challenged the authority of reformist or socialist governments. The bloodless coup in Brazil in 1964 was largely a consequence of the army's suspicions about President Goulart's left-wing leanings. The Chilean president, Salvador Allende, the world's first democratically elected Marxist head of state, was overthrown and killed in 1973 by the army, which was led by General Pinochet. While the military is usually anxious to demonstrate that its intervention in politics is motivated by, for example, a desire to end corruption, heal divisions, or defend the nation, narrow selfish considerations are never entirely absent. Military coups are often an attempt to preserve the privileges, independence and prestige of the armed forces, or they may be a vehicle for the pursuit of political ambition.

Finally, the military's decision to seize power may also be affected by international considerations. There are few countries in which a military takeover does not have implications for neighbouring states, regional and international organisations, or the larger international community. In some cases, international pressures undoubtedly encourage military action. This was clearly the case with the Pinochet coup in Chile. The US Central Intelligence Agency (CIA) viewed Allende as a pro-Cuban communist whose economic reforms threatened the interests of US multinational corporations in Chile and elsewhere in Latin America. Not only did Pinochet receive covert advice and encouragement from the CIA, but he was also guaranteed US diplomatic support once his new military regime was established.

On other occasions, the prospect of an adverse diplomatic reaction has discouraged military plotters. In eastern Europe in 1989, for example, militaries remained largely passive as communist regimes collapsed in the face of mass demonstrations and popular pressure. In addition to a loss of political will on the part of communist leaderships, the armed forces recognised that military action would receive no support from President Gorbachev and the USSR, and that it would be fiercely condemned by the USA and the West. It would be wrong, however, to overstate the sensitivity of military regimes to diplomatic pressure. Saddam Hussein was little affected by international criticism of his military repression of the Kurds and the Shi'ite Moslems following the 1991 Gulf War. Similarly, General Abacha of Nigeria was unmoved by Commonwealth pressure in 1995 intended to prevent the execution of Ken Saro-Wiwa and other human rights protesters.

◼ The police and politics

The police force, like the military, is part of the coercive state. However, whereas the principal function of the military is to uphold national defence, the central purpose of a police force is to maintain domestic order. Police forces came into existence in the nineteenth century, largely as a result of the higher levels of social unrest and political discontent that industrialisation unleashed. For instance, in the UK, a paid, uniformed, full-time and specially trained police force was established by Robert Peel in London in 1829 following the Peterloo Massacre of 1819 in Manchester, when cavalry had been used to break up a large but peaceful working-class demonstration. This type of police system was introduced throughout the UK in 1856 and was later adopted by many other countries. Although police forces and militaries are similar in that they are both disciplined, uniformed, and (if to different degrees) armed bodies, important differences can be identified.

In the first place, whereas the military's essentially external orientation means that it is called into action only rarely, for example, in times of war, national emergency, and national disaster, the police force's concern with domestic order means that it has a routine and everyday involvement in public life. The police force is also more closely integrated into society than is the military; its members and their families usually live in the communities in which they work, although, as discussed below, a distinctive police culture often develops. Furthermore, the police typically use non-military tactics: because of their reliance on at least a measure of consent and legitimacy, they are either usually unarmed (as in the UK), or their arms are primarily a form of self-defence. To some extent, however, modern developments have tended to blur the distinction between the police and the military. Not only have armed forces been called in to deal with domestic disorder, as during the Los Angeles riots of 1992, but police forces have also tended to develop an increasingly paramilitary character. This is reflected in their access to progressively more sophisticated weaponry, and, in many states, their adoption of a quasi-military mode of operation.

Roles of the police

There are three contrasting approaches to the nature of policing and the role that it plays in society: the liberal, conservative and radical perspectives. The liberal

---

Concept

Order

The term order, in everyday language, refers to regular and tidy patterns, as when clothes are arranged in an 'orderly' fashion. As a political principle, order refers to stable and predictable forms of behaviour and, above all, to ones that safeguard personal security. Disorder therefore implies chaos and violence. Although order is universally valued, it has two very different political associations. Most commonly, it is linked with political authority and is thought to be achievable only if imposed 'from above' through a system of law. 'Law and order' thus become a single fused concept. The alternative view links order to equality and social justice, and emphasises that stability and security may arise naturally 'from below', through cooperation and mutual respect.

Crime

A crime is a breach of criminal law, which is law that establishes the relationship between the state and the individual, and thus lays down the conditions for orderly and peaceful social interaction. Criminals (persons convicted of a crime) are usually seen as being motivated by self-gain of some kind, rather than broader political or moral considerations, as in the case of civil disobedience (see p. 265). Crime is often viewed as an indication of the general level of social disorder and personal insecurity. However, the causes of, and remedies for, crime are hotly contested. The general divide is between those who blame individual corruption and place their faith in punishment, and those who blame deprivation and thus look to reduce crime through social reform.

perspective regards the police as an essentially neutral body, the purpose of which is to maintain domestic order through the protection of individual rights and liberties. In this view, police forces operate within a broad consensus and enjoy a high measure of legitimacy, based on the perception that policing promotes social stability and personal security. The police are essentially concerned with protecting citizens from each other. As policing is strictly concerned with upholding the rule of law (see p. 284), it has no broader political function.

The conservative perspective stresses the police's role in preserving the authority of the state and ensuring that its jurisdiction extends throughout the community. This view, which is rooted in a more pessimistic view of human nature, emphasises the importance of the police as an enforcement agency capable of controlling social unrest and civil disorder. In this light, police forces are inevitably seen as mechanisms of political control.

The radical perspective advances a much more critical view of police power. This portrays police forces as tools of oppression that act in the interests of the state, rather than the people, and serve elites rather than the masses. In the Marxist version of this theory, the police are seen specifically as defenders of property and upholders of capitalist class interests.

The role of the police force is also shaped by the nature of the political system in which it operates and the ways in which the government uses the police. Civil policing tends to be distinguished from political policing, and divisions are usually identified between liberal states and so-called police states.

Civil policing

Civil policing refers to the role of the police in the enforcement of criminal law. This is the aspect of police work with which the general public is usually most familiar and which dominates the public image of the police force: the police force exists to 'fight crime'. Clearly, however, the maintenance of civil order is a very different undertaking in, say, rural India than it is in modern cities such as New York, Paris and St Petersburg. It is widely accepted that, while small and relatively homogeneous communities are characterised by a significant level of self-policing, this changes as societies become more fragmented (socially and culturally), and as large-scale organisation depersonalises relationships and interaction. The spread of industrialisation in the twentieth century therefore brought about a measure of convergence in police organisation and tactics in different parts of the world. Police forces everywhere tend to confront similar problems in the form of, for example, traffic infringements, car theft, burglary, street crime and organised crime.

However, various contrasting styles of civil policing have been adopted. On the one hand, there is the idea of community policing. This relies on a constant police presence within the community to ensure public cooperation and support in the investigation of crimes, and to encourage the development of values and attitudes that help to prevent law breaking in the first place. This system has traditionally been exemplified by the UK concept of policing – the 'bobby on the beat' – and has been particularly well developed in Japan. Japanese police officers are expected to know and visit the various families and workplaces that fall within their area of jurisdiction, operating either from police boxes (*koban*) or residential police stations (*chuzaisho*). The success of this method, however, depends on the police being regarded as respected members of the local community and citizens accepting that their lives will be closely monitored. Pressure for efficiency and cost cutting led to the phasing out of community policing in the UK in the 1960s and 1970s, although it was reintroduced in a limited fashion after the urban riots of the early 1980s.

On the other hand, there is what is called 'fire brigade' policing. This emphasises the capacity of the police to react to breaches of law when they occur, in the hope that crime will be prevented by the effectiveness of the police response. Fire-brigade policing, or reactive policing, requires the adoption of harder, even paramilitary, tactics, and a greater emphasis on technology and arms. This type of approach has plainly been adopted in authoritarian and totalitarian states, but it is also found to some degree in liberal democracies. In an attempt to instil fear in potential offenders, the police in New York carry large-calibre revolvers and batons. Parisian police officers carry small-calibre semi-automatic pistols, batons and leaded capes, and the Cairo police carry submachine guns or automatic rifles.

Political policing

Policing can be 'political' in two senses. First, policing may be carried out in accordance with political biases or social prejudices that favour certain groups or interests over others. Secondly, policing may extend beyond civil matters and impact on specifically political disputes. The first concern has traditionally been raised by radicals and socialists, who dismiss the idea that police forces (or any other state body) act in a neutral and impartial fashion. From this perspective, the training and discipline of the police force and the nature of police work itself tend to breed a culture that is socially authoritarian and politically conservative. The working classes, strikers, protesters, women and racial minorities are therefore likely to be amongst the groups treated less sympathetically by the police.

Despite mechanisms of public accountability and protestations of impartiality, there is undoubtedly evidence to support these allegations, at least in particular circumstances. For instance, the US National Advisory Commission on Civil Disorders, set up by Lyndon Johnson to investigate the urban unrest that broke out in the USA during the 'long hot summer' of 1967, found that many of the disturbances were linked to the grievances of black ghetto dwellers about abusive or discriminatory police actions. The attack on Rodney King by four white Los Angeles police officers, whose acquittal in 1992 sparked two days of rioting, kept this image alive. Similarly, in the UK, the Scarman Report on the 1981 Brixton riots identified police racism as one of the reasons for the breakdown in police–community relations. Amongst its recommendations were that procedures be adopted to screen out racists, and that more black people and women be encouraged to join the force.

The level of political policing, meaning the use of the police as a political, rather than civil, instrument, has increased as societies have become more complex and fragmented. Some observers challenge the very distinction between civil and political areas of police work, arguing that all crime is 'political' in the sense that it springs from the distribution of wealth, power and other resources in society, and thus that all policing is 'political' because it defends the prevailing distribution of resources. The neutrality of the police force in the eyes of the public is particularly compromised when it is used to control strikes, demonstrations and civil unrest that stem from deep divisions in society. This certainly applies to the policing of areas riven by ethnic or national rivalry, such as the Basque region of northern Spain and Northern Ireland, where the police have been viewed as an illegitimate force by significant sections of the population.

In many cases, specially trained paramilitary police units have been set up specifically to carry out politically sensitive operations. The classic example of this is the widely feared Compagnie Republicaine de Securité (CRS) in France, which is organised along military lines and whose members live in barracks. In the UK, the Special Patrol Group (SPG) was set up for similar purposes. In addition, virtually all states have intelligence or security agencies that are usually shrouded in secrecy. Their role is deeply political in that it includes the surveillance and sometimes destabilisation of groups classified as a threat to the state or as opponents of the existing social system. These internal-security agencies include the Special Branch and MI5 in the UK, the FBI and the CIA in the USA, and the KGB in Russia.

Police states

The term police state refers to a form of rule in which the liberal balance between police powers and civil liberties has been entirely abandoned, allowing a system of arbitrary and indiscriminate policing to develop. The police force therefore operates outside a legal framework and is accountable to neither the courts nor the general public. Police states have totalitarian features (see p. 27), in that the excessive and unregulated power that is vested in the police is designed to create a climate of fear and intimidation in which all aspects of social existence are brought under political control. However, a police state is not run by the police force in the same way as a military regime is controlled by the armed forces. Rather, the police force acts as a private army that is controlled by, and acts in the interests of, a ruling elite.

This was clearly the case in Nazi Germany, which spawned a vast apparatus of political intimidation and secret policing. The SA, or 'Brownshirts', operated as political bullies and street fighters, the Gestapo was a secret police force, the SD (Sicherheitsdienst) carried out intelligence and security operations, and the SS developed, under Himmler, into a state within a state. The USSR also relied heavily on the activities of the secret police. Lenin formed the Cheka in 1917 to undermine his political opponents, and this mutated into the OGPU (which was responsible for, amongst other things, forcible collectivisation), then the NKVD (Stalin's personal instrument of terror), and eventually in 1953 into the KGB. In addition to political policing, the KGB took control of frontier and general security and the forced-labour system. Other examples of communist secret police agencies were the Stasi in East Germany and the Securitate in Romania. Both of these operated tools of political repression, building up vast networks of civilian informers, infiltrating all areas of society, and, when required, 'neutralising' opponents of the regime.

However, systems of security policing may operate alongside more 'orthodox' policing methods and machinery. For example, during the Nazi period in Germany, a conventional locally-organised police force survived, albeit uncomfortably, and took responsibility for the more mundane and less political aspects of law enforcement. In the USSR, the militia, which was separate from the KGB and ultimately responsible to the Ministry of Internal Affairs, was charged with the detection of crime, the apprehension of criminals, the supervision of the internal passport system, and the general maintenance of public order.

At the same time, some states usually classified as 'liberal' have also found a role for the secret police. The CIA in the USA has certainly engaged in a range of covert external operations, including the Pinochet coup in Chile, the attempted assassination of the Cuban leader Fidel Castro, and the supply of arms to the Contra rebels in El Salvador. It has also been subject to allegations of interference in domestic affairs, not least in the form of the still unsubstantiated claim that it played a role in the assassination of President Kennedy in 1962. A form of terroristic policing was used in Northern Ireland in the late 1960s in the form of the B-Specials. This was an auxiliary unit of the Royal Ulster Constabulary formed to control civilian demonstrations and fight the IRA. The B-Specials engaged in partisan and routine intimidation of the Catholic community and were disbanded in 1969, but only as the British army took on a more prominent role in policing 'the troubles'.

Political control and accountability

The issue of the control of the police is often posed in terms of Aristotle's question '*quis custodiet ipsos custodes?*' ('who will guard the Guardians?'). The issue of political control is highly sensitive, and conjures up two contrasting images. In a positive sense, it suggests accountability, oversight and scrutiny, a police force constrained by and loyal to properly instituted authority. In a negative sense, however, it implies politicisation and the possibility of police power being harnessed to the needs of the government of the day.

The key factor in determining where the balance lies between accountability and politicisation in practice is whether the police force is organised on a centralised or decentralised basis. The attraction of decentralisation is that a bottom-up structure allows the police a healthy independence from central government, whilst building in responsiveness to local needs and interests. This is why a decentralised, locally accountable police force is often considered to be the ideal. However, the pressures for centralisation are considerable, even irresistible. Not only does centralisation better meet the needs of national governments, but it holds out the prospect of greater administrative efficiency and increased political effectiveness.

Most continental European states have centrally controlled national police forces, the French policy often being identified as the classic example of this model. France has two national police forces: the National Police, under the civilian control of the Ministry of the Interior, and the Gendarmerie, under the military control of the Ministry of Defence. Although the former is responsible for maintaining law and order in large towns and cities, and the latter is primarily responsible for policing rural areas, the jurisdiction of the two commonly overlaps, giving rise to a traditional 'police war'. Particular concern, however, has been expressed about the level of political control exercised over the National Police. Interior ministers are personally responsible for the appointment of senior officers; the prefects who head the forces in each of the 96 *départements* act simply as agents of the Ministry of the Interior, and police chiefs are allowed to exercise only limited operational autonomy.

These problems have been compounded by the relative weakness of the French Department of Justice, meaning that the accountability of the police to the judiciary has traditionally been weak. The National Police were therefore often seen as a mere instrument of government, insensitive to civil liberties and justice, with senior officers who were prepared publicly to express sympathy for right-wing parties such as the Rassemblement pour la République (RPR) and the Union pour la Démocratie Française (UDF). However, when a socialist government was formed in 1981 after the election of President Mitterrand, sweeping changes were made. These involved a shakeup of senior personnel, including the replacement of the Prefect of Police and the Director-General of the National Police, and the imposition of tighter restrictions on the power of the police to interfere with citizens' rights through practices such

Concept

Accountability

Accountability means answerability, that is, a duty to explain one's conduct and be open to criticism by another. Accountability requires that the duties, powers and functions of bodies be defined in such a way that the performance of subordinate ones can be effectively monitored and evaluated. In this sense, accountability can only operate in a context of constitutionalism and respect for rules; being accountable does not mean being subject to arbitrary authority or capricious punishment. However, accountability may also amount to a weak form of responsibility (see p. 300), since it establishes a duty to answer and explain, but not necessarily to bear guilt and accept punishment.

as unauthorised telephone tapping.

On the other hand, the experience in Scandinavian countries suggests that it is possible to combine a unified police service with a high level of public accountability. In Denmark, the central government appoints the Commissioner of Police, a post that has broad strategic responsibilities, and the 72 local chief constables act as independent commanders of the personnel and resources placed at their disposal. In Sweden, a nationally administered police force has existed since 1965, but a system of local police committees ensures that representatives of local government can review police budgets and discuss policy and operational issues with police chiefs.

Perhaps the most decentralised police system in the world is that in the USA. The multi-layered US federal system results in no fewer than five major types of police agency. These include federal bodies attached to the Department of Justice (such as the FBI, the Bureau of Internal Revenue, and the Drug Enforcement Administration), the police forces of the 50 US states, sheriffs and deputy sheriffs at county level, city and township police forces, and, finally, a system of village and borough policing. The strength of this system is that it ensures that there is a high level of local responsiveness, the police being organised and operating according to the wishes of the communities they serve. The major drawbacks are that the system leads to considerable duplication and overlap amongst approximately 40 000 separate police agencies, and the balance between effective public accountability and unwarranted political interference is difficult to maintain.

In major US cities such as New York and Los Angeles, political pressure on the operational decisions of police departments is almost unavoidable, in view of the fact that police commissioners, usually career police officers, are appointed by mayors for fixed terms, and are, in most circumstances, keen to be reappointed. In other cases, however, decentralised systems have been abandoned altogether. In both West Germany and Japan, a shift towards decentralisation in police organisation was a major feature of democratic reconstruction after 1945. However, the resulting inefficiency and confusion soon led to a reversal of these policies. By 1950, West Germany had re-established provincial (*Länder*) police forces, with national bodies, such as the Federal Criminal Police Bureau and the Frontier Police Force, being set up shortly afterwards. In Japan, all the police forces were amalgamated into a single national service in 1954, responsible to the National Public Safety Commissioner, but it continues to be administered at the level of prefectural districts.

The UK is also usually considered to be an example of decentralised policing as it has never had a national police force. Apart from the Metropolitan Police in London, who are directly responsible to the Home Secretary, the police forces are locally organised and accountable, through their chief constables, to police committees that include magistrates and local councillors. However, this image of commendable decentralisation is often not realised in practice. In the first place, the Home Secretary's powers extend well beyond responsibility for the Metropolitan police force and include all matters related to law enforcement. Through guidelines, directions and circulars, as well as legislation steered through Parliament, the Home Office exercises a continuing influence on both police authorities and chief constables. In addition, there has been a trend towards increased centralisation through the establishment of national data storage and retrieval systems, such as the National Police Computer, and the National Reporting Centre, used during the 1984–85 miners' strike to coordinate police operations across the country. Centralisation was also fostered in the 1990s by the reduction of the influence of elected members of police authorities. Moreover, much politically sensitive policing is subject to little or inadequate democratic control. This is particularly true of MI5, whose remit was extended in 1996 to include intelligence related to crime and law enforcement as well as 'national security'. All MI5 operations are secret, its budget is not subject to parliamentary oversight, and alone amongst UK security agencies it is allowed to be 'self-tasking'. This means that, in theory, it can target who it likes, when it likes.

Summary

◆ The military is a political institution of a very particular kind. It is distinguished by its virtual monopoly of weaponry and substantial coercive power, its high level of internal discipline and strict hierarchical organisation, a set of values and a culture separate from those of civilian society, and the perception that it embodies the national interest and so is 'above' politics.

◆ The central purpose of the military is to be an instrument of war that can be directed against other political societies. However, the military may also operate as a powerful interest group that influences defence and foreign policy in particular. In addition, it may help to maintain domestic order and stability when civilian mechanisms are unable or unwilling to act, and it may, in particular circumstances, displace civilian government with a form of military rule.

◆ Two contrasting mechanisms have been used to exert control over the military. Liberal, or 'objective', methods rely on keeping the military out of politics by ensuring that it is subordinate and accountable to civilian leaders. Penetration, or 'subjective', methods, on the other hand, attempt to bind the armed forces to the civilian leadership by imbuing them with the leadership's political values and ideological goals.

◆ Military coups have tended to be associated with particular circumstances. The most significant of these are economic backwardness (which weakens support for the incumbent government), a loss of legitimacy on the part of existing institutions and the ruling elite, a conflict of interests or political values between military and civilian leaderships, and an international context that favours, or at least tolerates, the advent of a military regime.

◆ The central role of the police is to enforce criminal law and maintain civil order. The police force may nevertheless have a political character if social or other biases operate within it, if it is deployed in the event of civil unrest or political disputes, and if there is a police state in which the police force is turned into a private army that only serves the interests of the ruling elite.

◆ The control of the police relies on an appropriate balance between accountability and politicisation, which, in turn, depends on whether the police force is organised on a centralised or a decentralised basis. Decentralised police forces enjoy a healthy independence from central government and a high measure of local responsiveness. However, centralisation better meets the needs of national governments, and also holds out the prospect of greater administrative efficiency and increased police effectiveness.

▮ Questions for discussion

▶ If all states rest on coercive power, why do armed forces so rarely intervene directly in politics?

▶ When, if ever, it is justifiable to use the military as an instrument of domestic policy?

▶ Does the military–industrial complex pose a threat to the democratic process?

▶ Is it inevitable that the military will be wedded to right-wing or authoritarian values?

▶ Is all policing political?

▶ Is a decentralised police force always to be preferred to a centralised one?

▮ Further reading

Brewer, J., A. Guelke, I. Hume, E. Moxon-Browne and R. Wilford *The Police, Public Order and the State* (Basingstoke: Macmillan, 1988). A good comparative introduction to the role of the police in eight states.

Nordlinger, E. *Soldiers in Politics: Military Coups and Governments* (Englewoods Cliffs, NJ: Prentice Hall, 1977). An insightful introduction to the role of the military in politics and to means of achieving civilian control.

Pinkney, R. *Right-Wing Military Government* (London: Pinter, 1990). A useful study of military regimes in various parts of the world.

Roach, J. and J. Thomaneck *Police and Public Order in Europe* (London: Croom Helm, 1985). A collection of contributions that examine policing in various parts of Europe.

Policy and Performance

Policy Process and System Performance

CHAPTER

19

'My policy is to have no policy.'

Remark made by ABRAHAM LINCOLN to his secretary (1861)

In a sense, policy is the aspect of politics which concerns most people. In crude terms, policy consists of the 'outputs' of the political process. It reflects the impact of government on society, that is, its ability to make things better or to make things worse. Indeed, during the 1960s and 1970s, a distinctive area of study, policy analysis, was developed. This set out to examine how policy was initiated, formulated and implemented, and how the policy process could be improved. Policy analysis, however, is not just concerned with issues of efficiency and effectiveness, with the 'how' of policy making. It also addresses the 'what' of policy making: the nature of government 'outputs' and their 'outcomes' for the larger society. At the heart of policy analysis lie normative questions such as 'what is government *for*?' and 'what is the nature of the "good society"?'. Any attempt to evaluate the performance of government or the political system must therefore consider some of the deepest political and ideological divisions in the discipline itself.

The key issues discussed in this chapter are as follows:

Contents

Key issues

▶ What is policy?

▶ How are decisions made? What theories have been developed to explain decision-making?

▶ What are the key stages in the policy process, and what is their significance?

▶ What are the desirable 'outcomes' of the policy process?

▶ How do particular states and political systems perform in relation to these 'outcomes'?

Concept

Policy

A policy, in a general sense, is a plan of action adopted by, for example, an individual, group, business or government. To designate something as a policy implies that a formal decision has been made, giving official sanction to a particular course of action. Public policy can therefore be seen as the formal or stated decisions of government bodies. However, policy is better understood as the linkage between intentions, actions and results. At the level of *intentions*, policy is reflected in the stance of government (what government says it will do). At the level of *actions*, policy is reflected in the behaviour of government (what government actually does). At the level of *results*, policy is reflected in the consequences of government action (the impact of government on the larger society).

▉ The policy process

The policy process relates to the mechanisms through which public (government) policy is made. Policy making is a *process* in two senses. First, it involves a linked series of actions or events. These commence with the germination of ideas and the initiation of proposals, continue with some form of debate, analysis and evaluation, and conclude with the making of formal decisions and their implementation through designated actions. Policy making is therefore similar to the process of digestion in the human body: it links certain 'inputs' to particular 'outputs'. Secondly, it is a process in the sense that it distinguishes the 'how' of government from the 'what' of government, that is, it focuses on the way in which policy is made (process), rather than on the substance of policy itself and its consequences (product). Ultimately, policy can only be evaluated in the light of its impact, according to 'what actually happens', for good or ill. The first section of this unit considers how decisions are made, and examines the significance of the various stages in the policy process.

Theories of decision-making

The making of **decisions**, and specifically of bundles of decisions, is clearly central to the policy process. Although policy making also relates to the acts of initiation and implementation, the making of decisions and reaching of conclusions is usually seen as its key feature. However, it may be difficult to establish how and why decisions are made. Decisions are undoubtedly made in different ways by individuals and by groups, within small bodies and within large organisations, and within democratic and authoritarian structures. Nevertheless, a number of general theories of political decision-making have been advanced. The most important of these are the following:

* rational actor models
* incremental models
* bureaucratic organisation models
* belief system models.

Rational actor models

Decision-making models that emphasise human rationality have generally been constructed on the basis of economic theories which have themselves been derived from utilitarianism. Such ideas provide the basis for public choice theories (see p. 258), developed by thinkers such as Anthony Downs (1957), and enthusiastically taken up by the New Right. At the heart of such theories lies the notion of so-called 'economic man', a model of human nature that stresses the self-interested pursuit of material satisfaction, calculated in terms of utility. In this light, decisions can be seen to be reached using the following procedures:

* The nature of the problem is identified.
* An objective or goal is selected on the basis of an ordering of individual preferences.
* The available means of achieving this objective are evaluated in terms of their effectiveness, reliability, costs and so on.
* A decision is made through the selection of the means most likely to secure the desired end.

Decision: An act of choice; a selection from a range of options.

This type of process assumes both that clear-cut objectives exist, and that human beings are able to pursue them in a rational and consistent manner. For this to occur, utility must be homogeneous: it must be possible to compare the amount of satisfaction (pleasure or happiness) that each action would bring with that which would result from any other action. The best example of such an approach to decision-making is found in the use of cost–benefit analysis in the making of business decisions.

The rational actor model is attractive, in part, because it reflects how most people believe decisions *should* be made. Certainly, politicians and others are strongly inclined to portray their actions as both goal-orientated and the product of careful thought and deliberation. When examined more closely, however, rational calculation may not appear to be a particularly convincing model of decision-making. In the first place, the model is more easily applied to individuals, who may have an ordered set of preferences, than it is to groups, within which there are likely to be a number of conflicting objectives. Organisations may therefore only be said to make rational decisions if they are highly centralised and possess a strict command structure.

A second problem is that, in practice, decisions are often made on the basis of inadequate and sometimes inaccurate information, and the benefits of various actions may in any case not be comparable. Is it possible, for instance, to compare the 'costs' of raising taxes with those of reducing healthcare provision? Such difficulties encouraged Herbert Simon (1983) to develop the notion of 'bounded rationality'. This acknowledges that, as it is impossible to analyse and select all possible courses of action, decision-making is essentially an act of compromising between differently valued and imprecisely calculated outcomes. Simon described this process as 'satisficing'. The final drawback of rational actor models is that they ignore the role of perception, that is, the degree to which actions are shaped by belief and assumptions about reality, rather than by reality itself. Little or no importance is thus attached to the values and ideological leanings of decision makers.

Incremental models

Incrementalism is usually portrayed as the principal alternative to rational decision-making. David Braybrooke and Charles Lindblom (1963) termed this model 'disjointed incrementalism', neatly summed up by Lindblom (1959) as the 'science of muddling through'. This position holds that, in practice, decisions tend to be made on the basis of inadequate information and low levels of understanding, and this discourages decision makers from pursuing bold and innovative courses of action. Policy making is therefore a continuous, exploratory process; lacking overriding goals and clear-cut ends, policy makers tend to operate within an existing pattern or framework, adjusting their position in the light of feedback in the form of information about the impact of earlier decisions. Indeed, incrementalism may suggest a strategy of avoidance or evasion, policy makers being inclined to move away from problems, rather than trying to solve them.

Lindblom's case for incrementalism is normative as well as descriptive. In addition to providing a more accurate account of how decisions are made in the real world, he argued that this approach also has the merit of allowing for flexibility and the expression of divergent views. In this sense, it has a distinctly anti-utopian character and is well suited to policy making in pluralist democracies; 'muddling through' at least implies responsiveness and flexibility, consultation and compromise. However, the model has also been criticised as profoundly conservative, in that it justifies a bias against innovation and in favour of inertia. Policy makers

Concept

Utilitarianism

Utilitarianism is a moral philosophy that was developed by Jeremy Bentham (see p. 71) and James Mill (1773–1836). It claimed to propound a reliable, even scientific, ethical theory by equating 'good' with pleasure or happiness, and 'evil' with pain or unhappiness. Individuals are therefore assumed to act so as to maximise pleasure and minimise pain, these being calculated in terms of utility or use value, usually seen as satisfaction derived from material consumption. A principle of general or social utility can be used to evaluate laws, institutions and political systems in the form of 'the greatest happiness for the greatest number'. In political terms, utilitarianism has been linked to classical liberalism and free-market economics, providing, as it does, a theoretical and moral basis for egoistical individualism.

Incrementalism: The theory that decisions are not made in the light of clear-cut objectives, but through small adjustments dictated by changing circumstances.

who embrace incrementalism are more likely to be concerned with day-to-day problems than with indulging in long-term visionary thinking. Their energy is channelled into keeping the ship on course, not on reflecting on where that course is leading.

A further difficulty is that incrementalism sheds little light on those political decisions that are radical, even revolutionary, in character. For instance, Stalin's decision to launch the USSR's First Five Year Plan in 1928, Castro's decision to seize power in Cuba in 1959, and even Thatcher's decision to 'roll back the state' in the UK in the 1980s, can hardly be described as incremental adjustments. In view of such difficulties, Amitai Etzioni (1967) proposed the idea of 'mixed scanning', which attempts to bridge the gap between the rational approach and incrementalism. Mixed scanning allows for decision-making being carried out in two distinct phases. First, decision makers broadly evaluate, or scan, all the available policy options in terms of their effectiveness in meeting pre-existing objectives. Then, a narrower and more incremental approach is adopted as the details of a selected policy option are reviewed. In this way, for example, a broad decision to cut public spending must be accompanied by a series of more narrowly focused decisions relating to the specific areas or programmes that may be affected.

Bureaucratic organisation models

Both rational actor and incremental models are essentially 'black box' theories of decision-making; neither pays attention to the impact that the structure of the policy making process has on the resulting decisions. Bureaucratic or organisational models, on the other hand, try to get inside the black box by highlighting the degree to which process influences product. This approach was pioneered by Graham Allison (1971) in his examination of US and USSR decision-making during the Cuban Missile Crisis of 1962. Two contrasting, but related, models emerged from this study. The first, usually called the 'organisational process' model, highlights the impact on decisions of the values, assumptions and regular patterns of behaviour that are found in any large organisation. Rather than corresponding to rational analysis and objective evaluation, decisions are seen to reflect the entrenched culture of the government department or agency that makes them. The second theory, the 'bureaucratic politics' model, emphasises the impact on decisions of bargaining between personnel and agencies each pursuing different perceived interests. This approach dismisses the idea of the state as a monolith united around a single view or a single interest, and suggests that decisions arise from an arena of contest in which the balance of advantage is constantly shifting.

Although these models undoubtedly draw attention to important aspects of decision-making, they also have their drawbacks. In the first place, the organisational process model allows little scope for political leadership (see p. 330) to be imposed from above. It would be foolish, for example, to suggest that all decisions are shaped by organisational pressures and perceptions, for this would be to ignore the personal role played by F. D. Roosevelt in initiating the New Deal, or Hitler's influence on Germany's decision to invade Poland. Secondly, it is simplistic to suggest, as the bureaucratic politics model does, that political actors simply hold views that are based on their own position and on the interests of the organisations in which they work. Although the aphorism 'where you stand depends on where you sit' may often be applicable, personal sympathies and individual goals cannot be altogether discounted. Finally, to explain decisions entirely in terms of black-box considerations is to fail to give any weight to the external pressures that emanate from the broader economic, political and ideological context.

Belief system models

Models of decision-making that place an emphasis on the role of beliefs and ideology (see p. 41) highlight the degree to which behaviour is structured by perception. What people see and understand is, to an extent, what their concepts and values allow them, or encourage them, to see and understand. This tendency is particularly entrenched because, in most cases, it is largely unconscious. Although decision makers may believe that they are being rational, rigorous and strictly impartial, their social and political values may act as a powerful filter, defining for them what is thinkable, what is possible, and what is desirable. Certain information and particular options are therefore not appreciated or even considered, while other pieces of information and other courses of action feature prominently in the calculus of decision-making. Indeed, Kenneth Boulding (1956) underlined the vital importance of this process by pointing out that, without a mechanism to filter information, decision makers would simply be overwhelmed by the sheer volume of data confronting them.

However, there are different views about the origin and nature of this filtering process. Robert Jervis (1968), for instance, drew attention to evidence of consistent misperception on the part of decision makers in international affairs. In his view, this largely stemmed from ethnocentrism. The inclination of Anthony Eden and the UK government to view General Nasser as a 'second Hitler' during the 1956 Suez Crisis, and the tendency of the USA in 1959 to regard Fidel Castro as a Marxist revolutionary, may be examples of this phenomenon. Irving Janis (1972), on the other hand, suggested that many decisions in the field of international relations could be explained in terms of what he called 'groupthink'. This is the phenomenon in which psychological and professional pressures conspire to encourage a group of decision makers to adopt a unified and coherent position, with contrary or inconvenient views being squeezed out of consideration.

An attempt to combine different approaches to decision-making that takes account of the impact of belief systems has been made by Paul Sabatier (1988). Sabatier's principal concern was to explain how policy changes occur. In particular, he drew attention to the role of 'policy subsystems', that is, collections of people who in some way contribute to influencing policy in a particular area. A policy system may include not only interlocking groups of politicians, civil servants and interest groups, but also researchers, academics and journalists concerned with that area. Sabatier maintained that, within these subsystems, 'advocacy coalitions' emerge that comprise collections of individuals who share broadly similar beliefs and values. These beliefs nevertheless operate on three different levels:

- deep core beliefs (fundamental moral or philosophical principles)
- near-core beliefs (policy preferences)
- secondary beliefs (views about implementation or application).

The importance of such beliefs is that they provide what Sabatier called the 'glue' of politics, binding together people on the basis of shared values and preferences. However, while core beliefs are highly resistant to change, a greater measure of disagreement and flexibility is usually found at the near-core and secondary levels. Using this framework, Sabatier proposed that policy change could largely be understood in terms of the shifting balance of forces within a policy subsystem, in particular through the dominance of one advocacy coalition over others. This process may nevertheless be seen to be rational insofar as debate within a belief system, and rivalry between belief systems, promotes 'policy-orientated learning'.

In the hands of Marxists and feminists, however, such ideas can be used to draw very different conclusions (Hann, 1995). Marxists have argued that the core beliefs within any policy subsystem, or indeed amongst policy makers and opinion formers at large, are structured by ruling-class ideology and so favour the interests of dominant economic interests. Feminists, for their part, may argue that a preponderance of men amongst policy makers ensures that the 'glue' of politics is provided by patriarchal ideas and values. This results in policy biases that help to sustain a system of male power.

Stages in the policy process

Policy making cannot be understood simply in terms of how decisions are made. Policy not only involves clusters of decisions, in the sense of a number of related decisions concerning a particular policy area, but also different *kinds* of decisions. For instance, in the first place, there is the 'decision to make a decision'. Such decisions arise from the perception that there are problems to solve and issues to address; in short, 'something must be done'. The policy process then moves on to a different set of decisions about exactly *what* should be done, *how* it should be done, and *when* it should be done. The matter does not stop there, however. Even when the 'doing' has been done and the decisions have been put into effect, other questions emerge and other decisions must be taken. These relate to whether policy outcomes match policy intentions, and whether the content of policy, as well as the process of decision-making, can be improved in the future. The policy process can thus be broken down into four distinct stages:

* policy initiation
* policy formulation
* policy implementation
* policy evaluation.

Initiation

Where does policy come from? How do policy proposals arise in the first place? Such questions are significant not only because policy must start somewhere (without initiation there can be no formulation, implementation, and so on), but also because this stage in the policy process structures all subsequent debate, discussion and decision-making. Policy initiation, then, is crucial in that it sets the political agenda by both defining certain problems as **issues** and by determining how those issues are to be addressed. Why, for example, did environmental protection, largely ignored up to that point, arise on the political agenda in the 1980s, and how did this occur? Also, why has unemployment, commonly understood in the 1950s and 1960s to imply a need to boost public spending, come to be linked with ideas such as labour flexibility and the weakening of trade union power? Why do other political options (for example, the extension of worker's self-management) fail to become issues at all?

The difficulty of studying policy initiation is that policy can originate in literally

Issue: A matter recognised as part of the policy agenda, over which there is public debate or disagreement.

any part of the political system. Policy can stem 'from above', that is, from political leaders, cabinets, government agencies and so forth, and it can arise 'from below', through pressure from public opinion, the mass media, political parties, interest groups, 'think tanks' and the like. In the form of political leadership, policy initiation consists of mobilising support for initiatives emanating from the personal vision of the leader or the ideological priorities of a ruling party or group. This is most clearly seen in cases of transformational leadership (exemplified by Lenin and the Bolsheviks in Russia, Hitler and the Nazis in Germany, and even Thatcher and the Conservatives in the UK), in which leaders set out to 'create a story' that has broad, popular resonance in order to carry through a major restructuring of society.

However, political leaders are rarely original thinkers and are seldom the source of genuine policy innovation. It is in this area that writers, academics and philosophers seemingly unconnected with the world of practical politics may play a vital role in the process of policy initiation by developing 'core' values and theories, later developed into specific policy proposals by leaders and parties. Much of the economic policy in developed western states during the early post-Second-World-War period emanated from the ideas of John Maynard Keynes (see p. 172). Similarly, New Right policies aimed at 'rolling back the state', reducing taxes, targeting welfare spending and so on, originally sprang from the writings of, for example, Friedrich Hayek (see p. 48) and Milton Friedman (see p. 173).

Policy initiation 'from below' is significant in all political systems. As Harold Macmillan replied, when asked about the decisive factors in political life, 'Events, dear boy, events'. These events can range from strikes, riots and natural disasters to stock-market crashes in foreign states and investment decisions made by multinational corporations. As a general rule, however, the more democratic and pluralistic the political system, the more significant are bottom-up pressures on policy initiation. Indeed, democracy could be understood in this sense to imply that the political agenda is shaped 'from below' rather than 'from above'.

Public opinion clearly plays a significant role in this process insofar as regular and competitive elections force aspiring leaders to form policy proposals that take account of popular concerns and aspirations. However, these concerns and aspirations often remain shapeless and unformed until they are articulated by groups claiming to represent sections of the public. The mass media – newspapers, magazines, the radio and particularly television – undoubtedly make a major contribution to this process, both by selecting and prioritising the information available to the public, and by digesting and interpreting it through the process of editorialisation. Political corruption, for instance, became an issue in Italy and Japan largely through the publicity given to it by the print media.

Political parties and interest groups also play a key role in **agenda setting**. Opposition parties, for example, do not merely criticise government policy; they also develop alternative policies in an attempt to appear to be viable parties of government. Interest groups, for their part, highlight a broad array of grievances and concerns, promote causes and ideals, and give expression to the interests of diverse groups and sections of society. In the case of 'think tanks', interest groups have been formed specifically to develop policy proposals and to campaign for their acceptance amongst key players in the policy process.

Since the 1970s, researchers have tended to play down the role of formal, representative institutions, and to give greater prominence to the informal processes

Agenda setting: The ability to structure policy debate by controlling which issues are discussed or establishing a priority amongst them.

Concept

Policy network

A policy network (or policy community) is a systematic set of relationships between political actors who share a common interest or general orientation in a particular area. These relationships typically cut across formal institutional arrangements and the divide between government and nongovernmental bodies. A policy network may therefore embrace government officials, key legislators, well-placed lobbyists, sympathetic academics, leading journalists and others. The recognition of the existence of policy networks highlights the importance of informal processes and relationships in policy making, and particularly in policy initiation. Policy networks have been criticised for being relatively impervious to external influence, and for reducing the impact of the public, via representative institutions, on the policy process.

through which policy is initiated and developed. This highlights the importance of policy networks, that is, communities of policy actors that crisscross the public and private sectors.

From a technical point of view – that is, taking account of the effectiveness of the policy process, not the quality of its outputs – policy initiation can suffer from two contrasting weaknesses. First, it can be stifled by a paucity of policy proposals and innovative ideas; in other words, there can be too few policy 'inputs'. This could be seen in the state socialist systems of the USSR and eastern Europe. In the absence of competitive elections, a free press, opposition parties and autonomous groups, policy initiation was largely left to networks of officials working within the party–state apparatus. The problem this caused was that, since those who initiated policy had a vested interest in maintaining the system of central planning, the issue of economic reform did not appear on the political agenda until the system itself was beyond salvation. The Gorbachev reforms in the late 1980s, for example, were simply 'too little, too late'.

The other weakness of policy initiation relates to the opposite problem. The policy process can, quite simply, be overwhelmed by the weight and diversity of policy 'inputs', bringing about stagnation and paralysis. This has been seen as the problem of government 'overload', a phenomenon associated with interventionist policies that heighten expectations of government. Expanding popular and interest group demands thus outstrip the capacity of government to respond. Samuel Beer (1982) termed this problem 'pluralistic stagnation'. As a consequence, in the 1980s and 1990s, New Right governments tried to reduce popular expectations of what the state can do, thus, to some extent, wresting back control of policy initiation.

Formulation

Once an issue, or set of issues, is on the political agenda, a process of detailed elaboration and analysis is required to develop systematic policy proposals. Conventionally seen as the most crucial stage in the policy process, policy formulation entails not only the translation of broad proposals into specific and detailed recommendations, but also the filtering out of proposals and perhaps even the fundamental recasting of the issue under consideration. In their analysis of the policy cycle, Hogwood and Gunn (1984) identified a number of stages in the formulation process, following the initiation of policy through to a 'decision to decide'. The first stage is the decision about how to decide, that is, a decision about which mechanisms or procedures and which political actors should be involved in the analysis and elaboration of policy. Should a particular policy be formulated by civil servants or by ministers? Should it be carried out through established processes, or should a special committee or commission be set up? Should interest groups and think tanks be consulted, and, if so, which ones? These decisions are clearly vital in that they determine the sympathies and interests that will be brought to bear on the policy as it is developed and discussed.

The second stage involves issue definition and forecasting. This stage allows considerable scope for reinterpretation, as those who formulate policy may view 'the problem' very differently from those who raised the issue in the first place. Thirdly, there is the setting of objectives and priorities. Although public opinion and the concerns of bodies such as the media, political parties and interest groups are likely to influence objective setting, there is, of course, no guarantee that the priorities identified by priority formulators will be the same as those advanced by policy initiators.

Finally, there is the analysis and review of the policy options, leading to the selection of a preferred option. This, in effect, means that an authoritative decision is taken. Various factors are likely to be taken into account at this stage in policy formulation, the political and electoral ramifications of particular options being no less important than considerations of administrative efficiency and effectiveness. It is important to note, however, that the final decision, which brings the formulation process to an end, may be little more than a formality, decisive argument and debate having happened at a much earlier stage. Cabinets, legislatures and international summits thus often ratify or 'rubber stamp' decisions that have effectively been *made* elsewhere.

It would be foolish to imply that the task of formulation has the same character in different systems and different states. Richardson (1984) attempted to unravel different policy-formulation processes by identifying contrasting national 'policy styles'. In particular, he drew attention to two main dimensions: whether policy formulation is based on consultation or imposition, and whether governments engage in long-term planning or react to events on a more or less day-to-day basis. In this light, Sweden and Japan can perhaps be classified as states with policy styles that broadly favour both consultation and long-term planning. In both cases, there is an elaborate and formalised system of group consultation orientated around a widely agreed set of policy objectives and priorities. On the other hand, in the USA, although the fragmented nature of the federal government requires a high level of consensus for policy to be accepted, it also virtually rules out longer-term planning, and so entrenches a reactive, 'fire brigade' policy style.

The UK provides an example of how a policy style can shift over time. The style identified by Richardson highlighted both a British predilection for consultation, and a tendency to react to problems, rather than anticipate them. However, under Margaret Thatcher in the 1980s, an attempt was made to alter both these characteristics. First, a much clearer set of long-term policy goals was outlined in the form of a commitment to what Andrew Gamble (1988) described as 'the free economy and the strong state'. The pursuit of these goals was, in turn, accompanied by a shift from consultation to imposition, reflected in developments such as the growth of prime-ministerial power, the declining independence of local government and the end of corporatism (see p. 257). Although John Major in the 1990s may have adopted a more collegiate and consensual leadership style, the policy process in the UK has been no less ideologically driven (Savage, Atkinson and Robins, 1994).

A key feature of formulation, regardless of differences in national policy styles, is that it substantially reduces the range of actors involved in the policy process. While a broad variety of interests, groups and movements may play a role in policy initiation, policy formulation is the job of 'insiders' (government officials, key advisers, politicians and consulted groups), those who are either part of the machinery of government or have institutionalised access to it. This has left the formulation process open to a number of criticisms. One of these arises from the undue influence civil servants supposedly exert by virtue of their role as policy advisers. Politicians, at best, set broad policy priorities and leave specific objectives and the review of policy options largely in the hands of government officials. Public choice theorists have argued that policy therefore tends to reflect the career interests of professional civil servants, while Marxists have pointed out that radical policy alternatives tend to be discounted because of the social and educational backgrounds of senior public officials.

Other criticisms relate to the growth in the level of consultation and thus in the number of groups and actors involved in policy formulation. New Right theorists in particular have argued that the drift towards corporatism has allowed policy to be shaped by powerful sectional interests rather than by the broader public good (Olson, 1982). From this perspective, corporatism can be seen to be a breach in the divide between initiation and formulation that allows groups that should be merely setting the political agenda to shape instead the content of government policy. A final set of criticisms are based on the general 'democratic deficit' in policy formulation. In democratic systems, although elected politicians oversee the policy process and make the final decisions, the process itself often guarantees that their contribution is marginal. Because it is time-consuming and exacting, policy formulation requires professionalism, specialist knowledge and a concern for detail, qualities that politicians, democratic or otherwise, rarely possess in abundance.

Implementation

One of the major advances made in the discipline of policy analysis has been to underline the importance of the implementation stage. Traditionally, implementation was taken for granted, being seen as an aspect of administration (see p. 345), not as a feature of politics. Analyses of the Great Society programme in the USA in the mid1960s, however, destroyed illusions about the politics–administration divide, and graphically illustrated how far policy 'outputs' may differ from the intentions of policy makers. For this reason, Wildavsky (1980) described policy analysis as 'speaking truth to power'. The conditions required to achieve 'perfect' implementation, in the sense of ensuring that policy is delivered exactly as intended, were outlined by Hood (1976) as follows:

- a unitary administrative system with a single line of authority to ensure central control
- uniform norms and rules that operate throughout the system
- perfect obedience or perfect control
- perfect information, perfect communication and perfect coordination
- sufficient time for administrative resources to be mobilised.

In view of the difficulty of achieving any of these conditions, let alone all of them, it is not surprising that the gap between decision and delivery is often a gulf. Indeed, not only may central control and strict obedience be unfeasible, they may also be undesirable. Although those who make policy may enjoy democratic legitimacy, those who implement it (civil servants, local government officers, teachers, doctors, police officers and so on) may have a better 'street level' understanding of what will work and what will not work. Such considerations have led to a 'bottom-up' tradition of policy analysis that stresses the need for flexibility as well as the value of leaving discretion in the hands of policy executors. This contrasts with the more conventional 'top-down' view of implementation that emphasises uniformity and control. Most commentators, however, now recognise the trade-off between central control and flexibility in application as the major dilemma in the area of policy implementation (Barrett and Fudge, 1981).

Although perfect implementation may be neither possible nor desirable, most of the concerns expressed about policy implementation have focused on the dangers of flexibility in application. This was underlined by Pressman and Wildavsky's (1973) pioneering study of implementation, subtitled *How Great Expectations in Washington Are Dashed in Oakland Or Why It's Amazing That Federal Programs Work At All....* Flexibility may arise for a number of reasons. One of these is that those who execute policy may not merely be anxious to use their experience and 'street-level' knowledge to ensure that implementation is effective, they may also, as public choice theorists point out, wish to protect their career and professional interests. Civil servants and public-sector professionals will then have an obvious incentive to filter out or reinterpret aspects of public policy that seem to be threatening or inconvenient.

Other concerns about policy implementation arise less from the inadequacy of political control from above and more from the absence of consumer pressure from below. From this perspective, poor implementation, especially in the delivery of public services, results from the fact that government typically operates outside the market mechanism and is usually a monopoly supplier of its 'goods'. Civil servants, local government officers and public-sector workers can in general afford to be sloppy and inefficient because, unlike in private businesses, they do not have to keep the customer satisfied. One response to this has been the wider use of performance indicators that bind public services to a set of 'delivery standards' that effectively mimic market competition by penalising sub-standard performance. This idea was enthusiastically taken up in the UK by the Major government in the form of the Citizen's Charter initiative, launched in 1991.

The initiative, which drew on experiments in local government in York and elsewhere, led to a proliferation of charters laying down explicit standards of service for all government departments, the National Health Service, nationalised industries, privatised utilities, local government and universities. Services that meet delivery standards can be rewarded with a charter mark, and ones that fail are obliged to put things right or, in some cases, offer financial compensation. The philosophy behind such performance indicators is the 'empowerment' of the citizen as a consumer, that is, someone whose needs and interests have to be taken into account in the delivery of services. Amongst the criticisms of such schemes are that they risk substituting the writing of charters for the provision of adequate services, and that they are based on a narrow and inadequate concept of citizenship (see p. 397).

Evaluation

The policy process culminates with the evaluation and review of policy, leading, in theory at least, to decisions being made about the maintenance, succession or termination of the policy in question. This stage completes the policy cycle in the sense that information acquired through evaluation can be fed back into the initiation and formulation stages. This process can throw up new policy proposals and help to refine and improve existing ones (see Figure 19.1).

As well as addressing substantive issues related to the appropriateness or effectiveness of public policy, evaluation may also shed light on procedural issues, such as how the formulation stage is organised, who is consulted and when, and how implementation is controlled. However, unfortunately, despite its manifest importance, governments have usually been reluctant to allocate funds for policy evaluation. In the USA in the late 1970s, President Carter's insistence that 1 per cent of the funds for any project should be devoted to evaluation may have been a bold innovation, but it generated an enormous amount of paperwork without bringing about a

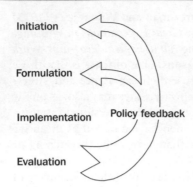

Fig. 19.1 Policy-feedback process

noticeable improvement in either the policy process or its products. The only states that take policy evaluation seriously are the few, usually consensual, democracies that are geared to long-term planning.

Academics have taken more interest in evaluation through policy output studies, widely undertaken, especially in the USA, since the late 1960s. Empirical research is used to examine both what government does, in terms of laws, taxes, programmes and so on (outputs), and the consequences or impact of such policies (outcomes). As Dye (1995) put it, this form of policy analysis is concerned with 'who gets what'.

What is clear is that the outcomes of the policy process are often very different from what was intended by those who formulated or made policy decisions. There are many examples of this. Welfare policies designed to alleviate poverty and enable

Focus on . . .

Open government: for and against

Open government is the principle that what happens in government should be open to public scrutiny and criticism on the basis of a free flow of information from public bodies to representative institutions, the mass media and the general public. As it is universally accepted that some information should be kept secret (on the grounds of national security, privacy and so on), open government is normally understood to imply a bias in favour of the public's 'right to know'. This is usually enshrined in a freedom of information act that forces the government to defend secrecy before the courts.

The advantages of open government include the following:

- It places a check on incompetence, corruption and tyranny.
- It promotes political argument and debate, and results in improved policy outcomes and a better-informed electorate.

Its drawbacks include the following:

- It hampers the efficiency of policy making by exposing the formulation process to the glare of publicity.
- It discourages the consideration of unpopular, but nevertheless important, ideas and proposals.

all citizens to participate in the life of the community have led, according to Le Grand (1982), to the cushioning of the middle classes, or, in the view of Murray (1984), to the growth of a welfare-dependent underclass. In their case study of the poll tax in the UK, Butler, Adonis and Travers (1994) highlighted a catalogue of failures and oversights in government, the cabinet and Parliament which allowed a policy primarily designed to control local government spending to result in widespread civil unrest. This contributed to the downfall of Margaret Thatcher and the swift reversal of the policy under her successor, John Major. For many, such policy failures highlight the pressing importance of open government and public accountability (see p. 375). For the policy process to work effectively in translating inputs into appropriate outputs, it must be open, at all times, to scrutiny and criticism. All too frequently, a culture of secrecy merely conceals incompetence and provides scope for arbitrary and self-serving behaviour.

System performance

The policy process has been analysed above in largely 'managerial' terms. How are decisions made? What stages are there in the policy process? How effective, efficient and economical (the 'three Es') is policy making? However, a series of deeper 'political' issues underlie these questions. These are not so much concerned with what government *does* as with what government *should* do, that is, with what government is 'for'. The problem is that this uncovers those intractable normative questions that lie at the heart of politics. It is impossible to know what government is for without understanding such issues as the nature of justice and the desirable balance between freedom and authority, without, in other words, having a vision of the 'good society'.

Since views about such matters differ fundamentally, the standards against which governments and political systems can be judged also vary. Four widely held such standards can nevertheless be identified, each shedding a very particular light on system performance. These performance criteria are as follows:

- stability and order
- material prosperity
- citizenship
- democratic rule.

Stability performance

It can reasonably be claimed that the maintenance of stability and order (see p. 371) is the most basic function of government. With the exception of anarchists, who argue that social order will emerge from the spontaneous actions of free individuals, all political thinkers and philosophers have endorsed government as the only means of keeping chaos and instability at bay. In Thomas Hobbes's (see p. 285) words, in the absence of government, life would be 'solitary, poor, nasty, brutish and short'. From this perspective, the core purpose of government is to govern, to rule, to ensure stability through the exercise of authority. This, in turn, requires that government is able to perpetuate its own existence and ensure the survival of the broader political system. System performance can thus be judged on the basis of criteria such as longevity and endurance, as the simple fact of survival indicates a regime's ability to contain or reconcile conflict. However, there are differing views about how this goal can best be achieved.

These views fall into two broad categories. The first stems from the essentially liberal belief that stable government must be rooted in consensus and consent. In this view, what ensures the long-term survival of a regime is its responsiveness to popular demands and pressures. This is expressed in the language of systems theory as the ability to bring the 'outputs' of government into line with the various 'inputs'. This has often been identified as a particular strength of western liberal democracies. Advocates of liberal democracy (see p. 28) stress that, as it is based on consent, it embodies mechanisms that ensure that it is responsive, and so guarantees a high degree of systemic equilibrium. Government power is won through a competitive struggle for the popular vote, and can be lost when that support diminishes. A vigorous civil society allows citizens to exert influence through autonomous groups and associations.

To some extent, it has been the ability of liberal democracy to generate political stability that explains the wider adoption in the postcommunist and developing worlds of liberal-democratic practices such as electoral democracy and party competition. Nevertheless, liberal democracy also has its drawbacks in this respect. Chief amongst these is that responsiveness may generate instability, insofar as it heightens popular expectations of government and fosters the illusion that the political system can meet all demands and accommodate all 'inputs'. From this perspective, the central dilemma of stable government is that responsiveness must be balanced against effectiveness. Government must be sensitive to external pressures, but it must also be able to impose its will on society when those pressures threaten to generate irreconcilable conflict.

This latter fear underpins the alternative view of stability and order. Conservative thinkers have traditionally linked stability and order not to responsiveness but to authority. Thomas Hobbes presented this idea as a stark choice between absolutism and anarchy, between the acceptance of an unquestionable and sovereign power and a descent into the chaos and disorder of the state of nature. However, conservatives have been particularly concerned to stress the degree to which political authority is underpinned by shared values and a common culture. In this view, stability and order are largely the product of social and cultural cohesion, the capacity of society to generate respect for authority and maintain support for established institutions.

This position is clearly reflected in neoconservative fears about permissiveness and moral and cultural relativism (see p. 395), leading to calls for the restoration of 'traditional', 'family' or 'Christian' values. It is also possible, from this perspective, to suggest that East Asian states which subscribe to some form of Confucianism (see p. 34), as well as Islamic states, have a greater capacity to maintain political stability than do western liberal-democratic regimes. However, the weakness of this view of stability is that, since it relies on authority being exerted from above, it may not place effective constraints on the exercise of government power. If stability is seen as an end in itself, divorced from considerations such as democratic legitimacy, social justice and respect for human rights, the result may simply be tyranny and oppression. Saddam Hussein, after all, has been able to perpetuate the existence of his Iraqi regime, despite opposition from Shi'ite Moslems and Kurds, largely through systematic terror and brutal repression.

Focus on . . .

The welfare debate

The most general meaning of the term welfare is happiness, prosperity and well-being; welfare implies not mere physical survival, but some measure of health and contentment as well. As a political principle, however, welfare has come to be associated with a particular means of achieving general well-being: collectively provided welfare, delivered by government through the mechanism of a so-called welfare state.

Supporters of welfare argue that its benefits include the following:

- It promotes national efficiency by creating a healthier and better educated workforce.
- It encourages personal development by safeguarding individuals from social deprivation.
- It fosters social cohesion by guaranteeing everyone a stake in society.

Critics of welfare have nevertheless opposed it for the following reasons:

- It breeds dependency by reducing the fear of poverty and thus the incentive to work.
- It undermines economic growth by adding to the tax burden.
- It ameliorates hardship and poverty without dealing with structural disadvantage and inequality.

> ## Concept
>
> ### Relativism
>
> Relativism is a position that denies the existence of objective or 'absolute' standards, and so holds that statements can only be judged in relation to their contexts. *Moral* relativism rejects the notion that there are, or can be, authoritative ethical principles, usually on the grounds that the individual is a morally autonomous being. *Cognitive*, or epistemological, relativism holds that different modes of knowing are equally valid, and thus dismisses the universalist pretensions of, say, science (see p. 16). Relativism has been criticised for both weakening the moral cement of society (creating a 'pathless desert'), and for being intellectually self-defeating (the denial of objective standards is itself relative). Relativism contrasts starkly with all forms of fundamentalism (see p. 61).

Material performance

The idea that political systems can and should be judged by their material performance is a familiar one. Electoral politics, for example, is invariably dominated by economic issues and the so-called 'feel good' factor. Governments are usually re-elected in periods of growth and widening prosperity, and defeated during recessions and economic crises. Similarly, there can be little doubt that the success of the broader political system is linked to its capacity to 'deliver the goods'. Widespread poverty and low levels of economic growth in developing states have deepened social and ethnic tensions, fuelled corruption, and undermined attempts to establish constitutional and representative government. The collapse of the state socialist regimes of eastern Europe and the USSR was also linked to the failure of central planning and, in particular, to its inability to deliver the levels of material prosperity and range of consumer goods that were available in the capitalist West. Moreover, it is no co-incidence that advanced industrialised states have enjoyed both the greatest levels of political stability and the highest living standards in the world; hence their classification as first-world regimes.

Considerable debate has taken place about the most reliable means of generating wealth and achieving material prosperity. In some senses, this debate reflects the traditional ideological divide between capitalism and socialism; the former places its faith in the market (see p. 167) and competition, and the latter relies on nationalisation and planning (see p. 174). However, the eastern European revolutions of 1989–91 dramatically changed the terms of this debate by (apparently) undermining the validity of any form of socialism qualitatively distinct from market capitalism. In

► Concept

Equality

Equality is the principle of uniform apportionment, but does not imply identity, or sameness. The term equality has differing implications, depending on what is being apportioned. *Formal* equality means the equal distribution of legal and political rights, and is usually based on the assumption that human beings are 'born' equal. Equality of *opportunity* means that everyone has the same starting-point, or equal life chances, but may justify social inequality because talent and the capacity for hard work are unequally distributed. Equality of *outcome* (the most controversial manifestation of equality) means that there is an equal distribution of income, wealth and other social goods. Its supporters argue that it promotes justice and community (see p. 135); its detractors view it as 'levelling downwards' and a form of social engineering.

other words, even socialists came to accept that the market, or at least some form of market competition, is the only reliable mechanism for generating wealth. The 'capitalism or socialism?' debate has therefore developed into a 'what kind of capitalism?' debate. This issue is not merely about how wealth can be *generated*, but also about how it is *distributed*, that is, who gets what. This is closely linked to the balance between the market and the state, and the degree to which government can, and should, modify market outcomes through a system of welfare (see p. 395) and redistribution.

The central dilemma that arises from the use of material prosperity as a performance indicator is that growth must be balanced against fairness. This is the difficulty of being concerned both about the size of the cake and about how the cake is cut. Two contrasting views of this problem can be identified. The free-market view, advanced by theorists such as Hayek and Friedman, holds that general prosperity is best achieved by a system of unregulated capitalism. This is what Titmuss (1968) referred to as the 'industrial–achievement' performance model. From this perspective, economic growth is best promoted by material incentives that encourage enterprise and endeavour and penalise laziness. The welfare state should therefore act only as a safety net that protects individuals from absolute poverty in the sense that they lack the basic means of subsistence. Although this system is likely to increase social inequality, the theory holds that it benefits even the less well-off, who receive a smaller proportion of a much larger cake, so ending up better off. Free-market economists refer to this theory as the 'trickle down' effect. Such policy priorities have guided New Right governments since the 1970s in their attempts to break away from the 'fiscal crisis of the welfare state'. In this view, burgeoning social budgets led to a growing tax burden which, in turn, merely hampered the process of wealth generation.

The rival social-democratic view, which Titmuss called the 'institutional–redistributive' model, highlights the moral and economic benefits of equality. Not only is unregulated competition condemned for promoting greed and conflict, but it is also seen as inefficient and unproductive. The virtue of social justice is that, by taking the distribution of wealth away from the vagaries of the market, it ensures that all citizens have a stake in society and that each of them has an incentive to contribute. In tolerating wide social inequality, free-market policies thus run the risk of promoting social exclusion, reflected in the growth of an underclass that is a breeding ground for crime and social unrest. Long-term and sustainable prosperity therefore requires that material incentives operate within a broader framework of fair distribution and effective welfare.

Citizenship performance

The idea that citizenship is the proper end of government can be traced back to the political thought of Ancient Greece. For instance, in 431 BCE, in his famous funeral oration, Pericles stated that:

An Athenian citizen does not neglect the state because he takes care of his own household; and even those of us who are engaged in business have a very fair idea of politics. We alone regard a man who takes no interest in public affairs, not as harmless, but as a useless character; and if few of us are originators, we are all sound judges of policy.

A citizen is a member of a political community or state, endowed with a set of rights and a set of obligations. Citizenship is therefore the 'public' face of individual existence. People are able to participate in the life of their communities to the extent that they possess entitlements and responsibilities. Civil participation is, in turn, linked to the advance of constitutional government, as reflected in the extension of political rights and civil liberties (see p. 365).

In his classic contribution to the study of citizenship rights, T. H. Marshall (1950) distinguished between three 'bundles of rights': civil rights, political rights and social rights. Civil rights were defined by Marshall as 'rights necessary for individual freedom'. These include freedom of speech, freedom of assembly, freedom of movement, freedom of conscience, the right to equality before the law and the right to own property. Civil rights are therefore rights that are exercised within civil society; they are 'negative' rights in the sense that they limit or check the exercise of government power. Political rights provide the individual with the opportunity to participate in political life. The central political rights are thus the right to vote, the right to stand for election and the right to hold public office. The provision of political rights clearly requires the development of universal suffrage, political equality (see p. 67), and democratic government. Finally, and most controversially, Marshall argued that citizenship implied social rights which guarantee the individual a minimum social status and therefore provide the basis for the exercise of both civil and political rights. Marshall defined these 'positive' rights, rather vaguely, as the right 'to live the life of a civilised being according to the standards prevailing in society'.

As the concept of citizenship is usually seen as a distinctively western invention, it is perhaps not surprising that liberal democracies perform particularly well in this respect. Civil and political rights clearly imply the form of constitutional and representative government commonly found in the industrialised West. The idea of social rights, however, has stimulated significant divisions, because it implies a level of welfare provision and redistribution that classical liberals and the New Right have regarded as both unjustifiable and economically damaging. Marxists and feminists have also criticised the idea of citizenship, the former on the grounds that it ignores unequal class power, and the latter because it takes no account of patriarchal oppression.

A major dilemma nevertheless confronts those who employ citizenship as a performance criterion: the need to balance rights against duties and thereby to apportion responsibilities between the individual and the community. Since the early 1980s, this issue has been taken up in the growing debate between liberalism and communitarianism. Communitarian theorists such as Alisdair MacIntyre (1981) and Michael Sandel (1982) have dismissed the idea of an unencumbered self, arguing that the 'politics of rights' should be replaced by a 'politics of the common good'. In this view, liberal individualism, in effect, eats itself. By investing individuals with rights and entitlements, it simply breeds atomism and alienation, weakening the communal bonds that hold society together. From this perspective, nonwestern societies that may appear to perform poorly in relation to citizenship indicators (with, for example, poor records on human rights) may nevertheless succeed in creating a stronger sense of community and social belonging.

Democracy performance

Whereas stability, material prosperity and citizenship are all outcomes or products of government, democracy is essentially concerned with the process itself, with *how* decisions are made, rather than *what* decisions are made. Democracy means popular

Concept

Citizenship

Citizenship is a relationship between the individual and the state in which the two are bound together by reciprocal rights and duties. Citizens differ from subjects and aliens in that they are full members of their political community or state by virtue of their possession of basic rights. Citizenship is viewed differently depending on whether it is shaped by individualism (see p. 178) or communitarianism (see p. 136). The former, linked to liberalism, advances the principle of a 'citizenship of rights', and places particular stress on private entitlement and the status of the individual as an autonomous actor. There are socialist and conservative versions of communitarianism, but each advances the principle of a 'citizenship of duty'; they also highlight the role of the state as a moral agency and the importance of community or social existence.

◆ **Concept**

Autonomy

The term autonomy (from the Greek, meaning 'law to oneself') literally means self-rule. States, institutions or groups can be said to be autonomous if they enjoy a substantial degree of independence, although autonomy in this connection is sometimes taken to imply a high measure of self-government, rather than sovereign independence. Applied to the individual, autonomy is closely linked with freedom (see p. 282). However, since it suggests not merely being 'left alone' but being rationally self-willed, autonomy is classified as a form of positive freedom. By responding to inner or 'genuine' drives, the autonomous individual is seen to achieve authenticity. Autonomy is often linked with democracy, but may nevertheless also limit the jurisdiction of democracy, as it emphasises individuality rather than collective or majority rule.

rule, in crude terms, the widest possible dispersal of political power and influence. From the democratic perspective, the purpose of politics is to empower the individual and enlarge the scope of personal autonomy. Autonomy has been seen as both an end in itself and a means to an end. Classical theorists of democracy, such as J.-J. Rousseau (see p. 73) and J. S. Mill (see p. 44), portrayed political participation as a source of personal development and self-realisation. Democracy is thus the stuff of freedom, or, as Rousseau put it, freedom means 'being one's own master'.

Taken to its logical extreme, the idea of popular self-government implies the abolition of the distinction between the state and civil society through the establishment of some form of direct democracy (see p. 68). For example, Athenian democracy, described in Chapter 4, amounted to a form of government by mass meeting, in which citizens were encouraged to participate directly and continuously in the life of their *polis*, or city-state. Modern notions of democracy, however, have shifted away from this utopian vision, and instead embrace democracy more as a means to an end. The more familiar machinery of representative democracy (see p. 68) – universal suffrage, the secret ballot, and competitive elections – has tended to be defended on the grounds, for example, that the existence of voting rights checks the abuse of government power and that party competition helps to generate social consensus. The ability of the people to 'kick the rascals out' therefore helps to ensure that government is limited and that there is at least a measure of public accountability.

However, most political systems fare poorly by the standards of personal autonomy and popular rule. What passes for democracy in the modern world tends to be a limited and indirect form of democracy: liberal democracy. This operates as little more than what Joseph Schumpeter (see p. 211) referred to as an 'institutional arrangement for arriving at political decisions in which individuals acquire the power to decide by means of a competitive struggle for the people's vote' (Schumpeter, 1942:269). This 'institutional arrangement' has been criticised by radical democrats for reducing popular participation to a near meaningless ritual: casting a vote every few years for politicians who can only be removed by replacing them with another set of politicians. In short, the people never rule, and the growing gulf between government and the people is reflected in the spread of inertia, apathy and the breakdown of community.

This perspective is therefore linked to calls for radical, even revolutionary, political and social change. For example, government power should be decentralised so as to bring power 'closer' to the people. This could, for instance, require the break-up of the nation-state, as it is difficult, in practical terms, to see how a community the size of a modern nation could govern itself through direct and continuous participation. Similarly, insofar as the democratic principle is applied in modern societies, it is confined to a narrowly 'political' set of decisions. If democracy is understood as self-mastery, the ability to shape decisions that affect one's life, surely economic power must also be democratised, presumably through the machinery of worker's control and self-management.

As with the performance criteria examined above, democracy also poses its own set of dilemmas. The most important of these is the need for a balance between the twin goals of government *by* the people and government *for* the people. This highlights the tension between the competing virtues of popular participation and rule in the public interest. The most fundamental objection to participation, and thus to all forms of direct democracy, is simply that ordinary people lack the time, maturity and specialist knowledge to rule wisely on their own behalf. The earliest version of this argument was put by Plato (see p. 13), who advanced the idea of rule by the virtuous, that is, government by a class of philosopher kings. In this form, the case for government *for* the people amounts to an argument in favour of an enlightened despotism. The concern about the capabilities of ordinary people can, however, be dealt with more modestly, through the provision of representative processes that allow for a division of labour in political life. A further dilemma is that the empowerment of the individual must be balanced against the empowerment of the community. To give priority to personal autonomy is necessarily to place limits upon public authority. However, to extol the virtues of popular rule is to risk subordinating the individual to the will of the public or the majority. The tension between the individual and society not only raises major practical difficulties, but also highlights what some would argue has always been, and remains, the central issue in political theory.

■ Summary

◆ Public policy consists of the formal and stated decisions of government bodies. Policy making should be thought of as a process in two senses. First, it involves a linked series of actions through which policy intentions are translated into policy outputs. Secondly, policy making primarily relates to how governments make decisions, rather than to the substance of the decisions they make.

◆ A decision is an act of choosing one of a range of options. Decisions have been explained in terms of the goal-directed behaviour of rational actors, incremental adjustments made in the light of changing circumstances, the bureaucratic or organisational factors that shape the decision-making process, and the beliefs and values held by decision makers.

◆ The policy process can be broken down into four distinct stages. In the initiation stage, policy proposals are originated and the policy agenda is set. In the formulation stage, policy is developed in the sense that broad proposals are translated into specific and detailed recommendations. The implementation stage consists of the processes through which policy decisions are put into effect. The evaluation stage takes the form of critical reflection on policy outputs designed to improve the policy process in the future.

◆ Ultimately, policy can only be judged in terms of the impact it has on the larger society, for good or ill. However, as this raises normative questions, there is no consensus about the desirable 'outcomes' of government. The most commonly used indexes of a government's or system's performance include its ability to maintain stability and order, deliver material prosperity, promote citizenship, and foster democratic rule.

◆ Evaluating political systems is difficult because each performance indicator embodies complexities. Stability can be promoted through consent and popular responsiveness, or a shared culture and respect for authority. The generation of wealth may be hampered by policies designed to ensure that it is more equally distributed. The spread of citizenship rights may undermine civic duty and a sense of community. The extension of democratic rule may simply lead to restrictions on individual freedom or personal autonomy.

Questions for discussion

▶ Do people generally make decisions in a rational and calculating fashion?

▶ What is the most important stage in the policy process, and why?

▶ Is there a moral or economic case for greater social equality?

▶ Can the 'politics of rights' threaten the 'politics of the common good'?

▶ Is there an inevitable tension between democracy and liberty?

▶ Are people the best judges of what is good for them?

▶ Which political system comes closest to achieving the 'good society'?

Further reading

Anderson, J. *Public Policy Making* (Orlando, FL: Holt, Rinehart & Winston, 1984). A useful introduction to the field of policy analysis.

Bertsch, G., R. Clarke and D. Wood *Comparing Political Systems: Power and Policy in Three Worlds* (4th ed.) (New York: Macmillan, 1992). A detailed analysis of the policy process in various parts of the world.

Heidenheimer, A., H. Heclo and C. T. Adams *Comparative Public Policy* (3rd ed.) (New York: St Martin's Press, 1990). A good discussion of public policy and the performance of political systems.

Parsons, W. *Public Policy: Introduction to the Theory and Practice of Policy Analysis* (Aldershot: Edward Elgar, 1995). An up-to-date and thorough analysis of policy and the policy making process.

Glossary of Political Terms

When a term is discussed more fully in a box in the main text of the book, a page reference is given after the definition in the glossary.

Absolutism The theory or practice of absolute government, typically based on a claim to an unlimited right to rule (see p. 26).

Accountability Answerability; having a duty to explain ones conduct and being subject to monitoring and evaluation by a higher authority (see p. 375).

Administration The task of coordinating or executing policy; more narrowly, dealing with information and monetary control (see p. 345).

Administrative law Law that regulates the exercise of executive power and policy implementation.

Adversary politics A style of politics characterised by ideological antagonism and an ongoing electoral battle between major parties (see p. 308).

Agenda setting The ability to structure policy debate by controlling which issues are discussed or establishing a priority amongst them.

Alienation Separation from one's genuine or essential nature; for Marxists, the reduction of labour to a mere commodity.

Altruism A concern for the welfare of others, based on either enlightened self-interest or a recognition of a common humanity.

Anarchism An ideology committed to the abolition of the state and the outright rejection of political authority, based on an unqualified belief in liberty and equality.

Anarchy Literally, without rule; anarchy is often used pejoratively to suggest instability or even chaos.

Ancien régime (*French*) Literally, old order; usually linked with the absolutist structures that predated the French Revolution.

Anomie A weakening of values and normative rules, associated with feelings of isolation, loneliness and meaninglessness.

Anthropocentrism The belief that human needs and interests are of overriding moral and philosophical importance; the opposite of ecocentrism.

Antiparty parties Parties that set out to subvert traditional party politics by rejecting parliamentary compromise and emphasising popular mobilisation.

Anti-politics Disillusionment with formal and established political processes, reflected in nonparticipation, support for antisystem parties, or the use of direct action.

Anti-Semitism Prejudice or hatred towards Jews; anti-Semitism may take religious, economic or racial forms (see p. 115).

Association A group formed by voluntary action, reflecting recognition of shared interests or common concerns.

Athenian democracy A form of direct democracy, based on government by mass meetings and the allocation of public offices through lot or rota.

Atomism The belief that society is made up of a collection of largely self-sufficient individuals; or a tendency towards social breakdown and isolation.

Authoritarianism The belief in or practice of government 'from above'; the exercise of authority regardless of the consent of the governed (see p. 36).

Authority The right to influence the behaviour of others on the basis of an acknowledged duty to obey; authority may be traditional, charismatic or legal–rational (see p. 6).

Autonomy Literally, self-rule; an autonomous person is rationally self-willed by virtue of his or her independence of external authority (see p. 398).

Balance of power A pattern of interaction amongst states that tends to curb aggression and expansionism by rendering them impracticable.

Balkanisation The fragmentation of a political unit into a patchwork of antagonistic entities (as has often occurred in the Balkans).

Behaviouralism The belief that social theories should be constructed only on the basis of observable behaviour, providing quantifiable data for research.

Bias Sympathies or prejudices that (often unconsciously) affect human judgement; bias implies distortion.

Bicameralism The fragmentation of legislative power, established through the existence of two (co-equal) chambers in the assembly; a device of limited government (see p. 303).

Big government Interventionist government, usually understood to imply economic management and social regulation.

Bill Proposed legislation in the form of a draft statute; if passed, a bill becomes an act.

Bill of rights A constitutional document that specifies the rights and freedoms of the individual, and so defines the legal extent of civil liberty.

Bipolarity The tendency of the international system to revolve around two poles (major power blocs); bipolarity implies equilibrium and stability.

Bonapartism A style of government that fuses personal leadership with conservative nationalism; for Marxists, it reflects the relative autonomy of the state.

Bourgeois ideology A Marxist term, denoting ideas and theories that serve the interests of the bourgeoisie by disguising the contradictions of capitalist society.

Bourgeoisie A Marxist term, denoting the ruling class of a capitalist society, the owners of productive wealth.

Bureaucracy Literally, rule by officials; the administrative machinery of the state or, more broadly, a rational and rule-governed mode of organisation (see p. 341).

Cabinet A group of senior ministers that meets formally and regularly, and is chaired by the chief executive; cabinets may make policy or be consultative.

Cabinet government A system of government in which executive power is vested in a cabinet, each member having (in theory) equal influence and being subject to collective responsibility (see p. 328).

Cadre A group of elite members of a party, distinguished by their ideological commitment and quasi-military discipline.

Capitalism A system of generalised commodity production in which wealth is owned privately and economic life is organised according to market principles.

Caucus A meeting of party members held to nominate election candidates or to discuss legislative proposals in advance of formal proceedings.

Censorship The control or suppression of publications, expressions of opinion, or other pubic acts; censorship may be formal or informal.

Centralisation The concentration of political power or government authority at the national level.

Charisma Charm or personal power; the ability to inspire loyalty, emotional dependence, or even devotion, in others (see p. 195).

Chauvinism An irrational belief in the superiority or dominance of one's own group or cause.

Checks and balances Internal tensions within the governmental system that result from institutional fragmentation.

Christian Democracy An ideological tradition within European conservatism, characterised by a commitment to the social market and qualified interventionism.

Citizenship Membership of a state; a relationship between the individual and state based on reciprocal rights and responsibilities (see p. 397).

Civic culture A culture that blends popular participation with effective government; supposedly, the basis for stable democratic rule.

Civil liberty The private sphere of existence, belonging to the citizen not to the state; freedom from government (see p. 365).

Civil society The realm of autonomous groups and associations; a private sphere independent from public authority (see p. 6).

Civil war An armed conflict between politically organised groups within a state, usually fought either for control of the state or to establish a new state.

Class consciousness A Marxist term, denoting an accurate awareness of class interests and a willingness to pursue them; a class-conscious class is a class for-itself, (see p. 199).

Class dealignment A weakening of the relationship between social class and party support (see p. 226).

Clientelism A relationship through which government agencies come to serve the interests of the client groups they are responsible for regulating or supervising.

Coalition A grouping of rival political actors, brought together through the perception of a common threat or to harness collective energies (see p. 246).

Coalition government A government in which power is shared between two or more parties, based on the distribution among them of ministerial portfolios.

Cohabitation An arrangement in a semi-presidential system in which the president works with a government and assembly controlled by a rival party or parties.

Cold War The period of rivalry between the USA-dominated West and the USSR-dominated East that extended from 1945 to the collapse of communism in the revolutions of 1989–91 (see p. 146).

Collective responsibility The doctrine of cabinet government that holds that all ministers are obliged to give public support to government policies.

Collective security The theory or practice of resisting aggression through united action by a number of states (see p. 159).

Collectivisation The abolition of private property in favour of a system of common or public ownership.

Collectivism   A belief in the capacity of human beings for collective action, based on cooperation not self-striving; collectivism implies that social entities are meaningful (see p. 178).

Colonialism   The theory or practice of establishing control over a foreign territory, usually by settlement and economic domination (see p. 116).

Committee   A small work group composed of members drawn from a larger body and charged with specific responsibilities (see p. 304).

Common law   Law based on custom and precedent; law that is supposedly 'common' to all.

Commune   A small-scale collective organisation based on the sharing of wealth and power, possibly also extending to personal and domestic arrangements.

Communism   The principle of the common ownership of property; communism often refers to movements or regimes based on Marxist principles (see p. 33).

Communitarianism   The belief that the self or person is constituted through the community in the sense that there are no 'unencumbered selves' (see p. 136).

Community   A principle or sentiment based on the collective identity of a social group; bonds of comradeship, loyalty and duty (see p. 135).

Concept   A general idea about something, usually expressed in a single word or short phrase.

Confederation   A qualified union of states in which each state retains its independence, typically guaranteed by unanimous decision-making.

Conflict   Competition between opposing forces, reflecting a diversity of opinions, preferences, needs or interests.

Confucianism   A system of ethics derived from the philosophy of Confucius which emphasises respect and loyalty in human relationships and the cultivation of the self (see p. 34).

Consensus   A broad agreement on fundamental principles, allowing for disagreement on matters of emphasis or detail (see p. 10).

Consensus politics   A style of politics based on compromise and conciliation; or an overlap of policy and ideological priorities between parties.

Consent   Assent or permission; in politics, usually an agreement to be governed or ruled.

Conservatism   An ideology characterised by support for tradition, duty, authority and property, extending from Tory paternalism to the New Right.

Consociational democracy   A form of democracy that operates through power-sharing and a close association amongst a number of parties or political formations.

Constitution   A set of rules that establish the duties, powers and functions of the institutions of government and define the relationship between the state and the individual (see p. 274).

Constitutional government   Government that operates within a set of legal and institutional constraints that both limit its power and protect individual liberty.

Constitutional law   Law that regulates the relationship between branches of government and between the state and the individual.

Constitutionalism   The theory or practice of limited government brought about by the existence of a constitution and the fragmentation of power (see p. 279).

Contested concept   A concept over which there is theoretical or political debate; concepts are 'essentially contested' when no settled definition can ever be developed.

Contract   A voluntary agreement that is morally, and perhaps legally, binding.

Convention   A rule of conduct or behaviour; a nonlegal constitutional rule (see p. 276).

Convergence thesis   The theory that politico-economic factors dictate that capitalist and socialist states will become increasingly similar.

Cooperation   Working together; achieving goals through collective action.

Corporatism   The incorporation of organised interests into the processes of government; corporatism may have a liberal or a fascist character (see p. 257).

Corruption   A failure to carry out 'proper' responsibilities as a result of the pursuit of private (and usually material) gain (see p. 347).

Cosmopolitanism   Literally, a belief in a world state; more usually, a commitment to fostering harmony and understanding amongst nations (see p. 111).

Coup d'état   (*French*) A forcible seizure of power through illegal and unconstitutional action carried out (unlike in a revolution or rebellion) by a small group (see p. 369).

Cult of personality   A propaganda device through which a political leader is portrayed as a heroic or God-like figure (see p. 333).

Cultural nationalism   A form of nationalism that places primary emphasis on the regeneration of the nation as a distinctive civilisation (see p. 106).

Culture   A people's attitudes, beliefs, symbols and values; broadly, that which is acquired through learning, rather than inheritance.

Decentralisation   The expansion of local autonomy through the transfer of powers and responsibilities away from national bodies.

Decision   An act of choice; a selection from a range of options.

Deindustrialisation   A contraction of the economy's manufacturing base, reflected in the decline of 'heavy' industries.

Deliberative democracy   A form of democracy that emphasises the need for discourse and debate to help define the public interest.

Demagogue   A political leader whose control over the masses is based on the ability to whip up hysterical enthusiasm.

Democracy   Rule by the people; democracy implies both popular participation and government in the public interest, and can take a wide variety of forms (see Chapter 4).

Democratic centralism   The Leninist principle of party organisation, based on a supposed balance between freedom of discussion and strict unity of action.

Democratisation   The advance of liberal-democratic reform, implying, in particular, the granting of basic freedoms and the widening of popular participation and electoral choice.

Departmentalism   The tendency for government agencies to pursue their own interests and resist political control or broader administrative disciplines (see p. 348).

Détente   (*French*) Literally, loosening; the relaxation of tension between previously antagonistic states.

Determinism   The belief that human actions and choices are entirely conditioned by external factors; determinism implies that free will is a myth.

Devolution   The transfer of power from central government to subordinate regional bodies, without (unlike federalism) leading to shared sovereignty (see p. 131).

Dialectic   A process of interaction between two competing forces, giving rise to a higher stage of development.

Dialectical materialism   The crude and deterministic form of Marxism that dominated intellectual life in orthodox communist states.

Dictatorship   Rule by a single individual; the arbitrary and unchecked exercise of power (see p. 363).

Dictatorship of the proletariat   A Marxist term, denoting the transitory phase between the collapse of capitalism and the establishment of full communism.

Direct action   Political action taken outside the constitutional and legal framework; direct action may range from passive resistance to terrorism.

Direct democracy   Popular self-government, characterised by the direct and continuous participation of citizens in the tasks of government.

Discourse   Human interaction, especially communication; discourse may disclose or illustrate power relationships.

Divine right   The doctrine that earthly rulers are chosen by God and thus wield unchallengeable authority; a defence for monarchical absolutism.

Ecocentrism   A theoretical orientation that gives priority to the maintenance of ecological balance rather than the satisfaction of human interests.

Ecologism   An ideology based on the belief that there is an essential link between humankind and the natural world, and that the health of the ecosystem has priority over human interests.

Ecology   The study of the relationship between living organisms and their environment; ecology highlights the interconnectedness of nature (see p. 60).

Economic liberalism   A belief in the market as a self-regulating mechanism tending naturally to deliver general prosperity and opportunities for all.

Economic man   A model of human nature that stresses the self-interested pursuit of material satisfaction, individuals being seen as utility maximisers.

Egalitarianism   A theory or practice based on the desire to promote equality; or the belief that equality is the primary political value.

Election   A device for filling an office or post through choices made by a designated body of people: the electorate.

Elective dictatorship   A constitutional imbalance in which executive power is checked only by the need to win subsequent elections.

Electoral college   An indirect electoral mechanism; a body of electors charged with responsibility for filling a party or public office.

Elite   A minority in whose hands power, wealth or prestige is concentrated.

Elitism   The belief in, or practice of, rule by an elite; the theory that political power is concentrated in the hands of the few (see p. 78).

Empire   A structure of political domination comprising diverse cultures, ethnic groups and nationalities held together by force or the threat of force.

Empirical   Based on observation and experiment; empirical knowledge is derived from sense data and experience.

Empiricism   The belief that experience is the only basis for knowledge and therefore that all hypotheses and theories should be tested by observation and experiment.

Environmentalism A concern with protecting or conserving nature, ultimately (unlike ecologism) for the benefit of humankind.

Equality The principle of uniform apportionment, rather than 'sameness'; equality may be applied to rights, opportunities or outcomes (see p. 396).

Ethnic cleansing The forcible expulsion or extermination of 'alien' peoples; often used as a euphemism for genocide.

Ethnic group A group of people who share a common cultural and historical identity, typically linked to a belief in common dissent.

Ethnic nationalism A form of nationalism that is fuelled primarily by a keen sense of ethnic distinctiveness and the desire to preserve it.

Ethnicity A sentiment of loyalty towards a distinctive population, cultural group or territorial area; bonds that are cultural rather than racial (see p. 132).

Ethnocentrism The application of values and theories drawn from one's own culture to other groups and peoples; ethnocentrism implies bias or distortion (see p. 385).

Eurocommunism A form of deradicalised communism that attempted to blend Marxism with liberal-democratic principles.

Exceptionalism The features of a political system that are unique or particular to it, and thus restrict the application of broader categories.

Executive The branch of government that is responsible for implementing or carrying out law and policy (see p. 316).

Expansionism A policy of military aggression designed to secure territorial gains, a phenomenon closely linked to imperialism.

Fact A truth verified by experience or observation; something that is known to have happened or to be the case.

Faction A section or group within a larger formation, usually a party; a faction is distinguished by common policy commitments or ideological leanings (see p. 230).

Factionalism The proliferation of factions within a party or government; or the bitterness of factional rivalry or infighting.

False consciousness A Marxist term, denoting the delusion and mystification that prevents subordinate classes from recognising the fact of their own exploitation.

Fascism An ideology characterised by a belief in anti-rationalism, struggle, charismatic leadership, elitism and extreme nationalism; Fascism refers specifically to the Mussolini regime in Italy.

Federalism A territorial distribution of power based on the sharing of sovereignty between central (usually national) bodies and peripheral ones (see p. 125).

Feminism An ideology committed to promoting the social role of women and, in most cases, dedicated to the goal of gender equality.

Feudalism A system of agrarian-based production characterised by fixed social hierarchies and a rigid pattern of obligations.

Fiscal crisis of the welfare state The crisis in state finances that occurs when expanding social expenditure coincides with recession and declining tax revenues.

Fiscal policy Government tax and spending policies, aimed primarily at influencing aggregate demand.

Franchise The right to vote.

Fraternity Literally, brotherhood; bonds of sympathy and comradeship between and amongst human beings.

Free market The principle or policy of unfettered market competition, free from government interference.

Free trade A system of trading between states not restricted by tariffs or other forms of protectionism.

Freedom (or liberty) The ability to think or act as one wishes; freedom implies either noninterference (negative freedom) or personal self-development (positive freedom) (see p. 282).

Fundamentalism A movement or style of thought which holds certain principles to be essential and unchallengeable 'truths' (see p. 61).

Gemeinschaft (*German*) Community; social bonds based on organic ties and mutual respect.

Gender A cultural distinction between females and males, based on their different social roles and positions (see p. 183).

General will The genuine interests of a collective body, equivalent to the common good; the will of all provided each person acts selflessly.

Gerrymandering The manipulation of electoral boundaries so as to achieve political advantage for a party or candidate.

Gesellschaft (*German*) Association; artificial and contractual social bonds based on a recognition of overlapping interests.

Glasnost (*Russian*) Literally, openness; the relaxation of censorship and cultural repression.

Globalisation A complex web of interconnectedness

through which life is increasingly shaped by decisions or events taken at a distance (see p. 140).

Government   The mechanism through which ordered rule is maintained; the machinery for making and enforcing collective decisions in society and elsewhere (see p. 24).

Government gridlock   Paralysis resulting from institutional rivalry within government or the attempt to respond to conflicting public demands.

Great power   A state deemed to rank amongst the most powerful in a hierarchical state system, reflected in its influence over minor states.

Gross domestic product   The total financial value of final goods and services produced in an economy over one year.

Head of state   The leading representative of the state, usually either a president or monarch; a title of essentially symbolic significance (see p. 317).

Hegemony   The ascendency or domination of one element of a system over others; for Marxists, hegemony implies ideological domination (see p. 190).

Hierarchy   A gradation of social positions or status; hierarchy implies structural or fixed inequality in which position is unconnected with individual ability.

Historical materialism   A Marxist theory that holds that material or economic conditions ultimately structure law, politics, culture and other aspects of social existence.

Human nature   The essential and immutable character of all human beings; that which is innate to humankind rather than socially or culturally produced.

Human rights   Rights to which people are entitled by virtue of being human; universal and fundamental rights (see p. 284).

Ideal type   A mental construct designed to draw out meaning from a complex reality through the presentation of a logical extreme (see p. 18).

Idealism   A view of politics that emphasises the importance of morality and ideals; philosophically, idealism can imply that ideas are more 'real' than the material world.

Ideology   A more or less coherent set of ideas that provides the basis for some kind of organised political action (see p. 41).

Immobilism   Political paralysis stemming from the absence of a strong executive, caused by multiple divisions in the assembly and (probably) society.

Impartiality   The absence of bias; the capacity to prevent political sympathies from intruding into professional or public responsibilities.

Impeachment   A formal process for the removal of a public official in the event of personal or professional wrongdoing.

Imperialism   The policy or practice of extending the power or rule of a state beyond its borders; imperialism can be an ideology of expansionism (see p. 145).

Incrementalism   The theory that decisions are not made in the light of clear-cut objectives, but through small adjustments dictated by changing circumstances.

Individual responsibility   See *ministerial responsibility*.

Individualism   A belief in the supreme importance of the human individual rather than any social group or collective body (see p. 178).

Industrialism   An economic theory or system based on large-scale factory production and the relentless accumulation of capital.

Initiative   A type of referendum through which the public is able to raise legislative proposals.

Integral nationalism   An intense, even hysterical, nationalist enthusiasm that absorbs individual identity into that of the nation.

Interest   That which benefits an individual or group; interests (unlike wants or preferences) are usually understood to be objective, or 'real', as opposed to 'felt'.

Interest group (or pressure group)   An organised association that aims to influence the policies or actions of government; interest groups may have a sectional or promotional character (see p. 254).

Intergovernmentalism   Interaction between or amongst states that takes place on the basis of sovereign independence (see p. 154).

International law   A system of rules that is binding on states, and thus defines the formal relationships between them (see p. 160).

Internationalism   A theory or practice of politics based on transnational or global cooperation; the belief that nations are artificial and unwanted formations (see p. 142).

Interventionism   Government policies designed to regulate or manage economic life; more broadly, a policy of engagement or involvement.

Iron triangle   A policy network that comprises executive agencies, legislative committees and interest groups, typically found in the USA.

Isolationism   The policy of withdrawal from international affairs and, in particular, avoiding political or military commitment to other states.

Issue   A matter recognised as part of the policy agenda, over which there is public debate or disagreement.

Jingoism   A mood of public enthusiasm and celebration provoked by military expansion or imperial conquest.

Judicial activism   The willingness of judges to arbitrate in political disputes, as opposed to merely saying what the law means.

Judicial independence   The constitutional principle that there should be a strict separation between the judiciary and other branches of government; an application of the separation of powers.

Judicial review   The power of the judiciary to review the laws, decrees and actions of other branches of government, and to declare them invalid (see p. 288).

Judiciary   The branch of government that is empowered to decide legal disputes and adjudicate on the meaning of the law.

Junta   Literally, a council; a (usually military) clique that seizes power through a revolution or *coup d'état*.

Justice   The morally justifiable apportionment of rewards or punishments, each person being given what he or she is 'due'.

Keynesianism   The theory (developed by John Maynard Keynes) or policy of economic management, usually associated with the goal of full employment.

Laissez-faire   (*French*) Literally, to leave to do; the principle of the noninterference of government in economic life (see p. 171).

Law   A set of public and enforceable rules that apply throughout a political community; law is usually recognised as binding.

Leadership   Influence exerted over a larger group or body, or personal qualities that foster willing obedience in others (see p. 330).

Left   A broad ideological disposition characterised by sympathy for principles such as liberty, equality, fraternity and progress (see p. 234).

Legislature   The branch of government that is empowered to make law through the formal enactment of legislation.

Legitimacy   Rightfulness; a quality that confers on a command an authoritative or binding character, implying a duty to obey (see p. 193).

Leninism   Lenin's theoretical contributions to Marxism, notably his belief in the need for a revolutionary or vanguard party.

Liberal democracy   A form of democracy which incorporates both limited government and a system of regular and competitive elections; liberal democracy is a regime type (see p. 28).

Liberalisation   The introduction of internal and external checks on government power and/or shifts towards private enterprise and the market.

Liberalism   An ideology based on a commitment to individualism, freedom, toleration and consent; modern liberalism differs from classical liberalism.

Libertarianism   The belief that the realm of individual liberty should be maximised, usually associated with attempts to minimise the scope of public authority.

Liberty   See *freedom*.

Licence   Excessive liberty; the abuse of or disregard for others or the law.

Limited government   Government operating within constraints, usually imposed by law, a constitution or institutional checks and balances.

Lobby   *Verb*: to make representations to policy makers; *noun*: an interest group that influences the policy process (see p. 263).

Local democracy   A principle that embodies both the idea of local autonomy and the goal of popular responsiveness.

Machiavellianism   Cunning and manipulative behaviour, usually aimed at personal or political advancement (after Niccolo Machiavelli) (see p. 6).

Machine politics   A style of politics in which party 'bosses' control a mass organisation through patronage and the distribution of favours.

Majoritarianism   A theory or practice in which priority is accorded to the will of the majority; majoritarianism implies insensitivity towards minorities and individuals.

Maladministration   Bad administration; the improper use of powers, biased application of rules, failure to follow procedures, or simple incompetence.

Managerialism   The theory that in modern society class divisions have been replaced by ones based on managerial position and bureaucratic power; technocracy (rule by experts or specialists).

Mandate   An authoritative instruction or command; a mandate can be a legal order or a moral obligation (see p. 210).

Manifesto   A document outlining (in more or less detail) the policies or programme a party proposes to pursue if elected to power.

Market   A system of commercial exchange shaped by the forces of demand and supply, and regulated by the price mechanism (see p. 167).

Market socialism An economic system based on self-managing cooperative enterprises operating in a context of market competition.

Marxism The theoretical system devised by Karl Marx, characterised by a belief in historical materialism, dialectical change and the use of class analysis.

Mass media Social institutions in print and electronic publishing and broadcasting that channel communication towards a large and undifferentiated audience (see p. 188).

Mass society A society characterised by atomism and cultural and political rootlessness; the concept highlights pessimistic trends in modern societies.

Materialism An emphasis on material needs and satisfaction; philosophically, either the belief that only matter is 'real' or that economic factors are fundamental to historical explanations.

McCarthyism The use of witch hunts and unscrupulous investigations, as practised in the 1950s against 'communists' by US Senator Joseph McCarthy.

Meritocracy Rule by the talented; the principle that rewards and positions should be distributed on the basis of ability.

Meta-ideology A higher or second-order ideology that lays down the grounds on which ideological debate can take place.

Militarism The achievement of ends by military means; or the spread of military ideas and values throughout civilian society (see p. 362).

Military–industrial complex A symbiotic relationship between the armed forces and defence industries, based on a common desire to increase military spending.

Military regime A regime in which political office is allocated on the basis of the holder's position in the military hierarchy.

Minimal state A state whose functions are restricted to the maintenance of domestic order and the protection of property; a 'nightwatchman' state.

Ministerial (or individual) responsibility The doctrine that ministers are responsible or accountable for the actions (and mistakes) of their civil servants (see p. 354).

Model A theoretical representation of empirical data that aims to advance understanding by highlighting significant relationships and interactions.

Monarchy An institution in which the post of head of state is filled through inheritance or by dynastic succession; monarchy may be absolute or constitutional (see p. 324).

Monetarism The theory that inflation is caused by an increase in the supply of money; 'too much money chases too few goods'.

Monetary policy A government's influence over the supply and value of money, principally exercised through the mechanism of interest rates.

Monism A belief in only one theory or value; monism is reflected politically in enforced obedience to a unitary power and is thus implicitly totalitarian.

Multiplier The mechanism through which a change in aggregate demand has an increased effect on national income as it circulates through the economy.

Nanny state A state with extensive social responsibilities; the term implies that welfare programmes are unwarranted and demeaning to the individual.

Nation A group of people who share a common cultural inheritance and regard themselves as a natural political community (see p. 104).

Nation-state A sovereign political association within which citizenship and nationality overlap; one nation within a single state (see p. 117).

National self-determination The principle that the nation is a sovereign entity; self-determination implies both national independence and democratic rule.

National Socialism (or Nazism) A form of fascism practised in Hitler's Germany and characterised by totalitarian terror, genocidal anti-Semitism, and expansionist racism.

Nationalism An ideology that takes the nation to be the central principle of political organisation; nationalism can be associated with a wide range of ideals and goals (see Chapter 6).

Natural aristocracy The idea that talent and leadership are innate or inbred qualities that cannot be acquired through effort or self-advancement.

Natural law A moral system to which human laws do, or should, conform; natural law lays down universal standards of conduct.

Natural rights God-given rights that are fundamental to human beings and are therefore inalienable (they cannot be taken away).

Negative freedom Noninterference, the absence of external constraints on the individual; sometimes seen as freedom 'from'.

Negative rights Rights that mark out a realm of unconstrained action, and thus check the responsibilities of government.

Neocolonialism   Control exercised over a foreign territory through economic (and sometimes cultural) domination rather than formal political direction.

Neoconservatism   An updated version of social conservatism that emphasises the need to restore authority and return to traditional values.

Neocorporatism   A tendency found in western polyarchies for organised interests to be granted privileged and institutionalised access to policy formulation.

Neo-idealism   A perspective on international politics that emphasises the practical value of morality and, in particular, respect for human rights and national independence.

Neoliberalism   An updated version of classical political economy, dedicated to market individualism and minimal statism.

Neo-Marxism   An updated and revised form of Marxism that rejects determinism, the primacy of economics, and the privileged status of the proletariat (see p. 90).

Neopluralism   A revised form of pluralism that takes account of the imbalances of the market and the disproportionate power of private business (see p. 88).

Neo-realism   A perspective on international politics that modifies the power-politics model by highlighting the structural constraints of the international system.

Neutrality   The absence of partisanship or commitment; a refusal to 'take sides' (see p. 287).

New Left   An ideological movement that sought to revitalise socialist thought by developing a radical critique of advanced industrial society, stressing the need for decentralisation, participation and personal liberation (see p. 266).

New public administration   The incorporation of private-sector management techniques into government and the transfer of public functions to private bodies.

New Right   An ideological trend within conservatism that embraces a blend of market individualism and social authoritarianism.

Nightwatchman state   A state with minimal responsibilities, primarily linked to the maintenance of domestic order and personal security.

Noblesse oblige   (*French*) Literally, the obligations of the nobility; in general terms the responsibility to guide or protect those less fortunate or less privileged.

Nomenklatura   (*Russian*) A system of vetted appointments that operates through a list of approved candidates.

Normative   The prescription of values and standards of conduct; what 'should be' rather than what 'is'.

Objective   External to the observer, demonstrable; untainted by feelings, values or bias.

Oligarchy   Government or domination by the few (see p. 238).

Ombudsman   An officer of the state appointed to safeguard citizens' rights and investigate allegations of maladministration (see p. 355).

One-nation conservatism   A principle of conservative reformism, born out of a belief in paternal duty and a fear of social inequality.

Open government   A free flow of information from government to representative bodies, the mass media and the electorate, based on the public's 'right to know' (see p. 392).

Order   A stable and predictable pattern of behaviour associated, in particular, with personal security and public safety (see p. 371).

Organicism   The belief that society operates like an organism or living entity, the whole being more than a collection of its individual parts.

Pacifism   The principled rejection of war and all forms of violence as fundamentally evil.

Pan-nationalism   A style of nationalism dedicated to unifying a disparate people through either expansionism or political solidarity ('pan' means all or every).

Paradigm   An intellectual framework, comprising interrelated values, theories and assumptions, within which the search for knowledge is conducted (see p. 20).

Parliament   A forum for debate and deliberation; parliament is equivalent to assembly or legislature.

Parliamentary democracy   A form of democracy that operates through a popularly elected assembly and emphasises the importance of deliberation (see p. 74).

Parliamentary government   A system in which government governs in and through the assembly or parliament, thereby 'fusing' the legislature and executive (see p. 295).

Parliamentary sovereignty   The absolute and unlimited authority of a parliament or assembly, reflected in its ability to make, repeal or amend any law (see p. 283).

Partisan dealignment   A weakening in the strength and extent of party identification, reflected in an increase in electoral volatility (see p. 225).

Party democracy   The principle of the wide and even distribution of power within a party, or its concentration in the hands of its elected members (see p. 239).

Party government   A system in which a party is able to govern alone and carry out a programme of policies (see p. 243).

Party system   A relatively stable network of relationships between political parties that is structured by their number, size and ideological orientation.

Paternalism   An attitude or policy that demonstrates care or concern for those unable to help themselves, as in the (supposed) relationship between a father and a child.

Patriarchy   Literally, rule by the father; a system of male domination and female subordination in society at large (see p. 92).

Patriotism   Literally, love of one's fatherland; a psychological attachment and loyalty to one's nation or country (see p. 113).

Peak association   A group recognised by government as representing the general or collective interests of businesses or workers.

Perestroika   (*Russian*) Literally, restructuring; a slogan that refers to the attempt to liberalise and democratise the Soviet system within a communist framework.

Permissiveness   The willingness to allow people to make their own moral choices; permissiveness suggests that there are no authoritative values.

Planning   A system of economic organisation that relies on a rational allocation of resources in line with clearly defined goals; planning may be directive or indicative (see p. 174).

Plebiscitary democracy   A form of democracy that operates through an unmediated link between rulers and the ruled, and is conducted through plebiscites (referendums) (see p. 69).

Pluralism   A belief in, or commitment to, diversity or multiplicity; or the theory that power in modern societies is widely and evenly distributed (see p. 76).

Pluralist democracy   A form of democracy that operates through the capacity of organised groups to articulate popular demands and ensure government responsiveness (see p. 77).

Plurality   The largest of a collection of numbers; a 'relative' majority.

Police state   A form of rule characterised by arbitrary and terroristic policing, in which the police act as a private army controlled by a ruling elite.

Policy   Formal decisions made by public bodies; the 'outputs' of government (see p. 382).

Policy network   A systematic set of relationships between political actors who share a common interest or general orientation in a particular area (see p. 388).

Polis   (*Greek*) City-state; classically understood to imply the highest or most desirable form of social organisation.

Political culture   A pattern of psychological orientations towards political objects; a people's political attitudes, beliefs, symbols and values (see p. 186).

Political equality   The equal distribution of political power and influence, usually understood to imply 'one person, one vote; one vote, one value' (see p. 67).

Political obligation   The duty of the citizen towards the state; the basis of the state's right to rule.

Political party   A group of people organised to gain formal representation or win government power; a party usually displays some measure of ideological cohesion (see p. 230).

Political philosophy   The systematic analysis of the normative and methodological aspects of the study of politics.

Political pluralism   The existence of a range of political values, philosophies and movements; in particular, a competitive party system.

Political science   The study of government, the state and politics; more narrowly, the application of empirical theory and scientific methods to the analysis of political matters.

Political socialisation   The process through which individuals acquire political beliefs and values, and by which these are transmitted from generation to generation.

Political system   A network of relationships through which government generates 'outputs' (policies) in response to 'inputs' (demands or support) from the general public.

Politics   The activity through which people make, preserve and amend the general rules under which they live (see Chapter 1).

Polity   A society organised through the exercise of political authority; for Aristotle, rule by the many in the interests of all.

Polyarchy   Literally, rule by the many; an approximation of democracy based on the accountabiliy of power holders through regular and competitive elections (see p. 31).

Popular sovereignty   The principle that there is no higher authority than the will of the people (the basis of the classical concept of democracy).

Populism   The belief that the instincts of the masses are the only legitimate guide to political action; or a movement that appeals to popular instincts, resentments or aspirations (see p. 335).

Positive freedom   Freedom as personal development, self-realisation or self-mastery; sometimes seen as freedom 'to'.

Positive law   A system of enforceable commands that operates irrespective of their moral content.

Positive rights   Rights that make demands of government in terms of the provision of resources and support, and thus extend its responsibilities.

Positivism   The theory that social and indeed all forms of enquiry should adhere strictly to the methods of the natural sciences.

Post-Fordism   The transformation of modern society resulting from the shift away from large-scale, factory-based production methods (see p. 180).

Postindustrial society   A society no longer dependent on manufacturing industry, but more reliant on knowledge and communication; an 'information society'.

Postmaterialism   The theory that as material affluence spreads 'quality of life' issues and concerns tend to displace economic ones (see p. 193).

Postmodernism   An intellectual movement that rejects the idea of absolute and universal truth, and usually emphasises discourse, debate and democracy (see p. 61).

Power   The ability to influence the behaviour of others, typically through the power to reward or punish (see p. 7).

Power politics   An approach to politics based on the assumption that the pursuit of power is the principal human goal; the term is sometimes used descriptively.

Pragmatism   A theory or practice that places primary emphasis on practical circumstances and goals; pragmatism implies a distrust of abstract ideas.

President   A formal head of state, the republican equivalent of a monarch; executive presidents also serve as heads of government.

Presidential government   A system of government in which executive authority is concentrated in the hands of a president, whose office is politically and constitutionally separate from the legislature (see p. 320).

Pressure group   See *interest group*.

Primary election   An intraparty election held to select a candidate to contest a subsequent 'official' election (see p. 236).

Prime minister   A head of government whose power is derived from the leadership of the largest party (or coalition of parties) in the assembly.

Prime-ministerial government   A system of government in which executive power is concentrated in the prime minister's hands through the suppression of collective cabinet government (see p. 326).

Privatisation   The transfer of state assets from the public to the private sector, reflecting a contraction of the state's responsibilities.

Progress   Moving forwards; the belief that history is characterised by human advancement based on the accumulation of knowledge and wisdom.

Proletariat   A Marxist term, denoting a class that subsists through the sale of its labour power; strictly speaking, the proletariat is not equivalent to the working class.

Propaganda   Information disseminated in a deliberate attempt to shape opinions and, possibly, stimulate political action; communication as manipulation.

Proportional representation   A principle or system in which parties are represented in an assembly in proportion to their overall electoral strength (see p. 220).

Protectionism   Import restrictions such as quotas and tariffs, designed to protect domestic producers.

Public choice theory   A subfield of rational-choice theory concerned with the provision of public goods (see p. 258).

Public goods   Goods and benefits which individuals or groups who do not contribute to their provision cannot be prevented from enjoying.

Public interest   The general or collective interests of a community; that which is good for society as a whole (see p. 222).

Quango   An acronym for quasi-autonomous nongovernmental organisation: a public body staffed by appointees rather than politicians or civil servants (see p. 350).

Race   A group of people (supposedly) distinguished from other groups by physical or biological differences (see p. 182).

Racialism (or racism)   The doctrine that political and social organisation should be based on racial categories; racism may refer to prejudice or hostility towards members of other races (see p. 114).

Radical democracy   A form of democracy that favours decentralisation and participation, the widest possible dispersal of political power.

Radical feminism   A form of feminism that holds gender divisions to be the most politically significant of social cleavages, and believes that they are rooted in the structure of domestic life.

Radicalism   A commitment to thorough-going change that challenges basic or fundamental structures not merely superficial ones.

Rational choice   An approach to politics based on the assumption that individuals are rationally self-interested actors; an 'economic' theory of politics.

Rationalism   The belief that the world can be understood and explained through the exercise of human reason, based on assumptions about its rational structure.

Realism   A view of politics that emphasises the importance of power and self-interest, and disregards moral or normative considerations.

Rebellion   A popular uprising against the established order, usually (unlike a revolution) aimed at replacing rulers rather than the political system itself.

Recall   A process whereby the electorate can call unsatisfactory public officials to account and ultimately remove them.

Referendum   A vote in which the electorate can express a view on a particular issue of public policy; referendums may be advisory or binding (see p. 209).

Reform   Change brought about within a system, usually by peaceful and incremental measures; reform implies improvement.

Regime   A system of rule; a political system.

Representation   Standing for, or acting on behalf of, a larger body of people; representation can involve trusteeship, delegation or resemblance (see p. 206).

Representative democracy   A limited and indirect form of democracy based on the selection (usually by election) of those who will rule on behalf of the people.

Repression   A state of subjugation brought about through systematic intimidation or open violence (see p. 369).

Republicanism   The principle that political authority stems ultimately from the consent of the people; the rejection of monarchical and dynastic principles.

Reserve army of labour   An available supply of labour easily shed in times of recession; the 'army' enjoys no security and exercises little market power.

Responsibility   Sensible or morally correct behaviour; or accountability to a higher authority (see p. 300).

Responsible government   A government that is answerable or accountable to an elected assembly and, through it, to the people.

Revisionism   The modification of original or established beliefs; revisionism can imply the abandonment of principle or a loss of conviction.

Revolution   A popular uprising that involves extra-legal mass action aimed at changing the political system, not merely the ruling elite (see p. 198).

Rhetoric   The art of using language to persuade or influence; rhetoric can imply high-sounding but essentially vacuous speech.

Right   A broad ideological disposition characterised by sympathy for principles such as authority, order, hierarchy and duty (see p. 234).

Rights   Legal or moral entitlements to act or be treated in a particular way; civil rights differ from human rights.

Rule of law   The principle that law should 'rule' in the sense that it establishes a framework within which all conduct or behaviour takes place (see p. 284).

Ruling class   A Marxist term, denoting a class that dominates other classes and society at large by virtue of its ownership of productive wealth.

Science   The field of study that aims to develop reliable explanations of phenomena through repeatable experiments, observations and deductions (see p. 16).

Scientism   The belief that the scientific method is the only source of reliable knowledge, and is applicable to all fields of learning.

Secularism   The belief that religion should not intrude into secular (worldly) affairs, usually reflected in a desire to separate church from state.

Semi-presidential system   A system of government in which a separately elected president presides over a government drawn from, and accountable to, the assembly.

Separation of powers   The principle that legislative, executive and judicial power should be separated through the construction of three independent branches of government (see p. 297).

Separatism   The quest to secede from a political formation with a view to establishing an independent state.

Shari'a   Islamic law, believed to be based on divine revelation, and derived from the Koran, the Hadith (the teachings of Muhammad), and other sources.

Social capital   Cultural and moral resources that help to promote social cohesion, political stability and prosperity.

Social class   A group of people who share a common social position and economic interests; classes can reflect unequal economic power or occupational status (see p. 179).

Social contract   A voluntary agreement through which an organised society or state is (supposedly) brought into existence; usually used as a theoretical device (see p. 87).

Social democracy   A moderate or reformist brand of socialism that favours a balance between the market and the state, rather than the abolition of capitalism.

Social justice   The morally justifiable distribution of material rewards; social justice is often seen to imply a bias in favour of equality.

Social market An economy structured by market principles but underpinned by effective social provision designed to maintain cohesion (see p. 169).

Social movement A collective body distinguished by a high level of commitment and political activism, but often lacking clear organisation (see p. 266).

Socialism An ideology characterised by a belief in community, cooperation, equality and common ownership; socialist theories range from communism to social democracy.

Sovereignty Absolute and unlimited power; sovereignty can imply either supreme legal authority or unchallengeable political power (see p. 143).

Stalinism Economic and political structures that resemble those constructed by Stalin in the USSR, particularly central planning and brutal political discipline.

State A political association that establishes sovereign jurisdiction within defined territorial borders, characterised by its monopoly of legitimate violence (see Chapter 5).

State capitalism A system of state ownership which replicates capitalist class relationships by concentrating economic power in the hands of a party–state elite.

State of nature A society devoid of political authority and of formal (legal) checks on the individual; usually employed as a theoretical device.

State socialism A form of socialism in which the state controls and directs economic life, acting, in theory, in the interests of the people.

Statism The belief that the state is the most appropriate means of resolving problems and guaranteeing economic and social development (see p. 96).

Status A position within a hierarchical order; a person's role, rights and duties in relation to others (see p. 179).

Subjective Internal to the observer; related to or emanating from a person's feelings, values and opinions.

Subsidiarity The transfer of decision-making from central to peripheral bodies; the principle that decisions should be taken at the lowest appropriate level (see p. 158).

Suffrage The right to vote, or the exercising of that right.

Superpower A state with preponderant nuclear military capacity and global territorial influence; a superpower is higher than a 'great' power.

Supranationalism The ability of bodies with transnational or global jurisdiction to impose their will on nation-states (see p. 154).

Sustainability The ability of a system to maintain its health and continue to exist; the central principle of Green economics.

Systems theory The theory that treats the political system as a self-regulating mechanism, responding to 'inputs' (demands and support) by issuing authoritative decisions or 'outputs' (policies).

Thatcherism The free-market/strong-state ideological stance adopted by Margaret Thatcher; the UK version of the New Right political project.

Theocracy Literally, rule by God; the principle that religious authority should prevail over political authority through the domination of church over state (see p. 35).

Theory A systematic explanation of empirical data, usually (unlike a hypothesis) presented as reliable knowledge.

Think tank An interest group specifically formed to develop policy proposals and campaign for their acceptance amongst opinion formers and policy makers.

Tiger economies Fast-growing and export-orientated economies modelled on Japan; for example, South Korea, Taiwan and Singapore.

Toleration Forbearance; a willingness to allow people to think, speak and act in ways of which one disapproves.

Toryism An ideological stance within conservatism characterised by a belief in hierarchy, an emphasis on tradition, and support for duty and organicism.

Totalitarian democracy An absolute dictatorship that masquerades as a democracy, typically based on the leader's claim to a monopoly of ideological wisdom.

Totalitarianism An all-encompassing system of political rule established through pervasive ideological manipulation and open brutality; the abolition of civil society (see p. 27).

Tradition Continuity with the past, reflected in the transmission of institutions, values and practices from one generation to the next (see p. 195).

Tribalism Group behaviour characterised by insularity and exclusivity, typically fuelled by hostility towards rival groups.

Tripartitism The construction of bodies that represent government, business and the unions, designed to institutionalise group consultation.

Underclass A classification of people who are socially and politically marginalised by virtue of a combination of material and cultural deprivation.

Unicameralism The concentration of legislative power in a single-chamber assembly.

Utilitarianism A moral philosophy that equates pleasure with 'good' and pain with 'evil', and aims to achieve the greatest happiness for the greatest number (see p. 383).

Utility   Use value; satisfaction derived from material consumption.

Utopia   Literally, nowhere or good place; an ideal or perfect society (see p. 25).

Utopianism   A style of political theorising that develops a critique of the existing order by constructing a model of an ideal or perfect alternative.

Value   A moral principle that prescribes an accepted standard for individuals or groups.

Vanguardism   The Leninist belief in the need for a party to lead and guide the proletariat towards the fulfilment of its revolutionary destiny.

Veto   The formal power to block a decision or action through the refusal of consent.

Volksgeist   (*German*) Literally, the spirit of the people; the organic identity of a people reflected in their culture and particularly their language.

War   A condition of open conflict between two or more parties, usually states (see p. 361).

Welfare   Well-being in general; politically, the term is usually associated with collectively provided welfare delivered through the mechanism of the welfare state (see p. 395).

Westminster model   A system of government in which the executive is drawn from, and (in theory) accountable to, the assembly or parliament.

Written constitution   A single authoritative document that allocates duties, powers and functions amongst the institutions of government, and so constitutes 'higher' law.

Xenophobia   A fear or hatred of foreigners; pathological ethnocentrism.

Zionism   The movement for the establishment of a Jewish homeland, now linked to the defence of the interests and territorial integrity of Israel.

Bibliography

Abercrombie, W., S. Hill and B. Turner (1980) *The Dominant Ideology Thesis* (London: Allen & Unwin).

Albrow, M. (1970) *Bureaucracy* (London: Macmillan).

Allison, G. (1971) *Essence of Decision* (Boston: Little, Brown).

Almond, G. (1989) *A Discipline Divided: Schools and Sects in Political Science* (Newbury Park, CA: Sage).

Almond, G. A. and S. Verba (1963) *The Civic Culture: Political Attitudes and Democracy in Five Nations* (Princeton: Princeton University Press).

Almond, G. A. and S. Verba (eds) (1980) *The Civic Culture Revisited* (Boston: Little, Brown).

Alter, P. (1989) *Nationalism* (London: Edward Arnold).

Anderson, B. (1983) *Imagined Communities: Reflections on the Origins and Spread of Nationalism* (London: Verso).

Anderson, J. (1984) *Public Policy-Making* (Orlando, FL: Holt, Rinehart & Winston).

Arblaster, A. (1984) *The Rise and Decline of Western Liberalism* (Oxford: Basil Blackwell).

Arblaster, A. (1994) *Democracy* (2nd ed.) (Milton Keynes: Open University Press; Minneapolis: University of Minnesota Press).

Arendt, H. (1958) *The Human Condition* (Chicago: University of Chicago Press).

Aristotle (1948) *Politics* (Oxford: Clarendon Press) (ed. E. Baker).

Arrow, K. (1951) *Social Choice and Individual Values* (New York: Wiley).

Babbington, A. (1990) *Military Intervention in Britain* (London: Routledge).

Bachrach, P. and M. Baratz (1962) 'The Two Faces of Power', in F. G. Castles, D. J. Murray and D. C. Potter (eds) *Decisions, Organisations and Society* (Harmondsworth: Penguin).

Bagehot, W. ([1867] 1963) *The English Constitution* (London: Fontana).

Ball, A. and F. Millward (1986) *Pressure Politics in Industrial Societies* (London: Macmillan).

Barber, J. (1988) *Politics by Humans: Research on American Leadership* (Durham, NC: Duke University Press).

Barrett, S. and C. Fudge (1981) *Policy and Action* (London: Methuen).

Barry, N. P. (1987) *The New Right* (London: Croom Helm).

Beard, C. (1913) *Economic Interpretation of the Constitution of the United States* (New York: Macmillan).

Beer, S. (1982) *Britain Against Itself* (London: Faber).

Beetham, D. (1987) *Bureaucracy* (Milton Keynes: Open University Press).

Beetham, D. (1991) *The Legitimation of Power* (Basingstoke: Macmillan).

Bell, D. (1960) *The End of Ideology?: On the Exhaustion of Political Ideas in the 1950s* (New York: Free Press).

Bell, D. (1976) *The Cultural Contradictions of Capitalism* (London: Heinemann).

Bentham, J. ([1776] 1948) *Fragments on Government and an Introduction to the Principles of Law and Legislation* (Oxford: Blackwell) (ed. W. Harrison).

Bentley, A. ([1908] 1948) *The Process of Government* (Evanston, IL: Principia).

Berger, S. (ed.) (1981) *Organising Interests in Western Europe: Pluralism, Corporatism and the Transformation of Politics* (New York: Cambridge University Press).

Berlin, I. (1958) *Four Essays on Liberty* (Oxford: Oxford University Press).

Bernstein, E. ([1898] 1962) *Evolutionary Socialism* (New York: Schocken).

Bertsch, G., R. Clarke and D. Wood (1992) *Comparing Political Systems: Power and Policy in Three Worlds* (4th ed.) (New York: Macmillan).

Birch, A. H. (1993) *Concepts and Theories of Modern Democracy* (London and New York: Routledge).

Birch, A. H. (1972) *Representation* (London: Macmillan; New York: Praeger).

Blau, P. and M. Meyer (eds) (1987) *Bureaucracy in Modern Society* (3rd ed.) (New York: Random House).

Blondel, J. (1973) *Comparative Legislatures* (Englewood Cliffs, NJ: Prentice Hall).

Bodin, J. ([1576] 1962) *The Six Books of the Commonweal* (Cambridge, MA: Harvard University Press) (trans. R. Knolles).

Bogdanor, V. (1979) *Devolution* (Oxford: Oxford University Press).

Bogdanor, V. (ed.) (1988) *Constitutions in Democratic Politics* (Aldershot: Gower).

Bogdanor, V. and D. Butler (eds) (1983) *Democracy and Elections* (Cambridge: Cambridge University Press).

Bookchin, M. (1989) *Remaking Society* (Montreal: Black Rose).

Bottomore, T. (1991) *Classes in Modern Society* (London: Allen & Unwin).

Boulding, K. (1956) *The Image* (Ann Arbor: University of Michigan Press).

Boulding, K. (1989) *Three Faces of Power* (Newbury Park, CA: Sage).

Brandt Commission (1980) *North–South: A Programme for Survival* (Cambridge, MA: MIT Press).

Brandt Commission (1983) *Common Crisis: North–South Cooperation for World Recovery* (London: Pan).

Braybrooke, D. and C. Lindblom (1963) *A Strategy of Decision: Policy Evaluation as a Political Process* (New York: Collier Macmillan).

Breitenbach, H., T. Burden and D. Coates (1990) *Features of a Viable Socialism* (London and New York: Harvester Wheatsheaf).

Bretherton, C. and G. Ponton (eds) (1996) *Global Politics: An Introduction* (Oxford: Blackwell).

Brewer, J., A. Guelke, I. Hume, E. Moxon-Browne and R. Wilford (1988) *The Police, Public Order and the State* (Basingstoke: Macmillan).

Brittan, S. (1977) *The Economic Consequences of Democracy* (London: Temple Smith).

Brown, M. B. (1995) *Models in Political Economy: A Guide to the Arguments* (2nd ed.) (Harmondsworth: Penguin).

Bryson, V. (1992) *Feminist Political Thought: An Introduction* (Basingstoke: Macmillan).

Budge, I. and D. Mackie (eds) (1994) *Developing Democracy* (London: Sage).

Bull, H. (1977) *The Anarchical Society* (London: Macmillan).

Burchill, S. and A. Linklater (1996) *Theories of International Relations* (Basingstoke: Macmillan).

Burgess, M. and A.-G. Gagnon (eds) (1993) *Comparative Federalism and Federation* (London and New York: Harvester Wheatsheaf).

Burke, E. ([1790] 1968) *Reflections on the Revolution in France* (Harmondsworth: Penguin) (ed. C. C. O'Brien).

Burke, E. (1975) *On Government, Politics and Society* (London: Fontana) (ed. B. W. Hill).

Burnham, J. (1941) *The Managerial Revolution* (Harmondsworth: Penguin).

Burns, B. (1978) *Leadership* (New York: Harper & Row).

Burton, J. (1972) *World Society* (Cambridge: Cambridge University Press).

Butler, D. and D. Stokes (1969) *Political Change in Britain* (2nd ed.) (London: Macmillan).

Butler, D., H. Penniman and A. Ranney (eds) (1981) *Democracy at the Polls* (Washington DC: American Enterprise Institute).

Butler, D., A. Adonis and T. Travers (1994) *Failure in British Government: The Politics of the Poll Tax* (Oxford: Oxford University Press).

Calvocoressi, P. (1991) *World Politics Since 1945* (London and New York: Longman).

Campbell, A., P. Converse, W. E. Miller and D. Stokes (1960) *The American Voter* (New York: John Wiley).

Capra, F. (1983) *The Turning Point: Science, Society and the Rising Culture* (London: Fontana).

Carr, E. H. (1939) *The Twenty Years' Crisis, 1919–1939* (London: Macmillan).

Castle, B. (1980) *The Castle Diaries 1974–1976* (London: Weidenfeld & Nicolson).

Castles, F. and R. Wildmann (eds) (1986) *The Future of Party Government – Vol. 1* (Berlin: Gruyter).

Chamberlain, H. S. ([1899] 1913) *The Foundations of the Nineteenth Century* (New York: John Lane).

Chomsky, N. (1994) *World Order, Old and New* (London: Pluto Press).

Cigler, C. and B. Loomis (eds) (1985) *Interest Group Politics* (Washington DC: Congressional Quarterly Press).

Clarke, S. (ed.) (1991) *The State Debate* (London: Macmillan).

Cohen, A. (1975) *Theories of Revolution: An Introduction* (London: Nelson).

Connolly, W. (ed.) (1984) *Legitimacy and the State* (Oxford: Blackwell).

Cox, A. (1987) *The Court and the Constitution* (Boston: Houghton Mifflin).

Crewe, I. and D. Denver (eds) (1985) *Electoral Change in Western Democracies* (Beckenham: Croom Helm).

Crick, B. (1993) *In Defence of Politics* (Harmondsworth and New York: Penguin).

Crosland, C. A. R. (1956) *The Future of Socialism* (London: Jonathan Cape).

Crossman, R. (1963) 'Introduction to W. Bagehot', in *The English Constitution* (London: Fontana).

Crossman, R. (1979) *The Crossman Diaries* (London: Methuen) (ed. A. Howard).

Dahl, R. (1956) *A Preface to Democratic Theory* (Chicago: Chicago University Press).

Dahl, R. (1961) *Who Governs? Democracy and Power in an American City* (Newhaven, CT: Yale University Press).

Dahl, R. (1971) *Polyarchy: Participation and Opposition* (Newhaven, CT: Yale University Press).

Dahl, R. (1984) *Modern Political Analysis* (4th ed.) (Englewood Cliffs, NJ: Prentice Hall).

Dahl, R. (1985) *A Preface to Economic Democracy* (Cambridge: Polity Press).

Dahl, R. (1989) *Democracy and its Critics* (New Haven, CT: Yale University Press).

Dahl, R. and C. Lindblom (1953) *Politics, Economics, and Welfare* (New York: Harper & Row).

Daly, M. (1978) *Gyn/Ecology: The Mathematics of Radical Feminism* (London: The Women's Press).

Davidson, R. H. (ed.) (1992) *The Post-Reform Congress* (New York: St Martin's Press).

Davidson, R. H. and W. J. Oleszek (1993) *Congress and Its Members* (4th ed.) (Washington DC: Congressional Quarterly Press).

Davies, J. (1971) *When Men Revolt and Why* (New York: Free Press).

Decalo, S. (1976) *Coups and Army Rule in Africa* (Newhaven, CT: Yale University Press).

Devlin, P. (1968) *The Enforcement of Morals* (Oxford: Oxford University Press).

Diamond, L., J. Linz and S. Lipset (eds) (1989) *Democracy in Developing Countries* (Boulder, CO: Lynne Rienner) (4 vols).

Dicey, A. V. ([1885] 1939) *Introduction to the Study of the Law of the Constitution* (London: Macmillan) (ed. E. C. S. Wade).

Djilas, M. (1957) *The New Class: An Analysis of the Communist System* (New York: Praeger).

Dobson, A. (1990) *Green Political Thought* (London: Routledge).

Downs, A. (1957) *An Economic Theory of Democracy* (New York: Harper & Row).

Drewry, G. (ed.) (1989) *The New Select Committees* (rev. ed.) (Oxford: Oxford University Press).

Duchacek, I. (1973) *Power Maps: The Politics of Constitutions* (Santa Barbara, CA: ABC Clio).

Duncan, G. (ed.) (1983) *Democratic Theory and Practice* (Cambridge: Cambridge University Press).

Dunleavy, P. (1991) *Democracy, Bureaucracy and Public Choice: Economic Explanations in Political Science* (Hemel Hempstead: Harvester Wheatsheaf).

Dunleavy, P. and C. Husbands (1985) *British Democracy at the Crossroads* (London: Allen & Unwin).

Dunleavy, P. and B. O'Leary (1987) *Theories of the State* (London: Macmillan).

Dunn, J. (ed.) (1992) *Democracy: The Unfinished Journey 508 BC to AD 1993* (Oxford: Oxford University Press).

Duverger, M. (1954) *Political Parties* (London: Methuen).

Dworkin, R. (1986) *Law's Empire* (London: Fontana).

Dye, T. (1995) *Understanding Public Policy* (London: Prentice Hall).

Easton, D. (1979) *A Framework for Political Analysis* (2nd ed.) (Chicago: University of Chicago Press).

Easton, D. (1981) *The Political System* (3rd ed.) Chicago: University of Chicago Press).

Eccleston, B. (1989) *State and Society in Post-War Japan* (Cambridge: Polity Press).

Elgie, R. (1995) *Political Leadership in Liberal Democracies* (Basingstoke: Macmillan).

Etzioni, A. (1967) 'Mixed Scanning: A Third Approach to Decision Making', *Public Administration Review*, vol. 27, pp. 385–92.

Etzioni, A. (1995) *The Spirit of Community: Rights Responsibilities and the Communitarian Agenda* (London: Fontana).

Eysenck, H. (1964) *Sense and Nonsense in Psychology* (Harmondsworth: Penguin).

Finer, S. (1975) *The Man on Horseback: The Role of the Military in Politics* (Harmondsworth: Penguin).

Finn, J. E. (1991) *Constitutions in Crisis: Political Violence and the Rule of Law* (New York: Oxford University Press).

Foley, M. (1993) *The Rise of the British Presidency* (Manchester: Manchester University Press).

Forsyth, M. (1981) *Union of States: The Theory and Practice of Confederation* (London and New York: Leicester University Press).

Freud, S. and W. Bullitt (1967) *Thomas Woodrow Wilson: A Psychological Study* (Boston: Houghton Mifflin).

Friedan, B. (1963) *The Feminine Mystique* (Harmondsworth: Penguin).

Friedman, M. (1962) *Capitalism and Freedom* (Chicago: Chicago University Press).

Friedrich, C. J., M. Curtis and B. Barber (1960) *Totalitarianism in Perspective* (New York: Praeger).

Friedrich, C. J. and Z. Brzezinski (1963) *Totalitarian Dictatorships and Autocracy* (New York: Praeger).

Fromm, E. *The Fear of Freedom* (London: Ark).

Fukuyama, F. (1989) 'The End of History?', *National Interest*, Summer.

Fukuyama, F. (1992) *The End of History and the Last Man* (Harmondsworth: Penguin).

Fukuyama, F. (1996) *Trust* (Harmondsworth: Penguin).

Galbraith, J. K. (1992) *The Culture of Contentment* (London: Sinclair Stevenson).

Gallie, W. B. (1955/56) 'Essentially Contested Concepts', *Proceedings of the Aristotelian Society*, vol. 56, pp. 167–97.

Gamble, A. (1981) *An Introduction to Modern Social and Political Thought* (London: Macmillan and New York: St Martin's Press).

Gamble, A. (1988) *The Free Market and the Strong State* (Basingstoke: Macmillan).

Gardner, H. (1996) *Leading Minds* (London: HarperCollins).

Gellner, E. (1983) *Nations and Nationalism* (Ithaca, NY: Cornell University Press).

Gibbins, J. (ed.) (1989) *Contemporary Political Culture: Politics in a Post-Modern Age* (London: Sage).

Giddens, A. (1994) *Beyond Left and Right: The Future of Radical Politics* (Cambridge: Polity Press).

Gill, S. and D. Law (1988) *The Global Political Economy: Perspectives, Problems and Policies* (Brighton: Harvester Wheatsheaf).

Ginsberg, B. (1982) *The Consequences of Consent* (Reading, MA: Addison–Wesley).

Glazer, N. and D. Moynihan (1975) *Ethnicity: Theory and Experience* (Cambridge, MA: Harvard University Press).

Gobineau, J.-A. ([1855] 1970) *Gobineau: Selected Political Writings* (New York: Harper & Row) (ed. M. D. Biddiss).

Graham, B. D. (1993) *Representation and Party Politics: A Comparative Perspective* (Oxford: Blackwell).

Graham, C. and T. Prosser (1988) *Waiving the Rules* (Milton Keynes: Open University Press).

Gramsci, A. (1971) *Selections from the Prison Notebooks* (Chicago: International Publishing Corporation) (ed. Q. Hoare and G. Nowell-Smith).

Grant, W. (1989) *Pressure Groups, Politics and Democracy in Britain* (Hemel Hempstead: Philip Allan).

Gray, J. (1993) *Post-Liberalism: Studies in Political Thought* (London: Routledge).

Griffen, R. (1991) *The Nature of Fascism* (London and New York: Pinter).

Griffiths, J. A. G. (1991) *The Politics of the Judiciary* (4th ed.) (London: Fontana).

Groz, A. (1982) *Farewell to the Working Class* (London: Pluto Press).

Gurr, T. (1970) *Why Men Rebel* (Princeton: Princeton University Press).

Habermas, J. (1973) *Legitimation Crisis* (Boston: Beacon).

Hague, R., M. Harrop and S. Breslin (1992) *Comparative Government and Politics: An Introduction* (3rd ed.) (Basingstoke: Macmillan) (US ed.: *Political Science: A Comparative Introduction* (New York: St Martin's Press)).

Hailsham, Lord (1976) *Elective Dictatorship* (BBC Publications).

Halliday, F. (1986) *The Making of the Second World War* (2nd ed.) (London: Verso).

Hamilton, A., J. Jay and J. Madison ([1787–89] 1961) *The Federalist Papers* (New York: New American Library) (ed. C. Rossiter).

Hampden-Turner, C. and F. Trompenaars (1993) *The Seven Cultures of Capitalism* (New York: Doubleday).

Hann, A. (1995) 'Sharpening up Sabatier: Belief Systems and Public Policy', *Politics*, February.

Harrop, M. and W. L. Miller (1987) *Elections and Voters: A Comparative Introduction* (Basingstoke: Macmillan).

Hart, H. L. A. (1961) *The Concept of Law* (Oxford: Oxford University Press).

Hartz, L. (1955) *The Liberal Tradition in America* (New York: Harcourt Brace Jovanovich).

Hayek, F. (1948) *The Road to Serfdom* (Chicago: University of Chicago Press).

Heady, F. (1979) *Public Administration: A Comparative Perspective* (New York: Marcel Dekker).

Hegel, G. W. F. ([1821] 1942) *The Philosophy of Right* (Oxford: Clarendon Press) (trans. T. M. Knox).

Heidenheimer, A., H. Heclo and C. T. Adams (1990) *Comparative Public Policy* (3rd ed.) (New York: St Martin's Press).

Held, D. (1993) *Prospects for Democracy: North, South, East, West* (Oxford: Polity Press).

Held, D. (1996) *Models of Democracy* (2nd ed.) (Oxford: Polity Press; Stanford: Stanford University Press).

Hennessy, P. (1986) *Cabinet* (Oxford: Blackwell).

Hennessy, P. (1990) *Whitehall* (rev. ed.) (London: Fontana).

Herder, J. G. (1969) *J. G. Herder on Social and Political Culture* (Cambridge: Cambridge University Press) (ed. F. M. Barnard).

Hess, S. (1988) *Organising the Presidency* (Brookings Institution).

Heywood, A. (1994) *Political Ideas and Concepts: An Introduction* (Basingstoke: Macmillan).

Heywood, A. (1997) *Political Ideologies: An Introduction* (2nd ed.) (Basingstoke: Macmillan).

Hill, R. and P. Frank (1983) *The Soviet Communist Party* (London: Allen & Unwin).

Himmelveit, H. T., P. Humphreys and M. Jaeger (1985) *How Voters Decide* (Milton Keynes: Open University Press).

Hitler, A. ([1925] 1969) *Mein Kampf* (London: Hutchinson) (trans. R. Mannheim).

Hobbes, T. ([1651] 1968) *Leviathan* (Harmondsworth: Penguin) (ed. C. B. Macpherson).

Hobsbawm, E. (1983) 'Inventing Traditions', in E. Hobsbawm and T. Ranger (eds) *The Invention of Tradition* (Cambridge: Cambridge University Press).

Hobsbawm, E. (1993) *Nations and Nationalism since 1780* (2nd ed.) (Cambridge: Cambridge University Press).

Hocking, B. and M. Smith (1995) *World Politics: An Introduction to International Relations* (London: Harvester Wheatsheaf).

Hogwood, B. and L. Gunn (1984) *Policy Analysis for the Real World* (Oxford: Oxford University Press).

Holden, B. (1993) *Understanding Liberal Democracy* (2nd ed.) (London and New York: Harvester Wheatsheaf).

Hondrich, T. (1992) *Conservatism* (Harmondsworth: Penguin).

Hood, C. C. (1976) *The Limits of Administration* (London: John Wiley).

Hough, J. (1977) *The Soviet Union and Social Science Theory* (Cambridge, MA: Harvard University Press).

Huntington, S. (1957) *The Soldier and the State: The Theory and Practice of Civil–Military Relations* (Cambridge, MA: Harvard University Press).

Hutchinson, J. and A. D. Smith (eds) (1994) *Nationalism* (Oxford and New York: Oxford University Press).

Hutton, W. (1995) *The State We're In* (London: Jonathan Cape).

Hyman, H. (1959) *Political Socialisation: A Study in the Psychology of Political Behaviour* (New York: Free Press).

Inglehart, R. (1977) *The Silent Revolution: Changing Values and Political Styles Amongst Western Publics* (Princeton: Princeton University Press).

Inglehart, R. (1990) *Cultural Shift in Advanced Industrial Society* (Princeton: Princeton University Press).

Inter-Parliamentary Union (1986) *Parliaments of the World* (Aldershot: Gower) (2 vols).

Janis, I. (1972) *Victims of Groupthink* (Boston: Houghton Mifflin).

Jenkins, S. (1995) *Accountable to None* (Harmondsworth: Penguin).

Jervis, R. (1968) 'Hypotheses on Misperception', *World Politics*, vol. 20, pp. 454–79.

Jessop, B. (1982) *The Capitalist State* (Oxford: Martin Robertson).

Jessop, B. (1990) *State Theory: Putting Capitalist States in Their Place* (Oxford: Polity Press).

Johnson, C. (1966) *Revolutionary Change* (Boston, MA: Little, Brown).

Jones, G. (ed.) (1991) *Western European Prime Ministers* (London: Frank Cass).

Kant, I. (1970) *Political Writings* (Cambridge: Cambridge University Press) (ed. H. Reiss).

Keating, M. (1988) *State and Regional Nationalism: Territorial Politics and the European State* (London and New York: Harvester Wheatsheaf).

Keith, M. (1993) *Race Riots and Policing* (London: UCL Press).

Kellas, J. (1991) *The Politics of Nationalism and Ethnicity* (London: Macmillan).

Kellner, P. and Lord Crowther-Hunt (1980) *The Civil Servants* (London: Macdonald).

Kennedy, P. (1989) *The Rise and Fall of the Great Powers* (London: Fontana).

Key, V. O. (1966) *The Responsible Electorate* (New York: Vintage).

Keynes, J. M. ([1936] 1965) *The General Theory of Employment, Interest and Money* (San Diego: Harcourt Brace).

King, A. (1975) 'Overload: Problems of Governing in the 1970s', *Political Studies*, vol. 23, pp. 284–96.

King, A. (ed.) (1985) *The British Prime Minister* (2nd ed.) (London: Macmillan).

Kirchheimer, O. (1966) 'The Transformation of the Western European Party Systems', in J. la Palombara and M. Weiner (eds) *Political Parties and Political Development* (Princeton, NJ: Princeton University Press).

Knott, J. and G. Miller (1987) *Reforming Bureaucracy: The Politics of Institutional Choice* (Englewood Cliffs, NJ: Prentice Hall).

Koh, B. (1989) *Japan's Administrative Elite* (Berkeley, CA: University of California Press).

Kolko, G. (1968) *The Politics of War* (London: Weidenfeld and Nicolson).

Kolko, G. (1988) *Restructuring the World Economy* (New York: Pantheon Books).

Kressel, N. J. (ed.) (1993) *Political Psychology: Classic and Contemporary Readings* (New York: Paragon House).

Kristol, I. (1983) *Two Cheers for Capitalism* (New York: Basic Books).

Kropotkin, P. (1912) *Fields, Factories and Workshops* (London: Nelson).

Kuhn, T. (1962) *The Structure of Scientific Revolutions* (2nd ed.) (Chicago: Chicago University Press).

Laclau, E. and C. Mouffe (1985) *Hegemony and Socialist Strategy: Towards a Radical Democratic Politics* (London: Verso).

Lafont, R. (1968) *Sur la France* (Paris: Gallimard).

Laqueur, W. (ed.) (1979) *Fascism: A Reader's Guide* (Harmondsworth: Penguin; Berkeley, CA: University of California Press).

Lane, J.-E. (1996) *Constitutions and Political Theory* (Manchester: Manchester University Press).

Lasswell, H. (1930) *Psychopathology and Politics* (New York: Viking).

Lasswell, H. (1936) *Politics: Who Gets What, When, How?* (New York: McGraw–Hill).

Le Bon, G. ([1895] 1960) *The Crowd* (New York: Viking Press).

Le Grand, J. (1982) *The Strategy of Equality: Redistribution and the Social Services* (London: Allen & Unwin).

LeDuc, L., R. G. Niemi and P. Norris (eds) (1996) *Comparing Democracies: Elections and Voting in Global Perspective* (London: Sage).

Lees, J. D. and M. Shaw (eds) (1979) *Committees in Legislatures: A Comparative Analysis* (Durham, NC: Duke University Press).

Leftwich, A. (ed.) (1984) *What is Politics? The Activity and Its Study* (Oxford and New York: Blackwell).

Lehmbruch, G. and P. C. Schmitter (1982) *Patterns of Corporatist Policy-Making* (London: Sage).

Leigh, D. and E. Vulliamy (1997) *Sleaze: The Corruption of Parliament* (London: Fourth Estate).

Lenin, V. I. ([1902] 1968) *What is to be Done?* (Harmondsworth and New York: Penguin).

Lenin, V. I. ([1916] 1970) *Imperialism: The Highest Stage of Capitalism* (Moscow: Progress).

Lichtheim, G. (1961) *Marxism* (London: Routledge & Kegan Paul).

Lijphart, A. (1984) *Democracies: Patterns of Majoritarian and Consensus Government in Twenty-One Countries* (New Haven, CT: Yale University Press).

Lijphart, A. (1990) 'Democratic Political Systems', in A. Bebler and J. Seroka (eds) *Contemporary Political Systems: Classifications and Typologies* (Boulder, CO: Lynne Reinner) pp. 71–87.

Lijphart, A. (ed.) (1992) *Parliamentary Versus Presidential Government* (Oxford: Oxford University Press).

Lijphart, A. and B. Grofman (eds) (1984) *Choosing an Electoral System* (New York: Praeger).

Lindblom, C. (1959) 'The Science of Muddling Through', *Public Administration Review*, vol. 19, pp. 79–88.

Lindblom, C. (1977) *Politics and Markets* (New York: Basic Books).

Lipset, S. and S. Rokkan (eds) (1967) *Party Systems and Voter Alignments* (New York: Free Press).

Little, R. and M. Smith (1991) *Perspective on World Politics* (London: Routledge).

Lively, J. (1975) *Democracy* (Oxford: Blackwell).

Locke, J. ([1690] 1965) *Two Treatises of Government* (New York: New American Library).

Loewenberg, F. and S. C. Patterson (1979) *Comparing Legislatures* (Boston, MA: Little, Brown).

Lovelock, J. (1979) *Gaia* (Oxford: Oxford University Press).

Lukes, S. (1974) *Power: A Radical View* (London: Macmillan; Atlantic Highlands, NJ: Humanities Press).

Machiavelli, N. ([1531] 1961) *The Prince* (Harmondsworth: Penguin) (trans. G. Bau).

MacIntyre, A. (1981) *After Virtue* (Notre Dame, IL: University of Notre Dame Press).

Mackintosh, J. P. (1977) *The British Cabinet* (London: Stevens).

Macpherson, C. B. (1962) *The Theory of Possessive Individualism* (Oxford: Oxford University Press).

Macpherson, C. B. (1972) *The Real World of Democracy* (New York and Oxford: Oxford University Press).

Macpherson, C. B. (1977) *The Life and Times of Liberal Democracy* (Oxford: Oxford University Press).

Mair, P. (1990) *The West European Party System* (Oxford: Oxford University Press).

Mao, Z. (1971) *Selected Readings from the Works of Mao Zedong* (Peking: Foreign Languages Press).

Marcuse, H. (1964) *One-Dimensional Man: Studies in the Ideology of Advanced Industrial Society* (Boston: Beacon).

Marquand, D. (1988) *The Unprincipled Society* (London: Cape).

Marsh, D. and R. A. W. Rhodes (eds) (1992) *Policy Networks in British Government* (Oxford: Oxford University Press).

Marsh, D. and G. Stoker (eds) (1995) *Theory and Methods in Political Science* (Basingstoke: Macmillan).

Marshall, P. (1991) *Demanding the Impossible: A History of Anarchism* (London: HarperCollins).

Marshall, T. H. (1950) 'Citizenship and Social Class', in T. Marshall (ed.) *Sociology at the Crossroads* (London: Heinemann).

Marty, M. E. and R. S. Appleby (1993) *Fundamentalisms and the State: Remaking Polities, Economies, and Militance* (Chicago: University of Chicago Press).

Marx, K. ([1845] 1968) 'Theses on Feuerbach', in *Selected Works in One Volume* (London: Lawrence & Wishart), pp. 28–31.

Marx, K. ([1852] 1963) *The Eighteenth Brumaire of Louis Bonaparte* (New York: International Publishers).

Marx, K. ([1867, 1885, 1894] 1970) *Capital* (London: Lawrence and Wishart) (3 vols).

Marx, K. and Engels, F. ([1846] 1970) *The German Ideology* (London: Lawrence & Wishart) (ed. C. J. Arthur).

Marx, K. and Engels, F. ([1848] 1967) *The Communist Manifesto* (Harmondsworth: Penguin).

Mayes, P. (1986) *Gender* (London: Longman).

Mayo, H. (1960) *An Introduction to Democratic Theory* (New York: Oxford University Press).

McCarthy, J. D. and M. N. Zald (1973) *The Trend of Social Movements in America: Professionalisation and Resource Mobilisation* (Morristown, NJ: General Learning Press).

McCauley, M. (1983) *The Origins of War* (London: Longman).

McDowell, L. and R. Pringle (eds) (1992) *Defining Women: Social Institutions and Gender Divisions* (Cambridge: Polity Press).

McGrew, A. G. *et al.* (eds) (1992) *Global Politics: Globalisation and the Nation-State* (Oxford: Policy Press).

McKenzie, R. T. (1955) *British Political Parties* (London: Heinemann).

McLellan, D. (1986) *Ideology* (Milton Keynes: Open University Press; Minneapolis: University of Minnesota Press).

McLennan, G., D. Held and S. Hall (eds) (1984) *The Idea of the Modern State* (Milton Keynes and Philadelphia, PA: Open University Press).

Meinecke, F. ([1907] 1970) *Cosmopolitanism and the National State* (Princeton: Princeton University Press).

Meny, Y. and V. Wright (eds) (1985) *Centre–Periphery Relations in Western Europe* (London: Croom Helm).

Mezey, M. (1979) *Comparative Legislatures* (Durham, NC: Duke University Press).

Michels, R. ([1911] 1962) *Political Parties: A Sociological Study of the Oligarchical Tendencies of Modern Democracy* (New York: Collier).

Miliband, R. (1969) *The State in Capitalist Society* (London: Weidenfeld and Nicolson).

Miliband, R. (1972) *Parliamentary Socialism* (London: Merlin).

Mill, J. S. ([1859] 1982) *On Liberty* (Harmondsworth: Penguin).

Mill, J. S. ([1861] 1951) *Considerations on Representative Government*, in H. B. Acton (ed.) *Utilitarianism, Liberty, and Representative Government* (London: Dent).

Millett, K. (1970) *Sexual Politics* (London: Granada).

Mills, C. W. (1956) *The Power Elite* (New York: Oxford University Press).

Montesquieu, C.-L. ([1748] 1949) *The Spirit of the Laws* (New York: Hafner) (trans. T. Nugent).

More, T. ([1516] 1965) *Utopia* (Harmondsworth: Penguin) (trans. P. Turner).

Morgenthau, H. (1948) *Politics Amongst Nations: The Struggle for Power and Peace* (New York: Knopf).

Mosca, G. ([1896] 1939) *The Ruling Class* (New York: McGraw–Hill) (trans. A. Livingstone).

Murray, C. (1984) *Losing Ground: American Social Policy (1950–80)* (New York: Basic Books).

Murray, C. and R. Herrnstein (1995) *The Bell Curve: Intelligence and Class Structure in American Life* (New York: Free Press).

Neumann, S. (1956) *Modern Political Parties* (Chicago: University of Chicago Press).

Neustadt, R. ([1964] 1980) *Presidential Power: The Politics of Leadership from FDR to Carter* (New York: John Wiley).

Nietzsche, F. (1982) *Thus Spoke Zarathustra* (New York: Random House) (trans. R. J. Hollingdale).

Niskanen, W. A. (1971) *Bureaucracy and Representative Government* (Chicago: Aldine–Atherton).

Nordlinger, E. (1977) *Soldiers in Politics: Military Coups and Governments* (Englewoods Cliffs, NJ: Prentice Hall).

Nordlinger, E. (1981) *On the Autonomy of the Democratic State* (Cambridge, MA: Harvard University Press).

Norton, P. (ed.) (1990a) *Legislatures* (Oxford: Oxford University Press).

Norton, P. (ed.) (1990b) *Parliaments in Western Europe* (London: Frank Cass).

Norton, P. (1993) *Does Parliament Matter?* (London: Harvester Wheatsheaf).

Nove, A. (1983) *The Economics of Feasible Socialism* (London: Macmillan).

Nozick, R. (1974) *Anarchy, State and Utopia* (Oxford: Basil Blackwell).

Nugent, N. (1991) *The Government and Politics of the European Community* (2nd ed.) (Basingstoke: Macmillan).

Oakeshott, M. (1962) *Rationalism in Politics and Other Essays* (London and New York: Methuen).

O'Brian, D. (1986) *Storm Centre: The Supreme Court in American Politics* (New York: Norton).

Offe, C. (1984) *Contradictions of the Welfare State* (London: Hutchinson).

Olson, M. (1968) *The Logic of Collective Action: Public Goods and the Theory of Groups* (Cambridge, MA: Harvard University Press).

Olson, M. (1982) *The Rise and Decline of Nations* (Newhaven, CT: Yale University Press).

Osborne, D. and T. Gaebler (1992) *Reinventing Government* (New York: Addison–Wesley).

Ostrogorski, M. (1902) *Democracy and the Organisation of Political Parties* (London: Macmillan).

O'Sullivan, N. (1976) *Conservatism* (London: Dent).

Paddison, R. (1983) *The Fragmented State: The Political Geography of Power* (New York: St Martin's Press).

Paine, T. ([1776] 1987) 'Common Sense', in M. Foot (ed.) *The Thomas Paine Reader* (Harmondsworth: Penguin).

Pakulski, J. (1990) *Social Movements: The Politics of Protest* (Melbourne: Longman).

Parry, G. and M. Moran (eds) (1994) *Democracy and Democratization* (London: Routledge).

Parsons, A. (1995) *From Cold War to Hot Peace: UN Interventions, 1945–1994* (London: Michael Joseph).

Parsons, W. (1995) *Public Policy: Introduction to the Theory and Practice of Policy Analysis* (Aldershot: Edward Elgar).

Pateman, C. (1970) *Participation and Democratic Theory* (Cambridge: Cambridge University Press).

Peele, G., C. Bailey, B. Cain and B. G. Peters (eds) (1994) *Developments in British Politics 2* (Basingstoke: Macmillan).

Pinkney, R. (1990) *Right-Wing Military Government* (London: Pinter).

Piore, M. J. and C. Sabel (1984) *The Second Industrial Divide: Possibilities for Prosperity* (New York: Basic Books).

Plant, R. (1991) *Modern Political Thought* (Oxford: Oxford University Press).

Plato (1955) *The Republic* (Harmondsworth: Penguin) (trans. H. D. Lee).

Poggi, G. (1990) *The State* (Cambridge: Polity Press).

Polsby, N. (1963) *Community Power and Political Theory* (Newhaven, CT: Yale University Press).

Poulantzas, N. (1968) *Political Power and Social Classes* (London: New Left Books).

Pressman, J. and A. Wildavsky (1973) *Implementation* (Berkeley, CA: University of California Press).

Proudhon, P.-J. ([1840] 1970) *What is Property?* (New York: Dover).

Pulzer, P. (1967) *Political Representation and Elections in Britain* (London: Allen & Unwin).

Putnam, R. (1996) 'Who Killed Civic America?', *Prospect*, March, pp. 66–72.

Randall, V. (ed.) (1988) *Political Parties in the Third World* (London: Sage).

Rawls, J. (1971) *A Theory of Justice* (Oxford: Oxford University Press).

Reiner, R. (1993) *The Politics of the Police* (2nd ed.) (Hemel Hempstead: Harvester Wheatsheaf).

Rex, J. and D. Mason (eds) (1992) *Theories of Race and Ethnic Relations* (Cambridge: Cambridge University Press).

Rhodes, R. A. W. (1988) *Beyond Westminster and Whitehall* (London: Unwin Hyman).

Richardson, J. (ed.) (1984) *Policy Styles in Western Europe* (London: Allen & Unwin).

Roach, J. and J. Thomaneck (1985) *Police and Public Order in Europe* (London: Croom Helm).

Robins, L., H. Blackmore and R. Pyper (eds) (1994) *Britain's Changing Party System* (London and New York: Leicester University Press).

Rokkan, S. (1970) *Citizens, Elections, Parties* (New York: McKay).

Rose, R. (ed.) (1980) *Challenge to Governance: Studies in Overloaded Politics* (London: Sage).

Rose, R. (1987) *The Postmodern Presidency: The White House Meets the World* (New York: Chartham House).

Rousseau, J.-J. ([1762] 1913) *The Social Contract* (London: Dent) (trans. G. D. H. Cole).

Rowat, D. (ed.) (1988) *Public Administration in Developed Democracies: A Comparative Study* (New York: Marcel Dekker).

Rush, M. (1992) *Politics and Society: An Introduction to Political Sociology* (Hemel Hempstead: Harvester Wheatsheaf).

Sabatier, P. (1988) 'An Advocacy Coalition Model of Policy Making and Change and the Role of Policy Orientated Learning Therein', *Policy Sciences*, vol. 1, pp. 129–68.

Sandel, M. (1982) *Liberalism and the Limits of Justice* (Cambridge: Cambridge University Press).

Sartori, G. (1976) *Parties and Party Systems: A Framework for Analysis* (Cambridge: Cambridge University Press).

Sartori, G. (1987) *The Theory of Democracy Revisited* (Chatham, NJ: Chatham House).

Saunders, P. (1990) *Social Class and Stratification* (London: Routledge).

Savage, S., R. Atkinson and L. Robins (1994) *Public Policy in Britain* (Basingstoke: Macmillan).

Schlesinger, A. (1974) *The Imperial Presidency* (New York: Popular Library).

Schumacher, E. F. (1973) *Small is Beautiful: A Study of Economics As If People Mattered* (London: Blond & Briggs).

Schumpeter, J. (1942) *Capitalism, Socialism and Democracy* (London: Allen & Unwin).

Schwarzmantel, J. (1991) *Socialism and the Idea of the Nation* (London: Harvester Wheatsheaf).

Schwarzmantel, J. (1994) *The State in Contemporary Society: An Introduction* (London and New York: Harvester Wheatsheaf).

Sedgemore, B. (1980) *The Secret Constitution* (London: Hodder & Stoughton).

Self, P. (1994) *Government by the Market? Politics of Public Choice* (Basingstoke: Macmillan).

Seliger, M. (1976) *Politics and Ideology* (London: Allen & Unwin).

Simon, H. (1983) *Models of Bounded Rationality – Vol. 2* (Cambridge, MA: MIT Press).

Skocpol, T. (1979) *States and Social Revolutions* (Cambridge: Cambridge University Press).

Smith, A. ([1776] 1930) *The Wealth of Nations* (London: Methuen).

Smith, A. D. (1986) *The Ethnic Origins of Nations* (Oxford: Basil Blackwell).

Smith, B. C. (1985) *Decentralisation: The Territorial Dimension of the State* (London: Allen & Unwin).

Social Trends, 1993 (London: HMSO).

Suleiman, E. (ed.) (1984) *Bureaucrats and Policy Making* (New York: Holmes & Meier).

Sun Tzu (1963) *The Art of War* (New York: Oxford University Press) (trans. S. B. Griffith).

Talmon, J. L. (1952) *The Origins of Totalitarian Democracy* (London: Secker & Warburg).

Thatcher, M. (1993) *The Downing Street Years* (London: HarperCollins).

Titmuss, R. M. (1968) *Essays on the Welfare State* (London: Allen & Unwin).

Tocqueville, A. de ([1856] 1947) *The Old Regime and the French Revolution* (Oxford: Blackwell) (trans. M. W. Patterson).

Trotsky, L. (1937) *The Revolution Betrayed* (London: Faber & Faber) (trans. M. Eastman).

Truman, D. (1951) *The Governmental Process* (New York: Knopf).

Waltman, J. and K. Holland (eds) (1988) *The Political Role of Law Courts in Modern Democracies* (New York: St Martin's Press).

Waltz, K. N. (1979) *Theory of International Politics* (Reading, MA: Addison–Wesley).

Weber, M. (1948) *From Max Weber: Essays in Sociology* (London: Routledge & Kegan Paul).

Weller, P. (1985) *First Among Equals: Prime Ministers in Westminster Systems* (Sydney: Allen & Unwin).

White, S., J. Gardner, G. Schopflin and T. Saich (1990) *Communist and Postcommunist Political Systems* (Basingstoke: Macmillan).

Wildavsky, A. (1980) *Art and Craft of Policy Analysis* (Macmillan: London).

Wilson, G. (1990) *Interest Groups* (Oxford: Blackwell).

Wilson, W. ([1885] 1961) *Constitutional Government: A Study in American Politics* (New York: Meridian).

Wollstonecraft, M. ([1792] 1985) *A Vindication of the Rights of Women* (Harmondsworth: Penguin).

World Bank (1985) *World Development Report 1985* (Washington DC: World Bank).

World Bank (1986) *World Development Report 1986* (Washington DC: World Bank).

Wright, A. (1987) *Socialisms: Theories and Practices* (Oxford: Oxford University Press).

Yergin, D. (1980) *Shattered Peace: The Origins of the Cold War and the National Security State* (Harmondsworth: Penguin).

Zimmerman, J. F. (1992) *Contemporary American Federalism* (London and New York: Leicester University Press)

Index

Numbers in **bold** refer to pages on which there is boxed information. Numbers in *italics* refer to pages on which a term is defined in the text, in the margin, or in the glossary.